OXFORD MONOGRAPHS IN
INTERNATIONAL LAW

General Editor: Professor Vaughan Lowe, *Chichele Professor
of Public International Law in the University of Oxford and
Fellow of All Souls College, Oxford*

PEREMPTORY NORMS IN INTERNATIONAL LAW

OXFORD MONOGRAPHS IN
INTERNATIONAL LAW

The aim of this series is to publish important and original pieces of research on all aspects of international law. Topics that are given particular prominence are those which, while of interest to the academic lawyer, also have important bearing on issues which touch upon the actual conduct of international relations. Nonetheless, the series is wide in scope and includes monographs on the history and philosophical foundations of international law.

RECENT TITLES IN THE SERIES

PEREMPTORY NORMS IN INTERNATIONAL LAW

ALEXANDER ORAKHELASHVILI

Fellow, Jesus College, Oxford

OXFORD

UNIVERSITY PRESS

OXFORD

UNIVERSITY PRESS

Great Clarendon Street, Oxford OX2 6DP

Oxford University Press is a department of the University of Oxford.
It furthers the University's objective of excellence in research, scholarship,
and education by publishing worldwide in

Oxford New York

Auckland Cape Town Dar es Salaam Hong Kong Karachi
Kuala Lumpur Madrid Melbourne Mexico City Nairobi
New Delhi Shanghai Taipei Toronto

With offices in

Argentina Austria Brazil Chile Czech Republic France Greece
Guatemala Hungary Italy Japan Poland Portugal Singapore
South Korea Switzerland Thailand Turkey Ukraine Vietnam

Oxford is a registered trade mark of Oxford University Press
in the UK and in certain other countries

Published in the United States
by Oxford University Press Inc., New York

British Library Cataloguing in Publication Data

Data available

Library of Congress Cataloging in Publication Data

Orakhelashvili, Alexander
Peremptory norms in international law/Alexander Orakhelashvili.
   p. cm.—(Oxford monographs in international law)
Includes bibliographical references and index.
ISBN-13: 978-0-19-929596-8 (hardback : alk. paper)
1. Customary law, International.   2. Jus cogens (International law).
3. International obligations.   I. Title.   II. Series.
KZ1261.O73 2006
341—dc22   2006009868

Typeset by RefineCatch Ltd.
Printed in Great Britain
on acid-free paper by
Biddles Ltd., King's Lynn

ISBN 978–0–19–929596–4 (Hbk.)
ISBN 978–0–19–954611–4 (Pbk.)

1 3 5 7 9 10 8 6 4 2

General Editor's Preface

It is well known that norms of *jus cogens* admit of no derogation. It is much less well known what the legal consequences of that principle, and of breaches of *jus cogens*, might be. This study breaks new ground by analysing these issues and throws light on a neglected, but crucial, aspect of this important topic. Dr Orakhelashvili, through a masterly survey of the literature and practice, develops a view of *jus cogens* as a system, rather than a static concept. His study is a valuable foundation for the refinement and development of this fundamental element of the international legal system.

IB
AVL

Acknowledgments

This monograph is the expanded version of the PhD thesis that I defended at Cambridge University in December 2004. The idea of writing a comprehensive study on peremptory norms was born during my LLM studies in Public International Law at the University of Leiden, where I was taught and supervised by Professor John Dugard LLD, Professor of Public International Law at Leiden University and the ILC Special Rapporteur on Diplomatic Protection. Professor Dugard had himself championed a doctrinal move towards constructing the conceptual basis for the extension of the scope of *jus cogens*, namely its application to the law of recognition, and the law of extradition. Professor Dugard's efforts have been invaluable in enabling me to do a doctorate in Cambridge.

After I started to work on my thesis in Cambridge, I was in the privileged position of being supervised by Professor James Crawford, Whewell Professor of International Law, the Chair of the Law Faculty, and formerly the ILC Special Rapporteur on State Responsibility. Professor Crawford's efforts made it possible to enable me to pursue doctoral studies, his thoughtful remarks and criticisms have been challenging all the time and very helpful and invaluable in enabling me to improve my argument.

Thanks are also due to the examiners of my PhD thesis, Dr Christine Gray, Reader in International Law at the Faculty of Law (Cambridge), and Professor Giorgio Gaja, Professor of International Law at the University of Florence and the ILC Special Rapporteur on Responsibility of International Organisations. Their remarks have benefited the further progress of the work on the monograph. I would also like to thank Mr Daniel Bethlehem, Director of the Lauterpacht Centre in Cambridge, for making the Centre available for me to complete this monograph.

This monograph includes and refers to some material that has been published by this writer in periodicals, namely in *EJIL, AJIL, ICLQ, GYIL, LJIL, JCSL, Baltic YIL, CLJ, CYELS, CWILJ, AVR, and IOLR*. Wherever relevant, permissions have been sought and obtained to reproduce the relevant work in this monograph. More generally in this context, thanks are due to Malcolm Evans, Bernard Oxman, Stephen Scher, Philip Alston, Anny Bremner, Philip Kunig, Rainer Hoffman, Andreas Zimmermann, Christian Tams, Christiane Wandscher, Holger Scheel, Thomas Skouteris, Steven Blockmans, Niels Blokker, John Bell, Alan Dashwood, Catherine Bedford, Loretta Malintoppi, Cheryl Dunn, Nigel White, Christine Gray, Ineta Ziemele, and Carin Laurin.

For writing and completing this work, the financial assistance of the Open Society Institute (OSI), New York, as well as the Cambridge Overseas Trust has been indispensable. My immense gratitude goes to Mr Aryeh Neier, President and Ms Julie Hayes, Executive Associate, OSI, and Dr Anil Seal, Director, Cambridge Overseas Trust, for their very helpful and constructive approach.

In the process of considering and processing this book at the Oxford University Press, my thanks go to the Delegates and Mr John Louth, the Law Commissioning Editor, as well as Dr Gwen Booth, Ms Rebecca Smith and Mrs Dédé Tété-Rosenthal, for their helpful approach directed towards complete understanding of all the issues that were faced in the process of preparation of the final manuscript of this monograph.

This study attempts to cover all relevant material, including international treaty practice, judicial practice, the practice of individual States, and the documents of international organizations. It is, however, important that this study has been written and is published at a time when several issues of the operation and effect of international *jus cogens*, whether related to judicial practice or codification, are being dealt with by international and national bodies, and this study therefore covers only such material as was publicly available at the time of completion. Some material that has become available after the completion of the monograph but responds to the issues raised in it is considered in the Appendix. Another significant problem is that several documents, notably the decisions of domestic courts, are not available publicly or other than in the language in which they were issued. Therefore, this study unfortunately makes no reference to the full or official versions of some decisions from Greece, Italy or Latin American States. The content of some of these decisions has been ascertained through secondary sources that elaborated upon them, and some decisions or reports simply remained beyond our attention for the reasons noted above.

AO
Jesus College, Oxford

Contents—Summary

**Part V—The Effect of Peremptory Norms in
National Legal Systems**

Contents

**Part V—The Effect of Peremptory Norms in
National Legal Systems**

Tables of Treaties, Reports and Decisions

TREATIES

Multilateral treaties

UNITED NATIONS MATERIALS

The United Nations General Assembly Resolutions

General Comments of the UN Human Rights Committee

Resolutions of the UN Human Rights Commission

The UN International Law Commission

SPECIAL RAPPORTEURS

REPORTS OF THE COMMISSION

REPORTS AND WORKING PAPERS OF THE UN RAPPORTEURS ON HUMAN
RIGHTS

The Institute of International Law

Permanent Court of International Justice

International Court of Justice

International Criminal Tribunal for the Former Yugoslavia

International Criminal Tribunal for Rwanda

UN Human Rights Committee

European Commission of Human Rights

European Court of Human Rights

African Commission of Human Rights

European Court of Justice

Special Court for Sierra Leone

DECISIONS OF NATIONAL COURTS

Introduction

The subject-matter of the present study relates to peremptory norms of international law (*jus cogens*), also known as international public order, the principal purpose of which is to maintain the integrity of the fundamental norms of international law and set limits on how far States and other subjects of international law can go in treating each other, as well as non-State actors such as individuals and peoples. The aim is to provide a comprehensive study of peremptory norms, something which is lacking so far in international legal doctrine. Peremptory norms, although often criticized or approached with sceptical nihilism, nevertheless attract growing doctrinal and practical attention and have increasing importance in determining the permissible limits on the action of State and non-State actors in different areas. In view of this overriding impact on what might otherwise be instances of the law-making process, peremptory norms concern a constitutional aspect of international law.

Despite the growing relevance of peremptory norms in practice, doctrine has failed to treat the issue comprehensively, even though it has noticed most of the developments in the field. Most of the existing literature is limited to examining specific aspects of the problem. The monographs of Christos Rozakis, *The Concept of* Jus Cogens *in the Law of Treaties* (1969) and Jerzy Sztucki, Jus Cogens *and the Vienna Convention on the Law of Treaties* (1974) examine the issue from the viewpoint of the law of treaties. Lauri Hannikainen's *Peremptory Norms of International Law* (1988) focuses mostly on identifying the individual peremptory norms and briefly examines some issues of *jus cogens* related to the law of treaties and State responsibility; this latter task is performed through analysing normative provisions and with little focus on State practice. From the literature written in French one must single out Robert Kolb's *Théorie du ius cogens international* (2001), which examines theoretical problems of peremptory norms but says little about their practical effects. The same holds true for the chapter on peremptory norms in Pierre-Marie Dupuy's General Course at the Hague Academy in 2002. The 1974 monograph of Nicoloudis, *La nullité de jus cogens et le developpement contemporain de droit international public* has a broader profile, focusing on pertinent issues of voidness, but it is 30 years old and hardly known to English-speaking readers. In German, Stefan Kadelbach's *Zwingendes Völkerrecht* (1994) makes a systematic effort to examine both theoretical and practical aspects of peremptory norms and presumably takes matters further than any other existing contribution. Nevertheless, he gives predominant place to theoretical issues.

The last few decades have witnessed the expansion of the debate regarding the identification, scope and effects of peremptory norms. In practice, several international controversies, such as the conflicts in Palestine, Cyprus, Iraq, the former Yugoslavia, the human rights abuses in African and Latin American States, the legacy of the Second World War involving the issues of prosecution of international criminals and compensation of the war victims, as well as the functioning of the collective security system within the United Nations, raise the relevance of peremptory norms in such a way as to make the outcome of the relevant controversy impacted upon by the effect of pertinent peremptory norms. The doctrinal developments in the same period have not properly accounted for this situation, still less have attempted to set up the comprehensive doctrinal framework enabling academics and practitioners to ascertain both the impact of peremptory norms and the reasons behind that impact. Most contributions in this period are written in the form of journal or yearbook articles and focus on one or another issue related to international public order, which causes them to be fragmented in their analysis, being unable to account for the entire framework on the subject.

This state of scholarship justifies the evaluation that there seems to be no general analysis which provides answers to many questions that arise in terms of the operation of peremptory norms,[1] and necessarily requires a fresh effort to examine and explain the phenomenon of peremptory norms in every possible area where they may be relevant. The literature must keep pace with practical developments. This study is intended to fill an important doctrinal gap through presenting in a systematic way the effects of peremptory norms and reappraising the significance of such effects bearing in mind the overall nature of peremptory norms.

There is a variety of ways in which *jus cogens* can be looked at. This study aims to demonstrate that the hierarchical superiority of peremptory norms is not limited to the primary legal relations but becomes most crucially relevant after a specific peremptory norm is breached, through its hierarchically superior effects with regard to these breaches. A norm's peremptory character is relevant not only for its substance but also for its consequential operation; it consists not in their substance but primarily in their capacity, so far very imperfectly realized in the literature, to impact through their effects and consequences upon conflicting acts, situations and agreements.

The purpose of this study is not to restate the issues extensively examined in doctrine, but to focus on the most acute and problematic issues related to the application of peremptory norms, by approaching the problem of *jus cogens* from the aspects which may look controversial or unresolved, examining in a systemic way the issues which have so far received only marginal attention from the viewpoint of peremptory norms, and thus consolidating

---

[1] H. Fox, *The Law of State Immunity* (2002), 525.

the approach to peremptory norms by reference to doctrinal and practical trends reflecting their character and effects. This represents the central purpose of this study: it is concerned with the effects of peremptory norms as a *system*. Such systematic analysis is necessary for the proper understanding of the phenomenon of *jus cogens*, because some aspects of this phenomenon can be explanatory of its other aspects. Drawing conclusions on the basis of the fragmented treatment of the phenomenon of *jus cogens* runs the risk of improper understanding.

The proper examination of this field necessarily involves the positive and systemic approach towards the phenomenon of peremptory norms. It is the widespread occurrence that in contributions dealing with various international law topics to which the concept and operation of peremptory norms is more or less relevant, writers deal with the issues of peremptory norms arising within the limits of few sentences or paragraphs and come up with quite straightforward conclusions about the relevance and impact of *jus cogens* in the relevant field without having properly examined the phenomenon of *jus cogens* itself. This monograph, on the other hand, offers its conclusions on the basis of the positive approach, which is necessary to properly comprehend the essence of the phenomenon. At the same time, any decent academic exercise needs to address the questions that may possibly arise, rather than dismissing the concepts because of the questions that may arise in relation to them. This last option leads to obscurity and academic stalemate and, in adhering to it, writers would remain isolated from how the law develops. Therefore, the focus of this monograph is constructive in its attempt to search.

This monograph consists of four parts, focusing on individual aspects of the problem. Part I examines what peremptory norms are, which factors make them peremptory, and in what this peremptory character actually consists. The argument developed in Part I is a single and interconnected one: it examines the rationale and basis of a norm's peremptory character, and also how the sources of international law respond to that rationale and basis.

Part II works out the effects of peremptory norms, such as non-derogability and non-reciprocity, in the variety of fields of general international law. The purpose this part serves is also to demonstrate that the effects of *jus cogens* in one field can be explanatory of its effects in other fields.

Unlike Part II, which focuses on simple legal relations involving the State-to-State or State-to-individual dimensions, Part III elevates the analysis to the more complex level of legal relations, where, apart from the above-mentioned factors, the additional factors such as the powers of international organizations come into play as relevant in terms of determining the effects of *jus cogens*. Part IV is also engaged in the analysis at the same level as it examines the effect of peremptory norms in the context of additional factors related to the implications of the character of international judicial competence. Finally, Part V will examine the effect of peremptory norms in national legal systems, thus complementing the analysis in previous parts by highlighting the practical issues and concerns related to the effective implementation of the relevant norms and standards as a matter of national law.

PART I
The Concept and Identification of Peremptory Norms

1

Peremptory Norms as International Public Order

I. PEREMPTORY NORMS AS AN ASPECT OF THE HIERARCHY OF NORMS

The hierarchy of norms in international law raises a variety of questions.[1] One norm could prevail over another because it emerged later in time; or because it applies as between certain States in contrast to general international law; or because the States which established that norm have so intended, for example by stipulating that the parties to a given treaty shall not consent to any treaty obligation contradicting that treaty,[2] and if they nevertheless do so, the original treaty will prevail, as specified, for instance, in Article 103 of the UN Charter which gives the Charter obligations primacy over inconsistent agreements. The precise scope of Article 103 is a subject of debates in doctrine and practice, but it is indisputable that it establishes the case of normative hierarchy by giving precedence to certain norms over others.

A specific kind of normative hierarchy is observable in international institutional law between constitutive instruments of international organizations and acts enacted within those organizations.[3]

These instances of hierarchy are based on the conception of international law as a consent-based system of norms derived from the will of States. Assumptions that a later norm prevails over an earlier one or that it does not so prevail because the States concerned have so wished, or that a norm applicable between a limited number of States can trump general international law all imply that the will of States determines the priority of norms. This means that there is no categorical hierarchy of international instruments, for no instrument is inherently superior to another. The issues of hierarchy arise only in the specific cases when the clauses of different instruments come into conflict with each other and the rule which prevails does so because this was so wished by the relevant States for this specific case.

---

[1] On hierarchy of norms in general, see Akehurst, The Hierarchy of Norms in International Law, *BYIL* (1974–75), 273–286; Pauwelyn, *Conflict of Norms in Public International Law* (2003), 13, 96–98; Shelton, International Law and 'Relative Normativity', Evans (ed.), *International Law* (2003), 145–172; Thirlway, The Sources of International Law, Evans (ed.), *International Law* (2003), 136–137.

[2] For examples see Sztucki, *Jus Cogens and the Vienna Convention on the Law of Treaties* (1974), 29–40.

[3] eg UN Charter, Articles 24–25; see further Jenks, The Conflict of Law-Making Treaties, 30 *BYIL* (1951), 440; Guggenheim (1949), 198, 201.

The only visible exception can be found in Article 53 of the 1969 Vienna Convention on the Law of Treaties,[4] stating that treaties in conflict with peremptory norms[5] are void and defining a peremptory norm as 'a norm accepted and recognised by the international community of States as a whole as a norm from which no derogation is permitted and which can be modified only by a subsequent norm of general international law having the same character'. Peremptory norms prevail not because the States involved have so decided but because they are intrinsically superior and cannot be dispensed with through standard inter-State transactions. The specific character of such hierarchy is also manifested by the nullity that is attached to the transactions conflicting with peremptory norms.

The rationale behind the distinction between peremptory and ordinary rules is described by the Special Rapporteur of the UN International Law Commission Fitzmaurice:

> The rules of international law in this context fall broadly into two classes—those which are mandatory and imperative in all circumstances (*jus cogens*) and those (*jus dispositivum*) which merely furnish a rule for application in the absence of any other agreed regime, or, more correctly, those the variation or modification of which under an agreed regime is permissible, provided the position and rights of third States are not affected.[6]

In other words, the rules of *jus cogens* have to apply whatever the will and attitude of States, while the applicability of the rules of *jus dispositivum* can

---

[4] Kadelbach, *Zwingendes Völkerrecht* (1992), 26–30; Akehurst (1974–75), 281–282; Dupuy, L'unité de l'ordre juridique international, 297 *RdC* (2002), 281, speaking of the new type of hierarchy; Pauwelyn (2003), 22, 98, speaking of 'the only instance of *a priori* hierarchy'; Thirlway, The Law and Procedure of the International Court of Justice, *BYIL* (1990), 143.

[5] Also denoted as imperative, absolute, mandatory, categorical, cogent, overriding, inalienable, compelling, conclusive, fundamental, self-determined norms, *Black's Law Dictionary* (1990), 1136; Hannikainen, *Peremptory Norms in International Law: Historical development, criteria, present status* (1988), 21; Eek, Peremptory Norms and Private International Law, 139 *RdC* (1973), 10–11; Parker and Neylon, *Jus Cogens*: Compelling the Law of Human Rights, 12 *Hastings International and Comparative Law Review* (1989), 415; Bassiouni, *Crimes Against Humanity in International Criminal Law* (1999), 210. All these terms point to the rigidity of these norms and their ability to produce legal effects irrespective of, and even against, the will of the relevant legal persons. As for the term *jus cogens*, which originates from the Roman law where it denoted the norms which cannot be derogated from by private contracts, it is used interchangeably with the term 'peremptory norms'. It has been so used in the work of the UN International Law Commission on the law of treaties. For an overview see Sztucki (1974), 103–106.

[6] Fitzmaurice, Third Report on the Law of Treaties, II YbILC 1958, 40. See also Fitzmaurice, The Law and Procedure of the International Court of Justice, *BYIL* 1959, 224. As Judge Verdross pointed out in the *Ringeisen* case before the European Court of Human Rights, Article 26 of the European Convention on Human Rights, dealing with the exhaustion of local remedies with regard to the cases submitted to the European Convention organs, can be considered to prevail over the rules and practices related to the exhaustion of local remedies as accepted under general international law. This is so, because the rule requiring the exhaustion of local remedies is not part of *jus cogens*. Separate Opinion of Judge Verdross, *Ringeisen*, para. 1, further stressing that it was 'superfluous to undertake an analysis of international practice on the matter'. In other words, Article 26 applied as *lex specialis*.

be excluded or modified in accordance with the duly expressed will of States.

Such regulation causes peremptory norms to prevail over treaties, thereby creating an exception to the *lex specialis* rule. This is a hierarchy related to international public order as a phenomenon of general international law and hence different from any institutional *lex superior*.[7] As Rozakis affirms, one of the effects of the introduction of peremptory law in the international legal system is that it partly transforms international law—a horizontal and consensual legal order—into a vertical system of law. Such a system includes rules with different hierarchical standing, that is superior and inferior rules. The superior rules determine the frame within which the inferior rules can be valid, while the inferior rules must comply with the content of superior rules.[8] In domestic law, peremptory norms are not necessarily hierarchically superior to other norms:[9] positive law, whatever its rank, can prevail over contracts. But in international law there can be no *jus cogens* unless it is superior to ordinary norms because the latter constitute positive law, not just transactions between legal persons.

In international law where legal norms are produced by the agreement of States no cases should arguably be admitted where one norm by itself, and not because of the relevant States' will and determination, prevails over another norm. This means that the factors must be sought for which make the relevant norm so special as to enable it to effectuate an exception from the otherwise valid and dominant consensual pattern.

Peremptory norms as defined in the Vienna Convention on the Law of Treaties can have multiple functions, bearing in mind the nature of the international community.[10] They operate as peremptory norms proper, constraining the contractual capacity of legal persons. Conceivably, they also operate as constitutional norms.[11] In national law, *jus cogens* and constitutional norms can be distinguished, even if they overlap in substance, because constitutional norms establish the overall framework for legislative and administrative regulation while peremptory norms relate to private contracts. In

---

[7] Meron, *Human Rights Law-Making in the United Nations* (1986), 177, suggests that the reach of hierarchically superior instruments adopted within an institution is limited to the legal system of the parent organization and should not be confused with *jus cogens*. See also Pauwelyn (2003), 99.

[8] Rozakis, *The Concept of* Jus Cogens *in the Law of Treaties* (1976), 19–20; see also Joint Dissenting Opinion, *Al-Adsani*, para. 1; Christenson (1988), 600–601. In another context involving *jus cogens*, the Joint Separate Opinion in *Arrest Warrant (Congo v Belgium)* emphasized that, in prosecuting crimes affecting the community interest, States act as community agents and this vertical notion of authority is significantly different from otherwise the horizontal pattern of international law, para. 51.

[9] Hannikainen (1988), 11.

[10] The notion of such functions can be borrowed from national law, Virally, Reflexions sur le 'jus cogens', 12 *Annuaire Français de Droit International* (1966), 7.

[11] *Per contra* Hannikainen (1988), 11.

the decentralized international legal system, agreements expressly or tacitly concluded by individual States are the primary source of positive law. Peremptory norms, prevailing over such agreements, necessarily implicate a constitutional element.[12] Given that individual States appear in international law as law-makers, the concept of *jus cogens* resembles conceptually not merely peremptory norms limiting the contractual freedom legal persons but also the constitutional limitations in terms of on what the law-makers can freely enact. Such constitutional character of a norm is a matter of the substance of that norm, whether enshrined in written or unwritten sources of law.

All said on this subject is only to indicate that peremptory norms can have the potential to build the constitutional element in international law, not that they necessarily have this potential. The constitution of the international community would conceivably encompass, apart from *jus cogens*, the UN Charter, the international bill of human rights, and the Vienna Convention on the Law of Treaties, that is the instruments which regulate in international relations the subject-matters which are regulated in national law by national constitutions. But there is no clear evidence that the international community as a whole views these instruments as its constitution.

The identification of international *jus cogens* with legislative norms is also a tempting option, as it reflects the subjection of contractual agreement to the legislative will.[13] However, this analogy would assume the logically anterior factors that simply do not occur in international law. Legislation is a process of the enactment of juridical instruments by an organ that has been specifically authorized to perform its function as a legislator. The absence of such in the international legal system makes it impossible to see *jus cogens* as an element of international legislation. Moreover, many peremptory norms are based on unwritten law.

Finally, peremptory norms operate as a public order protecting the legal system from incompatible laws, acts and transactions. As with every legal system, international law can be vulnerable to infiltration of the effect of certain norms and transactions which are fundamentally repugnant to it. It seems that the general concept of public order most suitably reflects the basic

---

[12] 'With public international law developing into much more than a law of bilateral and multilateral treaty relationships the threshold to a constitutional structure has long been crossed.' Frowein, Reactions by Not Directly Affected States to Breaches of Public International Law, 248 *RdC* (1994), 365; Münch, Bemerkungen zum ius cogens, *Voelkerrecht als Rechtsordnung—Internationale Gerichtsbarkeit—Menschenrechte: Festschrift Mosler* (1983), 617, affirms that even an unorganized society can have a constitution. It is also generally true that, as Jenks writes, 'The hierarchic principle represents the transposition to international life of the principle which determines the validity of legislation governed by a written constitution.' Jenks, The Conflict of Law-Making Treaties, 30 *BYIL* (1951), 436. As Janis suggests, the compelling law, *jus cogens*, 'is not a form of customary international law, but a form of international constitutional law, a norm which sets the very foundations of the international legal systems'. Janis, The Nature of *Jus Cogens*, 3 *Connecticut JIL* (1988), 363.

[13] Domb, *Jus Cogens* and Human Rights, 6 *Israel Yearbook of Human Rights* (1976), 108.

characteristics of international *jus cogens*. This concept not only reflects the domestic law analogy, but it is the most suitable, if not the only, analogy that can be adapted, without the disruption of the inherent character of the concept itself, to the decentralized character of the international legal system.

2. PUBLIC ORDER IN NATIONAL LEGAL SYSTEMS

2.1. The concept and essence of public order

The development of public order, or public policy, as a well-established concept in private law in general and private international law in particular has undergone substantial transformation and serious debates as to its suitability and relevance. Its open-ended nature and uncertainty caused scepticism as to its nature and scope. It has been attempted to deconstruct this concept or split it into the specific norms. But all attempts to expel the concept of public order from the area of private international law have proved unsuccessful.[14]

More than a century ago Zitelmann, a leading German scholar of private international law, affirmed that public order clauses are indispensable in every legal order.[15] As Judge Lauterpacht emphasized in the *Guardianship of Infants* case before the International Court of Justice, the concept of public order 'has often been exposed to criticism. But it is seldom, if ever, suggested that it is not an indispensable instrument of the interpretation, application and development of the law.'[16]

In national legal systems, public policy imposes limitations on the validity of certain regular, or even fundamental, principles of law. In private law, the freedom of contract is fundamental. A free-standing body of norms—private international law—makes it possible for national courts to apply foreign laws to situations involving foreign elements. In both these areas, the function of public policy in national legal systems is to prevent, due to some public interest factors, the otherwise permissible legal outcomes from having their effect either by nullifying contracts against good morals or by refusing to apply foreign laws that are unacceptable to the conceptions of the forum's legal systems. In the *Guardianship of Infants* case, Judge Moreno-Quintana defined public order as 'the whole body of laws and legal instruments whose legal principles cannot be set at naught either by special conventions or by a foreign law'.[17]

In referring to such phenomena, the terms 'public policy' and 'public order' (or its French equivalent *ordre public*) are used interchangeably and are

---

[14] Nussbaum, *Deutsches Internationales Privatrecht* (1974), 61–62.
[15] Zitelmann, *Internationales Privatrecht* (Bd. I, 1897), 319.
[16] Separate Opinion of Judge Lauterpacht, *ICJ Reports*, 1958, 456.
[17] Separate Opinion of Judge Moreno-Quintana, *ICJ Reports*, 1958, 105.

essentially identical concepts.[18] In other words, the concept has different names but the same essence in different legal systems. The meaning behind the terminology does not necessarily coincide with its literal appearance. To begin with, public policy is a concept derived from law, not from politics. As emphasized, public policy is not the same as political policy.[19] Political grounds alone cannot justify the refusal to apply foreign laws if these laws are made applicable by the forum's rules of conflict.[20] Nor has the concept of public order the same meaning as the more general concept of 'law and order'. As Graveson suggests, English law adopts the term 'public policy' because 'order' is identified here with 'law and order'.[21] But in other legal systems too, the word 'order' in the context of public order has a stronger connotation than the general concept of law and order.[22]

Public order is indispensable to every legal system, and is based on a written or unwritten clause.[23] In Germany, its role is guaranteed by Article 138 of the German Civil Code, which outlaws private transactions against good morals, and Article 30 of the *Einführungsgesetz* to the same Civil Code, which bans incompatible foreign laws. In France, Article 6 of the Civil Code plays a similar role. But even in countries where no legislative clause guarantees the supremacy of public order, such as in France (with regard to foreign laws), Austria, Switzerland or the UK, it is applied as a self-explanatory concept, sometimes as part of customary law.[24]

The requirements of public policy do not coincide with and are considerably narrower in scope than purely and simply the requirements that follow from the forum's legal norms. As North and Fawcett emphasize, the fact that a foreign law and acts governed by it are incompatible with English law does not prevent the enforcement of that foreign law in England.[25] Otherwise, the system of private international law would be rendered meaningless.

There is a certain consensus among national legal systems as to the scope and conditions of applicability of public policy. Both French and German legal systems accept that the application of foreign law could violate the sentiments and undermine important objectives of the forum's legal

---

[18] The term *ordre public* originates from Article 6 of the French Civil Code, Schütz, *Der internationale ordre public* (1984), 6. Even in German law, which normally refers to the concept as *Vorbehaltsklausel* (literally translated as 'reservation clause'), the term *Vorbehalt zugunsten der öffentlichen Ordnung* (reservation in favour of public order) has also found some acceptance, Raape, *Internationales Privatrecht* (1961), 91; Kropholler, *Internationales Privatrecht* (1997), 223.

[19] Graveson, *Conflict of Laws* (1974), 165.

[20] Mann, *Foreign Affairs in English Courts* (1986), 149.

[21] Graveson, *Conflict of Laws* (1974), 165.

[22] Kropholler, *Internationales Privatrecht* (1997), 232.

[23] Niederer, *Einführung in die Allgemeine Lehren des Internationalen Privatrechts* (1956), 284.

[24] cf Raape, *Internationales Privatrecht* (1961), 91; Nussbaum, *Deutsches Internationales Privatrecht* (1974), 61, 65.

[25] North and Fawcett, *Cheshire and North's Private International Law* (1999), 124.

order.[26] According to the French approach, public order is there to prevent the application in the forum's legal system of foreign laws that offend the forum's social or juridical conceptions.[27] For example, if a bigamy marriage is allowed under a foreign norm, French courts will not accept the validity of such marriages, even if under collision norms marriage is governed by personal laws, and declare the second marriage void.[28]

In the German legal system, public order interferes with foreign norms that contradict domestic legal principles whose application the State cannot refuse.[29] Consequently, the applicability of foreign laws must be subjected to certain limitations, for example under Article 30 of the *Einführungsgesetz* to the German Civil Code, which prohibits the application of foreign laws offending against good morals or the objective of a German law.[30] To illustrate, there are norms that guarantee free expression of will in private law, or reflect the forum's conceptions of family and marriage. In German law the right of parents to have contact with their children cannot be renounced. If a foreign law allows such renunciation, it is to be excluded through the intervention of public order.[31]

The approach of the English legal system is similar. A transaction that is valid under foreign law must not be nullified in English law unless its enforcement would offend some social, moral or economic principle so sacrosanct in English eyes as to require its maintenance at all costs and without exception.[32] Public policy is a more or less indefinite concept relating to the 'matters regarded by Parliament or the courts as clearly of fundamental concern to the state and society at large'.[33] The House of Lords in *Kuwait Air Corp.* emphasized that English public policy requires disregarding a provision of foreign law 'when it would lead to a result wholly alien to fundamental requirements of justice as administered by an English court'.[34]

There is no absolutely uniform conception of what legal relations should be subsumed within national public policies. As the Permanent Court of International Justice clarified, the definition of public policy in any particular country is largely dependent on the opinion prevailing in the relevant country.[35] However, there is a certain common minimum denominator of defining the scope of public policy in different legal systems. The application of public

---

[26] Raape, *Internationales Privatrecht* (1961), 90; Meyer, *Droit International Privé* (1994), 139, 144.

[27] Batiffol, H., and Lagarde, P., *Traité de Droit International Privé* (Tome 1, Paris, 1993), 567.

[28] Meyer, *Droit International Privé* (1994), 140.

[29] Nussbaum, *Deutsches Internationales Privatrecht* (1974), 60.

[30] Raape, *Internationales Privatrecht* (1961), 91.

[31] Wolff, *Das Internationale Privatrecht Deutschlands* (1954), 65–67.

[32] North and Fawcett, *Cheshire and North's Private International Law* (1999), 123.

[33] Graveson, *Conflict of Laws* (1974), 165.

[34] *Kuwait Air Corp.*, HL, 16 May 2002, para. 16 (*per* Lord Nicholls).

[35] *Serbian Loans*, PCIJ Series A 20/21, 46.

order norms depends on a value judgment, or *überstaatliches Werturteil*.[36] The French *Cour de cassation* identifies public order with principles of universal justice possessing an absolute international value, denoted as *verité absolue*.[37] These are principles indispensable to safeguard, because they relate to fundamental conceptions, values and sentiments recognized within the French legal system.[38] As an English court suggested in similar terms, public policy is 'a restriction upon acts which are thought to be harmful to the community'.[39]

Depending on the priorities of individual countries, their public policies can encompass principles necessary to safeguard their and their allies' important national interests.[40] But it is also widely accepted that the function of public order is to impeach results that are immoral or contrary to the forum's fundamental values,[41] or ethical fundamentals and general morality of *lex fori*;[42] to outlaw foreign legal institutions that are immoral under the forum's conceptions.[43] Public policy is determined by the conceptions of law, justice and morality as understood in the courts.[44] The concept of good morals is most frequently included in the concept of public order.[45] National legislative clauses that define the scope and function of public order directly refer to moral criteria,[46] and even in legal systems without such clauses, public order outlaws immoral acts and transactions. For instance, in *Kuwait Air Corp.* the general conceptions of morality and humanity were identified as aspects of public policy.[47] Public order may refer both to the rules of positive law and generally recognized principles of morality which are not necessarily part of positive law.[48] This partly explains the statement of Judge Spender in the *Guardianship of Infants* case that it is impossible to ascertain any absolute

---

[36] Niederer (1956), 288.   [37] Meyer (1994), 140.

[38] Batiffol and Lagarde (1993), 567, 574, speaking of *conceptions françaises réputées indispensables à sauvegarder*. Meyer (1994), 140–141; Raape (1961), 90; Jaenicke (1967), 79

[39] *Bank voor Handel en Scheepvaart*, 1 QB 1953, 263.

[40] Carter, The Role of Public Policy in English Private International Law, 42 *ICLQ* (1993), 4–6.

[41] Pillet and Niboyet, *Manuel de Droit International Privé* (II-1924), 417. See also *Kuwait Air Corp.*, HL, 16 May 2002, para. 17 (*per* Lord Nicholls).

[42] Niederer, *Einführung in die Allgemeine Lehren des Internationalen Privatrechts* (1956), 287; Carter, The Role of Public Policy in English Private International Law, 42 *ICLQ* (1993), 6.

[43] Nussbaum (1974), 60–61, 64, 67.

[44] *Kuwait Air Corp.*, HL, 16 May 2002, para. 149 (*per* Lord Hope) referring to Upjohn J in *Helbert Wagg*. Jaenicke, Zur Frage des Internationalen Ordre Public, 7 *Berichte der Deutschen Gesellschaft für Völkerrecht* (1967), 79.

[45] Rolin, H., Vers un ordre public réellement international, in *Hommage d'une génération des Juristes au President Basdevant* (Paris, 1961), 442.

[46] Article 138 of the German Civil Code and Article 30 of the *Einführungsgesetz*, Article 6 of the French Civil Code (placing good morals and public order on the same footing), Article 12 of the Preliminary Provisions to the Italian Civil Code. Zweigert and Kötz (1998), 380–382.

[47] *Kuwait Air Corp.*, 116 ILR 571.

[48] Kegel, *Internationales Privatrecht* (1987), 326; Levi, The International Ordre Public, 62 *Revue de Droit International* (1994), 57, 66–67.

criteria of identification of public policy: 'it cannot be determined within a formula. It is a conception.'[49] It is arguably a naïve approach to circumscribe precisely the scope of public order or list exhaustively the norms that belong to it. The matter is one of judicial value judgment.[50] The eviction of foreign laws is caused not less frequently by general principles and sentiments than specific norms.[51]

This is, however, not to suggest that there are no criteria to identify the scope of public policy: legal systems have, as demonstrated above, clearly worked out the relevant criteria. But these criteria are, to a certain extent, open-ended, which is necessary to ensure the ability of national public orders to develop in terms of social developments.

Legal systems also differ in defining the scope of relevance of their public policies. An overt reliance on public policy in England has been comparatively rare in comparison with some countries of continental Europe.[52] English courts have been traditionally quite reluctant to reject foreign laws or acts on the basis of public policy if that would breach international comity. To illustrate, the *Luther v Sagor* case related to the confiscation of timber in Soviet Russia which was later sold to the defendants in England. The Court of Appeal refused to reject the Soviet confiscation decree on the basis of public policy. Scrutton LJ held that to do so would be a 'serious breach of international comity'.[53] Dutch courts adopted a similar approach. The District and Supreme Courts of the Netherlands held that the nationalization decrees of Soviet Russia did not offend against the Dutch public order, because 'a sovereign State is fully competent to enact such decrees'.[54] In another case, a Dutch court refused to challenge the Mexican expropriation decree which was based on Article 27 of the Mexican Constitution[55] as contrary to Dutch public order, having not felt at liberty to rule that this decree was 'at variance with what should be considered proper and permissible for a foreign legislature'.[56] French courts, on the other hand, have displaced Soviet Russian confiscatory laws which were otherwise applicable under French private international law. Thus, the English approach based on comity can be contrasted with the French public order approach. It is suggested that the idea of

---

[49]　*ICJ Reports* 1958, 122.

[50]　Niederer, *Einführung in die Allgemeine Lehren des Internationalen Privatrechts* (1956), 287–288.

[51]　Meyer, *Droit International Privé* (1994), 141.

[52]　Carter, The Role of Public Policy in English Private International Law, 42 *ICLQ* (1993), 3.

[53]　3 *KB* 1921, 558–559.

[54]　*Hanani Ltd v Vladikawkaz Railway Company*, 11 *Annual Digest* 21–23.

[55]　Article 27 of the 1917 Mexican Constitution has been an important provision to trigger the changes in the then dominant views of private property and the powers of a State with regard to nationalization and expropriation. For an analysis see Lowenfeld, *International Economic Law* (2002), 392–394.

[56]　*United States of Mexico v Batsafsche Petroleum Maatschappij*, 11 *Annual Digest* 16–17.

international comity, if carried too far, could neutralize the forum's public policy.[57]

But such fears should not encourage extreme solutions. It is understandable that national courts can decline in certain cases questioning the legality of sovereign acts of foreign States, such as expropriation. National courts ought not to interfere with economic and social processes in foreign countries and can be justified in adopting the comity-based approach, unless some exceptionally serious reasons make this necessary. Such exceptional reasons were involved, for example, in the judicial treatment of the effects of racially motivated confiscation laws in Nazi Germany. French courts remained faithful to their public order approach and refused to give effect to the Third Reich expropriation decree directed against non-Arians, because the equality of races was part of French public order.[58] Dutch courts, on the contrary, have recognized without any query the German legislation depriving German Jews of some of their rights.[59] A Dutch court has also refused to register the marriage between a German Jew and a German 'Aryan' woman, recognizing Nazi marriage laws designed 'for the protection of German blood'. The court stated that it

cannot endorse the view that the principle of equality of all men and women before the law forms such an essential part of the Dutch legal system and Dutch public order, that the Netherlands ought to guarantee even to foreigners, who stay on their territory for some time, that equality with regard to their right of contracting a marriage, even in cases where the national law of the foreigners concerned prohibits a marriage between them on the ground of race-distinctions.

The court refused to register the marriage as one of the partners was a Jew as defined by German, even if not by Dutch, law, stating that 'the matter is settled by the meaning which the German law attaches to the word "*Jude*" '.[60]

It is thus clear that while the approach based on comity and restraint is useful in some contexts, in other contexts it produces appalling outcomes. This seems to be understood in English courts: they treat foreign sovereign acts with a certain degree of tolerance, but once such acts cross the line separating the human from the inhuman and the decent from the indecent, they are ready to set limits to their tolerance, as confirmed by the decision of

---

[57] Enonchong, Public Policy in the Conflict of Laws: A Chinese Wall around Little England? 45 *ICLQ* (1996), 652–653, 658; Mann, The Consequences of an International Wrong in National and International Law, *BYIL* (1976–77), 53.

[58] *Jellinek v Levi*, 11 *Annual Digest* 24–25; see also another decision, Court of Appeals of Paris, 26 *ILR* 51.

[59] *Lidauer and Becker v Trading Company*, District Court of Breda, 11 *Annual Digest* 183–184.

[60] *Menkel and Muks v Registration Officer*, Decision of the District Court, 11 *Annual Digest* 23–24; this contrasts with the decision of a Polish court rejecting the South African law prohibiting interracial marriages as discriminatory and thus contrary to Polish public policy. *Bartholomeus T*, District Court of Krakow, 1970, 52 *ILR* 28–29.

the House of Lords in the case of *Oppenheimer v Cattermole* relating to the Nazi confiscation decree involving severe violations of human rights.[61]

2.2. Ordre public interne *and* ordre public international

Although national legal systems recognize a single concept of public order with single conceptual justification, they nevertheless differentiate the effects of public order depending on the character of the relevant legal relations. In France, the domain of public order in terms of private international law (*ordre public international*) does not coincide with that of public order in internal law (*ordre public interne*).[62] The scope of *ordre public international* is narrower than that of *ordre public interne*. If a principle is part of *ordre public international* then it is necessarily part of *ordre public interne*.[63] A similar distinction is reflected in English law where 'the court will be even slower to invoke public policy in the field of conflict of laws than when a purely municipal legal issue is concerned'.[64]

This distinction between the two 'subcategories' of public order of national legal systems is due to multiple factors. Public order is effective with regard to incompatible foreign laws and also, within the forum's legal system, to derogatory transactions between private persons. A national public order ought presumably to be more far-reaching with regard to purely domestic situations and less so to legal situations involving foreign elements. National legal systems are independent of each other. National legislators and courts accept that foreign legal systems may envisage different legal solutions and those solutions must not be rejected just because they are different from the forum's solutions, unless certain fundamental values require the opposite. Furthermore, while it is relevant that the norms and principles reinforcing public order are peremptory, the peremptory status of a norm is not always necessarily meant to trump foreign rules, but in the first place to operate with overriding legal force within the forum's legal system.

As for the substance of subcategories, *ordre public interne* and *ordre public international* are distinguished as the latter arguably refers to the order common to all nations under the law of nations. But such public order is still a national public order.[65] This approach emphasizes the national character of

---

[61] See below, Chapter 19.   [62] Meyer, *Droit International Privé* (1994), 143.

[63] Meyer, *Droit International Privé* (1994), 142–143; see also *Kuwait Air Corp.*, HL, 16 May 2002, para. 114 (*per* Lord Steyn) affirming the same principle with regard to English public policy.

[64] *Vervaeke v Smith* (HL), *AC* 1983, 164.

[65] Jaenicke, Zur Frage des Internationalen Ordre Public, 7 *Berichte der Deutschen Gesellschaft für Völkerrecht* (1967), 80; Schütz (1984), 8; Bucher, L'ordre public et le but social des lois en droit international privé, 239 *RdC* (1993-II), 24; Pillet and Niboyet, *Manuel de Droit International Privé* (II-1924), 418. Raape, *Internationales Privatrecht* (1961), 99–100 considers that public order is a 'home affair'.

public policy in terms of private international law. Although Judge Lauterpacht suggested that the public policy of individual States should be determined not by reference to their legal systems but 'in the same way as any
other general principle of law in the sense of Article 38 of the [International
Court's] Statute', he nevertheless admitted that this must be done 'by
reference to the practice and experience of the municipal law of civilised
countries'.[66] This reinforces the concept of *ordre public international* as a body
of principles accepted as fundamental in different national legal systems. In
France, for example, a foreign law is not considered as contrary to public
order just because it contradicts the imperative principles of French law, but
only if it offends the principles of universal justice that are considered in
France as absolute international values.[67] This confirms that even if public
order is essentially national, it nevertheless has some international or even
universal dimension, for example in terms of morality or decency. This factor
is translated, in its turn, into the categorization of peremptory norms that
reinforce the concept of every public order.

For example, the norms governing personal status in French law belong to
ordre public interne as an aspect of the forum's internal law, and contracts
contrary to such norms are prohibited. But such norms are not part of *ordre
public international* because under private international law the status of
foreigners is determined by their own law.[68] The same applies to norms on
custody which are peremptory in German law but would not prevent application of different custody rules of foreign law to situations involving a foreign
element.[69] Similarly, the rules on the conditions of marriage in French law are
imperative and hence part of internal public order. But they are not part of
ordre public international. The French legal system sets 18 years as the marriage age but considers null and void a marriage contracted by a foreigner
who is 18 years old and whose national law does not allow persons under 20
to marry. On the other hand, *ordre public international* would interfere with a
marriage contracted by a 13-year-old person even if this is legal under his
national law.[70]

Such differentiation is due to the categorization of peremptory norms. As
Raape explains, the distinction between *jus cogens* and *jus dispositivum* is
relevant for the concept of public order. But the *jus cogens* character of a
norm is relevant for the applicability of collision norms only exceptionally.[71]
According to Nussbaum, it is normal that a peremptory norm that prevails

---

[66] *ICJ Reports*, 1958, 92.
[67] Batiffol, H., and Lagarde, P., *Traité de Droit International Privé* (Tome 1, Paris, 1993), 584;
Meyer, *Droit International Prive* (1994), 140.
[68] Pillet and Niboyet, *Manuel de Droit International Privé* (II-1924), 417–418.
[69] Raape, *Internationales Privatrecht* (1961), 97.
[70] Meyer, *Droit International Privé* (1994), 143.
[71] Raape, *Internationales Privatrecht* (1961), 97.

over the derogatory will of parties does not necessarily prevail over an incompatible foreign norm. That part of peremptory law which applies both to internal and foreign legal relations is included in *ordre public international* and that part of it which is peremptory only with regard to transactions accomplished within the forum's legal system is subsumed within *ordre public interne*.[72] To clarify further, *ordre public interne* is a peremptory law of *lex fori* from which private parties cannot derogate. *Ordre public international* is a narrower group of peremptory norms to be observed even if the given legal relation is governed by foreign law. Not every peremptory norm has peremptory effect with regard to foreign laws in the ambit of private international law.[73]

This differentiation in the effect of peremptory norms is explained by the rationale of specific peremptory norms. Not all peremptory norms can justify the refusal to apply foreign laws, especially not those enacted for protecting persons who are bearers of relevant rights, such as norms governing personal status, but only those peremptory norms which are based on higher moral grounds. The distinction between these two groups of peremptory norms reinforces the distinction between *ordre public interne* and *ordre public international*.[74]

In private law, especially the law of contract, the purpose of public order is to ensure the supremacy of society over the individual by restricting the autonomy of contractual will.[75] Imperative, or peremptory, legal norms that protect good morals are a natural constituent of public order.[76] The rules of public order determine the validity of juridical acts; agreements contrary to public order are void.[77] Imperative, or peremptory, public order norms cannot be set aside by the will of the parties, and a direct reference in this regard is made to legislative provisions outlawing contracts which are against good morals and public order.[78]

There is an intrinsic link between public order which bans conflicting transactions and public order which excludes incompatible foreign laws. For

---

[72] Nussbaum, *Deutsches Internationales Privatrecht* (1974), 64–65.

[73] Niederer, *Einführung in die Allgemeine Lehren des Internationalen Privatrechts* (1956), 288; Kropholler, *Internationales Privatrecht* (1997), 224; Enonchong, Public Policy in the Conflict of Laws: A Chinese Wall around Little England? 45 *ICLQ* (1996), 659.

[74] Kegel, *Internationales Privatrecht* (1987), 328; Wolff, *Das Internationale Privatrecht Deutschlands* (1954), 61.

[75] Van der Meersch, Does the Convention have the Power of 'Ordre Public' in Municipal Law? Robertson (ed.), *Human Rights in National and International Law* (1968), 97.

[76] Nussbaum, *Deutsches Internationales Privatrecht* (1974), 60–61.

[77] Van der Meersch, Does the Convention have the Power of 'Ordre Public' in Municipal Law? Robertson (ed.), *Human Rights in National and International Law* (1968), 98.

[78] Batiffol and Lagarde (1993), 584; Nussbaum (1974), 60–61, referring to the link between peremptory norms and public order made by Savigny. References are made to Article 6 of the French Civil Code, Article 138 of the German Civil Code, Article 12 of the Preliminary Provisions of the Italian Civil Code. For public policy with regard to contract in English law see *Chitty on Contracts* (1999), 835–839.

example, the concept of good morals in Article 30 of the *Einführungsgesetz* to the German Civil Code, which bans incompatible foreign laws, is identical to the concept of the concept of good morals under Article 138 of the same Civil Code, which bans immoral transactions concluded by private persons within the forum's legal system.[79] Article 6 of the French Civil Code, which outlaws private transactions derogating from public order, is also based on the same conceptions as public order in terms of private international law.[80]

2.3. Doctrines of relativity of public order

The essentially national character of public order has not only caused a differentiation accepted in national legal systems as to the character of legal norms that trump incompatible foreign laws, but also contributed to formulate yet another qualification on the scope of public policy. This latter qualification relates not so much to the character of the norms involved but the type of situation addressed in the context of public order, and requires that public policy should extend only to situations having a significant link with the forum. The doctrines justifying such approach are known as doctrines of relativity.

The assumption of relativity of public order has been found helpful to reinforce the essentially national character of public order.[81] The relativist profile of English public policy has sometimes been taken so far as to justify its tolerating some foreign contracts prohibited in England, such as the contracts of slavery.[82] The German approach, on the other hand, has been stricter and emphasized that the immorality of a transaction can be a factor dispensing with the requirement of the link to the forum. As Zitelmann affirmed a century ago, the German legal system would not accept legal claims based on slavery even if the slave had never been in Germany. The German legal order would not accept immoral transactions.[83]

The relativity of public order is generally manifested by the requirement that a foreign law must be in some spatial proximity with the forum.[84] This is best known as the factor of *Inlandsbeziehung* or *Binnenbeziehung*, which requires that a foreign law can be rendered inapplicable if its application

---

[79] Kegel, *Internationales Privatrecht* (1987), 324–325; Wolff, *Das Internationale Privatrecht Deutschlands* (1954), 62. Bleckmann, A., *Sittenwidrigkeit wegen Verstoßes gegen den* ordre public international, 34 *ZaöRV* (1974), 114–116, 130, outlines how the interpretation and application of Article 138 BGB in German courts came to encompass the offences against German *ordre public* and affirms the interpretative link between Article 138 BGB and Article 30 of the *Einführungsgesetz*.

[80] Niederer, *Einführung in die Allgemeine Lehren des Internationalen Privatrechts* (1956), 297.

[81] Bucher (1993), 52.   [82] Graveson, *Conflict of Laws* (1974), 165.

[83] Zitelmann, *Internationales Privatrecht* (Bd. I, 1897), 365.

[84] Batiffol, H., and Lagarde, P., *Traité de Droit International Privé* (Tome 1, Paris, 1993), 576

produces a situation linked to the forum.[85] Arguably, public order should not extend to situations that are so remote from the forum's legal order that they can have no impact within it. The conceptual basis of *Inlandsbeziehung* is that domestic courts should not pass abstract judgments on foreign laws but judge them only if that will entail a practically realizable judgment.[86]

This requirement does not seem to be absolute and universal, as, for example, the French *Cour de cassation* has never formulated a rule that the public order exception is subordinated to the judicial clarification that the relevant situation is linked to France.[87] However, doctrinal opinion according to which a legal relation that develops abroad and between persons domiciled abroad will not be affected by French public order still persists.[88] Nevertheless, the requirement of the link to the forum is not absolute. Public order could still interfere, independently of the nationality of the parties, if the principles endangered by the application of foreign law are of fundamental character, such as those of human rights.[89]

Another expression of the relativity of public order is its mitigated effect (*L'effet atténné*), meaning that the public order should not oppose certain situations outside the forum's legal system as it would oppose them within that legal system.[90] For example, legal systems that consider divorce illegal could accept divorces performed in other legal systems. The conceptual basis of that is, as the French *Cour de cassation* suggested, the assumption that public order should not oppose in the same way the acquisition of a right within the forum's legal system and the effects produced within that legal system by a right that is acquired in good faith in another legal system in accordance with the forum's norms of private international law. For instance, if divorce is not allowed in France (as was the case in 1860), French courts would nevertheless recognize a divorce performed in England and allow the person thus divorced to re-marry in France.[91] If French law did not recognize paternity claims of a child against his natural father (as was the case before 1912), French courts would nevertheless recognize foreign judgments that ordered payment of alimony in a foreign country, on the basis of foreign law

---

[85] Batiffol, H., and Lagarde, P., *Traité de Droit International Privé* (Tome 1, Paris, 1993), 576; Kegel, *Internationales Privatrecht* (1987), 330; Kropholler, *Internationales Privatrecht* (1997), 225.

[86] Kropholler, *Internationales Privatrecht* (1997), 225.

[87] Batiffol, H., and Lagarde, P., *Traité de Droit International Privé* (Tome 1, Paris, 1993), 578.

[88] Meyer, *Droit International Privé* (1994), 144; Nussbaum, *Deutsches Internationales Privatrecht* (1974), 63.

[89] Batiffol, H., and Lagarde, P., *Traité de Droit International Privé* (Tome 1, Paris, 1993), 580.

[90] Batiffol, H., and Lagarde, P., *Traité de Droit International Privé* (Tome 1, Paris, 1993), 580; Enonchong, Public Policy in the Conflict of Laws: A Chinese Wall around Little England? 45 *ICLQ* (1996), 659–660.

[91] Batiffol, H., and Lagarde, P., *Traité de Droit International Privé* (Tome 1, Paris, 1993), 580–581; Meyer, *Droit International Privé* (1994), 144.

and with regard to foreigners.[92] Again, if French law does not recognize polygamy, it would nevertheless accept certain claims of or on behalf of persons born in polygamy, such as payment of alimony.[93] A similar approach in German law is explained by reference to tolerance of some foreign customs and traditions,[94] or to the requirement that in order to be affected by public policy, the application of foreign law must relate to the principal element (*Hauptpunkt*) of the relevant situation.[95] The most coherent way to explain this phenomenon is not some tolerance towards polygamy itself but a certain degree of humanitarian approach not to suppress the rights of a person who is not an accomplice to the transaction repugnant to the forum's sentiments and conceptions.

While the doctrines of relativity are generally accepted in national legal systems, they are neither uniform nor absolute and serve substantially diverging purposes. Such doctrines can, among others, be used in terms of the forum's implicit acknowledgment that its certain legal institutions, such as the French prohibition of divorce, are not acceptable in a transnational context. Consequently, the doctrines of relativity appear in some cases to be not so much independent doctrines or characteristics of the concept of public order as the implications of the nature of legal relations involved in specific cases, such as the distinction between *ordre public interne* and *ordre public international*. The outcomes arguably dictated by the remoteness between the relevant situation and the forum could also be arrived at by suggesting that the relevant legal principles were themselves not part of *ordre public international* and for this reason they were not imposable on foreign legal relations. To illustrate, divorce was prohibited in France, but it was prohibited as a matter of French values (as they then were) only and hence this prohibition did not qualify as an element of *ordre public international*. This approach would be different from the suggestion that even if a principle is part of *ordre public international* and trumps foreign laws and transactions, it still would not do so if the situations in which these laws and transactions are involved are not too closely linked to the forum. Finally, the doctrines of relativity, as developed in doctrine and judicial practice, are themselves relative and qualified by exceptions.

---

[92] Nussbaum, *Deutsches Internationales Privatrecht* (1974), 63.

[93] Batiffol, H., and Lagarde, P., *Traité de Droit International Privé* (Tome 1, Paris, 1993), 582.

[94] Raape, *Internationales Privatrecht* (1961), 95; Nussbaum, *Deutsches Internationales Privatrecht* (1974), 63.

[95] Kegel, *Internationales Privatrecht* (1987), 331: in such a case the inheritance claims of a child born in polygamy would not be the principal element of the situation, but the issue whether the polygamic marriage is contracted within or outside the forum's legal system would be such a principal element.

2.4. Effects of public order

The repressive effect of public order extends not only to foreign legislation, but also to acts and decisions of foreign governments: if public order can cause the eviction of the former, there is no reason why it cannot have a similar effect with regard to the latter.[96] For example, Article 30 of the *Einführungsgesetz* to the German Civil Code excludes the application of foreign laws that contradict good morals; Article 328 of the German Code of Civil Procedure excludes the application of similar foreign judgments.[97] The English legal system responds similarly. In *Oppenheimer*, public policy was applied to a legislative decree,[98] while in *Kuwait Airways Corp.* it was applied to an administrative act.[99]

In terms of private law, public policy applies not just to contracts but to other relations of private law including unilateral actions or other situations contrary to public policy.[100] The effect of national legislative clauses outlawing acts and transactions contrary to public order is not limited to agreements, but also extends to other acts without a limitation of their form or character.[101] The primary consideration is to protect the integrity of the legal system from certain unacceptable acts, whatever their formal character.

Public order in national legal systems has different but interconnected and mutually complimentary effects. The negative effect of public order means the eviction of the normally competent foreign law or the non-recognition and non-execution of incompatible judgments. If, for instance, an English court decides that English public policy is affected, 'then the incompatible foreign rule must, indeed, be totally excluded'.[102] French and German legal systems respond similarly, though not in terms of the intrinsic validity of an incompatible foreign norm but merely its applicability within the forum's legal system.[103]

This negative effect is not sufficient to deal with situations where a foreign law contradicts the forum's *ordre public international* and judges shall look for norms in the forum's legal system to replace the rejected foreign norm. This is

---

[96] Batiffol, H., and Lagarde, P., *Traité de Droit International Privé* (Tome 1, Paris, 1993), 573–574; Brundner, The Domestic Enforcement of International Covenants on Human Rights, 35 *University of Toronto Law Journal* (1985), 246; Kegel (1987), 334.

[97] Nussbaum, *Deutsches Internationales Privatrecht* (1974), 65; Kegel, *Internationales Privatrecht* (1987), 326.

[98] Such as the German decree depriving expatriate Jews of German citizenship, *Oppenheimer v Cattermole*, 27 ILR 446.

[99] Such as the confiscatory decree of the Revolutionary Command Council of Iraq, *Kuwait Air Corp.* (HL), 16 May 2002, para. 2 (*per* Lord Nicholls).

[100] Zweigert and Kötz, *Introduction to Comparative Law* (1998), 381.

[101] Jaenicke (1967), 78–79; Nussbaum (1974), 65; Bleckmann (1974), 113, 128; Niederer (1956), 297, referring to national public order clauses extended to non-contractual acts.

[102] North and Fawcett, *Cheshire and North's Private International Law* (1999), 124.

[103] Nussbaum, *Deutsches Internationales Privatrecht* (1974), 67; Battifol and Lagarde, 574.

referred to as the positive effect of public order.[104] For example, if a foreign couple cannot marry under the law of their country because this law prohibits marriage for confessional motives, the negative effect of French public order is to exclude the foreign law that prohibits the marriage in question, and its positive effect is the application of the relevant norms of French law governing marriages.[105] Positive effect of public order is also observable in the case of internal public order related to contractual derogations from laws protecting good morals and public order, as outlawed, for example, under Article 6 of the French Civil Code.[106]

2.5. Interim conclusions

The scope of public policy and the factors that inform it, as well as the peculiarities of its specific effects in different national legal systems, do not totally overlap. National legal systems can differ in understanding the function, scope and extent of the relevance of public order. Nevertheless, there is a certain core and minimum common denominator informing and reinforcing the concept of every national public order to protect the forum's fundamental interests and sentiments from the effects of acts accomplished both within and outside the forum's legal system.

3. THE PROPER INTERNATIONAL PUBLIC ORDER

3.1. The relevance of national public policy in international law

Private international law is part of the law of individual States. Subject only to the general standards of public international law, such as the general obligations related to the application of foreign laws, it is determined by the policies, traditions and standards of justice of the individual countries.[107] General international law, as opposed to particular treaties, is not concerned with the regulation of collision norms within national legal systems.[108] Every State is generally free to choose the collision norms it considers best suitable.

Public international law regulates the relations between States. The opposability of national public policies on an international plane, against an international obligation, is controversial. Some private international law

---

[104] Batiffol, H., and Lagarde, P., *Traité de Droit International Privé* (Tome 1, Paris, 1993), 591. referring to 'substitution de la loi française à la loi normalement compétente'. Pillet and Niboyet, *Manuel de Droit International Privé* (II-1924), 419; Meyer, *Droit International Privé* (1994), 145; Nussbaum, *Deutsches Internationales Privatrecht* (1974), 69; Kegel, *Internationales Privatrecht* (1987), 335; Kropholler, *Internationales Privatrecht* (1997), 233.

[105] Pillet and Niboyet, *Manuel de Droit International Privé* (II-1924), 419–420.

[106] Kropholler, *Internationales Privatrecht* (1997), 224.

[107] Lipstein, Principles of the Conflict of Laws: National and International (1981), 64, 80.

[108] Kropholler, *Internationales Privatrecht* (1997), 49–50.

conventions permit States to use their public order clauses, because its absence could endanger the prospects of ratification by States.[109] On the other hand, such clauses can easily endanger the purposes of such conventions.[110] According to one view, public order clauses in treaties enable States-parties to unilaterally influence the scope of treaty obligations and hence such clauses should be omitted from treaties wherever possible.[111]

Whatever the merits of conventional public policy clauses, it seems clear that if a convention contains no such clause, its scope cannot be influenced by national public policies. The application of public order can be excluded by a treaty and public order cannot be invoked if this would contradict a treaty obligation. When, for instance, a convention exclusively lists the conditions preventing marriage, the court of a State-party cannot invoke public order to justify a ground prohibiting marriage that is not mentioned in that convention. This would be contrary to international law.[112]

The issue of whether national public order can affect the scope of international treaty obligations arose in the *Guardianship of Infants* case between the Netherlands and Sweden before the International Court of Justice. Under the 1902 Convention, the guardianship of infants is governed by the national law of the infant and the issue was whether that Convention prohibited the application of laws such as the Swedish law on protective upbringing of children, which Sweden justified by reference to its *ordre public*. The Court avoided the issue of public order and decided the case on other grounds. It justified the Swedish law as an element of social progress to which the letter of the 1902 Convention should not be an obstacle.[113] Although Wilfried Jenks and Henri Rolin considered this as an implicit and concealed application of public policy as a factor qualifying the scope of treaty obligations,[114] it is still the case that the Court has not expressly based its decision on national public policy. The Court took its approach presumably because it considered that the protective upbringing of children was socially progressive as such, and not necessarily because it was part of domestic public order.

Individual judges have extensively dealt with the issue of public order. Judges Spender and Winiarski considered that the applicability of a treaty

---

[109] Judge Badawi in *Guardianship of Infants, ICJ Reports*, 1958, 75; Judge Spender, id., 124–130; Judge Cordova, id., 140.

[110] Raape, *Internationales Privatrecht* (1961), 100; Nussbaum, *Deutsches Internationales Privatrecht* (1974), 62. Cf also Kropholler, *Internationales Privatrecht* (1997), 234.

[111] Wolff, *Das Internationale Privatrecht Deutschlands* (1954), 70.

[112] Nussbaum, *Deutsches Internationales Privatrecht* (1974), 70; Kegel, *Internationales Privatrecht* (1987), 334. Only one author supports the view that public order can exclude the foreign rule that is applicable under the treaty, Niederer, *Einführung in die Allgemeine Lehren des Internationalen Privatrechts* (1956), 298–299.

[113] *ICJ Reports*, 1958, 71.

[114] Jenks, *The Prospects of International Adjudication* (1964), 432; Rolin, H., Vers un ordre public réellement international, in *Hommage d'une génération des Juristes au President Basdevant* (Paris, 1961), 447.

obligation is not qualified by national public policy which has no independent relevance in international law.[115] Judges Lauterpacht and Badawi saw, however, some room for national public order as qualifying the treaty obligations,[116] either because the Convention was deemed to contain an implied reservation allowing the public order laws to override the terms of the 1902 Convention, or because this followed from the character of the Convention as a private international law treaty. Judge Cordova dismissed the relevance of public order by pointing out that a treaty on private international law is in the first place an international treaty embodying the will of sovereign States and it is unclear how an exception that States-parties did not write into the Convention could be implicitly inferred from it.[117]

It seems that the national public policy, something that is not *per se* part of public international law and has no inherent normative value in the international legal system, should have no independent standing to qualify the scope of international obligations. This corresponds to the general principle that municipal laws are merely facts whose legality is to be judged in terms of international law.[118] According to Article 27 of the 1969 Vienna Convention on the Law of Treaties, a State cannot rely on its national law to justify non-compliance with its treaty obligations. As Fitzmaurice observes, even if the national public order exception can be viewed as a general principle of law, the *lex specialis* principle prevents it from superseding or overriding treaty obligations. Otherwise, the outcome could be reached that can be quite risky for the stability of treaty obligations.[119]

Even less is it permissible to allow the flexible and ever-changing concept of national public policy to serve as an exception to treaty obligations. This would grant States the power of auto-interpretation of their treaty obligations: international tribunals judging the compliance with the treaty cannot construe the scope of national public policies on their own but would instead have to rely on the construction made by the State, which means that the State could unilaterally modify the scope of its treaty obligations as it pleases.

---

[115] *ICJ Reports*, 1958, 128–129, 136–137.

[116] *ICJ Reports*, 1958, 74 ff., 94. For a detailed examination of the Judgment and individual opinions see Jenks, *The Prospects of International Adjudication* (1964), 432–441, and Eek (1973), 41–47.

[117] Judge Cordova, *ICJ Report* 1958, 141 also referred to the principle *pacta sunt servanda*, which makes it impossible for States to release themselves unilaterally from treaties they have signed.

[118] *Certain German Interests in Polish Upper Silesia*, PCIJ Series A, No. 7, 19. In *Free Zones*, the Permanent Court noted that a State cannot refer to its domestic legislation in order to limit the scope of its international obligations, PCIJ Series A/B, No. 46, 167.

[119] As Fitzmaurice further observes, 'Considered as a general principle of universal application, it [ie a national public order clause] would afford plausible ground for non-compliance with any public international law obligation, and would therefore, regarded as a generally applicable ground of exception to international law obligations, be quite unacceptable'. Fitzmaurice, The Law and Procedure of the International Court of Justice, *BYIL* 1959, 223–224.

3.2. The necessity of international public order

National courts would not normally apply the public policy of foreign legal systems,[120] but only their own public policy.[121] Given this, and also that national public orders have no inherent normative value in international law, the only public order to which international courts and tribunals competent to administer international law can refer is the public order of international law. The question thus arises whether there is a proper international public policy which, in a manner similar to the operation of national public policies in national legal systems, protects the fundamental interests of the international community, qualifies the scope and affects the validity of conflicting norms, acts and transactions.

It is contended that international courts can have their own public order to the extent that they have their own *lex fori*.[122] It is even contended that international courts do not have their own *lex fori* and the only public order that such courts could apply is natural law.[123] But international courts do have their own *lex fori* as determined by their constitutive instruments. The *lex fori* of some international courts is limited to a specific treaty (the European Court of Human Rights is competent to apply the European Convention on Human Rights), while the competence of the International Court of Justice extends to the entire body of international law as determined in Article 38 of its Statute. There is nothing precluding tribunals like these from identifying and applying public order following from their *lex fori*.

Teachings of private international law accept that there can be a proper international public order common to all nations in the sense of public international law. In this sense, a treaty authorizing slavery is contrary to international public order.[124] These teachings make a difference between public order as part of national law, and universal public order or *ordre public vraiment international* of the international community of States, which follows from *jus cogens* of supranational law, and this latter category can only

---

[120] Batiffol, H., and Lagarde, P., *Traité de Droit International Privé* (Tome 1, Paris, 1993), 589–590; Nussbaum, *Deutsches Internationales Privatrecht* (1974), 66–67; Kropholler, *Internationales Privatrecht* (1997), 236; Wolff, *Das Internationale Privatrecht Deutschlands* (1954), 71.

[121] Pillet and Niboyet, *Manuel de Droit International Privé* (II-1924), 421–422 speak of the 'reflexive' effect of foreign public order within the forum's legal system, as illustrated by the recognition by a French court of the marriage of a Polish couple in Belgium which recognized the secularity of marriage (which formed part of Belgian public order), contrary to Polish laws that regulated the matter differently. But this seems just an application of a foreign law that is consistent with French legal system and public order rather than any inherent reflexive effect of foreign public order. Batiffol, H., and Lagarde, P., *Traité de Droit International Privé* (Tome 1, Paris, 1993), 590, also consider this as a case where foreign public order overlapped with French public order and exactly this factor justified the solution that was adopted. For a similar outcome see Wolff, *Das Internationale Privatrecht Deutschlands* (1954), 71.

[122] Nussbaum, *Deutsches Internationales Privatrecht* (1974), 71.

[123] Niederer, *Einführung in die Allgemeine Lehren des Internationalen Privatrechts* (1956), 301.

[124] Pillet and Niboyet, *Manuel de Droit International Privé* (II-1924), 418.

exist as a genuine norm of international law and be applicable by international courts.[125]

In the domain of public international law, the existence of public order has been affirmed unambiguously. A minimum core of norms and principles safeguarding certain higher interests from being frustrated by transactions between legal persons is presumed to exist in every legal system. According to McNair,

> It is difficult to imagine any society, whether of individuals or of States, whose law sets no limit whatever to freedom of contract. In every civilised community there are some rules of law and some principles of morality which individuals are not permitted by law to ignore or to modify by their agreements. The maxim *modus et conventio vincunt legem* does not apply to imperative provisions of the law or of public policy; *pacta, quae contra leges constitutionesque vel contra bonos mores fiunt, nullam vim habere, indubidati juris est;* and *privatorum conventio juri publico non derogat*.
>
> The society of States—which acknowledges obedience to the rules of international law—forms no exception to the principles stated above.[126]

This statement refers to a legal necessity, to something indispensable for a legal order such as is assumed to exist in international law. These are 'imperative provisions of the law or of public policy' producing exceptional legal effects. McNair refers interchangeably to public policy and imperative law.

The similar reference to the factor of necessity can be seen in the pronouncement of the Japanese court, emphasizing that 'so long as international law is law, the legal effect of agreements between nations which are contrary to the "public order and good manners" as an ideal or fundamental value by which all legal systems of civilised nations are established, cannot be admitted.'[127]

Judge Moreno-Quintana suggested in the *Guardianship of Infants* case that there is a proper international public policy:

> International public order operates within the limits of system of public international law, when it lays down certain principles such as the general principles of the law of nations and the fundamental rights of States, respect for which is indispensable to the legal coexistence of the political units which make up the international community. ... These principles—we are all quite familiar with them because they are very limited—and these rights, too, have a peremptory character and universal scope.[128]

International public order is thus a body of rules deriving from international law as such,[129] and governs the relations between States.[130] It is something

---

[125] Niederer, *Einführung in die Allgemeine Lehren des Internationalen Privatrechts* (1956), 289.

[126] McNair (1961), 213–214; Verdross (1937), 572; Minagawa (1968), 18; Kolb (2001), 172; UNCLT Second Session (1969), 97 (UK).

[127] Decision of the Tokyo District Court, 28 February 1966, 13 *Japanese Annual of International Law* (1969), 115.

[128] Separate Opinion of Judge Moreno-Quintana, *ICJ Reports*, 1958, 106–107.

[129] Jaenicke (1967), 80; Virally (1966), 8.   [130] Van der Meersch (1968), 99.

more than national public orders, even as national public orders can overlap in substance.[131] Its character and scope is shaped by the system of international law.[132]

Arguably peremptory norms are not the only element of international public order. The latter could also include foundational principles of international law such as sovereign equality.[133] This solution would leave open the purpose of such categorization, as to be part of public order a norm must prevail over conflicting transactions.[134] Conceivably, international law adopts a different and original solution, but the whole question is outside the ambit of this work, which focuses on the public order character of peremptory norms only.

Some are reluctant to recognize that peremptory norms reflect international public policy, since public policy is said to protect the domestic law of a State through repelling the impact of incompatible norms and principles of foreign law.[135] Sztucki disputes the link between *jus cogens* and public policy on empirical grounds, suggesting that in drafting the Vienna Convention the ILC 'formally abandoned' the link between the two concepts: the concept of public policy appeared neither in Waldock's latest reports nor in the ILC's final report.[136] But the argument is unpersuasive, not least because the issues of *jus cogens* were dealt with by the ILC from the perspective of the law of treaties only. In any event, the ILC has never formally separated the two concepts. Sztucki himself emphasizes that such a separation is illogical.[137]

De-linking peremptory norms from the concept of public order is inadequate as it ignores the inherent rationale and scope of public policy, which encompasses both internal and external aspects with regard to conflicting acts and transactions. Along with overriding incompatible foreign laws, the function of public order is to ensure the imperative application of certain national laws in the face of conflicting acts and transactions of private persons.[138] Imperative, or peremptory, public order norms cannot be set aside by the will of the parties, and a direct reference in this regard is made to legislative provisions outlawing contracts which are against good morals and public order.[139] In line with this, Judge Moreno-Quintana understood public order

---

[131] Jaenicke (1967), 81.   [132] Levi (1994), 56.

[133] Jaenicke, International Public Order, 7 *EPIL* (Amsterdam, 1984), 315.

[134] Jaenicke accepts that, id., 316.

[135] Mosler, Ius Cogens im Völkerrecht, 25 *Schweizerisches Jahrbuch für Internationales Recht* (1968), 23; Sinclair, *The Vienna Convention on the Law of Treaties* (1986), 204.

[136] Sztucki (1974), 9–10.   [137] Id., 10.

[138] Suy, The Concept of Jus Cogens in International Law, *Lagonissi Conference: Papers and Proceedings*, vol II, Carnegie Endowment for International Peace (1967), 23–24; van der Meersch (1968), 97–98, especially referring to English law; Batiffol and Lagarde (1993), 569. For English law see Beatson, *Anson's Law of Contract* (2002), 352–353.

[139] Batiffol and Lagarde (1993), 584; Nussbaum (1974), 60–61, referring to the link between peremptory norms and public order made by Savigny. Münch (1983), 619. References are made to Article 6 of the French Civil Code, Article 138 of the German Civil Code, Article 12 of the Preliminary Provisions of the Italian Civil Code. For public policy with regard to contract in English law see *Chitty on Contracts* (1999), 835–839.

as 'the whole body of laws and legal instruments whose legal principles cannot be set at naught either by special conventions or by a foreign law'.[140] Also, extension of the effects of *jus cogens* beyond the law of treaties, especially its comprehension of the validity of acts accomplished within legal systems other than international law, conceptually reinforces its link with public order designed to repel incompatible laws or acts performed within another legal system.

The link between *jus cogens* and public policy was affirmed before the adoption of Article 53 of the Vienna Convention. Jenks considered that nothing in the nature of public international law precluded recourse to the concept of proper international public policy. It can have the effect of *jus cogens* precluding the consent of parties to agreements or wrongs inconsistent with international public policy, but also serve as a climate of interpretation of the intention of the parties to treaties.[141] Rolin has viewed the international law standard of the voidness of immoral treaties as an aspect of public order in international law. He made reference to doctrinal writings from eighteenth century onwards emphasizing that treaties and customs shall not have an immoral object and content.[142] Similar conclusions were suggested by Van der Meersch.[143] Jaenicke refers to international *ordre public* which is part of the international legal system as distinct from national legal systems. It is something more than national public orders, even as national public orders can overlap in substance. According to Jaenicke, international public order is possible only if *jus cogens* is accepted; in outlawing conflicting treaties, *jus cogens* operates as public order.[144]

As Dugard suggests, *jus cogens* inevitably reflects public policy.[145] Meron affirms that the underlying concepts of *jus cogens* and international public order are the same: both operate in an absolute way and are non-derogable.[146] According to Jaenicke, international public order is possible only if *jus cogens* is accepted; in outlawing conflicting treaties, *jus cogens* operates as public order.[147] The history of Article 53 of the Vienna Convention demonstrates

---

[140] Separate Opinion of Judge Moreno-Quintana, *ICJ Reports*, 1958, 105.

[141] Jenks, *The Prospects of International Adjudication* (1964), 457–458.

[142] Rolin, H., Vers un ordre public réellement international, in *Hommage d'une génération des Juristes au President Basdevant* (Paris, 1961), 451–454.

[143] Van der Meersch, Does the Convention have the Power of 'Ordre Public' in Municipal Law? Robertson (ed.), *Human Rights in National and International Law* (1968), 99–101.

[144] Jaenicke, Zur Frage des Internationalen Ordre Public, 7 *Berichte der Deutschen Gesellschaft für Völkerrecht* (1967), 80–81, 88–90, 96.

[145] Dugard, *Recognition and the United Nations* (1987), 149; Dhokalia (1972), 175–176.

[146] Meron (1986), 198; Dupuy (2002), 282–283.

[147] Jaenicke (1967), 96; Saladin, Völkerrechtliches Jus Cogens und Schweizerisches Landesrecht, Jenny and Kälin, *Die Schweizerische Rechtsordnung in Ihren Internationalen Bezügen* (1988), 70; Ford, Adjudicating *Jus Cogens*, 13 *Wisconsin International Law Journal* (1994), 147; Sudre, Existe-t-il un ordre public Européen? Tavernier, *Quelle Europe pour les droits de l'homme?* (1966), 41–42; Virally (1966), 11; Shelton (2003), 159; Sur, (1972), 175 suggests that international *jus cogens* is similar to national public orders voiding contracts.

that it refers to international public order. Special Rapporteur Lauterpacht linked the illegality of the object of treaties to violations of international public order,[148] and Special Rapporteur Waldock also emphasized that voiding treaties for their illegality of object in contradiction with a peremptory norm 'presupposes the existence of an international public order containing rules having the character of *jus cogens*'.[149] At the time when the Vienna Convention was drafted, the concept of *jus cogens* was essentially associated with international public order,[150] and at the Vienna Conference, the latter notion was preferred by some delegations to that of *jus cogens*.[151] Article 53 is anyway similar to the provisions in national legal systems outlawing agreements against good morals and public order.

In short, international public policy has the same conceptual basis and function as public policies in national legal systems, but with certain differences. International public order does not admit any differentiation between internal and external aspects of public order similar to *ordre public interne* and *ordre public international* in national legal systems, or any doctrines of relativity. National legal systems are territorially limited and designed to apply to persons and events within their territorial limits or the conduct of their nationals. That is why they are *national* legal systems. This is furthermore why they tolerate certain foreign laws or certain situations remote from the forum's legal system even if these *prima facie* contradict the forum's public policy. Therefore, national public orders are nationally and territorially oriented and sometimes limited by the doctrines of relativity. The international legal system is, on the other hand, designed to apply to the entire international legal community and no act or situation contradicting international law can be remote from that legal system. Hence, the doctrines of relativity can have no meaningful sense in terms of international public order. If an act or law enacted or performed within a national legal system contradicts international public order, it becomes directly relevant in terms of the operation of the international legal system and is subject to its sanctions.

National legal systems are independent of each other, but they are not similarly independent of international law. The law of one country does not bind other States, but international law binds all States. A provision of national law is not an excuse for non-compliance with international law. Hence, a true international public order cannot operate in a differentiated way: it has to apply with equal force to acts whether performed on a national or international plane.

---

[148] Report on the Law of Treaties, YbILC 1954(II), 154–155.
[149] YbILC 1963(II), 52.
[150] YbILC 1963(I), 63 (Yasseen), 65 (Pal), 66 (Bartos).
[151] UNCLT First Session (1969), 323 (Switzerland).

4. OBJECTIONS TO INTERNATIONAL PUBLIC ORDER

4.1. Objections to the concept of peremptory law

The idea of international public order has not met a unanimous doctrinal welcome.[152] Although the existence of *jus cogens* is clearly recognized in the Vienna Convention on the Law of Treaties as well as practice, it seems opportune to deal with some principal objections, as they are helpful in clarifying specific questions of the nature and effects of international public order.

Guggenheim considers that the concept of *jus cogens* or public order that causes the nullity of conflicting acts does not find any confirmation in customary international law.[153] Apart from the fact that this view is no longer in conformity with the state of customary law, it is unclear in which form or way customary law is supposed to reflect *jus cogens*. Whether or not the practice in customary law is reflective of *jus cogens*, its existence is linked with public order that is an inherent element of every legal system.

Schwarzenberger is concerned that *jus cogens* would interfere with bilateral legal relations based on the principles of consent and *pacta sunt servanda*, and could assist States unwilling to comply with their treaty obligations unilaterally to absolve themselves from those obligations.[154] This objection hints at the true function of *jus cogens*. According to Simma, the concept of *jus cogens* invests norms created in the community interest with the 'destructive capacity' to invalidate conflicting legal acts.[155] This is to deprive the authors of such acts of their ensuing legal security. As Frowein indicates, even if the dangers outlined by Weil should not be overlooked, no retreat would seem possible.[156]

Doctrinal concerns as to the possible detrimental impact of *jus cogens* on the stability of treaty relations have been overcome in practice also. The European Court of Human Rights faced a plea in *Soering* that the overriding impact of the prohibition of torture under Article 3 of the European Convention on Human Rights, justifying non-compliance with extradition requests based on bilateral extradition treaties, endangered the stability of treaty relations and involved adjudication on internal affairs of third States not parties to the proceedings.[157] But the Court upheld the overriding effect of Article 3 and by implication tolerated some dangers to legal stability and the routine expectations of the States concerned. *Soering* involved no issue of

---

[152] For the overview of objections see Dugard (1987), 147ff, and Virally (1966), 20ff.
[153] Guggenheim, La validité et la nullité des actes juridiques internationaux, *RdC* (I-1949), 196–197.
[154] Schwarzenberger, The Problem of International Public Policy, 18 *Current Legal Problems* (1965), 213–214.
[155] Simma, From Bilateralism to Community Interest, 250 *RdC* (1994), 285.
[156] Frowein (1994), 365.   [157] Soering, 98 ILR 300.

treaty validity and hence Article 53 of the Vienna Convention was not invoked, but in construing treaty rights and obligations, the Court nevertheless treated the prohibition of torture as a superior limitation.

Weil contends that the concept of *jus cogens* relativizes normativity and divides rules into 'norms and norms' with 'more or less' force.[158] But the differentiation of norms is accepted in all legal systems. Weil's description misrepresents the true state of things, because this differentiation does not question the normative force of ordinary norms as far as they go; it merely determines the limits on their ambit.

Schwarzenberger contends that '*jus cogens*, as distinct from *jus dispositivum*, presupposes the existence of an effective *de jure* order, which has at its disposal legislative and judicial machinery, able to formulate rules of public policy and, in the last resort, can rely on overwhelming physical force'.[159] This contention does not suffer from originality. Similar grounds were invoked as denying the legal character of international law itself, because of its decentralized character, but they are now abandoned as anachronistic.

There is nothing in the decentralized nature of international law to preclude the notion of international public order,[160] especially its invalidating effect on conflicting acts. As Judge Winiarski noted, 'The view that it is only possible to rely on the rule relating to nullities where some procedure for this purpose is established, finds no support in international law'.[161] As the ILC emphasized, 'whatever imperfections international law may still have, the view that there is no rule from which States cannot at their free will contract out has become increasingly difficult to sustain'.[162] Writing before the Vienna Convention on the Law of Treaties was adopted, Sir Robert Jennings accepted that the existence of *jus cogens* marks an entry into a more advanced state of development of the law, and concluded that 'that stage has been reached'.[163]

The Vienna Convention recognizes public order norms even though these do not fall within the competence of a centralized and impartial institutional body. Article 66 of the Convention states that disputes involving the *jus cogens* invalidity of treaties under Articles 53 and 64 may be referred to the

[158] Weil, Towards Relative Normativity in International Law? *AJIL* (1983), 421.

[159] Schwarzenberger, *A Manual of International Law* (1967), 29–30; Schwarzenberger (1965), 212; *per contra* van Hoof, *Rethinking the Sources of International Law* (1983), 155–156. As shown below, Schwarzenberger denies the existence of *jus cogens* in terms of public order as understood in national legal systems, but supports the concept of *jus cogens* as public order linked to the decentralized structure of international law.

[160] Levi (1994), 59.

[161] Opinion of Judge Winiarski, *Effect of Awards, ICJ Reports*, 1954, 65; this view effectively contradicts the view of Guggenheim (1949), 207–208, that nullity in international law is possible in the case of existence of the institutional body that makes constitutive declarations of nullity.

[162] YbILC 1963(II), 198; for Waldock's identical view see id., 52.

[163] Jennings, Nullity and Effectiveness in International Law, *Cambridge Essays in International Law* (1965), 74.

International Court, but this falls short of making substantive invalidity dependent on the functioning of dispute-settlement mechanisms. Articles 65–66 of the Vienna Convention relate to the settlement of treaty disputes only and not to the invalidity of a treaty as such.[164] At the Vienna Conference the notion of *jus cogens* was upheld and the arguments concerning the relevance of institutional safeguards were outweighed by the necessity to recognize the effect of certain overriding norms.[165] This latter view prevailed, reflecting the argument of necessity in the spirit of McNair's approach.

4.2. Objections to the relevance and character of peremptory norms

A separate group of objections raised against peremptory norms proceed from the acknowledgment that it is no longer realistic to challenge the concept of peremptory norms and argue that the character of the international legal system tolerates no public order norms. The normative and practical evidence makes these assumptions unworkable. Therefore, the reluctance towards international *jus cogens* is expressed not through its denial but through doubting its relevance and practical viability.

Some would consider *jus cogens* not as an operational concept but as an instrument of dissuasion.[166] According to Czaplinski and Danilenko, *jus cogens* does not play a major role in the international practice which relates to the conflict between international legal rules, because States are not willing to declare their own acts invalid. Therefore, *de lege lata* the concept of peremptory norms is 'more a theoretical concept rather than a practical regulation'.[167] According to Charlesworth and Chinkin, 'much of the importance of the *jus cogens* doctrine lies not in its practical application but in its symbolic significance in the international legal process'.[168]

The value of such objections does not exceed that of theoretical conjectures. To begin with, the attempt to distinguish between dissuasive and operational aspects of *jus cogens* is conceptually flawed. While it is perfectly true that peremptory norms are meant to dissuade States from entering into certain kinds of transaction, such dissuasion is possible only through the operative effects of peremptory norms. To illustrate, the prohibition of

---

[164] Simma (1994), 289.

[165] For instance, as the Israeli delegation noted, development of *jus cogens* does not depend on the existence of procedural rules, and compulsory settlement is not inherently tied to *jus cogens*, since the means of settlement are not compulsory under the UN Charter. UNCLT First Session (1969), 310.

[166] Sorel, L'avenir du 'crime' en droit international à la lumière de l'experience du *jus cogens*, 23 *Polish Yearbook of International Law* (1997–98), 72.

[167] Czaplinski and Danilenko, Conflicts of Norms in International Law, 21 *Netherlands Yearbook of International Law* (1990), 11, 42.

[168] Charlesworth and Chinkin, The gender of *jus cogens*, 15 *Human Rights Quarterly* (1993), 66.

derogation from peremptory norms would not dissuade States unless it is made clear that the transactions based on such derogation are null and void. The argument of Czaplinski and Danilenko that the unwillingness of States to invalidate their own acts deprives *jus cogens* of its practical meaning is also misguided. The viability of public order invalidity does not depend on the attitudes of States. The very fact that two States have entered into the agreement authorizing or condoning the breach of peremptory norms means that this transaction responds to their interests. It is therefore quite conceivable that they may resist the application of nullity. This, however, does not affect the principle that such agreements are null and void.

As for the more general contention about the theoretical or symbolic character of peremptory norms, the careful analysis of the fields of State practice in which *jus cogens* has found application will easily prove that the attempts to see *jus cogens* as the merely symbolic concept does not rest on sound conceptual or evidential basis. The concept of peremptory norms is accepted in several fields of international law as that of the norms of operative design producing specifically defined legal consequences in relation to specific legal relations. The will of the international community to view *jus cogens* in such a way is evidenced, among others, by the provisions of the 1969 Vienna Convention foreseeing the detailed legal consequences for treaties contradicting *jus cogens*, as well as for example by the adherence to the doctrine of non-recognition. This normative framework leaves little space for the viability of theories portraying peremptory norms as no more than aspirational norms.

2

The Identification of Peremptory Norms

I. GENERAL ISSUES

The identification of the peremptory character of a norm requires a multi-level analysis: the categorical argument focuses on the basic nature of peremptory norms, on factors that make a norm peremptory; the normative argument examines whether a norm categorically qualifying as part of *jus cogens* is so recognized under international law.

In national legal systems, public order norms can be enacted by the legislator or be accepted due to their subject-matter as self-evident even where the legislation does not expressly refer to it, as unwritten or customary law. In international law, a norm cannot become part of public order through legislation, as in this decentralized legal system the law-making is concentrated in the hands of legal persons and they can change the law by agreement. Public order operates as a matter of necessity and factors other than State will are necessary to comprehend this phenomenon.

This perhaps suggests that consensual positivism cannot be the proper approach for explaining the existence and operation of peremptory norms, and some alternative approach must be sought. There is strong doctrinal support for the idea that *jus cogens* has its roots in the natural law doctrine of classical international law,[1] or embodies natural law propositions applicable to all legal systems.[2]

The idea of the law that stands above inter-State transactions is indeed developed by classical writers. Wolff suggested the notion of 'the necessary law of nations which consists in the law of nature applied to nations'. The law of nature is immutable and hence 'the necessary law of nations also is absolutely immutable'. Consequently, 'neither can any nation free itself nor can any nation free another from it'.[3] This natural law of nations is, according to Vattel, '*necessary*, because Nations are absolutely bound to observe it'. The necessary law of nations 'is not subject to change'. 'Nations cannot alter it by agreement, nor individually or mutually release themselves from it.'[4]

---

[1] Dugard, *Recognition and the United Nations* (1987), 137.

[2] Charney, Universal International Law, *AJIL* (1993) 541.

[3] Wolff, *The Law of Nations Treated according to a Scientific Method*, in Scott (ed.), *Classics of International Law* (Oxford 1934), 10.

[4] Vattel, *The Law of Nations or the Principles of Natural Law applied to the Conduct and to the Affairs of Nations and of Sovereigns*, in Scott (ed.), *Classics of International Law* (Washington 1916), 4 (emphasis original).

It is clear that Wolff and Vattel effectively submit that the immutable norms of the law of nature admit of no derogation. This also implies that the 'positive law of nations which takes its origin from the will of nations' and consists of stipulative and customary law,[5] is subject to the immutable law of nature. Vattel expressly maintains this position by submitting that

It is by the application of this principle that a distinction can be made between lawful and unlawful treaties or conventions and between customs which are innocent and reasonable and those which are unjust and deserving of condemnation.

Things which are just in themselves and permitted by the necessary Law of Nations may form the subject of an agreement by Nations or may be given sacredness and force through force and custom. Indifferent affairs may be settled either by treaty, if Nations so please, or by the introduction of some suitable custom or usage. But all treaties and customs contrary to the dictates of the necessary law of nations are unlawful.[6]

Thus Vattel emphasized the principle of *lex specialis* which generally allows States to derogate from or modify general international law. However, the same principle no longer stands when the agreements between States conflict with the immutable law of nations. As Vattel's analysis of the essence of peremptory law in international relations could not be more precise, the basic question to be addressed is whether it is natural law that provides the foundation for that peremptory law.

There is also the argument both in doctrine and practice that the natural law reinforcement for international *jus cogens* was demonstrated in the Trials of the Major War Criminals at Nuremberg. The key for individual criminal responsibility of the perpetrators was not that those norms were binding on the State for which they acted on the basis of its consent, but on the character of the acts themselves whose prohibition and criminality were self-evident with or without State consent.[7]

The concept of *jus cogens* requires re-examination of the positivist approach,[8] and this is likewise affirmed by those who oppose the concept of international public order.[9] Verdross observed that the existence of *jus cogens* was not doubted before the positivist doctrinal takeover.[10] Arguably, 'the

---

[5] Wolff, 18–19.   [6] Vattel, 4–5.

[7] Belski *et al.*, Implied Waiver under the FSIA: A Proposed Exception to Immunity for Violations of Peremptory Norms of International Law, 77 *California Law Review* (1989), 385–387; *Siderman de Blake v Argentina*, US Court of Appeals (Ninth Circuit), 103 ILR 471.

[8] Visscher, Positivisme et 'jus cogens', 40 *RGDIP* (1971), 6; Lauterpacht, I *Collected Papers*, (1970), 357–358.

[9] Guggenheim, La validité et la nullité des actes juridiques internationales, *RdC* (I-1949), 197.

[10] Verdross, Forbidden Treaties in International Law, *AJIL* (1937), 571; see also Danilenko, *Law-Making in the International Community* (1993), 215–216; Parker and Neylon (1989), 419–422; Nieto-Navia, International Peremptory Norms (*Jus Cogens*) and International Humanitarian Law, L.C. Vorhah *et al.* (eds.), *Man's Inhumanity to Man, Essays on International Law in Honour of Antonio Cassese* (2003), 601.

conception of *jus cogens* will remain incomplete as long as it is not based on philosophy of values like natural law' as *jus cogens* grew out of the naturalist school.[11] Alternatively, *jus cogens* is not natural law but the expression of common legal order within the community of nations reflecting their historically created common conviction.[12] As Kolb points out, natural law relates to the creation and modification of law, while *jus cogens* relates to the derogation from a general legal regime.[13]

Jus cogens is similar to natural law in that it is not the product of the will of States and hence not comprehensible through a strict positivist approach. But, even if *jus cogens* resembles natural law, the crucial question still is not whether a norm is part of natural law, but whether it is of such character as to prevail over positive law. In this sense, *jus cogens* appears more cognate to *jus necessarium*—another concept developed in classical doctrine and denoting the body of rules binding without and despite the agreement of States.[14] However, *jus cogens* is not absolutely identical with any of these discussed notions, which were developed earlier than *jus cogens* in its present form emerged as a free-standing concept, and hence cannot explain all its peculiarities. Although it is correct that *jus cogens* requires the re-examination of the traditional positivist consensual approach, at least to the extent of the ambit within which *jus cogens* operates, this exercise does not necessarily entail the reversion to the classical natural law approaches, but rather requires consideration of the character and effects of public order norms.

2. GENERAL, REGIONAL AND BILATERAL NORMS

It is contended that peremptory law can be produced on an *inter se* basis,[15] that is there can be bilateral *jus cogens*. Such possibility would, however, involve a contradiction in terms. As Verdross submits, 'even if we admit the very improbable consensus of two States to the creation of such a norm,

---

[11] Simma, *The Contribution of Alfred Verdross to the Theory of International Law*, 6 *EJIL* (1995), 34, 51–54; Charney, Universal International Law, *AJIL* (1993), 541; Janis, The Nature of *Jus Cogens, Connecticut JIL* (1988), 361–362; Parker and Neylon, *Jus Cogens*: Compelling the Law of Human Rights, 12 *Hastings International and Comparative Law Review* (1989), 423; Gormley, The Right to Life and The Rule of Non-Derogability: Peremptory Norms of *Jus Cogens*, Ramcharan (ed.), *The Right to Life in International Law* (1985), 122.

[12] Scheuner, Conflict of Treaty Provisions with a Peremptory Norm of General International Law, 29 *Zeitschrift für ausländisches öffentliches Recht und Völkerrecht* (1969), 30.

[13] Kolb, Théorie du *ius cogens* international, *Revue Belge de Droit International* (2003/1), 14.

[14] Nussbaum, *The Concise History of the Law of Nations* (1964), 153; Abi-Saab, The Concept of *Jus Cogens* in International Law, 2 *Lagonissi Conference: Papers and Proceedings*, vol. II, Carnegie Endowment for International Peace (1967), 12–13.

[15] Rozakis, *The Concept of Jus Cogens in the Law of Treaties* (1976), 56; Kolb, Formal Source of *Ius Cogens* in Public International Law, 53 *Zeitschrift für öffentliches Recht* (1998), 99–102.

there is no doubt that its abrogation by the same parties is always possible. Consequently there is no room for its application at all.'[16]

The issue whether peremptory norms are part of general international law or there can also be a regional *jus cogens* is a subject of doctrinal debates. The desirability of regional *jus cogens* has been emphasized by a number of authors, but without adducing any significant normative or practical evidence to support this view. It is nevertheless contended that the formation of regional *jus cogens* is possible since within a limited group of States the concurrence of attitudes is more likely than at a universal level.[17] Such regional peremptory norms would bind only States belonging to a given regional group.[18]

The principal obstacle to the existence of regional *jus cogens* is that the definition of *jus cogens* under Article 53 of the Vienna Convention refers to norms of general international law accepted by the entire international community of States, which seems to exclude regional norms. The preparatory work of Article 53 is also clear that this provision covers only general international law.

To prove that regional *jus cogens* exists, Kolb insists that Article 53 defines peremptory norms 'for the purposes of the present Convention', which he understands as evidence that in the ILC work and later at the Vienna Conference, 'far from being excluded, regional *jus cogens* was simply not examined'. Consequently, the wording of Article 53 does not reject the notion of regional *jus cogens*.[19] However, the fact that Article 53 does not refer to regional *jus cogens* means that it does not admit that they have the force to invalidate incompatible treaties. Moreover, Kolb's account of the ILC's work is not quite accurate, because the ILC Drafting Committee made it clear that the reference to the norms of general international law was meant to exclude regional norms.[20]

Anyway, having regional *jus cogens* would introduce chaos into the international legal system. It would raise the conceptual possibility of conflict between different regional norms of *jus cogens*. It would further complicate the issue of how the validity of a treaty conflicting with such regional *jus cogens* must be judged. If a State belonging to the region which accepts a certain regional peremptory norm concludes a treaty with a State from another region in which the same norm is not regarded as peremptory, the legal consequences of such a treaty would be unclear and it would be

---

[16] Verdross, Jus Dispositivum and Jus Cogens in International Law, 60 *AJIL* (1966), 61.

[17] Sztucki, Jus Cogens *and the Vienna Convention on the Law of Treaties* (1974), 108–110.

[18] Jaenicke, Zur Frage des Internationalen Ordre Public, 7 *Berichte der Deutschen Gesellschaft für Völkerrecht* (1967), 87.

[19] Kolb (1998), 99. But see Domb, *Jus Cogens* and Human Rights, 6 *Israel Yearbook of Human Rights* (1976), 109–110, suggesting that if regional *jus cogens* were to emerge, it would be outside the scope of Article 53.

[20] II YbILC (1963), 199.

uncertain if nullity could follow. The first State could be acting contrary to regional *jus cogens* while the second State would be acting lawfully, its action being beyond the reach of the peremptory norm which operates in another region. General international law would have no reason to condemn the second State for entering into such a treaty and would thus fail to provide for nullity. This proves that in order to outlaw conflicting transactions, a peremptory norm must be established as unconditionally binding all relevant parties irrespective of their regional affiliation. Regional *jus cogens* simply cannot operate peremptorily.

As Virally considers, since the creation of *jus cogens* engages the whole international community, peremptory norms definitionally belong to general international law, and cannot be limited in terms of their geographical application.[21] Rozakis and Virally note that even if a regional *jus cogens* exists, it must be subordinated to universal *jus cogens*, to avoid the legal dualism intolerable to the latter.[22] As Hannikainen suggests, only universality ensures the fulfilment of the purpose of peremptory norms.[23] Despite doctrinal debates, no regional *jus cogens* has been identified[24] and the German *Bundesverfassungsgericht* clarified that peremptory norms are those which all members of the international community are required to observe.[25] There is anyway no authority on regional *jus cogens* comparable to Article 53 of the Vienna Convention.

3. ELEMENTS OF DEFINITION OF *JUS COGENS*

McNair considers it easier to illustrate peremptory norms than to define them.[26] Brownlie and Meron, by contrast, suggest that the category of *jus cogens* is clearer than its particular content.[27] It is also suggested that the inactivity of the international community to define peremptory norms and their catalogue, 'and the consequent uncertainty as to which norms are

---

[21] Virally, Reflexions sur le 'jus cogens', 12 *Annuaire Français de Droit International* (1966), 14, 25; Scheuner, Conflict of Treaty Provisions with a Peremptory Norm of General International Law, 29 *Zeitschrift für ausländisches öffentliches Recht und Völkerrecht* (1969), 31.

[22] Rozakis (1976), 56; Virally (1966), 14; Jaenicke (1967), 89.

[23] Hannikainen, *Peremptory Norms in International Law* (1988), 5; see also Meron, *Human Rights Law-Making in the United Nations* (1986), 193; Domb (1976), 108; Nieto-Navia, International Peremptory Norms (*Jus Cogens*) and International Humanitarian Law, L.C. Vorhah *et al.* (eds.), *Man's Inhumanity to Man, Essays on International Law in Honour of Antonio Cassese* (2003), 611.

[24] See, however, *Roach*, Resolution No. 3/87, Case No. 9647, 8 *HRLJ* (1987), 345.

[25] BVGE, 1965, 411.

[26] McNair, *The Law of Treaties* (1961), 215.

[27] Brownlie, *Principles* (2003), 490; Meron, *Human Rights in Internal Strife* (1987), 137; Brundner, The Domestic Enforcement of International Covenants on Human Rights, 35 *University of Toronto Law Journal* (1985), 250.

peremptory, constitute at present the main problem of the viability of *jus cogens*.[28]

It would be a misapprehension, however, to imagine that the existence and operation of public order necessarily requires the existence of the exclusive catalogue of the norms it encompasses. In national legal systems, too, the nature of public order makes it difficult to list its norms exhaustively.[29] But this is not a sufficient basis for rejecting the concept.[30] In international law, the vagueness of principles 'does not necessarily deprive them of their legal or even *jus cogens* character'.[31]

It has been repeatedly pointed out in doctrine that 'There appears to be no case on record in which an international court or arbitral tribunal decided that an international treaty was void because of a repugnancy to a peremptory rule, in which an international political organ made a decision or recommendation to this effect, or where, in settling a dispute, governments agreed to such a proposition'.[32] But, as McNair suggests, the society of States is subject to peremptory norms 'though judicial and arbitral sources do not furnish much guidance upon the application of these principles'.[33] Likewise, Special Rapporteur Lauterpacht suggested that public order norms may take their effect, 'although there are no instances in international judicial and arbitral practice, of a treaty being declared void on account of the illegality of its object'.[34]

Some references to peremptory norms are found in judicial practice. It is also mistakenly assumed that the International Court has never referred to the concept of *jus cogens*.[35] However, the International Court made clear and straightforward reference to the peremptory character of the prohibition of the use of force in the *Nicaragua* case,[36] and individual opinions have repeatedly affirmed the peremptory character of specific norms. It is especially inaccurate to state that neither international nor national tribunals have

---

[28] Hannikainen (1988), 724.

[29] Meyer, *Droit International Privé* (1994), 141.

[30] Nussbaum, *Deutsches Internationales Privatrecht* (1974), 61; Wolff, *Das Internationale Privatrecht Deutschlands* (1954), 61.

[31] Van Hoof, *Rethinking the Sources of International Law* (1983), 165.

[32] Schwelb, Some Aspects of International *Jus Cogens*, 61 *AJIL* (1967), 949–950. See also Sztucki (1974), 45 ff., Cassese, *Self-Determination of Peoples* (1994), 174; Janis (1988), 362; Aust, *Modern Treaty Law and Practice* (2000), 258.

[33] McNair, *The Law of Treaties* (1961), 213–214; UNCLT Second Session (1969), 97 (UK); Minagawa, *Jus Cogens* in Public International Law, 6 *Hirotsubashi Journal of Law and Politics* (1968), 18.

[34] Lauterpacht, Report on the Law of Treaties, 2 YbILC 1953, 155. The ILC followed the same approach in affirming the role of *jus cogens* as a limitation on the defence of consent even if practice provided with no evidence to support the principle, YbILC 1979, vol. II, Part 2, 114.

[35] Shelton, Righting Wrongs: Reparations in the Articles on State Responsibility, 96 *AJIL* (2002), 843; Hartmann, The Gillon Affair, *ICLQ* (2005), 754.

[36] *ICJ Reports*, 1986, 100–101.

discussed the concept of *jus cogens*.[37] It is furthermore inaccurate to read the *Nicaragua* judgment in such a way as to construe it as just referring to the ILC's emphasis on the peremptory character of the prohibition of the use of force and not itself expressing the similar attitude.[38]

But the crucial point is that the peremptory character of norms does not exclusively depend on judicial pronouncements. This is so in the first place because tribunals are going to refer to the concept of *jus cogens* only if the peremptory character of the norm is relevant for the resolution of the dispute, that is the dispute includes the pertinent issues of validity or other relevant question. In addition, the lack of reference to peremptory norms in a judicial decision where the governing law would require otherwise can be questioned in the same way as any judicial decision that does not conform to the governing law. It must be understood that international courts and tribunals are there not to make international law but to identify and apply the pre-existing law. The failure of the court to make proper references to the legal principle does not mean that that legal principle does not exist or is irrelevant to the pertinent dispute. Finally, there can be judicial references to the concept of *jus cogens* which do not quite relate to peremptory law and likewise there can be proper references to the peremptory law without mentioning the general concept of *jus cogens*.

The Arbitral Tribunal in *Najera* considered that the duty to register treaties under Article 20 of the League of Nations Covenant was based on *jus cogens*,[39] while the Permanent Court in *Wimbledon* labelled the right of passage through the Kiel Canal in accordance with Article 380 of the Versailles Peace Treaty as 'peremptory',[40] and the International Court in *Teheran Hostages* underlined 'imperative' requirements following from the rules on diplomatic immunity.[41] But this does not make any of these norms peremptory, nor does it necessarily prove that it was *jus cogens* proper that the respective tribunals had in mind.

Judicial practice also actually deals with peremptory norms without mentioning the concept, but underlining the special character or effect of norms. In the Advisory Opinion on *Reservations*, the International Court referred to the purpose of the Genocide Convention to safeguard community interest rather than individual State interest and accepted that the duties

---

[37] Shelton, above, states this but in fact refers to the *Nicaragua* case.

[38] Shelton (2002), 843 argues that the International Court cited 'the ILC assertion that the norm against assertion is a peremptory norm as evidence that it is an obligation under customary international law'. Shelton unfortunately misreads the *Nicaragua* judgment. What the Court did was to point to the ILC's qualification of the relevant norm as peremptory and then to use this factor as evidence of the relevant norm's customary character. Once the Court did this, it subscribed to the view that the prohibition of the use of force is part of peremptory law.

[39] RIAA, 1920, 470.

[40] PCIJ Series A, No.1, 21–22.   [41] *ICJ Reports*, 1980, 41.

imposed thereby on States are in fact peremptory.[42] Other instances are *Soering*[43] and the reference in the Joint Separate Opinion in *Arrest Warrant* to specific jurisdictional effects of war crimes and crimes against humanity.[44] These instances refer to the distinctive character of relevant norms and their difference from the regular pattern of ordinary norms, though not explicitly to *jus cogens*.

Therefore, each norm must be examined on the merits of its substantive content and practice cannot be an exclusive factor in identifying peremptory norms. The peremptory character of the prohibition of slavery or torture is independent from whether the freedom of information or prohibition of massive pollution of the seas is also peremptory. The absence of an exhaustive catalogue of peremptory norms is not an obstacle to clarifying a norm's peremptory character on an individual basis.

This requires not only the reference to practical evidence but also a categorical approach, enquiring into the content of every norm on its merits in the light of some predetermined category of identifying a norm's peremptory character. If merely evidentiary criteria were adopted, then the reason for which a given norm is peremptory would be unclear (as practice often denotes as peremptory norms those which are not and vice versa). This would be incompatible with Article 53, which formulates a category of peremptory norms as norms from which no derogation is permitted.[45] The task is to examine which norms are non-derogable and what makes them so. As Abi-Saab suggests, without having a category we cannot have consensus on which rules belong to this category.[46]

The International Court emphasized in *Nuclear Weapons* that 'The question whether a norm is part of *jus cogens* relates to the *legal character of the norm*',[47] but this category is too broad. The Article 53 definition of peremptory norms as norms from which no derogation is permitted is said to be formalistic, because it does not explain why a rule of *jus cogens* occupies a higher rank and takes precedence over other norms.[48] As Abi-Saab suggests, '*jus cogens* rules are defined by their effect, but the effect is the consequence

---

[42] *ICJ Reports*, 1951, 22.

[43] 98 ILR 300; see also above, Chapter 1, note 157.

[44] Joint Separate Opinion, para. 51, *Arrest Warrant*, 2002.

[45] Article 53 also requires that a norm must be accepted and recognized as peremptory. This is another, though complementary, aspect of the argument which is examined in Chapter 2.

[46] Abi-Saab, Discussion in Cassese and Weiler (eds) (1988), 96.

[47] *ICJ Reports*, 1996, 258 (emphasis added). The Court meant the character of a norm as opposed to its scope.

[48] Tomuschat, Obligations Arising for States without or against Their Will, 241 *RdC* (1993), 223; Arechaga, International Law in the Past Third of the Century, 159 *RdC* (1978), 64. The same can be said of the formal definition given by the Arbitral Tribunal in *Guinea-Bissau v Senegal*: 'From the point of view of the law of treaties, *jus cogens* is simply a peculiar feature of certain legal norms, namely that of not admitting derogation by Agreement,' 83 ILR 25.

and not the cause of the quality of the rules. This quality depends on the content of the rules.'[49] Therefore, the initial criteria must be found for material aspects of definition explaining the reason of a norm's peremptory character as distinct from the consequential aspect of non-derogability.

Different aspects of the definition do not result in different standards of identifying peremptory norms. A single legal concept can be defined in both material and in formal terms.[50] The two aspects are interdependent and mutually supportive. Formal characteristics depend on material elements, for there must be a clear reason why that norm is non-derogable. Arguably, this subject-matter must be something independent of the will of States. Otherwise it would be difficult to explain why a norm is not derogable—the very idea of non-derogability of peremptory norms implies a superior limit of permissibility of the exercise of State will in disposing the interests protected by peremptory norms.

The formal element itself is useful in establishing whether a norm is part of *jus cogens* by asking whether that norm would be derogable by agreement, whether such derogation would be compatible with the structure and substance of that norm. These factors could compensate for the lack of affirmative evidence of the peremptory nature of a given norm.

4. STRUCTURAL (SYSTEMIC) NORMS AND SUBSTANTIVE NORMS

Criteria for identifying peremptory norms aim at demonstrating that certain norms are more fundamental. One's criteria would depend on one's understanding of the nature of the international legal order. A distinction here can be made between structural and substantive approaches.

The structural approach links *jus cogens* to the norms and principles structural to or inherent in the international legal system and inseparable from it. Schwarzenberger suggests that 'A fundamental principle which can be eradicated from international law only at the price of destruction of international law itself forms necessarily part of the international public order'.[51] He further suggests that 'Rules of international law which give the character of a fundamental principle to the principle sustained by them and, in addition, are practically indestructible are indistinguishable from *jus cogens*'.[52]

---

[49] Abi-Saab (1967), 15.

[50] Nicoloudis, *La nullité de jus cogens et le développement contemporain de droit international public* (1974), 38–39, defining *jus cogens* according to object and effect, respectively as fundamentally important and non-derogable norms. Abi-Saab (1967), 9–10.

[51] Schwarzenberger, The Fundamental Principles of International Law, 87 *RdC* (1955), 326.

[52] Id., 288.

Consequently, principles such as *pacta sunt servanda*, recognition, consent and good faith are portrayed as part of *jus cogens*.[53]

To start with, Schwarzenberger's reasoning is defective as the crucial issue in determining a norm's peremptory character is not whether it is indestructible but whether it is non-derogable or can be split into bilateral relations.

There is little utility in considering 'structural' norms such as consent or good faith as part of public order. Not all rules which are important or even indispensable for the existence and operation of international law belong to the category of peremptory norms.[54] These norms do not need to be qualified as peremptory in order to fulfil their functions. For example, to consider *pacta sunt servanda* as part of *jus cogens* would make little sense, since a treaty can hardly be concluded denying the very norm serving as a basis of the bindingness of treaties.[55] The derogation from *pacta sunt servanda* involves the logical impossibility.[56] A provision in a treaty that it shall not be binding would be a contradiction in terms[57] and an absurdity.[58]

From a broader perspective also, structural norms cannot be peremptory due to their reach and scope. *Pacta sunt servanda* requires the respect of treaty obligations, but does not require States to respond to violations of those obligations in any particular way. Breaches of treaty, unless offending against a substantive peremptory norm embodied in a bilateral or multilateral treaty, normally leave injured States the choice whether and how to respond. If *pacta sunt servanda* were part of *jus cogens*, an injured State would have no such choice. This would result in an assertion that every conventional norm is peremptory, leave no room for the *inter se* doctrine, and would misrepresent the structure of international law.

The principle of good faith is not part of *jus cogens*, since it is an accessory to substantive legal norms.[59] As with *pacta sunt servanda*, an agreement providing for performance of obligations in bad faith would be an absurdity.

In national legal systems, norms structurally inherent to a legal system are not part of public order, but rather certain substantive principles prevailing due to their substance.[60] The application of public order norms in national legal systems depends on a value judgment, identifying public order with

---

[53] Id., 260–261, 287–289, 326; Kolb (2001), 211; Pauwelyn, *The Conflict of Norms in Public International Law* (2003), 37; Nieto-Navia (2003), 614–616; Rosenne, YbILC, 1963(I), 73. Janis (1987), 363, refers to the 'essential' character of *pacta sunt servanda* and stating that no rule fits better the definition of *jus cogens* than it. Fitzmaurice (1959), 196, considers that the principle of *pacta sunt servanda* 'is a principle of natural law in the nature of *jus cogens*'. Jaenicke (1967), 91–92, refers to the principle of sovereign equality and the basic principles of the law of treaties and State responsibility.

[54] Simma, From Bilateralism to Community Interest, 250 *RdC* (1994), 288.

[55] Virally (1966), 10; Simma (1994), 288.

[56] Sztucki (1974), 80.   [57] Simma (1994), 288; Barberis (1970), 26–27.

[58] Crawford, *The Creation of States in International Law* (1979), 79.

[59] Virally (1966), 10. *Armed Actions, ICJ Reports*, 1988, 69.

[60] Kegel, *Internationales Privatrecht* (1987), 325, 327; van der Meersch (1968), 98.

principles indispensable to safeguard, because they relate to fundamental conceptions, values and sentiments recognized within the forum legal system. Public order is meant as a restriction upon acts which are thought to be harmful to the community.[61]

Identification of the content of international public order as embodied in peremptory norms is only possible through identifying the substantive values and principles which are as fundamentally important to the international community as the principles embodied by national public orders are to national legal systems. Not all rules which are important, or even indispensable, for the existence and working of international law are peremptory. The peremptory character of a rule derives from the substantive importance of the interest protected by that rule.[62] The ILC, while drafting what became Article 53 of the Vienna Convention, determined that it is the subject-matter importance of a rule which makes it peremptory and proposed only substantive norms as examples of *jus cogens*, such as prohibitions of aggression, genocide, slavery, as well as basic human rights and self-determination.[63] The ICTY has emphasized that norms are peremptory because of the values they protect.[64] Such substantive value must be the value which is not at the disposal of individual States.[65] Otherwise it would be unclear why the given norm is non-derogable.

The purpose of *jus cogens* is to safeguard the predominant and overriding interests and values of the international community as a whole as distinct from the interests of individual States.[66] *Jus cogens* embodies 'a transcendent

---

[61] See Chapter 1. [62] Simma (1994), 288.

[63] YbILC 1966(II), 248; Kolb (1998), 77; see also Whiteman, *Jus Cogens* in International Law, with a Projected List, 7 *Georgia Journal of International and Comparative Law* (1977), 625–626. Scheuner, Conflict of a Treaty Provision with a Peremptory Norm of International Law and Its Consequences, 27 *Zeitschrift für ausländisches öffentliches Recht und Völkerrecht* (1967), 525–526 suggests that peremptory rules are the 'rules which deal with definite material questions in particular areas of international life, not consequences drawn from the legal structure of the international legal order'.

[64] *Furundzija*, 38 ILM 1999, 349. See also *Barcelona Traction, ICJ Reports*, 1970, 33.

[65] Zemanek, New Trends in the Enforcement of *erga omnes* Obligations, 4 *Max Planck Yearbook of United Nations Law* (2000), 8.

[66] Verdross, Jus Dispositivum and Jus Cogens in International Law, 60 *AJIL* (1966), 58; Frowein, *Jus Cogens*, 7 *EPIL* 329; Rozakis, *The Concept of* Jus Cogens *in the Law of Treaties* (1976), 2; Hannikainen, *Peremptory Norms in International Law* (1988), 2–5, 261; Hannikainen, The case of East Timor from the perspective of jus cogens, *International Law and the Question of East Timor* (1995), 103, 105; Abi-Saab, The Concept of *Jus Cogens* in International Law, 2 *Lagonissi Conference: Papers and Proceedings*, vol. II, Geneva, Carnegie Endowment for International Peace (1967), 13; Jaenicke, (1967), 85–87; Virally, Reflexions sur le 'jus cogens', 12 *Annuaire Français de Droit International* (1966), 21; Klein, A Theory of the Application of the Customary International Law of Human Rights by Domestic Courts, 13 *Yale Journal of International Law* (1988), 351; Gormley, The Right to Life and The Rule of Non-Derogability: Peremptory Norms of *Jus Cogens*, Ramcharan (ed.), *The Right to Life in International Law* (1985), 130; Zotiades, Staatsautonomie und die Grenzen der Vertragsfreiheit im Völkerrecht, 17 *Österreichische Zeitschrift für öffentliches Recht* (1967), 109; Nicoloudis (1974), 43; Schütz (1984), 13.

common good of the international community, while *jus dispositivum* is customary law that embodies a fusion of self-regarding national interests'.[67] Furthermore, 'there is virtually no disagreement that the purpose of international peremptory law is to protect overriding interests and values of the international community of States'.[68] Most importantly, *jus cogens* protects not common interests of a random group of States but the basic values of the entire international community.[69]

The link to community interest as distinct from individual interests of States should be a key factor in determining a norm's peremptory character. It must be asked whether a norm is intended to benefit a given actor in the interest of the community. It must also be asked whether a valid derogation would be possible from a given norm—whether it could be split into bilateral legal relations. These formal and material criteria are as complementary as the two sides of a coin. They refer to an objective standard of identification of *jus cogens* based on the substance of a norm and hence independent of the will of States or judicial practice as an exclusive factor determining whether a norm is peremptory. Thus, as Hannikainen suggests, if a norm protects the community interest and derogation from it would seriously offend that interest, its peremptory nature should be presumed.[70] Special Rapporteur Waldock suggested assuming the peremptory character of *jus ad bellum*, the prohibition of genocide and some principles of international criminal law, as their very existence implied their link to international public order.[71]

The emphasis on community interest as distinct from or opposed to the interests of individual States as the basis of peremptory norms reinforces their public order character. The very essence of public order in every legal system consists in ensuring that public interest is preserved in the face of private transactions motivated by individual interests of legal persons.

After all this, the contrast between structural and substantive approaches becomes clearer. The drawback of a structural approach is its categorical contradiction with the notions of *jus cogens* and public order as legal categories safeguarding public or community interest. Every emphasis on the peremptory nature of structural rules is a conscious or subconscious attempt to portray *jus cogens* as a notion perpetuating a bilateralist conception of international law with its paramount emphasis on individual State will and interests.

---

[67] Brundner, The Domestic Enforcement of International Covenants on Human Rights, 35 *University of Toronto Law Journal* (1985), 249–250.

[68] Hannikainen (1988), 4.

[69] Zemanek (2000), 6.   [70] Hannikainen (1988), 20; Pauwelyn (2003), 98.

[71] Second Report, 2 YbILC (1963), 52; the Commission's report 2 YbILC (1963), 198.

5. THE BASIS FOR THE PEREMPTORY CHARACTER OF NORMS

It is crucial to determine which factor causes a legal interest to become the community concern and be protected by a peremptory norm. It is widely accepted that the concept of public order is based on morality and its function is to outlaw the acts and transactions offending against the morality accepted in the given legal system.[72] Sentiments of the just and unjust impose themselves as absolute values.[73] National legislative clauses directly refer to moral criteria,[74] and even in legal systems without such clauses, public order outlaws immoral acts and transactions. For instance, in *Kuwait Air Corp.* the general conceptions of morality and humanity were identified as aspects of public policy.[75] Public order may refer both to the rules of positive law and generally recognized principles of morality which are not necessarily part of positive law.[76] Although the starting-point distinction can be made between the mere concept of morality and peremptory norms mentioned in Article 53 of the Vienna Convention as legal norms,[77] the crucial question is the relevance of the morality factor in conferring the peremptory character to legal norms.

In international law, it is arguable that when a right of a particular actor or entity is very important in terms of morality, it can be assumed to embody the community interest and hence limit the will and discretion of individual States. The Inter-American Commission affirmed that peremptory norms are accepted 'as necessary to protect the public interest of the society of nations or to maintain the levels of public morality recognised by them'.[78]

---

[72] Rolin, Vers un ordre public réellement international, in *Hommage d'une generation des Juristes au President Basdevant* (1961), 444; Nussbaum (1974), 60–61, 64, 67; Pillet and Niboyet, *Manuel de Droit International Privé* (1924), 417; Wolff (1954), 62; Kegel (1987), 325, emphasizing that the same considerations of morality apply to the nullity of contracts and application of foreign laws; Kropholler, *Internationales Privatrecht* (1997), 224; Niederer, *Einführung in die Allgemeine Lehren des Internationalen Privatrechts* (1956), 285–287; Bleckmann, *Sittenwidrigkeit wegen Verstoßes gegen den* ordre public international, 34 *ZaöRV* (1974), 112–113, 118, 128; Raape (1961), 95; Zitelmann (1897), 334; Blom, Public Policy in Private International Law and Its Evolution in Time, 50 *Netherlands International Law Review* (2003), 374.

[73] Meyer (1994), 140.

[74] Article 138 of the German Civil Code and Article 30 of the *Einführungsgesetz*, Article 6 of the French Civil Code (placing good morals and public order on the same footing), Article 12 of the Preliminary Provisions to the Italian Civil Code. Levi (1994), 58; Zweigert and Kötz, *An Introduction to Comparative Law* (1998), 380–382; Bernier, Droit Public and Ordre Public, 15 *Transactions of the Grotius Society* (1930), 90.

[75] *Kuwait Air Corp.*, 116 ILR 571.

[76] Kegel (1987), 326; Levi (1994), 57, 66–67.   [77] Domb (1976), 107–108.

[78] *Victims of the Tugboat '13 de Marzo'*, para. 79; *Roach*, Resolution No. 3/87, Case No. 9647, para. 55, 8 *HRLJ* (1987), 352; *Mangas*, para. 144; Gormley (1985), 123–124; Reuter, *Introduction to the Law of Treaties* (1972), 111.

Morality can arguably itself explain a norm's peremptory character. According to Special Rapporteur Lauterpacht, in order to operate as norms of public policy, these norms 'need not necessarily have crystallised in a clearly accepted rule of law'; they may alternatively 'be expressive of rules of international morality so cogent' that an international tribunal would consider them as part of the general principles of law in terms of Article 38 of the International Court's Statute.[79] Special Rapporteur Fitzmaurice attributed similar effects to *jus cogens* and humanity and good morals with regard to treaty invalidity, further emphasizing that

> it is not possible . . . to state exhaustively what are the rules of international law that have the character of *jus cogens*, but a feature common to them, or to a great many of them, evidently is that they involve not only legal rules but considerations of morals and international good order.[80]

Public policy is not determinable by mere reference to norms of positive law, but refers also to the prevailing social and moral attitudes of the community.[81] McNair refers in terms of *jus cogens* to 'some rules of law or some principles of morality which individuals are not permitted by law to ignore or to modify by their agreements'.[82] This is a reference to positive law and morality as two separate but mutually complementary concepts. Verdross explains *jus cogens* by reference to the ethics of the international community.[83] As Cassese submits, even if the content of *jus cogens* may be unclear on occasions, it may have effect due to its moral and psychological weight, and invalidate conflicting acts and transactions merely on the ground of their immorality.[84] According to Judge Schücking in *Oscar Chinn*, tribunals would never apply a legal instrument the terms of which are contrary to public morality.[85]

Lauterpacht also links public order to morality, emphasizing that States cannot change by treaties the rules of customary law by laying down immoral obligations.[86] At the same time, mere immorality is not sufficient, 'it must be such as to render its enforcement contrary to public policy and to socially imperative dictates of justice'.[87]

---

[79] YbILC (1953-II), 155.

[80] YbILC (1958-II), 41, treaties conflicting with one of these categories are similarly void even *inter partes*.

[81] Levi (1994), 56; Virally (1966), 11, stresses that the morality factor reinforces the link between international *jus cogens* and public order as recognized in national law.

[82] McNair (1961), 213. See also Hall, *A Treatise on International Law* (1924), 383.

[83] Verdross, Forbidden Treaties in International Law, *AJIL* (1937), 572.

[84] Cassese, *Self-Determination of Peoples* (1994), 174; cf Jaenicke (1967), 92, and the Swiss attitude at the Vienna Conference, UNCLT First Session (1969), 324.

[85] PCIJ Series A/B, No. 63, 150.

[86] Lauterpacht (1970), 234.   [87] Lauterpacht (1970), 358.

6. SPECIFIC NORMS OF INTERNATIONAL PUBLIC ORDER

In order to qualify as peremptory, a norm, while protecting a given actor, legal person or value, must safeguard interests transcending those of individual States, have a moral or humanitarian connotation, because its breach would involve a result so morally deplorable as to be considered absolutely unacceptable by the international community as a whole, and consequently not permitting division of these interests into bilateral legal relations. It remains to identify the norms and principles meeting these criteria.

6.1. The prohibition of the use of force

The fundamental importance of State interests to survive, exist independently and effectively protect its population can justify the elevation of such interests to the interests of the international community as a whole and their protection through peremptory norms.[88] The law related to the use of force in international relations which is based on the UN Charter and relevant customary law is the principal implication of those considerations.

The prohibition of the use of force by States undoubtedly forms part of *jus cogens*.[89] Judge Nagendra Singh emphasized that the principle of the non-use of force, being 'the very cornerstone of the human effort to promote peace', is part of *jus cogens*.[90] Judge Sette-Camara also pointed out that this principle is part of 'peremptory rules of customary international law which impose obligations on all States'.[91] In *Oil Platforms*, Judge Simma affirmed that the norms of general international law on the unilateral use of force are undeniably of a peremptory nature.[92] Judge Elaraby emphasized in his Separate Opinion in the *Palestinian Wall* case that the prohibition of the use of force, as the most important principle that emerged in the twentieth century, is undoubtedly part of *jus cogens*.[93]

The inherent right of States to self-defence is also part of *jus cogens*. The International Court considered in *Nuclear Weapons* that the right of a State to resort to self-defence follows from the fundamental right of every State to

---

[88] As the ILC emphasized, the prohibition of the use of force protects the interests of the international community as a whole even though it overlaps with protecting the survival and security of individual States, commentary to Article 48, para. 10, *ILC Report* 2001, 322; Jaenicke (1967), 86.

[89] As confirmed by ICJ, *Nicaragua, ICJ Reports*, 1986, 100–101 and ILC, YbILC (1966-II), 248; *ILC Report* 2001, commentary to Article 40, 283, para. 4. The German *Bundesverwaltungsgericht* has also confirmed that the prohibition of the use of force is part of *jus cogens*, BverwG 2 WD 12.04, para. 4.1.2.6. See also Dinstein (2001), 94.

[90] *ICJ Reports*, 1986, 153.

[91] *ICJ Reports*, 1986, 199.

[92] Separate Opinion, para. 9; see also Separate Opinion of Judge Koojmans, para. 44; Dissenting Opinion of Judge Elaraby, para. 1.1.

[93] Judge Elaraby, Separate Opinion, *Wall*, para. 3.1.

survival and hesitated to qualify this right even by reference to non-use of nuclear weapons.[94] Self-defence implies the right to defend itself and organize State machinery in a way necessary and sufficient for protecting life, property and well-being of citizens.[95]

It seems that *jus ad bellum* as a whole is peremptory. *Jus ad bellum* concerns the right of States to use force and defines the circumstances of such use. It thereby comes in touch with the outer limits of the very prohibition of the use of force and any judgment as to whether the use of force is legal has to do with the question whether that use of force is justified under Article 2(4) of the UN Charter and its customary counterpart. Therefore, if the very prohibition of the use of force is peremptory, then every principle specifying the limits on the entitlement of States to use force is also peremptory. To illustrate, in *Oil Platforms* the International Court in fact affirmed the peremptory character of the entire *jus ad bellum* as it examined and affirmed the limits these norms impose on the interpretation of bilateral treaties.[96]

6.2. The principle of self-determination and its incidences

The right of peoples to self-determination is undoubtedly part of *jus cogens* because of its fundamental importance,[97] even if its peremptory character is sometimes disputed.[98] The UN General Assembly made a number of statements based on the peremptory status of the right of peoples to self-determination. In the preamble of Resolution 1803(XVII), the General Assembly pointed out that 'economic and financial agreements between the developed and developing countries must be based on the principles of equality and of the right of peoples and nations to self-determination'. In Resolution 35/118, the General Assembly 'categorically reject[ed] any agreement, arrangement or unilateral action by colonial or racist Powers which ignores, violates, denies or conflicts with the inalienable rights of peoples

---

[94] *ICJ Reports*, 1996, 263.

[95] Verdross (1937), 574–575, refers to a memorandum of the Austrian Government of 2 March 1936 on the re-establishment of compulsory military service despite the limitations imposed by the peace treaties after the First World War. Verdross also suggests that 'It would be immoral to oblige a State to remain defenceless,' id. Mosler (1968), 10; Schwelb (1967), 966–967.

[96] See Chapter 6.

[97] Judge Ammoun, *Barcelona Traction, ICJ Reports*, 1970, 72, emphasized that the right to self-determination is based on the 'norm of the nature of *jus cogens*, derogation from which is not permissible under any circumstances'. See also Shaw, *Title to Territory in Africa* (1986), 91; Gros-Espiel, Self-Determination and *Jus Cogens*, Cassese (ed.), *UN Law/Fundamental Rights* (1979), 167–171; Dugard, *Recognition and the United Nations* (1987), 158ff; Cassese, *Self-Determination of Peoples* (1994), 171–172; Parker and Neylon (1989), 440–441.

[98] Crawford, *Creation of States in International Law* (1979), 81; Weisbrud, The Emptiness of *Jus Cogens*, as Illustrated by the War in Bosnia-Herzegovina 17 *Michigan Journal of International Law* (1995), 23–24; Scheuner, Conflict of a Treaty Provision with a Peremptory Norm of International Law and Its Consequences, 27 *Zeitschrift für ausländisches öffentliches Recht und Völkerrecht* (1967), 525; Scheuner (1969), 34.

under colonial domination to self-determination and independence'. This attitude clearly views the principle of self-determination as the limitation on the permissible content of treaties and hence the public order principle of peremptory status.[99] The ILC and the UN Human Rights Commission have likewise affirmed the peremptory character of the principle of self-determination.[100]

It seems that certain incidences of the principle of self-determination, such as permanent sovereignty over natural resources, are part of *jus cogens*.[101] As Brownlie suggests, the provisions of the UN General Assembly Resolution 1803 regarding the Permanent Sovereignty over Natural Resources constitute the part of the catalogue of peremptory norms.[102] Authors such as Sztucki and Schrijver contend that a State, in exercise of its permanent sovereignty, can conclude contracts which would derogate from the principle, and hence the principle is not peremptory.[103] The Arbitral Tribunal in *Aminoil* expressed a similar view, but only to assert that permanent sovereignty over natural resources does not prohibit the State's subscribing to the stabilisation clauses that are often included in State contracts.[104] The Arbitral Tribunal in *Texaco* does not deny the *jus cogens* character of permanent sovereignty and adopts a subtler solution that in entering into a concession contract a State does not necessarily contradict that sovereignty. *Jus cogens* would extend to the agreements concluded between States and foreign private companies if these agreements 'in fact alienate the sovereignty of the State over [its natural] resources'. Some State contracts are not alienations, but just the exercise of sovereignty over natural resources.[105]

But this reasoning is defective for several reasons. First, the principle of permanent sovereignty is an integral element of the principle of self-

---

[99] See also the attitude of the General Assembly with regard to the agreements violating the right of the Palestinian people to self-determination, below, Chapter 6, and see further Hannikainen (1988), 382.

[100] YbILC (1963-II), 22; UN Human Rights Commission Resolutions 1997/4, 1998/4, 2003/3. Craven, The European Community Arbitration Commission on Yugoslavia, *BYIL* (1995), 380–381, suggests that while the principle of self-determination is peremptory in the colonial context, it is unclear whether the same could be said of its non-colonial context. Craven refers to the statement of Judge Dillard in *Namibia* (*ICJ Reports* 1971) that self-determination as a norm applies to decolonization. But the scope of applicability is not the same thing as the normative quality. Today it is absolutely clear that the principle of self-determination benefits peoples also outside the colonial context, as was affirmed in *East Timor, ICJ Reports* 1995, 105–106, and *Palestinian Wall*, General List No. 131, paras 88, 122 (respectively on East Timor and Palestine). At the same time, the UN Human Rights Commission affirmed the peremptory status of this principle with regard to Palestine, that is in a non-colonial context.

[101] Jaenicke (1967), 94. Another peremptory incidence can be the special combatant status of armed defenders of self-determination, Brownlie, *Principles* (2003), 78.

[102] Brownlie (2003), 489.

[103] Scrijver (1997), 375; Sztucki (1973), 44; see also Paavistra, Internationalization and Stabilization of Contracts versus State Sovereignty, *BYIL* (1989), 340.

[104] *Aminoil*, 66 ILR 587–588.

[105] *Texaco*, para. 78, 53 ILR 482.

determination, and is so regarded by the UN General Assembly.[106] Second, it is the very essence of the principle that a State should be free to dispose of its natural resources in the exercise of its sovereignty. This normative core is the basis of the peremptory nature of the principle. Contracts concluded in the exercise of permanent sovereignty are not derogations from the principle; rather, there would be derogation if a State entered into an agreement through which it waived the right to take decisions on all or part of its natural resources.[107] Third, several peremptory norms, such as the prohibition of the use of force or the principle of self-determination itself, enable the actor protected by a given norm to exercise the choice in performance of rights under that norm: a State could invite another State to intervene; it could even decide to become part of another State, and none of these would contradict the relevant peremptory norms. The peremptory character of the above-mentioned norms has not been doubted because they give the protected actors the right to choose, and the validity of such argument with regard to sovereignty over natural resources should be assessed accordingly.

6.3. Fundamental human rights

Most of the cases of *jus cogens* are 'cases where the position of the individual is involved'.[108] Human rights norms protect not the individual interests of a State but the interests of mankind as such and the interests they protect are not at the disposal of States, nor can these interests be damaged by reprisals or reciprocal non-compliance.[109] This reflects the fact that, unlike individual rights pure and simple, human rights protect the individual as such, regardless of the link to the rights and interests of any State, and hence protect the community interest. Human rights are not just individual rights; they are rights not disposable by States, individually or in concert.

As Judge Tanaka proposed,

---

[106] In Resolution 1803(1962), the General Assembly stressed that permanent sovereignty over natural resources is 'a basic constituent of the right to self-determination'. Parker and Neylon (1989), 440, emphasize that in order to realize self-determination, political independence must be coupled with permanent sovereignty over natural resources. Sornarajah, *The International Law on Foreign Investment* (2004), 327 also emphasizes the intrinsic link between the right to self-determination on the one hand and the permanent sovereignty over natural resources, or economic sovereignty, on the other.

[107] In addition, the contracts disposing the natural resources concluded by unrepresentative rulers are also invalid, Sornarajah (2004), 42.

[108] Fitzmaurice, 2 YbILC 1958, 40; see also Barberis, La liberté de traiter des Etats et le *jus cogens*, 30 *Zeitschrift für ausländisches öffentliches Recht und Völkerrecht* (1970), 44.

[109] Barile, The Protection of Human Rights in Article 60, paragraph 5 of the Vienna Convention on the Law of Treaties, *International Law at the Time of its Codification, Essays in Honour of Roberto Ago*, vol. II (1987), 3–4.

if we can introduce in the international field a category of law, namely *jus cogens* . . . a kind of imperative law which constitutes the contrast to *jus dispositivum*, capable of being changed by way of agreement between States, surely the law of human rights may be considered to belong to the *jus cogens*.[110]

Verdross also considered that

a very important group of norms having the character of *jus cogens* are all rules of general international law created for a humanitarian purpose.[111]

The peremptory character of some human rights is affirmed in judicial practice. According to the Inter-American Commission, the right to life is part of *jus cogens*.[112] According to the ICTY, the prohibition of torture has acquired 'a particularly high status in the international normative system, a status similar to the principles such as those prohibiting genocide, slavery, racial discrimination, aggression, the acquisition of territory by force and the forcible suppression of the right of peoples to self-determination'. Consequently, the prohibition of torture is a peremptory norm, similar to 'the other general principles protecting fundamental human rights'.[113] The US and Canadian Courts of Appeal, as well as the Canadian Supreme Court, also accepted that the prohibition of torture is a peremptory norm of public international law.[114] The US court in *Xuncax v Gramajo* affirmed the peremptory character of the prohibition of summary execution, disappearance, torture and arbitrary detention.[115] The Court of Appeals for the Ninth Circuit similarly considered that forced labour, torture, murder and slavery are violations of *jus cogens*.[116]

The Inter-American Court affirmed that 'the principle of equality before the law, equal protection before the law and non-discrimination belongs to *jus*

---

[110] *ICJ Reports*, 1966, 298.

[111] Verdross, *Jus Dispositivum* and *Jus Cogens* in International Law, *AJIL* (1966), 59.

[112] *Victims of the Tugboat '13 de Marzo'*, para. 79; Parker and Neylon (1989), 431–432.

[113] *Furundzija*, Judgment of 10 December 1998, case no. IT-95-17/I-T, paras 147–155; see also *Delalic*, Judgment of 16 November 1998, case no. IT-96-2-T, para. 466; *Kunarac*, Judgment of 22 February 2001, case no. IT-96-23-T, para. 454.

[114] *Siderman de Blake*, Court of Appeals (Ninth Circuit), 103 ILR 472; *Bouzari* (Court of Appeal of Ontario), para. 36, *per* Goudge JA; *Suresh* (Supreme Court of Canada), paras 61–65; it should be noted that the Canadian Supreme Court's attitude regarding the peremptory status of the prohibition of torture is misrepresented in academic contributions, see Bourgon, The Impact of Terrorism on the Principle of '*Non-Refoulement*' of Refugees: The *Suresh* Case before the Supreme Court of Canada, 1 *Journal of International Criminal Justice* (2003), 174, 184. The Supreme Court, which decided the case on the basis of Canadian, not international, law, was not required to decide this issue in finalized terms, which is stated as a clear reason in para. 65 of the judgment. It is crucial, however, that the Supreme Court acknowledged the arguments in favour of the peremptory status of the prohibition of torture and did not contradict them and, most importantly, used the aforementioned position to interpret the Canadian and international provisions with the result that the return of the person to the country where torture may be faced contradicts Canadian 'principles of fundamental justice', id., paras 66 ff.

[115] *Xuncax v Gramajo*, 184.

[116] *Doe v Unocal*, 14208.

cogens, because the whole legal structure of national and international public order rests on it'.[117] A yet another firmly established peremptory norm related to the rights of an individual is the principle of *non-refoulement*, which is enshrined both in Article 33 of the 1951 Geneva Convention on the Status of Refugees, as well as in customary law.[118] The peremptory character of this principle is reinforced by its inseparable link with the observance of basic human rights such as the right to life, freedom from torture and non-discrimination. The UNHCR Executive Committee recognized in its Conclusion No. 25 that the principle of *non-refoulement* amounts to a norm of *jus cogens*.[119] Similarly, the Cartagena Declaration on Refugees affirms that this principle 'is imperative in regard to refugees and in the present state of international law should be acknowledged and observed as a rule of *jus cogens*'.[120] Goodwin-Gill opposes this attitude on the basis of lack of practice, referring to Article 53 of the Vienna Convention, which requires that the peremptory norm must be accepted and recognized by the international community,[121] and insists that 'little is likely to be achieved' by regarding the principle of *non-refoulement* as peremptory.[122] This position is difficult to sustain, because if this principle is not peremptory, then it is open to States to override it by treaties in which they will provide for the legality of the return of persons to the countries where serious violations of human rights may be faced.

As can be seen, judicial practice says enough about the peremptory character of individual human rights. However, the doctrinal treatment of the subject reveals the need to have independent criteria for identifying peremptory human rights, especially in terms of the doctrinal debate as to whether all human rights are peremptory or only some of them possess such status.

Several other writers hold that not all human rights are part of peremptory law.[123] But this view is taken as a premise and is based on routine and

---

[117] *Juridical Condition and Rights of the Undocumented Migrants*, Advisory Opinion, OC-18/03, para. 101; see also the identical view of the Inter-American Commission, *Maya Indigenous Community*, Case 12.053, para. 4.

[118] On peremptory character of *non-refoulement* see Alain, The *jus cogens* Nature of *non-refoulement*, 13 *International Journal of Refugee Law* (2002), 538–541; Parker and Neylon (1989), 435–436; de Wet, The Prohibition of Torture as an International Norm of *Jus Cogens* and Its Implications for National and Customary Law, 15 *EJIL* (2004), 101, especially focusing on the view of the Swiss Government that the prohibition of *refoulement* is peremptory.

[119] Conclusion No 25 (XXXIII-1982), para. (b).

[120] Cartagena Declaration, para. III.5.

[121] It should be emphasized in this regard that the requirements under Article 53 with regard to the acceptance and recognition of peremptory norms do not necessarily refer to recognition in the practice of individual States. For a more detailed analysis see Chapter 5 on sources of peremptory norms.

[122] Goodwin-Gill, *The Refugee in International Law* (1996), 168.

[123] Sinclair, *The Vienna Convention on the Law of Treaties* (1986), 217; Gormley (1985), 122. Special scepticism is expressed on freedom from debt imprisonment, Koji, Emerging Hierarchy in International Human Rights and Beyond: From the Perspective of Non-derogable Rights, 12 *EJIL* (2001), 920.

automatic repetition rather than a careful examination of the nature of specific human rights or their interaction with comparable standards and their effects in general international law. It is exactly this task that needs to be performed in order to find the correct view on the subject.

Arguably, not every right recognized in the Universal Declaration on Human Rights is part of *jus cogens*.[124] According to Frowein, the use of the word 'basic' instead of 'fundamental' in *Barcelona Traction* means that the Court had in mind a very narrow core of human rights—narrower than those enshrined in human rights instruments.[125] But according to Meron and Schindler, the difference between basic and other human rights as arguably distinguished in *Barcelona Traction* is no longer significant.[126]

There is a doctrinal view that peremptory norms cover all human rights,[127] which accords with Judge Tanaka's reference to the *jus cogens* nature of human rights law in general and without qualification.

Scheuner suggests that not all human rights belong to *jus cogens*, but only 'basic rules, which protect human dignity, life, personal and spiritual liberty, equality, family rights and the free exercise of those human activities which are derived from these highest principles'.[128] Under Scheuner's approach, *jus cogens* would encompass rights and freedoms to personal liberty, religion, equality, private and family life. This approach is qualitatively different from the approach referring to 'derogability' of a right in that it refers not to the text of human rights instruments, but to the essence of specific human rights.

Higgins considers that certain rights—the right to life, freedom from slavery or torture—are so fundamental that they are non-derogable. Treaty instruments contain norms binding as principles recognized by civilized States, not only as mutual treaty commitments; but not all the rights covered by treaty instruments have a status which is more than treaty-based. Neither

---

[124] Dinstein, The *erga omnes* Applicability of Human Rights, 30 *AVR* (1992), 17; Simma and Alston, The Sources of Human Rights Law: Custom, Jus Cogens, and General Principles, 12 *Australian Yearbook of International Law* (1992), 103.

[125] Frowein, Verpflichtungen *erga omnes* im Völkerrecht und Ihre Durchsetzung, *Voelkerrecht als Rechtsordnung – Internationale Gerichtsbarkeit – Menschenrechte: Festschrift Mosler* (1983), 243–244, 258.

[126] Meron, *Human Rights and Humanitarian Norms as Customary Law* (1989), 199, 227; Schindler, Erga omnes-Wirkung des humanitären Völkerrechts, Beyerlin, Bothe, Hofmann and Petersmann (Hrsg.), *Recht zwischen Umbruch und Bewahrung. Festschrift für Rudolf Bernhardt* (1993), 206.

[127] Zemanek, The Unilateral Enforcement of International Obligations, 47 *ZaöRV* (1987), 39–40; Parker and Neylon (1989), 441–443; Bryde, Verpflichtungen *Erga Omnes* aus Menschenrechten, Kälin, Riedel and Karl (eds.) *Aktuelle Probleme des Menschenrechtsschutzes, Berichte der Deutschen Gesellschaft für Völkerrecht*, Bd. 33, 1993 (1994) 167; Meron, *Human Rights Law-Making in the United Nations* (1986), 195–196, sees the International Law Institute's treatment of human rights and extradition as confirming that all human rights are peremptory.

[128] Scheuner (1969), 33–34.

the wording of human rights instruments, nor the practice hereunder, leads to the view that all human rights are *jus cogens*.[129]

The emphasis on non-derogation in times of emergency is also made. In *Furundzija* the ICTY linked the fact that the prohibition of torture 'can never be derogated from, not even in time of emergency', with its peremptory character.[130] Some would require more than just non-derogability in emergencies to consider a human right as peremptory. Meron considers that not all non-derogable treaty-based human rights have attained the status of categorical norms under customary law and are non-derogable under it.[131] For instance, the ICCPR's non-derogable rights are not *per se* peremptory (as only about half of all States are parties to the Covenant).[132] Meron suggests that perhaps the common core of non-derogable rights under different human rights instruments can be regarded as *jus cogens*.[133]

This is, however, not necessarily a correct methodological exercise. The common core and consensus between treaty frameworks that address the same subject-matter can also be inferred from a treaty framework which conceives that subject-matter in a broader way than others. This was the attitude of the ICTY as it repeatedly affirmed in *Delalic* and *Furundzija* that the definition of torture under the 1984 UN Convention was broader than those contained in the 1975 UN Declaration against Torture or the 1985 Inter-American Convention against Torture, and thus it constituted a consensus representative of customary international law.[134] It is thus worth asking why the broadest catalogue of non-derogable rights as opposed to the common core of non-derogable rights embodied in different treaties cannot represent peremptory law. Meron's criteria are based only on consensus about norms and not their inherent character. In addition, if Meron's approach were adopted, it would leave excluded from the scope of *jus cogens* important rights such as those embodied in the non-derogable provisions of the ICCPR as well as other human rights instruments. This perspective would not be free of problems because of the fundamental importance of those rights.

To focus exclusively upon the wording of a treaty instrument in clarifying whether a norm embodied in that treaty is peremptory is to imply that it is the text of a treaty, and the intention of the parties, which makes a rule

---

[129] Higgins, Derogations under Human Rights Treaties, *BYIL* (1976–77), 282; see also Goodwin-Gill, The Limits of the Power of Expulsion in Public International Law, *BYIL* (1976), 69. For linking the non-derogability of a right under a treaty instrument and its peremptory character see the Swiss court decision in BGE 109Ib 72.

[130] *Furundzija*, para. 144.

[131] Meron (1987), 137; Koji (2001), 928.   [132] Meron (1987), 59, 138–139.

[133] Meron (1987), 59. Meron (1986), 192, also doubts that, because it is not non-derogable under Article 4 ICCPR, the prohibition of prolonged arbitrary detention is peremptory.

[134] *Delalic*, para. 459; *Furundzija*, para. 160.

peremptory. This is incompatible with the nature of *jus cogens*, which serves as the guidance for the permissible content of treaties, and cannot depend on the intention of parties to a treaty. It was affirmed by the ILC and further reaffirmed at the Vienna Conference and in the literature that a norm is not *jus cogens* just because the parties stipulate that no derogation from it is permitted.[135] True, a nearly universal treaty might reflect a widespread view of States on non-derogability and be relevant in assessing peremptory status but this can only have an accessory significance and cannot exclude the peremptory character of other rights, if only because non-derogability under human rights treaties does not necessarily reflect or prejudice a norm's peremptory character.

The fact that certain rights are denoted as non-derogable under human rights treaties can in some cases provide the starting-point criteria to clarify whether the given right is part of *jus cogens*.[136] The non-derogability of certain human rights under treaties bears some similarity with peremptory norms as it emphasizes the special status of rights which cannot be set aside even in circumstances justifying derogation from other rights. However, the utility of these criteria is limited to the character of those rights only which are 'non-derogable' under human rights instruments and should not necessarily prejudice the status of other rights.

In clarifying whether a formally 'derogable' right can still be part of *jus cogens* the relevant criterion would be the content of specific rights and their status under general international law, namely their embodiment of the community interest as distinct from individual State interests.[137] Rights to personal liberty, fair trial and due process, private or family life, freedom of expression and religion, although 'derogable' under some human rights instruments, certainly protect the community interest going beyond the individual interests of States and it seems doubtful whether the mere fact of their derogability under human rights treaties precludes their peremptory nature.

Derogation under the Vienna Convention on the Law of Treaties and derogation under human rights instruments are different things. Derogation under Article 53 of the Vienna Convention is an attempt to nullify a peremptory

---

[135] YbILC II-1966, 248; UNCLT First Session (1969), 296 (Iraq), 303 (Austria); Dhokalia, R., *Problems Relating to Jus Cogens*, Agrawala (ed.), *Essays on the Law of Treaties* (1972), 168; Leonetti, Interprétation des traités et règles impératives du droit international général (*jus cogens*), 24 *ÖZÖR* (1973), 99; Domb (1976), 114.

[136] De Wet, The Role of Human Rights in Limiting the Enforcement Power of the Security Council: A Principled View, De Wet and Nollkaemper (eds.), *Review of the Security Council by Member States* (2003), 22.

[137] Treaty-based organs exercise control over derogations not only in accordance with treaty provisions proper, but also the status of specific rights under general international law. The Human Rights Committee can invalidate derogations from certain rights if they are part of *jus cogens*, on the basis of General Comment No. 29. This is comparable to the approach of General Comment No. 24 on reservations.

norm *inter se*. It is one thing to derogate from a 'derogable' human right such as the freedom of information by a bilateral agreement and it is another thing to derogate from the same right in terms of national emergency as provided in human rights instruments. In the latter case, 'derogation' is made within the system, the continuing operation of a given human right is unaffected, it is only temporarily limited (even if the suspension of a given right through derogation may be for a considerable period and may have substantial effects). But in case of derogation from *jus cogens* by a treaty, derogating States attempt to replace public order norms, to make them inapplicable and inoperative *inter se*, themselves deciding when and how to derogate.

By accepting that a right is 'derogable' under the conditions stated in a treaty instrument, States cannot be presumed to hold that they are entitled to exclude the operation of that right in their relations *inter se*, that is, consider it non-peremptory.

In addition, the fact that a given right is derogable in a treaty instrument does not exclude an inherent limitation on derogatory powers of States due to a norm's peremptory character. The attitude of the UN Human Rights Committee expressed in General Comment 29 confirms such an approach. According to the Committee,

The enumeration of non-derogable provisions in article 4 [ICCPR] is related to, but not identical with, the question whether certain human rights obligations bear the nature of peremptory norms of international law. . . . [T]he category of peremptory norms extends beyond the list of non-derogable provisions as given in article 4, paragraph 2 [ICCPR]. States-parties may in no circumstances invoke article 4 of the Covenant as justification for acting in violation of humanitarian law or peremptory norms of international law, for instance by taking hostages, by imposing collective punishments, through arbitrary deprivations of liberty or by deviating from fundamental principles of fair trial, including the presumption of innocence.

Therefore, categorization of rights into derogable and non-derogable is not the same as dividing human rights norms into *jus cogens* and *jus dispositivum*.

The argument that all human rights are part of *jus cogens* is not without merit and to what extent that is true should be demonstrated by individual examination of rights. Substantive criteria to identify peremptory human rights are the same as general criteria of identification of *jus cogens*: (1) whether a right protects the community interest transcending the individual State interests; (2) whether the derogation from such right is prevented by its non-bilateralizable character. This perspective does not exclude that all human rights can be part of *jus cogens*. In any case, it is clear that the scope of *jus cogens* in human rights law is not limited to rights designated as non-derogable under treaty instruments.

Therefore, certain 'derogable' rights can be peremptory. This is clear with regard to due process guarantees and the right to fair trial,[138] as well as the freedom from illegal deprivation of liberty.

Certain 'relative' rights can also be peremptory. They are not absolute in scope, but their core serves as a criterion of the peremptory character of rights such as the freedom to expression, religion, information, family and private life. It is one issue whether States could limit these rights through the margin of appreciation; it is quite another issue whether they could derogate from the core of these rights. For example, it is impossible to see how a treaty abolishing freedom of expression or assembly would be valid. Thus, the European Court of Human Rights examined in the *Slivenko* case whether the 1994 Russian–Latvian Treaty on the Withdrawal of Russian Troops from Latvia satisfied the criteria of the margin of appreciation under Article 8 of the European Convention on Human Rights and consequently whether it was compatible with that provision.[139] Such examination in principle affirms that the Court could have disregarded the 1994 Treaty and its effect in order to enable Article 8 of the European Convention to take effect.

Economic and social rights are part of the Universal Declaration of Human Rights and hence of 'basic' human rights. To say that they are peremptory is not to say that they are subject to immediate implementation like civil and political rights and deny their dependence on progressive realization. But they operate in a peremptory way as rights requiring progressive realization. States perhaps could claim that they are not bound to immediately implement these rights, but they cannot derogate by agreement from their duty to seek progressive implementation of every such right.

---

[138] The peremptory status of due process guarantee is doubted in Zappala, *Human Rights in International Criminal Proceedings* (2003), 9, 154. But judicial practice proves the opposite. *Tadic* (Allegations of Contempt), 2001 suggests that Article 14 ICCPR reflects *jus cogens*. The Special Court for Sierra Leone held that the right to have the criminal conviction against oneself reviewed by the higher tribunal as enshrined in Article 14(5) ICCPR is part of *jus cogens, Prosecutor v Sam Hinga Norman*, Case No. SCSL-2003-08-PT, para. 19. The Chernichenko and Treat Report, paras 127–159, affirms that while formally derogable, the due process guarantees are practically non-derogable and unrestricted in emergency situations because it is essential in observance of other rights, paras 133–159. See also IACtHR decisions on *Habeas Corpus*, paras 27–29 and *Judicial Guarantees in States of Emergency*, paras 23–25. Seiderman, *Hierarchy in International Law: The Human Rights Dimension* (2001), 74–84.

[139] *Slivenko*, paras 104–109; the Court held that the requirement of the withdrawal of Russian officers from Latvian territory satisfied the criteria of the margin of appreciation. The 1994 Treaty did not derogate from the core of Article 8 guarantees but was merely an exercise of margin of appreciation. But the Court found the breach of Article 8 on other grounds and ordered Latvia to pay compensation to victims. This case is also relevant in terms of the conflict of treaties as an aspect of the applicability of *jus cogens* to treaties as dealt with in Chapter 6 below. In extradition practice too, 'relative' rights can be affected insofar as the content of the right, as the margin of appreciation or similar circumstances permit, but never in their core. With regard to different categories of rights involved in the context of extradition see Van den Wyngaert, Applying the European Convention on Human Rights to Extradition: Opening Pandora's Box? 39 *ILCQ* (1990), 773.

6.4. Humanitarian law

The peremptory status of individual humanitarian norms is treated in practice in different ways. The Greek court in the *Distomo* case affirmed that the duty of the occupying power to respect the lives, property and family honour of the occupied population, as embodied in Article 46 of the 1907 Hague Regulations, is part of *jus cogens*.[140] The District Court of Tokyo denied the peremptory character of the principles of respect for private property and the prohibition of confiscation.[141] But, apart from individual decisions, the inherent character of humanitarian law also counts in terms of its peremptory character.

International humanitarian law is not intended to protect State interests; it is primarily designed to protect human beings *qua* human beings.[142] As the ICTY emphasized, the objective, or non-reciprocal, nature of obligations embodied in humanitarian law treaties stems from their *erga omnes* character in the sense of the *Barcelona Traction* dictum.[143] Humanitarian law standards such as the Martens clause directly incorporate the concept of morality. It seems generally agreed that the basic rules of humanitarian law are peremptory.[144] The non-reciprocal character of the humanitarian law obligations is a yet another factor supporting the peremptory status of these obligations. As emphasized, the rights granted to protected persons under the Geneva Conventions are inalienable rights and 'there could no longer be any question of those rights being liable to withdrawal or restriction as a result of a violation'.[145]

This view is reinforced by the fact that humanitarian law outlaws agreements adversely affecting its operation, and protects basic rights of human persons which is the classic feature of *jus cogens*.[146] According to the Common Article 6/6/6/7,

---

[140] Case No. 137/1997, Court of Levadia, 599.

[141] Decision of the Tokyo District Court, 28 February, 1966, 13 *Japanese Annual of International Law* (1969), 115; for the peremptory character of certain norms embodied in the Hague Regulations see *Re Koch* (Voivodship Court of Warsaw), 30 ILR 303.

[142] *Kuprsekic*, IT-95-16-T, Judgment of 14 January 2000, para. 518.

[143] *Kupreskic*, para. 519.

[144] *Nuclear Weapons, ICJ Reports* 1996, 257; Judge Bedjaoui, Declaration, *ICJ Reports* 1996, 273; Judge Weeramantry, Dissenting Opinion, 46; Judge Koroma, Separate Opinion, *ICJ Reports*, 1996, 574. This was also affirmed by German *Bundesverwaltungsgericht*, BverwG 2 WD 12.04, para. 4.1.2.6. See also *ILC Report* 2001, 284; Sassoli (2002), 413–414; Parker and Neylon (1989), 434; Barile (1987), 5–6.

[145] Pictet, Article 46, 346.

[146] Sassoli, State Responsibility for Violations of Humanitarian Law, 84 *International Red Cross Review* (2002), 414; E. de Wet, Human Rights Limitations to Economic Enforcement Measures under Article 41 of the UN Charter and the Iraqi Sanctions Regime, 14 *LJIL* (2001), 288; Werksman and Khalatschi, Nuclear weapons and the concept of *jus cogens*: peremptory norms and justice pre-empted? Boisson de Chazournes and Sands (eds), *International Law, the International Court of Justice and Nuclear Weapons* (1999), 194–196.

No special agreement shall adversely affect the situation of protected persons, as defined by the present Convention, nor restrict the rights which it confers upon them.

The Common Article 7/7/7/8 provides that

Protected persons may in no circumstances renounce in part or in entirety the rights secured to them by the present Convention.

Finally, Article 47 of the Fourth Geneva Convention provides that

Protected persons who are in the occupied territory shall not be deprived ... of the benefits of the present Convention by any change introduced, as the result of the occupation of the territory, into the institutions or governments of the said territory, nor by any agreements concluded between the authorities of the occupied territories and the Occupying Power, nor by annexation by the latter of the whole or part of the occupied territory.

The Common Article 6/6/6/7 is 'a landmark in the process of the renunciation by States of their sovereign rights in favour of the individual and of a superior juridical order'.[147] Article 7/7/7/8 also confirms the peremptory status of the rights of protected persons by prohibiting them to renounce in any circumstance their rights in part or in total. In other words, the rights of protected persons are so fundamental that they ought to apply even if the very same protected persons decide otherwise.

As for Article 47 of the Fourth Geneva Convention, it makes the Convention 'a higher law' that prevails over any conflicting agreement. 'No agreement between the occupying power and the authorities representing the occupied population may diminish the Convention-protected rights of members of the occupied population'.[148]

It is accepted that is the criterion of derogation, not of adverse effect, which provides the best basis for deciding whether the special agreement mentioned in the relevant provisions of the Geneva Conventions is or is not in conformity with the Geneva Conventions.[149] This means that the Geneva Conventions are in principle non-derogable in their entirety. When their terms are strict and allow no deviation or special agreements, they must be deemed to have peremptory application. The non-derogability of the provisions of the Geneva Conventions is therefore a clear incidence of the non-bilateralizable character of these provisions and their superior legal status.

According to Meron, the clause in Common Article 6/6/6/7 is supposed, like *jus cogens*, to bring about the nullity of conflicting agreements, but unlike

---

[147] Pictet, *Commentary to the First Geneva Convention of 1949* (1952), 75.

[148] Quigley, The Israel–PLO Agreements versus the Geneva Civilians Convention, 7 *Palestinian Yearbook of International Law* (1992–1994), 58, 61.

[149] Pictet (1952), Article 6, 74; see also Nieto-Navia, International Peremptory Norms (*Jus Cogens*) and International Humanitarian Law, L.C. Vorhah *et al.* (eds), *Man's Inhumanity to Man, Essays on International Law in Honour of Antonio Cassese* (2003), 635–636.

jus cogens it derives from express provisions of the Geneva Conventions. Such agreements can in some cases violate *jus cogens*.[150] According to Quigley, the effect of Articles 6/6/6/7 and 7/7/7/8, as well as Article 47 of the Fourth Geneva Convention, is that the renunciation of the rights under the Geneva Conventions either by the State or by the affected individuals is invalid.[151]

The non-derogability and non-absolution provisions in Geneva Conventions evidence the intention of States-parties to lay down the law in a qualitatively different way from *jus dispositivum*.[152] As is clear from the clauses, this intention covers the totality of rights enshrined in these instruments. These clauses also cover the safeguards which are not as such absolute, but may be balanced against military necessity. Of course, the conventional prohibition of derogatory agreements would not as such be enough to qualify Geneva Conventions as *jus cogens*. But such prohibition, in combination with the structure of denunciation clauses, criminalization of breaches, and limits on reciprocity evidenced by prohibition of reprisals could perhaps cumulatively confirm that these obligations are part of *jus cogens*.

Some provisions of humanitarian law are absolute in scope, such as prohibitions of mistreatment of civilians and war prisoners, while other provisions apply in terms of civilian/military distinction. But the core of provisions referring to military necessity can nevertheless be seen as peremptory as by protecting civilian objects and persons from unnecessary attack, they protect transcendent community interest and are not bilateralizable.

The peremptory status of basic humanitarian law norms was affirmed in jurisprudence with regard to the issue of belligerent reprisals as a broader issue of reciprocity in humanitarian law. The ICTY in *Kupreskic* confronted the issue whether the attacks committed by Croatian forces against the Muslim population were justifiable because similar attacks were allegedly being perpetrated against the Croat population. The Tribunal considered it as a defining characteristic of humanitarian law that the key standards must be upheld regardless of the conduct of enemy combatants. This entails the irrelevance of reciprocity, particularly in relation to obligations under humanitarian law 'which have an absolute and non-derogable character'.[153] The *tu quoque* argument is not only universally rejected but also flawed in principle because it envisages humanitarian law as based upon a narrow bilateral exchange of rights and obligations. However, humanitarian law

---

[150] Meron, The Humanisation of Humanitarian Law, 94 *AJIL* (2000), 252.

[151] Quigley (1992–1994), 46.

[152] Those guarantees strengthen the effects of *jus cogens*, Münch, Bemerkungen zum ius cogens, *Voelkerrecht als Rechtsordnung—Internationale Gerichtsbarkeit—Menschenrechte: Festschrift Mosler* (1983), 623, and affirm the non-bilateral character of the obligations, Provost, Reciprocity in Human Rights and Humanitarian Law, *BYIL* (1995), 388.

[153] *Kupreskic*, para. 511.

lays down absolute obligations that operate unconditionally and cannot be broken in response to the previous breaches. Instead, the general erosion of reciprocity in the application of humanitarian law follows.[154]

The ICTY emphasized that as a consequence of its absolute character humanitarian law imposed not synallagmatic obligations but obligations towards the international community as a whole. Most humanitarian norms such as those prohibiting war crimes, crimes against humanity and genocide, are peremptory norms. The Tribunal's reasoning clearly linked the absence of reciprocity in humanitarian law to the peremptory character of the relevant norms as it confirmed that the impermissibility of reciprocal breach as well as the limitations on the reciprocal termination of a treaty in case of its breach under Article 60(5) of the Vienna Convention on the Law of Treaties follow from the peremptory character of the relevant norms.[155]

The peremptory character of certain humanitarian norms, such as the fundamental guarantees enshrined in Common Article 3, Article 149 of the Third Geneva Convention, Article 75 of the First Additional Protocol and Articles 4–6 of the Second Additional Protocol is reinforced by their link to fundamental human rights. These guarantees, especially Common Article 3, apply to both international and internal conflicts, and reaffirm in categorical terms certain rights which are derogable under human rights treaties, such as the right to fair trial.[156] As Common Article 3 applies to all armed conflicts, it is hardly possible to justify derogation from the right to fair trial in a less grave emergency situation.[157] The basic humanitarian norms are practically indistinguishable from fundamental human rights.[158] The compelling conclusion is that humanitarian norms which protect the human being as such are undoubtedly peremptory.

Furthermore, the prohibition under Article 49 of the Fourth Geneva Convention of the settlements in the occupied territories also seems to be part of *jus cogens*. Otherwise it is unclear why the International Court acknowledged the Israeli settlements in the Occupied Palestinian Territory as void. Instances like this make a strong case for the assumption that many provisions in Geneva Conventions have peremptory status. In more general terms, the UN General Assembly affirmed in its Resolution 2949(XXVII) that the changes introduced by Israel in the occupied territories in violation of the Geneva Conventions are null and void. This emphasis on nullity underlines also here the peremptory character of the pertinent norms of the Conventions.

---

[154] *Kupreskic*, paras 517–518.   [155] *Kupreskic*, paras 519–520.
[156] Chernichenko and Treat Report, para. 137.
[157] Stavros, Fair Trial in Emergency Situations, *ICLQ* (1992), 349.
[158] Meron (2000), 253.

6.5. Environmental law

Despite the lack of evidence, peremptory character could be attributed to certain norms of environmental law, namely to those prohibiting the large-scale pollution of the human environment. The principle of harm prevention, as embodied in *Trail Smelter*, has evolved from a bilateral principle into that obliging States to prevent environmental harm not only with respect to other States, but also with regard to the international community as a whole. According to Principle 2 of the 1992 Rio Declaration, States must prevent environmental harm within or outside their national jurisdiction.

The system of environmental law, like human rights law, protects community interests, not merely those of States *inter se*,[159] and the management by a State of its own environment affects the community interest independently of any transnational effects.[160] The obligation to prevent harm to the human environment 'is no longer solely bilateral but benefits the international community as a whole'.[161] This is not essentially different from recognizing the peremptory character of the relevant environmental law norms.

Nevertheless, Birnie and Boyle contend that there are no *jus cogens* rules in environmental law, and refer to *Gabcikovo-Nagymaros* to justify this view.[162] There, Hungary contended that 'subsequently imposed requirements of international law in relation to the protection of the environment precluded the performance [by Hungary] of the [1977] Treaty'. Obligations as to harm prevention had evolved into *erga omnes* obligations.[163] It is unclear whether Hungary spoke in terms of Article 64 VCLT. Slovakia argued that none of the environmental law rules gives rise to peremptory norms that could override the 1977 Treaty.[164] The Court concluded that 'Neither of the Parties contended that new peremptory norms of environmental law had emerged since the conclusion of the 1977 Treaty, and the Court will consequently not be required to examine the scope of Article 64'.[165] Thus, the Court did not pronounce on this issue and it is ill-founded to argue that it denied the existence of *jus cogens* in environmental law.[166] On the other hand, the Court perhaps implicitly accepted the peremptory nature of new rules of environmental law as it considered it necessary for the parties to consider them 'when agreeing upon the means to be specified in the Joint Contractual Plan',[167] ie, when concluding an agreement.

---

[159] Birnie and Boyle, *International Law and the Environment* (2002), 99.
[160] Birnie and Boyle, 81, 85, 97. [161] Birnie and Boyle, 111.
[162] Birnie and Boyle, 81. [163] *ICJ Reports*, 1998, 62.
[164] *ICJ Reports*, 1998, 62. [165] *ICJ Reports*, 1998, 76.
[166] Dupuy, L'unité de l'ordre juridique international, 297 *RdC* (2002), 292, suggests that the Court has not rejected the existence of new environmental *jus cogens*.
[167] *ICJ Reports*, 1998, para. 112.

7. EVALUATION

The analysis demonstrates that although there is no exhaustive catalogue of peremptory norms, there certainly are established criteria for identifying the norms of *jus cogens* in individual cases. It would be fruitless to consider the scope of peremptory law limited to the norms that are pronounced as peremptory—this would indeed be a denial of the criteria of identification of *jus cogens*. The proper way rather is to assess every single norm, on its merits and in the light of the criteria of identification, to clarify whether it qualifies as a peremptory norm.

3

Distinctive Characteristics of
Peremptory Norms

I. THE UNCONDITIONAL CHARACTER OF
PEREMPTORY NORMS

Peremptory norms are not just binding but operate in an absolute and unconditional way.[1] The International Criminal Tribunal for the Former Yugoslavia has stated in quite categorical terms that the *jus cogens* character of the prohibition of torture as one of the most fundamental standards of the international community is designed to produce a deterrent effect and it 'is an absolute value from which nobody must deviate'.[2] This is similar to the general concept of public order, which requires absolute validity and performance.[3] The very rationale of peremptory norms in international law is that the interests of the international community as a whole shall prevail over the conflicting interests of individual States and groups of States.[4] This rationale makes peremptory rules absolute. The other rules are relative, since they concern only individual State interests.[5]

---

[1] Fitzmaurice, Third Report (1958), 40; Virally, Réflexions sur le 'jus cogens', 12 *Annuaire Français de Droit International* (1966), 8; Verdross, Forbidden Treaties in International Law (1937), 571–572; Suy, The Concept of Jus Cogens in International Law, *Lagonissi Conference: Papers and Proceedings*, vol. II, Carnegie Endowment for International Peace (1967), 18; Paul, Legal Consequences of Conflict between a Treaty and an Imperative Norm of General International Law (*jus cogens*), 21 *Österreichische Zeitschrift für öffentliches Recht* (1971), 32; Domb, Jus Cogens and Human Rights, 6 *Israel Yearbook of Human Rights* (1976), 112; Saladin, Völkerrechtliches Jus Cogens und Schweizerisches Landesrecht, Jenny and Kälin, *Die Schweizerische Rechtsordnung in Ihren Internationalen Bezügen* (1988), 73.

[2] *Furundzija*, para. 154.

[3] Nussbaum, *Deutsches Internationales Privatrecht* (1974), 64–65; Meyer, *Droit International Privé* (1994), 141.

[4] Jaenicke, Zur Frage des Internationalen Ordre Public, 7 *Berichte der Deutschen Gesellschaft für Völkerrecht* (1967), 85–87; Hannikainen, *Peremptory Norms in International Law* (1988), 4. The British reply in the *Fisheries* case expounded the reasoning of the prevalence of the norms embodying the community interest over the norms and claims based on individual State interest when it maintained that if the view of the individual State as to the applicable law or legal position differs from the view of the international community, then the attitude 'preserving the interests of the international community as a whole must prevail over the view of an individual State', *ICJ Pleadings, Anglo-Norwegian Fisheries case*, vol. 1, 428. Although the pertinent norms of the law of the sea were not peremptory, the principle itself as expounded by the UK is the precise description of the rationale of the primacy of peremptory norms.

[5] Verdross, *Jus Dispositivum* and *Jus Cogens* in International Law, *AJIL* (1966), 58; Hannikainen (1988), 4; Hannikainen, The case of East Timor from the perspective of jus cogens, *International Law and the Question of East Timor* (1995), 103.

Jus cogens is an inherent attribute of norms which safeguard the public interest and envisages their special effect of non-derogability.[6] Since *jus cogens* protects the community interest, respective absolute obligations are imposed on States towards the international community as a whole and not to individual States.[7] Peremptory rules, as rules serving superior interests, operate in an imperative manner in virtually all circumstances.[8] Reciprocity is not admitted.[9]

Jus cogens not only postulates the hierarchy between conflicting interests, but provides, by its very essence, the legal tool of ensuring the maintenance and continuous operability of this hierarchy, depriving conflicting acts and transactions of States of their legal significance.

The absolute character of a peremptory norm relates not to its scope, but to its normative quality. Peremptory norms can be qualified in scope. While the prohibition of torture is absolute in scope, outlawing everything which may generically fall within this concept, prohibition of the use of force, right to life[10] and right to self-determination are qualified in scope. Some peremptory norms (such as those on use of force and self-determination) refer for their operation to the will of the protected actor. Certain humanitarian law norms, such as those distinguishing between civilian and military objectives, operate by reference to principles of military necessity and proportionality, outlawing only conduct performed in breach of these limitations. The peremptory character of a given norm does not expand or modify that norm's scope but relates to that scope as it stands.

To the extent of their substantive, even qualified, scope, peremptory norms apply despite any conflicting circumstance external to a norm in question, such as the conduct or the will and attitude of the actors involved. In *Corfu Channel*, the International Court held that the prohibition of the use of force

---

[6] Kolb, *Theorie du* ius cogens *international* (2001), 172–173; Dupuy, L'unité de l'ordre juridique international, 297 *RdC* (2002), 276–277, 282.

[7] Hannikainen (1988), 5; Gaja, *Ius Cogens*, Obligations *Erga Omnes* and International Crimes: A Tentative Analysis of Three Related Concepts, Weiler, Cassese and Spinedi (ed.), *International Crimes of State: A Critical Analysis of Article 19 of the ILC's Draft Articles on State Responsibility* (1989), 159; Simma, Bilateralism and Community Interest in the Law of State Responsibility, Y. Dinstein/M.Tabory (eds.), *International Law at a Time of Perplexity – Essays in Honour of Shabtai Rosenne* (1989), 299; Li Haopei, Jus Cogens and International Law, Sienho Yee and Wang Tieya (ed.), *International Law in the Post-Cold War World – Festschrift Li Haopei* (2001), 514; on correlation between *jus cogens* and *erga omnes* obligations see Gaja, First ILI Report on Obligations *Erga Omnes*, section 5, and see further Chapter 8.

[8] Fitzmaurice, The general principles of international law considered from the standpoint of the rule of law, RdC (II-1957), 125; Virally (1966), 11.

[9] Kadelbach, *Zwingendes Volkerrecht* (1992), 329; the absence of reciprocity is particularly manifested by the inadmissibility of countermeasures that violate peremptory norms, as confirmed in ILC's Article 50 on State responsibility and commentary thereto, *ILC Report 2001*, 333, 336–337.

[10] The right to life is part of *jus cogens* subject to the carefully controlled exceptions, Ramcharan (1985), 15.

outlawed the Respondent's action despite the purpose for which force was used.[11] In *Hostages*, the Court did not accept a justificatory plea for the use of force to rescue hostages. The European Court of Human Rights applies the prohibition of torture despite any circumstance external to the prohibition, such as the suppression of terrorism. The absolute character of this prohibition means that neither the conduct of the victim nor the potential threat to society is relevant in applying the prohibition. The principle of *non-refoulement* and a parallel effect of the prohibition of torture with regard to expulsion and extradition have a similar basis.[12] The overriding absolute applicability of human rights and humanitarian law is reflected in a number of anti-terrorist conventions, as well as UN Security Council resolutions.[13]

The absolute applicability of *jus cogens* makes irrelevant the pleas of reciprocity and circumstances precluding wrongfulness, such as necessity.[14] Fitzmaurice characterizes peremptory norms as norms to be complied with even in the case of the prior illegal action of another State. Breaches of *jus cogens* are not merely illegal, but *malum in se*, because *jus cogens* embodies 'obligations of an absolute character, compliance with which is not dependent on corresponding compliance by others, but is requisite in all circumstances, unless under stress of literal *vis major*'.[15] No gaps in the applicability of *jus cogens* are permitted: they bind States upon their succession to another State irrespective of the successor's consent.[16] This conceptual independence of *jus cogens* from individual State conduct and attitudes explains its non-derogability.

Absolute validity modifies some patterns of traditional international law in which obligations are normally relative. When a norm operates just because individual States want it to, it is relative, operating only if and to the extent that the given individual States, especially the State injured in consequence

---

[11] *ICJ Reports*, 1949, 35.

[12] *Chahal* (ECtHR), paras 79–80. For a similar reasoning on extradition see The ILI Resolution on 'New Problems of Extradition', para. IV, I-60 *ILI Yearbook* (1983), 306, specifying that when extradition must be refused to protect individual human rights, the contrary factors such as the nature of the offence are irrelevant. The Resolution refers to basic human rights and as the preceding reports and discussion demonstrate, was adopted with *jus cogens* in mind.

[13] For treaties see Chapter 3, section 4; UNSCR 1456(2003).

[14] Gaja, *Jus Cogens* beyond the Vienna Convention, 172 *RdC* (1981), 297–298; Lowe (1999), 408–409; Laursen, The Use of Force and (the State of) Necessity, 37 *Vanderbilt Journal of Transnational Law* (2004), 507–512; Some peremptory humanitarian norms refer to military necessity. Military necessity relates to *lawful* acts while necessity as a defence relates to *unlawful* actions whose wrongfulness is precluded because they are *performed in* the state of necessity. See in general *ILC Report* 2001, Article 26 and its commentary, and the commentary to Article 50, para. 9.

[15] Fitzmaurice (1957), 119–120, 125.

[16] 'The peremptory norms of general international law and, in particular, respect for the fundamental rights of the individual and of the rights of peoples and minorities, are binding on all parties to the succession.' Opinion 1 of the Arbitration Commission, para. 1(e).

of a breach, want it to operate. But if a norm is dictated by transcendent community interest, it is not dependent on whether individual States want it to operate with regard to a specific situation. If a norm affects only the interest of individual States, it is logical that reciprocity is permitted, and all ordinary obligations are open to the possibility of being violated, terminated, abrogated or modified *inter se*. All these issues are matters exclusively for bilateral relations of the States involved. According to Virally, States may, to the extent of their mutual relations, decide not to apply a given norm at all.[17] Although the norm would continue to exist on a general plane, whether or not it would take its effect *inter se*—either generally or in a specific situation—depends on the subjective, even if concordant, will of those States.

In ordinary legal relations based on *jus dispositivum*, rules may be treated as subjective. For instance, States may redefine in their *inter se* relations the regime of territorial sea and ensuing rights and obligations, even with regard to the same maritime space. A State may adopt a limit of twelve miles with one State, six miles with the second State and twenty miles with the third State. It would be the same territorial sea, yet involve different regimes for different States subject to their agreement wherever required. When a State infringes upon fishing rights in the maritime space of another State, the rules of the 1982 Convention on the Law of the Sea or relevant customary law are generally applicable to that wrongful act as a basis for possible claims. But if a directly affected State wishes not to regard foreign illegal fishing as a breach of its rights relating to maritime space, either generally, or with regard to a specific case, or with regard to a specific State, or, alternatively, not to insist upon implementation of the consequences of such a breach, its will constitutes the ultimate determinative factor of how that legal relationship is to be conducted. The same principle would apply to fields like diplomatic immunities, trade, or expropriation of property. All these legal relations are bilateral and the decision of States not to apply a given norm on a bilateral plane would not involve any legal interest other than the interests of the States directly involved. Subject to State attitudes and practice, illegality could translate into law on an *inter se* basis.

The rationale behind *jus dispositivum* is observable in *Anglo-Norwegian Fisheries*, where the International Court affirmed the legality of straight baselines as the inner boundary of Norwegian territorial waters even though that regime deviated from the general regime of territorial waters and the latter regime remained valid and unaffected on a general plane. The judgment indicates that the regime of the territorial sea can be regulated in more than one way with regard to specific States or situations and that was based in that case on the attitudes of the States involved towards Norwegian baselines,

---

[17] Virally (1966), 9.

their abstention and acquiescence. The overall reason for the finding in Norway's favour was that the baselines method was not contrary to international law,[18] even though it was different from general international law.[19]

Thus, *jus dispositivum* is relative and States are masters of norms in their *inter se* relations. State attitudes as to their interpretation, application and remedies for violation of *jus dispositivum* can qualitatively resemble derogation. The former may be a factor leading to the latter, or the very element of the latter, as embodying or evidencing an implicit or explicit will of the directly involved States to derogate from a given norm. *Jus dispositivum* is derogable in every aspect: substance, invocation, remedies, or validation of a breach. Derogability in substance is conceptually similar to derogability in other aspects.

Public order norms operate integrally and cannot be fragmented either through formal derogation or interpretation and application. They apply integrally in all circumstances with uniform scope and content. As peremptory norms protect the community interest distinct from individual State interests, their integrity is the concern of all and the determination of questions whether a given norm applies to a given legal situation, or whether a given norm is breached and what are the consequences of a breach, affects the community interest. That is also why they are non-derogable. As Kolb emphasizes, *jus cogens* is opposed to the fragmentation of an objective and integral juridical regime, by reason of the public interest it embodies.[20] If the *jus cogens* nature of norms follows from their importance for the entire community, it would be contradictory to recognize the right of individual States to interpret, apply, or modify peremptory norms in their mutual relations as they please.

In case of norms protecting individual State interests, States directly affected by an illegal act are free not to invoke the illegality at all, thus transforming the illegality into legality through State practice and attitudes.[21] But for the rules protecting the community interest such a model is no longer appropriate, because their breach is objectively illegal. As Jennings suggests, objective wrongs are breaches of *jus cogens* offending against the community

---

[18] Fitzmaurice (1965), 42. *ICJ Reports* 1951, 143. Geographical features of the coast were not decisive: Judge McNair referred to similar geographical features of other coasts, *ICJ Reports*, 1951, 170.

[19] The UK reply contended that 'Norway is not entitled to go beyond what is permitted by customary law unless she can show the acquiescence of other States either by particular agreement or by establishing an historic title', *ICJ Pleadings*, vol. 1, 429. The British position was thus clearly based on the *jus dispositivum* character of the pertinent norms that can be derogated from through the use of the variety of methods.

[20] Kolb (2001), 96; Kolb, *Jus Cogens*, Intangibilité, Intransgressibilité, Dérogation 'Positive' et 'Négative', *RGDIP* (2005), 323.

[21] Rozakis, *The Concept of Jus Cogens in the Law of Treaties* (1976), 25.

interest.[22] According to Rozakis, 'objective illegality means the objective recognition of an illegality, as such, which can, therefore, be invoked with a view of its extinction by all members of the international community regardless of whether there is a particular damage sustained by the invoking States'.[23] Objective illegality can be most conveniently and comprehensively defined as an illegality independent in its emergence and elimination of the attitudes of involved States.

The concept of objective illegality seems to have the following elements: (a) the act is objectively illegal, independently of the attitudes of individual States; (b) the illegality may be objectively invoked, independently of the attitudes of a directly injured State; (c) the illegality must be objectively eliminated, and may not be cured through the expression of the attitudes of States. The absence of any of the above-mentioned elements from the concept of objective illegality would negate its qualitative difference from the subjective illegality, since individual States would be left the choice to prevent, through one means or another, the enforcement of a given peremptory norm through treating any of the aspects of illegality as subjective.

The concept of objective illegality, which is indispensable for the operation of peremptory norms, is organically linked to the need for uniformity in interpreting, applying or remedying violation of peremptory norms which protect the community interest and whose violation affects the community as a whole.

2. THE CONCEPT OF DEROGATION FROM *JUS COGENS*

A breach of *jus cogens* is absolutely illegal and the prohibition of derogation prevents States from treating illegality as legal, legitimating violation and fragmentation of operation of integrally operating peremptory norms. Derogation is something conceptually different from the limitations, qualifications or exceptions that are included within the content of the relevant norm itself. Derogation is something that takes place outside, and despite the requirements of, the relevant peremptory norm, and on the basis of the agreement between States. That the prohibition of the use of force is qualified by some exceptions under the United Nations Charter is not the derogation from this prohibition, but the factor related to its substantive scope. There would be derogation if some States were to agree that as between themselves certain uses of force not fitting into the substantive exceptions of the prohibition of the use of force is legal and thus exempt themselves from

---

[22] Jennings, Nullity and Effectiveness in International Law, *Cambridge Essays in International Law* (1965), 74; see also Judge Cancado Trinidade in *Blake* (Merits), para. 25, stating that objective illegality is 'one of the concepts underlying *jus cogens*'.

[23] Rozakis (1976), 24.

the aspects of the prohibition of the use of force that applies on a general plane.

To derogate means to repeal or abrogate in part, to destroy and impair the force and effect of, to lessen the extent of authority of, take away or detract from, deteriorate, diminish, depreciate; it also means to curtail or deprive a person of any part of his rights. Derogation is a partial abrogation or repeal of a law, contract, treaty, legal right etc.[24] This definition mirrors the concept of derogation from international *jus cogens*. This can be conveniently defined as the fragmentation *ratione personae* of the objective or integral juridical regime into particular juridical relations. Derogation is an incidence of the principle *lex specialis derogat legi generali*.[25]

Derogation from *jus cogens* is an attempt at establishment of a divergent, contrary legal regime. It is an attempt to legitimize acts contrary to *jus cogens* on an *inter se* basis and thus to hinder the integral and non-fragmentable operation of a given peremptory norm, to aim at a result outlawed by that norm, to allow States to do what peremptory norms prohibit or abstain from what peremptory norms require. This confirms that although early debates on peremptory norms focused on derogation by treaties, the concept of derogation itself is considerably broader to include derogations in other contexts as well.

It is suggested that the distinction must be drawn between the violation of and derogation from peremptory norms. Violation is a material act of simple non-compliance with the content of the norm. Derogation is, on the other hand, the substitution of one normative regime by another, the replacement of *lex generalis* by *lex specialis* as between the specified parties. Therefore, violation is a simple fact while derogation is a juridical act.[26] However, while this distinction is correct in principle, in the context of the operation of peremptory norms it could turn out that the dividing line between these two concepts is not as strict as may appear at first glance.

Any derogation is based on the violation of the pertinent peremptory norms. Derogation itself is a violation, but of specific character: it is the violation by conspiracy, by agreement. While derogation from *jus dispositivum* is permitted, it is illegal in the case of *jus cogens* and gives rise to a violation. Derogation generates not only the specific consequences such as those related to validity but also the consequences applicable to violations of international law in general.

On the other hand, every violation is capable of giving rise to derogation. In the decentralized international legal system, it is a tolerated occurrence that illegality can be transformed into the law and this happens when the

---

[24] *The Oxford English Dictionary* vol. IV (1989), 504.

[25] Kolb, *Jus Cogens*, Intangibilité, Intransgressibilité, Dérogation 'Positive' et 'Négative', *RGDIP* (2005), 323.

[26] Id., 322.

original illegality is complemented by the agreement between the relevant States with the effect that the illegal situation is no longer considered as illegal as far as those States are concerned. An example is the development of the law of continental shelf. The original declarations claiming continental shelf made at the time when this institution was non-existent violated the principles regarding the freedom of the seas. However, agreement among the relevant States has legitimized this institution and made it part of the law. When illegality exists on a bilateral plane only, it is the concern only for those relevant States and does not exist outside their bilateral relations. This is among the basic reasons as to why the derogation making illegality legal is permissible. The absence of such factors in the case of breaches of *jus cogens* that involve objective illegality is the basic factor that puts the limitations on derogation.

At the same time, non-derogability is the factor that independently produces legal outcomes in specific situations. The scope of the effects of peremptory norms cannot be judged solely in terms of the individual instances of the affirmation of these effects in practice, but also involves the categorical approach based on the inherent character of peremptory norms. The individual incidences of such effects in practice obviously retain their important evidentiary function, but relying on them solely and using them as the only factor for constructing the framework of the effects of *jus cogens* runs the risk of neglecting the crucial question of what the hierarchical superiority of peremptory norms as based on their non-derogability actually means.

Article 53 of the Vienna Convention outlaws formal derogation from *jus cogens* through agreements, but also defines peremptory norms as norms from which no derogation is permitted, without expressly specifying the proscribed means of derogation, still less limiting the impact of *jus cogens* to the specific kinds of derogations to the effect of exclusion of other derogations from its impact. The Vienna Convention applies only to agreements and this does not deny that the general rationale for outlawing derogation lies with the function of *jus cogens* and not the form of derogation. Derogation from *jus cogens* is illegal as a broader phenomenon and may take a variety of forms.

While derogation veils violation, violation can itself cause derogation, unless adequately redressed, due to the law-creating role of facts in the decentralized international legal system. The conduct of States can cause an implicit or informal derogation from a peremptory norm, where acquiescence or waiver may result in an implicit or informal agreement. All cases of derogation are conceivable subsequent to the actual breach; they may relate either to the substance of a rule or its effects. The peremptory character of a norm would be incompatible with the existence of the faculty of States to derogate from it implicitly, informally or subsequently, because these very derogations would achieve the purpose explicitly outlawed by Article 53, namely the legitimation of breaches of peremptory norms.

Derogation from *jus cogens* can relate to a norm's different aspects. Derogation could take place through denial of the existence or applicability of a norm to a given situation on an *inter se* basis. In the case of *jus cogens* the obligation would apply even if the States concerned take the attitude that, or behave as if, it does not. For instance, Israel's attitude that the Fourth Geneva Convention does not apply to the occupied Palestinian territories[27] is void and cannot entail a new legal relationship. Other States are precluded from accepting that attitude—they are prevented from derogation through establishing an exemption from the applicable regime. A similar outcome applies to claims that certain territories are not occupied but liberated or incorporated,[28] that the people entitled to self-determination has no valid right to self-determination,[29] that persons that are accorded POW status under international humanitarian law are not POWs but something else. The outcome of such claims cannot depend on individual State attitudes. This is not just a State unilaterally determining which regime applies but also the value of the attitudes of other States; once a certain attitude is absolutely illegal and objectively wrong, it cannot be accepted by other States. *Jus cogens* applies integrally and States are precluded from adopting any contrary attitude.

The similar context of derogation can be seen in the limits on reconciliation of State attitudes as to the characterization of their actions as illegal. The *Oil Platforms* case witnessed the situation when Iran characterized the US attacks on Iranian oil platforms as acts of aggression, while the US characterized the same attacks as actions taken in the exercise of the right to self-defence.[30] Disputes like this are to be resolved objectively, not as a bilateral matter. As the context involves the objective illegality, one party cannot validly acquiesce to the qualification which the other party gives to the relevant actions, unless that qualification is what the relevant norms, in this case those of *jus ad bellum*, objectively require. In other words, the parties cannot agree on the qualification of an action contrary to *jus cogens* which diverges from the qualification that is objectively due for that action.

Derogation can be attempted by *inter se* denial by States of the peremptory

---

[27] Kwakwa, *The International Law of Armed Conflict: Personal and Material Fields of Application* (1992), 81; Imseis, On the Fourth Geneva Convention and the Occupied Palestinian Territory, 44 *Harvard International Law Journal* (2003), 67–138; Quigley, The Israel–PLO Agreements versus the Geneva Civilians Convention, 7 *Palestinian Yearbook of International Law* (1992–1994), 57.

[28] Therefore, as the Israeli annexation of East Jerusalem is void, the attitude of the USA and the consequent coincidence of the attitudes of the two States cannot establish the valid legal relationship, cf Quigley (1992–1994), 52.

[29] cf Hannikainen, The case of East Timor from the perspective of jus cogens, *International Law and the Question of East Timor* (1995), 113.

[30] cf Separate Opinion of Judge Koojmans, para. 14.

character of a norm, either explicitly or implicitly by conduct. As Rozakis confirms, the presumption of the peremptory character of a norm is not rebuttable. If it were, States and their groups thus acting would be entitled to deny a norm's peremptory character and create a contrary legal regime undermining the very rationale of *jus cogens*.[31]

As Fitzmaurice asserts, whether there is an illegal use of force must be objectively determined and does not depend exclusively on the views of the parties.[32] In the same spirit, *Nicaragua* dictates that 'There is no rule of customary international law permitting another State to exercise the right of collective self-defence on the basis of its own assessment of the situation'.[33] Here again, the resort to collective self-defence must be objectively justified under relevant norms, as an unjustified action would cause an absolute illegality offending the community interest. In *Oil Platforms*, the International Court refused to judge the legality of forcible actions just by reference to the attitude embodied in a bilateral treaty and examined the relevant *jus ad bellum* as a matter of general international law.[34]

This relates also to State attitudes regarding invocation of collective self-defence treaty clauses. It is not enough that the States-parties to a treaty collectively consider that such a clause applies to a given situation; the clause must be objectively applicable in a way that the condition authorizing the resort to self-defence must be objectively present. Otherwise, States could justify, by reference to such clauses, the uses of force unjustified under the *jus ad bellum*.

Within the realm of *jus cogens*, the legal regime applicable to a situation must be objectively determined by reference to applicable norms, because the rights, obligations and responsibilities arising from such regimes protect not individual State interests but the community interest, and diverging State attitudes are tantamount to derogation.

Derogation from *jus cogens* can be *general*, showing the intent that a given peremptory norm does not govern *inter se* relations, or *specific*, intended for a particular fact or situation, where a norm is formally maintained 'alive', but it is stipulated that it does not apply or its consequences shall not be enforced with regard to a given situation. Both situations fall within the concept of derogation as they purport to preclude a peremptory norm from applying where it is supposed to apply. The community interest safeguarded by *jus cogens* would be offended whether peremptory norms are derogated from on a general plane or with regard to a specific situation.

Derogation can be informal or formal. The difference would be merely one of form, not substance. A treaty which does not derogate formally can be

---

[31] Rozakis (1976), 78.　　[32] Fitzmaurice, RdC (II-1957), 122–123.
[33] *Nicaragua*, *ICJ Reports*, 1986, 104.　　[34] *Oil Platforms*, General List No. 90.

informally applied, through interpretation, in a way that a derogatory result would be achieved. States could agree through their conduct that a given peremptory norm has no effect *inter se* or with regard to a specific situation. As Judge *ad hoc* Fernandez suggested in *Right of Passage*, State practice diverging from *jus cogens* is derogation and has no effect.[35]

Derogation can be previous or subsequent to a breach, aiming respectively at validating a breach in advance or subsequently. Pfluger considers that occupation of a territory supplemented by absence of protest or tacit consent is a bilateral or multilateral transaction.[36] As Judge Fitzmaurice asserts, acquiescence or estoppel, on an occasion where there was a duty to speak or act, implies agreement, or waiver of right.[37] According to Judge Spender, recognition of title and situation implies a fresh conventional arrangement.[38] Agreement means derogation, despite the time factor, and is subject to the effect of *jus cogens*. This justifies Abi-Saab's statement that *jus cogens* cannot give place through recognition, acquiescence or prescription, to a new legal regime.[39] If peremptory norms outlaw derogations through explicit treaty, the same must hold true for any process of recognition or tolerance, leading to a tacit agreement.[40]

The integral application of peremptory norms in spite of conflicting transactions is dictated by the community interest.[41] A normal public order impact on derogations of whatever character is that it has the negative effect of barring conflicting acts or transactions and the positive effect of replacing them by compatible norms.[42] The equivalent effect of international public order is that the derogation is without legal effect and the norms of public order governing a given situation apply instead of the purported derogatory

---

[35] *ICJ Reports*, 1960, 135. See also Sztucki, Jus Cogens *and the Vienna Convention on the Law of Treaties* (1974), 111, 'Assuming that there is a peremptory norm of general international law, any practice of States contrary to that norm would be illegal'; Brownlie, *Principles* (2003), 85–86; Abi-Saab, The Concept of *Jus Cogens* in International Law, 2 *Lagonissi Conference: Papers and Proceedings*, vol. II, Carnegie Endowment for International Peace (1967), 10; Janis, The Nature of *Jus Cogens*, 3 *Connecticut JIL* (1988), 362; Ford, Adjudicating *Jus Cogens*, 13 *Wisconsin International Law Journal* (1994), 146, 152, suggesting that even the widespread or universal contrary practice cannot corrupt *jus cogens*. Schachter, *International Law: Theory and Practice* (1991), 30–31 excludes derogation through multiple States' practice.

[36] Pfluger, *Die Einseitigen Rechtsgeschäfte im Völkerrecht* (1936), 294, though such a transaction is not a treaty.

[37] Fitzmaurice, *ICJ Reports*, 1962, 62.   [38] Spender, *ICJ Reports*, 1962, 130.

[39] Abi-Saab (1967), 11; Kadelbach (1992), 335; Nieto-Navia, International Peremptory Norms (*Jus Cogens*) and International Humanitarian Law, L.C. Vorhah *et al.* (eds), *Man's Inhumanity to Man, Essays on International Law in Honour of Antonio Cassese* (2003), 623.

[40] Suy (1967), 75, 86.

[41] cf Jaenicke (1967), 94.

[42] Battifol and Lagarde, *Traité de Droit International Privé* (1993), 591; Pillet and Niboyet, *Manuel de Droit International Privé* (1924), 419–420; Niederer, *Einführung in die Allgemeine Lehren des Internationalen Privatrechts* (1966), 291; Kropholler, *Internationales Privatrecht* (1994), 224; Meyer, *Droit International Privé* (1994), 145–146.

outcome. To illustrate, while a treaty authorizing an armed attack *inter partes* is void, the peremptory norms of *jus ad bellum* would continue applying to situations covered by a purported *inter partes* relationship. A classical provision regarding the negative and positive effect of public order norms in international law is Article 47 of the Fourth Geneva Convention, which proclaims the invalidity of the annexation measures of the occupied territory, and also specifies that the status of the occupied territory continues intact.

Derogation from *jus cogens* is different from its modification as foreseen under Article 53 of the Vienna Convention: while the latter, subject to the heavy standard of evidence of the community acceptance, changes the peremptory norm as such, the former, whether on a bilateral or multilateral plane, attempts to undermine the peremptory norm without modifying it. Universal derogation is a contradiction in terms.

The final aspect is that related to the relationship between the concept of derogation and those of countermeasures (reprisals), reciprocal non-compliance, and related defences. If such defences are admitted with regard to a legal norm this means that the system of international law treats the relevant norm as bilaterally disposable between the relevant States. Such derogation is not the product of the agreement between States to derogate, but rather the unilateral decision of the aggrieved party. Nevertheless, it exempts the bilateral relations from the ambit of the affected norm and this process takes place on the basis of the systemic features of the entire international legal system. It is therefore possible to speak of the consensual derogation and reciprocal, or systemic, derogation.

3. THE EFFECT-ORIENTED CHARACTER OF PEREMPTORY NORMS

Jus cogens does nothing to alter the decentralized character of the international legal system. The enforcement of peremptory norms can suffer from the same deficiencies as the enforcement of international law in general. But the specificity of peremptory norms is their specific impact on conflicting acts and transactions and other legal norms manifested through their specific effects which cannot be produced by ordinary norms of international law.

Peremptory norms are peremptory and non-derogable not as aspirations, but as norms. The peremptory character of a norm means that its operation as a legal norm, including its capability to produce the effects of a legal norm, is peremptory in itself.

It is nevertheless contended that the substance and the enforcement of *jus cogens* are different things; that while peremptory norms may exist, they do not possess superior force with regard to their effect and enforcement.[43] It is also occasionally submitted that the decentralized nature of international law makes it impossible for *jus cogens* norms to have their full effect,[44] though there is no major source behind this argument. As Bianchi suggests, the endorsement of the consequences to which *jus cogens* gives rise

would necessitate the calling into question of some of the founding elements of the international system as currently perceived. . . . In particular, its consequences can be highly disruptive of the still primarily State-centred international legal system, and States are not willing to accept them.

However, Bianchi also points to the fact that States have indeed accepted the concept of *jus cogens* by subscribing to the Vienna Convention on the Law of Treaties.[45] In addition, the Convention accepts the concept of *jus cogens* as a category of multi-level effects. As for the argument that the full effects of peremptory norms are impeded by the decentralized nature of international law, it has not yet been demonstrated in which aspect this decentralized nature is opposed to the full operation of *jus cogens*. The effects such as, for instance, the non-recognition of illegal annexations or the refusal to grant immunity for the breaches of *jus cogens* are certainly possible in the State-centred, or decentralized, international legal system. There is nothing in those effects of *jus cogens* to require for their viability the existence of some centralized government or authority that would be authorized to create and administer international law. If, on the other hand, the accepted structure of international law means the paramount validity of certain principles and institutions in the scope and shape in which they exist at the certain fixed period of time or stage of development, it is beyond doubt that most if not all legal institutions are subject to change and modification in terms of what the prevailing community needs may require. Consequently, certain principles that were at some stage considered as fundamental to the character of international law need not be so considered forever.

Yet another conceptual construct aimed at limiting the effects of peremptory norms is the approach under which peremptory norms constitute merely the norms of primary conduct and do not encompass the aspects of the further operation and enforcement of the relevant norms, that is the 'secondary' aspect of the norm.

---

[43] As contended by Judge *ad hoc* Kreca in the *Bosnia* case, the legal nature of a norm and its enforcement are different things; *ICJ Reports*, 1996, 658 (Dissenting Opinion). Judge Kreca opposed the International Court's findings on the impact of the nature of a rule on its jurisdiction. But the Court held that the nature of a rule may influence the existence of its jurisdiction in a specific case; *ICJ Reports*, 1996, 116–117.

[44] Fox, *The Law of State Immunity* (2002), 540, speaking of the legal consequences of peremptory norms affecting 'the whole accepted structure of law'.

[45] Bianchi, Dismantling the Wall: The ICJ's Advisory Opinion and Its Likely Impact on International Law, 47 *German Yearbook of International Law* (2004), 386.

This approach, too, is merely theoretical. There is no general principle of international law according to which its norms ought to be divided into 'substantive' and 'consequential', 'primary' and 'secondary', or in any other comparable manner. Some national legal systems may be familiar with such categorizations, but international law is not, at least not more than in highly descriptive terms. Every norm of international law is a free-standing and full-fledged norm; it is, or can be, created and modified in the same way as other norms, subjected to the same processes of enforcement and, most importantly, undergo the same process of interaction with other legal norms as manifested by the cases of defences, derogation and reciprocal non-compliance. In this sense, every consequential or procedural norm of international law is, at the same time, a substantive norm, a rule of substance, embodying the substantive rights and obligations under international law.

The UN International Law Commission singled out 'primary' and 'secondary' norms in terms of the law of State responsibility, but it did so for descriptive purposes only, without attributing to this distinction any inherent impact on the character of relevant norms and the rights and obligations arising therefrom. On the contrary, what the ILC did was to reaffirm the applicability of peremptory norms exactly in the realm of the so-called 'secondary' norms, that is the norms on responsibility, reparation and enforcement.

Above all, the restrictive view of *jus cogens* neglects its general rationale. It is unclear why the norms are differentiated in terms of their substantive nature if this has no consequential effect, and why a norm should be specific in character because of embodying community interest and yet be unable to produce similarly specific consequences to safeguard the integrity of that community interest. It would be pointless if a norm was endowed with peremptory status, but its effects and legal consequences were governed by the criteria of ordinary rules.

A distinction in character between the norm and its enforcement is unfounded. Legal norms are there to be enforced. Non-peremptory norms protect individual State interests and their operation, including their enforcement, is left to the will of States. Peremptory norms operate in the community interest and the attitude of directly involved States is no longer decisive in whether and how they must be enforced. If the legal effects of *jus cogens* are not viewed as peremptory, then the distinction between *jus dispositivum* and *jus cogens* gets blurred; under such an approach, States would be free to regard in practice *jus cogens* as *jus dispositivum* and reduce the peremptory character of a norm to a dead letter.

Non-enforcement of a peremptory norm can offend the community interest in the same way as primary violations. Such community interest is present not only in avoiding torture, war crimes or genocide, but also in enforcing adequate remedies for such violations, such as the reparation and prosecution of perpetrators. When a norm operates on a bilateral plane, its further operation, including its effects, is also bilateral. But if a norm is peremptory the same holds true for its effects.

According to Pellet, '*Jus cogens* rules have no determinative form and are only recognisable by their effects: contrary provisions are null and void'.[46] According to Tomuschat, '*Jus cogens* as a higher-ranking group of legal rules comes into play only when the validity of a treaty is to be evaluated or when it has to be determined whether, by other means, a legal position can be created or maintained that is incompatible with such peremptory rules'.[47] As Nicoloudis submits, 'L'ordre juridique ne se contente pas de qualifier certaines de ses normes comme impératives, mais en plus organise leur protection juridique de sorte que leur nature de norme imperative se voit ainsi confirmée et assurée.'[48]

When a principle in question is peremptory, it would be artificial to attribute different legal force to various rules and principles specifying, elaborating and implementing that principle. 'The whole cluster of legal standards' emanating from a peremptory norm and supporting its enforcement must be regarded as peremptory.[49]

The prevailing pattern confirms the effect-oriented nature of *jus cogens*. Articles 53 and 64 of the Vienna Convention do not establish a substantive prohibition of concluding treaties conflicting with *jus cogens*, but say in consequential terms that a treaty conflicting with peremptory norms is void, or becomes void and terminates when a new conflicting peremptory norm emerges. Articles 53 and 64 themselves are peremptory.[50]

Peremptory norms possess the capacity to survive multiple levels of illegality and have a multiple consequential effect. Forcible territorial acquisitions cannot be recognized; they also cannot be validated through State succession.[51] The rule of non-recognition is also an illustration of the consequential and effect-oriented profile of *jus cogens*. This rule does not require that territories should not be acquired forcibly, but that such acquisitions are void and cannot be recognized.

The consequential profile of *jus cogens* seems to have been accepted in the codification of the law of State responsibility. As a matter of State attitudes,

---

[46] Pellet, The Normative Dilemma: Will and Consent in International Law-Making, 12 *Australian Yearbook of International Law* (1992), 38; Abi-Saab (1967), 15.

[47] Tomuschat, Obligations Arising for States without or against Their Will, 241 *RdC* (1993), 276.

[48] Nicoloudis, *La nullité de jus cogens et le développement contemporain de droit international public* (1974), 40.

[49] Cassese, *Self-Determination of Peoples* (1994), 140.

[50] Verhoeven, *Jus Cogens* and Reservations or 'Counter-reservations' to the Jurisdiction of the International Court of Justice, Wellens (ed.) *International Law: Theory and Practice: Essays in Honor of Eric Suy* (1998), 205.

[51] Zimmermann, *Staatennachfolge in völkerrechtlichen Verträgen* (2000), 27.

the Czech Republic considered that secondary rules applicable to peremptory norms 'must also be peremptory in nature, with no possibility of derogating from them by means of an agreement *inter partes*'.[52] This view has not been contradicted and later has been affirmed by the ILC.[53]

The analysis in the following chapters demonstrates that the difference between the substance and enforcement of legal norms in the case of *jus cogens* is often disapproved in practice as unworkable. Even in the cases where such distinction is adhered to, it is never justified by reference to the coherent conceptual basis.

---

[52] UN Doc. A/CN.4/488, 92.

[53] 'In certain cases the consequences that follow from a breach of some overriding rule may themselves have a peremptory character,' *ILC Report* 2001, commentary to Article 55, 357, para. 2.

4

Concepts Cognate to *Jus Cogens*

Certain instruments and concepts reveal characteristics not conceivable in terms of *jus dispositivum*. In order to understand whether they are cognate to peremptory norms, it must be examined whether they share its basic substantive characteristics of non-fragmentable protection of the community interest and the consequent constraining effect on the freedom of action of States. This section will examine the treaty obligations sharing the character of *jus cogens* and the concept of the object and purpose of a treaty.

I. TREATY OBLIGATIONS SHARING THE CHARACTER OF *JUS COGENS*

International law has long been familiar with the distinction between different kinds of treaties in terms of their substance.[1] The purpose of making this distinction has been the higher importance that States and their groups attached to the subject-matter of certain treaties and which they were thus keen to regard as higher law. This has been the case, for instance, with regard to the 1928 Paris Pact on the Renunciation of War, which has been regarded as higher law in a way giving rise to the duty of non-recognition of its violations,[2] or to certain treaties establishing territorial regimes,[3] or peace treaties. The reason behind this movement has been that the relevant treaties have somehow transcended the bilateral treaty relations. But only in some of these cases could some public order elements be identified in the relevant treaties, the other cases remaining placed within the conceptual framework of the bilateralist and individualist international legal system. The principal reason for this is that the multilateral or even so-called regime-creating character of the treaty is not necessarily the same as its embodiment of public order.

Certain kinds of multilateral treaties differ from the normally reciprocal pattern of multilateral treaties consisting of a multiplicity of bilateral relations. Arguably, there are two types of treaty obligations which do not involve a mutual exchange of benefits and performances on an individually

---

[1] McNair, Function and Differing Legal Character of Treaties, *BYIL*, 1930; Jenks, The Conflict of Law-Making Treaties, *BYIL* (1951); Jenks, State Succession in Respect to Law-Making Treaties, *BYIL* (1952).
[2] See below, Chapter 11.   [3] See below, Section 1.3.

reciprocating basis.[4] As Special Rapporteur Fitzmaurice suggests, it is 'necessary, in the case of multilateral treaties, to distinguish between types of obligations—on the one hand those based on contractual reciprocity consisting of a reciprocal interchange between the parties, each giving certain treatment to, and receiving it from, each of the others; or again, obligations of such a character that their performance by one party is necessarily dependent on performance by all the parties; and on the other hand, those which must be applied integrally or not at all.'[5]

Simma refers to treaty obligations that cannot be split into bilateral relationships. In the Nuclear Tests Ban Treaty, the rights and obligations of parties form an indivisible whole such that these obligations have to be performed vis-à-vis every other party. 'In other instances, multilateral obligations do not run between the States-parties at all but rather oblige the contracting States to adopt a certain "parallel" conduct within their jurisdiction which manifests itself as any tangible exchange or interaction *between* the parties', such as in the case of human rights treaties.[6] According to Simma, the Vienna Convention on the Law of Treaties accommodates this typology of treaty obligations.[7] But even if this Convention attaches some specific regulation to integral and interdependent obligations,[8] the core question for this analysis is whether such specific regulation and the character of these treaties follows from international public order.

1.1. Objective treaty obligations

As a rule, multilateral treaties, such as a multilateral extradition treaty, form merely a bundle of bilateral relations.[9] Their breach has effects only in relations between the State responsible for the breach and the injured State.[10] To give rise to a multilateral obligation, treaty rules must have an absolute

---

[4] The type of interdependent treaty obligations, along with integral or objective obligations, was first singled out by Special Rapporteur Fitzmaurice in the work on the law of treaties and further developed within the ILC both with regard to this topic and State responsibility. Fitzmaurice, Third Report, YbILC, 1958, vol. II, 44.

[5] Fitzmaurice, Second Report, II YbILC 1957, 53.

[6] Simma, Bilateralism and Community Interest in the Law of State Responsibility, Y. Dinstein/M.Tabory (eds.), *International Law at a Time of Perplexity – Essays in Honour of Shabtai Rosenne* (1989), 823–824 (emphasis original). See also Verdross and Simma, *Universelles Völkerrecht: Theorie und Praxis* (1984), §754.

[7] Simma (1989), 824.

[8] eg Articles 19, 31, 41, 58, 60.

[9] Dominice, The International Responsibility of States for Breach of Multilateral Obligations, 10 *EJIL* (1999), 354–355. Contrary to Kälin, Menschenrechtsverträge als Gewährleistung einer objektiven Ordnung, Kälin, Riedel and Karl (eds.) *Aktuelle Probleme des Menschenrechtsschutzes*, Berichte der Deutschen Gesellschaft für Völkerrecht, Bd. 33 (1994), 12, treaty obligations can be bilateral even if provided with the collective enforcement machinery. Pauwelyn, *Conflict of Norms in Public International Law* (2003), 68 ff., affirms that WTO obligations are bilateral. Orakhelashvili, Review on Pauwelyn (2003), *CLJ* 2004, 248.

[10] Dominice, 357.

value and 'it is precisely the intrinsic content of each obligation that may justify recognising it as incorporating a value important to the international community as a whole, thereby justifying the term multilateral obligation'.[11]

The most suitable candidates for the category of treaties that embody objective and non-bilateralizable obligations are treaties in the field of human rights and humanitarian law. It is argued that it is difficult to define what is meant by a humanitarian treaty and that there is no precise meaning behind this concept,[12] although the humanitarian treaty can conveniently, and simply, be defined as the treaty which protects the rights and interests of the individuals as distinct from those of the States-parties as such.

There are also doctrinal suggestions that humanitarian treaties are no exception from the normal bilateral pattern of treaty relations.[13] But these approaches are not approved in practice, which elaborates both on the special character of humanitarian treaties, as well as the reasons for which they are distinguished from other treaties.

The most appropriate explanation of the specific nature of humanitarian treaty obligations refers to their substantive character or 'intrinsic content'. According to Walter, 'Auch objektive Verpflichtungen sind subjektiv, insofern sie sich an die Subjekte richten, denen sie auferlegt sind. . . . Es sind die den Vertragstaaten *subjektiv* zugeordneten Pflichten, die die objektive Verpflichtungstheorie als objektiv qualifiziert.'[14] It is the substance of sub-jectively assumed treaty obligations which makes them objective.

International tribunals have repeatedly affirmed that humanitarian treaties have a specific objective character because they protect not the interests of contracting States but the fundamental rights of individuals or their groups. In the Advisory Opinion on *Reservations*, the International Court emphasized the special character of the 1948 Genocide Convention, stressing that 'In such a convention the contracting States do not have any interests of their own; they merely have, one and all, a common interest, namely, the accomplishment of those high purposes which are the *raison d'être* of the convention. Consequently, in a convention of this type one cannot speak of individual advantages or disadvantages to States, or of the maintenance of a perfect contractual balance between rights and duties.'[15] The European Commission of Human Rights has affirmed the similar character of the

---

[11] Dominice, 355–357.

[12] Pellet, *Second Report on Reservations to Treaties*, A/CN.4/477/Add.1, 12ff., paras 77 ff.; Hampson, Working Paper, para. 7.

[13] See eg Aust, *Modern Treaty Law and Practice* (2000), 122.

[14] Walter, *Die Europäische Menschenrechtsordnung* (1970), 55 (emphasis original); Craven, Legal Differentiation and the Concept of the Human Rights Treaty in International Law 11 *EJIL* (2001), 497, suggests that the overriding contractual paradigm is largely (if not wholly) inadequate for such treaties.

[15] *ICJ Reports*, 1951, 23. It must be pointed out in this regard that during the proceedings of the *Reservations* Opinion, the Court faced the argument, notably from the Government of

ECHR in *Austria v Italy*.[16] Later, in *Ireland v UK*, the European Court emphasized that

Unlike international treaties of the classic kind, the Convention comprises more than mere reciprocal engagements between contracting States. It creates, over and above a network of mutual, bilateral undertakings, objective obligations which, in the words of the Preamble, benefit from a 'collective enforcement'.[17]

These specific obligations are assumed by each State-party towards persons within its jurisdiction, not towards other States-parties.[18] The Inter-American Court of Human Rights has said much the same thing of the American Convention of Human Rights: 'The object and purpose of the Convention is not the exchange of reciprocal rights between a limited number of States, but the protection of the human rights of all individual human beings within the Americas, irrespective of their nationality.'[19] It further emphasized that

modern human rights treaties in general, and the American Convention in particular, are not multilateral treaties of the traditional type concluded to accomplish the reciprocal exchange of rights for the mutual benefit of the contracting States. Their object and purpose is the protection of the basic rights of individual human beings irrespective of their nationality, both against the State of their nationality and all other contracting States. In concluding these human rights treaties, the States can be deemed to submit themselves to a legal order within which they, for the common

---

Israel, that not all the provisions of the Genocide Convention are of normative character. It was submitted that 'the stipulations of the Convention are of three distinct kinds, that is to say, normative, contractual and ministerial', Written Statement of Israel, *ICJ Pleadings*, 1951, 200–201; Oral Statement by Rosenne, id., 333. The Genocide Convention 'contains stipulations of a normative character and stipulations of a contractual character. However, as is clear from its text and from the whole history of the United Nations dealing with the problem of genocide, the intention of its framers was equally to codify, at least in part, substantive international law and to establish international obligations to facilitate international cooperation in the prevention and punishment of the crime. Consequently, the Convention cannot be regarded as a single indivisible whole, and its normative stipulations are divisible from its contractual stipulations.' Rosenne, *ICJ Pleadings*, 1951, 356. Particular reference was made to contractual undertakings to implement the undertakings embodied in normative provisions, such as the duty to enact legislation under Article V, the duty of extradition under Article VIII, or the duty to submit to the jurisdiction of the International Court, Written Statement of Israel, *ICJ Pleadings*, 201–202, 202–203; Oral Statement by Rosenne, *ICJ Pleadings*, 337–338, 356–357. It should be pointed out that the Court itself did not uphold any such or related qualification of the Convention obligations into the commitments of different types. It rather made a general statement that 'The high ideas which inspired the Convention provide, by virtue of the common will of the parties, the foundation and measure of all its provisions,' *ICJ Reports*, 1951, 23. Furthermore, the submissions of Israel are devoid of essence as it is now increasingly recognized that the enforcement and implementation provisions of humanitarian conventions constitute the essential element of the object and purpose of those conventions. See below, Section 2.

[16] *Austria v Italy*, 4 *YB ECHR* (1961), 140.
[17] *Ireland v UK*, 58 ILR 188, at 291.
[18] *Cyprus v Turkey*, 8007/77, 13 *DR* 145, at 147 (1998), 40–41.
[19] *Effect of Reservations*, para. 27, 67 ILR 568.

good, assume various obligations, not in relation to other States, but towards all individuals within their jurisdiction.[20]

The Inter-American Court emphasized the similarity between regional human rights treaties and universal treaties such as the Genocide Convention.[21] Similarly, the UN Human Rights Committee emphasized that the ICCPR is not a web of inter-State obligations, but is designed to safeguard individual human beings.[22] Humanitarian law treaties also possess a similar character. They are not intended to benefit or protect State interests; they are primarily designed to protect human beings *qua* human beings. 'Unlike other international norms, such as those of commercial treaties which can legitimately be based on the protection of reciprocal interests of States, compliance with humanitarian rules could not be made dependent on a reciprocal or corresponding performance of those obligations by States.'[23] Geneva Conventions embody not merely engagements 'concluded on a basis of reciprocity, binding each party to the contract only in so far as the other party observes its obligations. It is rather a series of unilateral engagements solely contracted before the world as represented by the other contracting parties.'[24] An objective character may thus be attributed to obligations embodied in treaties on human rights, humanitarian and international labour law, whether of universal or regional scope.

Of course, objective treaty obligations are embodied in treaties accepted by States-parties and hence it is technically correct that such obligations are assumed by States-parties towards other States-parties, being invocable by the latter. But this must not lead us to overlook that the purpose and essence of such treaty obligations is to benefit and protect the interests of individuals rather than States.

Simma suggests that obligations under humanitarian treaties are assumed towards the 'circle of other contracting parties'.[25] But this ignores the objective character of obligations and the absence of contractual balance within them. If treaty obligations operate just as a matter of relations between parties, then parties can excuse their breach by a culprit State, exempt it from

---

[20] *Effect of Reservations*, para. 29, 67 ILR 568; the same was affirmed in '*Other Treaties*', 67 ILR 600, *Ivcher Bronstein*, Series C, No. 54, paras 43–45, *Constitutional Court*, Series C, No. 55, paras 41–44.

[21] Id., para. 30, 67 ILR 569; see also *Ivcher Bronstein*, IACtHR, Series C, No. 54, paras 39–41; *Constitutional Court*, IACtHR, Series C, No. 55, paras 42–44.

[22] General Comment 24(52), para. 17, 2 *IHRR* (1995), 10.

[23] *Kuprsekic*, Judgment of 14 January 2000, para. 518.

[24] Pictet, *Commentary to the First Geneva Convention of 1949* (1952), 17–18.

[25] Simma, From Bilateralism to Community Interest, 250 RdC (IV-1994), 370. But Bryde, Verpflichtungen *Erga Omnes* aus Menschenrechten, Kälin, Riedel and Karl (eds) *Aktuelle Probleme des Menschenrechtsschutzes, Berichte der Deutschen Gesellschaft für Völkerrecht* (1994), 169, stresses that even if such obligations are assumed towards other parties, they nevertheless relate to the international community interest.

them or breach them by reciprocity. The very reason that this is not possible[26] is that these treaty obligations go beyond contractual relations between the parties and are assumed towards the entire international community. In addition, even if, as a matter of treaty law, these obligations operate between a party and other parties, they have counterparts in general international law operating between a State and the entire international community.

A better characterization of objective or absolute treaty obligations is given by Fitzmaurice, suggesting that 'The obligation has an absolute rather than a reciprocal character—it is, so to speak, an obligation towards all the world rather than towards particular parties. Such obligations may be called self-existent, as opposed to concessionary, reciprocal or interdependent obligations.'[27] Fitzmaurice further specifies that these treaty obligations cannot be split into bilateral treaty relations. They are not, unlike, for instance, a multilateral treaty regulating commercial relations, a generalized set of bilateral agreements.[28] This is further confirmed by the character of the humanitarian treaties such as the Geneva Conventions as embodying 'unilateral engagements solely contracted before the world as represented by the other contracting parties'. This demonstrates that whatever the scope of the parties in the technical sense, the actual obligations operate towards each State-party and the entire international community. If Simma's approach were adopted, objective treaty obligations would still be subject to the principle of reciprocity which is definitionally incompatible with them.

The objective character of treaty obligations relates also to their subject-matter character. To illustrate, as Fitzmaurice does, under the Genocide Convention the parties 'did not undertake not to commit genocide only in relation to one another's subjects or citizens; they undertook not to commit genocide at all, even in relation to their own subjects and citizens, and irrespective of what other States were doing or of whether these could or could not be regarded as parties to the Conventions. In short, the Convention lays down a code of behaviour, to be conformed to invariably and *erga omnes*; and this is the characteristic feature of every norm-creating convention.'[29] This reflects also Fitzmaurice's observation about *jus cogens* generally as norms which cannot be violated even in response to their prior breach by other States.

Objective treaty obligations are invocable in relation to a State with whom the invoking State has no treaty relation on the subject. The Swiss *Bundesgericht* affirmed that peremptory norms of the European Convention on

---

[26] 'Interdependent' obligations are different; cf the next section.

[27] Fitzmaurice, Second Report, 2 YbILC 1957, 54.

[28] Fitzmaurice, Judicial Innovation: Its Uses and Its Perils, *Cambridge Essays in International Law* (1965), 33.

[29] Fitzmaurice (1965), 33–34. 'Norm-creating' meaning a convention that independently creates norms, or embodies the norms binding States even without any conventional obligation.

Human Rights must be observed in deciding on extradition whether or not Switzerland has treaty relations under the Convention with the requesting State.[30] As is recognized, 'the absence of a requirement for reciprocity means that relevant provisions of the Convention will apply in the case of extradition or deportation from party-States to third countries which are not party to the Convention'.[31]

Can obligations which are the product of the will of the contracting parties and whose continued existence is dependent solely on their will have an objective character? If a treaty obligation is there just because the parties have so wished, it is unclear why the same parties could not dispose of this obligation or split it into bilateral regimes. The extra-contractual relevance of such obligations should be demonstrated. As the International Court stressed in the *Reservations* Opinion, the objective character of the obligations embodied in the Genocide Convention is due to the fact that the Convention principles would bind States even in the absence of any conventional obligations as principles outlawing conduct shocking the conscience of mankind and contrary to moral law.[32] Treaties embodying objective obligations are obviously treaties and, subject to their own provisions or the Vienna convention on the Law of Treaties, States-parties can terminate them. But this is conceptually different from and does not imply any right to derogate from such treaty obligations and split them into bilateral legal relations while continuing to be a party to a relevant treaty: termination means ceasing being a party, while derogation implies continuing being a party on different terms with regard to different States-parties.[33]

---

[30] Auslieferung No. 10, *Entscheidungen des Schweizerischen Bundesgerichts*, 109. Band, I. Teil, 72. The Court referred to the ECHR prohibition of torture and its peremptory character but not to customary law of any kind (cf Simma and Alston, The Sources of Human Rights Law: Custom, Jus Cogens, and General Principles, 12 *Australian Yearbook of International Law* (1992), 106) or general international law. The Court's treatment of the issue conforms with the objective character of human rights treaty obligations as binding a State-party in an absolute way, independently of its treaty relations with other States. A similar reasoning was adopted by the same court in Auslieferung No. 47, *Entscheidungen des Schweizerischen Bundesgerichts*, 122. Band, I. Teil, 379–380. Hence the duty to observe is not limited to other States-parties.

[31] Stanbrook and Stanbrook, *Extradition: Law and Practice* (2000), 97–98.

[32] *ICJ Reports*, 1951, 22. In *Nuclear Weapons* the Court affirmed that a great many norms of humanitarian law are so fundamental that they have to be observed by all States whether or not they have ratified the conventions that contain them, *ICJ Reports*, 1996, para. 79. Barile, The Protection of Human Rights in Article 60, Paragraph 5 of the Vienna Convention on the Law of Treaties, *International Law at the Time of its Codification, Essays in Honour of Roberto Ago*, vol. II (1987), 8–9.

[33] This issue has practical relevance as all instances where tribunals assert the objective character of treaty obligations concern not the withdrawal from a treaty but derogatory action while the party concerned considers itself as continuing to be a party. See *Austria v Italy* and *Ivcher Bronstein*, and more generally Chapter 15. Furthermore, as Special Rapporteur Waldock submitted, it would be absurd to consider that the denunciation of the treaties like the Genocide Convention would free States from the obligations embodied in the Convention, I YbILC 1963, 131.

The difference of objective treaty obligations from reciprocal obligations embodied in multilateral treaties (community interest versus individual State interests) is the same as the difference between *jus cogens* and *jus dispositivum* in general international law. This may be an indication that the objective character of such treaty obligations mirrors their place and status under general international law.

As Verdross emphasized, conventions protecting human beings, banning slavery, abuse of prisoners, traffic in women and children are adopted in the interest not of individual States but of humanity as a whole.[34] According to Fitzmaurice, conventions on human rights and labour law embody obligations of an absolute and self-existent kind, the duty to perform which, once assumed, is not, unlike the commerce or disarmament treaties, dependent on the reciprocal or corresponding performance by other parties.[35] These qualities resemble *jus cogens*; they are, so to speak, a conventional equivalent.

Certain law-making treaties are declaratory of *jus cogens* such as the treaties on genocide, slavery, forced labour, discrimination and the 1949 Geneva Conventions.[36] The fundamental principles enshrined in the Geneva Conventions are of *jus cogens* character.[37] As such multilateral treaties embody non-reciprocal obligations giving a legal interest to all parties, such as basic human rights, these norms are anchored in general international law and possess the status of *jus cogens*, by reflecting peremptory norms of general international law.[38]

The specific execution structure of objective or integral treaty obligations also resembles *jus cogens*: obligations assumed by each party operate identically between that party and all other parties. Such obligations cannot be

---

[34] Verdross, *Jus Dispositivum* and *Jus Cogens* in International Law, *AJIL* (1966), 59.

[35] Fitzmaurice, The general principles of international law considered from the standpoint of the rule of law, RdC (II-1957), 125–126; Tanzi, Is Damage a Distinct Condition for the Existence of an Internationally Wrongful Act? Spinedi and Simma (ed.), *United Nations Codification of State Responsibility* (1987), 17; the ILC Study Group on Fragmentation of International Law emphasized in very similar terms that 'A human rights treaty gives rise to absolute obligations: the obligations it imposes are independent and absolute and performance of them is independent of the performance by the other parties of their obligations.' *Report of the ILC Study Group on Fragmentation of International Law*, A/CN.4/L.663/Rev.1, 18.

[36] Scheuner, Conflict of Treaty Provisions with a Peremptory Norm of General International Law, 29 *Zeitschrift für ausländisches öffentliches Recht und Völkerrecht* (1969), 30; Schwelb, Some Aspects of International *Jus Cogens*, 61 *AJIL* (1967), 953; Jaenicke (1967), 93–94; Capotorti, Possibilities of Conflict in National Legal Systems between the European Convention and Other International Agreements, Robertson (ed.), *Human Rights in National and International Law* (1968), 78.

[37] YbILC, 1963-II, 59; Meron, *Human Rights and Humanitarian Norms as Customary Law* (1989), 8–9.

[38] Dominice, The International Responsibility of States for Breach of Multilateral Obligations, 10 *EJIL* (1999), 355; Barile (1987), 6–9.

bilateralized or fragmented.[39] Such treaty obligations are assumed not by one party towards another as such, but objectively.[40] Also, as emphasized in the example of the European Convention on Human Rights, 'Die objektive Verpflichtungstheorie enthält die stillschweigende Voraussetzung daß sich die MRK nicht in subjektive Rechtsbeziehungen auflösen läßt.'[41] The law contained in the European Convention is not dispositive but peremptory. This *jus cogens* is not disposable on the basis of the concurring derogation (*Abweichung*) by the parties.[42] The code of obligations in humanitarian treaties is 'absolute and admits of no derogations'.[43] As human rights treaties merely reflect the pre-existing standard of *jus cogens*, the parties may not retract them in reciprocal relations.[44] As Kolb submits, the *erga omnes* aspect of integral treaties necessitates the interdiction of subsequent agreements which are incompatible with their object.[45] One consequence of a norm's peremptory character is that if it is embodied in a treaty it cannot be set aside in response to a material breach in line with Article 60 of the Vienna Convention.[46]

In historical perspective, the judicial emphasis on objective treaty obligations started when there was no uniformly consolidated concept of *jus cogens* in international law and this explains that judicial decisions fall short of directly referring to *jus cogens*.[47] However, tribunals since the International Court in *Genocide* and the European Commission in *Austria v Italy* referred

---

[39] Kolb, *Théorie du* ius cogens *international* (2001), 149–150. Kadelbach, *Zwingendes Völkerrecht* (1992), 77, suggests that in humanitarian conventions the principle of reciprocity is limited in a way resembling peremptory norms, and such treaties are sources of *jus cogens*. Provost, Reciprocity in Human Rights and Humanitarian Law, *BYIL* (1995), 404.

[40] Walter, *Die Europäische Menschenrechtsordnung* (1970), 56. The same is reiterated for the Geneva Conventions, Pictet, *Commentary to the First Geneva Convention of 1949* (1952), 18–19, Pilloud *et al*, *Commentary on the Additional Protocols of 8 June 1977 to the Geneva Conventions of 12 August 1949* (1987), 37–38: obligations under humanitarian treaties are not reciprocal but bind States even if another State breaches them.

[41] Walter (1970), 58.

[42] Walter (1970), 57, 99–100.

[43] Fitzmaurice, Judicial Innovation: Its Uses and Its Perils, *Cambridge Essays in International Law* (1965), 34. The Geneva Conventions, for instance, are the rights treaties that admit no derogation based on calculation, Quigley, The Israel–PLO Agreements versus the Geneva Civilians Convention, 7 *Palestinian Yearbook of International Law* (1992–1994), 61.

[44] Barile (1987), 9.

[45] Kolb (2001), 150. Sudre, Existe-t-il un ordre public Européen? Tavernier, *Quelle Europe pour les droits de l'homme?* (1996), 59, treating this problem in terms of *jus cogens*. In addition, Judge Ress emphasized in the *Bosphorus* case before the European Court of Human Rights that 'international treaties between the Contracting Parties have to be consistent with the provisions of the [European] Convention', Concurring Opinion, *Bosphorus*, para. 5. Why so, one wonders, unless the provisions of the Convention have peremptory status. See further Chapters 6 and 12.

[46] *Kupreskic*, para. 520; Simma, Reflections on Article 60 of the Vienna Convention on the Law of Treaties and Its Background in General International Law, 20 *Österreichische Zeitschrift für öffentliches Recht* (1970), 23, 54, making parallels, in terms of the impact of *jus cogens*, between the reciprocity measures in the law of treaties and reprisals.

[47] cf Orakhelashvili, 5 *CYELS* (2002–03), 244.

to the objective treaty obligations to emphasize their non-bilateralizable character. There is wide agreement in doctrine and practice that the first reference to the concept in the 1951 Opinion is identical to the character of *jus cogens* as developed subsequently.[48]

The European Commission of Human Rights has explicitly affirmed the peremptory character of ECHR obligations in an indiscriminate way.[49] In dealing with the question of the hierarchy of norms with regard to the freedom of action of States in cases of validity and termination of treaties, Special Rapporteur Fitzmaurice attributed to certain multilateral treaties—due to the character of obligations they embody—the same effects which are attributed to *jus cogens* by Article 53 of the Vienna Convention.[50] Special Rapporteur Waldock clearly emphasized that treaties like the Genocide Convention and the Geneva Conventions fall under the regime to avoid treaties conflicting with *jus cogens*.[51]

1.2. Interdependent or 'integral' treaty obligations

It is questionable whether all non-reciprocal treaties should be placed on the same footing in terms of international public order. Interdependent (or integral) treaties relate to the fields such as disarmament or territorial status in a broad sense. In his Second and Third Reports, Fitzmaurice stressed that in disarmament treaties the obligation of each party is dependent on a corresponding performance by all parties; in the case of a fundamental breach by one party, the obligation of the other parties would not merely cease towards the particular party, but would be liable to cease altogether in respect of all the parties and a really fundamental breach would ensure the end of a treaty.[52] It is clear that Fitzmaurice has allowed for reciprocity, not for a bilateralist reciprocity which could split treaty regimes into *inter se* relations, but for a kind of collective reciprocity, as the treaty obligations are not divisible, being assumed towards the totality of the parties. Fitzmaurice distinguished this case from humanitarian obligations, where the obligation of

---

[48] Suy, The Concept of Jus Cogens in International Law, *Lagonissi Conference: Papers and Proceedings*, vol. II, Carnegie Endowment for International Peace (1967), 20, 73; Gormley, The Right to Life and The Rule of Non-Derogability: Peremptory Norms of *Jus Cogens*, in Ramcharan (ed.), *The Right to Life in International Law* (1985), 129; Ford, Adjudicating *Jus Cogens*, 13 *Wisconsin International Law Journal* (1994), 164; Bassiouni, International Crimes: *Jus Cogens* and *Obligatio Erga Omnes, Law and Contemporary Problems* (1996), 73; Paul (1971), 25; Schwelb, Some Aspects of International *Jus Cogens*, 61 *AJIL* (1967), 955; UNCLT Second Session (1969), 96 (Ecuador); UNCLT First Session (1969), 296 (Kenya); *Jelisic*, para 60; Statement by the Secretary-General, ICJ Pleadings, 1951, 63.

[49] *M and Co v FRG*, Application No. 13258/87, 9 February 1990, 33 *YB ECHR* 1990, 51–52.

[50] Second Report, YbILC, 1957, vol. II, 54.

[51] YbILC, 1963–II, 59.

[52] Second Report, YbILC, 1957, vol. II, 54; Third Report, YbILC, 1958, vol. II, 44.

each party is altogether independent of performance by any of the others, and would continue for each party if defaults by others occurred.[53]

In its work on State responsibility, the ILC also singled out the concept of interdependent treaty obligations in the context of invocation of an internationally wrongful act and emphasized that the interdependent nature of treaty obligations which justifies assuming that in case of breach not only the directly injured State but also all parties to the regime can react to the breach.[54]

Interdependent obligations are not divisible but they are similar to ordinary obligations in that they cannot exist or survive a breach without the concordant will of States-parties. The very grant of a given status to a territory specified in a treaty, or a given regime of armaments, is there because States-parties have so agreed; it is not dictated by the community interest. Of course, such regimes may respond to the needs of peace and security and hence have a certain collective dimension but in legal terms such regimes protect the interests of parties and that interest is not independent of their will. Such obligations are just treaty obligations, without an extra-contractual basis. In case of their breach the attitude of States-parties or their collectivity is decisive for the continuation in force of treaties, not least because the interdependent treaty obligations are the product of the will of States.

As Fitzmaurice stressed, in cases of interdependent obligations 'the undertaking of each party is given in return for a similar undertaking by the others' and reciprocal non-observance can be justified.[55] This is so although the undertakings are given towards the parties in totality; they are nevertheless given towards the parties as such and do not relate to any transcendent community interest.

Derogation from interdependent treaty obligations is in principle possible, but must be authorized by all parties, because obligations are assumed towards all parties. For instance, if a given disarmament treaty prohibits possession of certain armaments above a certain quota, the parties may exempt a given State from that quota; although a treaty declares that a given territory should be demilitarized, States-parties may nevertheless authorize a certain State to maintain troops there. This is so, because although the parties have wished a certain result in a treaty, they could have wished otherwise and this is permitted under international law. Parties may grant such exemption authorizations either through a treaty, an additional protocol, or subsequent practice including waiver and acquiescence.

The situation is radically different with treaties embodying objective

---

[53] Third Report, YbILC, 1958, vol. II, 44.
[54] Commentary to Article 42, paras 6–14, *ILC Report* 2001, 297–300; Crawford, *Third Report*, A/CN.4/507, paras 82–98.
[55] Second Report, YbILC, 1957, vol. II, 54.

obligations. States-parties, even in their collectivity, cannot exempt any party from, for instance, the ICCPR or the Torture Convention in whatever form. When States adopt a treaty outlawing torture or genocide, this is not an exercise of free will, but a response to dictates of general international law and the laws of humanity. It is obviously open for States not to conclude treaties embodying peremptory norms, but it is not open for them to conclude treaties modifying their content as recognized in general international law.

Fitzmaurice spoke of the invalidity of treaties conflicting with 'interdependent' treaty obligations, but this is not, as also implicitly admitted by Fitzmaurice, a true invalidity, because the final result depends on the parties. They can either agree on treating the derogatory agreement as invalid, or terminate the fallback treaty. Not least due to this factor, at the later stage the ILC refused to accept that 'interdependent' treaties, unlike humanitarian treaties, can void agreements conflicting with them.

1.3. So-called 'objective' regimes

It is interesting to see whether the so-called 'objective' regimes are antecedents or concepts cognate to peremptory norms. As Judge McNair stated in his Separate Opinion in *International Status of South-West Africa,*

From time to time it happens that a group of great powers, or a large number of States both great and small, assume a power to create by a multipartite treaty some new international regime or status, which soon acquires a degree of acceptance and durability extending beyond the limits of the actual contracting parties, and giving it an objective existence.[56]

According to Waldock's proposal made to the ILC, treaty-based objective regimes

create in the general interest general obligations and rights relating to a particular region, State, territory, locality, river, waterway, or to a particular area of sea, sea-bed, or airspace, provided that a State having territorial competence with regard to the subject-matter of a treaty consents to such regime by becoming party to a treaty.[57]

Both statements, which are the most authoritative definitions of 'objective' regimes, refer to a certain general interest related to an area. Also, both statements imply that the origin of this very 'objective existence'—while dependent on commanding respective 'degrees of acceptance' by other States—is consensual and subjective. The basis of the so-called objective regimes is that, in addition to their treaty-based character, they are accepted, in one way or another, by States not parties to the relevant treaty.

Where an objective regime is established, whether creating a territorial

---

[56] Separate Opinion of Judge McNair, *ICJ Reports*, 1950, 128.
[57] 2 YbILC, 1964, 26.

status or a neutral State, it becomes operational only on the basis of sub-sequent explicit or tacit agreement by other States.[58] The position that third States are not legally bound to acquiesce in these 'objective settlements' but that they cannot interfere with the treaties establishing these settlements as long as these do not affect the rights and interests of their own,[59] explains the nature of these settlements in terms of the bilateralist model of international legal relations allocating rights and duties that regulate individual State interests.

The issue was examined by the Permanent Court in *Wimbledon*, when it had to apply Article 386 of the Versailles Treaty, under which 'any interested power' was entitled to seize the Permanent Court concerning the application of its Articles 380–386, dealing with the use by States of the Kiel Canal. The Court ruled that each of the applicant powers had a clear interest in the execution of the provisions concerning the Kiel Canal, 'since they all possessed fleets and merchant vessels flying their respective flags'.[60] The grant of protection on this basis means that this legal interest is strictly individual, and violations put individual benefits at risk.

The Court noted that Kiel Canal was 'permanently dedicated to the use of the whole world'.[61] This wording confirms that the regime was established to grant all States their individual legal benefits.

By contrast to the Kiel Canal, the regime of the Aaland Islands inter-nationalized the treatment by a State of a part of its own sovereign territory, without granting other States any individual right or interest as to the use of that territory. Also (as with the Kiel Canal), other States were entitled to demand the observance of that regime. That justified the Committee of Jurists' treatment of the regime based on the Convention of 30 March 1856 on the Aaland Islands as one going beyond the reciprocal interests of contracting States and safeguarding 'permanent international interests'.[62]

---

[58] For an overview see Subedi, The Doctrine of Objective Regimes in International Law and the Competence of the United Nations to Impose Territorial or Peace Settlements on States, 37 *German YIL* (1994), 176 ff.; Sztucki, Jus Cogens *and the Vienna Convention on the Law of Treaties* (1974), 52–54.

[59] Sztucki (1974), 21–22; as Sztucki further clarifies, 'Acquiescence of third States in such "objective regimes" is due either to their direct interest in supporting such settlements, or the lack of interest in opposing them, or, else, the lack of means to make their possible objections effective.'

[60] PCIJ Series A, No. 1, 20. For an overview of such regimes see Delbrück, Some Observations on the Foundations and Identification of *erga omnes* Norms in International Law, Götz, Selmer, Wolfrum (Hrsg.), *Liber Amicorum Günther Jaenicke – Zum 85. Geburtstag* (1998), 20 ff., 29 ff.; Subedi, (1994), 174 ff.

[61] PCIJ Series A, No. 1, 28.

[62] McNair, So-called 'State Servitudes', *BYIL* (1925), 114–115; Ragazzi, *The Concept of International Obligations* Erga Omnes (1997), 32; however, the status of the Islands was subjected to modification by several agreements, first in 1921, without participation of Russia, then in 1940 as between Finland and Soviet Union without participation of the Western Powers and the State under the 1940 Treaty was finally affirmed under the 1947 Peace Treaty with Finland, Sztucki (1974), 53.

However, like the regime of the Kiel Canal, the regime governing the Aaland Islands possessed the same status as ordinary norms: (1) the status of the Aaland Islands was the product of the will of the States-parties; (2) the States-parties were not prevented from waiving their right or legal interest in the observance of that status; (3) as subsequent developments demonstrated, the States-parties were entitled to abolish the status of the Aaland Islands, either explicitly or through acquiescence.

Certain observations on the concept of objective regimes can be made from the viewpoint of international public order. (1) Objective regimes are established on the basis of the intention and will of the States-parties to a given treaty. (2) A regime may penetrate into general customary law only on the basis of the will of States. Third States may prevent generalization of an objective regime into customary law by expressing timely protests and objections. (3) The concept does not distinguish between possible types of legal interest which the notion of 'general interest' confers on States-parties or non-parties. In some cases States may have an interest in situations where they are not directly prejudiced, but this interest would be based only on agreement. (4) It is possible that States or even groups of States renounce their rights to use and benefit from the area in question, or even terminate the whole regime, by withdrawing from a treaty, expressly waiving their rights or acquiescing to violations. (5) In case of such violation (as distinct from the abrogation of the regime), other States-parties to a treaty governing the regime may not interfere, since the legal relations, whether primary or secondary, operate exclusively at the bilateral level between the territorial and injured States.

It is thus clear that these regimes, established in a 'general interest', safeguard individual, even though collectivized, legal interests. The rules they embody are entirely subjective in all their aspects, do not protect transcendent community interests and form no antecedent or cognate concept to peremptory norms. Moreover, treaties establishing 'objective regimes' can be judged by reference to *jus cogens* (such as the norms on self-determination, the right of refugees to return home, or consequences of unlawful use of force) and possibly challenged as treaties contrary to *jus cogens*. If an 'objective' regime is established in breach of *jus cogens*, a wider, or extra-contractual, degree of its acceptance cannot immunize it from the impact of *jus cogens*. This last conclusion is reinforced by the overriding impact of *jus cogens* over customary law.

1.4. Evaluation

From the public order perspective, the international legal system is divided into two basic types of rules and obligations: those safeguarding the interests of individual States which are reciprocal or bilateral in character, and those safeguarding interests of the international community as a whole which possess an objective, integral character: *jus dispositivum* and *jus cogens*. The same distinction applies to treaty obligations. So-called interdependent obligations and 'objective regimes' do not share the fundamental characteristics of integral treaty obligations, still less of their counterpart in customary law—*jus cogens*. Their creation, continuation in force and termination is a matter of the will of the States-parties, and not of objective and transcendent community interest. States adhere to such treaties out of their individual interest-based calculations, and hence such treaty obligations are an exchange of mutual obligations of States—a phenomenon which has explicitly been excluded from the ambit of public order treaties in the advisory opinion on *Genocide*.

2. THE OBJECT AND PURPOSE OF A TREATY

It would seem on the face of it that once States decide to conclude a treaty, they do it for a reason and they intend to achieve certain results thereby, in their bilateral relations and beyond. It is therefore straightforwardly clear that treaties have their object and purpose as the important factor of their interpretation and application. The concept of the object and purpose of a treaty has, however, been criticized as a vague notion both in judicial practice and doctrine. The first reference to this concept in judicial practice took place in the *Reservations* Opinion of the International Court, which linked the permissibility of treaty reservations to their compatibility with the object and purpose of the relevant treaty. The Dissenting Opinion of Judges Guerrero, McNair, Read and Hsu Mo opposed the Court's approach by stressing the uncertainty of the concept of the object and purpose of the Genocide Convention. While it was clear to the Dissenting Judges that the object and purpose was to repress Genocide, it was unclear to them if it was more than that and comprised any or all enforcement provisions of the Convention. The whole concept was 'difficult to apply'.[63] Similar objections have been voiced in doctrine, labelling the concept of the object and purpose as an indeterminate, elusive and uncertain concept.[64]

These criticisms notwithstanding, the concept of the object and purpose of a treaty is nevertheless a concept of positive law, being mirrored in several conventions and judicial decisions as a factor relevant for specific juridical

[63] *ICJ Reports*, 1951, 43–44.

[64] Klabbers, Some Problems Regarding the Object and Purpose of Treaties, 8 *The Finnish Yearbook of International Law* (1998); Buffard and Zemanek, The 'Object and Purpose' of a Treaty: An Enigma? 3 *Austrian Review of International and European Law* (1998); for an overview of these objections and the debates as to the relevance of the treaty's object and purpose see Pellet, Tenth Report on Reservations to Treaties, Addendum 1, A/CN.4/558/Add.1

outcomes. The better, and conceivably the only viable, way is not to ignore or dismiss the relevance of this notion—which would be fruitless—but to examine its effects and scope and its impact on conflicting transactions.

Under the Vienna Convention on the Law of Treaties, the notion of a treaty's object and purpose limits the contractual freedom of States and bars ensuing transactions.

(1) Article 19 of the Convention outlaws treaty reservations that contradict the object and purpose of the treaty; in such cases, object and purpose is protected from being endangered in a normative sense and not merely in terms of a single case of application of a treaty.

(2) Articles 31 and 33 require that the outcome of the interpretation of a treaty must correspond to its object and purpose; the vulnerability of the object and purpose consists here not in the likelihood of a single violation of a treaty, but of a construction of a treaty hampering the furtherance of the object and purpose and its likely application in that way.

(3) Article 41 prohibits the agreements whereby treaty provisions are suspended *inter se* if these agreements contradict the object and purpose of the treaty; Article 58 similarly outlaws the agreements suspending treaty provisions. This is a case very much similar to the above-described situations.

These provisions confirm the relevance of the object and purpose of the treaty in determining whether certain transactions between the parties to the treaty are lawful. This, in its turn, implies that the object and purpose place certain relations under the relevant treaty above the derogatory power of States-parties. Therefore, this notion seems to be at least *prima facie* different from *jus dispositivum* as it operates even in disregard of a contrary agreement between the parties to a treaty. The limits the notion of the object and purpose imposes on the subject-matter of the conflicting transactions seem to be somehow similar to the prohibition of derogation.

It has been suggested in the ILC's work, most recently by Special Rapporteur Pellet, that the determination of the treaty's object and purpose involves a certain degree of subjectivity on the part of States-parties to the relevant treaty.[65] This approach is not satisfactory, above all because of its lack of clarity, especially in the question of the extent to which the States-parties are allowed the margin of auto-interpretation. It is also worth asking whose subjective judgment is referred to in this context: that of one individual party or more? At the same time, the perception of subjectivity does not accord with the very process of providing the guidelines of the identification of the object and purpose and its perception as a limit of inter-State transactions. Once the criteria of identification of the object and purpose are

---

[65] Pellet, Tenth Report on Reservations to Treaties, Addendum 1, A/CN.4/558/Add.1, 7, 12–13, also elaborating upon the doctrinal scepticism as to the objective determination of the treaty's object and purpose. See also Wei, Reservations to Treaties and Some Practical Issues, 7 *Asian Yearbook of International Law* (1997), 129–130.

ascertained, it is quite possible, indeed necessary, to perceive those as objective criteria, because they refer to something that is objectively there: the text of the treaty, its title, preamble and specific provisions.

Treaties, whether bilateral or multilateral and whatever their character, can have an object and purpose.[66] This is contested by Riphagen, suggesting that if a multilateral treaty is a 'unification' of independent bilateral relationships, one might even say that the multilateral treaty as such does not have an object and purpose of its own. Riphagen asserts that 'The very notion of an object and purpose of a treaty as a whole already implies some measure of extra-State interest, if only in the form of an inseparable common interest of the parties. In addition a treaty may envisage interests of "*third*" States and even of "entities" *other* than States, such as individual human persons.'[67]

But the governing legal framework does not support the view that the object and purpose can exist only in treaties that embody something more than bilateral obligations. Article 18 of the Vienna Convention prohibiting performance before the entry into force of a treaty of actions that defeat the object and purpose of that treaty and Article 60 of the same Convention, which defines the material breach of a treaty as the breach encroaching upon its object and purpose, certainly envisage the situations related to bilateral treaties. The better view therefore is that even bilateral treaties can have object and purpose and this notion serves the maintenance of legal certainty in reciprocal treaty relations of the parties and the respect for their legitimate expectations. This is further confirmed by the International Court's treatment of the object and purpose of bilateral treaties in the cases of *Nicaragua* and *Oil Platforms*.[68]

But the presence of the object and purpose in a treaty does not by itself produce limitations upon the consensual autonomy of parties. The relevance of the factor of whether the object and purpose of a treaty is a matter of bilateral relations between parties is not the issue whether such object and purpose exists, but whether that object and purpose can protect the treaty from incompatible *inter se* agreements. As Rolin stresses, the object and purpose of certain treaties is to assure mutual advantages to parties,[69] while other treaties are aimed at protection of a transcendent community interest. In some cases the object and purpose can be fragmentable and divisible, or derogable, protecting interests of individual parties only, but the link to community interests can make it indivisible and cause conflicting *inter se* transactions to have no force.

[66] Hutchison, Solidarity and Breaches of Multilateral Treaties, *BYIL* (1988).

[67] Riphagen, Preliminary Report, para. 64; Riphagen, Third Report, YbILC II-1982, Part One, 43, para. 35 (emphasis original).

[68] *Nicaragua, ICJ Reports*, 1986, 136–138; *Oil Platforms*, General List No. 90, paras 37–38, 41; see also *Fisheries Jurisdiction, ICJ Reports*, 1973, 17.

[69] Rolin, Vers un ordre public réellement international, in *Hommage d'une génération des Juristes au President Basdevant* (1961), 457; Hutchison (1988).

Owing to the manner in which the Vienna Convention in its several provisions introduces the concept of the object and purpose, it recognizes the community interest with a standing in the law.[70] Therefore, the object and purpose of a treaty assumes particular importance in humanitarian treaties.[71]

In the ILC's work the object and purpose of the treaty has been defined as 'the essential provisions of the treaty, which constitute its *raison d'être*'.[72] The object and purpose of a treaty has most preferably to be inferred from the plain meaning and text of a treaty.[73] But this approach would also mean treating the text in its entirety or specific provisions not as isolated rules, but as a unity of interrelated and interconnected legal provisions. In addition, such an approach still makes it necessary to examine whether the object and purpose has to be understood as:

(i) a notion narrower than provisions of a treaty in its entirety, relating to its most essential elements necessary to ensure that a treaty works;

(ii) a notion wider than provisions of a treaty in their entirety, relating to the aims a treaty pursues;

(iii) a notion reducible to certain provisions of a treaty; or

(iv) a unified notion comprising more than one of the above-mentioned aspects.

To understand which of the above criteria are correct, one should examine the factors helping to identify the object and purpose in specific cases. These factors may be categorized in the following ways.

(1) *What a treaty is about*, as inferred from its preamble or specific provisions.

(2) *What a treaty adds to obligations of States-parties which would otherwise bind them*. This refers to the rationale of the independent operation of a treaty. Already in 1951, the International Court stated that the principles embodied in the 1948 Genocide Convention bind States without any conventional obligation, which is an affirmation of their customary status. As treaties are independent sources of law, their object and purpose can be determined by reference to norms they embody independently of customary law and identified with the rationale of a treaty as such. This criterion may give different results at different times, depending on the state of customary law at a given point in time. If, in 1948 or 1951, the substantive provisions of the Convention were part of customary law, its object and purpose must have

---

[70] Rosenne, Bilateralism and the Community Interest in the Codified Law of Treaties, Friedmann, W., Henkin, L., and Lyssitzin, O., (eds.), *Transnational Law in a Changing Society: Essays in Honor of Philip C. Jessup* (1972), 224.

[71] Lauterpacht and Bethlehem, The Scope and Content of the Principle of *Non-Refoulement* (2001), 17.

[72] Pellet, Tenth Report on Reservations to Treaties, Addendum 1, A/CN.4/558/Add.1, 14.

[73] Jennings, Treaties, Bedjaoui (ed.), *International Law: Achievements and Prospects* (1991), 145.

been to oblige States to take measures for prevention and prosecution of genocide. This is confirmed by the preamble of the Convention stating that genocide *is* a crime under international law requiring international cooperation to liberate mankind from this odious scourge.

In *Pinochet*, the House of Lords examined the Convention against Torture. As Lord Hutton emphasized, the purpose of the Convention is not to reaffirm substantive prohibitions, but to provide it with supportive measures.[74] Lord Lloyd held that the purpose of the conventions like those against torture and hostage-taking is that States shall make these crimes offences in their domestic law and establish extra-territorial jurisdiction to prosecute them.[75] According to Lord Browne-Wilkinson, the overall objective of the Torture Convention was to ensure a general jurisdiction so that the torturer cannot evade prosecution if moving from one State to another. Also, prosecution for torture would not be precluded even if a government passes an amnesty law: 'hence the demand for some international machinery to repress State torture which is not dependent upon the local courts where the torture was committed.' The Torture Convention was agreed not to create an international crime which had not previously existed but to provide a system under which a torturer can find no safe haven.[76] Lord Browne-Wilkinson added that the purpose of the Torture Convention was to introduce the principle *aut dedere aut punire* with regard to the crime of torture,[77] and Lord Millett emphasized that this purpose is to permit States to punish an offender whom other States decline to punish.[78] The German Constitutional Court, while interpreting the Genocide Convention, emphasized that the object and purpose of this Convention is the effective criminal prosecution of the perpetrators of genocide.[79]

Thus, enforcement provisions may be part of a treaty's object and purpose and limit the consensual freedom of parties. Where substantive treaty obligations are objective and go beyond protection of individual State interests, the understanding of enforcement provisions as part of the object and purpose

---

[74] cf Lord Hutton, *Pinochet*, 2 All ER (1999), 163–164.

[75] Lord Lloyd, *Pinochet*, 4 All ER (1998), 928.

[76] Lord Browne-Wilkinson, *Pinochet*, 2 All ER (1999), 109, 115.

[77] Lord Browne-Wilkinson, *Pinochet*, 2 All ER (1999), 110.

[78] Lord Millett, *Pinochet*, 2 All ER (1999), 179.

[79] 1290/99, para. 40. This is actually confirmed by the German attitude in a different context, namely with regard to the reservation of Vietnam to the 1988 Convention against Illicit Traffic of Narcotic Drugs and Psychotropic Substances. Germany considered that the Vietnamese reservation to Article 6 of the Convention embodying the *aut dedere aut judicare* principle jeopardized the intention of the Convention to promote the cooperation of States-parties in addressing more effectively the international dimension of drug trafficking, and raised doubts 'as to the commitment of the Government of the Socialist Republic of Viet Nam to comply with fundamental provisions of the Convention', I *Multilateral Treaties Deposited With the Secretary-General. Status as at 31 December 2003*, 433. This confirms that the prosecution and jurisdictional clauses in multilateral treaties can be viewed as part of the object and purpose of the treaty.

is even more important, as in such cases those enforcement provisions are required in the public, or community, interest.[80] As the *Genocide* Opinion clarified, 'The high ideas which inspired the Convention provide, by virtue of the common will of the parties, the foundation and measure of all its provisions',[81] which include enforcement provisions. In line with this, Riphagen concludes that 'The element of the "object and purpose" of a treaty is particularly important in the context of "secondary" rules, if that object and purpose includes the creation or recognition of *extra-State interests* involved in the treaty and its implementation.'[82]

(3) *What is the status of specific provisions in general, or customary, international law?* If a principle is peremptory under general international law, States-parties could not intend to treat it as *jus dispositivum* for the purposes of their treaty and allow it to be subjected to derogatory transactions; otherwise, that would be an attempt to derogate from *jus cogens*. This would link such provisions to a treaty's object and purpose. For instance, the UN Human Rights Committee affirmed that reservations offending against peremptory norms are contrary to the object and purpose of the ICCPR.[83]

(4) *What is the position of a particular provision in a treaty as compared to the position of similar provisions in other treaties?* This factor can evidence the intention of States-parties to attach a certain function to a specific clause in achieving goals pursued by a treaty, while a similar provision may have a different role under another treaty. For example, the roles of Article IX of the Genocide Convention and Article 22 of the Convention on Elimination of All Forms of Racial Discrimination (CERD) may be compared. While the former regulates the only means of dispute settlement and treaty interpretation under the Genocide Convention, the latter regulates only one such means under the CERD. Conceivably, the more indispensable a provision is to the operation of a treaty, the better its standing to form part of the object and purpose.

(5) *What is the framework in which a treaty or its clauses operate?* A treaty may be adopted pursuant to another treaty or within a broader institutional framework, which is determinative of its object and purpose. This factor is relevant in considering the object and purpose of the ICJ Statute in relation to the UN Charter, and the Optional Clause declarations and treaties with compromissory clauses in relation to the ICJ Statute. The same holds true for the optional protocols to the International Covenant on Civil and Political Rights and the European Convention on Human Rights in relation to those instruments.

---

[80] Similar analysis can apply to jurisdictional provisions such as Article IX of the Genocide Convention or Article 22 of the Torture Convention. See Chapter 7.

[81] *ICJ Reports*, 1951, 23.

[82] Riphagen, Third Report, para. 34 (emphasis original).

[83] General Comment 24(52), 1994.

(6) *Which obligations in a treaty are 'stricter', or safeguarded in a heightened way?* This factor refers to either the specific intent of States-parties to safe-guard a given obligation more strictly, or to the level of protection afforded to an identical obligation under general international law. Human rights treaties single out certain non-derogable human rights; the 1949 Geneva Conventions evidence the intention not to allow fragmentation of their provisions through conflicting mutual arrangements related both to State and non-State actors; the 1951 Refugees Convention prohibits reservations to some of its provisions.

These criteria are not exhaustive. They should be treated as mutually supportive and not mutually exclusive. For example, Article 33 of the 1951 Refugees Convention may be part of the object and purpose on multiple grounds: the 1951 Convention allows no reservations to it and it is part of *jus cogens* under general international law.

5

Sources and Modification of Peremptory Norms

I. SOURCES OF PEREMPTORY NORMS

1.1. General questions

The question of the way in which the international community of States as a whole manifests its acceptance and recognition of peremptory norms as required under Article 53 of the Vienna Convention is among the most pertinent issues of the problem. The examination of this process is necessary to answer the questions that are logically anterior to the questions regarding the operation and effect of peremptory norms.

Sources of international law that embody rules of international law are normally based on evidentiary considerations; their existence must be proved. This is explainable in terms of the classical position on this subject as expounded by the Permanent Court of International Justice in *Lotus* that the restrictions on the sovereign freedom of States cannot be presumed.[1]

But if the international community realizes that a given conduct is an evil as such and shall be absolutely prohibited, this could perhaps impact upon the standard of proof and justify the assumption that the norm in question is legally binding. The existence of *jus dispositivum* has no inherent justification, except that individual States, whatever their number, consider that particular norms respond to their interests. But peremptory norms protect transcendent community interests not necessarily overlapping with the individual interests of States, and it is doubtful whether the latter have a monopoly in deciding whether and how such norms emerge.

The normal position seems suitable in the case of *jus dispositivum*; it seems that in the case of *jus cogens* the position can and indeed ought to be different.

For instance, once the international community realized that genocide is an absolute evil, in terms proclaimed in the preamble of the 1948 Convention, State attitudes could change little in the capacity of the norms outlawing genocide to bind all States. This factor is essential in understanding which sources of law may give rise to *jus cogens*.

This approach is consistent with the view of van Hoof, who emphasizes the need for an integral approach to combine traditional requirements of

---

[1] *Lotus*, Series A, No. 10, 19.

law-making and explain newer developments in a structural way.[2] According to Scheuner, *jus cogens* involves considerable changes in the theory of sources of international law.[3]

This approach is largely approved in the doctrine. According to Simma, once recognition of a rule by the international community as a whole is established, the question from which formal source peremptory norms flow is more or less irrelevant.[4] Tomuschat affirms that *jus cogens* rules evolve from the common values of all nations. 'To establish them is therefore less a constitutive than a declaratory process.'[5] Furthermore, 'Certain deductions from the constitutional foundations of the international community provide binding rules that need no additional corroboration by practice,' though the regular criteria of custom-generation keep an important evidentiary function.[6] Therefore, the question to which sources peremptory norms belong is not crucial from conceptual and practical perspectives as the peremptory character of a norm can be proved without proving the specific source.

Article 53 of the Vienna Convention requires that a peremptory norm be accepted and recognized as a non-derogable norm by the international community as a whole. At the Vienna Conference, Chairman of the Drafting Committee Yasseen suggested that under what subsequently became Article 53 of the Vienna Convention, the acceptance of a norm as peremptory by all essential components of the international community was required. A unanimous consent and acceptance within the community of States is not necessary: acceptance by 'a very large majority' suffices.[7] This in principle admits that a norm can become binding on a State as a peremptory norm without that State's consent.

It has been suggested that the Article 53 formulation, while requiring 'acceptance and recognition', abandons the Verdross–Lauterpacht approach

---

[2] Van Hoof, *Rethinking the Sources of International Law* (1983), 282, 288.

[3] Scheuner, Conflict of Treaty Provisions with a Peremptory Norm of General International Law, 29 *Zeitschrift für ausländisches öffentliches Recht und Völkerrecht* (1969), 30.

[4] Simma, From Bilateralism to Community Interest, 250 *RdC* (VI-1994), 292; see also Czaplinski and Danilenko, Conflicts of Norms in International Law, 21 *Netherlands Yearbook of International Law* (1990), 11; and Sztucki, Jus Cogens *and the Vienna Convention on the Law of Treaties* (1974), 73. As Kolb further submits, the hierarchical value of peremptory norms follows from the relevant norm and its substance, not its source, Kolb, Formal Source of *Ius Cogens* in Public International Law, 53 *Zeitschrift für öffentliches Recht* (1998), 77, 80, 94.

[5] Tomuschat, Obligations Arising for States without or against Their Will, 241 *RdC* (1993), 307.

[6] Tomuschat, (1993), 307. Thirlway, The Law and Procedure of the International Court of Justice (1990), 147 affirms that practice is not crucial according to the Article 53 definition. See also Blum and Steinhardt, Federal Jurisdiction over International Human Rights Claims: the Alien Tort Claims Act after *Filartiga v Pena-Irala*, 22 *Harvard JIL* (1981), 82. *Per contra* Gormley, The Right to Life and The Rule of Non-Derogability: Peremptory Norms of *Jus Cogens*, Ramcharan (ed.), *The Right to Life in International Law* (1985), 125.

[7] I UNCLT 472.

to *jus cogens* as an indispensable public order based on the community inter-est and the dictates of morality in favour of consensual law-making.[8] The consensual approach to *jus cogens* was voiced by State delegations at the Vienna Conference. The US held that if a State establishes that it has not recognized a norm's peremptory character, that would be a material factor clearly weighing in the balance.[9] The UK referred to the requirement of 'the absence of dissent by any important part of the international community'.[10] Switzerland asked whether a norm should contain an express declaration concerning its peremptory character or whether that follows from the norm's nature.[11] It is true, as Sztucki suggests, that 'a peremptory norm must be known as peremptory'.[12] But the real question is whether it has to be so known as recognized by the consent of States or on the basis of the norm's character.

This consensual view is supported in the doctrine. Turpel and Sands submit that 'The requirement of acceptance by the international community of States as a whole in Article 53 obviously implies consent for peremptory norms.'[13] Some argue that Article 53 requires a double consent: recognition of a norm and its peremptory character.[14] But it is broadly accepted that *jus cogens* reflecting community values should bind all States without exception notwithstanding their possible dissent. According to van Hoof, strict adherence to the consensual approach runs counter to the essence of *jus cogens* and makes it difficult to see how it would perform its function if

---

[8] Weisburd, The Emptiness of *Jus Cogens*, as Illustrated by the War in Bosnia-Herzegovina 17 *Michigan Journal of International Law* (1995), 33–34. For contrasting the two approaches see Styrdom, *Ius Cogens*: Peremptory Norm of Totalitarian Instrument? 14 *South African Yearbook of International Law* (1988–89), 45. On the UNCLT proceedings dealing with the issue of double consent and consensual basis of *jus cogens* see Rozakis, *The Concept of* Jus Cogens *in the Law of Treaties* (1976), 72–76.

[9] UNCLT Second Session (1969), 98 (UK).

[10] UNCLT Second Session (1969), 102 (US).

[11] UNCLT 22nd Plenary Meeting, 1969. Hannikainen, *Peremptory Norms in International Law* (1988), 20, denies that any express declaration is required and emphasizes the need that 'a norm fulfils the criteria of peremptory norms'. Von der Heydte, Die Erscheinungsform des zwischenstaatlichen Rechts: jus cogens und jus dispositivum im Völkerrecht, 16 *Zeitschrift für Völkerrecht* (1932), 470–471, suggests that any norm itself determines whether it is peremptory.

[12] Sztucki, Jus Cogens *and the Vienna Convention on the Law of Treaties* (1974), 188.

[13] Turpel and Sands, Peremptory International Law and Sovereignty: Some Questions, 3 *Connecticut JIL* (1988), 367; Weisburd (1995), 33; *per contra* Ford, Adjudicating *Jus Cogens*, 13 *Wisconsin International Law Journal* (1994), 152, and Scheuner (1969), 30 suggesting that the strictly binding norms can only have an objective basis, as independent from State consent.

[14] Rozakis, *The Concept of* Jus Cogens *in the Law of Treaties* (1976), 54; Rozakis, The Conditions of Invalidity of International Agreements, 26–27 *Revue Hellénique de Droit International* (1973–74), 250; Christenson (1988), 593; Kadelbach, *Zwingendes Volkerrecht* (1992), 178; Hannikainen, *Peremptory Norms in International Law* (1988), 12; Danilenko, *Law-Making in the International Community* (1993), 227–228.

States can avoid its peremptory status in specific cases.[15] It is emphasized that 'while consent gives authority to *jus dispositivum, jus cogens* is founded on a deeper moral consensus, and is merely illustrated by such acquiescence'.[16] The concept of such systemic consensus is reflected by the Inter-American Commission, stating that a norm achieves peremptory status precisely because it would shock the conscience of mankind and standards of public morality for a State to protest.[17] The US court affirmed in *Siderman* that while customary law derives from consent, *jus cogens* as a body of fundamental community norms transcends the requirement of consent.[18] The Court of Appeals for the Ninth Circuit also considered that peremptory norms are 'norms of international law that are binding on nations even if they do not agree to them'.[19] Therefore, individual States can be bound by *jus cogens* without and despite their agreement.[20]

How does Article 53 respond to that? Does its requirement of acceptance and recognition by the international community as a whole imply consent by States individually for a norm and its peremptory character, or acceptance by the international community as a whole that a given norm, due to its substance, is part of public order? 'Acceptance' of a norm can be based on consent, but then it may also be based on a belief of the international community that the interest protected by that norm is so essential that the norm binds States even if they have not consented to it. The international community of States as a whole can be understood as different from individual States or even their commonality and can conceivably enjoy standing in lawmaking in fields related to the community interest as distinct from individual State interests.

The Article 53 formulation of community acceptance does not require 'a State by State acceptance or even recognition' of a norm and its peremptory

---

[15] Van Hoof, *Rethinking the Sources of International Law* (1983), 161–162; Pauwelyn, *The Conflict of Norms in Public International Law* (2003), 67; Li Haopei, Jus Cogens and International Law, Sienho Yee and Wang Tieya (eds), *International Law in the Post-Cold War World – Festschrift Li Haopei* (2001), 511–522; Malanczuk, First ILA Report, 43, considers that the non-derogability of *jus cogens* implies its non-consensual character.

[16] Klein, A Theory of the Application of the Customary International Law of Human Rights by Domestic Courts, 13 *Yale Journal of International Law* (1988), 353; Henkin, *International Law: Politics and Values* (1995), 39, also suggests that for peremptory norms State practice and consent is not necessary, they are the product of systemic consensus. Randall, Universal Jurisdiction under International Law, 66 *Texas Law Review* (1988), 823, considers that individual States cannot object to peremptory norms. The Canadian Supreme Court in *Suresh* also affirmed that peremptory norms develop on the 'general consensus of the international community', para. 61.

[17] *Roach*, Resolution No. 3/87, Case No. 9647, para. 55, 8 *HRLJ* (1987), 352.

[18] *Siderman de Blake v Argentina*, 103 ILR, 470.

[19] *Doe v Unocal*, 14214.

[20] Charney (1993), 541, states that *jus cogens* binds States regardless of their timely objections. See also Stein (1985), 457.

character.[21] Perhaps a peremptory norm can be established through such double consent: different norms could be the subject of different historical processes of acceptance. But this cannot be a requirement. Article 53 could logically also admit an outcome requiring recognition by the international community as distinct from individual States. The requirement of double consent for *jus cogens* is incompatible with the moral basis of *jus cogens* and its necessity as public order, as well as with the ILC's view that *jus cogens* exists because of its necessity and that its subject-matter makes it peremptory. This looks like a categorical assumption and the text of Article 53 permits that interpretation.

The character of certain norms makes it difficult to portray them as other than peremptory. According to Dugard, once self-determination is *jus*, it would necessarily follow that it is *jus cogens* in the light of the pivotal position it occupies in the international public order.[22] Cassese also confirms regarding the example of the right to self-determination that the acceptance by the community of nations of the notion of *jus cogens* in general, and the fundamental and universal nature of a given rule automatically entails the recognition of a given norm as peremptory.[23]

Alternatively, it is plausible that the peremptory nature of a rule is recognized by the international community if the latter accepts that rule through a source which at least *prima facie* expresses the community will. After this condition is met, the moral character of the norm and its link to the community interest transcending individual State interests would be relevant in determining whether a norm thus accepted is peremptory. These factors dictate that the relevant sources of law are reappraised to reflect the dictates of public order.

1.2. Jus cogens *as an autonomous source of law*

Traditional sources of international law such as treaty and custom are generally regarded as the product of the consent of States. This could work against the conclusion that those sources give rise to peremptory norms. The conceptual difficulty thus arising is how consensual sources can give rise to norms that apply to States despite their consent and are concerned with the *a priori* hierarchy of norms which can operate despite and above the will of States expressed in traditional sources of law. These concerns could entail a logical necessity to consider that peremptory norms are not subsumable

---

[21] Pellet, The Normative Dilemma: Will and Consent in International Law-Making, 12 *Australian Yearbook of International Law* (1992), 38; Virally, Reflexions sur le 'jus cogens', 12 *Annuaire Français de Droit International* (1966), 25; Reuter, *Introduction to the Law of Treaties* (1972), 110.

[22] Dugard, *Recognition and the United Nations* (1987), 159, 161.

[23] Cassese, *Self-Determination of Peoples* (1994), 140.

under traditional sources but can only be based on a specific source of international law which covers only those norms which the international community considers so fundamental that it endows them with the superior peremptory status.

This situation has been addressed doctrinally as raising both categorical as well as evidence-based concerns. In terms of categorical concerns, the relevance of the autonomous source is stressed because of the alleged unsuitability of traditional sources to embody peremptory norms. According to Wolfke, none of the sources mentioned in Article 38 can generate *jus cogens*, as they are consensual.[24] Furthermore, in none of its pronouncements on what can be regarded as *jus cogens* in the field of human rights has the International Court identified the norms in question with the sources enumerated in Article 38 of the Statute.[25] This may not be a decisive argument because, as shown below, the International Court identified the customary prohibition of the use of force as part of *jus cogens* and national and international tribunals have identified the customary status of peremptory human rights and humanitarian law norms. Nevertheless, this may provoke the question whether peremptory norms can be based on sources other than those listed in Article 38.

Therefore, it may be suggested that *jus cogens* is based on an autonomous body of superior rules, independent of any source of international law. This suggestion is intended not to provoke a discussion on the relationship between natural and positive law, but to emphasize the special character of peremptory norms. Also, the affirmation that peremptory norms can be created through the autonomous source does not necessarily operate to the exclusion of the relevance of other sources in the same process. It is only meant to address the question of possible lack of relevance of the traditional sources of law in giving rise to peremptory norms, and suggest the viable alternatives of comprehending the international public order in the context of the process of international law-making.

The arguments advanced against the relevance of an independent source of *jus cogens* are no less significant. The view that the hierarchy of norms can establish itself only through the specific source of law and not through the norm proper, or, in other words, that the hierarchy rests outside rather than within norms, is considered wrong.[26]

Kolb denies that *jus cogens* is a group of material and autonomous norms

---

[24] Wolfke, *Jus Cogens* in International Law (Regulation and Prospects), 6 *Polish Yearbook of International Law* (1974), 154.

[25] Simma, From Bilateralism to Community Interest, 250 *RdC* (1994), 291. The ICJ did not identify customary law in this field, Simma and Alston, The Sources of Human Rights Law: Custom, Jus Cogens, and General Principles, 12 *Australian Yearbook of International Law* (1992), 105.

[26] Kolb, Formal Source of *Ius Cogens* in Public International Law, 53 *Zeitschrift für öffentliches Recht* (1998), 76.

of a higher rank and suggests that they can be found within each source of law.[27] Kolb clarifies that the alleged incapacity of an 'inferior' source to carry *jus cogens* does not follow from the hierarchic argument, for the problem is not one of production of norms (hence a 'sources problem'), but one of collision of norms.[28] But the autonomous source argument goes beyond the simple distinction between the question of sources of law and the question of collision of norms. It rather requires confronting a broader issue of whether the norms of the kind which prevail and invalidate norms that emerge through normal sources of law can be made through identical sources. If the answer is negative, then peremptory norms can only be conceived as product of the autonomous source of law specifically designed to produce superior norms; if the answer is positive, then further reasons must be sought as to why one norm produced within the given source of law is inherently better and prevails over another norm produced within the same source. The answer to this last question is beyond the scope of the problem of the sources of law.

Nevertheless, this conceptual framework evidences that the option of the autonomous source of peremptory norms cannot be lightly dismissed. Its relevance follows both from the decentralized process of law-making in international law which is generally based on the consent of States, and also from the public policy character of peremptory norms. The inherent justification behind public policy norms in municipal law could raise the question of relevance of the source of law which could provide for public policy norms independently of the consent of the relevant legal persons.

This attitude has significant doctrinal support. Lauterpacht's suggestion that peremptory 'principles need not necessarily have crystallised in a clearly accepted rule of law'[29] could mean that they do not have to be confirmed through a particular source of law and hence constitute an autonomous body of norms. According to Sur, Article 53 admits that *jus cogens* can be based on an original, autonomous mode of formation of the law which does not necessarily require a corresponding practice.[30] This reflects the character of *jus cogens* and its function to serve as a measure for general law-making techniques, to determine the permissible content of conventional and customary norms.

The formulation in Article 53 of the Vienna Convention makes it likely that a new source of general norms is emerging. That new source, to the extent it exists, manifestly involves the community intention to create general

---

[27] Kolb, *Théorie du* ius cogens *international* (2001), 140; Kolb (1998), 103; also Van Hoof, *Rethinking the Sources of International Law* (1983), 157 ff. *ILC Report* 2001, Commentary to Article 12, 128, para. 7.

[28] Kolb (1998), 81.

[29] YBILC II-1953, 154.

[30] Sur, discussion in Cassese and Weiler (1988), 128.

norms directly.[31] This is even referred to as a constitutional source.[32] If the autonomous nature of *jus cogens* is accepted, it must be explained by extra-positivist factors, such as morality and humanity, and their link to transcendent community interest.

The option of an autonomous source of peremptory norms is not the only and inescapable option, but nevertheless a viable option in explaining the origins of peremptory norms. The necessity and validity of the argument whether *jus cogens* is derived from a free-standing and autonomous source of law very much depends on the understanding of the relevance and conceptual basis of traditional sources of law in giving rise to *jus cogens* and the latter's impact on their development. If the approach is taken that traditional sources can embody only those rules that strictly satisfy their traditional requirements, the relevance of the autonomous source of peremptory norms acquires increased relevance. If, however, we are ready to concede that traditional sources can still give rise to peremptory norms even at the cost of some of their strict requirements, then the relevance of the concept of such an autonomous source would be significantly reduced.

1.3. Treaties as sources of jus cogens

The ILC has endorsed the idea that general multilateral treaties can give rise to peremptory norms,[33] and there is some doctrinal and practical support for the view that multilateral treaties can be among the sources of *jus cogens*.[34] The reference to the rules of general international law in Article 53 of the Vienna Convention raises the issue of whether treaty norms can fall into that category.

The suggestion that general multilateral treaties can give rise to *jus cogens* endorses the assumption that treaties can bind non-parties, which has no basis in international law, as confirmed in Articles 34–36 of the Vienna Convention on the Law of Treaties. Treaties embodying *jus cogens* would, to the extent of their *jus cogens* provisions, constitute an exception to the general *pacta tertiis* rule. This assumption is consistent with the nature of *jus cogens* in terms of its universal applicability and hierarchical primacy, but ignores its non-consensuality and independence from the will of States-parties to a treaty. The assumption that a peremptory rule binds non-parties merely

---

[31] Onuf and Birney, Peremptory Norms of International Law: Their Source, Function and Future, 4 *Denver Journal of International Law and Policy* (1974), 194–195.

[32] Janis, The Nature of *Jus Cogens*, 3 *Connecticut JIL* (1988), 363.

[33] II YbILC 1963, 211.

[34] Verdross, *Jus Dispositivum* and *Jus Cogens* in International Law, *AJIL* (1966), 61. The Government of the Netherlands has observed that the rules of *jus cogens* can be created and amended only by multilateral treaties, *NYIL* 215.

because it is embodied in a multilateral treaty implies that it is the will of the parties to that multilateral treaty which makes the peremptory provision binding on non-parties. This conclusion would be inescapable because any other view would admit the existence of peremptory norms which bind only the parties to the multilateral treaty. This would contradict the very essence of *jus cogens* and in this sense it appears unjustified to consider that treaties can give rise to peremptory norms.

But multilateral treaties may be vehicles for peremptory norms to be established as part of general international law. For example, the Genocide Convention marked the definitive recognition by the international community that the prohibition of genocide was fundamental to world order and therefore binding on all States. The passage in the 1951 Advisory Opinion that the obligations embodied in the Convention are so fundamental that they are binding even without any conventional obligation can be read as saying (1) that the obligations are part of general international law and would be so even if the Convention were non-existent, or (2) that the principles underlying the Convention are so important that they bind also non-parties. The Opinion is not clear as to which interpretation is preferable and the answer must be sought in the surrounding factors including the general character of treaty obligations.

Another example related to extra-conventional applicability of standards embodied in multilateral treaties—the Martens Clause—favours the first interpretation of the *Reservations* Opinion: the preamble of the 1907 Hague Regulations states that inhabitants and belligerents in any case 'remain' under the protection of the laws of humanity and dictates of public conscience, not that the treaties bring them under such protection. This factor indicates that multilateral treaties are merely evidence of *jus cogens* and not its source.

As Schwarzenberger claims, the Martens clause does not relate to the issue of how the rules of the law of war come into existence. Its purpose merely is 'to forestall an unintended and cynical argument *a contrario*. Its only function was to preserve intact any pre-existing rules of warfare, on whatever law-creating process they happened to rest.'[35] Such a static view is, however, too minimalist. The Martens clause implies that the laws of humanity and dictates of public conscience are not the products of the consensual will underlying treaties, but rest on another basis, on general international law. The reason that these apply even if treaties do not apply means that it is not the treaties that create them.

As Scheuner explains, the creation and existence of *jus cogens* is independent from law-making treaties; such treaties can only be declaratory of

---

[35] Schwarzenberger, *International Law* (1957), vol. I, 10–11, vol. II, 361–365.

them.[36] Thus, the norm's peremptory status is distinct from the status it may have *qua* treaty provision. This reasoning is consistent with the objective character of treaty obligations with peremptory counterparts in general international law: that character is due to something transcending the contractual will of States-parties. Therefore, even if a multilateral humanitarian treaty embodies *jus cogens*, it cannot be a direct source of *jus cogens*, but merely its reaffirmation and codification.

1.4. Custom as a source of jus cogens

Customary law is consistent with the nature of *jus cogens* in that it gives rise to the norms of general international law and is hence in principle accepted and recognized by the international community as a whole, in accordance with the requirements of Article 53 of the Vienna Convention. Article 38 of the International Court's Statute refers to customary law as a general practice accepted as law, thus singling out the material element of State practice and psychological element of acceptance of the norms thus practised as legally binding.

Custom is the most commonly recognized source of peremptory norms. Brownlie regards peremptory norms as norms of customary law.[37] Kolb considers that no long explanations are needed to justify considering custom as a formal source of *jus cogens*, because most of its norms such as the prohibition of the use of force, genocide or slavery belong to customary law.[38] This propensity of academics to place emphasis on custom seems to follow from the general acknowledgment of the unsuitability of treaties to create peremptory norms, in which case customary law, because of its generality and flexibility, is often considered as an easy fallback source. This should not justify overlooking several conceptual problems that may arise in the line of such reasoning.

The first, and most straightforward, problem is that many peremptory norms would conceivably fail to satisfy the State practice requirement of the custom-generation process. The prohibition of aggression, torture, genocide, slavery or disappearances is indisputably 'accepted as law'. But it is questionable if these norms are based on 'general practice', because of too high a non-compliance rate.[39]

---

[36] Scheuner (1969), 30; Abi-Saab, The Concept of *Jus Cogens* in International Law, 2 *Lagonissi Conference: Papers and Proceedings*, vol. II, Carnegie Endowment for International Peace (1967), 12. See Byers, Conceptualising the Relationship between Jus Cogens and Erga Omnes Rules, 66 *Nordic Journal of International Law* (1997), 226–227 for examining *jus cogens* in terms of custom-generation.

[37] Brownlie, *Principles* (2003), 488; similarly, the Canadian Court of Appeal described *jus cogens* as 'a higher form of customary law', para. 86.

[38] Kolb, Formal Source of *Ius Cogens* in Public International Law, 53 *Zeitschrift für öffentliches Recht* (1998), 94.

[39] Wolfke, *Jus Cogens* in International Law (Regulation and Prospects), 6 *Polish Yearbook of International Law* (1974), 155.

There is also a theoretical and conceptual objection against the customary nature of *jus cogens*. While customary norms are built through practice, peremptory norms follow directly from a judgment as to the moral or social values predominant for the international community.[40] Customary law by its nature is not an apt instrument for the development of non-derogable rules that are superior even to treaties. The special definition of peremptory norms in Article 53 does not refer to custom, although it could if the drafters had so wished, but to special non-derogable norms of their own character.[41] Calling peremptory norms customary distorts the concept of custom beyond recognition.[42] As Simma and Alston point out, 'The customary law-making process may be unable to provide logical and sound devices to identify peremptory norms of abstention.'[43] More specifically custom, unlike *jus cogens*, can be corrupted by contrary practice or persistent objection.[44]

These factors and concerns do not resolve the conceptual problem in any way or direction. But at least they point to the conceptual difficulty to find 'the existence of widespread rules entrenched in the legal conscience of the international community of States, difficult to measure empirically and easily confused with *opinio juris* in determining ordinary rules of customary international law'.[45] While concerns based on these factors are justified on their face because they draw on the generally recognized criteria of custom-generation, it must be examined how these concerns are met in practice, namely how international and national courts and tribunals deal with the conceptual obstacles posed by the traditional criteria of custom-generation to the process of emergence of peremptory norms.

International and national courts examine the customary status of peremptory norms as part of their establishment of the law applicable to the cases they decide. The trends established in the relevant jurisprudence with regard to the general criteria of custom-formation demonstrate that the relevance of State practice is, on the face of it, an obstacle for treating *jus cogens* as part of custom. But there can be, as *Gulf of Maine* acknowledges, different standards for identification of different customary norms. Customary law comprises a 'limited set of norms for ensuring the co-existence and vital co-operation of the members of the international community, together with a set of customary rules whose presence in the *opinio juris* of States can

---

[40] Visscher, Positivisme et 'jus cogens', 40 *RGDIP* (1971), 9; see also Byers (1997), 222–223.

[41] Akehurst, *The Hierarchy of Norms in International Law* (1974–75), 283; Janis, The Nature of *Jus Cogens*, 3 *Connecticut JIL* (1988), 360–361.

[42] Onuf and Birney, Peremptory Norms of International Law: Their Source, Function and Future, 4 *Denver Journal of International Law and Policy* (1974), 193.

[43] Simma and Alston, The Sources of Human Rights Law: Custom, Jus Cogens, and General Principles, 12 *Australian Yearbook of International Law* (1992), 103–104.

[44] Ford, Adjudicating *Jus Cogens*, 13 *Wisconsin International Law Journal* (1994), 152.

[45] Christenson, *Jus Cogens*: Guarding Interests Fundamental to the International Society, 28 *Virginia Journal of International Law* (1988), 593.

be tested by induction based on the analysis of a sufficiently extensive and convincing practice, and not by deduction of preconceived ideas'.[46] This seems to accept that not all customary norms can be judged and proved in the same way and that the norms fundamental to the international community are established in a way different from other norms. This is further evidenced by the approach of the ILA Committee on Formation of Customary International Law, which formulated the principles and elements applicable to normal cases of custom-formation, such as State practice and *opinio juris*, but decided not to focus on *jus cogens*, as it has 'some distinctive characteristics which merit separate examination'.[47]

In the *Asylum* case, the International Court asserted that the party which relies on custom 'must prove that this custom is established in such a manner that it has become binding on the other Party', that is prove 'that the rule invoked by it is in accordance with a constant and uniform usage practised by the States in question', and that this usage is expression of a right appertaining to one State and corresponds to the duty incumbent on the other.[48]

It is clear that the Court requires more than just a usage—it requires the usage which expresses rights and duties of the States involved, those rights and duties being either the factors external from and additional to that usage, or the factors related to the requirement as to the character of such usage. In other words, the mere usage is clearly insufficient. The factor that makes the usage expressive of rights and obligations must arguably be something expressive of the will and attitude of relevant States, as it is hardly possible to think of any other factor. In addition, the Court's statement requires the qualification of the conduct of the parties in terms of the type of conduct, that is *ratione materiae*, and in terms of requiring that the States that invoke custom must have participated at its creation, that is *ratione personae*. Such complex requirements are not easy to meet.

The criteria of the *Asylum* case relate to purely bilateralist contexts as they require that customary norms must be established in a way providing the rights for the one State and corresponding obligations for another State, that is they must be established in a way providing for reciprocal relationships between States. It is dubious if this model can operate with regard to norms that involve the obligations towards the international community as a whole. Peremptory norms do not, or not exclusively, allocate rights and obligations to one State conditioning them on similar or corresponding undertakings by another State. As the structure of obligations and compliance with them is different, the proof of the norms themselves at customary law must probably be different as well.

---

[46] *ICJ Reports*, 1982, 126.
[47] ILA Report, 5–6, para. 8.   [48] *Asylum, ICJ Reports*, 1950, 266 at 276.

This is further confirmed by the treatment of the custom-formation criteria in the *North Sea Continental Shelf* case where the *Asylum* criteria were developed and in fact reappraised. In *North Sea*, the Netherlands and Denmark contended that Article 6 of the 1958 Convention on Continental Shelf had become binding on the Federal Republic of Germany 'because by conduct, by public statements and proclamations, and in other ways, the Republic has unilaterally assumed the obligations of the Convention; or has manifested its acceptance of the Convention regime; or has recognised it as being generally applicable to the delimitation of continental shelf areas'.[49] This attitude indicates that those standards would not be binding on a State without its acceptance.

The Court responded to this attitude by adding its own strict criteria for identifying whether a norm is binding on a given State and considered that the proof would be 'only a very definite, very consistent course of conduct on the part of a State'.[50] Thus, *North Sea* required affirmative evidence that certain norms embodied in a convention had acquired customary status. This had to be proved by reference to the practice consisting in the actual behaviour of States. The customary law nature of the norms involved may hardly be inferred from the conduct of parties 'acting actually or potentially in the application of the Convention'.[51]

Meron considers it far from certain that the Court in *North Sea* intended to extend its reasoning to universally accepted conventions whose object is not so much the reciprocal exchange of rights and obligations as the protection of the rights of individuals.[52] But having drawn this distinction, Meron still examines the problem within the framework of traditional law-making methods, contending that the actual practice of non-compliance can weaken the customary status of a norm, even in case of humanitarian instruments. 'To illustrate, the fact that, in most cases, States fail either to prosecute or to extradite perpetrators of grave breaches of the Geneva Conventions weakens the claim of the obligations to prosecute or to extradite perpetrators of grave breaches to customary law status. Cumulatively, frequent evasions of the Conventions' norms by States through reliance on the specific circumstances

---

[49] *ICJ Reports*, 1969, 25.   [50] *ICJ Reports*, 1969, 25.

[51] *ICJ Reports*, 1969, 43. The application of such strict standards can probably explain why in the *Libya–Malta* case, where only Malta was party to the 1958 Convention, it was not directly suggested that Article 6 embodied customary law. *ICJ Reports*, 1985, 29. The Court, having analysed State practice in a number of delimitation agreements, concluded that this practice fell short of proving that the equidistance method was even a *prima facie* method of delimitation. *ICJ Reports*, 1985, 38 Malta insisted that the equidistance was dictated by the sovereign equality of States, regardless of the size of their coasts. The Court responded that the principle of sovereign equality was in itself insufficient evidence of existence of a norm dictating the equidistance method in delimitation. *ICJ Reports*, 1985, 275, 288; see also *Gulf of Maine, ICJ Reports*, 1982, 297, emphasizing that despite its being embodied in the 1958 Convention, the equidistance method has not become part of customary law.

[52] Meron (1989), 51.

of particular situations (*sui generis* claims) may erode the position of the Conventions as crucial instruments of humanitarian law, and *a fortiori* to *jus cogens*, status.' According to Meron, 'concordant practice is, of course, the best indicator of expectations about binding prescriptions on State behaviour'. In conclusion, 'the decisive factor is whether or not States observe Geneva Conventions'.[53] This view not only overemphasizes the role of actual State practice in creation and operation of peremptory norms, but in fact implicitly admits the possibility of persistent objection to *jus cogens*. The relevance of State practice cannot, of course, be excluded but it cannot be a factor excluding the relevance of other factors including the relevance of a norm's peremptory character and the community interest it embodies.

Actual non-compliance with human rights and humanitarian law instruments necessarily involves acts affronting laws of humanity and public conscience. Such acts cannot express any *opinio juris* of a State. A State which asserts its entitlement, as a matter of customary law, to torture a suspected terrorist could technically express what it believes to be the law but such view cannot be a valid *opinio juris* because it would contradict the community attitude outlawing torture.

Judge Schwebel accepted in *Nicaragua* that the rules governing the use of force are part of *jus cogens* and States not members of the UN can be bound by principles embodied in the UN Charter. But Judge Schwebel emphasized that to regard these rules as customary would run 'into the profound difficulty that the practice of States does not demonstrate that Article 2, paragraph 4, in fact reflects customary international law'.[54] But can a rule bind a State which is not party to a treaty unless it is part of customary law (unless we accept that *jus cogens* is based on either an autonomous source or general principles of law)? Judge Schwebel recognized the peremptory character of the rule, but still judged the question according to the traditional criteria of custom-generation in terms of *North Sea*.

The Court, however, took an attitude different from that expressed in *North Sea*. It affirmed the general principle embodied in *North Sea* that treaty rules may at the same time operate on a basis independent of that treaty, as customary rules.[55] In addition, nothing in *Nicaragua* suggests that the Court

---

[53] Meron (1989), 61–62; Meron, *AJIL* (1987), 348 at 363–370.

[54] Dissenting Opinion of Judge Schwebel, *ICJ Reports*, 1984, 615. The view that the Charter principles governing the use of force are part of customary law 'is widely and authoritatively accepted, despite the fact that the practice of States manifests such irregular support for the principles of law which the Charter proclaims. Indeed, it could even be argued that the practice, in contrast to the preachment, of States indicates that the restrictions on the use of force in international relations found in the Charter are not part of customary international law'. But despite the earlier view, Judge Schwebel considered it generally accepted that the Charter restrictions on the use of force have been incorporated into the body of customary law. Dissenting Opinion of Judge Schwebel, *ICJ Reports*, 1986, 303–304.

[55] *ICJ Reports*, 1986, 95.

intended to depart from the principle embodied in *North Sea* that strict and convincing evidence must be provided in order to infer the existence of a customary rule.[56] The Court stressed that it would appraise the practice of States in the light of a subjective element as emphasized in *North Sea*.[57] However, a striking difference is that in *North Sea* the Court applied this subjective element of norm-creation as an element additional to the practice of States consisting in their actual behaviour.[58] But in *Nicaragua*, the Court just applied the subjective criterion, without attempting to apply it to the objective and material behaviour and practice of States or their attitudes.

The subjective element, or *opinio juris*, was deduced in *Nicaragua* from the attitude of States towards technically non-binding General Assembly resolutions.[59] The Court found a further confirmation of the validity of the rules relating to the non-use of force as customary law in the fact that they are part of *jus cogens*.[60] The Court reached this conclusion without examining the actual practice and attitudes of States.

If it had applied in *Nicaragua* the criteria of the proof of norm-creation

---

[56] *ICJ Reports*, 1986, 96, the Court emphasizing that it 'must satisfy itself that the Parties are bound by the customary rule in question'. See also id., 97, the Court directing 'its attention to the practice and *opinio juris* of States', and 432, again emphasizing the role of the general practice of States.

[57] *ICJ Reports*, 1986, 98.

[58] *ICJ Reports*, 1969, 44. In *Gulf of Maine*, too, the Court considered that the presence of customary rules 'in the *opinio juris* of States can be tested by induction based on the analysis of a sufficiently extensive and convincing practice, and not by deduction from preconceived ideas'. Therefore, in an area where the actual practice of States is either absent or is not uniform, customary rules are unlikely to be found, *ICJ Reports*, 1982, 299. The Chamber held that the 1958 Convention was merely a special international law and did not generate customary norms, since that Convention had no force for non-parties, *ICJ Reports*, 1982, 303. The Court had to examine whether the actual conduct of parties over a given period of their relationship evidenced the acceptance of the equidistance principle laid down in the Convention. The principal disagreement between parties was about whether the conduct of a party could have the effect of consent to a certain legal principle, *ICJ Reports*, 1982, 303 ff. This is a standard different from *Nicaragua* and corresponds to, and further crystallizes, the standard adopted in *North Sea*. The Court in *Gulf of Maine* seems to have considered that not only actual practice, but specifically the practice of contending parties is crucial.

[59] *ICJ Reports*, 1986, 99–100. The US attitude in voting for that resolution was that it would be merely a statement of political intention and not a formulation of law, *ICJ Reports*, 1986, 107. Scheuner (1967), 527 suggests that *jus cogens* can be established by GA resolutions. In *Nuclear Weapons*, the arguments before the Court related to the identification of *opinio juris* from the actual behaviour of the States involved, *ICJ Reports*, 1996, 253–254. The Court suggested that the emergence of a customary rule on the subject is precluded by the still-strong adherence to the practice of deterrence. The Court concluded so despite several General Assembly resolutions attempting to outlaw the use of nuclear weapons, *ICJ Reports*, 1996, 255. By contrast, in *Reservations*, the Court referred to the General Assembly resolution for clarifying the nature of obligations under the Genocide Convention and for examining whether the obligations embodied in the Convention were also valid on an extra-conventional basis, *ICJ Reports*, 1951, 22–24.

[60] *ICJ Reports*, 1986, 100–101; Separate Opinion of President Nagendra Singh, *ICJ Reports*, 1986, 153; Separate Opinion of Judge Sette-Camara, *ICJ Reports*, 1986, 199–200; Christenson (1987), 93; Dupuy (2002), 291.

adhered to in *North Sea* (consisting in the assessment of the actual practice and behaviour of States), the Court would hardly find that the rules governing the use of force were customary. Perhaps the nature of rules involved was relevant for the Court in choosing different methods of custom-identification. Having been confronted with indisputable reality that the rules governing the use of force are peremptory, it would not have been a proper judicial exercise to hold that customary rules did not exist on the subject merely because actual State practice was lacking. Arguably, a norm recognized and accepted by the international community of States as a norm from which no derogation is permitted would pass the test of custom, but then the Court in fact treated the norm's peremptory character as an alternative to traditional custom-generation criteria.

Thirlway suggests that 'the Court must be taken to have been ruling implicitly that only customary law can produce obligations of *jus cogens*'.[61] But the Court has not suggested any reasoning exclusive of other possible sources. In fact, Thirlway himself suggests such exclusive reasoning by claiming that 'if a rule which is one of *jus cogens* must be one of general, non-treaty, law, rules of *jus cogens* are a sub-category of customary law rules'.[62] But the Court in *Nicaragua* has not adopted the exclusionary reasoning, particularly against the relevance of general principles of law or the autonomous source of *jus cogens*. What the Court did, or so it would seem, was merely to choose among several ways available to prove the peremptory status of the prohibition of the use of force. Given the Court's past jurisprudence, the Court seems to have felt inclined to locate its criteria of identification of *jus cogens* in the context of its prior findings on custom-generation, even though resort to sources other than custom could have been possible and consistent given the Court's treatment of law-making processes other than custom in the cases of *Corfu Channel, Anglo-Norwegian Fisheries* and the *Reservations* advisory opinion.

Commenting on *Nicaragua*, Thirlway suggests that 'to prove that a rule is one of customary law by demonstrating that it is one of *jus cogens* appears to be putting the cart before the horse', and consequently caution 'is necessary [in the approach to] claims that a particular rule is one of *jus cogens*'.[63] But what the Court's judgment affirms is that once a norm is part of *jus cogens*, its customary status can be proved by criteria different from those applicable to other norms and the consent by individual States as opposed to the community acceptance is not crucially relevant. In other words, the norm's peremptory status does not by itself make it customary—partly due to the above-mentioned absence in the Court's judgment of the exclusion of the relevance of other sources—but merely impacts the criteria of proof of its customary status. As for the need for caution, it is already implied in the fact

---

[61] Thirlway (1990), 108. [62] Thirlway (1990), 109. [63] Thirlway (1990), 109–110.

that the *Nicaragua* test is used in limited circumstances where public order norms are involved, and this does not affect the correctness of the principle.

This approach of identification of customary *jus cogens*, different as it is from traditional methods of custom-identification, was also applied to humanitarian law. In deciding whether the Geneva Conventions embody customary law, the Court did not enquire into the actual practice of their application. It referred to the provisions governing denunciation of the Conventions—purely conventional provisions—for demonstrating that the Conventions are in some respects merely an expression of customary international law. The same method was applied to Common Article 3 of the Geneva Conventions, which has been considered by the Court as customary law simply because it embodies 'elementary considerations of humanity'.[64] No doubt, the Court implies that these considerations can outweigh the factor of State practice.

By referring to *Nicaragua*, the ICTY concluded in *Furundzija* that Common Article 3 is a well-established part of customary law.[65] Again, there was no reference to actual practice of States and this evidenced the unanimity between the two tribunals in assuming that the substantive value of a conventional norm may be sufficient evidence for holding that that norm is also binding as part of customary law.

As in *jus ad bellum*, general recognition of principles is contrasted to the insufficiency of State practice also in human rights law.[66] But judicial practice does not seem to be deterred by that. *Furundzija* suggests that 'a general prohibition against torture has evolved in customary international law'. But the Tribunal supported this statement by analysing provisions of certain humanitarian treaties and referred to the wide participation in them, and to the norm's peremptory character. The Tribunal further emphasized, as part of its argument about custom, that the wide participation of States in such treaties is indicative of the attitudes of States towards the prohibition of torture. It was therefore incontrovertible that torture in time of armed conflict is prohibited by a general rule of international law.[67] The same approach was categorically reiterated in *Delalic* and *Kunarac*. In *Delalic*, the Tribunal supported its view by reference to the relevant treaty provisions and the attitude of the UN Special Rapporteur for Torture.[68] *Kunarac* affirmed the customary character of the prohibition of enslavement by 'the almost universal acceptance' of the 1926 Slavery Convention and other anti-slavery

---

[64] *ICJ Reports*, 1986, 113–114.

[65] *Furundzija*, IT-95-17/I-T, para. 138; *Aleksovski*, para. 50; Akayesu, para. 608.

[66] Simma and Alston (1992), 104.

[67] *Furundzija*, IT-95-17/I-T, para. 137–139. The Tribunal used absolutely the same approach in considering the customary character of the definition of torture. It found the customary international law reflecting the definition of torture just by analysing treaty provisions, para. 160, and the right to physical integrity, para. 170.

[68] *Delalic*, 452–453, 459; *Kunarac*, para. 466.

treaties.[69] This reasoning would hardly satisfy traditional requirements of custom-creation, from the viewpoint of which it would seem rather odd to refer to the undisputed acceptance of a rule in conventional law in order to demonstrate that it is also part of customary law; for treaties and custom are separate sources of law and the Tribunal referred to no actual State practice supporting the customary nature of the prohibition embodied in the treaty.

The same Tribunal affirmed the customary character of the Martens clause even without the support of State practice.[70]

The ICTY also emphasized that individual criminal responsibility for war crimes and crimes against humanity are indisputably part of customary law[71] and specifically reaffirmed this with regard to the crimes such as rape, torture and outrages upon personal dignity which constitute serious violations of Common Article 3 of the 1949 Geneva Conventions.[72] In the same spirit, the Joint Separate Opinion in *Arrest Warrant* underlines that the provisions of the Geneva Conventions dealing with the duty to prosecute war criminals are part of customary law.[73] No reference is made to actual State practice and behaviour. All international crimes elude strict positivistic requirements in terms of transformation into customary law (even if there is practice supporting the customary law basis of some crimes). Written provisions qualifying these crimes in general conventions on genocide, slavery and apartheid, usually transform after a short period into customary law.[74]

In the *Reservations* Opinion, the Court equally did not refer to any State practice or attitudes to support the view that the provisions of the Genocide Convention were binding even without any conventional obligation. Rather, it referred to the nature of the respective rules and their link to moral laws and the conscience of mankind.

Kwakwa asserts, in view of traditional custom-generation criteria such as State practice *stricto sensu*, that the prohibition of reprisals against civilians under Article 52 of the First Additional Protocol of 1977 does not reflect customary law and even encourages to some extent the right to take reprisals against civilians.[75] However, in *Kupreskic* the ICTY inferred the absence of the *tu quoque* defence as flawed in principle because 'it envisages humanitarian law as based upon a narrow bilateral exchange of rights and obligations', but these obligations are unconditional and not based on reciprocity.[76]

The Tribunal affirmed that Articles 57 and 58 of the First Additional

---

[69] *Kunarac*, para. 520.   [70] *Kupreskic*, para. 525.

[71] *Furundzija*, IT-95-17/I-T, para. 140.

[72] *Kunarac*, para. 408.

[73] Joint Separate Opinion, *Arrest Warrant*, ICJ General List No. 121, para. 46.

[74] Degan, Responsibility for International Crimes, Sienho Yee and Wang Tieya (eds), *International Law in the Post-Cold War World—Festschrift Li Haopei* (2001), 205.

[75] Kwakwa, *The International Law of Armed Conflict: Personal and Material Fields of Application* (1992), 142–143, 150, 157.

[76] *Kupreskic*, paras 511, 515.

Protocol of 1977 which prohibit indiscriminate attacks against civilians as part of customary law, mainly because no State contested them.[77] The Tribunal spoke only about treaty provisions and State attitudes with regard to them, not attitudes with regard to their customary status specifically. As for reprisals against civilians, the Tribunal stated that under customary international law they are prohibited as long as civilians find themselves in the hands of the adversary. With regard to civilians in combat zones, reprisals against them are prohibited by Article 51(6) of the First Additional Protocol of 1977, whereas reprisals against civilian objects are outlawed by Article 52(1) of the same instrument. But for the Tribunal the question nevertheless arose as to whether these provisions, assuming that they were not declaratory of customary international law, have subsequently been transformed into general rules of international law; were those States which have not ratified the First Protocol (including the US, France, India, Indonesia, Israel, Japan, Pakistan and Turkey), nevertheless bound by general rules having the same purport as those two provisions? The Tribunal thus elaborated upon the constituents of customary law and specified that

Admittedly, there does not seem to have emerged recently a body of State practice consistently supporting the proposition that one of the elements of custom, namely *usus* or *diuturnitas* has taken shape. This is however an area where *opinio iuris sive necessitatis* may play a much greater role than *usus*, as a result of the aforementioned Martens Clause. In the light of the way States and courts have implemented it, this Clause clearly shows that principles of international humanitarian law may emerge through a customary process under the pressure of the demands of humanity or the dictates of public conscience, even where State practice is scant or inconsistent. The other element, in the form of *opinio necessitatis*, crystallising as a result of the imperatives of humanity or public conscience, may turn out to be the decisive element heralding the emergence of a general rule or principle of humanitarian law.[78]

The Tribunal supported this approach by referring to the inherently barbarous character of reprisals against civilians and their contradiction with fundamental human rights, as well as to the 1970 General Assembly resolution emphasizing that civilians must not be the object of reprisals, and further overruled the concerns regarding the lack of consensus in State practice.[79]

Thus the Tribunal admitted that in certain cases customary law could come into existence even without the requirement of State practice being adequately satisfied. This attitude was parallel to the affirmation that the obligations under humanitarian law are assumed towards the entire international community and most of them are part of *jus cogens*. At the same time, this attitude is completely opposite to what the International Court of

---

[77] *Kupreskic*, para. 524.   [78] *Kupreskic*, para. 527.
[79] *Kupreskic*, paras 528–529, 532.

Justice held in an analogous situation in *North Sea Continental Shelf*, where it required clear and definite evidence of State practice for proving the customary character of treaty norms which have not previously possessed customary status. In *Kupreskic* the ICTY found a different solution but also stated the basis for that was linked with the substantive character of the relevant norms.

The ICTY's analysis of the sources of humanitarian law does not quite accord with Meron's attitude on the customary law status of the provisions of the Geneva Conventions. However, Meron notes in the later contribution that *Kupreskic* does not satisfy the traditional custom-generation test but is inclined to support its findings by reference to the general non-reciprocal character of humanitarian law requiring objective application.[80]

US courts under the Alien Tort Claims Act, in order to exercise jurisdiction over violations of international law, have to demonstrate that the rule in question forms part of general international law, in other words they are, as consistently emphasized in jurisprudence, 'universal, definable and obligatory'. In several cases, US courts emphasized the peremptory status of certain rules to prove that they were generally recognized norms of international law.[81] State practice in the traditional sense is not examined. In *Siderman*, the US court affirmed that 'the right to be free from official torture is fundamental and universal, a right deserving of the highest stature under international law, a norm of *jus cogens*', the violations of which the international order will not tolerate.[82] In *Trajano v Marcos* the US court reaffirmed the peremptory character of the prohibition of torture along similar lines.[83] In *Hilao v Marcos*, the US court has affirmed that the *jus cogens* prohibition of torture was part of general international law, mainly by reference to treaty and UN declaration texts which it considered as the evidence of universal agreement regarding torture. On similar grounds, the same court considered that the prohibition of summary execution and causing disappearance is also universal, definable and obligatory.[84] The case of *Xuncax v Gramajo*, which dealt with the claims arising out of the torture and mistreatment committed in Guatemala, provides a quite comprehensive justification of the attitude that the customary status of the relevant norms, as the basis of jurisdiction of the US court was found among others in their peremptory status. As the wrongs involved were of international character, there appeared 'little warrant to look to municipal law exclusively for guidance in redressing those violations', and the Court had to engage in identifying the international

---

[80] Meron, The Humanisation of Humanitarian Law, *AJIL* (2000), 250–251.

[81] *Filartiga*, 77 ILR 169. *Siderman* suggests that although *Filartiga* did not explicitly refer to *jus cogens*, its reasoning affirmed the peremptory character of the prohibition of torture, 103 ILR 473; contrary to Shelton (2003), 157.

[82] *Siderman*, 103 ILR 473.   [83] *Trajano v Marcos*, 103 ILR 527.

[84] *Hilao v Marcos*, 104 ILR 128.

standards whose violations can support jurisdiction under §1350 ATCA.[85] To provide jurisdictional basis under ATCA as a universal and obligatory norm, a norm should be 'non derogable and therefore binding at all times upon all actors'.[86] That is in fact a definition of *jus cogens*. The court affirmed that the prohibitions of summary execution, disappearances, torture and arbitrary detention possessed such status. As a matter of fact the Court affirmed the universal character of these prohibitions by reference to treaties and other instruments, not State practice. It consequently maintained jurisdiction over those breaches.[87] In some cases US courts expressly link the issue to *jus cogens* and in other cases not,[88] but all cases are common in affirming the general international law status of respective fundamental human rights without the examination of State practice proper.

The Australian Federal Court in *Nulyarimma* has largely followed the attitude that the evidence of customary *jus cogens* must be sought in the UN General Assembly resolutions and also further crystallized and consolidated the approach that the 1951 Opinion of the International Court links peremptory norms, in that case the prohibition of genocide, to general international law. The court affirmed that the prohibition of genocide, which is 'a peremptory norm of customary international law, giving rise to a non-derogable obligation by each nation State to the entire international community', is an obligation independent of the Genocide Convention; it existed before the Convention was adopted, probably at least from the time of the United Nations General Assembly Resolution in December 1946.[89]

In general, the criteria for identifying a norm in case of *jus cogens* are essentially different from the criteria applicable to ordinary rules. *Nicaragua* embodies standards essentially different from traditional approaches to custom-generation. The general attitude of the judgment makes it appear that the Court acts within the scope of that traditional perspective, but the manner in which rules are identified and the result achieved are radically different. The judgment suggests that the Court perhaps intended to place *jus cogens* into the cage of positivism, similar to all other norms, but it seems to have at least implicitly ascertained that the cage would not suit the size of the animal.

The *Nicaragua–Furundzija–Filartiga* standard differs from the traditional

---

[85] *Xuncax*, 183–184.

[86] *Xuncax v Gramajo*, 104 ILR 184, actually considering these violations under the heading of 'Peremptory Norms of International Law'.

[87] Id., 184–186, 189.

[88] Dodge, Which Torts in Violation of the Law of Nations? 24 *Hastings International and Comparative Law Review* (2001), 356–359; Seiderman, *Hierarchy in International Law: The Human Rights Dimension* (2001), 254–256. But also for cases not directly mentioning *jus cogens* such as probably *Filartiga*, the courts' reference to universal, definable and obligatory norms is understood as the reference to non-derogable norms, Blum and Steinhardt (1981), 88–89.

[89] *Nulyarimma v Thompson*, 165 ALR 627.

approach also because it refers to specific manifestations of the community will, notably in terms of the General Assembly resolutions and multilateral conventions. The latter can evidence that the international community considers a given norm as customary and peremptory. This practice may provoke a question: why search for *opinio juris cogentis* where the norm's peremptory character can itself evidence a norm's customary law status?

As Blum and Steinhardt suggest, the international community has de-emphasized the significance of contrary State practice in instances where there is sufficient confirmatory State practice to support the claim that a norm of customary *jus cogens* exists. In other words, contrary State practice has been stripped of some of its capacity to undermine international norms.[90] This view seems to attempt striking the balance of the relevant factors in assessing the relevance of State practice in the formation of customary *jus cogens*. There are also more straightforward views. As Dugard points out, it is possible to categorize the rules of *jus cogens* as customary rules under Article 38(1)(b) of the International Court's Statute 'provided that the requirement of *usus*, in the sense of State practice outside the United Nations, is not given superior status over *opinio juris*, as evidenced by the expression of the intention of States within the political organs of the United Nations'.[91]

Such treatment of human rights and humanitarian law as customary law can also be explained by Baxter's statement made decades ago that the provisions of treaties of humanitarian character, insofar as they are directed at protecting human beings rather than individual State interests, have a wider claim of application as customary norms.[92]

Unlike the traditional framework, the emergence of customary *jus cogens* hardly requires examination of behaviour or attitudes of specific States. Certain norms are there simply because they belong to public order and not because States specifically consented to them through their actual practice. Traditional elements of custom-generation could be useful in explaining the emergence of *jus dispositivum*, which States recognize as suiting their individual interests, but not of *jus cogens*, whose existence and operation serves the fundamental community interest.

1.5. General principles of law as a source of jus cogens

A possible link of *jus cogens* to general principles of law in terms of Article 38(1)(c) of the ICJ Statute[93] would require understanding them not as

---

[90] Blum and Steinhardt (1981), 82.
[91] Dugard, *Recognition and the United Nations* (1987), 168.
[92] Baxter, Multilateral Treaties as Evidence of Customary Law, *BYIL* (1963), 286.
[93] The relevance of this question is noted by Thirlway, The Law and Procedure of the International Court of Justice, *BYIL* (1990), 147.

principles recognized in domestic legal systems, but as principles recognized by nations as guiding their behaviour in international relations. Article 38(1)(c) mentions just general principles, not the ways of their recognition.[94] If peremptory norms embody the standards of morality, ethics and humanity, it is easier to demonstrate that they are subsumable under the notion of general principles. Perhaps the nature of principles capable of binding States even in the absence of any conventional obligation, as specified in the *Genocide* Opinion, could resemble general principles of law.[95] Some authors suggest that international acceptance as general principles of law is more suitable than customary law for meeting the requirements of the formation of *jus cogens*.[96] As Judge Tanaka affirmed the peremptory character of human rights law, he considered that the concept of human rights and of their protection is included in the general principles of law mentioned in Article 38 of the International Court's Statute.[97]

The link to general principles is helpful in understanding the non-consensuality of *jus cogens*. In this context, it would have to be assumed that the 'recognition' of general principles in terms of Article 38(1)(c) takes place in a way different from recognition of customary norms, that is, without an otherwise necessary element of State practice. In other words, it would be possible to assume that such general principles are recognized by States, or civilized nations, due to the necessity of their presence and operation within the international law and not as a result of their practice or agreement. In addition, such principles would meet the criteria laid down in Article 53 of the Vienna Convention that a peremptory norm must be accepted and recognized by the international community as a whole.

1.6. Conclusions on sources of jus cogens

The outcome of this chapter reflects the categorical criteria of identification of *jus cogens* as norms protecting the community interest and the impact of their distinctive character.

The character of *jus cogens* is compatible with the law-making processes through custom and general principles. The nature of *jus cogens* can influence, adapt to itself or even predetermine, totally or partly, these

---

[94] Thirlway, (1990), 114–115, suggests that the general principles referred to in jurisprudence are not limited to principles recognized in national legal systems, though he adopts the working assumption that Article 38(1)(c) is limited to principles accepted *in foro domestico*.

[95] See also Lauterpacht's observation on principles reflecting international morality which can be applied by international courts, 2 YbILC 1953, 155, and the treatment of elementary considerations of humanity in *Corfu Channel, ICJ Reports*, 1949, 22.

[96] Simma and Alston, The Sources of Human Rights Law: Custom, Jus Cogens, and General Principles, 12 *Australian Yearbook of International Law* (1992), 107; Domb, *Jus Cogens* and Human Rights, 6 *Israel Yearbook of Human Rights* (1976), 106.

[97] *ICJ Reports*, 1966, 298.

law-making processes, such as the case of custom-generation, and even justify the autonomous mode of law-making. The relevant sources of *jus cogens* should be treated as mutually complementary and not as mutually exclusive.

In practice, the prevailing trend consists in recognition of the inevitability of the need to affirm the existence of peremptory norms in specific cases. The ways to find a specific source are accessory to that primary task. The consistent application of certain peremptory norms by tribunals and their failure to identify certain elements of specific sources of international law in these norms is also reminiscent of Lauterpacht's characterization of public order principles that 'these principles need not clearly be crystallised in a clearly accepted rule of law', but could be applied by a tribunal merely as principles cogently expressing dictates of international morality.

2. THE MODIFICATION OF PEREMPTORY NORMS

The judgment on the ways and means of how *jus cogens* can be modified must be undertaken in full understanding of the context in which such modification would take place. First, the process of modification of *jus cogens* is not necessarily identical to the process of emergence of *jus cogens*. A kind of majoritarian view of the decision-making process that has been admitted at the Vienna Conference with regard to the emergence of peremptory norms, as illustrated by the irrelevance of the persistent objection by States and the possibility that a very large majority of States may impose a peremptory norm on dissenting States,[98] is relevant in the context where a peremptory norm emerges where none exists and applies to the relevant legal relations. This should not be viewed as the ready-made outcome for situations where the relevant peremptory norms already exist and apply. Secondly, the modification of *jus cogens* must also be distinguished from the emergence of *jus cogens superveniens*, whose function is not to modify existing norms of *jus cogens* but to retrospectively outlaw certain treaties. These two distinctions are essential for understanding the proper role and options of modification of peremptory norms.

Article 53 of the Vienna Convention admits that a peremptory norm can be modified by the norm of the same character. The modification of a norm can mean different things: it can refer to the development or expansion of the scope of the norm; it might as well refer to the abolition or replacement of the norm. It must be enquired whether all such options are subsumable under Article 53.

---

[98] Statement by Yasseen, Summary Records UNCLT, First Session (1969), 472.

In the context of Article 53, 'there is modification when a norm is replaced by another which regulates the same subject in a different way'.[99] But is such regulation 'in a different way' necessarily the regulation contrary to what the norm required before modification? In other words, does modification refer to, or include the option of, abrogation of peremptory norms?

The natural law writers, notably Wolff and Vattel, subscribed to the view of immutability of *jus necessarium*[100]—the law that cannot be derogated from through inter-State transactions, the conceptual antecedent of the concept of *jus cogens*. A different perspective prevailed during the process of adoption of what is now Article 53. Special Rapporteur Waldock submitted that 'it would be clearly wrong to consider rules now accepted as rules of *jus cogens* as immutable of abrogation or amendment in the future'.[101] The ILC reiterated the same principle but used the term 'modification' instead of 'abrogation or amendment',[102] which could indicate to the Commission's intent not necessarily to imply that the modification of a peremptory norm means its abrogation. The text of the Vienna Convention does not include these specific terms but the broader concept of 'modification'. It cannot be taken for granted that this 'modification' necessarily includes abrogation of peremptory norms or their essential elements. Instead, as Nicoloudis suggests, it could be assumed that abrogation of *jus cogens* is excluded by the Vienna Convention.[103]

As for the means of modification, the definition of *jus cogens* in Waldock's 1963 Report on the Law of Treaties referred to the likelihood of its modification or annulment 'only by a subsequent norm of general international law'.[104] Accordingly, Article 13 proposed by Waldock exempted from *jus cogens* invalidity 'a general multilateral treaty which abrogates or modifies a rule having the character of *jus cogens*',[105] which admits that peremptory norms can be modified by multilateral treaties. Article 53 of the Vienna Convention refers to norms of general international law, not treaties, in terms of modification of *jus cogens* and, consistently with that, Article 53 extends the voidness to every treaty conflicting with *jus cogens*, whether bilateral or multilateral.[106]

Doctrinal views diverge as to the means through which *jus cogens* can be modified. It is submitted, on the one hand, that peremptory norms are more likely to be changed by treaty than by custom.[107] Brownlie, however, refers to

---

[99]   Ragazzi, *The Concept of International Obligations* Erga Omnes (1997), 59.

[100] Above, Chapter 2.

[101] Second Report, YbILC, II-1963, 53.

[102] II YbILC 1963, 199; see also the final Report on the Law of Treaties, II YbILC 1966, 248.

[103] Nicoloudis, *La nullité de jus cogens et le développement contemporain de droit international public* (1974), 39.

[104] Waldock, Second Report, II YbILC 1963, 39.   [105] Id., 52.

[106] Below, Chapter 6.

[107] Paul, Legal Consequences of Conflict between a Treaty and an Imperative Norm, 21 *ÖZÖR* (1971), 42–43. For the inherent problems relating to both options see Dinstein, *War, Aggression and Self-Defence* (2001), 96–98.

jus cogens as 'rules of customary law which cannot be set aside by treaty or acquiescence but only by the formation of a subsequent customary rule of contrary effect'.[108] It is also held that peremptory norms can sink into desuetude or be transformed into non-peremptory norms,[109] and further asserted that a peremptory norm may be replaced by a non-peremptory norm. The essential question is how widespread the acceptance of such a change by the international community would have to be.[110] This last option is clearly incompatible with what Article 53 of the Vienna Convention requires.

Writers also refer to the specificity of *jus cogens*. Abi-Saab suggests that as a peremptory norm, the prohibition of the use of force, as partly embodied in Article 2(4) of the UN Charter, cannot fall into desuetude.[111] The practice directed towards the change of *jus cogens* by way of custom would be invalid.[112] According to van Hoof, changes of peremptory norms cannot be lightly assumed, since they lay down the basic norms of the society.[113] States are not at liberty to withdraw *opinio juris cogentis*. Such change would require the same overwhelming majority which is necessary for the acceptance and recognition of the rule and this is confirmed by the requirement of the rule of the same character under Article 53 of the Vienna Convention. Until this happens, any attempt to withdraw *opinio juris cogentis* must be considered to be a violation.[114]

Bearing in mind the character of *jus cogens*, it should be asked what can amount to the norm which can satisfy requirements of Article 53 of the Vienna Convention to modify *jus cogens*. It does not seem that a State practice purely and simply would be enough. Unilateral acts conflicting with *jus cogens* would be void and so would be derogatory agreements. In case of the latter, the very first derogatory agreement would be void and generate no legal consequences whatsoever; the next agreement would likewise be void, without in any way being supported by a previous one, itself void. Such sequence of things could last indefinitely but bring no legally tangible results. It is hardly serious to think about modification of *jus cogens* through acts for which *jus cogens* itself constitutes a standard and measure of legality, determining their right to existence.

---

[108] Brownlie, *Principles* (2003), 488.

[109] Minagawa, *Jus Cogens* in Public International Law, 6 *Hirotsubashi Journal of Law and Politics* (1968), 27.

[110] Riesenfeld, *Jus Dispositivum* and *Jus Cogens* in International Law in the Light of a Recent Decision of the German Supreme Constitutional Court, 60 *AJIL* (1966), 514–515, submitting that 'The rule accomplishing this change would itself be non-peremptory'.

[111] Abi-Saab, The Concept of International Crime and Its Place in Contemporary International Law, in Weiler, Cassese and Spinedi (eds), 146.

[112] Czaplinski and Danilenko (1990), 11.

[113] Van Hoof, *Rethinking the Sources of International Law* (1983), 166–167.

[114] Id., 167.

It can be concluded that while it may seem theoretically possible to abrogate the existing peremptory norm, in practice this is hardly conceivable. At least the practice offers no visible and credible examples in this regard. It is therefore worth asking whether the process foreseen under Article 53 of the Vienna Convention includes the processes other than the abrogation of a norm.

The process of modification of peremptory norms might as well include the development of new aspects of the existing peremptory norms, which is in essence an enlargement of the scope of a peremptory norm rather than its abrogation. This can be seen by the example of the scope of the prohibition of torture and inhumane treatment. In order to qualify as torture or ill-treatment, at least for the purposes of the European Convention on Human Rights, the treatment in question must attain the required minimum degree of severity.[115] As Judge Fitzmaurice suggested, the European Convention 'made no provision against lesser forms of ill-treatment than such as would amount to torture, or fall into the category of the inhuman' and thus 'these lesser forms were not intended to be covered'.[116] These were those which 'amount *recognisably* to torture or inhuman treatment'.[117] Also, the US District Court did not consider that so-called 'constructive expulsion', based on fears only and not on actual suffering, constituted cruel, inhuman and degrading treatment in violation of international law and to recognize it as such would involve the exercise of the law-making function by the court.[118]

It is possible that the practice of States, international organizations, and tribunals may, at some stage and in response to the contemporaneous attitude, bring about some developments which would expand the limited scope of certain peremptory norms in a way that makes them extend to the conduct to which they do not currently extend. Such an evolution of rules would change the scope of the relevant peremptory norm and would amount to its modification, but not to its abolition or abrogation. Modification would take place through the enlargement in scope.

It can be concluded that there are plenty of options which may adduce a reasonable meaning to the notion of modification of peremptory norms under Article 53 of the Vienna Convention. The modification of peremptory norms does not necessarily imply the abrogation of the norm or the abolition of its peremptory character.

---

[115] *Ireland v UK*, 58 ILR 264; *Soering*, 98 ILR 107, para. 100.
[116] Separate Opinion, 58 ILR 316, para. 17.
[117] Id. (emphasis original).   [118] *Xuncax v Gramajo*, 104 ILR 187–189.

PART II

The Effect of Peremptory Norms in General International Law

6

The Effect of *Jus Cogens* in the Law of Treaties

The mainline problems of the impact of *jus cogens* in the law of treaties relate to the transactions of different kinds that purport to derogate from peremptory norms. It is generally accepted that the voidness of treaties procured by force under Article 52 is an aspect of *jus cogens*,[1] but it is really the incidence of the broader issue of the voidness of the consequences of the unlawful use of force. The following analysis will thus concentrate on the issues related to derogation as a matter of the law of treaties.

I. CONFLICT OF A TREATY WITH *JUS COGENS*

Article 53 of the Vienna Convention, which voids treaties conflicting with *jus cogens*, is based on the general principle of law that the agreements conflicting with international public order have illegal object and are void.[2] In more practical terms, voidness is the necessary requirement if the objective illegality arising out of conflict with *jus cogens* is to be properly redressed. In the case of normative conflicts involving ordinary norms of international law, the conflict can in principle be decided in any way that the directly involved States agree upon. The public order invalidity transcends the agreement of the States involved. The following analysis will work out the modalities of this process in the international legal system.

1.1. Article 53 of the Vienna Convention and objective illegality

Positivists such as Jellinek have contended that a treaty can elevate every illegality to legality, as States have an unlimited treaty-making power and their will is predominant in determining what is illegal.[3] As treaties can normally transform any actual or possible illegality into *lex specialis*, they are illegal only if they offend against public order norms. As Special Rapporteur Fitzmaurice pointed out, 'Neither the mere fact of departure from general rules of international law, nor of conflict with the previous treaty, will of themselves necessarily have the effect' of causing the object of the treaty 'to

---

[1] Waldock, I YbILC (1963), 52; Virally, Réflexions sur le 'jus cogens', 12 *Annuaire Français de Droit International* (1966), 13; Dissenting Opinion of Judge Schwebel, *ICJ Reports*, 1984, 615.

[2] Lauterpacht, Report on the Law of Treaties, II YbILC 1953, 155; Fitzmaurice, Third Report on the Law of Treaties 1958, 39.

[3] Jellinek (1880), 59.

be illegal in such a way as to invalidate the treaty'.[4] Treaties can derogate from *jus dispositivum*, but not from peremptory norms of what Fitzmaurice considered an 'absolute and non-rejectable character', or 'absolute and imperative prohibitions of international law in the nature of *jus cogens*', the conflict with which will give rise to invalidity.[5]

Article 53 of the Vienna Convention governs public interest invalidity.[6] It refers to the defect of a treaty *qua* treaty, not the defect of a party's consent;[7] not to the conduct of one party in relation to another, but to the common conduct of parties with regard to a peremptory norm and the community interest it protects. Restriction of the contractual autonomy of States inherently implies that the will of States cannot transform certain illegalities into legal rules, because these illegalities are *objective*, not depending on the will and attitudes of States. Objective invalidity ensues even if all parties to a treaty take the opposite view. The assessment of the conflict of a treaty with *jus cogens* in an objective sense, not merely according to the attitudes of States, is a logical corollary of the system of invalidity under Article 53. If the view of the parties as to whether a conflict occurs—eg whether a norm in question is peremptory and whether a treaty clashes with it—is decisive, the purpose of Article 53 would be frustrated. If only the parties were to determine whether a treaty is illegal, this would be an implicit recognition of their faculty of actual derogation from peremptory norms.

1.2. *Necessary distinctions*

The content of a treaty can violate international law in various ways, for instance if it affects the rights of third parties or conflicts with previous treaty obligations. But none of these entail invalidity. As Fitzmaurice submits, treaties offending against the *pacta tertiis* rule and those conflicting with *jus cogens* have in common that none of them can affect the rights and obligations of third States.[8] However, a treaty is not void merely because it offends against the rights of third States, because this causes no objective illegality, but only relative and subjective illegality, which exists as between the States concerned and depends in its continuation upon the will of those States. By contrast, once *jus cogens* is affected, this involves community interest and leads to an objectively unacceptable result, which could not stand under international law whether or not it infringes upon the rights of a non-party, or even any State at all.

---

[4] Fitzmaurice, Third Report, II YbILC 1958, 39. The ILC adopted the identical view, II YbILC 1963, 198.

[5] 2 YbILC 1958, 27, 40.

[6] Rozakis, *The Concept of* Jus Cogens *in the Law of Treaties* (1976), 108; Rozakis, The Law on Invalidity of Treaties, 16 *Archiv des Völkerrechts* (1974), 171.

[7] Rozakis (1974), 171.

[8] Fitzmaurice, Third Report on the Law of Treaties, 2 YbILC 1958, 40.

The *pacta tertiis* rule is subsidiary to Article 53; once a treaty falls within the scope of the latter, the former is overtaken by it. A treaty contemplating unlawful use of force would infringe the rights of third States and *prima facie* fall within the ambit of Articles 34–36 of the Vienna Convention, but a simultaneous offence against public order would make the *pacta tertiis* rule irrelevant. As the latter rule protects the individual interests of a third State, while *jus cogens* protects the community interest, the priority must be given to the voidness under Article 53 and there could be no room for the application of Articles 35–36 of the Vienna Convention, which foresee the legitimation of a treaty affecting the rights of third parties through their consent. The treaty in question would be void not because an armed attack is contemplated against a third State, or genocide or enslavement is contemplated against the population of that third State, but simply because they *are contemplated*, no matter against whom, because a treaty contemplates acts prohibited by *jus cogens*. As Special Rapporteur Lauterpacht remarked, 'The object of a treaty may be illegal—and the treaty correspondingly void— even if it does not affect third States.'[9] This is so, because peremptory norms are absolute and the identity of an injured party is not decisive when the illegality involved is objective. As Hannikainen points out, 'to invalidate an *inter se* treaty between two States, which does not violate the rights of third States, implies that the interests of a larger community are predominant.'[10]

As Special Rapporteur Waldock stressed, 'The problem of resolving conflicts with successive treaties dealing with the same matters may sometimes overlap with the question of conflict with a *jus cogens* rule; but the rule in the present article [a draft article which subsequently became Article 53 of the Vienna Convention] is an overriding one of international public order, which invalidates the later treaty independently of any conclusion that may be reached concerning the relative priority to be given to treaties whose provisions conflict.'[11] The conflict of a treaty with a prior treaty obligation does not necessarily render a treaty objectively illegal (as the issue can still be resolved as between parties to a prior treaty), and does not by itself trigger Article 53. As Elias submits, if a treaty forbids parties from entering in the future into a conflicting treaty, 'the party acting thus might be guilty of a breach resulting in its international responsibility, but not guilty of any rule of *jus cogens*'.[12] As soon as a treaty conflicts with *jus cogens* embodied in a treaty clause, Article 53 is triggered, and the more bilateral-conciliatory approach foreseen under Article 30 of the Vienna Convention is overtaken by the public order invalidity regime under Article 53.

---

[9] Lauterpacht, Report on the Law of Treaties, 2 YbILC 1953, 154. See also Domb (1976), 105.
[10] Hannikainen, *Peremptory Norms in International Law* (1988), 4.
[11] YbILC, 1963–II, 53.
[12] Elias, Problems concerning the Validity of Treaties, 134 *RdC* (1971), 391.

1.3. The scope of Article 53

A 'treaty' under Article 53 is defined by Article 2 of the Vienna Convention as 'an international agreement concluded between States in written form and governed by international law, whether embodied in a single instrument or in two or more interrelated instruments and whatever its particular designation'. Invalidity applies to all conflicting treaties despite their form or designation. No limitation is admitted in terms of the subject-matter of a treaty or the number of parties.[13]

While working on the topic of the law of treaties, Special Rapporteur Waldock, and later the ILC, proposed that the invalidating capacity of *jus cogens* should not apply to general multilateral treaties.[14] But Article 53 is nonetheless clear in not admitting any exception, even if the ILC thought of one. Preparatory work has only secondary value in treaty interpretation, where a treaty is ambiguous, which is not the case in terms of Article 53. Article 53 covers all treaties, whether bilateral or multilateral. Moreover, as the methods of international law-making evolve, it becomes possible that multilateral regime treaties can also conflict with *jus cogens*, even as they enjoy the support of important parts of the international community including major powers, such as treaties of collective disposition of territory, establishment of territorial regimes or States, or post-conflict settlement; Article 53 would apply even to such cases. Furthermore, as the Vienna Convention applies to treaties founding international organizations, such treaties can also be voided if they trigger Article 53.[15]

1.4. The concept of normative conflict under Article 53

The characteristics of the conflict of treaties with *jus cogens* that brings about the nullity have been elaborated upon differently at different times. Special Rapporteur Lauterpacht considered that a treaty is void if its performance involves an act which is contrary to international law.[16] Special Rapporteur Fitzmaurice considered that 'it is essential to the validity of a treaty that it should be in conformity with or not contravene, or that its execution should not involve an infraction of those principles and rules of international law which are in the nature of *jus cogens*'.[17] Special Rapporteur Waldock likewise referred to the object of the treaty or its execution.[18]

Under Article 53 of the Vienna Convention, pursuant to the approach adopted in the 1966 Final Report on the law of treaties, a treaty is void if 'it'

---

[13] This is further confirmed by the wording of the French text of Article 53: 'Est nul tout traite.' See also Verdross (1966), 60.

[14] Second Report, YbILC, II-1963, 52; YbILC, II–1966.

[15] Nicoloudis, *La nullité de jus cogens et le développement contemporain de droit international public* (1974), 122.

[16] II YbILC 1953, 154.   [17] II YbILC 1958, 26.   [18] II YbILC 1963, 52.

conflicts with a peremptory norm. But the issue of the logical and normative elements in the notion of conflict under Article 53 has hardly been system-atically examined. The clarification of this concept is necessary for the proper construction of the scope of Article 53.

The meaning of 'conflict' with *jus cogens* involves the ordinary meaning of the term;[19] this refers to what is prohibited by a peremptory norm, what is contrary to it, aiming at a result outlawed under a peremptory norm, allowing or obliging States to do what peremptory norms prohibit or abstain from what peremptory norms require them to do. It is just as much as Article 53 requires, because it does not contain any qualification as to the type of conflict of treaties with *jus cogens* or any other factor.

A normative conflict involves operation of two different sets of norms—in our case a peremptory norm and a treaty norm. These may conflict on their face as read narrowly, but also in terms of the effects they have and the results they necessarily require. This practical and operative aspect is predominant in understanding whether there is a normative conflict, as in this area the emergence of conflicting rights and duties of States is most likely.

Consequently, whether there is a conflict of a treaty with *jus cogens* depends upon an objective and dynamic interplay between a treaty and a relevant peremptory norm. Not only the clear wording and the stated intent should be studied, but also the necessary result of the possible application of relevant clauses, because parties may conceal their intent to derogate through adopting totally innocent and neutral wording. For example, a bilateral treaty involving resettlement of a whole ethnic group in the context of a large regional economic project without respecting the will of the persons con-cerned, and foreseeing no adequate settlement or compensation, may create the appearance that the parties are pursuing a goal of economic development and do not intend genocide or crimes against humanity. This requires an objective examination of how an actual treaty provision and a given peremp-tory norm interact with each other, ie of the reality and not only the form.

The word 'it' with respect to a treaty under Article 53 indicates that the treaty is meant in its totality, including the text, object and purpose, or direct effects (necessary consequences if it is enforced). If any of a treaty's elements conflicts with *jus cogens*, so does the treaty itself. It is emphasized that one cannot pronounce upon the validity of a treaty unless one considers its object

---

[19] To be in conflict means 'To come into collision, to clash; to be at variance, be incompatible (now the chief sense)', *The Oxford English Dictionary* vol. III (2nd edition, 1989), 713. For a similar definition see Pauwelyn, *Conflict of Norms in Public International Law* (2003), 174–176; Orakhelashvili, Review on Pauwelyn (2003), *CLJ* 2004, 248. As Jenks points out at the example of conflicts between treaties but in a way relevant in the present context, the conflict between two normative standards exists 'where a party to the two treaties cannot simultaneously comply with its obligations under both treaties'. Jenks, The Conflict of Law-Making Treaties, 30 *BYIL* (1951), 426.

and purpose.[20] This seems exaggerated, for what matters in terms of Article 53 is not the purpose of a treaty but the actual conflict between a specific treaty provision and *jus cogens*. If the object and purpose of a treaty is not offensive to international public order, this cannot prevent the nullity of a treaty whose substantive provisions conflict with *jus cogens*.

A normative conflict with *jus cogens* may also result from the very identity of contracting parties if a treaty is concluded by a party not having necessary and adequate treaty-making power to conclude that treaty, because under a peremptory norm this power rests with another actor. This may hold true for situations where a party in question does not have a right to be in a given territory, because it is a colonial power or alien occupying power, and concludes a treaty with regard to such territory or its resources.

It may be contended that Article 53 invalidates only treaties conflicting with the substance of *jus cogens* as primary norms, authorizing the actual acts contrary to *jus cogens*, but not treaties related to the consequential aspect of breaches of *jus cogens*, such as the issues of accountability or waiver. Such a view was voiced during the ILC's preparatory work on the law of treaties,[21] and would be most acceptable in terms of a 'traditional' bilateralist approach to international law, as it would keep the public order limitations on contractual freedom of States to a minimum. But this seems far too formalistic. If we define 'conflict' with *jus cogens* in terms of the natural meaning of the word, then Article 53 refers to 'conflict' in general, without specifying or excluding any of its types or categories. In fact, the distinction that Fitzmaurice makes between 'direct' or 'material conflict' with treaty provisions embodying *jus cogens* and the agreement between States not to insist on the implementation of those or agreement 'actually not to perform the treaty obligations', in other words, 'a renunciation or modification by some of the parties of their rights, or of parts of their rights', is actually a distinction without difference. If parties agree that certain rules or obligations are not to be implemented on an *inter se* basis and the relevant rights are renounced accordingly, they in fact agree that the relevant norms are excluded from their bilateral *inter se* relations. Such agreement gives rise to normative conflict not less than any 'direct' or 'material' conflict would.

As Cassese submits, it is implausible for States to conclude a treaty in which their intention to act contrary to *jus cogens* is recorded for all to see;

---

[20] Leonetti, Interprétation des traités et règles impératives du droit international général (*jus cogens*), 24 *ÖZÖR* (1973), 97.

[21] Special Rapporteur Fitzmaurice has elaborated upon this issue in terms of treaties embodying objective obligations (*jus cogens*), and submitted that only material, or direct, conflict should matter for the purposes of invalidity. If a number of the parties to a treaty containing objective obligations agree not to insist, so far as they are concerned, on the performance of it by another, this may weaken the force of the treaty, and may be inconsistent with its spirit, but it is not in direct conflict with the treaty so long as they do not actually agree not to perform the treaty obligations. Fitzmaurice, Third Report on the Law of Treaties, 2 YbILC 1958, 44–45.

'there are more subtle, consequential or indirect ways in which a treaty can come into conflict with *jus cogens*'.[22] In fact, whether or not a peremptory norm may be violated and whether or not its violation can go unpunished or unaccounted for are not very different questions from the normative point of view, as both relate to the question whether a peremptory norm operates as a legal norm (as distinct from a mere hypothetical standard of conduct). An agreement not to perform a peremptory norm or to ignore the effects of that norm in *inter se* relations is itself an attempt to make a peremptory norm *inter se* inoperable and to deprive it of its legal force. A consequential derogation undermines the primary prohibition, and it is difficult not to qualify this as a conflict with *jus cogens*. A conflict between two different normative sets is here perfectly observable and entails voidness. Such an understanding of conflict with *jus cogens* under Article 53 of the Vienna Convention is required both by a general concept of normative conflict and a broader nature of *jus cogens*, which requires absolute compliance.

1.5. Consequences of voidness

The early proposals regarding the consequences of treaty invalidity did not elaborate upon the specific case of the *jus cogens* invalidity.[23] The Vienna Convention contains, however, the specific provision in this regard. Article 71(1) VCLT imposes specific obligations on States in terms of invalidity of a treaty conflicting with *jus cogens*: to 'eliminate as far as possible the consequences of any act performed in reliance on any provision which conflicts with the peremptory norm of general international law; and bring their mutual relations into conformity with the peremptory norm of general international law'.

The regime of treaty invalidity under the Vienna Convention is differentiated in accordance with degrees of illegality involved. Some illegalities affect a co-contracting party only, while others affect the public interest. 'The law of invalidity should treat therefore different types of violations differently according to their significance with respect to the interest involved.'[24] This distinction provides a ground for differentiating between relative and absolute nullity.[25] Article 53 of the Vienna Convention involves a degree of illegality substantially higher than in other cases of invalidity. Hence it produces the nullity *ab initio*. The preference for absolute and *ab initio*

---

[22] Cassese, *Self-Determination of Peoples* (1994), 173.

[23] Waldock, Second Report, Articles 27–28, II YbILC 1963, 93–94, and the ILC's 1963 Report, Articles 52–53, id., 216.

[24] Rozakis (1974), 154.

[25] Jaenicke, Zur Frage des Internationalen Ordre Public, 7 *Berichte der Deutschen Gesellschaft für Völkerrecht* (1967), 94, notes that the integral application of the given peremptory norm excluded even the relative validity of the impugned treaty *inter partes*.

invalidity has been maintained since the proposals of the Special Rapporteur Fitzmaurice.[26]

The nullity under Article 53 is a special case of nullity. The illegality which causes it is not simply the illegality subsumable within the bilateral relations of the parties, but the objective illegality requiring objective elimination. As the ILC remarked, it is not about mutual adjustment of positions between parties, but about their obligation to bring the situation concerned into full conformity with *jus cogens*.[27] As Nicoloudis suggests, the invalidity regime under Article 71(1) relates to elimination of consequences which are fundamentally antisocial, and requires parties to re-establish their relations in terms of public order requirements. This is an absolute sanction for violations of public order.[28]

Consequently, invalidity under Article 53 entails a different regime of (a) invocation of invalidity and (b) consequences of invalidity. This regime of invalidity reflects a link between substance and legal consequences. When a treaty 'is void', more imperative consequences apply than in the case of voidable treaties.

1.5.1. Procedural aspects of voidness

The very emergence of the concept of *jus cogens* caused a fear of instability in treaty relations. As Lauterpacht noted, 'the supposed invalidity of immoral treaties is a standing invitation to the law-breaker to disengage himself uni-laterally—in a heroic manner—from an inconvenient duty.'[29] Arguably, decision-making by an impartial agency was necessary.[30] According to Arechaga, no unilateral application of grounds of invalidity is permissible and though States may invoke these grounds, invalidation may take place on the basis of either an agreement with other parties or a decision of an international organ.[31]

Concerns about possible abuses are legitimate. But such concerns have arisen in other fields of the law of treaties too, and there as well the cogency of principle has prevailed.[32] In this field, if invalidity is objective, it should not

---

[26] Fitzmaurice, Fourth Report, II YbILC 1959, 46.
[27] (1966–II) YbILC, 266.   [28] Nicoloudis (1974), 108.
[29] Lauterpacht, *Collected Papers*, vol. I (1970), 358.   [30] Lauterpacht (1970), 358–359.
[31] Arechaga, International Law in the Past Third of the Century, 159 *RdC* (1978), 59.
[32] As Special Rapporteur Fitzmaurice suggested, the principle that States can reciprocally refuse the compliance with treaty obligations or even terminate the treaty is 'not without danger in the international field, where it is all too easy to allege fundamental breaches of the treaty as a ground for claiming to terminate it', and furthermore the merits of the issue cannot in many cases be tested before a tribunal. Fitzmaurice, Second Report, II YbILC 1957, 52–53. Neverthe-less, Fitzmaurice has supported the principle of reciprocal non-compliance which has later been embodied in Article 60 of the Vienna Convention. Even this provision can appear to some as imprecise as it defines the material breach of the treaty entitling its termination as a breach impeding the realization of the object and purpose of the treaty. This requires identifying such object and purpose in the case of specific treaties.

depend on recognition by parties involved or any other actor. If Arechaga's approach is accepted and followed, then although a treaty conflicting with *jus cogens* is absolutely and objectively void, it is nevertheless still valid unless declared otherwise and validly authorizes acts contrary to *jus cogens*. This assumption not only sins against the clear wording of the Vienna Convention, but also justifies fragmentation of *jus cogens*, and hence it must be rejected.

It may be contended that invalidity under Article 53 is not automatic,[33] but subject to dispute settlement procedures under Part V of the Vienna Convention. Article 69 of the Convention, dealing with the consequences of treaty invalidity in general, states that a treaty whose invalidity is established under the Convention is void. This provision can be read as requiring that invalidity must be established through application of Articles 65–68 of the Convention on dispute settlement procedures. Frowein suggests that under Article 69, only an agreement whose invalidity is established under the Convention is void, and no party may treat an agreement as a nullity before the procedure is terminated.[34] But then, the words 'established under the present Convention' in Article 69 do not necessarily refer to establishment of invalidity through dispute settlement procedures, but to its establishment as such under the Convention which distinguishes between nullity and voidabilty. Gaja is concerned that if Article 65 procedures are applied to invalidity under Article 53, 'conflict with a peremptory norm would not make a treaty void unless one of the parties took some action to this end', and this approach is hardly reconcilable with Article 71 of the Convention.[35] As Nicoloudis suggests, the *erga omnes* character of invalidity under Article 53 loses its importance if the Vienna Convention procedures of application of nullity are treated as prerequisites.[36] Moreover, invalidity under Article 53 does not fall within the Article 69 regime. Article 71 specifically and imperatively establishes the *lex specialis* required by the special nature of the *jus cogens* invalidity.

This approach accords with a more general approach of international law to nullity. As Jennings suggests, while relative nullity often needs institutional determination to be set in motion, absolute nullity, such as nullity for conflict with *jus cogens*, follows the operation of law automatically and institutional

---

[33] cf Czaplinski and Danilenko, Conflicts of Norms in International Law, 21 *Netherlands Yearbook of International Law* (1990), 10.

[34] Frowein, *Jus Cogens*, 7 EPIL 329; Frowein, Nullity, 7 EPIL 364; Stein, Collective Enforcement of International Obligations, 47 *ZaöRV* (1987), 77.

[35] Gaja, *Jus Cogens* beyond the Vienna Convention, 172 *RdC* (1981), 283.

[36] Nicoloudis (1974), 113.

determinations, if any, can only be declaratory of it.[37] Therefore, to consider institutional determination as a precondition for voiding a treaty under Article 53 of the Vienna Convention is to undermine its regime of nullity.

Another implication of objective invalidity under Article 53, which is a matter for the community interest, is that standing to invoke invalidity is not limited to the parties to a treaty.

According to Tomuschat, the authors of the Vienna Convention made conflict of a treaty with *jus cogens* a legal occurrence that should be settled exclusively between the parties to the treaty, no third State being allowed to invoke the nullity.[38] But neither the Vienna Convention's text nor preparatory work confirms that. At early stages of the ILC's work, a Memorandum by Yepes endorsed the idea that all States have standing to challenge treaties conflicting with *jus cogens*.[39] At the Vienna Conference, the view was put forward that the invalidity of treaties conflicting with *jus cogens* is an objective invalidity and can thus be asserted by any State or organization aware of the invalidity. That is inherent in the very nature of *jus cogens*.[40] The Convention text does not contradict that.

This furthermore corresponds to the principle of objective illegality in the case of *jus cogens* invalidity that a treaty conflicting with public order 'cannot be enforced by an international tribunal even if the State which stands to benefit from the judicial nullification of the treaty does not raise the issue'.[41]

According to Simma, it is a bilateralist approach to consider that the invalidity of a treaty is invocable by parties to that treaty only.[42] Sztucki considers that the role of third States to challenge a treaty conflicting with *jus cogens* follows from the idea of international public order.[43] The view that

---

[37] Jennings, Nullity and Effectiveness in International Law, *Cambridge Essays in International Law* (1965), 67. Also, 'The view that it is only possible to rely on the rule relating to nullities where some procedure for this purpose is established, finds no support in international law.' Judge Winiarski, Effect of Awards, ICJ Reports, 1954, 65.

[38] Tomuschat, Obligations Arising for States without or against their Will, 241 *RdC* (1993), 363; Cassese, *International Law* (2005), 203–204; Li Haopei, Jus Cogens and International Law, Sienho Yee and Wang Tieya (eds), *International Law in the Post-Cold War World—Festschrift Li Haopei* (2001), 520; Czaplinski and Danilenko (1990), 10.

[39] YbILC, 1953, 166.

[40] UNCLT First Session (1969), 310 (Israel).

[41] Lauterpacht, Report on the Law of Treaties, YbILC 1954, 155.

[42] Simma, Bilateralism and Community Interest in the Law of State Responsibility, Y. Dinstein and M.Tabory (eds), *International Law at a Time of Perplexity—Essays in Honour of Shabtai Rosenne* (1989), 821; Rozakis (1974), 171, 190; Reuter, *Introduction to the Law of Treaties* (1972), 143; Scheuner, Conflict of Treaty Provisions with a Peremptory Norm of General International Law, 29 *Zeitschrift für ausländisches öffentliches Recht und Völkerrecht* (1969), 31.

[43] Sztucki, Jus Cogens *and the Vienna Convention on the Law of Treaties* (1974), 130.

invalidity cannot be invoked except by parties to a treaty is incompatible with the notion of peremptory norms.[44] Customary rules reflecting the Vienna Convention invalidity provisions also admit that any State can invoke the voidness of a treaty conflicting with *jus cogens*.[45]

If the standing to invoke the invalidity of the treaty conflicting with *jus cogens* was limited to the parties to the treaty only, then non-State actors would also be left without protection. For instance, treaties like the 1989 Timor Gap Treaty would not be challengeable except by its two parties, none of which would do so, and States or entities like East Timor would not be entitled to challenge the Treaty that legitimized the exploitation of their resources.

When a treaty conflicts with *jus cogens*, third States are under a duty to recognize such nullity. This is also the consequence of a legal duty not to recognize illegalities such as forcible territorial acquisitions and to treat unlawful annexations as void.[46]

1.5.2. Substantive aspects of voidness

(1) Under Article 69.2(a) of the Vienna Convention, which deals with the relative invalidity of treaties in the context of reciprocity and bilateralism, 'each party may require any other party to establish as far as possible in their mutual relations the position that would have existed if the acts had not been performed'. Article 71(1), dealing with public order invalidity operating in the interests of the international community as a whole, does not leave invalidity to the discretion of any, even an injured party, but imperatively declares that 'the parties shall' remove any illegality produced by a treaty conflicting with *jus cogens*. It is not the parties—even all of them—who decide on the invalidity, but the latter is imperatively predetermined under the law.

(2) Article 71(1) does not, unlike Article 69(1), simply require that the situation that would have existed before the conclusion of a treaty has to be restored; rather, it requires that parties bring their mutual relations into conformity with the relevant peremptory norm. Under Article 69(1), restoration of a situation which would have existed before the conclusion of a voidable treaty is a bilateral concern of the parties only, depending on their subsequent agreement. But bringing *inter se* relations in compliance with *jus cogens* is no longer a matter of the discretion of the parties, but their imperative duty, required by an equally imperative duty to avoid fragmentation of *jus cogens*.

(3) Under Article 69.2(b) of the Vienna Convention, invalidity of a treaty

[44] Nicoloudis (1974), 116.   [45] Cassese (2005), 177.
[46] Frowein, Nullity, 7 EPIL 363; Stein (1987), 77.

does not render invalid acts performed in good faith before the invocation of invalidity of a voidable treaty. Under Article 69(3), in cases of invalidity based on fraud, error, corruption or coercion, the party which performed acts pursuant to the invalid treaty cannot benefit from those acts. This also demonstrates that the only illegality such invalidity involves is the injury to the individual interests of parties.

Article 71 does not allow a party to benefit from acts performed pursuant to a treaty conflicting with *jus cogens*. No party, not even the injured one, may claim a legal benefit from *bona fide* acts performed pursuant to a void treaty. If a treaty is invalid for offending against the public interest, the consequences of invalidity are determined by reference to the public interest and not to the individual interest of a party. As Article 71 requires the parties to 'eliminate ... the consequences of *any* act performed in reliance on any provision which conflicts with the peremptory norm', it matters that the act is contrary to *jus cogens* and not whether it is performed in good faith, as invalidity in such cases is absolute.

(4)   Article 69(2) requires, 'as far as possible', the re-establishment of the position in the mutual relations of the parties which would have existed if the acts pursuant to an invalid treaty had not been performed. Article 71(1) requires elimination of acts contrary to *jus cogens* also 'as far as possible'. However, the relevance of the words 'as far as possible' in Articles 69(2) and 71(1) should be understood differently.

The word 'possible' may have factual or legal connotations; certain juridical factors can be relevant in determining whether it is 'possible' to wipe out all the consequences of an invalid treaty. In the case of Article 69(2) what is possible is not least to be determined by the parties *inter se*. In the case of Article 71(1), the words 'as far as possible' should be understood in terms of the overarching legal framework. The parties hardly possess any discretion in determining what is possible and what is not when they act in terms of Article 71(1). Furthermore, this duty is accompanied by another duty under Article 71.1(b)—stated in more imperative terms and not referring to what is 'possible'—to bring their mutual relations into conformity with peremptory norms. Therefore, what is 'possible' and what is not is already predetermined by the law—specific peremptory norms applicable to a given situation—and is not subject to the attitudes of the parties.

It seems that Article 71 also incorporates certain legal consequences normally relevant in the law of State responsibility. These consequences are similar to restitution in kind and thus Article 71 reinforces the principle—although in context of the Vienna Convention only—that the legal effects of *jus cogens* are themselves peremptory.

It is submitted that the operation of Article 71(1) of the Vienna Convention should be interpreted restrictively in the case of State creation. The status of a State created by a treaty conflicting with *jus cogens* would not in principle be affected by its invalidation, because Article 71 arguably applies to the parties to an illegal treaty and does not govern the status of a State established by that treaty unless the latter itself is party to it; and because 'it is hard to imagine a situation actually arising in which a treaty creating a State (as distinct from one providing for its termination) could be a breach of a *jus cogens* norm'.[47]

This question has substantive and consequential aspects closely inter-related to each other. As for the substantive aspect, States could be established by a treaty in violation of *jus cogens*, in consequence of the use of force, in breach of the right to self-determination and basic human rights. Such statehood and the treaty establishing it would be void. States are not created in a legal or physical vacuum, but in a specific space, endowed with authority over a specific population. Thus, in at least a substantive number, if not in the majority, or even all, of the cases, a State established by a treaty conflicting with *jus cogens* would be based on the termination or modification of another State. This means that a newly established State would be a direct consequence of a breach of *jus cogens* with regard to an earlier State.

As for the consequential aspect, the fact that Article 71 mentions only parties to a treaty does not make a State established by that treaty immune from the effects of *jus cogens*. If it is so immune, this would mean that a State continues to exist, although its legal basis—an illegal treaty—is void *ab initio*. In such a case, parties would have to assume that 'statehood' is legitimate and opposable to them (which could mean the recognition of such statehood, or at least a failure to apply to it the duty of non-recognition). This would be directly contrary to the duties of parties under Article 71. The very duty to 'bring mutual relations into conformity with the peremptory norm' and eliminate as far as possible the consequences of its breach includes the duty to withdraw any support from an illegal State, not to recognize it, to take a legal attitude favouring the voidness of its 'statehood' and to take steps towards its elimination. It is hard to imagine how the parties to an invalid treaty can 'bring mutual relations into conformity with the peremptory norm' and eliminate as far as possible the consequences of its breach, if they are precluded under international law from taking steps towards the annihilation of those very consequences—the entities claiming 'statehood' under the illegal treaty.

(5) The Second Report of Special Rapporteur Waldock included the provision regarding the loss of the right to insist on the invalidity of a treaty, which envisaged the cases of waiver and preclusion through acquiescence, and made no special provision for the cases of *jus cogens* invalidity.[48]

---

[47] Crawford, *Creation of States in International Law* (1979), 83.
[48] II YbILC 1963, 38.

However, the Commission subsequently adopted Article 47 in which it excluded the relevance of the subsequent validation in the cases of *jus cogens* invalidity.[49] In its Final Report on the Law of Treaties the Commission reaffirmed this approach by emphasizing that the principle that invalid treaties can be validated through subsequent waiver or acquiescence would be inappropriate to admit in cases of *jus cogens* or supervening *jus cogens*.[50]

Article 45 of the Vienna Convention precludes validation of a treaty conflicting with *jus cogens* through waiver and acquiescence. According to Jennings, 'if the *injuria* is truly a breach of a *jus cogens*, whether or not there be also a wrong in respect of a particular legal person, there should in principle be no question of qualifying the resulting nullity by waivers or estoppels resulting from the conduct of a particular legal person'.[51] This suggestion accords with the principle that breaches of *jus cogens* objectively injure the international community and the attitude of individual States cannot validate such illegality.

Some writers nevertheless attempted to qualify this principle. Rozakis considers that in view of the inadequacy of international machinery, 'the likelihood of a totally unhindered operation of an illegal treaty is not to be precluded. A long-lasting operation could eventually amount to a *de facto* validation of a treaty.'[52] It is recognized that the possibility of such validation reduces the objective invalidity to a private inter-State concern to be settled *inter partes*,[53] which reveals the conceptual controversy between the concept of *jus cogens* and such validation. According to Rozakis, States cannot validate treaties conflicting with *jus cogens* but the international community can, by its attitude and conduct, including acquiescence. That is qualitatively different from validation by the parties, because the community as a whole is the beneficiary of peremptory norms and has the exclusive right to decide whether to validate the treaty.[54]

According to Jennings, as the international community is decentralized, the attitude of third States may qualify the nullity.[55] But that is something the Vienna Convention does not confirm, as Article 45 relates to validation by a State-party only. The third-party or community validation issue depends on a more general question of whether peremptory norms tolerate the community acquiescence.

Another practical question is how the community validation, if admitted outside the Vienna Convention, interacts with the irrelevance of the attitude of the State-party under Article 45 of the Vienna Convention. Would com-

---

[49] II YbILC 1963, 212–213.   [50] II YbILC 1966, 240.   [51] Jennings (1965), 74.
[52] Rozakis (1974), 172, also emphasizing that this can be precluded through non-recognition; Rozakis (1976), 128–129.
[53] Rozakis (1976), 129.   [54] Rozakis (1976), 128.   [55] Jennings (1965), 74.

munity acquiescence work if the State-party refuses to validate? That cannot be assumed.

The Vienna Convention provisions were drafted with a view of imposing some limits on the relevance of State attitudes. The Convention is clear in distinguishing between what can and what cannot be accomplished through waiver or acquiescence. The very function of *jus cogens* is to operate in a considerably more rigid manner than *jus dispositivum* and that includes a limitation on any subsequent validation process. The very reasoning recognizing that *jus cogens* is in principle not susceptible to subsequent validation through acquiescence, waiver or prescription, but its effects may nevertheless be qualified by the same factors, appears circular.

If the drafters of the Vienna Convention had wished to accept Rozakis' approach, they could have done so. In addition, as treaties void under Article 53 are null and void *ab initio*, that is non-existent, it is questionable if one may validate an act which has never existed. One may perhaps validate subjective and relative illegality, but not acts involving objective illegality. So far, no single suggestion has been made in practice that a treaty contrary to *jus cogens* was to be validated through waiver or acquiescence by an interested State or third States, or even the entire international community, and it is unsound to affirm the existence of legal options directly excluded by the Vienna Convention. Furthermore, the decentralized nature of the international community makes it impossible to find a general acquiescence to the illegality, as it is difficult to find evidence of the community attitude.

Confirmation of validity is *a fortiori* incompatible with the *jus cogens* invalidity. The treaty which transgresses *jus cogens* cannot continue existing and producing effects.[56] Even if a State does not invoke the cause of nullity, nothing prevents it from doing so later.[57] In terms of prescription, Nicoloudis considers that non-invocation of voidness for a long time does not imply either validation of a treaty or its effects. In short, prescription of invalidity is impossible in the case of *jus cogens* and a treaty offending against *jus cogens* is imprescriptible.[58] A bilateral or multilateral confirmation is nothing but a new synallagmatic relationship,[59] and this raises the question of compatibility with *jus cogens* of such a new synallagmatic relationship as such, which would be nothing but a fresh attempt to derogate from *jus cogens*.

A treaty conflicting with *jus cogens* cannot be validated through State succession either, as the latter is without prejudice to any issue of validity (Article 11 of the 1978 Vienna Convention on State Succession).

(6) Special Rapporteur Lauterpacht considered that the principle of severability should apply to the *jus cogens* invalidity of treaties, 'namely, that

---

[56] Nicoloudis (1974), 188.
[57] Nicoloudis, (1974), 189–190.
[58] Nicoloudis, (1974), 191.
[59] Nicoloudis, (1974), 190.

any single provision involving an illegality, does not entail the nullity of the treaty if the latter, taken as a whole, can be upheld'. But this would not be possible 'if the provision in question constitutes an essential part of the treaty'.[60] Special Rapporteur Waldock also considered it wrong to hold 'a treaty totally void by reason of a minor inconsistency with a *jus cogens* rule' and proposed 'to allow the severance of illegal provisions from a treaty in cases where they do not form part of the principal objects of the treaty and are clearly severable from the rest of its provisions'.[61]

Within the ILC, however, the approach prevailed that the 'rules of *jus cogens* are of so fundamental character that, when parties conclude a treaty which conflicts in any of its clauses with an already existing rule of *jus cogens*, the treaty must be considered totally invalid'. Therefore, in its proposed Article 37 dealing with the *jus cogens* invalidity of treaties the Commission did not admit the principle of separability.[62] The ILC Final Report on the Law of Treaties subscribes to the same approach and further specifies that it must be open to States-parties to revise the treaty so as to bring it into conformity with the relevant peremptory norm. 'If they did not do so, the law must attach the sanction of nullity to the whole transaction.'[63]

In the case of relative invalidity not entire treaties but only those clauses to which the ground of invalidity relates are invalid. They are separable from the rest of a treaty if such separation is possible. But in case of conflict with *jus cogens* the entire treaty is invalid; Article 44(5) does not allow separability. Such a strict approach is questioned by some. A number of States at the Vienna Conference considered that a total invalidation of a treaty and non-separability of impugned clauses was too grave a consequence.[64] In theory, the ILC's attempt to provide for a uniform formula of entire invalidity and non-severability is criticized.[65] Gaja contends that non-separability and entire invalidity is hardly an effective sanction and is hence unreasonable,[66] and Cassese submits that even if severability is banned under the Vienna Convention in relation to Article 53, this rule is unreasonable and general inter-

---

[60] YbILC 1954, 155

[61] Waldock, Second Report, II YbILC 1963, 52–53: Waldock's Article 13 provides for the severability accordingly.

[62] II YbILC 1963, 198–199.   [63] II YbILC 1966, 239.

[64] UNCLT Second Session (1969), 98 (UK); UNCLT First Session (1969), 323 (Canada).

[65] Rozakis (1976), 126; Scheuner, Conflict of a Treaty Provision with a Peremptory Norm of International Law and Its Consequences, 27 *Zeitschrift für ausländisches öffentliches Recht und Völkerrecht* (1967), 532; Scheuner (1969), 35; Dhokalia, Problems Relating to *Jus Cogens*, Agrawala (ed.), *Essays on the Law of Treaties* (1972), 172–173; Minagawa, *Jus Cogens* in Public International Law, 6 *Hirotsubashi Journal of Law and Politics* (1968), 28, suggesting also that specific situations should be resolved independently of any general principle.

[66] Gaja (1981), 285. It is contended that Article 71(1) in fact permits separability as it only requires bringing mutual relations of contracting parties with peremptory norms, Nicoloudis (1974), 104. But this is not to qualify the scope of Article 44(5).

national law perhaps admits severability in relation to non-parties to the Vienna Convention.[67]

On the other hand, the ILC suggested that peremptory norms are so fundamental that States must be aware of the consequences of concluding treaties in conflict with them.[68] At the Vienna Conference, a number of States submitted that it is not sufficient to condemn fundamental violations; it is necessary to lay down a preventive sanction of absolute nullity of the treaty which constitutes a preparatory act of the violation.[69] The reason for repudiating the entire treaty is that peremptory norms are of such fundamental and humanitarian character that none of them can form an unimportant and secondary provision of a treaty, even if incorporated in some isolated (and *prima facie* severable) provision.[70] The text of the Vienna Convention follows this reasoning and there is little to oppose it. But with regard to non-parties to the Convention or treaties concluded before the Convention entered into force, severability perhaps could apply as it does not hamper the effects of *jus cogens* with regard to provisions conflicting with it.

The entire law of treaty invalidity reflects an indispensable link between the substance of the primary principles and their legal effects. In a case of relative invalidity the regime of invalidity depends in its operation on the will and attitudes of the parties to the contested treaty, whereas in the case of absolute invalidity ensuing from objective illegality, the Vienna Convention establishes absolute invalidity independent of the attitudes of States, and defines its implications. Consequently, the system of invalidity under the Vienna Convention effectively refutes the perception that under international law nullity cannot produce its full effects.

2. TERMINATION OF TREATIES UNDER ARTICLE 64 OF THE VIENNA CONVENTION

2.1. Substantive questions

Under Article 64 of the Vienna Convention, a treaty conflicting with a new peremptory norm becomes void and terminates. As the ILC Final Report specified, the new rule of *jus cogens* 'does not annul the treaty; it forbids its further existence and performance'.[71] This is however the only case of the

---

[67] Cassese (2005), 205.

[68] 2 YbILC 1966, 243; Pauwelyn (2003), 282.

[69] UNCLT Second Session (1969), 105 (Uruguay); UNCLT First Session (1969), 303 (Uruguay), 449 (USSR).

[70] Fahmi, Peremptory Norms as General Rules of International Law, 22 *Österreichische Zeitschrift für öffentliches Recht* (1971), 399; Rozakis (1976), 124.

[71] II YbILC 1966, 261.

termination of a treaty due to general international law without reference to any act of the parties.[72] Unlike other grounds of termination, which protect the interests of individual parties, Article 64 protects general interests of the international community through safeguarding the uniform operation of *jus cogens*,[73] and offers a special public order type of termination—compulsory termination independent of the will of parties.[74]

Article 64 differs from what was proposed at earlier stages of the codification of the law of treaties. Special Rapporteurs Fitzmaurice and Waldock proposed that it should be open to any party to call for the termination of a treaty or violate it reciprocally if it conflicts with a new peremptory norm.[75] Waldock himself recognized that such treaties are incapable of application due to the subsequent emergence of relevant *jus cogens*,[76] but the language of his draft article was defective in that it referred to the discretion of parties and hence to relative invalidity. This was remedied by the ILC, which adopted the formulation now reflected in Article 64 of the Vienna Convention.[77]

As the ILC emphasized, a treaty conflicting with a new norm of *jus cogens* becomes void 'after having been valid and applied during some, perhaps quite long, period of time'. Therefore, what subsequently attaches to such a treaty is not nullity *ab initio*, but nevertheless, the rule of *jus cogens* being an overriding rule of international law, 'any situation resulting from the previous application of the treaty could only retain its validity after the emergence of the rule of *jus cogens* to the extent that it was not in conflict with that rule'.[78]

As the view prevailing at the Vienna Conference has demonstrated, Article 64 is a corollary to Article 53, both from the viewpoint of its supporters and opponents.[79] However, Article 64 does not void *ab initio* treaties conflicting with *jus cogens*, but only prohibits their future existence or performance.[80] The ILC originally intended that invalidity is to attach only as from the time of the establishment of the relevant peremptory norm. In other words, there would be no retroactive invalidity.[81] Peremptory norms have arguably no retroactive effect within the law of treaties.[82]

---

[72] Possibly apart from desuetude, which is anyway not mirrored in the Vienna Convention.

[73] Rozakis (1976), 138, 148–149.

[74] Rozakis (1974), 174–175.

[75] Fitzmaurice, Fourth Report, YbILC (II-1959), 46; Draft Article 21 proposed by Waldock, YbILC, II–1963, 78.

[76] See commentary to Article 21, id., 79.   [77] YbILC II-1963, 211.

[78] 2 YbILC 1963, 216–217. The Commission accordingly adopted the provision in Article 53(2).

[79] UNCLT First Session (1969), 386 ff. ILC took a similar view, YbILC, II-1963, 211.

[80] Elias, Problems concerning the Validity of Treaties, 134 *RdC* (1971), 393.

[81] II YbILC 1966, 249, 267.

[82] Gaja (1981), 292; Schwelb, Some Aspects of International *Jus Cogens*, 61 *AJIL* (1967), 969.

The scope of Article 64 is very much the same as that of Article 53: it extends to 'any treaty'. The criteria for establishing normative conflict under Article 64 are likewise the same as under Article 53: an objective contradiction between the treaty and a peremptory norm.

2.2. Legal consequences of treaty termination under Article 64 of the Vienna Convention

According to Article 71(2) of the Vienna Convention:

In the case of a treaty which becomes void and terminates under Article 64, the termination of the treaty:

(a)   releases the parties from any obligation further to perform the treaty;

(b)   does not affect any right, obligation or legal situation of the parties created through the execution of the treaty prior to its termination; provided that those rights, obligations or situations may thereafter be maintained only to the extent that their maintenance is not in itself in conflict with the new peremptory norm of general international law.

This provision reflects the attitude expressed in the ILC Final Report that 'a right, obligation or legal situation valid when it arose is not to be made retroactively invalid; but its *further* maintenance after the establishment of the new rule of *jus cogens* is admissible only to the extent that such further maintenance is not in itself in conflict with that rule.'[83] Article 71(2), together with the ILC's commentary, makes is quite clear that, as far as the legal relations after the establishment of the new peremptory norm are concerned, the effect of invalidity under Article 64 is identical to that under Article 53 of the Vienna Convention. A crucial, and most complex, issue is that of the impact of the new peremptory norm on the acts and situations that arose before its emergence.

A new peremptory rule terminates a treaty *ipso facto*. This is not a treaty termination in a strict sense, but occurs imperatively and not by the will of the parties, whether on an *ad hoc* basis or as agreed in a treaty itself; the consequences are more similar to the consequences of voidness. Such specific regulation is required by *jus cogens superveniens*. The law of treaty termination is inherently bilateral and reciprocal, and hence cannot embrace all the effects of peremptory norms. On the other hand, a strict application of the principles of nullity would hardly suit situations where a treaty was not intended to conflict with *jus cogens* but came into contradiction with it only after the latter emerged.

It has been argued that Article 71(2) does not provide for genuine nullity as its sanction is less absolute and categorical, being posterior in nature.[84]

---

[83]   II YbILC 1966, 267 (emphasis original).   [84]   Nicoloudis (1974), 109.

According to Elias, the case of Article 64 is special both with regard to invalidity and termination, especially because invalidity does not operate *ab initio*.[85]

Elias and Nicoloudis seem to assume implicitly that the rights, obligations or legal situations invalidated by Article 71(2) can be maintained legally alive if the parties so agree.[86] But Article 71(2) does not allow that acts or situations contrary to *jus cogens* are maintained in force, and in this aspect Article 64 gives rise to a regime of invalidity, as does Article 53. The abolition of situations contrary to *jus cogens* definitionally implies bringing the mutual relations of parties in accordance with *jus cogens superveniens*, and to that extent the regimes under Articles 71(1) and 71(2) are essentially identical. Legal relations in situations under Article 64 of the Vienna Convention are not reducible to the rights and attitudes of parties, but relate to public order, and hence the decision of parties to maintain the treaty alive could have little effect in law.

In addition, Article 45 does not permit acquiescence or waiver with regard to a treaty void under Article 64.[87] Were the reading of Article 71(2) by Elias and Nicoloudis correct, a treaty voluntarily maintained alive would be under a constant threat of invalidation. Even if the parties could maintain a treaty in force, none of them could be deprived of the right to challenge the rights subsequently.

The effect of Article 64 is limited *ratione temporis*, in terms of the effect of *jus cogens superveniens* on acts performed under a void treaty. According to Elias, Article 71(2) allows only completed acts and situations not to become void, and not the acts continuing after the treaty has become void.[88] Gaja considers that in the case of termination of a treaty under Article 64, under Article 71(2), while damages may be due for earlier breaches of the treaty, the other forms of reparation would be inapplicable 'if they involve an action or omission which is contrary to the new peremptory norm'.[89] But to require payment of damages for non-compliance with a treaty retrospectively voided under Article 64 is to frustrate the purpose of this provision, which extends to all incomplete acts and situations, as Elias suggests, and situations where damages have yet to be paid are clearly incomplete.

In terms of the invocability of voidness, views are divided in the same way as with regard to the effects of Article 53. According to Rozakis, it is only the parties who can invoke illegality.[90] But Elias suggests that third States may freely invoke the invalidity.[91] For reasons set out above in relation to the effects of Article 53, it seems that the view of Elias must be preferred.

---

[85] Elias (1971), 408.   [86] Elias (1971), 408–409; Nicoloudis (1974), 109.
[87] But see Rozakis (1976), 145–146 on community acquiescence.
[88] Elias (1971), 409.   [89] Gaja (1981), 291–292.
[90] Rozakis (1976), 145.   [91] Elias (1971), 409.

Neither the Vienna Convention's text nor its preparatory materials exclude severability in case of invalidity under Article 64.[92] The ILC's Final Report expressly emphasized that if the provisions of a treaty conflicting with *jus cogens superveniens* 'can properly be regarded as separable from the rest of the treaty ... the rest of the treaty ought to be regarded as still valid'.[93] Hence, severability may perhaps be presumed.[94] According to Elias, the principle of separability applies because when first concluded the treaty was entirely valid but some of its provisions are later found to be void on the ground because of a conflict with a newly established rule of *jus cogens*.[95] Perhaps separability ought to be permitted because the parties to a treaty have not intentionally contradicted *jus cogens*, and this should be reflected in terms of voidness. But separability could not be implied at least under the Vienna Convention. According to Article 71(2), the rights and obligations before invalidation are maintained, not the treaty provisions themselves, and this seems to contradict the idea of severability, as Article 71 is *lex specialis* in relation to Article 44. But this does not affect severability under general international law.

3. STATE PRACTICE

Jus cogens invalidity of a treaty because of inconsistency with a higher legal standard is the only ground of substantive invalidity, all other invalidities being based on defects of will. Therefore, the instances of the practice of application of *jus cogens* invalidity of treaties can be the ones that involve the claims of invalidity related to the substance of treaties, as distinct from the other grounds of invalidity. Even if some contend that States are not willing to apply the *jus cogens* invalidity to treaties,[96] the practice can prove the opposite.

The practice involving claims of the nullity of treaties also encompasses cases of conflict with previous treaty obligations or the rights of third parties. These are the cases where nullity would have been conducive to the interests of the States that claimed that nullity and was hence claimed.[97] This practice,

---

[92] For the ILC's position see II YbILC 1963, 212, admitting the severability in the case of *jus cogens superveniens*.

[93] II YbILC 1966, 261.

[94] Schwelb (1967), 972; *per contra* Li Haopei (2001), 519, referring to the fact that Article 71(2) refers to 'the treaty' as a whole.

[95] Elias (1971), 393; see also Rozakis (1976), 145.

[96] Czaplinski, Concepts of *jus cogens* and Obligations *erga omnes* in International Law in the Light of Recent Developments, 23 *Polish Yearbook of International Law* (1997–1998), 89.

[97] Such as, for instance, with regard to the Rapallo Treaty between Germany and Soviet Russia, as well as the decisions of Western powers with regard to Germany as incompatible with the Yalta Agreements, Sztucki (1974), 30–32.

however, demonstrates the attitudes of the respective States perceiving the so-called nullity as a phenomenon following from the expression of their will, rather than the inherent capacity of the relevant norms to produce such nullity. Therefore, this practice is not directly relevant in terms of the application of *jus cogens* invalidity. The analysis should be limited to the cases of *jus cogens* invalidity proper.

Some practice of tribunals relevant in terms of Article 53 affirms the validity of the principle that treaties conflicting with *jus cogens* are void, but falls short of declaring the treaty in question void. For instance, the Military Tribunal at Nuremberg in *Krupp* faced a defendant's plea that German exploitation of French POWs was justified under the Agreement between the German and French Governments at Vichy obliging French prisoners to work for German factories. The Tribunal found no credible evidence of the existence of such an agreement, but nevertheless pronounced on a hypothetical question of its validity, stating that even if concluded, it would be void as *contra bonos mores*.[98] It seems that the Tribunal dealt with a hypothetical agreement for the sake of conceptual coherence: it would be conceptually wrong to convict individuals and at the same time permit the inference that the criminal acts would be legitimate if supported by a treaty.[99] In *Aloeboetoe*, the Inter-American Court had to determine reparations due by Surinam to persons belonging to the Saramakas tribe and for that it had to ascertain family structures among the Saramakas to award proper compensation to relatives. For proving that Surinamese family law does not apply to the issue, the Inter-American Commission referred to a treaty of 19 September 1762 whereby Surinamese authorities granted them the right to be governed by their own laws. But the Court noted that this treaty, even if it were an international treaty, provided for cooperation between the tribe and the authorities in arresting fleeing slaves and payment of reward by the Surinamese Governor. The Court noted that 'the treaty would today be null and void because it contradicts the norms of *jus cogens superveniens*', and refused to apply it.[100] The Court refused to apply the treaty despite the fact that the impugned clauses were separate from the clauses related to family law and effectively took the non-severability view with regard to a treaty voided by *jus cogens superveniens*.

Tribunals sometimes hesitate to pronounce nullity because of their doubt of a norm's peremptory character. In *Guinea-Bissau/Senegal*, the Arbitral Tribunal faced the plea that the agreement concluded by a colonial power

---

[98] 15 ILR, 626–627; Paul, Legal Consequences of Conflict between a Treaty and an Imperative Norm of General International Law (*jus cogens*), 21 *Österreichische Zeitschrift für öffentliches Recht* (1971), 26; Schwelb (1967), 950–951.

[99] This point is reflected in Waldock's report on the law of treaties, linking the issue of *jus cogens* to the criminality of an act, 2 YbILC 1963, 52–53.

[100] Ser. C, No. 15 (1993), paras 56–57.

with regard to colonial territory was invalid because the colonial power had no *jus tractatus* with regard to colonial territories on the way to their self-determination. The Tribunal refused to avoid the agreement, holding that the rule in question was not peremptory,[101] which itself is the affirmation of *jus cogens* invalidity as a principle. In treating the argument of Guinea-Bissau that Senegal had no right to confirm the agreement concluded by France in relation to the territory of Senegal because that agreement conflicted with peremptory norms the Tribunal reiterated its assertion that the relevant norm was not peremptory,[102] and thereby implicitly affirmed the principle that the subsequent will of the State-party cannot cure the treaty that conflicts with *jus cogens*. The Tribunal's reasoning affirmed that if the rule were peremptory, it would not hesitate to declare the treaty invalid.[103] *Jus cogens* invalidity was also accepted but not applied in *Aminoil*, where the Arbitral Tribunal rejected the plea that permanent sovereignty over natural resources retrospectively annulled stabilization clauses in a 1948 Concession Agreement concluded with the Sheikh of Kuwait. The Tribunal denied the peremptory character of the norm, but not *jus cogens* invalidity as such.[104] The concept of the *jus cogens* invalidity of treaties was further affirmed by the Special Court for Sierra Leone in *Prosecutor v Kallon*, in which the Court held that it could declare the provision of the treaty by which it is established void if it contradicted the relevant peremptory norm.[105]

Classical international law recognized that treaties may provide for a right of forcible intervention. But after the use of force came to be considered a matter of community concern as distinct from a subject of private contract, such agreements are no longer lawful.[106] It is true that the right of inter-vention did not disappear from treaty practice after the First World War, when the Peace Treaties provided for intervention to enforce treaty obliga-tions and so did the Soviet–Persian Treaty.[107] Brownlie contends that, in general, the right of forcible intervention may still be lawfully conferred by a treaty.[108] But this is contradictory in face of the general prohibition of the use

---

[101] 83 ILR 23.   [102] Id., 26–27.   [103] Cassese (1994), 168; Cassese (2005), 205.

[104] 66 ILR 586–588.

[105] *Prosecutor v Kallon*, 13 March 2004, para. 61; the provision in question is Article 10 of the Statute of the Court (which in its turn forms part of the 2002 Agreement between the UN and Sierra Leone) related to the irrelevance of the amnesties for crimes falling within the Court's jurisdiction. Similarly, the Court emphasized in *Prosecutor v Taylor* that 'Article 6(2) of the Statute [related to the irrelevance of immunities] is not in conflict with any peremptory norm of general international law and must be given effect by this court', Decision of 31 May 2004, para. 53.

[106] Brownlie, *International Law and the Use of Force by States* (1963), 318–319.

[107] Id., 319.

[108] Brownlie (1963), 321. Other authors qualify this by suggesting that this cannot happen through the treaty concluded during the civil war because it would be done without the acqui-escence of the considerable number of citizens, cf Doswald-Beck, The Legal Validity of Military Intervention by Invitation of the Government, 56 *BYIL* (1985), 245. Doswald-Beck considers that 'a treaty authorising intervention to support any regime is of dubious worth', id., 250.

of force, which Brownlie himself recognizes as a limitation on intervention agreements. But it is also important to note that when the treaties that Brownlie mentions were concluded there was still no general ban on the use of force.

A treaty whereby a State is invited to intervene in a specific situation or whereby foreign troops are permitted to be stationed or to pass through a State's territory would not fall within the ambit of Article 53 of the Vienna Convention, it would not involve an actual breach of the prohibition of force or an authorization to commit such a breach; a breach arises where the victim State is not asked. In the case of intervention or guarantee treaties, there would be an authorization to commit a breach; a treaty would operate as if the ban of force were not in force between the contracting States and would derogate from it.

The *Treaty between Soviet Russia and Persia* (1921)[109] was intended as the framework treaty redefining relations between the two States as they existed between Tsarist Russia and Persia, and regulating territorial issues as well as issues of communication and navigation. Article 6 of the Treaty dealt with possible situations of using Persian territory as a base for preparing and performing aggressive military operations against Russia, and stipulated that if, after a warning, Persia was unable to deal with the situation so as to prevent any menace to Russia, the Russian Soviet Government would be entitled to deploy its armed forces on Persian territory to deal with the menace, and would withdraw as soon as this was accomplished. This provision is said to have granted Russia a unilateral discretion in determining if and when the conditions justifying intervention had been fulfilled.[110] On 5 November 1979, Iran announced the abrogation of Article 6.[111]

State practice treated the Treaty as valid for years,[112] though caution has been urged to assume that this indeed resulted in the validity of the Treaty, because of diplomatic acquiescence.[113] Indeed, practice must be viewed as of limited relevance. It was only the USSR which expressly affirmed its validity and it is impossible to infer consensus between the parties on this issue except by resorting to the doctrine of acquiescence: Iran was silent during the time the USSR was affirming the validity of the Treaty. Nevertheless, acquiescence cannot be validly invoked in a case where a treaty contradicts *jus cogens*.

It seems that the basis of abrogation of Article 6 is *jus cogens superveniens* under Article 64 of the Vienna Convention. Reisman noted that at the time

---

[109] No. 268, LNTS 1922, 394.
[110] Reisman, Termination of the USSR's Treaty Right of Intervention in Iran, 74 *AJIL* (1980), 148.
[111] Reisman, 145; Gaja (1981), 288.
[112] Brownlie (1963), 320–321, especially notes a continuous Soviet attitude affirming the validity of the Treaty over about 40 years.
[113] Reisman, (1980), 145.

of its conclusion the Treaty may have been lawful,[114] and this view may be justified, as at that time international law did not prohibit the use of force. However, after such prohibition emerged, notably under the UN Charter and related customary law, the operation of Article 6 became more problematic as there was a clear conflict between this Article and the peremptory prohibition of force. Reisman correctly suggests that the rights acquired in Article 6 could not survive developments in international law since 1945.[115] But this also suggests that the correct stance is to regard Article 6 not as abrogated by Iran in 1979, but as voided in consequence of the emergence of modern *jus ad bellum* in 1945.[116] In addition, under Article 71.2(b), voidness affected the whole Treaty and not just Article 6, but left intact the rights and situations created through its execution, such as arrangements regarding territorial status, communication and navigation.

Ronzitti argues that Article 6 did not offend against *jus cogens* as it entitled Russia not to commit an act of aggression against Persia but just to carry out operations to eliminate a menace to itself which existed on Persian territory. Ronzitti reaches this conclusion by assuming that Article 2(4) outlaws aggression only, not each and every use of force.[117] But such a reading cannot be reconciled with the plain meaning of Article 2(4), and especially with the fact that, as Reisman suggests, the use of force under Article 6 would necessarily infringe the territorial integrity of Iran, and its political independence, by virtue of being carried out without Iran's consent.[118]

The *Treaty of Guarantee between Cyprus and Greece, United Kingdom and Turkey* (1960)[119] served as one of the framework agreements for the statehood of Cyprus and prohibited it from participating 'in any political or economic union with any State whatsoever' (Article I). Greece, Turkey and the UK assumed the role of guarantor of Cyprus's independence (Articles II–III). Most problematically, Article IV, in case of a breach of the Treaty's provisions and the impossibility of common or concerted action, provided that 'each of the three guaranteeing Powers reserves the right to take the action with the sole aim of re-establishing the state of affairs created by the present Treaty'.

This provision became problematic in the early 1960s as Turkey launched armed attacks on Cyprus with the stated intention of supporting Turkish Cypriots, and was alleged by Turkey to confer on each of the three guarantors powers to intervene in Cyprus in order to ensure observance of the treaty. In 1963, Cyprus questioned the validity of that treaty as contrary to *jus cogens*, namely the prohibition of the use of force.[120] In 1964, Cyprus

---

[114] Reisman, 151.   [115] Reisman, 153.

[116] Abrogation would not hold on its own as USSR has maintained that Article 6 is still in force, Ronzitti, Use of Force, Consent and *Jus Cogens*, Cassese (ed.), *The Current Legal Regulation of the Use of Force* (1986) 158.

[117] Ronzitti (1986), 159.   [118] Reisman, 152.   [119] UNTS No. 5475.

[120] Paul (1971), 28; Schwelb (1967), 952–953; Gaja (1981), 288; Ronzitti (1986), 159; Li Haopei (2001), 506–508.

made such a submission to the UN Security Council. The Council never expressed its view on that argument. Jacovides correctly notes that the Council did not follow the proposal of Turkey to affirm the Guarantee Treaty, but simply noted the views of the parties in relation thereto and referred to Article 2(4) of the Charter,[121] which could also be interpreted as negating the validity of claims of forcible intervention.

The debate in the Security Council concerning the legality, validity or otherwise of the Guarantee Treaty has involved the expression of different, sometimes mutually contradictory, attitudes.[122] Turkey has arguably claimed that Article IV gave it the right to military intervention in Cyprus.[123] The British Representative considered that the principal aim of the Guarantee Treaty was to ensure the proper protection of the rights and interests of both communities in Cyprus.[124] The US Representative went further by expressly suggesting that Article IV of the Treaty was the means of maintaining the proper balance of the rights of the communities, without specifying, however, whether all available means were acceptable for this purpose.[125] But as the context of the case involved military intervention, there is some room for assuming that the US expressed some approval of the treaty that authorizes forcible interventions.

This was more expressly emphasized by the British Representative, suggesting that the purposes of the Guarantee Treaty were in accordance with Article 2(4) of the Charter because the right to intervention under Article IV was not unlimited but related only to the 'action with the sole aim of re-establishing the state of affairs created by the present Treaty'. He added that 'a right to intervention for this purpose, and for this purpose alone, is provided for in the Treaty'. There was 'nothing in Article IV to suggest that action taken under it would necessarily be contrary to the United Nations Charter'.[126] The British Representative's reading of the Treaty and its context was based on the narrow understanding of the prohibition of the use of force under Article 2(4) according to which not every use of force is outlawed, only those which impair the territorial integrity and political independence of the State.

The Soviet Representative opposed the idea advanced by the British Representative that the Security Council should approve the reading of the Treaty that justifies military intervention in Cyprus. This would 'in reality amount to

---

[121] Jacovides, *Treaties Conflicting with Peremptory Norms of International Law and the Zurich-London 'Agreements'* (1966), 25; Roth, The illegality of 'pro-democratic' invasion pacts, Fox and Roth (eds), *Democratic Governance and International Law* (2000), 339; Roth, *Governmental Illegitimacy in International Law* (1999), 193–194.

[122] For the summaries of discussion both in the Security Council and General Assembly see GAOR Official Supplement No. 1, 1963–1964, A/5801 (NY 1964), and *YBUN* 1964, 151–155.

[123] cf SCOR 1097th meeting, 27.

[124] SCOR 1095th meeting, 7–8.

[125] SCOR 1096th meeting, 13.   [126] SCOR 1098th meeting, 11.

a ratification by the Security Council of the inequitable treaties which have been imposed on Cyprus'.[127]

The Soviet Representative noted the fact that Article IV was in practice the most conveniently invoked basis to justify the intervention in Cyprus. At the same time, as Soviet and Czechoslovak Representatives pointed out, Article IV conflicted with the prohibition of the use of force under the UN Charter and hence that prohibition prevailed over it by virtue of Article 103. The Czechoslovak Representative further emphasized that 'no agreement can, in fact, legalise something which is illegal under the terms of the Charter'.[128] This pronouncement relates of course to the Charter provisions and not *jus cogens* in general international law. However, what is crucial is that the Soviet and Czechoslovak Representatives saw the normative conflict between Article IV and the Charter provision. *A fortiori* Article IV must be presumed to conflict with the prohibition of the use of force in general international law which has the same content as Article 2(4) of the Charter and this factor raises the issue of the invalidity of the relevant treaty clause.

The Cyprus Representative also pointed out that the operability of the intervention clauses under the Guarantee Treaty was problematic in terms of Articles 2(4) and 103 of the Charter.[129] Cyprus rejected the interpretation of Article IV as authorizing unilateral military intervention and pointed out that if interpreted that way it would be contrary to *jus cogens*, with the absolute prohibition of the use of force and void.[130] The Cyprus Representative suggested instead a more harmless interpretation of Article IV, construing its use of the word 'action' as referring to the 'representations and measures' mentioned in the same Article and thus excluding the use of force.[131]

The Representative of Greece likewise rejected the view that Article IV of the Guarantee Treaty authorized military intervention in Cyprus, pointing out that this had not been the intention of the drafters. In addition, the independence, sovereignty and unity of a State could not be subject to a treaty which may be interpreted as authorizing unilateral armed interventions against it.[132]

However, the Cyprus Representative took a different view before the General Assembly, contradicting the contentions that the Agreement was valid, describing it as 'invalid, unworkable and unrealistic', conflicting with the Charter and with inherent rights of Cyprus such as freedom, sovereignty, equality and independence. He clearly viewed these Agreements as exempted as illegal from the scope of the principle of *pacta sunt servanda*.[133] The

---

[127] SCOR 1096th meeting, 7.   [128] Id.; SCOR 1097th meeting, 11.
[129] SCOR 1097th meeting, 27–28.
[130] SCOR 1098th meeting, 16–19, including the heavy references to the ILC's work on the law of treaties.
[131] Id., 19.   [132] SCOR 1097th meeting, 32.   [133] GAOR 19th Session, 10–11.

concepts to which the Cyprus Representative referred confirm that he had the public order invalidity in mind.

On the one hand, the silence of UN organs such as the Security Council on claims of voidness, coupled with the fact that Article IV empowered guarantor States 'to take action' and mentioned no authorization of force, could indicate that the Treaty did not empower armed intervention and hence UN organs saw no need to pass judgment on its validity. The right 'to take action' does not necessarily imply the use of force and a wide variety of non-forcible action could have been available to the guarantor powers to promote re-establishment of the state of affairs in accordance with the Treaty. It is possible to hold that Article IV had envisaged exactly that, and, due to over-riding *jus ad bellum*, the parties would have been prevented from holding a different view, or from having the original intention to authorize the use of force.[134]

There is a conceptual possibility that interpretative methods can spare a treaty like the Cyprus Guarantee Treaty of invalidity, for instance if its terms as construed in a way authorizing armed intervention are viewed as absurd under Article 32 of the 1969 Vienna Convention. But while this conceptual possibility remains, the diverse views of States expressed in the process of interpretation and application of the Treaty confirm that it cannot be excluded that the Treaty indeed purported to authorize the use of force. In other words, if the wording of the Treaty construed as authorizing forcible interventions appeals as much to Governments as it did during the discussions before the United Nations organs, then its continuous validity and operation becomes—especially in the cases where compulsory jurisdiction is absent—dangerous in terms of the operation of public order, and it must be considered as invalid.

The view of the General Assembly was clear. In 1965, in Resolution 2077(XX), the General Assembly asked the guarantor powers not to intervene in Cyprus without pronouncing on the validity of the Guarantee Treaty. The General Assembly affirmed that the Republic of Cyprus was entitled to enjoy full sovereignty and independence without outside interference. It called upon all States to refrain from any intervention directed against the independence or territorial integrity of Cyprus.[135] The Assembly, aware of the existence of the Guarantee Treaty and its clauses on intervention, appeared to ignore them and demanded conduct opposite to the right to intervene under that Treaty, thus in fact treating the Treaty, or at least its intervention clause, as non-existent.

But the issue of the validity of Article IV in case it authorizes force is

---

[134] For suggested outcomes of interpretation see Doswald-Beck (1985), 244–250. But Ronzitti, 158, holds that Article IV does not exclude the use of force.

[135] Jacovides (1966), 26; Paul (1971), 28; Schwelb (1967), 952–953.

nevertheless pressing. Ronzitti interprets the *jus cogens* prohibition of force to apply to acts of aggression only, not to actions to safeguard multi-ethnic arrangements under a treaty.[136] But Ronzitti's analysis fails in the face of modern *jus ad bellum*. The peremptory prohibition of force encompasses *any* armed attack on a State, whatever its purpose, unless it is justified under Article 51. To hold that a Treaty can make armed intervention lawful is to assume that States can, by concluding a treaty, determine the content and scope of the peremptory *jus ad bellum* on each occasion as they please. Were this so, the *jus ad bellum* would no longer be peremptory. In addition, an armed attack can constitute aggression despite its purpose, as confirmed by the Definition of Aggression in UNGA 3314(1974), and the terms of this Definition easily cover the action by Turkey against Cyprus.[137]

Furthermore, the narrow reading of the prohibition of the use of force under Article 2(4) of the UN Charter limiting its scope only to the uses of force which threaten political independence and territorial integrity of the State has never been generally approved and is rejected as unfounded.[138] All in all, if such a narrow reading of Article 2(4) of the Charter were accepted, every use of force would be legal irrespective of its purpose as soon as it would be aimed at less than the overthrow of the Government, annexation of the country or its partition. This is what Article 2(4) would suggest by its terms if its narrow reading were adopted, which makes clear that such interpretation must be rejected as absurd and unreasonable.

The *Treaty between USSR and Afghanistan* (1978)[139] was arguably used by the USSR to justify its intervention into Afghanistan, with the consequent overthrow of the Afghan Government and the instalment of the Government it supported.[140] But no provisions in the Treaty actually authorized forcible intervention in Afghanistan. The Treaty provided for non-interference and required agreement between the parties to take appropriate measures to ensure their security and independence (Articles 1 and 4).

The US Government nevertheless held that if the Treaty 'actually does lend itself to support of Soviet intervention of the type in question in Afghanistan, it would be void' for conflict with *jus cogens*.[141] Cassese states that, to the extent it would support the Soviet intervention, the Treaty was to

---

[136] Ronzitti, 157–158.

[137] If the 1960 Treaty is contrary to *jus cogens*, this does not entail that the Republic of Cyprus is illegal, as the treaty was concluded before the VCLT and the severability may well apply to it, see Section 1.5.2(3) above. This point is misunderstood by Müllerson, *Ordering Anarchy* (2000), 158–159.

[138] Henkin, The Legality of Pro-democratic Invasion, 78 *AJIL* (1984), 642.

[139] Treaty of Friendship, Good Neighbourliness and Cooperation, December 5, 1978, 19 ILM (1980), 1.

[140] Nash, US Contemporary Practice Relating to International Law, 74 *AJIL* (1980), 418.

[141] Nash, 419.

be regarded null and void for conflict with *jus cogens*.[142] Although it is difficult to accept that the 1978 Treaty actually offended against *jus cogens*, this case has nevertheless been useful for its reaffirmation in practice of the voidness of treaties conflicting with peremptory norms. In addition, the US invoked voidness despite the fact that it was not a party to the Treaty.

After the Second World War, Japan concluded several treaties with States with which it had been at war to normalize relations, provide for reparations and other arrangements due upon termination of war. Article 14(b) of the Treaty of Peace with Japan of 8 September 1951 provided for waiver of the war damage claims of the Allies against Japan. Similarly, Article IV(1) of the Agreement on the Settlement of the Problem Concerning Property and Claims between Japan and the Republic of Korea[143] provides that:

The Contracting Parties confirm that problems concerning property, rights and interests of the two Contracting Parties and their nationals (including juridical persons) and concerning claims between the Contracting Parties and their nationals . . . is settled completely and finally.

These provisions are drafted categorically and comprehensively. On their face they exclude each and every claim against Japan. However, it is questionable if this could close the issue with regard to claims of persons abused and raped by Japanese forces during the Second World War, as these claims involve issues of *jus cogens*, such as freedom from arbitrary killing, torture and cruel treatment.

It is recognized that if Japanese treaties were to bar the claims of war victims, they would be in conflict not with substantive peremptory prohibition, but only with the consequential duty to make reparation. This latter duty is peremptory itself,[144] and the treaties, if so construed, would constitute an attempt to waive war claims on behalf of individuals. In this case, the validity of these treaties depends on the substantive response of international law to the issue of whether waiver can operate in the face of *jus cogens*.[145]

Conversely, an overriding *jus cogens* or *jus cogens superveniens* could require that treaty waiver clauses should be interpreted restrictively as not encompassing waivers for fundamental human rights and humanitarian law violations, which would lead to the view that the validity of these treaties is not affected.[146] The parties arguably have not intended to affect claims based on fundamental norms, bearing in mind their *jus cogens* character and ensuing constraints on contractual autonomy.

General Assembly Resolution 34/65 B of 29 November 1979 declared the Camp David Agreements void 'in so far as they purport to determine the future of Palestinian People and of Palestinian territories occupied by Israel

---

[142] Cassese (1994), 138.
[143] 22 June 1965, 10 *Japanese Annual* (1966), 284.
[144] See below, Chapter 8.
[145] See below, Chapter 11.
[146] cf below, Section 4.

since 1967' (para B4). This is consistent with the fact that the United Nations regards Palestine as a self-determination unit and its occupation by Israel as void and unable to generate a territorial title over the territories concerned. This justifies Gaja's suggestion that the most likely cause of the declaration of invalidity was a conflict with *jus cogens*,[147] and even as the General Assembly rejected the provisions violating the right of Palestinian refugees to return home and tied the issue of validity of accords to the observance of this right (para B1-2). All in all, it is a question of interpretation whether the institutional arrangements provided for Palestine under the Agreements affect the self-determination of Palestinians, but this conclusion is implied in the fact that the arrangements were concluded without the participation of Palestine, and do not provide for full self-determination. True, the Agreement (Article A1) provides for Palestinian participation in negotiations but it does not specify what standing it gives to Palestine.

The language of the General Assembly resolutions that the Camp David Agreements are invalid not *in toto* but only insofar as they affect the self-determination of the Palestinian people seems to be premised on a view of the severability of impugned clauses as a matter of general international law.[148] Furthermore, the unequivocal attitude of the General Assembly as to the invalidity refutes the contention of Czaplinski that the idea of invalidity of treaties was rejected in the case of the Camp David Agreements.[149]

The Timor Gap Treaty between Australia and Indonesia (1989)[150] was concluded after Indonesia's unlawful annexation of East Timor with a view to establishing a regime of joint disposal by parties of oil resources in maritime areas adjacent to East Timor. The Treaty established the Australia–Indonesia Zone of Cooperation and the Ministerial Council and Joint Authority for the area. The revenues were to be shared equally between Australia and Indonesia.

The Treaty is aimed at cooperation for the mutual benefit of the peoples of Indonesia and Australia and strengthening relations between the two countries,[151] and is silent about the interests of East Timor. Australia arguably had strong and pressing economic reasons for entering into the Treaty.[152]

On its face, the purposes of the Treaty are innocent as it expresses no intention to contradict *jus cogens*. But there is a systemic and consequential contradiction—the whole Treaty regime conflicts with the right of the East

---

[147] Gaja (1981), 282.

[148] Kadelbach, *Zwingendes Völkerrecht* (1992), 89–90 suggests that the voidness should not be presumed and the question is whether the Agreements can be interpreted in a way which hampers the exercise of the Palestinian right to self-determination.

[149] Czaplinski (1997–1998), 89.

[150] See text and comments in Charney and Alexander, *International Maritime Boundaries* (1993), 1245 ff.

[151] Charney and Alexander (1993), 1256.   [152] Charney and Alexander (1993), 1249.

Timorese people to self-determination and the norms incident to it and it hampers the exercise of inalienable rights of the people of East Timor through disposing of East Timor's natural resources without its consent.

Indonesia's title in East Timor was null and void for breaches of peremptory norms and it had no right to enter into treaty relations that extended to East Timor. The very conclusion of this Treaty contradicted the principle of self-determination in relation to the people of East Timor as it was aimed at exploiting East Timorese natural resources for Indonesia's own purposes.[153]

The Treaty incorporates and expresses Australia's *de jure* recognition of annexation. This is inferable from Australia's then-expressed view that there is no binding obligation in international law not to recognize acquisitions of territory by force.[154] The Preamble and Article 2 refer to the 'Indonesian Province of East Timor',[155] which is *de jure* recognition of East Timor's annexation. Such recognition is furthermore implicit in the establishment of the Ministerial Council (Articles 5–6) and the Joint Authority (Articles 7–8) for the management of the Timor Gap resources.

All this presents a clear case of the voidness of the whole treaty without allowing separability of the impugned clauses: the whole treaty is based on the breach of the peremptory right to self-determination of East Timor and its permanent sovereignty over its oil resources. In line with such voidness, the Timor Gap Treaty has been replaced by a new treaty between East Timor and Australia which allocates 90 per cent of revenues from the joint area to East Timor.

Treaties providing impunity for international crimes could possibly trigger Article 53. This issue arises with the 1962 Evian Treaty or the Lomé Agreement providing for amnesty for perpetrators. This issue depends on logically anterior issues of whether such amnesties are permitted in the first place, though if an amnesty conflicts with *jus cogens*, any agreement granting it would be null and void under Article 53 of the Vienna Convention, as an agreement derogating from *jus cogens*.[156]

4. *JUS COGENS* AND INTERPRETATION OF TREATIES

States do not often conclude treaties directly or apparently contrary to peremptory norms.[157] But situations not involving a direct conflict between a

---

[153] Hannikainen, 'The case of East Timor from the perspective of *jus cogens*', *International Law and the Question of East Timor* (1995), 103, 115–116.

[154] Charney and Alexander (1993), 1248.   [155] Charney and Alexander (1993), 1256.

[156] Domb, Treatment of War Crimes in Peace Settlements – Prosecution or Amnesty? Dinstein and Tabory (eds), *War Crimes in International Law* (1996), 311, 316–317.

[157] Rosenne, *Developments in the Law of Treaties 1945–1986* (1989), 287. See also Rosenne, *Breach of Treaty* (1985), 64–65; Minagawa (1968), 17.

treaty and a peremptory norm are no less problematic. If States apply an innocent treaty in a way offending *jus cogens*, this could result in derogation from *jus cogens*. In the absence of express derogation, these issues are normally approached by way of treaty interpretation.

Generally, for the purposes of interpretation, a treaty provision may mean whatever it means in accordance with the parties' intention as established through the normal interpretive methods, irrespective of what general international law says on the subject. If a treaty obligation conflicts with ordinary norms, this cannot excuse non-compliance with the treaty in relation to treaty partners, as treaties can derogate from general international law. States must exercise their rights under general international law in a way which is not detrimental to their treaty obligations.[158] It does not matter whether the conflict is substantive, following from a provision of a treaty, or incidental, following from the application or interpretation of treaty provisions.

Treaties are normally not supposed to be affected by general international law in terms of interpretation, unless there is a specific circumstance allowing a rule of general international law to trump a treaty and cause construction of its meaning in accordance with the rule.[159] The *lex specialis* principle is, as Jenks points out, unimpeachable and continuously affirmed since the times of classical writers as one of the basic principles of the resolution of normative conflicts.[160] Furthermore, this is the principle that reflects the character of the law-making system in international law where States themselves appear as law-makers.

There could obviously be factors that militate in favour of the construction of treaty obligations in accordance with general law. But this approach could be viable only if the text of treaty clauses as they stand does not require an outcome different from that provided under general international law. The primacy of *lex specialis* is the direct implication of the role of the will of States-parties to the relevant treaty as the basis of legal obligations. As Jenks writes,

---

[158] *Wimbledon*, PCIJ, Series A, 1923; *Free Zones of Upper Savoy and the District of Gex*, PCIJ Series A/B, No. 46, 167.

[159] The idea of the impact of general international law on treaty interpretation is mirrored in the *North Atlantic Coast Fisheries* arbitration, Cheng, *General Principles of Law* (1953), 114–118, 123–132; Lauterpacht (1970), 234–235 supports the interpretation of treaties in terms of applicable customary law. On the varying practice of the Iran–US claims tribunal see Kontou, *The Termination and Revision of Treaties in the Light of New Customary International Law* (1994), 127–132. For Kontou's moderate preference for the *lex specialis* principle see id. 137–144. For a stronger preference for *lex specialis* see Waldock, Third Report, 2 YbILC 61, and Fitzmaurice, The Law and Procedure of the International Court of Justice, *BYIL* 1959, 224, pointing out that 'the existence of a general rule on a subject (unless in the nature of *jus cogens*) is perfectly consistent with its non-application, as between two or more States who by treaty have specially so agreed'.

[160] Jenks, The Conflict of Law-Making Treaties, 30 *BYIL* (1951), 446.

the presumption against conflict is not, however, of an overriding character. It is one of the elements to be taken into account in determining the meaning of a treaty provision, but will not avail against clear language or clear evidence or intention. Such a presumption will not suffice to reconcile clearly irreconcilable provisions.

In other words, 'the presumption against conflict may eliminate certain potential conflicts; it cannot eliminate the problem of conflict'.[161] As Pauwelyn further comments, 'the presumption against conflict is a presumption in favour of continuity, not a prohibition of change. It ought not to lead to a restrictive interpretation of the new, allegedly conflicting, norm'.[162] All this is to effectively affirm the primacy of conventional arrangements over inconsistent general international law.

Treaty norms are unlikely to be affected by the rights of States under general international law, despite the importance of such rights. In *The Wimbledon*, the Permanent Court considered that even 'important rights' of States under general international law cannot qualify treaty provisions.[163] This is logical, as a treaty is an *inter se* consensus to modify or qualify such rights. To constitute an exception from this principle, the rights or norms must not be susceptible to derogation, and this brings us to peremptory norms, under which States are no longer in a position to claim that they may override the operation of *jus cogens* rules by reference to their treaty rights. In practical terms, it is worth asking why general international law was irrelevant in *The Wimbledon* in the face of Article 386 of the Versailles Treaty, but crucially relevant, for instance, in the *Namibia* case for construing the purposes of the Mandate Agreement. In *Namibia*, the International Court emphasized that 'an international instrument has to be interpreted and applied within the framework of the entire legal system prevailing at the time of interpretation'.[164]

Articles 53 and 64 of the Vienna Convention—which relate to the substance of a treaty—do not govern exhaustively the interplay between a treaty and *jus cogens*. In its work on the law of treaties, the ILC had long been preoccupied with this matter.[165] Later, the ILC rejected the proposal of Special Rapporteur Waldock that invalidity from conflict with *jus cogens* would also have covered cases of conflict between the execution or implementation of a treaty and *jus cogens*. The Commission adopted the view that invalidity under the Convention should follow only the issue of incompatibility of a treaty with *jus cogens* as to its content and not its execution.[166]

---

[161] Jenks, The Conflict of Law-Making Treaties, 30 *BYIL* (1951), 429.

[162] Pauwelyn, *Conflict of Norms in Public International Law* (2003), 242.

[163] PCIJ Series A, No. 1, 15.   [164] *ICJ Reports* 1971, 50.

[165] The proposals that the validity of a treaty could be affected in cases where it offends against *jus cogens* either by its content or its execution were submitted by Special Rapporteurs Lauterpacht and Fitzmaurice, YbILC (1954-II), 154–156, YbILC (1958-II), 26.

[166] Rozakis (1976), 98–100, for the attitudes within and of the ILC in detail.

Articles 53 and 64 constitute a warning directed to States that if they insert in treaties clauses conflicting with *jus cogens*, such treaties will be void. It would be unsound to argue, however, that if no issue arises under Articles 53 and 64, *jus cogens* is no longer relevant. States may offend against *jus cogens* not only by inserting explicit clauses in treaties, but also—and predominantly—by the manner in which they attempt to exercise rights and prerogatives under a treaty which does not itself explicitly conflict with *jus cogens* but can prejudice it in the course of its application.

Article 53 of the Vienna Convention 'does not refer at all to the possible incompatibility of the execution of a treaty with the content of a *jus cogens* norm and does not sanction a treaty in that case. The above-mentioned arrangement may leave unhindered a number of treaties which do not violate a *jus cogens* norm directly by their content, but which, nevertheless, violate that rule in the course of their execution. . . . A perfectly legitimate content may produce, through the execution of a treaty, illegal results violating a *jus cogens* norm.'[167]

The issue of compatibility of the execution of a treaty with *jus cogens* cannot be raised *a priori*, but must be tested in specific cases of application. Otherwise, as Rozakis explains, 'an unbearable burden to the presumption of validity' would emerge.[168] The principle is that 'the law should be less severe towards treaties (and their parties) which did not intend to violate a peremptory norm'.[169] In such cases it is not the inherent validity of the treaty which is the concern from the viewpoint of public order, but merely the execution of such treaty, which by itself remains valid.[170] The issue of consistency with peremptory norms of a treaty in its execution lies outside the law of the invalidity of treaties.

The rules applicable in such situations are those of treaty interpretation. An inherent goal of treaty interpretation is the preservation of the integrity of treaty obligations. Also, treaty interpretation is a process to be performed in accordance with international law, as confirmed by Article 31.3(c) of the Vienna Convention requiring that together with the text and context of a treaty, 'any relevant rules of international law applicable in the relations between the parties' shall be taken into account.[171] While Article 31.3(c) refers to applicable norms, it must be borne in mind that in international law some norms are applicable because they are made applicable by the parties, others

---

[167] Rozakis (1976), 97.
[168] Id., 100–101.   [169] Id., 124; Sztucki (1974), 124.   [170] Nicoloudis (1974), 161.
[171] The ILC considered that that formulation should refer not to the relevance of the so-called inter-temporal law, but simply to the rules of international law applicable between the parties, YbILC, 1966, vol. II, 222. Earlier, Special Rapporteur Waldock, when submitting to the ILC what is now Article 31.3(c) VCLT, clearly emphasized that the interpretation of treaties in the light of applicable rules of international law involved the interpretation of a treaty in conformity with *jus cogens*, Third Report, YbILC (1964-II), 8–9.

because the parties have not made them inapplicable, and still others are applicable whether or not the parties want them to be applicable.

The norms protecting the community interest qualify each and every treaty instrument and this is relevant in the interpretive process. To use the method that Judge McNair suggested, the choice has to be made among the methods of interpretation when more than one interpretation equally make sense.[172] Interpretative methods should ensure that the outcome reflects the primacy of 'the consistent meaning to the meaning inconsistent with generally recognised principles of international law'.[173] As Vattel pointed out, 'It is not to be presumed that sensible persons, in treating together, or transacting any other serious business, meant that the result of their proceedings should prove a mere nullity. The interpretation, therefore, which would render a treaty null and inefficient, cannot be admitted.' In particular, restrictive interpretation is required in the case of clauses which on their face would lead to something unlawful.[174] A treaty leading to something unlawful involves its conflict with non-derogable peremptory norms.

Thus, *jus cogens* is relevant not only in terms of the validity but also in terms of the interpretation of treaties. As Jenks submits, *jus cogens* may operate not only as a body of rules from which no explicit derogation is permitted, but also 'as a climate of interpretation of the intention of the parties'.[175] According to Cassese, 'a court may be led to *construe* a treaty provision possessing a dubious scope in a sense consistent with a peremptory norm on the matter, rather than in any other sense'.[176] States cannot disregard peremptory norms through treaty interpretation based on Article 31 of the 1969 Vienna Convention.[177] The voidness of a treaty can be avoided if it is interpreted and performed in a way compatible with *jus cogens*, which involves the prevention of conduct contrary to *jus cogens*.[178] *Jus cogens* would be devoid of its essence if States were entitled to use their treaty rights in disregard of it.

The rule under Article 31.3(c) of the Vienna Convention also includes the possibility of new rules of *jus cogens* becoming the rules applicable between the parties. Situations may arise where, if a treaty is interpreted in terms of the law contemporary to its conclusion, it may conflict with a peremptory norm and be void. To avoid such a consequence, we have to abandon the *tempus regit actum* rule and establish that a treaty is not meant to conflict

---

[172] Individual Opinion, *ICJ Reports*, 1952, 117–118.
[173] Oppenheim, *International Law* vol. I (7th ed., 1947), 859.
[174] Vattel (1916), Book II, chapter 12, para. 283.
[175] Jenks, *The Prospects of International Adjudication* (1964), 458.
[176] Cassese (2005), 206 (emphasis original).
[177] Separate Opinion of Judge Bedjaoui, *Gabcikovo*, para. 6; Fitzmaurice (1963), 138.
[178] Kadelbach (1992), 326; Sztucki (1974), 124; de Wet, The Prohibition of Torture as an International Norm of *Jus Cogens* and Its Implications for National and Customary Law, 15 *EJIL* (2004), 99.

with a peremptory norm. One such case is *Namibia*, where the International Court interpreted the Mandate agreement as implicitly incorporating the reference to the principle of self-determination established after the Mandate agreement was concluded. Such an interpretation takes into account the evolution of law to the extent compatible with the judicial function to interpret and not to revise treaties.

The Court held in *Namibia* that the interpretation of the Mandate Agreement must take into account the principles that have developed after the Agreement was concluded, such as those on 'the self-determination and independence of the peoples concerned'.[179] It retrospectively incorporated these principles into the Agreement as its object and purpose even though they were not even extant at the time of its conclusion. Otherwise, it might have been difficult to assert that the Agreement was still valid, given the right of Namibia to self-determination.

The practice of enforcing treaty obligations in compliance with some external standards subsequently having achieved peremptory status dates back to the nineteenth century. The 1858 Treaty between Britain and China obliged Britain to surrender to China any offender taking refuge in Hong Kong. But as Britain became aware that persons thus surrendered might be subjected to torture, it demanded from China an express assurance that this would not happen, even though the Treaty provided for no such obligation. Britain even considered suspending the respective provision of the Treaty, but the law officers advised to refuse to perform that obligation as the consequences of such fulfilment were objectionable.[180] It is clear that the law at that time was not familiar with *jus cogens* but Britain nevertheless referred to the need to avoid torture as some overarching extra-contractual standard justifying an impact on treaty rights and obligations. The reasons could have been the then nascent concept of public order or higher moral standards eventually reinforcing peremptory norms.

A typical case of interpretative impact of peremptory norms is extradition treaties. The US Court of Appeals held by reference to humanitarian grounds of non-extradition that 'while extradition treaties obligate the parties to extradite according to their terms, nearly all extradition treaties have some room—at least by implication—for discretion by the requested State not to extradite in certain cases'.[181] Swiss courts also interpret extradition treaties in terms of peremptory norms and refuse extradition if these are likely to be

---

[179] *ICJ Reports*, 1971, 50.

[180] McNair, Severance of Treaty Provisions, *Hommage d'une génération des Juristes au Président Basdevant* (1961), 352–353.

[181] *Extradition of Atta*, 104 ILR 96; the Court also pointed out that 'when conditions change after an extradition treaty is concluded, without formal denunciation or suspension of the treaty, the executive of the requested State—here the Secretary of State—may refuse to extradite', id. For a more moderate attitude see Van den Wyngaert (1990), 308.

violated.[182] Such an inherent qualification would not defeat the object and purpose of a given treaty but ensure its viable application.

Although extradition treaties do not expressly contradict *jus cogens* and hence do not trigger Articles 53 and 64 of the Vienna Convention, the Report on Extradition of the International Law Institute emphasizes that the application of these treaties can still cause the violation of *jus cogens* because in most cases they do not contain the provision justifying the non-compliance with the extradition request on the basis of human rights. The Report observes that Articles 53 and 64

would not give any direct answer to the question whether the fulfilment of a treaty may be refused if it is to be expected that the behaviour of a party would in future lead to non-observance of the rules of *jus cogens*. Nevertheless, it seems appropriate to apply *per analogiam* those rules of the Convention on the Law of Treaties because of the corresponding interests in both cases. It would be hard to accept that a treaty must be performed if it is foreseeable that its performance would violate *jus cogens* since, on the other hand it is recognised that a treaty violating *jus cogens* is void and that even a validly enacted treaty can be voided by a subsequently established rule of *jus cogens*.[183]

It is against this background that the Institute's Resolution on 'New problems of extradition' contains the clause with an absolute requirement that in cases where there is a well-founded fear for the violation of fundamental human rights in the requesting State, extradition may be refused whatever the nature of the offence committed by the relevant person.[184]

The International Law Association Report on Extradition and Human Rights also affirms that human rights as *jus cogens* prevail over the requirements of extradition treaties and this is parallel to the effect of Article 53 of the Vienna Convention. If the extradition treaty contains no clause justifying the refusal to extradite on human rights grounds, 'extradition should not be granted if this would violate a human rights norm *external* to the treaty. This argument, premised on the notion that there are certain higher norms in the field of human rights, which take precedence over extradition treaties, owes its origin to the notion of *jus cogens* which received recognition in Article 53 of the Vienna Convention on the Law of Treaties.' Consequently, jurisprudential links between extradition and human rights are provided by a high-ranking *jus cogens*.[185]

It seems that such a jurisprudential link affirms the peremptory character

---

[182] BGE 108 Ib 408; BGE 109 Ib 72; Saladin, Völkerrechtliches Jus Cogens und Schweizerisches Landesrecht, Jenny and Kälin, *Die Schweizerische Rechtsordnung in Ihren Internationalen Bezügen* (1988), 91.

[183] Doering, Preliminary Report, I–59 ILI Yearbook (1981), 150.

[184] II-60 ILI Yearbook (1983), 306.

[185] Dugard and Van den Wyngaert, First Report (1994), para. 14 (emphasis original); ILA Resolution 1/98 on 'Extradition and Human Rights', para. I. Goodwin-Gill (1999), 221; Stein, Terrorists: Extradition versus Deportation, 19 *Israel Yearbook of Human Rights* (1989), 290.

of the entire body of human rights. It is recognized in practice that extradition can be impeded in cases of violations not only of so-called absolute rights which admit of no exception as to their scope, such as the freedom from torture, but also of those rights which are qualified in scope, such as the rights related to fair trial and due process, and family rights.[186] The European Court of Human Rights repeatedly affirmed that the right to fair trial can limit the power of a State to extradite suspects, among others in the context where the extradition treaty requires extradition.[187] As for the rights that admit a margin of appreciation, the extradition and related measures are permissible only within the scope of that margin of appreciation on the basis of the qualifications stated in the relevant provisions of the Convention,[188] but in no way at the expense of the core of the relevant rights. If the jurisprudential link between extradition and human rights is provided by *jus cogens*, and if the likelihood of violation of the given human right bars extradition, among others in the face of treaty obligations to extradite, it is difficult to understand how that very human right is not part of *jus cogens*.

Some treaties, including those establishing frameworks of interstate cooperation through exchange of mutual rights and obligations in a bilateralist way, stipulate that they are not intended to prejudice superior *jus cogens* as could otherwise happen in the course of their performance.[189] The presence of such 'no prejudice' clauses is not an exclusive source of validity for principles safeguarded by those clauses and their applicability to the subject-matter of a treaty. As soon as the principles safeguarded by those clauses are peremptory, they would anyway apply with their sanctioning power (in terms of validity and interpretation). By inserting such clauses, parties act *ex abundanti cautela* to demonstrate the absence of their intent to contradict a given peremptory norm, and avoid any normative conflict as this might possibly hinder the proper enforcement of the treaty.

---

[186] This contradicts the earlier view of Van den Wyngaert, Applying the European Convention on Human Rights to Extradition: Opening Pandora's Box? 39 *ILCQ* (1990), 762, 769, suggesting that only those rights that in her opinion 'beyond any doubt belong to *jus cogens*', such as the freedom from torture, can bar extradition.

[187] *Soering*, 98 ILR 270; *Einhorn v France*, para. 34, 22 *HRLJ* (2001), 276, where the European Court admitted that Article 6 can prevent extradition if there is evidence that the suspect will face trial in the requesting country incompatible with the requirements of Article 6.

[188] Van den Wyngaert (1990), 773.

[189] Anti-terrorist conventions defer to fundamental human rights, providing that the measures and obligations they provide for are not meant to supersede the enjoyment by individuals of fundamental human rights, eg Article 12, the 1998 Convention on Terrorist Bombing, Article 15, the 1999 Convention on the Financing of Terrorism, Article 15, the 2002 Inter-American Convention against Terrorism. The Vienna Conventions on State Succession of 1978 and 1983 defer to the principle of self-determination, eg Articles 13 and 38(2), respectively. The 1988 Drugs Convention defers to sovereign equality and territorial integrity, Article 2. *Alvarez-Machain* 41 ILM 139. For other examples see Goodwin-Gill, Crime and International Law: Expulsion, Removal, and the Non-Derogable Obligation, Goodwin-Gill and Talmon (eds), *The Reality of International Law, The Essays in Honour of Ian Brownlie* (1999), 211.

The Oil Platforms *Case*

The interpretative relevance of *jus cogens* was affirmed in the judgment of the International Court of Justice in the *Case concerning Oil Platforms*,[190] which arose out of forcible action by US naval forces in the Persian Gulf against certain Iranian oil platforms. In October 1987, US naval forces attacked the Reshadat and Resalat oil production complexes of Iran, and destroyed some of their platforms. In April 1988, US naval forces attacked and destroyed the Nasr and Salman oil production complexes. The United States considered this a response to missile and mine attacks on Kuwaiti and US shipping in the area, which it attributed to Iran. Before the Court, the US defended its actions by placing reliance on Article XX.1(d) of the Treaty, which stipulates that the Treaty as a whole 'shall not preclude application of measures . . . necessary to protect [the] essential security interests' of a contracting party.[191]

The Court decided to interpret the essential security exception under Article XX.1(d) of the 1955 Iran–US Treaty in the light of the 'relevant rules of international law applicable in the relations between the parties', as required by Article 31.3(c) of the Vienna Convention, and refused to accept that it should be examined outside the framework of the rules of general international law concerning the use of force. Thus the legality of the US actions fell to be assessed with reference to Article XX.1(d), in the light of the rules of international law regarding the use of force in self-defence.[192] Although the Court stressed that it was not judging the conduct of any State under general international law as such, it did think it necessary to examine the action of the US in the light of *jus ad bellum* in order to establish whether they were indeed performed in self-defence and thus were measures necessary to protect essential security interests under the terms of the Treaty.[193] The Court concluded that

when Article XX, paragraph 1 *(d)*, is invoked to justify actions involving the use of armed force, allegedly in self-defence, the interpretation and application of that Article will necessarily entail an assessment of the conditions of legitimate self-defence under international law.

The Court cannot accept that Article XX, paragraph 1 *(d)*, was intended to operate wholly independently of the relevant rules of international law on the use of force, so as to be capable of being successfully invoked, even in the limited context of a claim for breach of the Treaty, in relation to an unlawful use of force.[194]

Consequently, the United States had to show that in order to be justifiable under Article XX, its attacks against Iran were the response to the prior

---

[190] *Oil Platforms (Islamic Republic of Iran v United States of America)*, Merits, Judgment of 6 November 2003.
[191] ibid., paras 32, 36.
[192] ibid., paras 41–45.   [193] ibid., para. 39.   [194] *Oil Platforms*, paras 40–41.

Iranian attack which justifies action pursuant to Article 51 of the UN Charter and relevant customary law. It had furthermore to demonstrate that its actions were necessary and proportionate such that they could constitute acts of legitimate self-defence.[195] These factors ultimately led the Court to rejecting the plea of the United States.

In its submissions Iran treated the matter as one of *jus cogens*, arguing that because the prohibition of the use of force was peremptory, Article XX.1(d) could not authorize conduct contrary to *jus cogens*, since States were not free to authorize such acts. Iran argued that since a treaty conflicting with *jus cogens* is invalid totally and unconditionally, a strict interpretative approach was needed to preserve the validity of the 1955 Treaty and that this required it to be read in such a way as to ensure that it did not purport to authorize acts contrary to *jus cogens*.[196] The US did not directly contest this, but argued that the jurisdiction of the Court was limited to the interpretation of the Treaty and did not extend to issues of general international law.[197] The Court did not directly address the issue of *jus cogens*, but its analysis of the Treaty resulted in very much the same sort of outcome as might have been expected had it been explicitly relied upon. The Court, together with Judges Simma and Al-Khasawneh, affirmed that *lex specialis* is irrelevant in the face of the interpretive relevance of *jus cogens*.

Judge Simma referred to the fact that the outcome of the interpretation of Article XX.1(d) of the 1955 Treaty necessarily affected the operation of the general rules of *jus ad bellum*. Consequently, Judge Simma pointed out, 'If these general rules of international law are of peremptory nature, as they undeniably are in our case, then the principle of interpretation just mentioned turns into a legally insurmountable limit to a permissible treaty interpretation.'[198] Not to observe those limits 'would be destructive because it would allow a mutual "emancipation" from some of the most cogent of all rules of international law'.[199]

Judge Al-Khasawneh supported the Court's interpretation of Article XX.1(d) and rejected the view that it was exceeding its jurisdiction. He defended the Court's approach, emphasizing that it did not offend against the

---

[195] *Oil Platforms*, para. 51.

[196] See Reply of Iran, 164–165, para. 7.75; CR 2003/8, 15–17 (Crawford); CR 2003/16, 13, 16 (Crawford).

[197] CR 2003/18, 17–18 (Weil); Judgment, para. 39; although the US position can also be interpreted as regarding Article XX of the 1955 Treaty as *lex specialis* in relation to *jus ad bellum*. As the US submitted, 'the standard for determining the lawfulness under the 1955 Treaty of the United States action is not self-defence; it is the need to take these actions to protect essential security interests, see CR 2003/12, 19 and see further Separate Opinion of Judge Koojmans, para. 47.

[198] Separate Opinion, para. 9, also expressly linking this issue to the relevance of Article 31.3(c) of the 1969 Vienna Convention.

[199] Id., para. 10.

principle of *lex specialis* because that concept did not exclude the operation of peremptory rules of international law.[200]

The Court's approach to the interpretation of Article XX.1(d) was consistent with the rule that in cases of occasional (or incidental) conflict between a treaty and *jus cogens* the treaty must be interpreted as being in conformity with *jus cogens*. The question was whether something categorically and imperatively outlawed under general international law—to the extent that it cannot be justified by an express term in a treaty—could be construed as legitimate as a matter of treaty interpretation and the Court's judgment indicates that it could not.

The Court's approach to the hierarchy of norms is in fact similar to that of Judge Al-Khasawneh, and Judge Simma (though it does not explicitly address his concern that the Court should have taken the opportunity to make its views on the peremptory nature of the *jus ad bellum* clear) and produced the outcome Judge Simma thought necessary since the Court's treatment of Article XX.1(d) demonstrates the integral character of the rules governing the use of force. However, Judge Simma's criticism is justified in part because it would have been better if the Court had made its approach more explicit, at least with regard to the terminology it employed.

Some individual judges have disapproved the Court's reasoning in *Oil Platforms*. Judge Owada blamed the Court for shifting the problem from the issues related to Article XX to the one of self-defence under international law.[201] Judge Owada argued that 'certain measures can be undertaken' under Article XX of the 1955 Treaty, 'as being "necessary to protect [the] essential security interests" of the United States'.[202] Judge Owada gave no definition or scope of those 'certain measures', but if these 'certain measures' include forcible measures as well, then Article XX in fact amounts to the clause that purports to derogate from peremptory *jus ad bellum*. In fact, Owada's reasoning leads to the outcome that the requirements of the application of force in self-defence can be disregarded if the terms of the treaty lead to such an outcome. This is effectively to conceive the 1955 Treaty as operating in a legal vacuum, which cannot be a proper judicial exercise of the legal system that clearly acknowledges the public order limitations on the content of treaty provisions.

Judge Higgins advanced a double objection, on the one hand by holding that it was beyond the Court's jurisdiction to pronounce on the issues of *jus ad bellum* within the framework of the pertinent dispute, and on the other hand by criticizing the Court that it had 'not interpreted Article XX by reference to the rules on treaty interpretation. It has rather invoked the

---

[200] Judge Al-Khasawneh, Dissenting Opinion, paras 8–9.
[201] Separate Opinion of Judge Owada, para. 34.
[202] Separate Opinion of Judge Owada, para. 34.

concept of treaty interpretation to displace the applicable law.'[203] But to accuse the Court of having displaced the applicable law under the guise of the use of interpretative methods is to argue that the 1955 Treaty could itself be seen as validly displacing *inter partes* the relevance of the peremptory *jus ad bellum*.

Judge Koojmans considered that it was immaterial whether the measures justified by the United States were justified as acts of self-defence, and that the only relevant question was whether those measures were in breach of the Treaty.[204] But this ignores the fact that the Court itself treated as the basic question before it the issue whether those measures were in breach of the 1955 Treaty. What the Court did, however, was to clarify the meaning of the Treaty through interpretation, in order to ascertain which actions are its breaches and which are not. In order to ascertain whether the pertinent uses of force were in breach of the 1955 Treaty, the Court had to clarify whether the Treaty itself authorized or justified the actions of that kind. This is exactly what the Court did, no more and no less.

Judge Koojmans' distinction between the illegality under the Treaty and illegality under general international law is not helpful either to properly resolve disputes like that in *Oil Platforms*. It is technically true that treaty rules and customary rules are separate from each other. But in this case the factual basis of the breach was single, consisting of identical facts. If the Court had, through the interpretative methods other than those it actually used, pronounced the US attacks as legal under the 1955 Treaty and declared the 1955 Treaty as the sole standard against which those attacks must be judged, it would in fact issue the decision that would legalize what is illegal under *jus ad bellum*. Thus, even if the Court were to limit its discussion to the terms of the Treaty, it would effectively pronounce on the legality of acts governed by general international law. This would be to exempt the actions governed by *jus ad bellum* from its scope, that is approve the derogation from it. Therefore, the technical difference between various sources of law does not

---

[203] Separate Opinion of Judge Higgins, paras 42, 49.

[204] Separate Opinion of Judge Koojmans, para. 25. In other places Judge Koojmans suggested mutually exclusive arguments. On the one hand he agreed with the United States that if its measures were 'deemed to be necessary to protect its essential security interests, there is no need to ask whether these measures were *also* taken in the exercise of self-defence', but then continued that 'in order to come to the first conclusion, the law on the right of self-defence cannot be disregarded', Separate Opinion of Judge Koojmans, para. 49 (emphasis original), the very self-defence he had just considered irrelevant. In another place, Judge Koojmans reaffirmed that the Court had no jurisdiction to pronounce on whether the US actions were justified as self-defence, but then added that the legality test of the Article XX measured must be based 'on the presumption that the use of force is prohibited unless it can be justified under general international law of which the principle of legitimate self-defence is an important element'. Separate Opinion of Judge Koojmans, para. 52. These two outcomes also contradict each other, at least in the context of this case.

always lead in practice to straightforward distinctions in terms of the legality of State actions that happen to be governed by those sources.

In sum, the judges that opposed the Court's treatment of Article XX of the 1955 Treaty give the impression that the relevant treaty clauses exist and operate in a vacuum, which is by no means the case.

Finally, there seems to have been no useful alternative to the use of general international law. To judge on the measures protecting essential security interests would have been a complicated task.[205] The Court would have either to find a workable definition for essential security measures, which is difficult, or to follow the auto-interpretation made by the United States. This would not have been a viable alternative to the use of the defined set of *jus ad bellum* and this is what explains the Court's attitude towards the interpretation of the 1955 Treaty.

5. IMPLICIT SAFEGUARDS AGAINST DEROGATION FROM *JUS COGENS* UNDER THE VIENNA CONVENTION

Articles 53 and 64 of the Vienna Convention safeguard *jus cogens* from conflicting treaties. But *jus cogens* could also be vulnerable to acts and transactions of States endangering the integrity of humanitarian treaties embodying objective obligations. Such treaties and their object and purpose cannot be split into reciprocal relations between States and this makes it worthwhile to enquire into the effect of the peremptory norms embodied in them.

5.1. Jus cogens *and reservations to treaties*

5.1.1. Substantive questions

Reservations can offend against multilateral treaty provisions embodying *jus cogens* and be subject to the overriding effect of peremptory norms as conflicting transactions. In order to see the implications thereof in the law of reservations, it is important to see how this ever-changing field of law has developed over the decades. The original dominant pattern of the law of treaties was that reservations were valid only if permissible under the respective treaty and also accepted by all parties. This was based on the character of reservations as an offer made by the reserving State to other contracting

---

[205] As particularly admitted by Judge Koojmans, 'The evaluation of what essential security interests are and whether they are in jeopardy is first and foremost a political question and can hardly be replaced by a judicial assessment. Only when the political evaluation is patently unreasonable (which might bring us close to an "abuse of authority") is a judicial ban appropriate.' Separate Opinion of Judge Koojmans, para. 44.

parties to modify the terms of the treaty by the additional contractual agreement, and unless the latter States accepted that, the reserving State could make no reservation. This approach of absolute integrity was accepted by the League of Nations Secretariat. The Pan-American Union, however, chose to follow a more flexible approach, according to which the reserving State can become a party in relation to those States which accept its reservations and, in principle, regardless of the character of reservations.[206]

The conceptual clash between the integrity approach and the flexibility approach is often conceived as the clash between the ideas of the integrity of treaty obligations and the universality of participation in treaties. The latter approach allows compromising the integrity of obligations for the sake of widest possible participation in treaties. At the same time, the approach of absolute integrity could be seen, and was indeed so seen, as incompatible with the sovereign capacity to make reservations. Nor is the flexibility view free of shortcomings because it can potentially ruin and undermine treaty obligations effectively freeing States-parties from the obligation to comply with treaties. What is more is that both 'schools' imagine themselves universal, that is applicable to each and every kind of treaty.

In addition, from the perspective of both 'schools' the basic question is not so much whether reservation can modify or affect treaty obligations, but whether the reserving State may still be seen as a party.[207] However, the concerns that arise specifically with regard to humanitarian treaties embodying objective obligations are rather different, namely to ensure the integrity of the relevant obligations as they cannot be split into bilateral relations. The unsuitability of old 'schools' in the context of objective treaty obligations is further demonstrated by Sir Robert Jennings, emphasizing that any compromise towards the participation of the reserving State in a treaty with its reservation kept intact 'must result in some fragmentation of obligations'.[208]

That none of these approaches is absolutely sinless on its merit and that, moreover, the view that any single principle can apply to all kinds of treaties is not without problems became clear when the International Court of Justice was requested to deal with the legal consequences of making reservations to the Genocide Convention. The 1951 *Reservations* Opinion, widely considered as referring to *jus cogens*,[209] contains the foundations of the modern law of

---

[206] Brownlie, *Principles* (2003), 584.

[207] This was at least so perceived at that time, as demonstrated by the UK submission to the International Court in the *Reservations* case: 'The real issue is not the right of countries to seek or to attempt to make reservations—*but their right to become parties to the Convention* while at the same time maintaining reservations to which *objection* has been offered by other interested States.' Written Statement of the UK, *ICJ Pleadings*, 51 (emphasis original).

[208] Jennings, General Course on Principles of International Law, II *RdC* (1967), 535.

[209] See above, Chapter 4, Section 1.1.

reservations to humanitarian treaties, in that it confirms the specific character of objective treaty obligations and the impact thereof on reservations.[210]

The basic premise embodied in the Opinion is that the reservations are permissible if compatible with the treaty's object and purpose. The International Law Commission criticized this notion as 'subjective' and upheld the old standard of the 'doctrine requiring unanimous consent for the admission of a State as a party to a treaty subject to a reservation'. At the same time, the Commission held that 'no single rule uniformly applied could be wholly satisfactory to cover all cases'.[211]

It is crucial, however, that the requirement of the compatibility of reservations with the object and purpose of a treaty survived serious opposition and found its place in Article 19 of the Vienna Convention on the Law of Treaties as one of the basic requirements for the legality of reservations. Even if referred to at earlier stages as 'subjective', the concept of the object and purpose is effectively the requirement referring to the objective criteria.[212] Apart from this Opinion, the adoption of the Vienna Convention[213] and the further practice of human rights treaty bodies have contributed to the development of the law of reservations to humanitarian treaties.

The Vienna Convention regime provides for the criteria of permissibility of reservations under Article 19 and then, subject to the type of the reservation and its permissibility, elaborates in Articles 20–23 upon the issue of legal consequences. This model seems to mirror the ILC's statement made at the stage when the Vienna Convention was being drafted that no single rule uniformly applied could provide satisfactory guidance for all cases.

It is debated whether reservations to humanitarian treaties are subject to the general Vienna Convention regime of reservations. Simma contends that the Vienna Convention does not specifically address the issue of reservations to humanitarian treaties.[214] By contrast Special Rapporteur Pellet suggests that the regime for reservations is uniform and consensual, applying to every kind of treaty despite its nature.[215] But the Vienna Convention regime,

---

[210] But see Fitzmaurice, Judicial Innovation: Its Uses and Its Perils, *Cambridge Essays in International Law* (1965), 34, emphasizing that though the Court recognized the impact of objective and non-derogable treaty obligations, the regime of the consequences of the reservations it upheld is vague, leaving room for radically different outcomes, some of which do and others do not reflect the substantive character of obligations. If Fitzmaurice's conclusion is correct, this means that the Opinion's outcomes may in some cases allow for the bilateralization of legal relations in integral multilateral treaties.

[211] ILC Final Report on the Law of Treaties, II YbILC 1966, 204.

[212] See above, Chapter 4.

[213] Articles 19–23. For the ILC's final commentary on reservations see 2 *YbILC* (1966), 202–209.

[214] Simma, From Bilateralism to Community Interest, 250 *RdC* (VI–1994), 370.

[215] Pellet, Second Report, 16–45; The 1997 ILC Report, paras 75–76; see also Aust (2000), 122; Wei, Reservation to Treaties and Some Practical Issues, 7 *Asian Yearbook of International Law* (1997), 136–138.

especially the reference in Article 19 to the object and purpose of a treaty, allows for differentiated solutions depending on the nature of the case.[216] The issue whether the object and purpose of a treaty is divisible into bilateral relations can influence the regime of reservations. Arguably in this spirit, the UN Human Rights Committee has developed its severability view with regard to reservations incompatible with humanitarian treaties with clear reference to the Vienna Convention regime (General Comment No 24). This approach and the opposite ILC approach dominate the debate on the reservations regime in situations where integrity of *jus cogens* is at stake.

In general terms, it seems that the issue whether humanitarian treaties are subject to the special reservations regime is purely academic. Alternatively, it can be asked whether that special regime of reservations is defined from the perspective of the law of treaties or from the perspective of special character of human rights conventions.

On the other hand, it must be clarified whether humanitarian conventions being subjected to the special regime of reservations means that the reservations entered to them are judged by criteria different from those applicable to other treaties; or that this means that the actual outcome with regard to the reservations entered are specific and different from what is the case for other treaties.

If the legal framework is analysed from the perspective of the Vienna Convention, it becomes clear that the permissibility criteria under Article 19, especially that of compatibility with the object and purpose of the treaty, can accommodate the special requirements of humanitarian treaties whose object and purpose entails requirements different from that of the other treaties. From this perspective, the answer is that humanitarian treaties are not subject to any special regime and the reservations entered to them can be judged by reference to the requirements under the general law of treaties.

If, however, the same question is posed from the perspective of the outcome with regard to the reservations entered, then it becomes clear that humanitarian treaties contain provisions that cannot be split into bilateral relations and hence their object and purpose will not tolerate reservations entered to them. From this perspective, humanitarian treaties are indeed subject to the special regime of reservations.

When, therefore, this question whether humanitarian treaties are subject to the specific reservations regime is asked, it must be made clear what is actually meant by humanitarian treaties being subjected to any specific regime of treaty reservations, which is not always done by those who ask this question.

---

[216] To illustrate, the IACtHR emphasized the specificity of the reservations regime of IACHR due to its object and purpose, even though its Article 75 expressly refers to VCLT reservations regime, *Effect of Reservations*, 67 ILR, 564–565, emphasizing that VCLT reservations regime provides for 'different rules for different categories of treaties', and then affirmed specificity of reservations regime applicable to IACHR as a human rights treaty, 568–569.

A reservation has no self-explanatory legal consequences; its effect is determined not by the fact of making it but by juridical circumstances external to it; it takes its effect, or it does not, because certain governing rules so determine.[217] Article 2.1(d) of the Vienna Convention defines reservations as acts governed by the law and not acts above the law, not as acts modifying the extent of treaty obligations, but merely as acts which 'purport' to do so.[218] Therefore, the validity, compatibility, or opposability of a reservation must be determined by reference to external legal factors. And the very fact that reservations may constitute *inter se* agreements naturally invites the argument that a reservation 'purporting' to achieve its effect cannot do so if the result would be contrary to a peremptory norm.

Pellet considers that reservation is a unilateral act and the applicability of *jus cogens* to unilateral acts constitutes 'the only intellectually convincing argument for not transposing to reservations to peremptory provisions the reasoning that would not exclude, in principle, the ability to formulate reservations to treaty provisions embodying customary rules.' However, Pellet also suggests that the nullity of reservations contradicting *jus cogens* follows *mutatis mutandis* from the principle set out in Article 53 of the Vienna Convention.[219] This is in fact to put the emphasis on the factor of non-derogability and affirm that reservations purport to establish the contractual relations between the relevant States-parties, which contradicts Pellet's identification of the relevance of *jus cogens* in the field of unilateral acts as 'the only intellectually convincing argument'.

A reservation as such may indeed be similar in nature to a unilateral act, but it eventually leads to *inter se* consensual or contractual relations as between the reserving State and other States-parties to the relevant treaty.[220] *Jus cogens* can in principle be understood as an autonomous set of rules influencing, as *lex superior*, the compatibility of treaty reservations and their consequences independently of the terms and object of a treaty, attitudes of States-parties or even the governing provisions of the law of treaties. There is

---

[217] HRC General Comment 24, para 18, states that the compatibility of a reservation must be established objectively, by reference to legal principles.

[218] Similarly, the UK pointed out in the *Reservations* case that 'a reservation consists and must consist of an attempt *(a)* to *restrict* (not enlarge) the scope of the Convention, and *(b)* to do so in relation to the obligations *of the reserving State itself* (not other States)'. Written Statement of the UK, *ICJ Pleadings*, 51–52 (emphasis original).

[219] Pellet, Tenth Report on Reservations to Treaties, Addendum 1, A/CN.4/558/Add.1, 35–36.

[220] As can be seen, reservations are denoted on some occasions as contractual transactions and on other occasions as unilateral acts. But whichever option is chosen, the relevance of peremptory norms as the framework governing the permissibility and validity of reservations is not affected. This is moreover so because, as further shown in Chapter 7, the rationale of the applicability of peremptory norms to unilateral acts and actions in most cases is linked exactly to the likelihood of the establishment of the new *inter se* legal relation contradicting peremptory norms. Therefore, even if reservations can be viewed as unilateral acts, they are such unilateral acts whose ultimate effects, or indeed lack of effect, depend on the contractual relations that they entail.

sufficient evidence that *jus cogens* limits the faculty of making reservations. According to Judge Padilla Nervo in *North Sea*, 'customary rules belonging to the category of *jus cogens* cannot be subjected to unilateral reservations'.[221] In case of *jus dispositivum* the parties could excuse each other's non-compliance not only with a treaty norm, but also (*inter se*) with its customary counterpart. But when a norm is peremptory, then a reservation may demonstrate the intent of parties to derogate from *jus cogens*, and hence be invalid.

As Judge Lachs remarked, 'a general rule which is not of the nature of *jus cogens*' cannot prevent some States from adopting an attitude apart.[222] Judge Sorensen contended that there is no incompatibility between the faculty of making reservations and the recognition of the provisions subjected to reservations as part or expression of general customary law.[223] Judge Padilla Nervo went even further by suggesting that if the convention expressly permits reservation to a specific provision, that provision is not an expression of the general law.[224]

Compliance with customary law consisting predominantly of *jus dispositivum* is substantially different from compliance with *jus cogens*. This can be seen in the statement of Judge Sorensen suggesting that 'Provided the customary rule does not belong to the category of *jus cogens*, a special contractual relationship of this nature is not invalid as such'.[225] But as Judge Tanaka suggested, if a reservation is against a norm of *jus cogens*, that reservation itself is null and void.[226] The UN Human Rights Committee held a similar view, in General Comment 24(52), stating that while reciprocal treaties allow States to reserve *inter se* application of general international law, the position is different in cases where peremptory norms and human rights treaty provisions are concerned.[227] Sinclair affirmed this view with the reasoning based on contractual analogy: 'If States cannot enter into a treaty contrary to a norm of *jus cogens*, it seems only logical that they should not be permitted to make reservations to those treaty provisions which embody the norms of *jus cogens*.'[228]

An outcome naturally dictated by the nature of *jus cogens* would be to ensure that no attempt to derogate is effective and that the integral operation of peremptory norms is left intact. To translate this into the language of the

---

[221] Separate Opinion of Judge Padilla Nervo, *ICJ Reports*, 1969, 97.

[222] Dissenting Opinion of Judge Lachs, *ICJ Reports*, 1969, 229.

[223] Dissenting Opinion of Judge Sorensen, *ICJ Reports*, 1969, 248.

[224] Separate Opinion of Judge Padilla Nervo, *ICJ Reports*, 1969, 97–98.

[225] Dissenting Opinion of Judge Sorensen, *ICJ Reports*, 1969, 248.

[226] Dissenting Opinion of Judge Tanaka, *ICJ Reports*, 1969, 182. Judge Tanaka considered that the continental shelf rule was part of *jus cogens*.

[227] General Comment 24(52), para. 8.

[228] Sinclair, *The Vienna Convention on the Law of Treaties* (1986), 65–66.

law of reservations: a reservation contrary to *jus cogens* must be void and the norms it purports to amend, limit or modify must be left intact even in *inter se* relations.

Buergenthal suggests that in the case of human rights treaties the non-derogability of a provision and the incompatibility of reservations are linked.[229] But as the Human Rights Committee suggests, there is no automatic correlation between the non-derogable provisions of a treaty and its object and purpose.[230] The fact that a right is 'derogable' under a treaty is not *per se* evidence that it is not peremptory. The fact that peremptory provisions cannot be subjected to reservations is due to their inherent character and not to the fact that the parties designated them as non-derogable.

'Derogable' provisions in human rights treaties can perhaps be subjected to reservations to the extent they warrant some limitation due to their terms[231] (eg having regard to the margin of appreciation), to applicable general standards embodied in specific treaties, such as Article 64 ECHR and Article 75 ACHR, and above all to the object and purpose of a given human rights instrument. But a reservation to a 'derogable' provision can never injure the substance of a right as the core of every human right is non-fragmentable and indivisible into bilateral relations of States, and hence part of *jus cogens*.

Reservations contrary to *jus cogens* can be impermissible on several grounds. The common intention of parties to a treaty may result in (directly or indirectly) safeguarding peremptory norms from incompatible reservations, in terms of paragraphs (a)–(b) Article 19 of the Vienna Convention.[232] A reservation could also conflict with *jus cogens* as being incompatible with

---

[229] Buergenthal, Advisory Practice of the Inter-American Court of Human Rights, 79 *AJIL* (1985), 25.

[230] General Comment 24(52), para. 10. Burgenthal's view is also incomplete as derogability means different things in different contexts, cf above, Chapter 2. In this regard, the criteria suggested in Draft Guideline 3.1.12 of Special Rapporteur Pellet make better sense as they allow judging the relevance of every individual right on its merits rather than applying the stigmatizing criteria of 'derogability'. According to this Draft Guideline, 'To assess the compatibility of a reservation with the object and purpose of a general treaty for the protection of human rights, account should be taken of the indivisibility of the rights set out therein, the importance that the right which is subject of the reservation has within the general architecture of the treaty, and the seriousness of the impact the reservation has upon it.' Pellet, Tenth Report on Reservations to Treaties, Addendum 1, A/CN.4/558/Add.1, 21. See, further, Pellet's comment regarding the Danish objection to US reservations to Articles 6 and 7 of the ICCPR that Denmark objected not because the provisions were non-derogable, but because the reservations emptied them of their substance, id., 38–39.

[231] eg the European Court would accept a reservation to Articles 5–6 ECHR if it has a precise scope and is not ambiguous, *Belilos*, A132, 26, *Chorcherr*, para. 18. *X v Austria*, 2765/66, YBECHR 1967, 412.

[232] Article 33 (*non-refoulement*) of the 1951 Refugees Convention is expressly made immune from reservations, but the peremptory character of *non-refoulement* could also ensure the same result.

the object and purpose of a treaty[233] when the object and purpose as such excludes reservations, ie when it is non-fragmentable and protects a community interest different from individual State-party interests, that is, embodies *jus cogens*. If and to the extent that the object and purpose of a treaty is divisible into bilateral relations, reservations to such a treaty are not contrary to its object and purpose and may be considered legitimate agreements between reserving and objecting States.

Finally, *jus cogens* can have an autonomous effect on conflicting reservations. The question of reservations to treaty provisions embodying *jus cogens* is not necessarily the same as that of reservations to treaty provisions embodying customary law. Customary law is derogable by treaties and reservations could in principle modify custom *inter se*. But *jus cogens* is not derogable and reservations cannot achieve this result even *inter se*. It may be objected that a reservation would modify the norms in question only as treaty norms, not as part of general international law.[234] But such an argument is circular, as giving effect to a reservation contrary to *jus cogens*, even only as a matter of the treaty regime in question, would imply an *inter se* derogation from *jus cogens* on the basis of that very treaty regime. This, in turn, would imply that the given treaty, notably its object and purpose, allows for an *inter se* agreement contrary to *jus cogens*, and the issue of the compatibility with *jus cogens* of the object and purpose of a treaty, and consequently of a treaty as such, would arise, triggering Article 53 of the Vienna Convention. This could not be presumed in the absence of the conclusive evidence and interpretative methods can ensure that the object and purpose of a treaty is construed in a way banning any reservation contrary to *jus cogens*. For, if a treaty cannot derogate from *jus cogens*, it cannot authorize reservations contrary to *jus cogens* either.

Therefore, while in certain cases *jus cogens* is an autonomous limitation on the faculty of States to make reservations independent from, and external to, provisions of a treaty in question or the Vienna Convention (if the context of a treaty demonstrates that a given provision embodying *jus cogens* does not pertain to the object and purpose of a treaty, nor is made immune from reservations by an explicit treaty clause), it also can be understood as a notion implicit in the object and purpose of a treaty, thus indirectly impacting compatibility and consequences of a reservation.

'A reservation is incompatible with the object and purpose of a treaty if it intends to derogate from provisions the implementation of which is essential

---

[233] The General Comment No. 24 of the UN Human Rights Committee, para. 8 suggests that a reservation conflicting with *jus cogens* is as such incompatible with the ICCPR's object and purpose.

[234] *ILC Report* 1997, para 106; see also Pellet, Tenth Report on Reservations to Treaties, Addendum 1, A/CN.4/558/Add.1, 35; Wei, Reservation to Treaties and Some Practical Issues, 7 *Asian Yearbook of International Law* (1997), 133–134.

to fulfilling its object and purpose.'[235] That could happen through reservations to substantive prohibitions or consequential duties. The enforcement provisions related to jurisdiction and extradition in humanitarian treaties, such as the Genocide Convention, Geneva Conventions and the Torture Convention, are integrally linked to criminalization under substantive prohibitions. If a State attempts to limit any of its enforcement obligations under such conventions by way of reservations, it thereby attempts to repudiate the original duty to prevent and punish the crimes concerned and thus it contradicts the object and purpose of the given treaty.

5.1.2. Legal consequences of reservations offending against *jus cogens*

In doctrine, the legality, compatibility, validity or otherwise of treaty reservations is judged from the perspective of different conceptual approaches. The permissibility approach requires assessing the legality of reservations in the light of their compatibility with some objective standards, such as Article 19 of the Vienna Convention. The opposability school, however, puts emphasis on the will of States-parties to the respective treaty and the possibility of their acceptance of certain reservations that may not pass the test of the permissibility approach. The validity of a reservation depends, under this view, solely on the acceptance of that reservation by other contracting parties.[236]

As Bowett rightly emphasizes, the issue of permissibility is a preliminary issue and 'must be resolved by reference to the treaty and its interpretation'.[237] This confirms that the permissibility of a reservation is to be objectively determined by reference to the treaty text and meaning. Bowett goes on to explain that the issue of permissibility 'has nothing to do with whether, as a matter of policy, other parties find the reservation acceptable or not'. This latter issue is that of opposability and 'pre-supposes that the reservation is permissible'. Whether a party chooses to accept the reservation, object to it or both to the reservation and entire participation of the reserving State is a matter for policy decision by States.[238] As for impermissible reservations, they are according to Bowett 'a request for a waiver which the treaty does not permit'.[239]

It seems that there is no inherent contradiction between permissibility and opposability views. There are reservations which are permissible *because* other States-parties accept them and such reservations become opposable to them. There are, on the other hand, some inherently permissible reservations which are not opposable to other States-parties because they choose not to

---

[235] Austrian objection to Malaysian reservation to the 1989 Convention on the Rights of the Child.
[236] For an overview see A/CN.4/470, paras 100–102, at 48–49.
[237] Bowett, Reservations to Non-Restricted Multilateral treaties, *BYIL* (1975–76), 88.
[238] Id.   [239] Id., 84.

accept them. Thus in some cases permissibility and opposability of a reservation go hand in hand and this happens above all in situations where the legal relations covered by the respective reservation are matters for bilateral relations between reserving and accepting/objecting States.

If, as Bowett writes, the opposability of a reservation presupposes its permissibility, it seems that the relevance of the opposability doctrine is not unlimited—it can work only if the reservation is permissible in the first place. It seems that permissibility thus means different things in different contexts, depending above all on the type of treaty obligations, especially whether they are subsumable into bilateral relations of parties. It seems that reservations to bilaterally disposable provisions are in principle permissible, while the situation may be different with reservations to provisions that regulate rights and duties going beyond such bilateral relations.

In the case of multilateral treaties which are bundles of bilateral obligations, every reservation can be judged by the opposability criterion; as obligations are reciprocal, reservations are addressed to States individually. States, being masters of their treaty relations, are also masters of the effect of a reservation and the impact of that effect on the continuing operation of entire treaty relations (including the option that a treaty is not in force between reserving and objecting States).[240]

But a reservation to an integral treaty provision is aimed not at limiting or modifying a reserving State's obligations towards individual parties, but towards the entire international community. The outcome cannot depend upon the individual assessment of States-parties; as treaty provisions are integral, they would not tolerate different regimes of their applicability in relation to different States; they must run identically towards all parties. If a treaty provision, or the object and purpose, do not tolerate a reservation, the latter is invalid in relation to all parties, and must be judged from the perspective of objective validity and compatibility.

As the Inter-American Court of Human Rights asserted in *Effect of Reservations*, 'the principles enunciated in Article 20(4) reflect the needs of traditional multilateral international agreements which have as their object the reciprocal exchange, for the mutual benefit of the States-parties, or bargained rights and obligations. . . . It permits States to ratify many multilateral treaties and to do so with the reservations they deem necessary. It enables the other contracting parties to accept or reject the reservations and to determine whether they wish to enter into treaty relations with the reserving State.'[241] But the Court concluded that this regime cannot apply to a humanitarian instrument of a non-reciprocal type.

---

[240] Fitzmaurice (1965), 33, notes that in conventions reflecting a set of bilateral agreements parties can bilateralize their treaty relations through reservations and withhold treaty benefits from the reserving State to whose reservations they object.

[241] 67 ILR 568.

The consequences of reservations to non-reciprocal treaty provisions are not governed by Articles 20–22 of the Vienna Convention.[242] If reservations are contrary to the object and purpose of a treaty, they do not fall within the regime of Articles 20–22: according to Article 21 of the Vienna Convention, a reservation can take effect only if permissible under Article 19. Thus, the Vienna Convention regime of consequences of reservations is conceptually unsuitable to humanitarian treaty obligations.

According to the joint effect of Articles 20(4) and 21(1) of the Vienna Convention, a reservation made by one State can be accepted by another State and this causes modification of treaty provisions affected by a reservation as between reserving and accepting States. When a treaty comprises a bundle of bilateral and reciprocal relations only, it is perfectly possible that some parties could accept a reservation diverging from the terms of a treaty on an *inter se* basis. Examples could be diplomatic immunities, trade relations or other fields governed by bilateralism, and such diversification of regimes would not offend against the object and purpose of the given treaty. However, in the case of treaties embodying *jus cogens*, notably humanitarian treaties, the non-reciprocal and non-fragmentable nature of the treaty obligations militate against acceptance. In such treaties, every obligation is assumed towards all parties, not towards each party as such, and should run to all parties in a similar way. 'Acceptance' of a reservation offending against the object and purpose of a humanitarian treaty attempts to establish a special contractual relationship as between reserving and 'accepting' States, while both of them remain bound towards all other parties in accordance with the original treaty standard, in a direct contradiction to the 'accepted' reservation they regard as valid *inter se*.

The fact that a reservation incompatible with the object and purpose of a humanitarian treaty is explicitly or implicitly accepted by other States is not a conclusive evidence of its compatibility. As Bowett states, parties may accept an incompatible reservation. But the Vienna Convention does not affirm that reservations contrary to the object and purpose may have the effect of accepted reservations, for the simple reason that none of its provisions govern this issue.[243]

Absence of protest or objection does not validate an incompatible reservation.[244] 'If other States not merely failed to object but positively indicated

---

[242] For example, Belgium and Denmark have clearly considered that the 12-month limit under Article 20(5) does not apply to incompatible reservations or those which are null and void.

[243] As Bowett remarks, 'The contradiction in the conduct of a party which accepts a treaty and then "accepts" a reservation which it acknowledges to be contrary to the object and purpose of that same treaty is self-evident. Thus, the conclusion ought to be that impermissible reservations cannot be accepted.' Bowett (1975–76), 83. Bowett remarks that such an 'acceptance' should be regarded as a nullity, id., 84. See also McGoldrick, The Human Rights Committee, Capps, Evans and Konstadinidis (eds), *Asserting Jurisdiction* (2003), 205.

[244] General Comment 24, para. 17.

their acceptance of the reservation, this collective view would no doubt be regarded as important by the enforcement/monitoring body, but it would not be binding upon it.'[245] Monitoring bodies are bound to apply the law, and if such 'collective views' are not binding on them, then they are purely and simply not the law. In practice, views on this subject are hardly ever expressed collectively.

Article 20(4) of the Vienna Convention, together with Article 21(3), suggests that an objection to a reservation without the stated intent to prevent establishment of treaty relations between reserving and objecting States excludes applicability of affected treaty provision as between reserving and objecting States. Unlike the situations of 'acceptance', the desired effect here is to exclude the respective provision in *inter se* relations without any substitute. That can work only with synallagmatic treaty obligations, and is in fact only intended under the Vienna Convention for compatible reservations, not for reservations attempting to fragment the operation of objective treaty obligations.

Article 20(4) of the Vienna Convention suggests that an objection to a reservation may preclude the entry into force of a treaty as between reserving and objecting States if the objecting State clearly expresses such an intention. In the case of reciprocal treaties based on a system of reciprocal benefits, a reservation to a particular provision may directly affect rights, benefits and interests of other parties which on their side are entitled to object to it and even exclude the reserving State from treaty relations. In the case of treaties embodying objective obligations, a reservation does not affect the rights, benefits or interests of specific States but those of the international community as a whole. The significance of a State becoming a party to such a treaty is not that it acquires any benefits, but merely that it undertakes obligations invocable by other States-parties. The only consequence of exclusion through entire invalidity is to free a reserving State from the burden of its obligations.

Furthermore, as treaties embodying objective obligations bind all parties towards all parties in the same way, an objecting State cannot claim that there are no treaty relations as between itself and the reserving party, because such treaties are not about reciprocal treaty relations and an objecting State cannot exclude that which is non-existent; a treaty will fully apply to the objecting State whatever its attitude or the position of the reserving State, not least because the objecting State is objectively bound towards other parties to the full extent of treaty obligations. In addition, States-parties, while having excluded a reserving State from the treaty, cannot consider that they are no longer bound to observe treaty obligations in relation to that State's nationals. This would be incompatible with the objective character of such treaty obligations. With human rights and humanitarian treaties, the position

---

[245] Hampson, Working Paper, E/CN.4/SUB.2/1999/28, para. 21.

where the State is party to the treaty in relation to some but not the other parties is simply irrelevant.

So far in practice, States objecting to reservations under Article 20(4) have not expressed the attitude that a humanitarian treaty would not enter into force as between reserving and objecting States.[246] Moreover, according to the Inter-American Court of Human Rights, objections cannot prevent a humanitarian treaty from entering into force.[247]

What happens in the absence of objections? Three States commenting on HRC General Comment 24(52)—France, UK, and the USA—and ILC Special Rapporteur Pellet have considered that if a reservation is incompatible, it must be up to a reserving State either to change or revoke a reservation or to withdraw from the entire treaty. At the final stage, the ILC suggested a division of competences between monitoring bodies and States, so that the former would judge the compatibility while the latter decided on the consequences. This approach, unlike the options specified in Articles 20–22 of the Vienna Convention, applies to incompatible reservations, and is conceptually based on the principles of consent and State sovereignty. A major problem with this option is that it is not featured in the Vienna Convention with regard to *any* type of treaties.[248] Nor has any tribunal endorsed such a view, despite the pleas that reservations are an essential condition of acceptance of treaty obligations.[249]

Acknowledging that the Vienna Convention does not support the 'entire invalidity view', Pellet referred to the principle of consent to support the idea of invalidity of an entire acceptance:

According to some opinions based on the principle of the 'severability' of the reservation (the possibility of severing it from the rest of the expression by a State of its consent to be bound), only an 'impermissible' reservation should be regarded as null and void, whereas the State continued to be a party to the treaty. However, this approach was contrary to the consensual principle, the basis of any treaty undertaking.[250]

---

[246] Vierdag, Special Features of Human Rights Treaties, Barnhoorn and Wellens (eds) *Diversity in Secondary Rules and the Unity of International Law* (1995), 134.

[247] *Effect of Reservations*, 67 ILR 570.

[248] Apart from the fact that none of the VCLT's provisions apart from Article 19 govern the regime of incompatible reservations, Article 20(4), if it were applicable to such reservations, requires that the attitude of the objecting and not the reserving State is decisive, which contradicts the approach of Pellet and ILC.

[249] The category of 'essential condition of acceptance' has merely been referred to in cases before the International Court and European Court by respondent governments and dissenting judges. In *Chrysostomos*, 12 *HRLJ* (1991), 123, para. 43, and *Loizidou*, Series A, 310, 30–31, para. 90; Judge Lauterpacht in *Norwegian Loans, ICJ Reports*, 1957, 57; Judges Petitti and Gölcüclü in *Loizidou*, Series A, 310, 36–37. But it has never seriously been applied so as to form the basis of a judicial decision. It is also relevant that the International Court emphasized that 'the complete exclusion from the [Genocide] Convention of one or more States would not only restrict the scope of its application, but would detract from the authority of the moral and humanitarian principles that are its basis'. *ICJ Reports*, 1951, 15.

[250] YbILC, 1996, vol. II, Part Two, 82, para. 130.

And further:

> although the withdrawal of a State from a treaty was not provided for in the Vienna Convention, it was based on the underlying principle of consent. . . . [I]f the State did not intend to become a party to the treaty, its original reservation and its initial consent had to be regarded as null and void.[251]

These comments demonstrate that the Special Rapporteur failed to identify any specific rule or principle dictating that the incompatibility of a reservation causes the invalidity of an entire acceptance; hence the abstract reference to 'consensual principle'. Simma supported this approach, emphasizing the incompatibility of the Human Rights Committee's severability approach with the fact that even human rights treaties are based on contractual consent.[252] But Simma ignores the fact that human rights organs do not deny that humanitarian treaties are also treaties; rather they emphasize that the obligations they embody are different, having an objective non-bilateralizable character.[253]

Bowett considers that 'when the impermissibility arises from the fundamental inconsistency of the reservation with the object and purpose of the treaty, the reservation and the whole acceptance of the treaty by the reserving States are nullities'.[254] However, Bowett considers that only such reservations, impermissible under Article 19(c) of the Vienna Convention may invalidate the whole acceptance, while reservations 'impermissible on other grounds'—obviously those prohibited under Articles 19(a) and 19(b) of the Vienna Convention—may be struck down and severed.[255] This approach is inconsistent, for it attributes to Articles 19(a) and 19(b) legal consequences different from those of Article 19(c). Such a differentiation is not warranted under Article 21 or otherwise. Bowett simply says that his view is 'the better view', without providing any sound legal argument for supporting it. But Horn states in his classic treatise that 'Incompatible reservations are to be treated in the same manner as expressly prohibited reservations'.[256]

Human rights bodies, both on a general plane and in dealing with specific cases, have insisted that a reservation incompatible with a humanitarian treaty's object and purpose is void without affecting the entire acceptance. As Cassese comments, the severability view, 'although some major Powers have attacked it, is in keeping with the object and purpose of human rights law.

---

[251] YbILC, 1997, vol. II, Part Two, 52, para. 110.

[252] Simma (1994), 346–349. Simma also speaks of the 'adequate division of labour' between the reserving State and the monitoring body.

[253] cf Partly Dissenting Opinion of Judge Valticos, *Chorcherr v Austria*, suggesting that due to ECHR's nature the principle of exclusion of a reserving State from a treaty cannot apply to that instrument and incompatible reservations must be treated as non-existent.

[254] Bowett (1975–76), 84, 89.

[255] Id., 83–84.

[256] Horn, *Reservations and Interpretative Declarations to Multilateral Treaties* (1988), 127.

It therefore commends itself as appropriate'.[257] In general, the severability view is preferable, because it follows the objective or integral character of humanitarian treaty obligations, which require absolute compliance and bar bilateralization of treaty relations—the factor which confirms that they share the nature of *jus cogens* and have superiority over reciprocal deals.

Some opposition to this principle has been vigorously expressed,[258] despite the fact that only three States—France, UK, and the USA—have registered their disapproval of the approach of the Human Rights Committee. These States have done so partly because their reservations of doubtful validity were at stake before the human rights treaty bodies and to that extent their approach is of doubtful normative value.

Another factor diminishing the weight of objections to the severability view is that the proponents of these objections (Special Rapporteur Pellet and three Governments) do not accept the objective nature of respective treaty obligations.[259] Consequently, those who oppose the severability view implicitly concede that there is a link between the substance of norms and the legal consequences of offending acts and transactions such as reservations. So far, one has only suggested that the severability view is unfounded *because humanitarian treaties are no exception from normal reciprocal pattern of multi-lateral treaties*, but not that it is impossible *despite the objective nature of the respective treaty obligations*. As a matter of fact, the objective and non-reciprocal character of certain treaty obligations is widely accepted despite such opposition.

The severability view seems to be in accordance with the Vienna Convention. Tribunals do not consider that the severability view is contrary to, or an exception from, the Vienna Convention. Rather, they are guided by the Vienna Convention in the very process of considering that incompatible reservations are to be severed. The Vienna Convention is not an obstacle, but a factor assisting tribunals in performing this task. This holds true for the Human Rights Committee,[260] the European Commission[261] and European Court of Human Rights,[262] and the Inter-American Court of Human

---

[257] Cassese (2005), 175; Higgins, Introduction, Gardner (ed.), *Human Rights as General Norms and a State's Right to Opt Out* (1997), xxvii, also considers that 'the special character of human rights treaties militates in favour of severability without the setting aside of general acceptance'.

[258] Simma (1994), 347–348.

[259] Pellet, Second Report, 14–15, 37–38, 65, disputing pronouncements of human rights organs on the specific nature of humanitarian treaties, even if he accepts the relevance of *jus cogens*; UK view, McGoldrick (2003), 218. Wei, 137.

[260] *Rawle Kennedy*, 7 *IHRR* (2000), 321ff. paras 6.5 ff., and more generally, General Comment No. 24(52), para. 6.

[261] *Temeltasch*, 5 *EHRR* (1983), 423 ff., paras 32 ff., 431 ff., paras. 68 ff.; *Chrysostomos*, 12 *HRLJ* (1991), 120–121, paras 12, 23.

[262] *Belilos*, Series A, 132, 21 ff. para. 42; *Loizidou*, Series A, 310, 27, paras 72 ff.; van Dijk and van Hoof (1998), 776, emphasize that the outcome of severability in *Loizidou* was dictated by the need for compatibility with the object and purpose under Article 19 VCLT.

Rights.[263] The perception of the alleged unsuitability of the Vienna Convention for the policy chosen by the tribunals is artificial.

The final remaining objection to the severability view is that while it is legitimately applied at the European level, it is unsuitable at the universal level, as the latter is not based on the same degree of solidarity as the former. But such a difference between the European and the universal does not seem to be tenable. The ECHR organs do not consider that their severability approach is different from that applicable at the global level; their reasoning indeed coincides with the Human Rights Committee's reasoning on the objective nature of ICCPR obligations. ECHR organs sever reservations not because this is allowed by the European character of the ECHR, but because of its objective public order character—a feature fully shared by a number of universal human rights treaties. In addition, on the issue that incompatible reservations are severable, the European Court of Human Rights has never referred to the special European character of the ECHR.[264]

In practice, States do not consider that the severability view is limited to the European context. Finland and Sweden objected to the Kuwaiti reservation to ICCPR, stating that 'this objection does not preclude the entry into force in its entirety' between them and Kuwait. Finland objected to Guyana's reservation to the First Optional Protocol to the ICCPR, stating that while the objection does not preclude entry into force of the Protocol between the two States, it 'will thus become operative between the two States without Guyana benefiting from the reservation'. Similarly, both Finland and Sweden objected to Azerbaijan's reservations to the Second Optional Protocol to the ICCPR, and stated that the 'Optional Protocol will thus become operative between the two States without Azerbaijan benefiting from the reservation'. Furthermore, Sweden and Finland objected to US reservations to the CAT, stating that these reservations 'do not relieve the United States of America as a party to the Convention from the responsibility to fulfil the obligations undertaken therein'. Denmark objected to Malaysia's and Brunei's reservations to the CRC and considered that while the reservation is null, the Convention 'remains in force in its entirety' as between Denmark and Brunei and Malaysia. Austria objected to Pakistan's reservation to the CEDAW and considered that it does not preclude 'the entry into force in its entirety of the Convention between Pakistan and Austria'. On identical terms Austria also

---

[263] *Effect of Reservations*, Advisory Opinion OC-2/82, paras 21 ff.; *Restrictions to the Death Penalty*, OC-3/83, paras 48 ff., 60 ff.

[264] cf *Second Report* by Pellet, A/CN.4/477/Add.1, 66–67, para. 209. The Court inferred *its own power to sever reservations* from the two other circumstances: the interplay between the respondent's intention and the jurisdictional requirements contained in Articles 25 and 46 ECHR (para. 95) and the fact that an examination of the respondent's declaration allowed the separation of impugned clauses from the remainder of acceptance (para. 97), Series A, 310, 31–32.

objected to Saudi Arabia's reservation to CERD. Sweden objected to Yemen's reservation to CERD, stating that the objection does not prevent the entry into force of the Convention and 'the reservations cannot alter or modify, in any respect, the obligations arising from the Convention'. It also objected to the Saudi reservation to CERD, stating that the Convention 'will thus become operative between the two States without Saudi Arabia benefiting from this reservation'. Portugal objected to the reservations of the Maldives to the CEDAW, stating that 'these reservations cannot alter or modify in any respect the obligations arising from the Convention for any State-party thereto'.[265] Therefore, State practice demonstrates that the severability view is acceptable both at European and at universal levels, and follows the approach of General Comment No. 24.

5.2. Jus cogens *and application of successive treaties*

Article 30 of the Vienna Convention, which deals with the application of treaties conflicting with each other, does not make the conclusion of a treaty conflicting with another treaty inherently impermissible; nor does it speak of normative hierarchy as a matter of *lex superior*. It regulates treaty relations through designating which treaties prevail in which circumstances: it is not axiomatic why one treaty commitment undertaken towards one State should be inherently better than a commitment undertaken towards another State. If treaties embody reciprocal obligations, it cannot be assumed that an interest protected in one treaty is more important than that protected in another and prevails over it; it is perfectly possible that the same party has different treaty obligations in relation to non-parties, or even other parties, because treaty obligations are bilateralizable. But this is impossible in case of objective treaty obligations operating integrally in relation to all parties, because they are indivisible and non-fragmentable, admitting of no different *inter se* regulation.

The issue of the consequences of the conflict of different treaty obligations has received most diverse treatment in the process of the codification of the law of treaties, and has been treated sometimes as an issue of validity and in other cases as an issue of the application of treaties. Special Rapporteur

---

[265] In a different context, Finland and Sweden objected to Pakistan's declaration on Article 19 of the Convention against Terrorist Bombings (which in fact amounted to a reservation), stating that 'the Convention will thus become operative between the two States without Pakistan benefiting from its declaration'. Sweden objected on identical terms to Turkey's reservation to the same Convention. Furthermore, Norway and Sweden objected to North Korea's reservation to the 1999 Convention on the Financing of Terrorism, stating that the Convention enters into force without the reserving State benefiting from its reservation. Finland objected to the Guatemalan reservation to Article 27 VCLT, stating that it reflects customary law, the reservation to it is contrary to the VCLT object and purpose and that the instrument 'will thus become operative between the two States without Guatemala benefiting from these reservations'.

Lauterpacht admitted in his Report on the Law of Treaties the case where a treaty conflicting with previous treaty obligations is void.[266] However, while dealing with the public order invalidity of treaties, Lauterpacht referred, alongside the cases of conflict with public order norms of general international law, to the cases of 'inconsistency of a subsequent treaty with rules of international law which, although originating from a treaty concluded between a limited number of States, subsequently acquire the complexion of generally accepted—and, to that extent, customary—rules of international law'. This was viewed as one of the categories of the conflict of treaties with overriding principles of international public policy.[267]

Article 18 on the Law of Treaties proposed by Special Rapporteur Fitzmaurice dealt with the legality of the object of a treaty conflicting previous treaty obligations and arrived at the same solutions as are laid down in Article 30(4) of the Vienna Convention. At the same time, Fitzmaurice took care to emphasize that 'the present article applies primarily to bilateral treaties, and to those pluri- or multilateral treaties which are of the reciprocating type, providing for a mutual interchange of benefits between the parties, with rights and obligations for each involving specific treatment at the hands of and towards each of the others individually.'[268] Such principles would not extend to treaties which either lay down interdependent obligations or those of 'absolute, self-existent and inherent' character. For such treaty obligations a special regime would apply and the nullity would be produced in the relevant circumstances of normative conflict.[269]

As Fitzmaurice explained, 'Even where a treaty is of general and so-called law-making character, and embodies rules in the nature of *jus cogens*, it remains *as such* technically *res inter alios acta* for non-parties. In so far therefore as it contains general international rules, this will be either because the treaty declares or codifies existing rules of international law, or because the rules it contains have come to be recognized as rules valid for and *erga omnes*, and have been received into general international law. It will be the underlying conflict with the latter, rather than the treaty, as such, which evidences them, that will be the cause of any invalidity in a later treaty.'[270]

Special Rapporteur Waldock pointed to the difference between the legal effect of a conflict with a prior treaty and that of conflict with a *jus cogens* rule, 'even although they may overlap when the *jus cogens* rule is embodied in a general multilateral treaty such as the Genocide Convention'. The same would be true for humanitarian treaties such as the Geneva Conventions.[271] Draft Article 14 on the conflict between inconsistent treaties proposed by

---

[266] Lauterpacht, Report on the Law of Treaties, YbILC 1953, 156.   [267] Id., 155.
[268] Fitzmaurice, Third Report, II YbILC 1958, 27.
[269] Id., 27–28.   [270] Fitzmaurice, Third Report, II YbILC 1958, 41.
[271] Waldock, Second Report, II YbILC 1963, 54, 59.

Waldock laid down the rules resolving the conflicts between different treaties but contained the exception under paragraph 4, which specified that those rules of conflict 'shall not be applicable if the provision of an earlier treaty with which a later treaty conflicts is a provision embodying a rule having the character of *jus cogens*', in which case the matter would be governed by the law of treaty invalidity.[272]

It seems that, while the context in which the conflict of inconsistent treaty obligations should be placed has been the principal issue in the debate, the specificity of treaties embodying indivisible, integral and objective obligations in the context of conflict between treaties has been accepted throughout the codification process.

In the Final Report on the law of treaties, the ILC refused to formulate a special rule for integral and interdependent treaty obligations, holding rather that these are relevant from the viewpoint of the responsibility of a State-party to such treaty which concludes the later incompatible agreement. Therefore, as Simma points out, Article 30 makes no provision 'for multi-lateral treaties of an integral performance structure'.[273] However, as the ILC emphasized, in some case treaty obligations 'by reason of their subject-matter, might be of a *jus cogens* character' and such cases fall within the ambit of the invalidity of treaties conflicting with peremptory norms.[274]

What happens where the integral treaty embodies norms of *jus cogens*? Is it superseded by the later agreement, the legal consequences being limited to the responsibility of the State concerned, or does it continue to impose integral obligations?

As Jenks pointed out, there is no direct conflict between the two treaties 'although a party may have different obligations to co-contractants under different instruments, if its obligations can be analysed into a complex of bilateral obligations which can be separated from each other and inde-pendently performed in relation to each of the other parties'. However, 'the position is different where the obligations resulting from an instrument are of an objective character and cannot be analysed as separable obligations towards individual parties.'[275] It is probably true for the 1961 Vienna Con-vention on the Law of Treaties or the Law of the Sea conventions that treaty obligations 'can be separated from each other and independently performed in relation to each of the other parties', but the same thesis would not stand in the case of treaties like the Genocide Convention, Torture Convention or any other humanitarian treaty.

Article 30.4.b of the Vienna Convention, which governs the application of successive treaties conflicting with each other, refers to mutual rights and

[272] Id., 53–54.
[273] Simma, From Bilateralism to Community Interest, 250 *RdC* (VI-1994), 349.
[274] YbILC, 1966-II, 217.
[275] Jenks, The Conflict of Law-Making Treaties, 30 *BYIL* (1951), 426.

obligations of States, that is *inter se* relations. Objective treaty obligations cannot be split in such a way, and it is logical that Article 30 of the Vienna Convention does not apply to a conflict of successive treaties where one of them embodies objective obligations having peremptory counterparts in general international law. Such conflicts are reserved for Article 53.

As the ILC Study Group Report on Fragmentation of International Law points out, Article 30 does not expressly address the question of the validity of the two inconsistent treaties, but only of their relative priority.[276] Nevertheless, the Study Group affirmed that there are some cases in which the relative priority between inconsistent treaty obligations gives rise to the absolute priority of one of the treaties. The core question thus is 'whether limits could be imposed on the will of States to choose between the inconsistent treaties to which it was a party which it would comply with and which it would have to breach'.[277]

The integral and objective character of a treaty obligation entails its primacy over other treaty obligations. If other treaty obligations can qualify integral treaties, they are no longer integral and non-fragmentable. The question of their objective character is in the final analysis a question of non-derogability.

Practice has developed accordingly and formulated an approach implicitly based on the hierarchical priority of human rights and humanitarian treaties, and has viewed other conflicting treaties as instruments subordinated to humanitarian treaties. As the UN Human Rights Committee observed with regard to the International Covenant on Civil and Political Rights, 'States-parties to the Covenant will often also be party to various bilateral obligations, including those under extradition treaties. A State-party to the Covenant is required to ensure that it carries out all its other legal commitments in a manner consistent with the Covenant', with a view of securing the rights enshrined in the Covenant to all persons within its jurisdiction.[278] Such construction of the interaction of treaty obligations is undertaken in order to emphasize that the State-party to the Covenant may find itself in violation of the Covenant if the person extradited will be deprived of some of the Covenant rights in the requesting State.

The choice between conflicting treaty obligations is one that does not confront human rights monitoring bodies as they apply their constituent instruments. Neither *Soering* nor *Ng* addresses the issue of conflict between

---

[276] *Report of the ILC Study Group on Fragmentation of International Law*, A/CN.4/L.663/ Rev.1, 15.

[277] *Report of the ILC Study Group on Fragmentation of International Law*, A/CN.4/L.663/ Rev.1, 16.

[278] *Kindler v Canada*, 98 ILR 444–445; *NG v Canada*, para. 14.1; with regard to the bilateral treaty the Committee expressed the approach in principle similar to *Kindler*, see *Evan Julian*, para. 8.2.

the ECHR or ICCPR and an extradition treaty; they simply examine whether the extraditing State would by extraditing violate a relevant human rights instrument.[279] The ECHR organs affirmed that this Convention prevails over other treaties because its obligations are peremptory. The European Commission emphasized that the States-parties to the European Convention are responsible for all acts violating the Convention 'regardless of whether the act or omission in question is a consequence of domestic law or of the necessity to comply with other international obligations'. It furthermore stressed that 'if a State contracts treaty obligations and subsequently concluded another international agreement which disables it from performing of its obligations under the first treaty it will be answerable for any resulting breach of its obligations under the earlier treaty. . . . Otherwise the guarantees of the Convention could be wantonly limited or excluded and thus be deprived of their peremptory character.'[280] Likewise, the European Court affirmed that the object and purpose of human rights treaties requires that the obligations under these treaties are not affected by the content of treaties under which powers are delegated to international organisations.[281] The Inter-American Court similarly affirmed its competence to examine any norm of international law, without the subject-matter limitation, in terms of its compatibility with the American Convention on Human Rights. In *Las Palmeras*, concerned with the facts of violation of the right to life under Article 4 of the American Convention, the Court considered itself 'competent to determine whether any norm of domestic or international law applied by a State, in times of peace or armed conflict, is compatible or not with the American Convention. In this activity, the Court has no normative limitation: any legal norm may be submitted to the examination of compatibility'. As for the way this is done, 'in order to carry out this examination, the Court interprets the norm in question and analyses it in the light of the provisions of the Convention. The result of this operation will always be an opinion in which the Court will say whether or not that norm or that fact is compatible with the American Convention.'[282] This policy set out by the Inter-American Court is essentially identical with the policies of other relevant tribunals.

---

[279] Dugard and van den Wyngaert, Reconciling Extradition with Human Rights, *AJIL* (1998), 195; *Soering*, 98 ILR 300, is the classical case where the ECHR was considered inherently superior to the bilateral extradition treaty and the latter was deemed simply irrelevant to the extent that it required conduct incompatible with ECHR.

[280] *M and Co v FRG*, Application No. 13258/87, 9 February 1990, 33 *YB ECHR* 1990, 51–52; *Matthews v UK*, ECHR 24833/94, 18 February 1999, paras 26–35; see also the Joint Concurring Opinion of Judges Rozakis *et al.* in *Bosphorus*, affirming that 'Member States are responsible, under Article 1 of the Convention, for all acts and omissions of their organs, whether they arise from domestic law or from the need to fulfil international legal obligations', para. 1. As Judge Ress emphasized in the same case, 'international treaties between the Contracting Parties have to be consistent with the provisions of the Convention', para. 5.

[281] *Waite and Kennedy v Germany*, 18 February 1999, para. 67.

[282] *Las Palmeras*, Series C, No. 67, paras 32–33.

Similarly, the Dutch Supreme Court confirmed that the duty to observe the European Convention on Human Rights prevails over the duty to observe the extradition clauses in the NATO Status of Forces Agreement (SOFA).[283] All this justifies Kolb's argument that the *erga omnes* aspect of integral treaties necessitates the interdiction of subsequent incompatible agreements which are incompatible with their object.[284]

The consequences of such normative conflict should be addressed. The ILC said that the breach of a treaty stipulation through another treaty entails responsibility, but 'does not, simply as such, render the treaty void'.[285] This is generally true, but the careful wording used by the Commission (especially the words 'simply as such') indicates that there still may be cases where agreements may be invalidated due to their conflict with certain kinds of multilateral treaties. The ILC explicitly noted that certain 'integral' treaties may embody *jus cogens* and hence treaties conflicting with them would fall within the scope of Articles 53 and 64 of the Vienna Convention,[286] and stated that 'in other cases' the question should be left to be dealt with in the framework of the international responsibility of States. Thus the Commission recognized that the Vienna Convention provisions on successive treaties relating to the same subject-matter are residual and do not preclude the superior applicability of treaties embodying *jus cogens* and the consequent invalidation of conflicting treaties. What is today Article 30 cannot be applied to treaty provisions embodying *jus cogens*. *Jus cogens* embodied in treaties can have the same sanctioning power as *jus cogens* in general international law.

As Nicoloudis suggests, this problem may be relevant not only in terms of operation of Article 53, but also Article 64 of the Vienna Convention.[287] The task here may also be linked to interpretation of treaties and result in a finding that the parties to a conflicting treaty could not have intended a conflict with objective treaty obligations. This task is quite similar to the interpretation of treaties in accordance with peremptory norms, dealt with above, and a similar set of principles seems to apply here as well. The outcome in specific cases would depend on the interpretation of the intent of the

---

[283] *Short v Netherlands*, 29 *ILM* (1990), 1378.

[284] Kolb (2001), 150, emphasizing that sanction is uncertain in such cases. But where a later treaty conflicts with a prior treaty embodying *jus cogens*, the outcome can be the invalidity of the later treaty. Specific reparation ordered by a tribunal could consist precisely in abrogation of, or in an order to abrogate, the later incompatible treaty, id. 152. The rules on conflict between treaties should be adapted to the existence of peremptory norms within the treaties. In this way, the norm of a subsequent incompatible treaty may become invalid. It is in this indirect and limited sense that *jus cogens* applies to the collision of treaties, id. 156.

[285] YbILC, 1966-II, 248.

[286] 'The problem of resolving conflicts with successive treaties dealing with the same matters may sometimes overlap with the question of conflict with a *jus cogens* rule.' YbILC, 1963-II, 53. YbILC, 1966-II, 217. Pauwelyn (2003), 60.

[287] Nicoloudis (1974), 101–102.

authors of a conflicting treaty. If the intent to conflict is confirmed through interpretation, then a normative conflict is present and invalidity ensues. The *Kindler* approach is relevant in terms of both interpretation and normative conflict.

There is thus sufficient practical evidence to refute the doubt raised by some scholars as to the point that human rights treaties are by their character superior to other treaties.[288] The practice consistently affirms that they are superior, as is required by the nature of the obligations they embody.

5.3. Impact of jus cogens *on modification of treaties*[289]

Article 41 of the Vienna Convention allows for the *inter se* modification of treaties through agreements. Arguably, the scopes of Articles 41 and 53 are different; Article 41 deals with modification of treaties and specifically the relationship between earlier and later treaties.[290] But Article 41(b)(ii) of the Vienna Convention prohibits modification by a treaty of a treaty provision 'derogation from which is incompatible with the effective execution of the object and purpose of the treaty as a whole'. Thus, the object and purpose of a treaty is a limit on the contractual freedom of States in effecting *inter se* modifications and the use in Article 41 of the word 'derogation' confirms that the object and purpose of the treaty is considered as something standing above the treaty-making power of States. This resembles, at least *prima facie*, the nature of peremptory norms.

It will be recalled that the ILC Study Group on Fragmentation emphasized that 'the *inter se* agreement thus *modifies* the operation of the original treaty without *amending* it. The relationship between the general and the particular is analogous to the relationship between the *lex generalis* and the *lex specialis*'.[291] If it is added that Article 41 effectively deals with the compatibility of *lex specialis* with the relevant *lex generalis*, it will become clear that in some contexts it involved the criteria of derogability. This is again explanatory of the phenomenon of the object and purpose of a treaty as a concept cognate to *jus cogens*.

The ILC introduced into its provision regarding the *inter se* modification of a treaty the limitation related to the treaty's object and purpose, because it felt that certain treaty obligations cannot be derogated from without frustrating the entire treaty. For example, 'an *inter se* agreement modifying

---

[288] Van den Wyngaert (1990), 762, but later Van den Wyngaert adopts a more moderate attitude, id., 763–764.

[289] This analysis applies to suspension of treaties under Article 58 VCLT as the two institutes are conceptually similar.

[290] Rumpf, Zur Lehre von den 'Zwingenden Völkerrechtsnormen' Brunner u.a. (Hrsg.), *Sowjetsystem und Ostrecht* (1985), 568.

[291] *Report of the ILC Study Group on Fragmentation of International Law*, A/CN.4/L.663/ Rev.1, 17 (emphasis original).

substantive provisions of a disarmament or neutralization treaty would be incompatible with its object and purpose'.[292] Similar considerations arise in the case of treaties that embody objective or absolute obligations, namely humanitarian treaties.

If a multilateral treaty is merely a set of bilateral relations between parties, its object and purpose would not preclude the parties from adopting *inter se* a different regulation.[293] But if a treaty involves public order obligations, such as humanitarian treaties protecting the community interest, it is arguable that Article 41 prohibits its *inter se* modification.

In no case would it make sense for States to modify or suspend humanitarian treaties *inter se* as the general standard of the fallback treaty would still apply with regard to all other States. Mutual modification or suspension would be ineffective unless all States-parties were in agreement.[294] States-parties to the modificatory agreement would still be bound by the original standard towards the other parties, which directly contradicts and negates the commitments under the modificatory agreement. The other parties, on their part, would still be fully entitled to demand from the derogating States the compliance with the original standard.

Sztucki considers that the conclusion of a treaty attempting to modify another treaty in violation of Article 41 involves a breach of the treaty in terms of Article 60 of the Vienna Convention, rather than invalidity.[295] But the applicability of Article 60 to treaties impermissible under Article 41 also supports the invalidity of certain treaties. If a treaty 'modified' contrary to Article 41 is a humanitarian treaty—a treaty stipulating objective and non-fragmentable obligations—its 'modification' may be a breach under Article 60, but its termination is excluded under Article 60(5). That means that all parties are obliged to treat an offended humanitarian treaty as continuing in force and unconditionally comply with it, which definitionally entails that they are obliged *erga omnes* to disregard a modificatory agreement as null. Perhaps all the parties could terminate a treaty embodying *jus cogens* but that is qualitatively different from derogatory modification.

Article 41(1)(b)(ii) supplements the function and effects of Article 53. True, the scope of applicability of the two provisions is not identical: the former safeguards treaty instruments only, while the latter safeguards both treaty and customary norms. But their function is similar in that both are designed to safeguard peremptory norms from derogatory agreements.

Assuming that Article 41(1)(b)(ii) precludes any modification of a treaty in a way conflicting with provisions embodying peremptory norms, the question is whether the sanction of invalidity foreseen under Article 53 could equally

---

[292] II YbILC 1966, 235.   [293] Pauwelyn (2003), 53.

[294] Craven, Legal Differentiation and the Concept of the Human Rights Treaty in International Law 11 *EJIL* (2001), 494.

[295] Sztucki (1974), 172–173.

apply to agreements unlawful under Article 41(1)(b)(ii). The invalidity of a later agreement may result if the rule it attempts to modify is part of *jus cogens* under general international law. But Article 41(1)(b)(ii) also mediates the sanctioning power of *jus cogens* where the latter is embodied in a previous treaty.

Sztucki emphasizes that the case of Article 41(b)(ii) of the Vienna Convention counts as a derogation and recognizes that 'derogation from a treaty is thus a sub-category within the institution of modification of multilateral treaties between some of the parties only', and 'the sanction of invalidity may be occasionally applied to such a derogation'.[296] This would be the invalidity due to the offending content of a derogatory agreement and it is hard to see what could be the substantive standard causing invalidity if not *jus cogens*. Furthermore, in the case of *jus cogens* invalidity, not even the derogating parties would be estopped from demanding from each other compliance with the original standard of treaty obligations.

5.4. Impact of jus cogens *on the law of treaty termination*

Fundamental or material breaches of treaty obligations do not as such have imperative and automatic consequences. They merely give rise to the faculty of States-parties to terminate it reciprocally.[297] The law of treaty termination is based on a bilateralist conception of international law. As Special Rapporteur Fitzmaurice pointed out,

The principle would in any event seem to be confined, mainly if not entirely, to the field of *bilateral* treaties. Indeed it is clear that in the case of a multilateral treaty, a breach by one party, however fundamental, could not *per se* give any right to bring the whole treaty to an end, though it might affect the position of that party, and the obligations of the other parties in their relations with the defaulting party, and might, in the case of treaties of a certain class to be noticed presently, lead to eventual termination of the treaty. On the other hand, there are other classes of multilateral treaties, of the law, system or regime creating, or 'social' categories, which have to be applied integrally, where a fundamental breach would not only not give any right of termination, but not even give a right to refuse its application in respect of the defaulting party.[298]

This statement admits the operation of the principle of reciprocal non-compliance in cases of bilateral treaties and those multilateral treaties under which the legal relations are bilateralizable. But it stresses the inherent limitations of the principle imposed by the integral, or non-bilateralizable, character of the treaty obligations.

The governing provision in terms of reciprocal treaty termination is

---

[296] Sztucki (1974), 174–175.   [297] Fitzmaurice, Second Report, II YbILC 1957, 52.
[298] Fitzmaurice, Second Report, II YbILC 1957, 53.

Article 60 of the Vienna Convention on the Law of Treaties which enables the State-party to the treaty to terminate it in response to the material breach committed by the other party. As Judge de Castro emphasized in the *ICAO* case, the general philosophy of Article 60 of the Vienna Convention follows from the contractual nature of treaties, and it entitles reciprocal non-performance.[299] Riphagen also confirms that Article 60 underlines the bilateral character of the breach/injury relationship.[300] According to Tomuschat, the material breach of a treaty and the consequent termination is a matter between the parties to a treaty only.[301]

While working on the law of treaties, the ILC took a unified approach towards all treaties and decided not to deal with the issue of multilateral treaties in this context.[302] The Vienna Conference has felt the necessity to single out certain non-reciprocal treaty obligations and consequently, Article 60(5) of the Vienna Convention exempts from the process of reciprocal termination the humanitarian treaties protecting individuals.[303] Like the law of countermeasures, the law of reciprocal treaty termination requires to maintain in force certain rules and obligations in the observance of which the international community as a whole has a legal interest.

Article 60(5) refers to humanitarian treaties. But this is just an empirical description; one still needs to clarify the factors which make humanitarian treaties insusceptible of reciprocal termination.

Simma suggests that there is a need to distinguish between multilateral conventions the integral application of which by all parties is essential to their value *erga omnes*, and other multilateral treaties which are bilateral in application and hence governed by the same rules of termination as bilateral treaties.[304] Article 60(5) of the Vienna Convention in principle follows the reasoning developed by Special Rapporteur Fitzmaurice with regard to

---

[299] Judge de Castro, *ICJ Reports*, 1972, 129.

[300] Riphagen, Third Report, YbILC II-1982, Part One, 43. Riphagen also considers that Article 60 VCLT is clearly inspired by the idea that a treaty is more than a barter transaction, and hence this provision requires not just existence of a breach, but a material breach impeding a treaty's object and purpose. Riphagen, State Responsibility: New Theories of Obligation of Inter-State Relations, in Macdonald and Johnston (eds), The Structure and Process of International Law: Essays in Legal Philosphy, Doctrine and Theory (1983) 601.

[301] Tomuschat, Obligations Arising for States without or against Their Will, 241 RdC (IV-1993), 363.

[302] *Inter alia* because treaties like the Genocide Convention and the Geneva Conventions expressly allow for denunciation, YbILC, 1966-II, 255. At the Vienna Conference, Expert Consultant Waldock expressed the similar view, I UNCLT Official Records, 359. But denunciation is a concept different from reciprocal termination, as the former is about whether an obligation exists and the latter, whether an existing obligation can be terminated by way of reciprocity.

[303] On the proceedings of the Vienna Conference regarding the adoption on the basis of Swiss proposal of what now is Article 60(5) of the Vienna Convention see Schwelb, Law of Treaties and Human Rights, 16 *Archiv des Volkerrechts* (1973) 16–21.

[304] Simma, Reflections on Article 60 of the Vienna Convention on the Law of Treaties and its Background in General International Law, 20 *Österreichische Zeitschrift für öffentliches Recht* (1970), 48.

termination of treaties in terms of different types of treaty obligations.[305] Fitzmaurice distinguished between reciprocal, interdependent and integral treaty obligations, and considered that although interdependent obligations require absolute performance, they depend in the final analysis on the will of States and their breach may justify their termination by States, but this cannot happen in case of integral treaty obligations of a humanitarian nature, whose performance does not depend on corresponding performance by other States and which are assumed towards the international community as a whole.[306] In addition, a violation of a treaty containing integral obligations would not even justify a refusal to apply the treaty vis-à-vis the offending party. A fundamental breach of a human rights or humanitarian law treaty could justify neither termination nor corresponding breaches even in respect of nationals of the offending party.[307]

The reason why humanitarian treaties cannot be terminated by reciprocity consists in their integral nature. Since obligations embodied in such treaties are objective and protect the community interest as different from individual State interests, their termination cannot be a proper response to a violation by a State of any of its treaty obligations. In practical terms, their violation by way of reciprocity towards a wrongdoer State would be a simultaneous violation towards the international community as a whole. This naturally resembles the nature of *jus cogens*, which may well be embodied in treaty provisions.

The view that it is the *jus cogens* nature of treaty obligations which makes them subsumable under Article 60(5) of the Vienna Convention has gained some recognition in literature. Above all, the parallel with the law of countermeasures is clear and, as Simma suggests, customary international law confines the operation of counter-actions arising from the law of treaties in the same way in which *jus cogens* limits the applicability of reprisals.[308]

In terms of the narrow conservative approach to *jus cogens*, the parallel between *jus cogens* and Article 60(5) may not appear self-evident to some. Having reviewed the literature, Simma submits that 'jurists do not exclude humanitarian agreements from the scope of application of the counter-measures with their *sedes materiae* in the law of treaties due to the fact that the obligations embodied therein might present themselves as a mere confirmation of already existing rules of (dispositive or peremptory) international law or as new *jus cogens* but because of the crucial importance of the obligations concerned and their absolute rather than reciprocal character'.[309] It has to be asked, however, what is the difference between peremptory character and absolute character of a norm? And Simma later admits that the

[305] Fitzmaurice, II YbILC 1957, paras 124–26, p. 54.   [306] Id., para. 126.
[307] Second Report, YbILC, 1957, vol. II, 54.
[308] Simma, (1970), 23.   [309] Simma, (1970), 23–24.

applicability of retaliatory measures under the law of treaties is confined exclusively by the character of rules belonging to international *jus cogens*.[310]

A breach of a peremptory norm embodied in a treaty cannot be invoked to justify the termination or suspension of the operation of that norm. Such treaty obligations arise not under treaty but general international law. 'If two parties cannot set that principle aside consensually, in their mutual relations, it must follow *a fortiori* that one party cannot set it aside unilaterally in its relations with another State that has failed to observe it.'[311]

A further, implicit but essential support of the link between Article 60(5) of the Vienna Convention and *jus cogens* follows from Fitzmaurice's reasoning, who noted that a collective will may not excuse the illegality arising out of breaches of certain norms; if a treaty 'requires absolute or integral performance, its character would be inconsistent with the existence of any faculty of general termination for such a cause, even if exercised by the joint body of the other parties'.[312] So Fitzmaurice linked non-reciprocity with the fact that certain obligations are superior even to the collective will of States— it is difficult to describe this as something other than *jus cogens*.

The restrictions on the collective will of States-parties to validate the breach of the treaty is conceptually identical to the restriction on the same will to derogate from the treaty. In other words, the treaty obligations in relation to which parties cannot collectively authorize reciprocal non-compliance are such from which they cannot derogate.

To conclude, Article 60(5) of the Vienna Convention confirms the *jus cogens* character of objective treaty obligations through exempting them from the regime of reciprocity in case of their breach. Such breaches encompass the conclusion of conflicting agreements and as the fallback humanitarian treaty cannot be terminated by way of reciprocity, this affirms that such treaties operate as *jus cogens*, making contrary provisions null and void.

6. CONCLUSION

The law of treaties contains multiple safeguards for the integral operation of peremptory norms whether as part of general international law or embodied in treaties. The Vienna Convention explicitly voids treaties conflicting with *jus cogens* but also implicitly safeguards peremptory norms from conventional transactions purported to undermine peremptory norms embodied in treaties. These conventional transactions, such as reservations, *inter se*

---

[310] Simma, (1970), 54.
[311] Plender, The Role of Consent in the Termination of Treaties, 57 *BYIL* 1986, 133, 164.
[312] Second Report, YbILC, 1957, vol. II, 54.

modification, and others, are essentially similar, or even identical, techniques and are constrained by the object and purpose of integral humanitarian treaties. There are in principle no bilateral relations under humanitarian treaties, which means that the derogatory agreements, whatever their form, must be treated as void and non-existent.

The framework of the law of treaties demonstrates that there is no inherent difference, either conceptually or in practical terms, between safeguarding peremptory norms embodied in treaties and safeguarding their integrity under general international law. While such inherent distinction does not stand the test of the law of reservations, the law of treaty termination disapproves it expressly: Article 60 does not allow the termination of absolute treaty obligations; it could not be simply contended that obligations would be suspended as treaty obligations without their integrity under general international law being affected. If treaty norms and customary norms address the same subject-matter, the derogation from treaty norms would inevitably undermine customary ones. So, if certain customary norms are non-derogable, their treaty counterparts must be similarly deemed non-derogable. What the Vienna Convention, as an instrument embodying general international law on the subject, does, is to implement this principle in the specific areas of the law of treaties.

7

Peremptory Norms and the Validity of the Actions of States

I. GENERAL QUESTIONS

Article 53 of the Vienna Convention is the only conventional provision on the invalidating effect of *jus cogens*. There is no comparable authority on the effect of *jus cogens* with regard to acts and transactions other than treaties. It has been suggested that the Vienna Convention is the sole legal basis for the superior authority of peremptory norms.[1] But the concept of invalidity for conflict with *jus cogens* is not an invention of the Vienna Convention; it is an aspect of general international law.[2] The approach that peremptory norms operate just due to Article 53 would reduce them to a form of conventional public policy, and would raise the question why a policy recognized in one convention should trump that included in another. Such an approach cannot explain the voidness of a treaty offending against *jus cogens* concluded between a party and a non-party to the Vienna Convention either, yet this is now established.

At the Vienna Conference, it was suggested that treaties cannot be used to conceal actions violating basic principles of international law.[3] The voidness of a treaty contradicting *jus cogens* emanates from its attempted legitimation of acts offending against *jus cogens*; such acts are also, and necessarily, subject to the effects of *jus cogens*.[4] Thus, the consequences of an act or action offending against peremptory norms must possess independent relevance if the concept is to have any intelligible meaning. The correct approach is not to enquire whether *jus cogens* applicable to treaties also applies to unilateral actions of States, but to acknowledge that *jus cogens* applies to treaties precisely because the fundamental illegality attached to certain acts is so grave

---

[1] Frowein, Reactions by Not Directly Affected States to Breaches of Public International Law, 248 *RdC* (1994), 365; Rozakis, *The Concept of* Jus Cogens *in the Law of Treaties* (1976), 31, but this contradicts Rozakis' view that *jus cogens* applies to unilateral acts as well.

[2] Nahlik, The Grounds of Invalidity and Termination of Treaties, 65 *AJIL* (1971), 745.

[3] USSR, meetings 843, 845, 910, in Schwelb, Some Aspects of International *Jus Cogens*, 61 *AJIL* (1967), 961–962.

[4] Arechaga, in Weiler, Cassese and Spinedi (1989), 240; Arechaga, International Law in the Past Third of the Century, 159 *RdC* (1978), 65; Gaja, *Jus Cogens* beyond the Vienna Convention, 172 *RdC* (1981), 295; Dinstein, *War, Aggression and Self-Defence* (2001), 95.

that it is not capable of being legitimized even if supported by a legal rule embodied in a derogatory agreement.[5]

Once peremptory norms are seen as the product of general international law rather than any specific instrument, it follows that there is no inherent limitation as to the types or categories of acts and transactions to which such norms may apply. And this is widely recognized in the doctrine. Thus Sir Robert Jennings considers that 'the content of *jus cogens* ranges far outside the scope of the law of treaties.'[6] According to Suy, if treaties conflicting with *jus cogens* are invalid, the acts they entail must be invalid as well, the treaty being a higher form of legal enactment than a unilateral enactment.[7] Crawford states that the prohibition of derogation from *jus cogens* as recognized under the Vienna Convention is a concept broad enough to include acts other than treaties: 'It is difficult to accept that a rule should be sacrosanct in one context and freely prescriptible in another.'[8] Meron states that the non-treaty aspect of *jus cogens* is even more important than its treaty aspect.[9] According to Nicoloudis, an act, even if based on the will of a single international person, can conflict with *jus cogens*, and there is a customary norm that every act conflicting with *jus cogens* is void.[10] The prohibition of derogation from *jus cogens* implies that it outlaws not just conflicting treaties but also any inconsistent legal act or situation.[11]

It seems that the very prohibition and voidness of the conventional agreements contrary to *jus cogens* is owed to the broader scope of peremptory norms causing the invalidity of any conflicting act including the non-treaty acts. While drafting the *jus cogens* provisions of the 1969 Vienna Convention,

[5] Müllerson, *Ordering Anarchy* (2000), 156–159, puts forward an extreme view that *jus cogens* in terms of Article 53 of the Vienna Convention is inapplicable to the law of treaties, and that the only question in terms of treaties allegedly offending against *jus cogens*, such as the 1960 Cyprus Guarantee Treaty, is not the illegality of a treaty but the acts performed under them. It seems that Müllerson's approach is unsustainable as Article 53 of the Vienna Convention expresses the community will and also, if a treaty expressly authorizes acts conflicting with *jus cogens*, it is impossible to separate the issue of legality of those acts from that of legality of the relevant treaty clauses.
[6] Jennings, General Course on Principles of International Law, II *RdC* (1967), 564; Allain, The *jus cogens* Nature of *non-refoulement*, 13 *International Journal of Refugee Law* (2002), 535.
[7] Suy, The Concept of Jus Cogens in International Law, *Lagonissi Conference: Papers and Proceedings*, vol. II, Carnegie Endowment for International Peace (1967), 75.
[8] Crawford, *Creation of States in International Law* (1979), 82; Ford, Adjudicating *Jus Cogens*, 13 *Wisconsin International Law Journal* (1994), 153–154; Gomez Robledo, Le ius cogens international: sa genèse, sa nature, ses fonctions, 172 *Recueil des cours* (1981), 194–196.
[9] Meron, *Human Rights Law-Making in the United Nations* (1986), 196–197.
[10] Nicoloudis, *La nullité de jus cogens et le développement contemporain de droit international public* (1974), 123, 134; Verhoeven, La reconnaissance internationale: déclin ou renouveau? 39 *Annuaire Français de Droit International* (1999), 38.
[11] Abi-Saab, The Concept of *Jus Cogens* in International Law, 2 *Lagonissi Conference: Papers and Proceedings*, vol. II, Carnegie Endowment for International Peace (1967), 10; Ford (1994), 146; Hannikainen, *Peremptory Norms in International Law* (1988), 7, 9; Saladin, Völkerrechtliches Jus Cogens und Schweizerisches Landesrecht, Jenny and Kälin, *Die Schweizerische Rechtsordnung in Ihren Internationalen Bezügen* (1988), 73.

the International Law Commission expressly emphasized that the *jus cogens* invalidity of treaties 'follows from the fact that a rule of *jus cogens* is an overriding rule depriving *any act or situation* which is in conflict with it of legality'.[12] As the Inter-American Court of Human Rights affirmed, '*Jus cogens* is not limited to treaty law. The sphere of *jus cogens* has expanded to encompass general international law, including all legal acts. *Jus cogens* has also emerged in the law of the responsibility of States and, finally, has had an influence on the basic principles of the international legal order.'[13]

The essence of the problem is clear but there are still some doctrinal objections. According to Weil, the applicability of *jus cogens* to unilateral acts is a logical impossibility, since unilateral acts involve no derogation from *jus cogens*.[14] Marek contends that the only question with regard to unilateral acts is whether they are legal or illegal and the concept of *jus cogens* is here irrelevant.[15] According to Kolb, *jus cogens* opposes the creation of a particular juridical regime intended to apply between certain legal subjects. A unilateral act is not capable of creating such a regime, because it only involves its author.[16] But Kolb acknowledges that the majority of writers uphold the applicability of *jus cogens* to unilateral acts by referring to the protection by *jus cogens* of the fundamental community interest. Since such superior interests are involved, *jus cogens* must, as a matter of hierarchy, apply to inferior unilateral acts in the same way it applies to treaties, in order to guarantee the integrity of the community interest it protects.[17]

Kolb concludes that whether or not *jus cogens* applies to unilateral acts, it is decisive that *jus cogens* deals with the validity of acts. Some unilateral acts may give rise to illegality pure and simple, while others can be intended as the sources of rights and obligations. *Jus cogens* applies to the latter type of unilateral act, ie to acts which are intended to be endowed with normative force.[18]

As Sztucki submits, the extension of *jus cogens* to non-treaty acts follows from the confusion between the notions of violation and derogation. The

[12] 2 YbILC 1966, 261 (emphasis added). Similarly, in Resolution 35/118, the General Assembly 'categorically reject[ed] any agreement, arrangement or unilateral action by colonial or racist Powers which ignores, violates, denies or conflicts with the inalienable rights of peoples under colonial domination to self-determination and independence'.

[13] *Juridical Condition and Rights of the Undocumented Migrants*, Advisory Opinion, OC-18/03, para. 99.

[14] Weil, Le droit international en quête de son identité. Cours général de droit international public, 237 *RdC* (1992), 261.

[15] Marek, 'Jus cogens' en droit international, *Recueil d'études de droit international en hommage à Paul Guggenheim* (1968), 441; see also Zimmerman, Sovereign Immunity and Violations of International *Jus Cogens*—Some Critical Remarks, 16 *Michigan Journal of International Law* (1995), 437–438.

[16] Kolb, *Théorie du ius cogens international* (2001), 89–90.

[17] Kolb (2001), 90.

[18] Kolb (2001), 90–91; Kolb, *Jus Cogens*, Intangibilité, Intransgressibilité, Derogation 'Positive' et 'Negative', *RGDIP* (2005), 322.

superiority of *jus cogens* does not mean that it cannot be violated, but that it cannot be derogated from, derogation being intended to produce effect only for derogating subjects.[19] Hannikainen, on the other hand, emphasizes that the prohibition of derogation under Article 53 of the Vienna Convention is to be understood to prohibit any acts conflicting with a given norm.[20]

Sztucki doubts the relevance of *jus cogens* for violations as a factor causing the nullity of actions of States, and considers that remedies attendant to nullity, such as restitution, are anyway available in the law of State responsibility.[21] Sztucki's reasoning is defective, as the law of State responsibility is not peremptory as such and nothing in it guarantees the voidness of certain acts, unless the peremptory character of a norm is resorted to in addition to what the law of State responsibility may require. In other words, unless the nullity is taken as the starting-point, the requirement of restitution could be bypassed in the law of State responsibility. The latter law is *jus dispositivum*, replaceable by *lex specialis*, and cannot by itself safeguard the public interest embodied in peremptory norms, unless it is clearly understood that *jus cogens* applies to wrongful acts, causing their nullity—a result which would derive from the law relating to peremptory norms, not that related to State responsibility more broadly.

The ILC codification process on unilateral acts has confirmed the relevance of *jus cogens* with regard to unilateral acts (declarations) of States. Special Rapporteur Rodriguez-Cedeno submitted that unilateral acts are subject to the same conditions of validity as treaties under the Vienna Convention on the Law of Treaties. Among these conditions is the lawfulness of the object in terms of compatibility with peremptory norms.[22] In the General Assembly Sixth Committee this analogy has been endorsed.[23] A unilateral act conflicting with *jus cogens* is absolutely invalid. This situation differs from a conflict with a previous unilateral act or a treaty.[24] Absolute invalidity in terms of *jus cogens* means that an act cannot be confirmed or validated[25] and that any State can invoke invalidity.[26]

But further qualifications to the applicability of peremptory norms to non-treaty acts are suggested. According to Rozakis, while the function of *jus cogens* may be fully effective with regard to treaties and unilateral acts of States considered as the source of normative commitments, it is less so with regard to other actions of States. The invalidating capacity of *jus cogens* is

---

[19] Sztucki, Jus Cogens *and the Vienna Convention on the Law of Treaties* (1974), 67–68; for a similar view see Talmon, The Constitutive versus the Declaratory Theory of Recognition: *Tertium Non Datur?, BYIL* (2004), 101 at 133–134.

[20] Hannikainen (1988), 7; see also Saladin (1988), 73.

[21] Sztucki (1974), 68; for a similar approach see Talmon (2004), 134.

[22] Rodriguez-Cedeno, *Fifth Report on Unilateral Acts*, A/CN.4/525, Add.1., 2, 7.

[23] Rodriguez-Cedeno, *Third Report on Unilateral Acts*, A/CN.4/505, 19, para. 135.

[24] Rodriguez-Cedeno, *Fifth Report on Unilateral Acts*, A/CN.4/525, Add.1., 5.

[25] Id., 6.   [26] Id., 9.

linked to prevention of the undesirable results of illegality, such as the declaration of invalidity of a normative instrument. 'But since the illegal effects of a unilateral action are nothing more than the action itself, a prevention of those effects is impossible.'[27] According to Hannikainen, while peremptory norms void actions aiming at creation of rights and titles, it serves no purpose to declare void the acts such as gross human rights violations that contradict *jus cogens*. 'There is little point in declaring void concrete violative acts which have produced their results by the time their validity is challenged—especially killings and, to a great extent, torture and brutalities.'[28]

This reasoning is too simplistic. Perhaps *jus cogens* cannot prevent the occurrence of certain actions, but it is quite another thing to say that *jus cogens* cannot prevent or influence their effects and consequences from a legal perspective. To suggest that the effect of an action is nothing but the action itself is incorrect. In a decentralized legal community, the actions of States can be a source of rights and obligations, and contribute to the formation and modification of legal relations through the establishment of *inter se* relations different from general international law. If such actions offend against *jus cogens*, the function of the latter is to prevent the former from becoming an element of a new *inter se* legal relation. As peremptory norms do not allow fragmentation of the relations they govern, the relevant acts and actions of States must be void, ie incapable of giving rise to new commitments inconsistent with the peremptory norm.

Furthermore, even as the gross violations of human rights (and also humanitarian law) do not bring the immediate benefit to the State that commits them, apart from the achievement of the purposes the atrocities were aimed at, their treatment as acts not compounding invalidity can affect a variety of legal relations through which the State that has committed these acts can gain legal benefits. This can have to do in some cases with the acquisition of the title over the relevant territory; this can affect the subsequent claims of the victims by opening the channels for the validation of the breaches based on gross violations; this can further enable the wrongdoer State to claim certain entitlements such as the immunity for sovereign acts[29]

---

[27] Rozakis (1976), 18.

[28] Hannikainen (1988), 9; Hannikainen, The case of East Timor from the perspective of jus cogens, *International Law and the Question of East Timor* (1995), 109; for a similar view see Talmon (2004), 134, contending that the *jus cogens* nullity cannot apply to actual socio-political events, physical actions or factual situations and that nullity in relation to genocide or slavery would be pointless.

[29] The Greek court construed the denial of immunity in terms of nullity of acts contradicting *jus cogens*. It emphasized that 'acts contrary to peremptory international law are null and void and cannot give rise to lawful rights, such as immunity (in application of the general principle of law *ex injuria jus non oritur*)'. Case No. 13/1997, Multi-member Court of Levadia, 30 October 1997, 50 *Revue Hellénique* (1997), 599.

and also enhance the relevance of the act of State defence before the foreign courts.[30] If the relevant norms are peremptory they have to ensure that the conduct of the wrongdoer State is judged in accordance with the principle *ex injuria jus non oritur*.

The same holds true for the acts of deportation, expulsion or extradition (this latter being also relevant in the context of the law of treaties) which are based on or lead to the breach of peremptory norms. Although the immediate results of those acts are expressed by their very performance, there are also subsequent effects related to the permissibility of further trials, issues of release and return as a matter of the observance of individual rights. In this context the absolute illegality or invalidity of the original act can be determinative of the legality of further measures in relation to the pertinent persons.

It seems that anything that can have the prospective effect in a way of modifying, amending or influencing the rights and entitlements of the actors protected by peremptory norms is subjected to the invalidating impact of *jus cogens*.

This reasoning fits perfectly into Sztucki's definition of derogation, by reference to which he denied the applicability of *jus cogens* to non-treaty acts. Fitzmaurice speaks of 'cases in which overriding rules of *jus cogens* produce a situation of irreducible obligation and demand that illegal action be ignored or not allowed to affect obligations of other States'.[31] This confirms at least implicitly that the issue is one of derogation. Furthermore, the International Law Commission has in fact affirmed that the derogation from *jus cogens* is likely to be attempted in contexts other than the law of treaties, while it emphasized in the context of State responsibility that peremptory norms 'defeat any attempt by two States to replace them in their relations by other rules having a different content'.[32]

Although there can be some difference between unilateral acts in the narrow sense (declarations) and the actions of States, they both have potential effects which are vulnerable to the operation of *jus cogens*, and sometimes the difference between the different categories of acts is blurred. In that context the formal designation of an act becomes less relevant.

As ILC Special Rapporteur Rodriguez-Cedeno suggests, will is a constituent of consent and necessary to the formation of the legal act; it should be seen as a psychological element (internal will) and as an element of externalization (declared will).[33] He defines a unilateral act as an 'unequivocal expression of will which is formulated by a State with the intention of producing legal

---

[30] See below, Chapter 19.

[31] Fitzmaurice, The general principles of international law considered from the standpoint of the rule of law, 92 *Recueil des cours* (1957), 122.

[32] II *YBILC* (1979), 115.

[33] Rodriguez-Cedeno, *Fifth Report on Unilateral Acts*, A/CN.4/525, 14.

effects'.[34] This definition does not include any requirement of a formal declaration of will and is broad enough to include acts whatever their formal features.

Doctrine does not distinguish *a priori* between different kinds of acts or actions either. Suy defines juridical acts as manifestations of will imputable to one or more international persons, to which legal consequences are attached by a legal norm.[35] Unilateral acts, or juridical acts in the strict sense, are manifestations of will producing legal effects in conformity with the will of the author.[36] This is broad enough to encompass acts other than unilateral acts (ie, declarations) proper.

Similarly according to Verzjil, international juridical acts are those which produce juridical effects in conformity with the will of the author.[37] According to Nicoloudis, an international juridical act is every act which manifests an international person's will to which international law attaches corresponding consequences.[38] These authors make no differentiation in terms of types of juridical acts.

Pfluger, although speaking of unilateral transactions, also focuses on the occupation of territory with a view to acquire the territorial title.[39] He defines occupation as an act of will. The unilateral will is not declared, but evidenced through assuming effective possession of a territory.[40] It is questionable whether such differences in form can be determinative of effects or of the governing rules. Indeed, the will and intention to achieve the relevant legal changes can be the element of an act or action of the State even if such intention is expressly disclaimed.[41]

---

[34] Id., 14, 18.   [35] Suy, *Les actes juridiques unilatéraux* (1962), 22.   [36] Suy (1962), 25.

[37] Verzjil, La validité et la nullité des actes juridiques internationales, 15 *Revue de droit international* (1935), 289.

[38] Nicoloudis (1974), 17–18.

[39] Pfluger, *Die Einseitigen Rechtsgeschäfte im Völkerrecht* (1936), 288 ff.

[40] Pfluger (1936), 291–293.

[41] For instance, the UN Special Rapporteur on Human Rights in the Occupied Palestinian Territory has seen the construction by Israel of the Wall in the Occupied Palestinian Territory as 'a case of de facto annexation in which the security situation is employed as a pretext for territorial expansion', Report of 17 December 2002, E/CN.4/2003/30, 14, para. 42. As the next Report further specified, 'there may be no official annexation of the Palestinian territory in effect transferred to Israel by the construction of the Wall, but it is impossible to avoid the conclusion that we are here faced with annexation of Palestinian territory,' Report of 8 September 2003, E/CN.4/2004/6, 6, para. 6. In the Advisory Opinion on the *Construction of a Wall in the Occupied Palestinian Territory*, the International Court noted that Israel had disclaimed the intention to annex the relevant territories or change their status in any way. The Court was not convinced by these submissions. It stated that it could not remain indifferent to certain fears expressed to it that the route of the Wall would prejudge the future frontier between Israel and Palestine, and the fear that Israel may integrate the settlements. The Court considers that the construction of the Wall and its associated regime create a 'fait accompli' on the ground that it could well become permanent, in which case, and notwithstanding the formal characterization of the Wall by Israel, it would be tantamount to *de facto* annexation. More so, as the planned route of the Wall would separate 16 per cent of the Palestinian territory from the rest of it. See the Opinion, paras 116, 121. The Court consequently applied the duty of non-recognition to the situation arising out of the construction of the Wall.

Therefore, the category of juridical acts intended to produce legal effects in accordance with the author's intention comprises not only unilateral acts (declarations) proper, but also acts of States consisting purely in their conduct which, if allowed to be valid and to go unchallenged, would produce the consequences desired by the acting State, either because this would follow from its own intent or because such consequences would ensue from that act due to the operation of some legal rule.

In principle, all acts or actions of States express the will of a State and are based on the intent to acquire, exercise or transfer rights, titles and obligations, to achieve certain legal consequences valid and opposable under international law. Acts performed within the sphere of sovereignty are normally presumed to be valid and opposable on the international plane with all intended effects. But any act or action can be at variance with the requirements of international public order by causing derogation.

A unilateral act is most often a transaction addressed to another State with a view to conducting or modifying legal relations between the respective States. Actions proper are perhaps acts not *per se* involving an element of transaction, the acting State arguably considering that it acts as permitted by international law or in the exercise of sovereign authority. However, if an act or action in question is at variance with international law, then intended effects may accrue only through an additional transaction with a State whose rights are thereby violated. The actual act or action, especially in cases where it involves the expression of will and intention, is the constituent element and subject-matter of this transaction, and is complemented by the will and acceptance by other State(s). This transaction can be explicit or conduct-based, but in either case it would be a derogation from the law applicable between the States concerned.

According to Pfluger, the consequences of a legally relevant action (*Rechtshandlung*) are determined by objective law, and the consequences of a transaction (*Rechtsgeschäft*) depend on the will to bring about certain consequences.[42] But this distinction is too strict: there can be an intention behind any action; equally, the effects of a transaction are necessarily circumscribed by the basic rules of the legal system within which it occurs or pursuant to which it has effect. Suy does not make such distinctions in stating that the will of a State cannot produce corresponding effects if the objective law does not permit this.[43] A manifestation of will is international where it involves a manifestation relevant in terms of a norm of international law.[44] Compliance with such norms is normally a matter between the acting and the affected State(s). But as Nicoloudis correctly suggests, the question with regard to every juridical act is whether it can by itself have the intended effect or it is

---

[42] Pfluger (1936), 5.   [43] Suy (1962), 21.   [44] Suy (1962), 23.

necessary for that act to conform to international public order (*jus cogens*) transcending the will of the author(s).[45]

By virtue of the principles of recognition or tolerance an unlawful act may begin to have legal effects: *ex factis jus oritur*.[46] Therefore, both categories of acts and actions can conflict with *jus cogens*. It is inherent in the idea of public order that it must apply to any conflicting act, whatever its form. In national legal systems, the principle of public policy applies both to foreign laws and acts, whether administrative or judicial.[47] Public policy is a factor which nullifies not just contract but legal acts of all kinds. It applies not just to contracts but to other relations of private law including unilateral actions.[48] The national public order clauses outlawing acts and transactions contrary to public order are not limited to agreements or legislative provisions, but also extend to other acts without a limitation of its form or character.[49] A primary consideration is to protect the integrity of the legal system from certain unacceptable acts, regardless of their formal character. In *Oppenheimer*, public policy was applied to a legislative decree,[50] while in *Kuwait Air Corp.* it was applied to an administrative act.[51]

There is also empirical evidence that the impact of *jus cogens* on non-treaty acts and actions is conceptually similar with, and often inherently linked to, its impact in the law of treaties. Article 71 of the Vienna Convention on the Law of Treaties, determining the regime of acts performed under treaties conflicting with *jus cogens*, confirms that acts or actions of States or situations created through their conduct can themselves conflict with peremptory norms and that the latter norms impact upon the legal consequences of such acts, actions or situations. Thus, contrary to some assertions,[52] the wording of Article 71 of the Vienna Convention expressly confirms that the nullity on the basis of conflict with *jus cogens* applies not only to treaties but also to the

---

[45] Nicoloudis (1974), 25–26.   [46] Suy (1967), 75.

[47] Batiffol and Lagarde, *Traité de Droit International Privé* (1993), 573; Kegel, *Internationales Privatrecht* (1987), 334.

[48] Zweigert and Kötz, *An Introduction to Comparative Law* (1998), 381.

[49] Jaenicke, Zur Frage des Internationalen Ordre Public, 7 *Berichte der Deutschen Gesellschaft für Völkerrecht* (1967), 78–79; Nussbaum, *Deutsches Internationales Privatrecht* (1974), 65; Bleckmann, *Sittenwidrigkeit wegen Verstoßes gegen den* ordre public international, 34 *ZaöRV* (1974), 113, 128; Niederer, *Einführung in die Allgemeine Lehren des Internationalen Privatrechts* (1956), 297, referring to national public order clauses extended to non-contractual acts.

[50] Such as the German decree depriving expatriate Jews of German citizenship, *Oppenheimer v Cattermole*, 27 ILR 446.

[51] Such as the confiscatory decree of the Revolutionary Command Council of Iraq, *Kuwait Air Corp.* (HL), 16 May 2002, para. 2 (*per* Lord Nicholls).

[52] Talmon (2004), 132, 135, argues that 'Article 71(1)(a) VCLT also shows that the concept of nullity is restricted to the bilateral or multilateral legal transaction, ie treaty, and does not extend to an ensuing factual situation,' and that the acts and situations that must be eliminated are not themselves declared void under Article 71. But view this misconceives the fact that the Vienna Convention is applicable to treaties only and its relevant provisions deal expressly with the cases

acts performed pursuant to them. These acts must be eliminated as far as possible.[53] The rationale of Article 52 of the same Convention which outlaws and voids the treaties imposed by the threat or use of force is inspired by the principle that the acts accomplished through coercion and use of force would be void in the first place, whatever the further characteristics of those acts. Following the similar rationale, Article 47 of the Fourth Geneva Convention reflects the comprehensive vulnerability and the consequent comprehensive effect of public order while it protects the rights of the population of occupied territories from the adverse effect of both the agreements between the sovereign and occupying powers and the unilateral action of the occupying power, such as annexation. Article 47 is indeed the classical public order clause which sets limits not only on treaty-making but also the law-creating force of facts and the ensuing principle of effectiveness.

In general, the difference between treaty and non-treaty relations does not seem to be inherent. The validity of the non-treaty act can be relevant in terms of treaty relations. For instance, the International Court ruled in *Oil Platforms* that the US actions did not constitute the valid self-defence and hence could not qualify as essential security measures under the 1955 Iran–US Treaty. In other words, the fact that the relevant actions contradicted *jus cogens* precluded their characterization in a way enabling the US benefiting from those actions in terms of the exercise of its otherwise lawful treaty rights. This was rightly treated as the issue of treaty interpretation,[54] but this is also an incidence of the principle *ex injuria jus non oritur* that operates at the scale broader than just the law of treaties.

All this justifies Dugard's view that 'The criticism of any attempt to extend *jus cogens* beyond the confines of the law of treaties is firmly premised on an outmoded perception of international public order'.[55]

Once the applicability of peremptory norms to an act is ascertained, the legal consequences should be examined. Breaches of *jus cogens* can perhaps have some effects. One should distinguish between general consequences foreseen under the law, such as bringing into operation certain legal rules and principles, and the consequences which are intended by the author. Illegal war or genocide can have certain consequences, such as the application of the laws of war or the rules on accountability; but whether these cover legal consequences intended by the author is another question.

---

of voidness of treaties only and not any other act. Moreover, Article 71 requires the elimination of the relevant acts because their legal basis, that is treaty, is null and void, and hence implies that they have no foundation in law, that is they are also invalid. Also, by requiring that the parties to the treaty conflicting with *jus cogens* bring their mutual relations into conformity with the relevant peremptory norm, Article 71 imperatively requires the total disregard of the relevant acts as acts that are legally non-existent. This is the most essential quality of the voidness and the differences between and play of words does not imply any difference in substance.

[53] See above, Chapter 6 for more detail.
[54] See above, Chapter 6.   [55] Dugard, *Recognition and the United Nations* (1987), 142.

Pfluger distinguishes between permitted and prohibited State actions: while the former produce their effect because they are in accordance with international law, the latter do not produce effects as they are not.[56] Such a classification can be relevant in terms of *jus cogens*, as it always deals with unlawful acts. But many illegal acts are not contrary to *jus cogens*, and their ultimate effect can be left to the States involved.

As Verzijl suggests, a juridical act, lawful or not, often involves multiple elements in terms of its validity, of responsibility for it and of its impacts in international and domestic law.[57] Within the law of treaties, *jus cogens* invalidates the conflicting transactions. As Guggenheim submits, the validity and nullity of international legal acts must be examined in terms of the conditions of validity of conventional norms.[58] While Guggenheim does not accept the existence of *jus cogens* in the first place and consequently of nullity in international law, such an approach is not only conceptually moot (because the existence of peremptory norms is not a matter of doubt), but also fails in the face of developments during the last few decades. The development of nullity in various fields governed by *jus cogens* justifies the alternative approach, the approach of Nicoloudis, according to which there exists the customary norm of *jus cogens* according to which all acts contradicting international public order are null and void.[59] The Vienna Convention regime of invalidity itself is an aspect of the more comprehensive legal effects *jus cogens* brings about with regard to different kinds of acts and actions.

Verzijl suggests that the question of validity can be relevant in terms of uni-lateral acts of all kinds.[60] Nicoloudis considers that the validity of juridical acts is not granted, but is subject to certain conditions whose non-observance results in invalidity, such as compliance with *jus cogens*.[61] Kolb submits that 'C'est uniquement sur le plan de la validité de l'acte juridique unilatéral que le droit impératif peut intervenir dans la mesure ou l'acte unilatéral n'est pas qu'un acte matériel mais aussi une source de droit.'[62]

The principal effect is that conflicting actions are without effect and void. If derogation from *jus cogens* is allowed in no circumstances, then a violation intended as an element of derogation is tainted with the same degree of illegality, and entails the same consequences as a derogation, that is, invalidity. The analogy with the law of treaties is justified both logically and empirically. The consequences of the unlawful use of force are void both within the law of treaties (Article 52 of the Vienna Convention) and outside it. In terms of Article 71 of the Vienna Convention *jus cogens* applies to acts

---

[56] Pfluger (1936), 5.   [57] Verzijl (1935), 292–293.
[58] Guggenheim, La validité et la nullité des actes juridiques internationaux, *RdC* (1949), 195; *per contra* Dinstein (2001), 153.
[59] Nicoloudis (1974), 134.   [60] Verzijl (1935), 306.
[61] Nicoloudis (1974), 26; Saladin (1988), 73.   [62] Kolb (2001), 91.

and actions of States primarily in terms of validity (though also in terms of remedies) and proceeds from the assumption that acts and actions contrary to *jus cogens* are void.

The logical and necessary consequence of the voidness of acts contrary to *jus cogens* is that, as they have no effect in law, the rules violated continue to operate as peremptory norms and therefore govern, in a peremptory manner, the legal relations which were intended by the author State(s) to be affected by the act, action or transaction.

Such consequences are necessary. *Jus cogens* voidness is only possible if it operates even despite the attitudes of States, so that the consequences of objective illegality are duly respected. Otherwise, owing to the decentralized nature of the international community, basic principles would be sacrificed. The effect of *jus cogens* must be multidimensional to maintain the integrity of peremptory norms. This can usually be achieved through the law of State responsibility or devices of subsequent validation, which require that *jus cogens* has to extend to these areas as well.

2. TYPES OF ACTS AND ACTIONS OF STATES SUBJECT TO *JUS COGENS*

The actions of States subject to peremptory norms can be of any type, consisting in the exercise of legislative, administrative or judicial competence of a State, where and when they are intended to produce effects on the national or the international plane, such as the acquisition, modification or relinquishment of a right, status or obligation.

Some actions of States are directly prohibited under *jus cogens*, such as aggression, genocide or crimes against humanity. Others involve more usual exercises of State authority and hence they do not as such conflict with peremptory norms, which are not intended to affect basic sovereign prerogatives. However, once the exercise of sovereign authority entails, or is consequential upon, a breach of a peremptory norm, the acts performed become subject to the overriding effect of *jus cogens*. Not only are they illegal—which would be the case for every wrongful act—but they are also void.

Peremptory norms apply to all kinds of acts and actions of States, whether performed on the domestic or the international plane. Normally all acts of States, even if performed within the framework of domestic or internal law, are subject to the overriding effect of international law. For instance, Virally considers that unilateral acts are acts of international significance, or 'acts done with intent to affect international legal relations. But they may be acts under municipal law, such as a statute or ordinance specifying the limits of the territorial sea, to the extent that their range or effects transcend the sphere of municipal law and affect that of international law'.[63] According to Verzijl, an act valid in national law can be devoid of validity in international law.[64] Normally this is a matter for bilateral relations but once falling within the scope of *jus cogens* it becomes a matter for community interest.

It is inherent in the very idea of public order that it should apply and invalidate acts originating both from within and outside the forum's legal system. Public policy can lead to the voidness of contracts within domestic private law, as well as of foreign laws and acts. International public order similarly applies to acts performed within the ambit of either national or international law, as soon as a pertinent act can have a detrimental effect for the operation of public order rules within the ambit of international law.

The ICTY in *Furundzija* examined both the conceptual and practical aspects of the problem. In a way responding to the general implications of the concept of public order, the Tribunal held that peremptory norms serve at the inter-State level to de-legitimize any legislative, administrative or judicial acts contrary to them.[65] If such national measures were taken, they would be null and void and in addition

would not be accorded international legal recognition. Proceedings could be initiated by potential victims if they had *locus standi* before a competent national or international judicial body with a view to asking it to hold the national measure to be internationally unlawful; or the victim could bring a civil suit for damage in a foreign court, which would therefore be asked *inter alia* to disregard the legal value of the national authorising act. What is even more important is that perpetrators of torture acting upon or benefiting from those national measures may nevertheless be held criminally responsible for torture, whether in a foreign State, or in their own State under a subsequent regime. In short, in spite of possible national authorisation by legislative or judicial bodies to violate the principle banning torture, individuals remain bound to comply with that principle.[66]

According to the Hungarian Constitutional Court, 'no domestic law confronted with a conflicting and express peremptory rule of international law (*jus cogens*) may be given legal effect'.[67] Arguably, such voidness operates only internationally, not necessarily in the legal system of the act's origin.[68]

It is now worth turning to specific incidences of the principles analysed so far. The relevant practice involves the acts and actions invalid on account of their substance—the conflict with a substantive peremptory norm.

---

[63] Virally, Sources of International Law, Sorensen (ed.), *A Manual of International Law* (1968), 154.

[64] Verzijl (1935), 292.   [65] Furundzija, 38 ILM 1999, 349.

[66] Furundzija, 38 ILM 1999, 349.   [67] Decision No. 53/1993, 13 October 1993, V.2.

[68] Meron (1986), 199. This reflects public order's impact precluding the operation within the forum's legal system of externally adopted acts, not their existence or validity.

2.1. Illegal territorial acquisitions

The law of territorial acquisitions is in principle bilateral, which means that much relevance is accorded to the actions and attitudes of individual States concerned in the process of title crystallization. Traditional rules are inspired by the rationale that the lack of due diligence by one State should not affect the legitimate interests of another. The principles governing territorial acquisitions are relative: they involve the individual interests of States, and their operation depends on the actions, and expression of attitudes, by these States. This classical approach is well illustrated in such well-known decisions as *Island of Palmas*, *Clipperton Island* and *Temple*, which are among those laying down the conceptual foundations of the law of territorial acquisitions.

But such bilateralism is overtaken in situations where an attempted territorial acquisition offends against the community interest, such as in situations of the unlawful use of force, or in cases where there is a breach of the principle of self-determination. The scope and effect of peremptory norms implies that the weight of actions and attitudes of States is diminished to ensure the integral operation of these norms. Traditionally, the capacity to acquire territory is among a State's basic sovereign prerogatives, but where a peremptory norm is engaged, these prerogatives are suppressed to that extent. Acquisitions offending against *jus cogens* are null and void.

As Sir Robert Jennings suggests, if the use of force is condemned as illegal, it cannot result in the acquisition of title.[69] Visscher agrees: if international law outlaws the use of force in an absolute way, it cannot treat the benefits ensuing from the use of force as valid.[70] Owing to the prohibition of the use of force, 'Neither conquest nor a cession imposed by illegal force of themselves confer title.'[71] This is an aspect of a more general principle of invalidity of forcibly acquired benefits, which applies specifically to territorial acquisitions.

These consequential effects are part of customary law. In practice, the OAS recommended as early as 1890 that forcible territorial cessions are void.[72] In the Joint Declaration of 1 November 1943, the Governments of Britain, the USA and the USSR regarded the annexation of Austria in 1938 as void *ab initio*, which is considered the case of nullity for conflict with *jus cogens*.[73] Both the ILC Declaration of Rights and Duties of States and the UN

---

[69] Jennings, *The Acquisition of Territory in International Law* (1967), 54.

[70] Visscher, *Les effectivités du droit international public* (1967), 115–116.

[71] Jennings (1967), 61; Brownlie, *Principles* (2003), 121 emphasizes the relevance of primary rules of *jus ad bellum* in determining the validity of forcible territorial changes. Dinstein (2001), 151.

[72] 1 Moore, *Digest*, 292.

[73] Suy (1967), 68–69. The Tripartite Declaration stated that the Three Powers 'regard the annexation imposed upon Austria by Germany on March 15, 1938, as null and void. They consider themselves in no way bound by any changes effected in Austria since that date.' 38 *AJIL Supplement* (1934), 7.

General Assembly Friendly Relations Declaration confirm the illegality of forcible territorial acquisitions. That this principle is part of customary law was reaffirmed in the International Court's Opinion on the *Construction of Wall in the Occupied Palestinian Territory*.[74]

Likewise, no title can be acquired in breach of the principle of self-determination.[75] This limitation applies both to populations of a State or its part, and communities not organized as a State.[76] The principle of self-determination requires that a territory cannot be acquired or transferred without the population expressing its will; otherwise a breach of *jus cogens* would be involved, voiding the transfer.[77]

There are territorial acquisitions in the narrow sense (where a State acquires a territory of another State), and in the broad sense (where territorial changes involve the emergence of a new State). In the latter case, it could be argued that a new State acquires the territory it is based on, while the State to which it belonged loses it. Peremptory norms impact both kinds of situations, due to a common principle according to which the actions in breach of *jus cogens* are void and can bring no rights to a wrongdoer. The relevance of the principle *ex injuria jus non oritur* is sometimes contested,[78] but all major cases involving the illegality, nullity, non-recognition or otherwise of the entities and situations established in violation of peremptory norms are based, in conceptual and normative terms, on that principle.

Nullity for contradicting *jus cogens* applies both to the acquisition of territory and the creation of States.[79] It is argued that nullity cannot apply to the creation of States because the illegally established State would be there even if it is considered as a nullity.[80] This view misconstrues the essence of nullity, which is a concept referring not to factual existence but to legal status. The acts that are void are not the same as non-existent acts. Non-existent acts are those that are either performed by the person with no requisite legal capacity or, most importantly, to the acts that are not performed as a matter of fact, such as the ineffective blockade whose enforcement would result in

---

[74] *Wall*, para. 87.　　[75] Cassese (1994), 188.

[76] *Western Sahara, ICJ Reports*, 1975, 13; Cassese (1994), 188–189.

[77] Cassese (1994), 188–190. *Per contra* Brownlie (2003), 161.

[78] cf Talmon (2004), 126–129. Among others, Talmon challenges the view of Sir Hersch Lauterpacht that the principle *ex injuria jus non oritur* is a general principle of law recognized by civilized nations, because domestic legal systems arguably recognize no such principle. However, it must be emphasized that general principles of law in terms of Article 38 of the International Court's Statute do not necessarily refer to the principles accepted in domestic legal systems but also incorporate the principles specific to the international community. cf Schachter, *International Law in Theory and Practice* (1991), 50.

[79] Dugard, Collective Non-Recognition: The Failure of South Africa's Bantustan States, *Boutros Boutros-Ghali—Amicorum Discipulorumque Liber—Peace, Development, Democracy*, vol. I (1998), 402. See also Crawford (1979), 420, on *jus cogens* in the law of the use of force as barring the extinction of States. This seems to be the other side of the coin in terms of preventing the validity of territorial changes contradicting *jus cogens*.

[80] Talmon (2004), 134–135, 137, 144.

the wrongful act. In difference to that, there are acts that exist in factual terms but attract absolute nullity, that is, they are null and void *ab initio*. The nullity of such acts refers to the lack of their legal effectiveness as opposed to their factual effectiveness. Nullity is attracted by those acts which are performed and brought about as a matter of fact.[81] If this is considered, then the illegally established entity can attract nullity even if it continues its factual existence.

It must be understood that nullity refers not to the reversal of the factual situation *per se*, but to its legal effect and the consequent legal requirement that it must be reversed. It refers to the normative requirements in relation to the factual situation. The reversal of the factual situation is the implication that follows, or must follow, from the nullity of the relevant act. In other words, nullity is the legal cause of reversal, and the fact that the factual situation is not reversed does not mean that it involves no nullity. This can be further seen in situations where a treaty conflicting with *jus cogens* is declared as void but the parties still apply it in their bilateral relations and maintain the situation established under it. In this context, the nullity is there, but the factual situation is not reversed, yet hardly can it be seriously contended that the treaty in such cases cannot be void. The situation is very much the same with regard to the creation of States and here too the issues of validity and factual existence must be separated from each other. In fact, the practice on the subject of entities and situations established in breach of peremptory norms confirms that the relevant sanction is nullity.

In practice, specific peremptory norms, such as the prohibition of force and the principle of self-determination, have voided several territorial changes. Jordan's occupation of Eastern Jerusalem since 1948 was a violation of Article 2(4) of the UN Charter and consequently Jordan was unable to acquire the sovereignty over that area.[82] The Israeli Occupation of the West Bank and East Jerusalem was similarly void for an identical reason. Therefore, despite the passage of time, the relevant territories are denoted as occupied territories, Israel as the occupying power and this has been so affirmed the UN Security Council in Resolution 672(1990),[83] and by the International Court in the *Wall* Advisory Opinion. This situation is due to the fact that, as Cassese emphasizes,

at present general international law has departed markedly from the principle of effectiveness: *de facto* situations brought about by force of arms are no longer automatically endorsed and sanctioned by international legal standards. At present the

---

[81] Jennings, Nullity and Effectiveness in International Law, *Cambridge Essays in International Law* (1965), 66–67. For the distinction between non-existent and void acts see also Guggenheim (1949), 202–210.

[82] Cassese, Legal Considerations on the International Status of Jerusalem, 3 *Palestinian Yearbook of International Law* (1986), 22.

[83] To which Israel has objected, contending that East Jerusalem is under its sovereignty, Quigley (1992–1994), 51.

principle of legality is overriding—at least at the normative level—and effectiveness must yield to it.[84]

The position at general international law is supplemented by the effect of the public order provision in the Fourth Geneva Convention—Article 47, which proclaims invalidity of the measures aimed at or following from the annexation of the occupied territory. As Quigley points out, despite the views of Israel and the USA, the steps taken by Israel to incorporate East Jerusalem are invalid and this territory remains an occupied territory.[85]

The voidness of the forcible territorial acquisition also brings about the nullity of acts ensuing from the illegal exercise of sovereign powers claimed in the process of or after the forcible territorial acquisition. The typical case could be when the occupying power legislates with regard to the occupied territory in a way exceeding its powers under Articles 42–56 of the 1907 Hague Regulations.[86] It is noteworthy that the UN Security Council referred to the inadmissibility of the acquisition of territory by force and regarded that the attempts of Israel to impose its laws, regulations and jurisdiction over the occupied Golan Heights are null and void.[87]

The International Court demonstrated in the *Wall* case that the Israel's legislative and administrative measures in the Occupied Palestinian Territory must be considered in the context of nullity. The Court referred to the lack of legal force and total invalidity of Israel's legislative and administrative measures to change the status of Jerusalem after its occupation, 'including expropriation of land and properties, transfer of populations and legislation aimed at the incorporation of the occupied section', as emphasized in UN Security Council Resolution 298 (1971). The Court further referred to Resolution 478 (1980), declaring null and void Israel's Basic Law making Jerusalem the 'complete and united' capital of Israel, as well as 'all legislative and administrative measures . . . which have altered or purport to alter the character and status of the Holy City of Jerusalem'.[88] The Court also examined the treatment by the Security Council of 'the policy and practices of Israel in establishing settlements in the Palestinian and other Arab territories occupied since 1967' in 'flagrant violation' of the provisions of the Fourth Geneva Convention dealing with the rights and responsibilities of the occupying power, especially Article 49. The Council had in its Resolutions 446 (1979), 452 (1979) and 465 (1980) affirmed that those settlements had 'no legal validity'.[89] The Court concluded that, all these actions being without legal effect, they have done nothing to alter the situation that these territories

---

[84] Cassese (1986), 32.

[85] Quigley, The Israel–PLO Agreements versus the Geneva Civilians Convention, 7 *Palestinian Yearbook of International Law* (1992–1994), 52.

[86] Schütz, Der internationale *ordre public* (1984), 30.

[87] UNSC Res 497 (1981).   [88] Opinion, paras 74–75.   [89] Opinion, para. 99.

(including East Jerusalem) remain occupied territories and Israel has continued to have the status of occupying power.[90] These findings corresponded to the context involving the breach of the prohibition of the use of force, serious breaches of humanitarian law and the ensuing illegality of forcible territorial acquisitions, and the Court has duly emphasized this link. These are in essence the findings as to the negative and positive effects of public order, the former being manifested in the nullity of Israel's actions, and the latter in the continuous operation of the law of occupation which is the applicable legal regime required by international public order.

The impact of the prohibition of the use of force was relevant in the cases of East Timor, East Jerusalem, and Northern Cyprus. Nullity and public order effects were implied in the European Court's treatment of the status of Northern Cyprus in *Loizidou* where the Court, having referred to the illegality of forcible territorial changes, considered the TRNC as legally nonexistent for the purposes of attribution of wrongful acts, and instead decided to attribute the relevant acts to Turkey.[91] As Cassese submits, the principle of self-determination has precluded Indonesia's acquisition of title over East Timor and of Israel over the occupied territories.[92] According to Hannikainen, Indonesia violated a number of peremptory norms in East Timor, such as the prohibition of aggressive use of force, the principle of self-determination and respect for human rights (through mass killings, torture and executions), and hence its title in East Timor was null and void.[93]

It seems that in all these cases the invalidity of titles as confirmed by UN organs is implementing and declaratory of the *jus cogens* nullity, not just a discretionary action.[94]

Arguably, in some cases forcible territorial acquisitions are treated as valid. It is suggested that 'India's successful annexation of Goa in 1961 may seem difficult to reconcile with the non-recognition of Israel's claims to Jerusalem and Golan heights'.[95] Brownlie considers that if force is used to gain a title over the territory in realization of the principle of self-determination, acquiescence and prescription can more easily cure ensuing illegality.[96] But this is contradictory: to require additional confirmation of title in such cases through the attitudes of States is to neglect the inherent effect of the primary norm on self-determination.

---

[90] Opinion, para. 78. This accords with the findings of the UN General Assembly and Security Council that the incorporation of Walvis Bay into South Africa was null and void and the territory continued to be the integral part of South West Africa, GA Res 32/9D, SCR 432 (1978).

[91] *Loizidou*, Merits ECtHR Reports 1996-VI (Grand Chamber), paras 39–44.

[92] Cassese (1994), 188; Imseis, On the Fourth Geneva Convention and the Occupied Palestinian Territory, 44 *Harvard International Law Journal* (2003), 92, 97.

[93] Hannikainen, (1995), 103, 111.   [94] Dugard (1998), 402.

[95] Dugard (1987), 115; the use of force by India was not justified as self-defence, 115–116.

[96] Brownlie (2003), 555.

The case of Goa was not a case of curing illegality through the process of recognition and prescription. The original illegality of the use of force remained and was subject to the duty of reparation, since it has been an illegality separate from the issue of the status of Goa and Indian or Portuguese presence there. But the principle of self-determination anyway required the Portuguese to withdraw. If the process was determined by prescription and acquiescence, then third States, had they so chosen, could protest and demand the restoration of Portuguese sovereignty over Goa. If the principle of self-determination is peremptory, this cannot be reasonable or correct.

It is preferable to attribute this phenomenon to the operation of primary norms. As Dugard states, 'It is the colonial context of India's invasion which distinguishes it from the cases of Jerusalem and the Golan Heights and explains why India had little difficulty in securing recognition of her conquest of Goa.'[97] Justification is thus based on the substance of primary norms, not in deviation from the regime of voidness applicable to breaches of *jus cogens*.

2.2. Amnesties for international crimes

International law has traditionally allowed States, as a matter of post-conflict settlement or otherwise, to free persons having committed crimes from criminal responsibility through amnesties, whether by inter-State agreement or unilateral act. The conceptual essence of such amnesties is to let the crimes concerned go unpunished,[98] in the interests of settlement of the underlying conflict or dispute. Vattel explained the conceptual underpinnings of amnesty, denoting it as 'a perfect oblivion of the past' and suggesting that, 'the end of peace being to extinguish all subject of discord, this should be the leading article of the treaty'.[99] If international law is viewed as a set of norms governing bilateralizable legal relations, such amnesties should pose no conceptual problem because under such view the will and attitude of States prevails, as the sole determinant of legal rights and obligations, over the need to prosecute the crimes against individuals.

As the South African Constitutional Court emphasized, amnesties for serious international crimes undoubtedly impact upon very fundamental rights. As all persons are entitled to the protection by the law against unlawful invasions of their right to life, right to dignity and freedom from torture, when these rights are invaded, those aggrieved have the right to obtain justice through the courts before which the perpetrators are to be held answerable

---

[97] Dugard (1987), 116.

[98] Cassese, *International Criminal Law* (2003), 312–313.

[99] Vattel, *The Law of Nations* (1811), 439.

and 'an amnesty to the perpetrator effectively obliterates such rights'.[100] As Judge Garcia-Ramirez emphasized, 'amnesty implies disremembering and remaining silent about acts that, in principle, are criminal in nature. However, this disremembrance and silence cannot be permitted to cover up the most severe human rights violations, violations that constitute an utter disregard for the dignity of the human being and are repugnant to the conscience of humanity.'[101]

Amnesties are sometimes viewed as an element of re-establishment of peace after an international or internal conflict or of the processes of national reconciliation and have been frequent occurrences in practice. An earlier example is the amnesty granted under the 1923 Lausanne Peace Treaty to the perpetrators of the Armenian massacres in 1915 during which one million Armenians were killed by Turkish forces. Subsequently, amnesty has been resorted to in the context of terminating international or internal conflicts. By the 1962 Evian Treaty between Algeria and France, which related to Algerian independence, the parties undertook to grant a complete amnesty for the conduct and actions performed during the war in Algeria that preceded the independence of that country. Similarly, in the India–Pakistan conflict regarding East Pakistan in which one million East Pakistanis were killed, the two States have, after initial intentions to try the perpetrators, agreed to grant them complete impunity.

The series of amnesties have followed the departure of dictatorial regimes in several countries. While after the colonels' regime in Greece no amnesty was offered and hundreds of perpetrators were prosecuted for torture and related acts, Latin American countries have widely embarked on the path of granting amnesties of various scope to the officials of dictatorial regimes. Such developments took place in Chile, Uruguay, Argentina, Haiti, Guatemala, and Honduras.[102] In some cases these amnesties were in fact self-amnesties, for instance in Chile after the departure of the Pinochet regime. During the Pinochet regime torture was a weapon of governmental policy and 'when the regime was about to end, it passed legislation designed to afford an amnesty to those who had engaged in institutionalised torture'.[103] Generally, amnesties for the perpetrators of serious violations of human rights and humanitarian law have promoted the sense of impunity and the conviction that the perpetrators of serious international crimes will be able to obtain impunity by, among others, reference to national or international peace and reconciliation, or simply as a matter of power. As Reisman observes,

---

[100] 4 SA 1996, 681.
[101] Concurring Opinion, Castillo Paez, 116 ILR, 524.
[102] For an overview see Roht-Ariaza (1990), 484–485; Roht-Ariaza and Gibson (1998), 843.
[103] Lord Browne-Wilkinson, *Pinochet*, 2 All ER (1999), 109.

Acts of kindness or grace to current violators, or, as is sometimes the case, convenient deals, may have high, long-term costs: Potential violators may assume that, threats of strict application of law notwithstanding, when the time comes for settlement, they, too, can strike a bargain in which they will be forgiven.[104]

It is this background against which Hitler's reference to the impunity of the perpetrators of Armenian massacres should be seen.

It can be stated with certainty that the Second World War, especially the affirmation through the Nuremberg and Tokyo Trials that certain crimes are prosecuted in the interest of the entire international community, has proved a turning point in the attitude of the international community that there should be some limitations as to the types of acts that can be subject to post-conflict amnesties.

Although amnesty has often accompanied and been embodied in the post-conflict arrangements such as peace treaties, it has not been viewed in practice as an indispensable element of terminating wars. After the Second World War, the 1947 peace treaties with Hungary, Romania, Bulgaria and Finland required the prosecution in these States of every person having committed, ordered or abetted war crimes and crimes against peace and humanity.[105]

After adoption of the 1949 Geneva Conventions regarding the protection of the victims of war, and the 1977 Protocols thereto, which impose the obligation to prosecute war criminals, amnesties for war criminals are viewed as contrary to these treaty obligations.[106] These instruments also seem to outlaw the amnesties and related measures that exclude the civil liability of the State. Amnesties of such kind would contradict the duty of States-parties to the Geneva Conventions not to absolve themselves or each other from the regime of liability of these Conventions. The development of human rights standards in conventional and customary law has been another, and independent, factor that operates as a limitation on the power of States to grant amnesty.

Once international law recognizes that certain crimes—genocide, torture, crimes against humanity, war crimes—are outlawed in the community inter-est and that their prosecution is required under the overriding *jus cogens*, then the above-mentioned traditional conceptual model becomes problematic. This is so because peremptory norms prevail over the very acts authorizing amnesties contradicting these norms.[107] An amnesty for international crimes

---

[104] Reisman, Legal Responses to Genocide and Other Massive Violations of Human Rights, 59 *Law and Contemporary Problems* (1996), 79.

[105] Art. 6, Peace Treaty with Hungary; Art. 5, Peace Treaty with Bulgaria; Art. 6, Peace Treaty with Romania; Art. 9, Peace Treaty with Romania.

[106] De Zayas, A., Amnesty Clause, 3 *EPIL* (1982), 17.

[107] Cassese, *International Criminal Law* (2003), 316.

would contradict the peremptory norm requiring the prosecution and punishment of war criminals, and hence it would be null and void.[108]

In *Furundzija* the ICTY gave a conceptual explanation for the invalidity and illegality of amnesties for perpetrators of *jus cogens* crimes:

> It would be senseless to argue, on the one hand, that on account of the *jus cogens* value of the prohibition against torture, treaties or customary rules providing for torture would be null and void *ab initio*, and then be unmindful of a State say, taking national measures authorising or condoning torture or absolving its perpetrators through an amnesty law.[109]

The Special Court for Sierra Leone adopted a similar approach with regard to international crimes to which universal jurisdiction extends by observing that

> it stands to reason that a State cannot sweep such crimes into oblivion and forgetfulness which other States have jurisdiction to prosecute by reason of the fact that the obligation to protect human dignity is a peremptory norm and has assumed the nature of obligation *erga omnes*.[110]

The Spanish court also approved the reasoning that amnesties contrary to *jus cogens* shall not be recognized by national courts.[111] The South African court implied the existence of the peremptory prohibition of the amnesty for crimes against humanity when it held that 'there is an exception to the peremptory rule prohibiting an amnesty in relation to crimes against humanity' contained in Article 6(5) of the Additional Protocol II to the Geneva Conventions.[112] This reference to the exception from a rule, which is considered below, confirms the existence of the rule itself.

The impermissibility of amnesties for core international crimes is contested by reference to the occurrence of amnesties in practice. As Scharf contends, 'notwithstanding an array of General Assembly resolutions calling for the prosecution of crimes against humanity and the strong policy and jurisprudential arguments warranting such a rule, the practice of States does not yet support the present existence of an obligation under customary inter-

---

[108] Domb, Treatment of War Crimes in Peace Settlements—Prosecution or Amnesty? Dinstein and Tabory (eds), *War Crimes in International Law* (1996), 311–317; Gattini, To What Extent are State Immunity and Non-Justiciability Major Hurdles to Individuals' Claims for War Damages? 1 *Journal of International Criminal Justice* (2003), 348–349.

[109] *Furundzija*, 38 ILM 1999, 349, para. 155.

[110] *Prosecutor v Kallon*, 13 March 2004, para. 71. The same Special Court reiterated in *Prosecutor v Gbao* (25 May 2004) that, owing to the effect of *jus cogens*, 'there is a crystallised international norm to the effect that a government cannot grant amnesty for serious crimes under international law,' para. 9.

[111] Carrasco and Fernandez, Case-note on *Pinochet* (Spanish National Court), 93 *AJIL* (1999), 696.

[112] [1996] All SA, 26–27.

national law to refrain from conferring amnesty for such crimes'.[113] Scharf further reiterates that 'since there is no international duty to prosecute crimes against humanity, or war crimes in an internal conflict, an amnesty for peace deal would not violate international law'.[114] This argument is flawed for several reasons.

First and foremost, this approach is based on dubious conceptual ground by demonstrating that the denial of the duty to prosecute core international crimes implies the affirmation of blanket permission for States to grant amnesties to the perpetrators of such crimes, whatever the types and conditions of the respective amnesty. If there is no duty to prosecute, then every blanket and unconditional amnesty would be lawful, including the amnesties proclaimed by dictatorial regimes to absolve themselves from crimes they have committed. Therefore, those who reject the existence of the duty to prosecute the core international crimes ought to consider the consequences of their assertions.

Second, this argument is flawed because if an act is void for its conflict with *jus cogens*, it is no longer necessary to find support in State practice for the existence of the additional duty of States to act in accordance with such nullity.

Third, what is material is not the positive existence of the prohibitive rule concerning amnesties specifically, but the analysis of the compliance of national legislative instruments with human rights and humanitarian law standards both under conventional and customary law. To illustrate, general human rights treaties do not expressly prohibit the amnesties that contravene the rights they protect, but this has not prevented treaty-based organs from declaring the relevant amnesties illegal.

Fourth, the assertion against the duty to prosecute core *jus cogens* crime fails also in the face of the principle of non-applicability of statutory limitations to these crimes which, as has been recognized among others by the Italian court in *Haas and Priebke*, is itself a peremptory principle. Otherwise, not only the duty to prosecute but also the very universal jurisdiction over *jus cogens* crimes would be rendered meaningless. Therefore, if international law does not accept as valid the enactment by States of legislation limiting the prosecutability of core crimes to a certain period of time, is it not

---

[113] Scharf, Swapping Amnesty for Peace: Was There a Duty to Prosecute International Crimes in Haiti? 31 *Texas International Law Journal* (1995–96), 59; Dugard, Possible Conflicts of Jurisdiction with Truth Commissions, in Cassese, Gaeta and Jones (eds), *The Rome Statute of the International Criminal Court—A Commentary* (2002), 698; Scharf, The Letter of the Law: The Scope of the International Legal Obligation to Prosecute Human Rights Crimes, 53 *Law and Contemporary Problems* (1996), 39–40. But Dugard accepts that amnesties for serious international crimes are prohibited, Dugard, Dealing With Crimes of a Past Regime: Is Amnesty Still an Option? 12 *Leiden Journal of International Law* (2000), 1005, 1015.

[114] Scharf, The Amnesty Exception to the Jurisdiction of the International Criminal Court, 32 *Cornell Journal of International Law* (1999), 526.

self-contradictory to argue that the same international law would accept the validity of laws that entirely bar the prosecution of the same core crimes?

Fifth, amnesty laws are territorial, as the prescriptive jurisdiction of the State that enacts them does not extend outside its territory. The recognition of such laws outside the enacting State's territory can only be envisaged in the context of the doctrine of the act of State. As the relevant evidence suggests,[115] the doctrine of the act of State is substantially qualified and cannot be used for recognition of the acts contradicting international *jus cogens* as an element of national public policies. In fact, there is hardly any case reported where the amnesty for *jus cogens* crimes has gained validity in another legal system. The possibilities of this remain limited because of the uniform disapproval of amnesties by the relevant international bodies.

The illegality and voidness of amnesties conflicting with *jus cogens* can also be established on alternative grounds such as the conflict with the right to fair trial and the right to remedies under international human rights instruments. The amnesties granted by States to the perpetrators of serious breaches of humanitarian law and human rights norms have mostly commanded condemnation and disapproval by the competent human rights organs which treat them as wrongful and void acts rather than valid practice. Tribunals and quasi-judicial bodies are practically unanimous in rejecting the legal force of amnesties which free perpetrators of *jus cogens* crimes as measures lacking legal force and validity.

The UN Human Rights Committee has emphasized in its General Comment 20 that amnesties for the perpetrators of torture are generally incompatible with the International Covenant on Civil and Political Rights.[116] Scharf contends that by emphasizing that amnesties are 'generally incompatible' the Committee has found certain kinds of amnesties acceptable.[117] But the fact remains that the Committee has not expressed any support for the legality under the Covenant of any kind of amnesty. Scharf's understanding as to how the Committee views the legality of amnesties not only reads too much into the phraseology chosen by the Committee but also fails in the face of the practice developed by this organ.

In *Hugo Rodriguez* the Human Rights Committee considered that the amnesty proclaimed by Uruguayan authorities violated several provisions of the Covenant such as the right to obtain adequate remedies. The amnesty law effectively excluded 'the possibility of investigation into past human rights

---

[115] Below, Chapter 19.

[116] General Comment No. 20, para. 15; according to *The Princeton Principles on Universal Jurisdiction*, 'Amnesties are generally inconsistent with the obligation of states to provide accountability for serious crimes under international law', and 'The exercise of universal jurisdiction with respect to serious crimes under international law ... shall not be precluded by amnesties which are incompatible with the international legal obligations of the granting state' (Principle 7).

[117] Scharf (1995–96), 27.

abuses and thereby prevents the State-party from discharging its responsibility to provide effective remedies to the victims of those abuses'. Furthermore, 'in adopting this law, the State-party has contributed to an atmosphere of impunity'.[118] On many occasions the Human Rights Committee has disapproved the amnesties enacted by States-parties to the Covenant as incompatible with the Covenant obligations to prosecute and punish the relevant violations.[119] The UN Committee against Torture has also rejected the legality and validity of amnesties for perpetrators of serious human rights violations.[120]

The organs of the American Convention on Human Rights have consistently opposed the amnesties granted in violation of that Convention. Even if some have assumed that the findings of these organs would not have the crucial practical impact on the conduct of States-parties in this field,[121] the Convention organs have persistently followed their approach.

The Inter-American Commission of Human Rights disapproved the amnesties hindering the victims' rights to achieve prosecution of the perpetrators of the massacre in the *Las Hojas* case related to the massacre perpetrated by the Salvadorian armed forces, where it considered that the Government of El Salvador has improperly used an amnesty law in violation of its obligations under international human rights law.[122] The case concerned the 1987 Amnesty Decree of the Legislative Assembly, which provided for impunity from prosecution for the perpetrators of the massacre and served as the basis on which the Supreme Court of El Salvador dismissed the case. The Court specified that this application of the Amnesty Decree constituted a clear violation of the duty of the Salvadorian Government to investigate and punish the violations of the rights of the Las Hojas victims, and to provide compensation to them. The amnesty 'legally eliminated the possibility of an effective investigation and the prosecution of the responsible parties, as well as proper compensation for the victims'.[123]

With regard to the amnesties for the perpetrators of atrocities during the

---

[118] *Hugo Rodriguez*, para. 12.

[119] The Committee disapproved on these grounds the amnesties enacted by Yemen, CCPR/C/79/Add.51; A/50/40, paras 242–265; El Salvador, CCPR/C/79/Add.34; A/49/40, paras 209–224; Congo, CCPR/C/79/Add.118; Chile, CCPR/C/79/Add.104; Peru, CCPR/CO/70/PER; Haiti, CCPR/C/79/Add.49; A/50/40, paras 224–241; Ecuador, CCPR/C/79/Add.92; Lebanon, CCPR/C/79/Add.78. On the other hand, the Committee commended Paraguay for not intending to enact the amnesty law, CCPR/C/79/Add.48; A/50/40, paras 192–223.

[120] The Committee has disapproved the amnesty laws of Croatia, A/54/44, paras. 61–71; Azerbaijan, A/55/44, paras 64–69; Kyrgyzstan, A/55/44, paras 70–75; Peru, A/55/44, paras 56–63; Senegal, A/51/44, paras. 102–119. The Committee has commended Paraguay for having not adopted the amnesty law, A/52/44, paras 189–213.

[121] Lutz, Responses to amnesties by the Inter-American system for the protection of human rights, in Harris and Livingstone (eds), *The Inter-American System of Human Rights* (1998), 370.

[122] *Las Hojas*, Report No. 26/92, Case 10.287, 24 September 1992, 14 *HRLJ* 1993, 167.

[123] Id., 168, 170.

Argentine 'dirty war', the Commission pronounced that these amnesties were incompatible with the right of victims to a fair trial, especially the right to bring criminal actions against the perpetrators. By enacting the amnesty law, Argentina failed to comply with its duty to investigate the violations under Article 1(1) of the Convention.[124] Identical violations were implicated in the enactment of the Uruguayan amnesty law.[125]

The Inter-American Court of Human Rights has repeatedly and unambiguously affirmed that approach in *Castillo Paez*, *Gangaram Panday*, *Loyaza Tamayo* and *Barrios Altos* on the ground that such amnesties prevent the punishment of those responsible for serious human rights violations. The Court's reasoning is clearly linked to the incompatibility of amnesties with the observance of basic human rights and emphasizes that such amnesties have no legal force.

In *Castillo Paez*, the Court dealt with the Peruvian law which granted an amnesty to all persons responsible for serious human rights violations committed in the course of what that State denoted as the 'fight against terrorism', whether or not they had been named, prosecuted, tried or investigated.[126] The Court emphasized that these amnesty laws violate international obligations of a State, in particular under human rights conventions, and lead to impunity.[127] Peru justified its amnesty laws by the 'difficult situation prevailing in the country', and emphasized that they were not an impediment for the compensation of victims.[128] The Court nevertheless considered that amnesty laws create 'internal difficulties' that prevent the identification of perpetrators of human rights violations, since they obstruct investigation and access to justice.[129] States retain in these circumstances the duty to prosecute those responsible for human rights violations.

In *Gangaram Panday*, the Inter-American Court was prepared to consider the amnesty laws freeing persons guilty of violations of the Convention of their responsibility as a violation of the Convention, if the sufficient evidence had been presented to it that such a law had indeed been adopted.[130] In *Loyaza Tamayo* the respondent State argued that the fulfilment of the duty to investigate the breaches of the Convention and punish victims was prevented by its legislation which granted general amnesty to military, police and civilian personnel involved in violations.[131] The Court held that the respondent's legislation precluded the implementation of the Convention obligations. Thus, amnesty laws could not be invoked as an excuse for avoiding compliance with international obligations.[132]

---

[124] Report No. 29/92 on Argentina, 13 *HRLJ* 1992, 339.
[125] Report No. 28/92 on Uruguay, 13 *HRLJ* 1992, 343–344.
[126] Castillo Paez, 116 ILR 516–517.
[127] Castillo Paez, 116 ILR 516.   [128] Castillo Paez, 116 ILR 517.
[129] Castillo Paez, 116 ILR 518.   [130] Gangaram Panday, 116 ILR 317.
[131] Loayza Tamayo, 116 ILR, 435.   [132] Loayza Tamayo, 116 ILR, 435.

In *Barrios Altos*, the Court held that the Peruvian amnesty law 'prevented the investigation, capture, prosecution and conviction of those responsible' for torture, extrajudicial, summary and arbitrary executions and forced disappearances, and hence violated Articles 1, 8 and 25 of the Convention and had no legal significance.[133]

This uniform approach of the human rights treaty organs has met no visible contradiction. The experience of these organs regarding amnesties for the perpetrators of serious human rights violations effectively disapproves the contentions that in order to view amnesties for international crimes as illegal the specific norms to that effect must be searched for. This means that in order for the 'secondary' process of amnesty to be outlawed, it is not necessary to have the specific norm aimed explicitly and exactly at that result; it is rather sufficient to point to primary human rights norms to which the relevant amnesty measures contradict. It seems that the similar logic of normative conflict can be applied to the amnesties contravening peremptory norms of general international law. Once the substantive peremptory norm is contravened, it is an artificial and superfluous requirement to search for the 'secondary' norm specifically dictating that the given amnesty is illegal.

A separate question arises in the case of amnesties which do not free perpetrators of international crimes in a blanket way[134] but establish an institutionalized procedure of finding the truth and relieving those recognizing their part in crimes of their criminal liability, as was the case of South African Truth and Reconciliation Commission.[135]

According to the South African Interim Constitution, in order to advance peace and reconciliation, 'amnesty shall be granted in respect of acts, omissions and offences associated with political objectives and committed in the course of the conflicts of the past'.[136] Pursuant to the Interim Constitution, the South African Parliament enacted in 1995 the Promotion of National Unity and Reconciliation Act, which embodies the policy of conditional amnesty. The Act established the Truth and Reconciliation Commission, whose mandate consists in establishing the complete picture of gross human rights violations during the apartheid period by means of hearings and investigations. The Truth Commission can grant an amnesty to each

---

[133] *Barrios Altos*, 41 ILM 2002, 852, 854.

[134] *Pinochet* (Spain), 344, dismissing the Chilean amnesty irrespective of whether it contradicted *jus cogens* because it was not a true pardon.

[135] Dugard (2002), 694–695; Byrnes and Kamminga, ILA Final Report on the Exercise of Universal Jurisdiction in Respect of Gross Human Rights Offences (2000), 15; on the South African TRC see Rakate, The South African Amnesty Process: Is International Law at the Crossroads? 56 *Zeitschrift für öffentliches Recht* (2001), 97; McGregor, Individual Accountability in South Africa: Cultural Optimum or Political Façade? 95 *AJIL* (2001), 32.

[136] Interim Constitution of 1993, quoted in Bell, *Peace Agreements and Human Rights* (2000), 273.

person having committed gross violations of human rights if they make full disclosure of the facts related to the crimes committed in the course of conflicts of the past. Persons granted amnesty are excluded, with regard to the pertinent acts, from criminal or civil prosecution.[137] The Commission is supposed to consider each applicant's case on individual basis.[138] The crimes the Commission is concerned with are 'the killing, abduction, torture or ill-treatment' committed in furtherance of political objectives, which fully meets the qualification for war crimes and crimes against humanity under international law.[139]

The case of the South African Truth and Reconciliation Commission presents us, so the argument goes, not with the case of impunity but with an alternative to criminal prosecution on the basis of the will of the relevant actors.[140] But the fact still remains that criminal prosecutions are set aside despite international requirements. That the standing of the South African amnesty arrangements is doubtful under international law can be seen in the arguments that South African courts used to uphold the legality of these arrangements. The Cape of Good Hope Provincial Division court, having noted the argument of the incompatibility with international *jus cogens* of the amnesty for war crimes, referred to the constitutional principle that the standing of customary international law in South African legal order is subject to the South African Constitution, and on these grounds the Constitution enabled the Parliament 'to pass a law even if such law would be contrary to *jus cogens*'.[141]

The South African Constitutional Court affirmed the legality of non-prosecution of perpetrators of serious international crimes as a consequence of the Truth Commission's procedures in *AZAPO*.[142] But the Court did not base its decision on international law.[143] This is clear from Judge Mahomed's reasoning, which considered the constitutionality of the Truth Commission, not its conformity with international law. The Court was asked to declare the amnesty law unconstitutional for its conflict with international law. But the Court identified the issue of the compatibility of the relevant legislation with the constitution as the only issue to be adjudicated upon. The Court noted that the relevant international treaties were not *per se* part of South African

---

[137] Dugard, Is the Truth and Reconciliation Process Compatible with International Law? The Unanswered Question. *South African Journal of Human Rights* (1998), 259; Dugard (2002), 700.

[138] Though the TRC has breached its mandate by granting the collective amnesty to 37 applicants, and this was overruled by the High Court, McGregor (2001), 39.

[139] Dugard (1998), 259–264.

[140] Dugard (1999), 1012.

[141] Case No 4895/96, 2 All SA [1996], 15.

[142] 4 SA 1996, 671.

[143] Dugard (1998) considers that international law factors were not central to the Court's reasoning.

law, nor was customary international law if it conflicted with the Constitution and therefore the outcome under those sources of law was irrelevant for judging the legality or constitutionality of the South African amnesty arrangements.[144]

That there is a *prima facie* difference between blanket amnesties and the option of truth commissions is clear. But this difference may still, one could suggest, fall short of establishing a difference in legal impact on the enforcement of peremptory norms on criminal responsibility. The relevant international instruments and customary norms which impose criminal accountability in perpetrators of *jus cogens* crimes do not seem to have a discriminating effect in requiring prosecution of one crime and not another depending on the type of measures excluding such accountability. The duty to prosecute still persists irrespective of whether the impunity obtains through a blanket amnesty or a truth and reconciliation mechanism. That is partly confirmed by the fact that the doctrinal supporters of Truth and Reconciliation Commissions in cases of *jus cogens* crimes try to doubt the existence of the duty to prosecute in the first place,[145] which implies that even the option of truth commissions is in at least potential contradiction with the duty to prosecute *jus cogens* crimes. For his part, Dugard concedes the absence of a clear rule exempting the Truth Commissions from the general *jus cogens* regime applicable to amnesties.[146]

That there can be differences between various types of amnesty in terms of their permissibility, but that this distinction cannot justify amnesties for most serious crimes, is illustrated by Judge Garcia Ramirez, who referred to self-amnesties promulgated by and for those in power and distinguished them from amnesties 'that are the result of a peace process, have a democratic base and a reasonable scope, that preclude prosecution of acts and behaviours of members of rival factions, but leave open the possibility of punishment for the kind of very egregious acts that no faction ever approves or views as appropriate'.[147] It is thus the scope of amnesties, and the type of crimes they cover, that remain the predominant criterion for judging their compatibility with international law.

The duties to prosecute the core international crimes both under conventional and customary law are stated in quite unconditional and imperative terms, thus leaving no room for some kind of margin of appreciation for considering alternative factors to justify the failures of prosecution. This is so with regard to *jus cogens* crimes for which the international community requires unconditional prosecution. This is further affirmed, as the Inter-American Commission emphasized with regard to Uruguayan amnesty law,

---

[144] 4 SA 1996, 688–689; for the relevance of Article 6(5) of the Second Geneva Protocol see below, note 150.

[145] Dugard (2002), 698; Dugard (1998), 267.

[146] Dugard (2002), 700.   [147] *Castillo Paez*, 116 ILR 525.

by the requirement that amnesties absolving the perpetrators of torture are impermissible even if they leave the victims the option to pursue civil remedies.[148] Truth Commissions can play a useful role provided that they are not used as a tool to avoid prosecution for core international crimes. That the establishment of the truth is not an alternative to the compliance with the duty to prosecute is reflected in the mandate of the Guatemalan Truth Commission under which the crimes against humanity, torture and genocide are exempted from the amnesty regime.[149]

It seems that the arguments favouring the legality, recognition or otherwise of certain 'limited' amnesties for international crimes fail to suggest any firm criteria of how the permissible amnesties should be distinguished from impermissible ones, and especially how any such distinction can avoid legitimating those amnesties which offer impunity to the perpetrators of serious international crimes.

This categorical and conceptual problem with the international validity of amnesties coupled with Truth Commissions is not unsettled in practice which, while denouncing amnesties with regard to *jus cogens* crimes, does not formulate a different regime applicable to institutionalized amnesties. All support for amnesties in favour of truth commissions stems from doctrinal writings or national court decisions which can hardly reach different conclusions because in most cases such institutionalized amnesties form part of constitutional arrangements. So far, international law does not accord recognition to any type of amnesty for perpetrators of *jus cogens* crimes irrespective of their institutional framework. If one perhaps should not make hasty conclusions that institutional amnesties are categorically outlawed, nor should the opposite hasty conclusion be prompted.

It is widely debated both in doctrine and practice whether international humanitarian law, particularly the Second 1977 Protocol to the Geneva Conventions allows the grant of amnesties for violations of humanitarian law. The reference in this regard is usually made to Article 6(5) of Protocol II, which requires that at the end of hostilities 'authorities in power shall endeavour to grant the broadest possible amnesty to persons who have participated in the armed conflict, or those deprived of their liberty for reasons related to the armed conflict, whether they are interned or detained'. The Cape Provincial Court saw Article 6(5) as the exception from the peremptory duty to prosecute international crimes.[150] The South African Constitutional Court construed Article 6(5) as allowing amnesty for international criminals.[151] But this construction distorts the true meaning of that clause

---

[148] Report No. 29/92 on Argentina, 13 *HRLJ* 1992; Report No. 28/92 on Uruguay, 13 *HRLJ* 1992.

[149] Roth-Ariaza and Gibson, The Developing Jurisprudence on Amnesty, 20 *Human Rights Quarterly* (1998), 852.

[150] 3 All SA [1996], 26–27.   [151] 689–690.

which requires merely that combatants shall not be tried for acts of war and has nothing to do with amnesties for international criminals.[152]

Amnesties are sometimes justified by reference to some extra-legal considerations of policy which have by themselves nothing to do with the legality of the amnesty measures. But it is worth considering them as they form the element of the pertinent debate. One such consideration is the democratic legitimacy of the measures on which amnesties and Truth Commissions are based. Nevertheless, a State act with intended international effects adopted through democratic participation is still a State act subject to international law and its validity depends on compliance with public order; its validity is not granted. To illustrate further, a treaty contravening *jus cogens* can be invalidated even if it is concluded by democratically elected governments and ratified by democratically elected parliaments. It is unclear why the case of amnesties should be otherwise.

The UN Human Rights Committee disapproved the Uruguayan Amnesty law even as the State-party contended that 'the notions of democracy and reconciliation ought to be taken into account when considering the laws on amnesty and on the lapsing of prosecutions'. On the contrary, the Committee considered that the law precluding prosecution for serious human rights violations was undermining the democratic order.[153] The contention of the State-party that the investigation of the past events 'is tantamount to reviving the confrontation between persons and groups . . . will not contribute to reconciliation, pacification and the strengthening of democratic institutions' was not considered relevant either.[154] The Inter-American Commission has disapproved the Argentine laws No. 23.521 and No. 23.492 which precluded the criminal responsibility of perpetrators of the 'dirty war', even though the respondent Government contended that these laws were the product of the democratic process, being 'actions taken by democratic bodies because of the compelling need for national reconciliation and consolidation of the democratic system'.[155] The identical argument was put forward by Uruguay, emphasizing that the amnesty law was supported by the necessary parliamentary majority and was also subject to plebiscite. Uruguay further asserted that 'the express will of the Uruguayan people to close a painful chapter in their history in order to put an end, as their sovereign right, to division among Uruguayans, is not subject to international condemnation'.[156]

---

[152] Byrnes and Kamminga (2000), 15; Bell, *Peace Agreements and Human Rights* (2000) 265; Gavron, Amnesties in the Light of Developments in International Law and the Establishment of the International Criminal Court, 51 *ICLQ* (2002), 100–103; Roht-Ariaza and Gibson (1998), 864–866.

[153] *Hugo Rodriguez*, paras 8.3, 12.4.

[154] Id., para. 8.4.   [155] Report No. 28/92, 13 *HRLJ* 1992, 338–340.

[156] The Commission in its Report No. 29/92 similarly considered them incompatible with the right to fair trial, id., 342–345.

The reliance on democratic legitimacy and popular will is beside the point when compliance by the State with its international obligations is assessed. Whatever the popular will, the State still remains bound by its international obligations and its sovereign powers are qualified accordingly. Individual rights would lose their meaning if the victims of their violations cannot assert and enforce them because of some legal position created by majoritarian decision-making process.

It is also argued, for instance by South African courts, that the conditional amnesty provided for the perpetrators of apartheid is the choice of South African society. It is furthermore alleged that the replacement of criminal accountability with truth commissions is based on the will of society.[157] But as prosecution of core international crimes is the matter of international public order and hence the peremptory choice of international society, it is conceptually incorrect to view national society attitudes as the crucial factor in the permissibility of amnesties for such crimes. In addition, the support of the relevant national societies for the amnesties is not always as clear as it is sometimes assumed. As Dugard emphasizes, the 'opaque origins' of the South African amnesty law, and 'the understandable desire for retribution that persists in many quarters, have made it the most controversial legislation of post-apartheid South Africa'.[158] Indeed, as most if not all international norms exist for a reason which is to meet certain social requirements of the time, the decision of a State not to observe the pertinent norms in its own legal order can hardly be expected to satisfy society as a whole.

On a more general plane, serious international crimes leave in people feelings totally opposite to political forgiveness. This explains why in many cases where amnesties were proclaimed, from the case of Armenian massacres in Turkey to the case of Haiti, the victims sought and enforced private justice through revenge.[159]

This confirms that, in addition to the irrelevance of extra-legal considerations invoked to justify amnesties for international crimes, the analysis of the relevant situations and practice demonstrates that those considerations are based on false generalizations and do not properly articulate the situation on the ground. Genuine peace and long-term reconciliation are possible only if the State takes up the relevant cases and prosecutes the perpetrators in accordance with relevant international obligations to the effect of avoidance of private retribution.

For all these reasons, instances like the South African Truth and Reconciliation Commission could not provide an exemplary model for post-conflict reconciliation in other countries. If the South African model

---

[157] Dugard (1999), 1012.   [158] Dugard (1998), 260.
[159] Bass, *Stay the Hand of Vengeance* (2002), 144–146; Scharf (1995–96), 14.

were to prevail as the dominant pattern of post-conflict arrangements, then probably no single international crime would ever be prosecuted.

One more factor that is invoked in doctrinal contributions to justify the amnesties for international crimes is that in some instances the United Nations has arguably supported the amnesty arrangements. As Scharf points out, the UN has closely worked towards achieving an amnesty in the context of several conflicts such as Cambodia and Haiti, and the Security Council has expressed its support for the process of the restoration of peace in Haiti, which included an amnesty for the perpetrators of the atrocities.[160]

It seems, however, that the expression of the UN attitude on questions of international law can be at most weighty, but by no means conclusive—it would certainly not be serious to imply that the United Nations can do no wrong. In addition, Scharf reads too much into the instances where the United Nations has arguably approved amnesties covering international crimes. The most that can be inferred from such practice is the general support of the UN for the processes of conflict-resolution, not necessarily support for amnesties specifically.

Furthermore, the attitude of the UN on this subject has evolved in the context of subsequent conflicts. On 8 July 1999, the UN Secretary-General announced that he would sign the Sierra Leone Peace Agreement, which provides in Article 9 for 'absolute and free pardon and reprieve to all combatants and collaborators in respect of anything done by them in pursuit of their objectives', but subject to the proviso that the amnesty would not apply to international crimes of genocide, crimes against humanity, war crimes and other serious violations of international humanitarian law.[161] Multilateral efforts of peace-building are also accompanied by the conviction that the perpetrators of serious international crimes shall not go unpunished. To illustrate, Article VI Annex 7 of the Dayton Agreement grants an amnesty to refugees or displaced persons with the exception of those having committed serious violations of international humanitarian law.

The proper consequence of amnesties that conflict with peremptory norms is their nullity. As Byrnes and Kamminga suggest, if amnesties for perpetrators of gross human rights violations are prohibited in international law, such amnesties are null and void and they cannot prevent proceedings in another State.[162]

The effect of amnesties contrary to human rights treaty obligations is dealt with in jurisprudence. In *Loyaza Tamayo* the respondent argued that the fulfilment of the duty to investigate the breaches of the Convention and punish victims was prevented by its legislation, which granted a general

---

[160] Scharf (1996), 41–42, 61.

[161] cf Byrnes and Kamminga (2000), 15; UN Daily Press Briefing, 5–7 July 1999.

[162] Byrnes and Kamminga, 14.

amnesty to military, police and civilian personnel involved in violations. The Court held that the Respondent's legislation precluded the implementation of the Convention obligations. Thus, amnesty laws could not be invoked as an excuse for avoiding compliance with international obligations.[163]

In *Barrios Altos*, the Inter-American Court of Human Rights, having concluded that the amnesty in Peru manifestly contradicted the American Convention, pronounced that 'the said laws lack legal effect and may not obstruct the investigation of the grounds on which this case is based or the identification and punishment of those responsible, nor can they have the same or a similar impact with regard to other cases that have occurred in Peru'.[164] It is relevant if the Inter-American Court meant that the amnesty law was null and void, since the lack of legal effect can refer to nullity and this is even more imperative from the perspective of contradiction with peremptory norms. On the other hand, it is arguable that the reference was made not to nullity but simply the pronouncement was made that the law enacted in violation of treaty obligations is an internationally wrongful act and the 'lack of legal effect' referred not, or at least not inherently, to nullity, but to the proclamation of its illegality and the affirmation of the continuation in force of the relevant treaty obligations by the competent institutional body charged with the application and enforcement of the American Convention. In this context nullity is different from the irrelevance of domestic law in terms of compliance with international obligations.

If an amnesty contrary to *jus cogens* is enacted, it would not be accorded international legal recognition and the perpetrators would nevertheless be prosecuted, for example in foreign States.[165] In terms of public order effects, international law is not concerned with the validity of amnesties contravening *jus cogens* on a national plane which depends on the status of international law in the country in which it was enacted, but their international validity and opposability.[166] The Special Court for Sierra Leone pronounced on this issue in terms reminiscent to the rationale of public order. The Court emphasized that whatever the effect of the amnesty granted in the Lomé Agreement for crimes covered by the Court's Statute, 'it is ineffective in removing the universal jurisdiction to prosecute persons accused of such crimes that other States have by reason of the nature of the crime'.[167] Given the Court's above reliance on *jus cogens*, this confirms not only the primacy of peremptory norms over inconsistent amnesties, but also the peremptory status of the universal jurisdiction itself.[168]

---

[163] Loayza Tamayo, 116 ILR, 435.

[164] *Barrios Altos*, para. 44 and operative para. 4, 41 ILM (2002), 106–108.

[165] *Furundzija*, para. 155.

[166] Judge Garcia-Ramirez, Concurring Opinion, *Castillo Paez*, 116 ILR, 523; Meron (1986), 199.

[167] *Prosecutor v Kallon*, 13 March 2004, para. 88.   [168] Below, Chapter 9.

In terms of the negative effect of international public order, amnesties are devoid of all legal validity and force internationally and cannot give rise to rights and obligations, *inter alia* as part of new *inter se* legal relations. In terms of its positive effect, international public order requires application to a given legal relation, of the norms of its choice, that is the norms requiring prosecution of perpetrators of *jus cogens* crimes, instead of potential legal norms relieving those perpetrators of their liability had the respective norms on accountability not possessed peremptory force.

2.3. Illegal imposition or deprivation of nationality

Imposition or deprivation of nationality is normally part of the sovereign power of a State and normally it would be a bilateral issue. But when a breach of *jus cogens* such as an unlawful use of force or racial discrimination is involved, it may generate objective illegality. This can relate both to imposition and deprivation of nationality. For instance, the grant by Germany of its nationality to the citizens of France and Luxembourg during the Second World War is an invalid act.[169]

O'Connell considers that denationalization is a matter of sovereign authority and can be effected as a penalty.[170] 'The only occasion where denationalisation would conceivably invite the interest of international law is where religious or racial minority groups are rendered stateless.' O'Connell acknowledges that a rule against denationalization is deducible from the conception of human rights.[171] A State may not evade its obligations under human rights law by using the sovereign prerogative of depriving them their nationality.[172] Similarly, the grant of nationality which involves a breach of *jus cogens* would be invalid.[173]

Measures of denationalization involving serious human rights violations are void and cannot be given international recognition. Alternative views are suggested, however. According to Lauterpacht, effect had to be given to the 1941 German denationalization decree, in order not to impose on persons a nationality which they are anxious not to possess.[174] But the voidness of a given act of denationalization does not by itself impose on persons a nationality they do not want; it merely ensures—through voidness of the denationalization act—that they can recover that nationality if they wish to. The recognition of a denationalization decree is not a logical precondition for allowing persons to refuse a certain nationality, and indeed prejudices the

---

[169] Guggenheim (1949), 211.

[170] O'Connell, *International Law* (1970), 683–684, particularly n. 63.   [171] Id., 684.

[172] Quigley, Displaced Palestinians and a Right to Return, 39 *Harvard International Law Journal* (1998), 197.

[173] Kadelbach, *Zwingendes Völkerrecht* (1992), 335–336.

[174] Quoted in Mann (1976–77), 45.

choice by affected individuals. It seems that Lauterpacht's view fails in face of public order requirements. The view of F.A. Mann has to be preferred, according to which no effect can be given to gross illegalities even if one is motivated by humanitarian considerations.[175]

---

[175] Mann (1976–77), 45.

8

Remedies for Breaches of Peremptory Norms

I. REPARATION FOR BREACHES OF PEREMPTORY NORMS

1.1. General questions

As the Permanent Court of International Justice emphasized in the *Chorzow Factory* case, 'it is a principle of international law that the breach of an engagement involves an obligation to make reparation in an adequate form'.[1] In other words, the duty to make reparation is an inherent and self-evident consequence of any failure to comply with international engagement, and no additional agreement between injured State and wrongdoer State is required.

The Permanent Court described the function of reparation in following terms: 'Reparation must, as far as possible, wipe out all the consequences of the illegal act and re-establish the situation which would, in all probability, have existed if that act had not been committed.'[2] The principle of reparation has a universal character and extends to every international legal relationship. Its function is to eliminate all injuries caused by the wrongdoer State, whether moral or material. The injured state is entitled to obtain various forms of reparation either singly or in combination according to the nature and extent of injury. According to the Permanent Court, reparation should cover 'restitution in kind, or, if this is not possible, payment of a sum corresponding to the value which a restitution in kind would bear; the award, if need be, of damages for loss sustained which would not be covered by restitution in kind or payment in place of it'.[3]

The Articles on State Responsibility of the International Law Commission (ILC) adopted in 2001 confirm that 'The responsible State is under an obligation to make full reparation for the injury caused by the internationally wrongful act'. It is further specified that 'injury includes any damage, whether material or moral, caused by the internationally wrongful act of a State'. The ILC's Articles further specify that reparation should be provided in the form of 'restitution, compensation and satisfaction, either singly or in combination'.[4]

As far as the traditional bilateralist framework of law enforcement is concerned, the duty of the author State to provide reparation exists only towards the directly injured State, similarly to substantive, or primary,

---

[1] PCIJ Series A, 1928, No. 17, 29.   [2] Ibid., 47.   [3] Ibid.
[4] Articles on State Responsibility, Article 31 (Reparation), in *ILC Report* (2001), 51.

obligations which operate on the basis of such bilateralist framework. However, there may be cases where the relevance of the problem transcends the limits of bilateral relations between the wrongdoer and injured States. The factor causing such alteration in the legal framework is the effect of the peremptory norms of general international law (*jus cogens*). Such norms impose on States obligations towards the international community as a whole, and not towards the individual States. Consequently, the duty to make reparation to a directly injured State or other victims is similarly owed by the author State not to the injured State(s) individually, but to the international community as a whole.

1.2. The general impact of peremptory norms on the law of reparation

The relevance of peremptory norms in relation to reparations follows from their general nature, namely from the fact that they are norms from which no derogation is permitted and which need to have absolute validity in order to meet their purpose. Such relevance of *jus cogens* influences the very concept of illegality in international law. Normally, in traditional bilateralist contexts, illegality may be relative or conditional, and even may be excluded as a consequence of bilateral relations determined by estoppel or acquiescence.[5] But for the rules and obligations involving the community interest such a model is no longer appropriate, because their breach shall be considered as objectively illegal. The concept of objective illegality follows from the need to protect the community interest embodied in peremptory norms and ensure that such interest is safeguarded in an integral way.

Therefore, in cases of breach of *jus cogens* the duty to make reparation has to be enforced objectively. Such objective performance is not the same as awarding reparations within a treaty-based institutional machinery. Such institutional machineries often fail to offer adequate compensation to the victims of human rights violations. For instance, in the *McCann* case, the European Court of Human Rights declined to award damages for unlawful killing contrary to Article 2 (right to life) of the European Convention on Human Rights,[6] even though the *Chorzhow Factory* principle would require the Court to award compensation. Even where remedies are awarded by tribunals, they are not necessarily adequate. In *Ogur*, the same Court awarded remedies clearly inappropriate in terms of a violent loss of life (100,000 French francs to be converted into Turkish lira), which prompted a following comment by Judge Bonello:

In this case, a State which had solemnly undertaken to cherish the right to life, has wantonly plucked and tossed away the being of a young man, paying the price of a

---

[5] Brownlie, *Principles* (2003), 486.
[6] *McCann and Others v the United Kingdom*, ECtHR, 18984/91 (27/09/95).

small car—almost an entertainment tax on homicide. In the Strasbourg market it seems that life comes cheap, and killing is a tremendous bargain.[7]

Therefore, the objective performance of the duty to make reparation means the measures taken to objectively satisfy the requirements of substantive peremptory norms and the duty of reparation they entail.

The peremptory nature of a norm may produce certain effects in a given legal relationship which would be absent in the case of *jus dispositivum*. The nature of a norm which gives rise to an obligation is important in determining which remedies are due and to what extent relevant actors enjoy discretion in deciding on remedies, and how imperative is the requirement to award a particular remedy. A starting-point is a general principle of international law that every breach of an international obligation gives rise to the duty to make reparation. If peremptory norms are non-derogable, the consequences thereof in terms of reparation must also be viewed as non-derogable. It lies thus beyond the power of directly interested States to determine whether and to what extent the reparation is due to the victims of breaches of *jus cogens*.

A suggestion that although certain norms are peremptory and thus non-derogable, the remedies for breaches may nevertheless be treated by States as non-peremptory and derogable, would in fact make the primary substantive *jus cogens* norms derogable. If States may by mutual agreement ignore the consequences of a breach, this means that they may in fact derogate from a peremptory norm by breaching it and not enforcing the respective consequences. Such an outcome is conceptually incompatible with the very concept of *jus cogens*. The entire regime of reparations in international law, as perhaps the entire law of State responsibility, is based on *jus dispositivum*, which means that it is up to the directly injured States whether and in which form the duty to make reparation is performed. But in the case of peremptory norms, this regime is overtaken by the operation of *jus cogens*. This is understandable since *jus dispositivum* is in any case derogable in all its aspects, while *jus cogens* is not.

The law of State responsibility is in line with such an approach. As early as 1985, the International Law Commission emphasized that although the rules on State responsibility may be replaced by a *lex specialis* and States may adopt different legal consequences, as between them, of the internationally wrongful act concerned, they cannot 'provide for legal consequences of a breach of their mutual obligations which would authorise acts contrary to peremptory norms of general international law'.[8] At the final stage of the ILC's work on State responsibility, this position has remained unchanged. The Commission emphasized in the commentary to the Articles that

---

[7] *Ogur v Turkey*, ECtHR, 21594/93 (20/05/99).
[8] Commentary to Article 37 of the ILC's draft, para. 2, YbILC 1985, vol. II, part 1, 4–5.

although the general regime of State responsibility may be replaced by *lex specialis*, States cannot, even as between themselves, provide for legal consequences authorizing acts against *jus cogens*.[9] This approach is well founded as a general principle and also, as we shall see in due course, by the regime of specific remedies or forms of reparation.

As the ILC's Special Rapporteur Crawford emphasized, 'A State whose right has been breached is entitled to protest, to insist on restitution or (even where restitution may be possible) to decide that it would prefer compensation. It may insist on the vindication of its right or decide in the circumstances to overlook it and waive the breach. But the position where the obligation is a multilateral one may well be different.'[10] Indeed, in the context of peremptory norms operating in the interest of the international community, and requiring, by their very nature, objective performance, the question must be not how States (whether or not directly injured) consider the problem of reparations can be resolved adequately, but what the content and nature of a violated peremptory norm demands to be done in order to ensure the proper vindication and continued operability of that norm.

The non-derogability and peremptory character of the norms governing and specifying the responsibility for violations of substantive peremptory norms is affirmed within specific normative regimes such as that of humanitarian law. In *Kupreskic*, the International Criminal Tribunal for the Former Yugoslavia, having emphasized the peremptory status of basic norms of humanitarian law and, among others by reference to the clauses in the 1949 Geneva Conventions whereby States-parties are not allowed to absolve each other from the liability incurred by the breaches of these conventions (Common Article 51/52/131/148), concluded that the 'liability for grave breaches [of the Geneva Conventions] is absolute and may in no case be set aside by resort to any legal means such as derogating treaties and agreements'. Such liability cannot be thwarted by recourse to reciprocity either.[11]

The specific character of human rights treaty obligations reflective of *jus cogens* also reinforces the regime of responsibility that cannot be split into bilateral relations. This has been reflected in the treatment of issues regarding the inter-country abduction that arose in the context of the European Convention on Human Rights. The European Court on Human Rights held in the *Stocke* case that

An arrest made by the authorities of one State on the territory of another State, without the consent of the State concerned, does not, therefore, only involve the State responsibility vis-à-vis the other State, but also affects that person's individual right to security under Article 5 para. 1. The question whether or not the other State claimed

---

[9] Articles on State Responsibility, Article 55 (*Lex specialis*) and Commentary, in *Report of the ILC* (2001), 357.

[10] Crawford, *Third Report on State Responsibility*, A/CN.4/507, 44.

[11] *Kupreskic*, para. 517.

reparation for violation of its rights under international law is not relevant for the individual right under the Convention.[12]

This approach is in accordance with the objective character of human rights treaty obligations which are there not for the benefit of States-parties, but individuals. Such objective character of treaty obligations is consequently inherently linked to the concept of objective illegality which is produced, among others, by the violation of rights that are designed to benefit individuals as such rather than States.

The approach of non-derogability of the State responsibility regime for the breaches of peremptory norms seems to be supported by the rules governing invocation of wrongfulness by States. In a bilateralist context, reparation can normally be claimed by the State whose individual rights and interests are encroached upon: either for its own injury or on behalf of its nationals. It is beyond doubt, however, that the above-mentioned requirement is not relevant when the obligation breached is a fundamental international obligation protected by peremptory norms. Insofar as *jus cogens* embodies the interests of the international community as a whole, the non-compliance with obligations established by those norms shall give rise to legal interest on behalf of the international community and therefore, all States shall have legal interest in protection and enforcement of these obligations.[13] It is inherent to the notion of *jus cogens* that its violation shall have *erga omnes* effects and be invocable by every State regardless of having suffered individual injury.[14]

The objective nature of the duty to make reparation for the breach of *jus cogens* refers *inter alia* to the objective circumstances underlying an actual situation of a given breach. In case of breach of norms protecting the community interest, reparation shall be consistent with the nature of the wrong.[15] Van Boven and Bassiouni, in their capacity as UN Special Rapporteurs, have affirmed that it is a paramount consideration that reparation should conform to the needs of victim,[16] be proportionate to the gravity of the violations and the harm suffered.[17] As the Inter-American Court of Human Rights stated

[12] *Stocke*, Series A, No. 199, at 24.

[13] Frowein, Reactions by Not Directly Affected States on Violations of Public International Law, *Recueil des cours*, 1994, vol. IV, 405.

[14] *Barcelona Traction, ICJ Reports*, 1970, p. 34; Gaja, Ius Cogens, Obligations *Erga Omnes* and International Crimes: A Tentative Analysis of Three Related Concepts, in Weiler, Cassese and Spinedi (eds), *International Crimes of State: A Critical Analysis of Article 19 of the ILC's Draft Articles on State Responsibility* (1989), 159; Bruno Simma, Injury and Countermeasures, ibid., 299 ff.

[15] Cassese, *International Law* (2005), 274.

[16] Theo van Boven, *Study concerning the right to restitution, compensation and rehabilitation for victims of gross violations of human rights and fundamental freedoms*, E/CN.4/Sub.2/1993/8, 2 July 1993, para. 137.

[17] Ibid., 57; van Boven, *Revised set of basic principles and guidelines on the right to reparation for victims of gross violations of human rights and humanitarian law*, E/CN.4/Sub.2/1996/17, para. 7; M. Cheriff Bassiouni, *Final Report on the right to restitution, compensation and rehabilitation for victims of gross human rights violations*, E/CN.4/2000, 62, 9 (para. 15).

in *Aloeboetoe*, reparation must reflect the nature of the right violated.[18] Such conformity of reparations with the damage caused is by itself the concern of the international community as a whole. Furthermore, the objective assessment of injury in case of breaches of peremptory norms may perhaps even take priority over the right of an injured party to elect among remedies and the amount of the award.[19] In *Suarez-Rosero*, the Inter-American Court, based on the extent of moral suffering caused to the victim and his family, decided to award compensation for moral damages in the amount substantially more than requested by the applicant.[20]

As emphasized above, the vast majority of situations dealing with reparation for violations of *jus cogens* deal with the rights of human beings. This is only natural, because most of the cases of *jus cogens* are 'cases where the position of the individual is involved, and where the rules contravened are rules instituted for the protection of the individual'.[21] In this context, Tomuschat has objected that international law knows no duty of States to make reparation for internationally wrongful acts committed not against other States, but against their own citizens. Tomuschat speaks about the traditional legal edifice of settling war claims in terms of inter-State relations.[22] This approach seems to be too formalistic. As reparation is an automatic consequence of an internationally wrongful act, and the need to award it does not have to be supported by practice, then it can be assumed, even in absence of sufficient practical evidence, that States owe the duty to provide reparations when their actions injure non-State actors. The *Chorzhow* principle contains not even the slightest indication that the duty to make reparation no longer operates when a wrongful act is committed towards individuals. Indeed, the Permanent Court spoke about the breach of 'every international engagement'.[23]

---

[18] *Aloeboetoe*, 116 ILR, 275; see also *Castillo Paez*, 116 ILR 499.

[19] For the contrary view see Crawford, *Third Report*, A/CN.4/507/Add.2, 11, referring to *Rainbow Warrior*. Also in *Corfu Channel*, the International Court refused to award more than claimed, *ICJ Reports*, 1949, 244, at 250.

[20] *Suarez-Rosero*, 118 ILR, 111.

[21] Fitzmaurice, Third Report on the Law of Treaties, YbILC 1958, vol. II, 40.

[22] Tomuschat, Individual Reparation Claims in Instances of Grave Human Rights Violations, in Randelzhofer and Tomuschat (eds), *State Responsibility and the Individual. Reparation in Instances of Grave Violations of Human Rights* (1999), 7. Tomuschat also refers to the non-subordination of States to each other and their sovereign immunity as an obstacle for awarding reparations to individuals, ibid., 14. For a similar approach to and a rather unfounded criticism of the reparations practice of national and international courts, such as the Inter-American Court, see Tomuschat, Reparation for Victims of Grave Human Rights Violations, 10 *Tulane Journal of International and Comparative Law* (2002) at 157, especially 166, 168 and 173. The practice of the Inter-American Court is duly dealt with below in the appropriate places.

[23] As Rolin commented on the *Chorzhow Factory* principle, 'Ce principe ne gouverne pas seulement la responsabilité interétatique, il s'entend également lorsque la responsabilité internationale d'un Etat est engagée directement ou indirectement a l'égard d'un individu'. See Rolin, La rôle du requérant dans la procédure prévue par la Commission Européenne des Droits de l'Homme, 9 *Revue Hellénique de Droit International* (1956), 6.

Some national courts uphold the inter-State approach on remedies, such as the Japanese courts on post-war compensation claims[24] and the German *Bundesgerichtshof* in *Distomo*.[25] This practice not only contradicts the applicable legal framework but also diminishes its value by the fact that it originates from the courts of States which are in some cases unwilling to compensate for the injuries and suffering they have caused to the victims of the Second World War.[26]

The reparation framework several decades ago could have been based on the bilateral inter-State approach, but owing to the current state of international law where bilateral relations are by no means exclusive and individual rights possess objective validity, such an approach is no longer tenable.

This is further confirmed by the Articles of the ILC on State responsibility. This is clear from Articles 35 to 37 on State responsibility, which, unlike their counterparts in the draft articles on State responsibility adopted in 1996, do not state that the injured State may demand remedies like restitution, compensation or satisfaction, but purely and simply emphasize that the wrongdoer State is under obligation to provide such remedies, without specifying the addressee of the remedies. Thus, these provisions do at least potentially cover individuals and their groups, and are in accordance with general international law. Furthermore, according to Article 48, 'Any State other than an injured State is entitled to invoke the responsibility of another State' if 'the obligation breached is owed to the international community as a whole', and claim 'performance of the obligation of reparation . . . *in the interest of the injured State or of the beneficiaries of the obligation breached.*'[27] Any State could, as the commentary to Article 48 confirms, claim restitution in the interest of beneficiaries of the obligation breached.[28] Therefore, there is

---

[24] Decisions on *X v State of Japan*, 39 Japanese Annual (1996), 265–266, *X et al. v The State of Japan*, 40 *Japanese Annual* (1997), 116–117, have considered that reparations for breaches of human rights and humanitarian law, particularly under Article 3 of the 1907 Hague Regulations, are due only at inter-State level reparations and not to individuals. *X et al. v The State of Japan*, 41 *Japanese Annual* (1999), 145 suggests that the damage to an individual is in all cases damage to the State of his nationality. See also Igarashi, Post-War Compensation Cases, Japanese Courts and International Law, 43 *Japanese Annual of International Law* (2000), 68; Frulli, When Are States Liable Towards Individuals for Serious Violations of Humanitarian Law? The *Markovic* Case, 1 *Journal of International Criminal Justice* (2003), 419–420. Pisillo-Mazzeschi, Reparation Claims by Individuals for State Breaches of Humanitarian Law and Human Rights: An Overview, 1 *Journal of International Criminal Justice* (2003), 341–342 suggests that Article 3 of the 1907 Regulations must be understood as covering individual reparation claims as well, due to the similarity between human rights and humanitarian law norms.

[25] III ZR 245/98, 26 June 2003, Section IV, para. 1. The Court examined the issue in terms of diplomatic protection and paid no attention to the humanitarian dimension of the case, 19–26.

[26] But there are exceptions, eg the Japanese court has compensated some Korean comfort women, Igarashi (2000), 54–55.

[27] Articles on State Responsibility, Article 48 (Invocation of responsibility by a State other than an injured State), in *Report of the ILC* (2001), 56 (emphasis added).

[28] *ILC Report* 2001, 323.

a duty to make reparation to the injured non-State actors, and it is invocable by all States, whether or not directly injured by a given breach.

The rationale of reparations in cases involving the rights of individuals can be formulated as follows. International law protects human rights and allocates the legal interest in this field to the international community as a whole. Since the avoidance of undue suffering by a human being is among the basic values and legal interests of the international community, the reversal of this human suffering caused in individual cases also forms part of the interest of the international community. The implementation of remedies goes thus far beyond the bilateral relationships between the victim and wrongdoer States, and acquires an important community dimension.

If *jus cogens* protects the rights of an individual in the interests of the international community as a whole, it is hardly justified to consider that the enforcement of these rights by way of reparation should be dependent upon the respective will of national States of victims or other States. Individuals' entitlement to reparation, which is independent from possible or actual claims by a State, is therefore a natural continuation of the peremptory status of basic human rights. The way of claiming reparation is to bring suits within national legal systems or international treaty mechanisms.[29]

The general impact of *jus cogens* on the law of reparations having been overviewed, it remains to examine the specific impact of *jus cogens* on particular kinds of remedies. The following analysis will demonstrate that along with the general concept of *jus cogens*, the context of operation of specific peremptory norms also can impact on the regime of specific remedies.

1.3. The impact of jus cogens on the regime of specific remedies

1.3.1. Restitution as a primary remedy

(a) The general primacy of restitution

The ILC's Articles on State Responsibility emphasize that 'A State responsible for an internationally wrongful act is under an obligation to make restitution, that is, to re-establish the situation which existed before the wrongful act was committed, provided and to the extent that restitution: (a) is not materially impossible; (b) does not involve a burden out of all proportion to the benefit deriving from restitution instead of compensation.'

Restitution is a remedy with retrospective effects. It is directed at the elimination of factual situations existing after commission of an internationally wrongful act. But sometimes in theory such a role of restitution is sceptically

---

[29] This is not to suggest that individuals have international legal personality, cf Orakhelashvili, *CWILJ*, 241–276.

assessed. Brownlie states that restitution is exceptional in practice and it is difficult to state conditions of its application with any certainty.[30] It is even suggested that restitution cannot be applied unless a specific provision is provided for in a compromise between the disputing parties,[31] and the rarity of the award of restitution dictates that it is not a primary remedy.[32]

Judicial practice concerning restitution as a remedy is not at all uniform. The starting-point in this regard is *Chorzhow Factory*, in which the PCIJ stated that 'restitution in kind or, if this is not possible, payment of a sum corresponding to the value which a restitution in kind would bear' is a proper material consequence of an internationally wrongful act.[33] The PCIJ affirmed thus the primacy of restitution notwithstanding the fact that in that concrete case restitution was not awarded. The ICJ took the same position in *Preah Vihear*, where it ordered Thailand to withdraw from the occupied Cambodian territory.[34] Arbitral practice is not totally clear, but hardly supports any view that restitution cannot be applied as a remedy when a party so requests.[35] Thus, judicial and arbitral practice does not reject

---

[30] Brownlie, *The System of the Law of Nations. State Responsibility* (1983), 211, 222; Gray, *Judicial Remedies in International Law* (1990), 13 ff., 95 ff.

[31] Gray, ibid., 16.

[32] Gray, The Choice between Restitution and Compensation, *European Journal of International Law*, vol. 10, 1999, 411 ff.

[33] PCIJ Ser. A. No. 13, 47.

[34] *ICJ Reports*, 1962, 6; see also *Tehran Hostages, ICJ Reports*, 1980.

[35] Reference is made to cases such as *Rhodophe Forests, Walter Fletcher Smith, Savarkar and Casablanca*, see Gray, above note 30, 15. But none of them rules out restitution. In *Rhodophe Forests* the arbitrator refused to award restitution because of the material impossibility of this remedy. The Tribunal did not rule out restitution as such, but indicated that it was impossible to restore confiscated forests in the state in which they were before confiscation, RIAA, vol. III, 1432. *Walter Fletcher Smith* might be invoked as an evidence of a somewhat liberal approach towards restitution. The Arbitrator awarded pecuniary compensation though he held that 'it would not be inappropriate that, according to law, the property should be restored to the claimant', *Walter Fletcher Smith Claim*, RIAA, vol. II, 918. According to the ILC, the Tribunal took into account the internal situation of the defendant State in deciding the appropriateness of certain remedies. *ILC Report* (1993), A/48/10, 149. The ILC treated *Walter Fletcher Smith* as a case supporting primacy of restitution over compensation, ibid., 153. It should also be kept in mind that the United States, in taking up the matter of Smith, did not use its right to insist on restitution as a sole remedy but considered it only as one of the options of settlement, RIAA, vol. II, 916. Nothing in the submissions made by the United States supports the idea that the United States ruled out restitution. They simply granted discretion to the Arbitrator to make choice between various remedies. From the reasoning of the Arbitrator it is clear that what he did was the exercise of that discretion, ibid., 918. Two other cases supply clearer evidence that restitution as a remedy cannot be ruled out. In *Casablanca*, the Tribunal condemned the non-respect of the German consular authority by French military officials in arresting deserters who were under the custody of the German consul. But the Tribunal did not declare that France's conduct in holding deserters was unlawful, *Affaire de Casablanca*, RIAA, vol. XI, 126. Consequently, restitution could not be ordered because of the absence of wrongfulness. *Savarkar* follows the same reasoning. The Tribunal refused restitution with regard to the Indian revolutionary Savarkar from Britain to France, because Britain obtained control over Savarkar not by violation of the French jurisdiction but as a consequence of error on the side of French authorities, *Case of Savarkar*, RIAA, vol. XI, 253–254.

restitution as a remedy in its own right, and nothing evidences that this remedy is exceptional rather than regular. Restitution is also a remedy widely used by treaty-based organs. It has been awarded by the European Court of Human Rights under Article 41 of the European Convention (just satisfaction),[36] and the Inter-American Court has held that restitution is expressly mandated under Article 63(1) of the American Convention, dealing with the remedial competence of that Court.[37]

The importance of restitution as a remedy increases in cases of violation of fundamental international obligations protecting the community interest, in the preservation of which all States have a legal interest. If under some circumstances restitution can be replaced by compensation in case of ordinary wrong (this consideration partly explains the frequent application of compensation in judicial and diplomatic practice), in the case of violations of peremptory norms no such approach could be tolerated. When a wrongful act affects the interests of the whole international community, the re-establishment of a situation before the breach has been committed goes beyond the interests of a directly injured State. Therefore, that State may not in such cases unilaterally refuse restitution. The nature of peremptory norms does not permit rejection of restitution. Aggression, genocide and massive violations of human rights by their very nature necessitate the application of restitution. Monetary compensation could only be a subsidiary remedy in such cases, as *Chorzow Factory* suggests. And as a matter of fact, there is no single judicial precedent denying restitution due to some exceptions or external circumstances in situations where a violation of *jus cogens* is involved. The toleration of automatic replacement of restitution by compensation in the case of violation of peremptory norms would defeat the object of those norms and jeopardize their very existence.

As Special Rapporteur Crawford noted, in certain cases the injured State is not entitled to waive restitution and prefer compensation, such as in the case of forcible invasion and annexation of a State's territory and illegal detention of persons.[38] Special Rapporteur Arangio-Ruiz also suggested that in the case of imperative rules, restitution cannot be renounced and in such situations the only justifiable solution would be to place on States a duty to provide full restitution in kind.[39] As the ILC noted, in such cases the vital interests of the international community as such are at stake.[40] In the same spirit, Professor Craefrath considers that while in the case of ordinary delicts the parties are free to determine the contents of the duty to reparation, in the case of a

[36] *Papamichalopoulos*, ECtHR, Series A-330B, 64.
[37] *Aloeboetoe*, 116 ILR, 275–276.
[38] Crawford, Third Report, A/CN.4/507/Add.1, 5.
[39] Arangio-Ruiz, Preliminary Report on State Responsibility, YbILC 1988-II(1), 37.
[40] *ILC Report* (2000), 56–58.

breach of *jus cogens*, legal restitution is a necessary part of the duty of reparation that cannot be disclaimed.[41]

In the specific context of human rights and humanitarian law, the primacy of restitution is more than clear. As Special Rapporteur Van Boven submits, restitution shall be performed in cases of serious and massive human rights violations, in order to ensure restoration of liberty, residence, citizenship, employment or property of victims, and is a most suitable remedy for human rights and humanitarian law violations.[42] Special Rapporteur Bassiouni affirmed the same view.[43] The Special Rapporteur on the impunity of perpetrators of human rights violations affirmed that restitution (seeking to restore victims to their previous state) is an indispensable consequence of serious human rights violations.[44]

It may be concluded that while the primacy of restitution may be subject to a different regulation by States in case of breaches of *jus dispositivum*, such primacy becomes peremptory as such in cases where a breach of *jus cogens* is involved and is no longer subject to the will of individual States. This general relevance of *jus cogens* for the primacy of restitution having been acsertained, it remains to move to the consideration of some specific legal contexts, and of the impact of specific peremptory norms, which definitionally affirm the unconditional primacy of restitution and the general principle just formulated.

(b) Specific legal contexts reinforcing the primacy of restitution

First and foremost, the law of treaty invalidity under the 1969 Vienna Convention on the Law of Treaties should be mentioned. Article 71 of the Convention deals with the consequences of invalidity of treaties conflicting

---

[41] Graefrath, in Weiler, Cassese and Spinedi (eds) (1989), 165.

[42] Van Boven, above, note 16, p. 57; van Boven, *Revised set of basic principles and guidelines on the right to reparation for victims of gross violations of human rights and humanitarian law*, E/CN.4/Sub.2/1996/17, para. 6; Paolilo, On Unfulfilled Duties: The Obligation to Make Reparation in Cases of Violation of Human Rights, in V. Götz, P. Selmer, R. Wolfrum (eds), *Liber Amicorum Günther Jaenicke—Zum 85. Geburtstag* (1998), 303.

[43] Cheriff Bassiouni, *Final Report on the right to restitution, compensation and rehabilitation for victims of gross human rights violations*, E/CN.4/2000/62, 10. The Resolution of the Human Rights Commission adopted on the basis of the report of Bassiouni subscribes to the same approach, emphasizing in particular that 'Restitution should, whenever possible, restore the victim to the original situation before the gross violations of international human rights law or serious violations of international humanitarian law occurred. Restitution includes, as appropriate: restoration of liberty, enjoyment of human rights, identity, family life and citizenship, return to one's place of residence, restoration of employment and return of property.' See Basic Principles and Guidelines on the Right to a Remedy and Reparation for Victims of Gross Violations of International Human Rights Law and Serious Violations of International Humanitarian Law, CHR res. 2005/35, UN Doc. E/CN.4/2005/ L.10/Add.11 (19 April 2005), para. 19.

[44] Lionel Joinet, *Revised final report on question of immunity of perpetrators of human rights violations*, E/CN.4/Sub.2/1997/20/Rev.1, para. 41 and principle 36.

with *jus cogens* in an imperative way, among others requiring that 'in the case of a treaty which is void the parties shall eliminate as far as possible the consequences of any act performed in reliance on any provision which conflicts with the peremptory norm of general international law'. This provision requires that the consequences of invalidity must be eliminated as such.[45] It is impermissible to waive this remedy or replace it with something else, such as monetary compensation. The situation existing before the conclusion of a void treaty has to be restored. As such treaties would offend against the community interest embodied in *jus cogens*, it would be in the interest, and power, of the international community as a whole that the consequences of such treaties are fully eliminated, which is tantamount to the full performance of *restitutio in integrum*.

Furthermore, certain acts or actions of States may themselves become invalid in cases of conflict with *jus cogens* and State practice is familiar with the invalidation of certain State actions as such, mostly dealing with the consequences of the unlawful use of force.[46] Both this voidness and the duty of non-recognition it entails are implications of the peremptory norms affected by violations.[47] This legal framework also supports primacy of restitution as the primary and irreplaceable remedy, because the duty to withdraw from the illegally occupied territory is restitution which is not negotiable.[48]

Another context of substantive law definitionally requiring performance of restitution is the right of displaced persons to return home. As emphasized, a forcible deportation or expulsion implies an intent to forbid return.[49] This means that the return to homes—and hence restitution—is the natural requirement for reversing the wrongfulness performed through deportation. As the Special Rapporteur on human rights and population transfer Al-Khasawneh affirmed, the remedy for the displaced persons is *restitutio in integrum*.[50]

This approach is even more appropriate if borne in mind that expulsion or deportation is defined as a crime against humanity or war crime. Under Article 18(g) of the ILC's draft code on crimes against peace and security of mankind and Article 7.1(d) of the ICC Statute, the arbitrary deportation

---

[45] See above, Chapter 6.

[46] For the overview of such practice see above, Chapter 7.

[47] Dugard, *Recognition and the United Nations* (1987), 137; see further below, Section 3.2.

[48] In particular, the General Assembly Resolution 32/9D declared the South African annexation of Walvis Bay as illegal, null and void, and the Security Council considered in Resolution 432 (1978) the reintegration of Walvis Bay as the ultimate remedy.

[49] Quigley, Displaced Palestinians and a Right to Return, 39 *Harvard Journal of International Law* (1998), 221.

[50] Al-Khasawneh, *Final report on human rights and population transfer*, E/CN.4/Sub.2/1997/23, paras 60–61.

or forcible transfer of population is a crime against humanity, and under Article 8.2(e VII) of the ICC Statute 'ordering the displacement of the civilian population for reasons related to the conflict' is an exceptionally serious war crime. This would naturally suggest that the violation of *jus cogens* is involved, with all due effects and consequences.[51]

The norm applicable to the right to return requires that the choice on return should lie with the victims themselves, and not with any other actor, including States. If this norm is peremptory, it is not subject to a derogation by agreement or other legal instrument. Therefore, under human rights law, an individual may have the right to return. Such a right would be independent of the will of the States involved, especially the State of sojourn, and would be valid even if the State of sojourn does not insist on return.[52] A logical consequence of the operation of rules protecting individuals as such, irrespective of the attitude of States in specific cases, is that these rules should operate and protect individuals irrespective of their nationality, and link their protection to the interests of the international community as a whole.

In line with such approach, the UN Security Council has repeatedly emphasized that the right of the displaced persons to return to homes is inalienable and imprescriptible,[53] and the similar view is taken in Dayton Peace Agreements.[54] Such a state of law would definitionally exclude replacement of restitution by compensation, above all in terms of a (bilateral) inter-State agreement.

Yet another situation which reflects the primacy of restitution in the case of breaches of peremptory norms is the position of persons abducted from foreign soil. The State-sponsored abduction of individuals violates two different sets of international norms: the international law of sovereignty and international human rights.[55] As the US Court of Appeals affirmed in *Toscanino*, there is 'a long standing principle of international law that abductions by one State of persons located within the territory of another violate the territorial sovereignty of the second State and are redressable usually by the return of the person kidnapped'.[56] According to FA Mann, a State committing official abduction is responsible for this wrongful act and is under

---

[51] As Special Rapporteur Waldock suggested, one of the criteria of determining a norm's peremptory status is the criminality of the conduct it outlaws, see YbILC 1963-II, 52–53.

[52] Quigley (1998), 196.

[53] UNSC Res. 1255(1999), 1287(2000), 1393(2002); for an overview of the relevant practice see Quigley (1998), 214–215.

[54] Annex 4, Article II (5) of the Dayton Peace Agreement confirms that refugees have the rights to have their property restored to them and to be compensated for the property which cannot be restored to them. This formulation is in line with the primacy of restitution. On the modalities of implementation of this and related provisions, and the difficulties and shortcomings of the process of return, see Cox (1998), 226–239.

[55] *Alvarez-Machain v US*, 41 ILM (2002), 132.

[56] 61 ILR 201.

a formal duty to return the person.[57] This principle is confirmed by State practice,[58] apart from the normal framework of State responsibility.

It is rightly suggested that if individual rights mean anything in this context, the abducting State must be under obligation to return the abductee[59] and must do so even without the request of the State in question.[60] This approach properly reflects the effect of the norms related to the use of force and human rights as peremptory norms. Particularly, human rights are not just individual rights in terms of persons separate from States as such, but the rights of individuals which cannot be prejudiced by the attitudes of States.

These regimes of individual norms incorporating restitution as a primary and inevitable remedy underline its role as the primary and imperative remedy in the case of breaches of *jus cogens*.

1.3.2. Compensation

Compensation is the most usual form of material responsibility, because it is easier to implement than restitution. As the ILC noted, the material damage caused by a wrongful act can always be evaluated in money and the gaps left after performance of relatively inflexible restitution in kind can be filed in this way.[61] Thus, Article 36 of the ILC states that:

1. The State responsible for an internationally wrongful act is under an obligation to compensate for the damage caused thereby, insofar as such damage is not made good by restitution.
2. The compensation shall cover any financially assessable damage including loss of profits insofar as it is established.

The flexibility of compensation as a remedy causes its most frequent application in treaty practice as well as in judicial and arbitral proceedings. Compensation is also less disputed in theory because it is beyond doubt that this remedy can be applied in all situations. At the same time, it is necessary to note that compensation can, in some cases, prove ineffective in wiping out the injury caused. Payment of money might be an artificial redress as compared with re-establishing the situation which existed before the wrongful act was committed, because the peculiarities of a legal relationship in context of

---

[57] Mann, Reflection on the Prosecution of Persons Abducted in Breach of International Law, Dinstein and Tabori (eds), *Festschrift Rosenne*, 407; Frowein, Male Captus Male Detentus: A Human Right, in Lawson and De Blois (eds), *Festschrift Schermers*, 183. It was recognized by the US Supreme Court in *Alvarez-Machain* that if the abduction were in breach of the US–Mexican extradition treaty, there would be a duty to return.

[58] For an overview of the relevant practice see Frowein, 183–184.

[59] Mann, Reflection on the Prosecution of Persons Abducted in Breach of International Law, in Dinstein and Tabori (eds), *Festschrift Rosenne*, 411.

[60] Frowein, Male Captus Male Detentus: A Human Right, in Lawson and De Blois (eds), *Festschrift Schermers*, 185.

[61] Commentary to Article 36, para. 3, *ILC Report* 2001, 244–245.

which a breach was committed always play an important role. These circumstances justify inclusion of provision in ILC's draft articles, according to which compensation is to be paid 'insofar as such damage is not made good by restitution', and another implicit reservation that there should be a further remedy for non-material injury.

Thus, compensation shall not be identified with material reparation of moral damage, the latter being an element of satisfaction[62] to be discussed below. All punitive aspects from compensation shall be excluded because it is remedy of purely compensatory character,[63] and includes only the economically assessable damage.[64]

As the Inter-American Court affirmed, compensation is due where restitution is impossible.[65] In case of human rights violations, compensation has to ensure that reparation fully matches the suffering caused to victims. For instance, the mere release of a person who unlawfully spent a long time in detention is hardly an adequate reparation. The suffering of deprivation of liberty and family, professional and other life needs to be repaired.[66] Treaty-based organs do regularly award compensation for materially assessable damage to victims of human rights violations. They even set objective conditions of such awards. For instance, the Inter-American Court emphasized in *Velasquez-Rodriguez* that compensation for the disappearance and death of a person 'must be calculated as a loss of earnings based upon the income the victim would have received up to the time of his possible death'.[67]

There is nothing more to add about this remedy and the impact on it of *jus cogens* is most usual. The only relevant issue from the perspective of *jus cogens* is that the amount of compensation should be objectively consistent with the breaches and suffering caused—a problem which was discussed above in a more general context. As Special Rapporteur Van Boven commented in respect of treaty-based human rights mechanisms, 'Any compensation or award granted to an injured party must not only be just towards that party itself, but also do justice to the purposes and principles of the human rights protection system.'[68] A more problematic issue is compensation for

---

[62] *Yearbook of the ILC*, 1993, vol. II, part 2, 67, 71. Here the relevant judicial practice is also analysed.

[63] Annacker, Part 2 of the International Law Commission's Draft Articles on State Responsibility, 37 *German Yearbook of International Law* (1994), 227; Crawford, *Third Report*, A/CN.4/507/Add.1, 18.

[64] The economically assessable damage covers: (i) damage caused to the State's territory in general, to its organization in a broad sense, its property at home and abroad, its military installations, diplomatic premises, ships, aircraft, spacecraft, etc. (so-called 'direct' damage to the State); (ii) damage caused to the State through the persons, physical or juridical, of its nationals or agents (so-called indirect damage to the state), *Yearbook of the ILC*, 1993, vol. II, part 2, 72.

[65] *Aloeboetoe*, 116 ILR 276; *Gangaram Panday*, 116 ILR 317–318.

[66] Paolilo, On Unfulfilled Duties: The Obligation to Make Reparation in Cases of Violation of Human Rights, in V. Götz, P. Selmer, R. Wolfrum (eds), *Liber Amicorum Günther Jaenicke—Zum 85. Geburtstag* (1998), 305.

[67] *Velasquez-Rodriguez* (Compenastion), 95 ILR 317.   [68] Van Boven, 36.

non-material injury, where the involvement of community interest acquires, as we shall see below, an additional relevance.

1.3.3. Satisfaction

(a) General impact of jus cogens on satisfaction

The ILC's articles on State responsibility treat satisfaction as one of the substantive consequences of a wrongful act, and stress its residual role, which consists in ensuring that reparation is full and effective, by stating in Article 37 that 'The State responsible for an internationally wrongful act is under an obligation to give satisfaction for the injury caused by that act insofar as it cannot be made good by restitution or compensation.' The ILC's Articles further specify that 'Satisfaction may consist in an acknowledgement of the breach, an expression of regret, a formal apology or another appropriate modality,' and the Commission adds in the commentary that the appropriate mode of satisfaction will be determined having regard to the circumstances of each case.[69] It is therefore clear that the modes of satisfaction listed in Article 37 are not exhaustive but merely illustrative, to be understood in the light of the overall goal of the reparations regime to effectively eliminate the harm and injury caused.

This entire framework confirms that satisfaction is the only form of reparation which has no self-explanatory concept and cannot, unlike restitution and compensation, be defined by reference to its title. It consists of specific headings of remedies, whose relevance has to be determined by reference to the overriding goals of reparation consisting in the elimination of the consequences of a wrongful act, as well as the governing legal framework. Consequently, peremptory norms protecting the community interest acquire their relevance here as well.

Satisfaction as a form of reparation is widely resorted to in international judicial practice and focused upon in doctrine, but this hardly ensures the existence of a uniform view on the subject. According to Article 41 of the European Convention on Human Rights, if 'there has been a violation of the Convention or the protocols thereto, and if the internal law of the High Contracting Party concerned allows only partial reparation to be made, the [European] Court [of Human Rights] shall, if necessary, afford just satisfaction to the injured party'. The Convention does not describe the kind and extent of satisfaction nor does it give distinction between satisfaction and other forms of reparation. In practice, the European Court has interpreted this provision quite extensively and awarded under the heading of 'just satisfaction' multiple remedies available under general international law and

---

[69] *ILC Report* 2001, 266 (commentary to Article 37, para. 5).

covered by the ILC's Articles, including restitution in kind, compensation for material and non-material injuries, as well as some modes of satisfaction, either singly, or in combination.[70] Thus, the concept of satisfaction under general international law, as mirrored in the ILC's Articles, is different from 'just satisfaction' in that it is not comprehensive, but residual, and covers only those remedies which are necessary to be awarded if the injury caused is not made good by restitution and compensation for material injury.

As a form of responsibility, satisfaction shall be applied to the acts of the State which cause moral injury to the State and which are not assessable in material terms. The modes or extent of satisfaction cannot be measured according to material criteria, because it reflects moral injury only. Even if residual, satisfaction is a fundamental form of reparation, since it is a corollary for the respect of fundamental principles of international law such as the sovereign equality of States and their dignity, and provides remedies for violation of those principles. In addition, with the introduction of humanitarian values into this legal system the importance of satisfaction has been established and gradually increased also in this area. Satisfaction is a suitable remedy in cases of human rights violations, because such violations involve a great deal of moral injury to human beings and the non-exhaustive nature of satisfaction is helpful in determining how such moral injury could be undone. Consequently, satisfaction is a remedy with multiple consequences, and it is no longer possible to keep its relevance within the traditional bilateralist understanding of State responsibility and to limit it to purely inter-State remedies such as expression of regret or apology. The open-endedness of the concept as mirrored in the ILC's articles shall be understood as allowing using satisfaction for effectively making good the injury caused to non-State actors in consequence of violation of *jus cogens*— the injury in whose redress the international community as a whole is deemed to have a legal interest. The relevance of community interest consists not only in making the satisfaction imperative and non-derogable, but also (again, because of the open-endedness of the concept) in determining which modes of satisfaction are suitable to meet the community interest in redressing the wrong caused. The reasons for the peremptory nature of the norms violated should be kept in mind. As most peremptory norms—such as those outlawing genocide, war crimes and crimes against humanity, torture, disappearance or unlawful killing—have such status because of outlawing conducts so immoral as to shock the conscience of mankind, the existence of community interest in a proper and objective redress of the harm caused also becomes

---

[70] In the practice of the ECtHR, 'satisfaction' in sense of Article 50 ECHR includes elements both of compensation and satisfaction in sense of the ILC's Articles, Crawford, *Third Report*, A/CN.4/507/Add.1, 24, n. 304.

clear. This, in its turn, is crucial in determining which modes of satisfaction are appropriate in a given particular case.

(b) Acknowledgment of a breach

Satisfaction may, under certain conditions, consist in a declaration that a certain act or conduct was wrongful. In *Corfu Channel*, the International Court of Justice stated that the actions by the British Royal Navy in Albanian territorial waters have violated sovereignty of Albania and that this declaration constituted itself an appropriate satisfaction. But it should not be overlooked that Albania itself limited its request to such remedy and did not ask for anything else, which the Court took note of.[71] In *Rainbow Warrior*, the Arbitral Tribunal stated that the condemnation of actions taken by France in violation of its obligations towards New Zealand constituted appropriate satisfaction,[72] but in the same case compensation was also awarded. If viewed pragmatically, declaration of wrongfulness is in fact the failure to award a remedy. Such an approach could be perfectly appropriate in disputes involving a traditional bilateralist legal framework, if this corresponds to the will of the parties. But in disputes involving peremptory norms protecting the community interest, such an approach is definitionally ill-founded, because to remedy violations of *jus cogens* is in the interest of the international community as a whole.

In a considerable number of cases involving non-pecuniary loss or moral damages, the European Court of Human Rights confines its ruling to holding that the finding of a breach in itself is an appropriate satisfaction (declaratory judgments),[73] using this option to justify its failure to award compensation.[74] But unlike the International Court, the European Court generally offers no explanation why a declaratory judgement should be regarded as an appropriate just satisfaction and this casts doubt upon the correctness of the Court's findings.[75] For the purposes of remedyng violations of peremptory norms (it may be routinely assumed that serious and grave human rights violations fall within that category), the option of declaratory judgments should be treated with caution and care, for it does not at all ensure that the

---

[71] *Corfu Channel, ICJ Reports*, 1948, 35.

[72] RIAA, vol. XX, 272–273, 275.

[73] *Kruslin* case 11801/85 (para. 39) and *Aquilina* case 25642/94 (para. 59); see also Robertson and Merrils, *Human Rights in Europe* (1993), 313–314.

[74] Kamminga, Legal Consequences of an Internationally Wrongful Act of a State against an Individual, Barkhuysen *et al.* (eds), *Execution of Strasbourg and Geneva Human Rights Decisions in National Legal Orders*, 67, 72; Pellonpää, Individual reparation claims under the European Convention on Human Rights, Randelzhofer and Tomuschat (eds), *State Responsibility and the Individual:* reparation in instances of grave violations of human rights (1999), 118; Dannemann, *Schadenersatz bei Verletzung der Europaeischen Menschenrechtskonvention* (1994), 365.

[75] Dannemann, *Schadenersatz bei Verletzung der Europaeischen Menschenrechtskonvention* (1994), 368.

wrongful consequences of a violation are objectively redressed. The approach of the Inter-American Court is better reasoned in that it recognizes that 'a condemnatory judgment does not suffice when the right to life is concerned, and the reparation for the moral suffering caused to the victim and to the family must take an alternative form, such as pecuniary compensation'.[76]

(c) Material compensation for moral injury

While in terms of compensation for material damage the concept of *jus cogens* operates as making the duty to make reparation imperative as such, in terms of compensation for moral damage *jus cogens* seems to have a further function, namely influencing the very cause of action and the extent and possible amount of compensation.[77] In case of material damage, the amount of compensation is determined in material terms depending upon the extent of material injury, but in terms of moral damage affronting the community interest the amount of compensation should be determined *inter alia* by reference to the fact that the conduct has been performed in detriment to what the international community as such considers to be a fundamental value or interest.

It must not be forgotten that certain norms are peremptory because they prohibit a conduct which is excessively brutal and causes unjustified suffering to human beings or their groups. Such an inherent link between the nature of the conduct prohibited and the community interest safeguarded by *jus cogens* justifies the assumption that award of adequate pecuniary compensation for non-material injury suffered by non-State actors also forms an inherent consequence of violations of peremptory norms.

At the earlier stage of the work on State responsibility, the ILC has noted that in practice satisfaction and compensation are frequently confused with each other.[78] Therefore, it specified that damages reflecting the gravity of infringement as part of satisfaction are awarded for the injury over and above actual, or material, loss.[79] This caused a strict delimitation between the concepts of compensation for material and non-material injuries, the latter concept being part of satisfaction. But the situation in the final version of the Articles on State Responsibility seems to be more confused and less clear. The Commission specified in the commentary to Article 36 that

Compensation corresponds to the financially assessable damage suffered by the injured State and its nationals. It is not concerned to punish the responsible State, nor does compensation have an expressive or exemplary character. . . . It is true that

---

[76] *Castillo Paez*, 116 ILR 511.
[77] See *inter alia* the Nicaragua's Memorial on Compensation in the *Nicaragua* case, *ICJ Pleadings* 1986, vol. V, 326, 334.
[78] *Yearbook of the ILC*, 1993, vol. II, part 2, 76; *ILC Report* 1996, 143.
[79] Ibid., 79.

monetary payments may be called for by way of satisfaction under article 37, but they perform the function distinct from that of compensation.... Satisfaction is concerned with non-material injury, on which a monetary value can be put only in a highly approximate and notional way.[80]

This function of satisfaction naturally is to make good a moral, or non-pecuniary, damage caused whether to a State or a non-State actor. The formulation is broad enough to cover both categories. However, in its commentary to Article 37, the ILC suggests that

Material and moral damage resulting from an internationally wrongful act will normally be financially assessable and hence covered by the remedy of compensation. Satisfaction, on the other hand, is the remedy for those injuries, not financially assessable, which amount to an affront to the State. These injuries are frequently of a symbolic character, arising from the very fact of the breach of the obligation, irrespective of its material consequences for the State concerned.[81]

If the ILC thereby means that satisfaction for not financially assessable injuries does not include an element of pecuniary compensation, this would contradict its own attitude just quoted above. But then, the ILC nevertheless seems to recognize the relevance of pecuniary compensation in terms of satisfaction, by stating, for instance, that satisfaction may include the arrangement of a 'trust fund to manage compensation payments in the interest of the beneficiaries';[82] it mentions the possibility of an award of 'symbolic damages for non-pecuniary injury' and refers in this respect to the *I'm Alone* case,[83] which can be taken as an authority supporting the notion of punitive damages. Furthermore, the ILC seems to acknowledge that in cases of serious breaches of peremptory norms, the payment of damages reflecting the gravity of infringement is not excluded since, as the ILC noted in the commentary, the author State remains under the duty to make reparation in accordance with the regime of reparations provided in the other provisions of the Articles on State Responsibility.[84]

Material compensation for non-material damage is a remedy widely recognized in the practice of different international tribunals and is unlikely to be abandoned as a remedy despite the possible scepticism, or even uncertainty, in the ILC's approach.[85] In case of *Rainbow Warrior* the UN Secretary-General decided to impose on France payment of a sum that was

---

[80] *ILC Report* 2001, 245–246 (commentary to Article 36, para. 4).
[81] Ibid., 264 (commentary to Article 37, para. 3).
[82] Ibid., 265–266 (commentary to Article 37, para. 5).
[83] Ibid., 266 (commentary to Article 37, para. 5).
[84] Ibid., 291 (commentary to Article 41, para. 12).
[85] Despite some sceptical views suggesting that State responsibility for non-material damage should be limited to non-material remedies, such as acknowledgment or a breach, expression or regret or apology, Wittich, Awe of the Gods and Fear of the Priests: Punitive Damages and the Law of State Responsibility, *Austrian Reviews of International and European Law*, vol. 3, 1998, 139, 155–156.

much higher than the material damage suffered from its action by New Zealand.[86] Although it is held that the European Court of Human Rights is generally reluctant to grant exemplary or punitive damages,[87] in a number of cases the clear distinction between the damages for pecuniary loss and the damages for non-pecuniary loss has been made, with pecuniary compensation in the amount higher than the material damage suffered by the applicant.[88] Similarly, the Inter-American Court concluded in *Velasquez-Rodriguez* and *Aloeboetoe* that fair compensation includes reparation of the material and moral damages suffered by victims, and that in case of moral damages caused by human rights violations, pecuniary indemnity must be awarded.[89] UN Special Rapporteurs have unanimously affirmed that in case of serious human rights and humanitarian law violations, compensation for non-material injury is a necessary consequence ro remedy the victims' mental harm, pain, suffering and emotional distress.[90]

As for the determination of quantum, the inter-American Court stressed in *Castillo Paez* that 'The pecuniary compensation should be determined on the basis of equity and by a prudent assessment of the moral damages.'[91] The Court went further and stressed that in cases of serious human rights violations, moral damages need not be shown, as they can be presumed. They are a natural consequence in cases of disappearances and abusive treatment of the victims, as well as in cases where their relatives experience terrible moral suffering.[92] This practice evidences that material reparation for non-material injury possesses the relevance of an independent remedy at least in the field here under consideration. The context of the norm and its breach determines what is full reparation in a given case and respectively what amount of moral damages should be paid.

The nature of a specific violation is crucial in determining the availability and extent of compensation for non-pecuniary injury. The Inter-American Court found the basis for compensation for moral damages in the fright, anguish and depression caused to the family members of the abducted persons.[93] In *Aloeboetoe*, the Court held that

---

[86] XX *RIAA*, 224, 271.

[87] Harris, O'Boyle and Warbrick, *The Law of the European Convention on Human Rights*, 1995, 687.

[88] *Aydin*, 23178/94, paras 127–130; *Aksoy*, 21987/93, para. 113.

[89] *Velasquez-Rodriguez*, 95 ILR 232; *Velasquez-Rodriguez* (Compensation), 95 ILR 314–316; *Aloeboetoe*, 116 ILR 277; *Castillo Paez*, 116 ILR 512.

[90] Van Boven, *Revised set of basic principles and guidelines on the right to reparation for victims of gross violations of human rights and humanitarian law*, E/CN.4/Sub.2/1996/17, para. 13; Bassiouni, *Final Report on the right to restitution, compensation and rehabilitation for victims of gross human rights violations*, E/CN.4/2000, 62, 10 (para. 23); Joinet, *Revised final report on question of immunity of perpetrators of human rights violations*, E/CN.4/Sub.2/1997/20/Rev.1, para. 41(b) and principle 36; Guy McDougal, *Report on systematic rape*, E/CN.4/Sub.2/1998/13, para. 88.

[91] *Castillo Paez*, 116 ILR 511.   [92] Ibid., 512; *Suarez Rosero*, 118 ILR 111.

[93] *Velasquez-Rodriguez* (Compensation), 95 ILR 318.

The beatings received, the pain of knowing they were condemned to die for no reason whatsoever, the torture of having to dig their own graves are all part of the moral damages suffered by the victims. In addition, the person who did not die outright had to bear the pain of his wounds being infested by maggots and of seeing the bodies of his companions being devoured by vultures.[94]

It must be emphasized that the practice of the Inter-American Court is most appropriate in terms of elimination of wrongful consequences of violation of peremptory norms. The Court fully takes into account the objective circumstances of particular breaches and also tries to award sums of compensation appropriate for redressing the actual suffering.[95] This practice illustrates that the Court tries to award damages in a way leading to objective elimination of wrongful consequences and the human suffering caused.

(d)   The question of punitive damages

Once it is clarified that material compensation for non-material injury is often an indispensable element of remedying violations of certain norms of *jus cogens*, it remains to clarify whether the violations of similar character permit to award punitive, or exemplary, damages to the victims of violations. The question of punitive damages may be prompted by the nature of a norm breached, or the breach itself and the extent and gravity of the injury suffered by a victim State or individuals.

As the ILC's Special Rapporteur submitted, 'there is no authority and very little justification for the award of punitive damages properly so-called, in cases of State responsibility, in the absence of some special regime for their imposition.'[96] The Inter-American Court also stated that Article 63(1) of the American Convention dealing with its remedial competence does not refer to punitive damages, but makes possible compensatory damages only,[97] but this may well be taken as an observation on the Court's remedial powers and not the substantive law of remedies. The Court in fact often awards compensation for moral injury in sufficiently high amounts, which are not very far from punitive damages.

Whether punitive damages are available could be clarified only after it is

---

[94] *Aloeboetoe*, 116 ILR 277.

[95] *Loayza Tamayo* (Reparations), 116 ILR 388; *Castillo Paez* (Reparations), 116 ILR 483; *Aloeboetoe*, 116 ILR 261; *Suarez Rosero* (Reparations), 118 ILR 92. In *Gangaram Panday*, the Inter-American Court awarded to the family members of the victim of deprivation of life $10,000, which it considered to be a nominal amount, 116 ILR 318. The reason for awarding nominal compensation was that the respondent State has not been found guilty of death of the victim, who died while imprisoned. The judgment makes clear that this essential sum is just nominal and would be insufficient to remedy fully the violation if it were attributed to the respondent State.

[96] Crawford, *Third Report on State Responsibility*, A/CN.4/507/Add.1, 40.

[97] *Velasquez-Rodriguez*, 95 ILR 306.

ascertained what is meant by the concept. Its difference from material compensation for moral injury is neither absolute nor strict. If material compensation is awarded for a moral injury, it is awarded to remedy moral suffering, but every material compensation form moral injury also has an exemplary or deterrent element. For example, it may be held that punitive damages have been awarded in *I'm Alone*[98] for the intentional sinking of a ship and in absence of any material damage to a State to which the damages were awarded. But it may then also be held that this was just compensation for the moral injury.

It is accepted that there is some scepticism both in theory and judicial practice regarding the imposition of punitive damages on States, but some authors hold that punitive damages are perhaps permitted.[99] A good example of a description of the purpose of punitive damages is the judgment of the District Court in the United States in *Filartiga*, whose criteria may apply to international law as well. The District Court considered that punitive damages are not justified by the desire to punish the defendant, but are designed to compensate for the greater pain caused by the atrocious nature of the act, to respond to 'human cruelty and brutality'.[100] In this context, the District Court focused upon the fact that 'it is essential and proper to grant the remedy of punitive damages in order to give effect to the manifest objectives of the international prohibition against torture', the breach of which, in the Court's view, cannot be remedied without punitive damages.[101] In addition, the deterrent impact of this remedy was emphasized.[102] The District Court's reasoning at the example of remedying breaches of the prohibition of torture, a profound example of *jus cogens*, is in accordance with the argument on what is the cause of a norm's peremptory character and what should be the consequence of such peremptory character. As the observance of the prohibition is in the interest of the international community as a whole and not merely of individual States, it is equally in the interest of the former to deter violations of that prohibition, and punitive damages, along with individual criminal responsibility (to be dealt with below), constitute a useful tool in achieving this task.

Whatever the term, the essence of punitive damages is therefore clear and it is hardly deniable that they have a unique function in redressing serious human rights violations. The ILC, which has sometimes been sceptical to the notion of punitive damages, nevertheless affirmed in its Report that if the egregious breaches of obligations owed to the international community are

---

[98] For the relevant passages from the case see Brownlie, *State Responsibility* (1983), 208–209.

[99] Brownlie, *International Law and the Use of Force by States* (1963), 148, referring also to Oppenheim and Briggs.

[100] *Filartiga v Pena-Irala*, 77 ILR 188, 190. The Court also emphasized that torture is viewed with universal abhorrence and a torturer is *hostis humani generis*, ibid., 187.

[101] Ibid., 188–189.   [102] Ibid., 190.

committed, the members of the international community must be able to seek aggravated damages on behalf of victims.[103] Viewed in this way, the commonality of the concept of punitive damages with the concept of pecuniary compensation for moral injury becomes clear. The very concept will become less unacceptable if one accepts the constructive and balanced view of Brownlie and Rosenne, submitting that punitive or exemplary damages are to be regarded more as a form of calculating and quantification, in the light of all the circumstances, of the amount of reparation due in monetary terms, than as punitive sanctions.[104] If this is accepted, one can conclude that the law of reparations would not sanction the award of punitive damages not responding to an actual injury, but on the other hand it would require the award of any amount of compensation responding to actual moral injury, however high in amount, even if it looks 'punitive' or 'exemplary' from an extra-legal point of view.[105] Therefore, the better way is not to categorize damages into 'punitive' and 'non-punitive' and thus judge on their permissibility in an aprioristic way, but to examine the nature of a breach and suffering in each specific case and thus find out what kind and amount of compensation is due.

(e) Individual criminal responsibility

The ILC's Articles on State Responsibility affirm that satisfaction includes 'disciplinary or penal action against the individuals whose conduct caused the internationally wrongful act'.[106] In practice it has been affirmed that the measures consisting in investigation of breaches and the punishment of those responsible is the part of reparation.[107] States must investigate serious human rights violations and punish the perpetrators, even if this is contrary to their domestic law.[108] Special Rapporteurs Van Boven, Bassiouni and Joinet consider that every State shall exercise universal jurisdiction over serious violations of human rights and humanitarian law.[109] The same principle has

[103] *ILC Report* 2000, 108, para. 358.

[104] Rosenne, War Crimes and State Responsibility, 24 *Israel Yearbook of Human Rights* (1994), 98; Brownlie (2003), 447.

[105] Despite the view that large sums of compensation may look as a punishment, Jorgensen, *Punitive Damages in International Law*, 68 *British Year Book of International Law* (1997), 266.

[106] *ILC Report* 2001, 265–266 (commentary to Article 37, para. 5).

[107] *Velasquez-Rodriguez* (Compensation), 95 ILR 315, emphasizing that measures consisting in investigation of breaches, the punishment of those responsible and a public statement condemning that practice constitutes the part of the reparation in accordance with Article 63(1) of the American Convention.

[108] *Loayza Tamayo*, 116 ILR 435.

[109] Van Boven, *Revised set of basic principles and guidelines on the right to reparation for victims of gross violations of human rights and humanitarian law*, E/CN.4/Sub.2/1996/17, para. 5; Bassiouni, *Final Report on the right to restitution, compensation and rehabilitation for victims of gross human rights violations*, E/CN.4/2000, 62, 7–8 (para. 5); Joinet, *Revised final report on question of immunity of perpetrators of human rights violations*, E/CN.4/Sub.2/1997/20/Rev.1, principle 20.

been upheld with regard to crimes against humanity and war crimes by the Special Rapporteur on systematic rape.[110]

From the perspective of *jus cogens*, this aspect of satisfaction acquires a specific importance. Prosecution of crimes against peace and security of mankind is a subject of interest to the international community as a whole. It seems to be established that universal jurisdiction is available in case of breaches of *jus cogens*.[111] States are in some circumstances under a duty to exercise universal jurisdiction through extraditing or prosecuting the accused, and it is submitted that individual criminal responsibility of perpetrators of war crimes and crimes against humanity is based on a peremptory norm.[112] In the same spirit, the ILC stated as early as 1976 that individual criminal responsibility for certain crimes 'testifies unquestionably to the exceptional importance now attached by the international community to the fulfilment of obligations having a certain subject-matter. It is, moreover, no accident that the obligations ... whose breach entails the personal punishment of the perpetrators, correspond largely to the certain rules of *jus cogens*.'[113]

Therefore, what is an ordinary element of satisfaction as a part of the duty to make reparation becomes peremptory as soon as a given violation involves the breach of peremptory norms. An otherwise bilateralist legal framework of this element of satisfaction is in such cases overtaken by the overriding effect of *jus cogens*.

1.4. Jus cogens *limitations on the duty to provide reparation*

Apart from providing the basis for some remedies in specific situations and making them as such peremptory, the function of *jus cogens* in the field of reparations also consists in providing some limitations upon the duty to make reparation, if that endangers the integral operation of peremptory norms. This can be explained by the fact that peremptory norms may be breached not only in the course of an original violation, but also of the consequential award of remedies. The purpose of such limiting function of *jus cogens* is to serve as a limitation both upon the concept of reparation in general, and specific remedies in particular, as well as to safeguard the fundamental

---

[110] McDougal, *Report on systematic rape*, E/CN.4/Sub.2/1998/13, para. 85.

[111] Crimes implicating breaches of *jus cogens* justify States in taking universal jurisdiction over them wherever committed, because offenders are common enemies of mankind and all nations have an equal interest in their apprehension and prosecution, Lord Browne-Wilkinson, *Pinochet*, 2 All ER (1999), 109; Lord Millett, ibid., 177–178. See also the Court of First Instance of Brussels, 119 ILR, 356–357; *Eichmann*, 36 ILR, 1; *Demjanjuk*, 79 ILR, 545.

[112] Lord Hope, *Pinochet*, 2 All ER (1999), 147, states that *jus cogens* imposes on all States an *erga omnes* obligation to punish certain international crimes. See also Dissenting Opinion of Judge van den Wyngaert, the *Arrest Warrant* case, ICJ General List No. 121, 2002, para. 46; Dissenting Opinion of Judge Al-Khasawneh, id., para. 7.

[113] YbILC, 1976, vol. II, part 2, 104.

interests guaranteed under peremptory norms both to States and non-State actors.

It is necessary to consider the inherent limitations on the remedy of pecuniary compensation. Some authors consider that compensation shall not endanger the existence and vital conditions of the population.[114] Article 42(3) of the ILC's draft articles adopted on first reading proclaimed the principle that reparation may not deprive a people of the means of subsistence. The commentary to that provision made it clear that its purpose was not to weaken the general regime of reparations, but to serve a specific purpose of not depriving the population of a State of the means of subsistence. The Commission noted that this provision was about extreme cases and applied in particular to cases where an injured State has to provide reparation by payment of sums of money by way of compensation. In this context, the commentary explained that this principle would not prevent such remedies as, for example, the return of a territory wrongfully seized.[115]

Though certain States considered that this principle would enable the wrongdoer State to refuse full reparation, others treated it as a valid principle,[116] and the principle was finally dropped from the ILC's Articles. The principle that a people shall in no way be deprived of the means of its subsistence is an important aspect of the right to self-determination, itself a *jus cogens* rule. It is further affirmed by the common Article 1 of the two human rights covenants of 1966. According to the General Comment 12(21) of the Human Rights Committee (para. 5), the right of peoples to self-determination entails corresponding duties for all States and the international community, and the duty to preserve the subsistence of peoples would have a similar effect. In addition, as the ILC emphasized, a crippling compensation could involve serious violations of human rights.[117] Consequently, in every bilateral relationship involving reparations the duty to preserve the subsistence of peoples would be a full-fledged limitation on the conduct of parties.

As the Special Rapporteur suggested, there is a difference between the delay of payment and the exclusion of it, between the quantum due and the method of payment. If a State for the time being is unable to pay, the provisions on circumstances precluding wrongfulness would govern this situation.[118] Therefore, reparation may still be refused to the extent that it may endanger the subsistence of peoples. But for a more legal security of protected actors, it would be better if the provision had not been dropped from the ILC's Articles, in which case the interested actors would be able to

---

[114] De Hoogh, *International Crimes and Obligations* Erga Omnes (1996), 190.
[115] Commentary to Article 42(3), para. 8(a) *ILC Report* 1996, 152.
[116] Crawford, A/CN.4/507, 13 (UK and Germany respectively).
[117] *ILC Report* 2000, 61, para. 191.
[118] Crawford, *Third Report*, A/CN.4/507, 21.

refer to a substantive principle rather than invoke circumstances precluding wrongfulness. But this latter circumstance does not affect their legal entitlement to refuse reparation insofar as the subsistence of peoples is endangered.

1.5. Evaluation

This analysis has demonstrated that *jus cogens* may influence the law of reparations in a variety of ways. This may take place through different modes:

(1) The otherwise bilateralist regime of reparations based on *jus dispositivum* is overtaken by the regime of consequences of operation of *jus cogens*. In cases of breach of *jus cogens* the duty to make reparation, or certain of its forms, such as *restitutio in integrum*, itself becomes peremptory and hence a subject of interest to the international community as a whole.

(2) Certain substantive norms of *jus cogens* may be crucial in determining whether specific remedies, such as the material compensation for non-material injury or punitive damages, are available and what should be their amount.

(3) Certain specific consequences of the operation of *jus cogens* may cause certain aspects of reparation to become peremptory as such. This holds true in case of restitution, as well as individual criminal responsibility as an element of satisfaction.

(4) *Jus cogens* operates not only as a cause for, but also as a limitation on reparations, when they are likely to result in breach of a peremptory norm.

Such effects of peremptory norms do supplement their role to safeguard the interests of the international community as a whole and to do so in an integral way, not allowing fragmentation of respective legal relations in any aspect. This underlines the consequential profile of *jus cogens* outlawing, in the context of responsibility and remedies, the acts that authorize the breaches of, and derogate from, peremptory norms. There are many ways that *jus cogens* operates in the law of reparations, and most of them are already widely recognized on their own merits, sometimes due to factors not totally or not clearly identical to *jus cogens*. But what is recognized in specific instances may be due to a more general phenomenon. *Jus cogens* may have a comprehensive impact on the law of reparations in the interest of the international community as a whole, and the respective effects of *jus cogens* should be examined in a consolidated way, thereby making clear the necessary link between the concept of peremptory norms and their specific effects.

2. THE INVOCATION OF BREACHES OF PEREMPTORY NORMS

That the observance of peremptory norms is a subject of interest to the international community as a whole indicates that the breach of such norms cannot be deemed to be a bilateral matter as between the injured and wrong-doer States. This raises the issue of the relationship between peremptory norms and another concept dealing with the community interest— obligations *erga omnes*. This latter concept can mean different things in different contexts. At the outset, the distinction made by Gaja appears quite useful, suggesting that 'the concept of obligation *erga omnes* should be used only with reference to the type of obligation and not to the type of the rules that impose these obligations'.[119] This implies that the *erga omnes* character of an obligation depends not on that obligation itself, but on some other factor.

In order to clarify what *erga omnes* obligations are, it must be clarified on what basis an obligation can be invocable *erga omnes*, that is invocable by States not having suffered individual injury or prejudice through the breach of that norm. One instance of such a phenomenon is where States decide, explicitly or implicitly, but mostly through a treaty, to endow the obligation in question with such status. These obligations are most conveniently denoted as obligations *erga omnes partes* and this is the case with regard to treaty regimes related to territory and disarmament.[120] Such obligations are said to be established in the common interest of the parties to a particular regime,[121] as arguably distinguished from the interests of the international community as a whole.

In other cases, the *erga omnes* character of an obligation is implied in the nature of obligation itself, as opposed to the consensual decision of States. This latter case suggests examining the content of norms on which respective obligations are based; if it is demonstrated that an obligation safeguards the interests of the international community as such, it should be deemed to be invocable *erga omnes*. The International Court in *Barcelona Traction* has indeed adopted such a substantive, as opposed to consensual-evidentiary, approach to certain *erga omnes* obligations, such as prohibition of aggression, genocide or racial discrimination, by pointing out that owing to the importance of the subject-matter of these obligations, all States have a legal interest in their protection.[122] It is this category of *erga omnes* obligations that is most significant for the present analysis.

It appears that *jus cogens* and obligations *erga omnes* are but two sides of

---

[119] Gaja, *Ius Cogens*, Obligations *Erga Omnes* and International Crimes: A Tentative Analysis of Three Related Concepts, in Weiler, Cassese and Spinedi (eds) (1996), 153.

[120] See further above, Chapter 4.   [121] Crawford, Third Report, A/CN.4/507, 47.

[122] *Barcelona Traction, ICJ Reports*, 1970, paras 33–34.

the same coin, as they both relate to the concern of all States.[123] Arguably, while obligations *erga omnes* follow from peremptory norms, the reverse is not always true. There can be *erga omnes* obligations not deriving from *jus cogens*, such as the right of passage in an international strait.[124] It seems that those *erga omnes* obligations which protect not just the interest of States-parties to a particular treaty but those of the international community as a whole, are based on peremptory norms. Such a parallel emphasizes the conceptual commonality between peremptory norms and *erga omnes* obligations of those kinds which were dealt with in *Barcelona Traction*. If Gaja's reasoning accepted that the concept of *erga omnes* relates to obligations not rules, then it must also be accepted that, as every obligation is based on a certain rule, the *erga omnes* character of an obligation is conceivably based on the character of a norm which gives rise to that obligation. In other words, the concept of *erga omnes* obligation is not an independent concept because there must be a reason *why* a given obligation has the *erga omnes* character and this issue cannot be clarified without clarifying the character of the underlying rule. If an obligation is specific in character, then it must be based on a rule which is also specific in character.

According to Frowein, the International Court implied the existence of *jus cogens*, without explicitly referring to it, when it spoke of *erga omnes* obligations in *Barcelona Traction*.[125] Even more clearly, Malanczuk suggests that *erga omnes* obligations are concerned with the enforceability of *jus cogens* norms, the violation of which affects not only individual States, but the international community as a whole.[126] This suggests that the *erga omnes* nature of an obligation is not a source or determinant of the public order nature of a norm but merely a consequence of such public order nature. The *erga omnes* nature of an obligation merely evidences the invocability of legal consequences of its violations as these consequences—especially those affecting the process of validity and interpretation—are determined by the *jus cogens* nature of a rule from which the obligation in question follows. Meron states in the specific context of human rights that the *erga omnes* character is a consequence, not the cause, of a right's fundamental character.[127]

---

[123] Simma, Injury and Countermeasures, in Weiler, Cassese and Spinedi (eds), 290; Simma, Bilateralism and the Community Interest in the Law of State Responsibility, *Festschrift Rosenne* (1989), 825; Dominice, The International Responsibility of States for Breach of Multilateral Obligations, 10 *EJIL* (1999), 358–359.

[124] Abi-Saab, The Uses of Article 19, 10 *EJIL* (1999), 348; Pellet, Can a State Commit a Crime? Definitely, Yes!, 10 *EJIL* (1999), 429.

[125] Frowein, *Jus Cogens*, 7 *EPIL* 328; Malanczuk, First ILA Report, 44–45, para. 141.

[126] Malanczuk, Counter-measures and Self-defence, in Spinedi and Simma (eds), 230–231.

[127] Meron, *Human Rights Law-Making in the United Nations* (1986), 183; Bassiouni, International Crimes: *Jus Cogens* and *Obligatio Erga Omnes, Law and Contemporary Problems* (1996), 73, considers that the *erga omnes* status in terms of international crimes is 'a consequence of a given international crime having risen to the level of *jus cogens*'.

The parallel between peremptory norms and *erga omnes* obligations is clear. As Special Rapporteur Crawford suggests, peremptory norms and *erga omnes* obligations are virtually coextensive.[128] It is further suggested that 'if a particular obligation can be set aside or displaced as between two States, it is hard to see how that obligation is owed to the international community as a whole'.[129] According to Simma, if the international community considers the observance of certain rules as imperative, individual States cannot be allowed to contract out of them in their relations *inter se*, and the performance of such essential obligations for the common benefit is naturally due to all members of the community, not just to one or more States *quid pro quo*.[130] This confirms that the *erga omnes* character of obligations under general international law is consequential upon the peremptory character of the norms under which those obligations are stipulated.

2.1. Third-party countermeasures

In the decentralized international legal system, the enforcement of international obligations depends to a great extent on the measures of reciprocity taken by individual States, such as reprisals or, in modern terminology, countermeasures.[131] The traditional pattern of international law requires that the faculty of countermeasures rests only with those States which are immediately injured by the breach of international law.

This predominant position of traditional international law has long been responsible for the reluctance of both doctrine and practice to accept the faculty of States to take countermeasures in response to the breaches of fundamental norms of international law, even if they are not directly affected by the respective breach. Thus Malanczuk argued that reprisals by third States in the case of violation of *erga omnes* obligations are not lawful countermeasures unless authorized by an international institution.[132] Having analysed the problem from different perspectives, Akehurst arrived at the conclusion that it was open to States to take third-party countermeasures only on one of these three cases: in enforcement of judicial decisions; as the affected party to the treaty under Article 60(2) of the 1969 Vienna Convention; or in response to the violation of rules prohibiting or regulating the use of force. In all other cases, Akehurst considered that 'there are sound policy reasons that third States are not, as a general rule, allowed to take reprisals'.

---

[128] Crawford, Third Report, A/CN.4/507, para. 106.

[129] Crawford, Third Report, A/CN.4/507, 46–47.

[130] Simma, Bilateralism and the Community Interest in the Law of State Responsibility, *Festschrift Rosenne* (1989), 825.

[131] The issue of countermeasures has been among the most important topics in the codification of the law of State responsibility in the UN International Law Commission, and is dealt with in Articles 49–54 on State responsibility, *ILC Report* 2001, 324–355.

[132] Malanczuk, Counter-measures and Self-defence, in Spinedi and Simma (eds), 234.

The principal concern against such a faculty is the danger of abuse and ensuing risks of instability.[133] As Frowein has suggested, the States that are not directly affected by the breach may limit their reaction to passive responses such as non-recognition of forcible territorial acquisitions.[134] But later Frowein seems to have reversed his view and considered that third-party countermeasures, such as trade embargoes, are permissible in response to the violation of fundamental international obligations.[135]

The actual or possible objections against the faculty of States to take third-party countermeasures in response to breaches of fundamental norms can thus be categorized into three groups: (a) the (conceptual) objection that points to the prevalence of bilateralism in the law of State responsibility; (b) the objection that, although certain international norms are established to safeguard the community interest, the insufficiency of State practice precludes the crystallization of the rule that would allow States to take third-party countermeasures; (c) the policy objection pointing to the ensuing risks of abuse and instability.

However, as Simma points out, it is a bilateralist approach to hold that only directly injured States can resort to countermeasures in response to the breaches of fundamental norms.[136] During the process of codification of the law of State responsibility within the ILC, Special Rapporteur Crawford suggested that States-parties to a community obligation should be allowed to take collective countermeasures in response to a gross and well-attested breach of that obligation.[137] As Gaja points out, in some cases, such as cases of human rights violations, even if no State seeks reparation, the counter-measures are still permissible as a safeguard for community interests.[138] In response to the breaches of *jus cogens*, such as torture and slavery, committed on a large scale, it may be openly and indisputably accepted that the use of reprisals is justified.[139]

The logical and consequential link between the nature of the relevant violations and the standing of third States to take countermeasures is quite clear. The International Law Commission, having originally intended to adopt the draft article regarding the faculty to take third-party counter-measures in response to breaches of community obligations, decided at the final stage of codification, due both to resistance from States and to lack of

---

[133] Akehurst, Reprisals by Third States, *BYIL* 1970, 15–18.
[134] Frowein, Verpflichtungen erga omnes im Völkerrecht und Ihre Durchsetzung, *Festschrift für Hermann Mosler* (1983), 260. This is said generally, also concerning *actio popularis*.
[135] Frowein, Staatengemeinschaftsinteresse—Probleme bei Formulierung und Durchsetzung, Hailbronner, Ress and Stein (Hrsg.), *Staat und Völkerrechtsordnung, Festschrift für Karl Doehring* (1989), 228.
[136] Simma, *Festschrift Rosenne* (1989), 821.
[137] Crawford, Third Report, A/CN.4/507/Add.4, 21 (practice reviewed, id., at 14–21).
[138] Gaja, in Weiler, Cassese and Spinedi (eds), 155–156.
[139] Stein, Collective Enforcement of International Obligations, 47 *ZaöRV* (1987), 76, 78.

uniformity and consistency in practice, not to adopt the clause explicitly authorizing States to take third-party countermeasures, but instead to adopt the neutral 'no-prejudice' clause.[140] The issue of third-party countermeasures is nevertheless of great conceptual and practical significance. The conceptual link between the nature of certain breaches of international law and the faculty to take third-party countermeasures, in other words the conceptual incompatibility between *erga omnes* obligations and the restriction of the standing to take countermeasures to the contexts of bilateralism, is the factor that can outweigh the lack of uniformity in State practice. In practical terms, limiting the standing to take countermeasures to bilateral contexts is effectively to leave many breaches without redress.

3. THE AGGRAVATED REGIMES OF RESPONSIBILITY

3.1. *Criminal responsibility of States*

The notion of aggravated, such as criminal, responsibility of States for exceptionally serious wrongful acts is underlined by social and juridical considerations. As a matter of social reality, the most heinous atrocities considered as criminal under international law—such as the Turkish massacre of Armenians in 1915, extermination of Jews in Nazi Germany, Japanese atrocities in China, Nazi atrocities in occupied territories, apartheid in South Africa, atrocities in Vietnam, South-Eastern Turkey, East Timor, Bosnia and Yugoslavia, and many others—have in their entirety been perpetrated with the direct participation of States in furtherance of their political or economic goals, even if the immediate perpetrators of these crimes were individuals. The problem is obvious: the law shall respond to a social reality dictating that it is both States and individuals which may commit acts criminal under international law. As the individual criminal responsibility is in this context indisputably recognized, it must be examined whether and to what extent international law responds to the pressing social need to regulate the legal framework governing the responsibility for criminal conducts in which States as such are implicated.

In juridical terms, the hierarchy of norms in international law poses a crucial question. As peremptory norms enjoy a heightened status, because they safeguard interests of the international community as distinct from those of individual States, it must be examined whether the violation of these norms gives rise to the specific regime of State responsibility.

At the same time, in situations that involve international crimes of States proper, the consequences of breaches of *erga omnes* obligations such as

---

[140] See ILC's Article 54 and commentary, *ILC Report* 2001, 349–355.

invocability and response through countermeasures are not sufficient. It is one thing who may invoke the breach; it is another thing what are the substantive rights and duties for the wrongdoer State and third States that come into play as a matter of aggravated responsibility.

The issue of aggravation of State responsibility because of the nature of the wrongful act has long been considered relevant in the context of general international law, as well as human rights and humanitarian law. To illustrate, in *Corfu Channel*, the United Kingdom defined the action of Albania as a wrongful act amounting in the circumstances of the case to an 'offence against humanity', which seriously aggravated that wrongful act.[141] Besides, the difference between single and massive violations of certain international obligations and the consequent aggravation of the wrongfulness is inherent to many international legal categories. For instance, the procedures before the Sub-commission of the UN Human Rights Commission under Resolution 1503 relate to gross and systematic human rights violations. In international criminal law, the concept of crimes against humanity definitionally involves the element of acts committed on a massive and systematic scale and as a matter of policy. While it is true that this qualification of the concept is to determine the threshold after the crossing of which individual perpetrators can be charged with crimes against humanity, it is also true that individuals in such cases are charged for something perpetrated as a matter of State policy.

As Van Boven points out, there is no generally accepted definition of gross violations of human rights and 'It appears that the word "gross" qualifies the term "violations" and indicates the serious character of the violations, but the word "gross" is also related to the type of human right that is being violated'.[142] It is nevertheless clear that

The term 'gross human rights offences' is employed as shorthand for certain serious violations of international humanitarian law and international human rights law that may qualify as crimes under international law and that are of such gravity as to set them out as deserving special attention, inter alia, through their being subjected to universal jurisdiction.[143]

Furthermore, gross violations affect both individuals and communities, such as indigenous peoples. Gross violations are likely to happen in the context of the land rights of indigenous peoples, the treatment of war prisoners, forced evictions and removals, environmental damage, violence against women, contemporary forms of slavery and slave-trade, and give rise to the duty to compensate.[144]

---

[141] *ICJ Pleadings*, 1949, 40, para. 72.

[142] Van Boven, Study Concerning the right to restitution, compensation and rehabilitation for victims of gross violations of human rights and fundamental freedoms, E/CN.4/Sub.2/1993/8, 6.

[143] Byrnes and Kamminga, ILA Final Report on the Exercise of Universal Jurisdiction in Respect of Gross Human Rights Offences (2000), 3.

[144] Van Boven, E/CN.4/Sub.2/1993/8, 8–12.

International tribunals also uphold the concept of massive and widespread breaches of human rights obligations. This concept is accepted in the jurisprudence under the European Convention of Human Rights under the category of 'administrative practice', although its establishment requires clear and convincing proof,[145] and also, on similar conditions, by the Inter-American Court of Human Rights. As this latter Court held in *Gangaram Panday*, 'the confirmation of a single case of violation of human rights by the authorities of a State is not in itself sufficient ground to presume or infer the existence in that State of widespread, large-scale practices to the detriment of the rights of other citizens'.[146] But in other cases the Inter-American Court considered it as established that during the period when the applicant was detained, 'there was a widespread practice in Peru of cruel, inhuman and degrading treatment during criminal investigations into the crimes of treason and terrorism'.[147] In a yet another case, the Court deemed it to have been proven that during the relevant period 'there existed in Peru a practice on the part of the forces of law and order which consisted in the forced disappearance of persons thought to be members of subversive groups, a practice well publicized by the press'.[148]

It is thus clear that the factor of gravity and seriousness of breaches of what are known as peremptory norms is part of the current social and juridical reality and needs to be reflected in the legal framework. The concept of international crimes can be among the concepts that reflect the required differentiation.

As the UN Human Rights Commission Working Paper suggests,

Since an international crime is a violation of international law, clearly it can be committed only by an entity subject to that law. While an international crime can in theory be committed by any subject of international law, it can in practice only be committed by an entity with the legal personality of a State.[149]

Although it is not quite accurate to limit the capacity to commit international crimes to States only—given the increased relevance in the international legal system of the actions of non-State actors such as armed factions and opposition groups—it is certainly correct that once the conduct designated as criminal under international law is committed by those who act as State agents and use State resources, the issue of responsibility of the relevant State for that crime is necessarily raised.

According to Pellet, the concept of international crimes is indispensable in contemporary international law and answers an indisputable need for dif-

---

[145] cf Orakhelashvili, *CYELS* (2002–2003), 248–249.

[146] *Gangaram Panday*, 116 ILR 316.

[147] *Loayza Tamayo*, Merits, 116 ILR 375.   [148] *Castillo Paez*, Merits, 116 ILR 468.

[149] Chernichenko, Working Paper, para. 24; see further Bos, Crimes of State: In Need of Legal Rules?, in Kreijen *et al.* (eds), *State, Sovereignty and International Governance* (2002), 237, suggesting that 'acts of State are often not those of a single individual, but of a whole system'.

ferentiating between different types of international wrong. Genocide cannot be considered an ordinary breach, like a breach of a trade agreement, since it offends against the community as a whole.[150] It is the reality of difference between various categories of wrongfulness which dictates the notion of State crimes.[151] Where actions such as gross human rights violations are perpetrated in a way to achieve the required degree of magnitude, they must at international level be regarded as international crime, that is a State action entailing State responsibility.[152]

The International Law Commission introduced the distinction between international crimes and international delicts in its draft articles on State responsibility adopted by first reading. In draft Article 19, the Commission defined the international crime as 'An internationally wrongful act which results from the breach by a State of an international obligation so essential for the protection of fundamental interests of the international community that its breach is recognized as a crime by that community as a whole'. This category, according to Article 19, encompasses the following wrongful acts:

a. a serious breach of an international obligation of essential importance for the maintenance of international peace and security, such as that prohibiting aggression;
b. a serious breach of an international obligation of essential importance for safeguarding the right of self-determination of peoples, such as that prohibiting the establishment or maintenance by force of colonial domination;
c. a serious breach on a widespread scale of an international obligation of essential importance for safeguarding the human being, such as those prohibiting slavery, genocide and apartheid;
d. a serious breach of an international obligation of essential importance for the safeguarding and preservation of the human environment, such as those prohibiting massive pollution of the atmosphere or of the seas.

There has been an emphasis on the existence of two completely different regimes of responsibility depending on the nature of a wrongful act and the obligations violated.[153] The criterion which distinguishes international crimes from international delicts is the legal interest of the international community in the violation.[154] Thus, the Commission's distinction was not based on abstract or theoretical considerations to distinguish between various categories of wrongful acts, but on the need to provide for the regimes of responsibility suitable to the nature and gravity of the wrongful acts in question. The

---

[150] Pellet, Can a State Commit a Crime? Definitely, Yes!, 10 *EJIL* (1999), 425–426.
[151] Pellet, Can a State Commit a Crime? Definitely, Yes!, 10 *EJIL* (1999), 434.
[152] Chernichenko, Working Paper, para. 41.
[153] YbILC, 1976, vol. II, part 2, 97; Mohr, The ILC's Distinction between International Crimes and International Delicts and Its Implications, Spinedi and Simma (eds), United Nations Codification of State Responsibility (1987), 116–117.
[154] Abi-Saab, The Uses of Article 19, 10 *EJIL* (1999), 347; Graefrath, International Crimes and Collective Security, *Festschrift Suy* (1998), 238.

basis of the difference between these categories is thus not purely notional, but practical, serving the practical purpose of implementing State responsibility in accordance with the gravity of a wrongful act.

The Commission was careful enough to emphasize that the concept of international State crimes is an independent concept and there is no intendment behind it to reproduce the categories of national criminal law into international law.[155] As Abi-Saab and Graefrath pointed out, the intention behind Article 19 was not to install a mirror-image of criminal law addressed to States, but 'simply to attach graver consequences to violations constituting international crimes'.[156] As Pellet further clarified, the analogies with domestic law are unhelpful; the concept of criminal responsibility of States is neither criminal nor civil as understood in national law—it is international.[157]

The Commission justified its approach by the parallelism between the category and examples of international crimes and those of peremptory norms. While accepting that there is no logically indispensable link between non-derogability and criminality, the Commission emphasized that

it would seem contradictory if the same consequences continued to be applied to the breach of obligations arising out of the rules defined as peremptory and to the breach of obligations arising out of rules from which derogation by special agreement is permitted.[158]

That the concept of international crimes of States is the outcome of the extension of the effect of *jus cogens* to unilateral acts or actions of States has been repeatedly affirmed in doctrine.[159] The fact that the breaches of *jus cogens* entail not only illegality but also nullity is a deviation from the unitary understanding of the State responsibility regime. This was the case of the non-recognition of the South Rhodesian Unilateral Declaration of Independence (UDI) as it constituted an international crime.[160] As Abi-Saab confirms, if one accepts the special effects of *jus cogens*, one cannot deny the existence of a special category of violations in the law of State responsibility.[161]

---

[155] YbILC, 1976, vol. II, part 2, para. 54.

[156] Abi-Saab, in Weiler, Cassese and Spinedi (eds) (1989), 146, Dupuy id., 184.

[157] Pellet, Can a State Commit a Crime? Definitely, Yes!, 10 *EJIL* (1999), 433.

[158] YbILC, 1976, vol. II, part 2, 102.

[159] Dugard, *Recognition and the United Nations* (1987), 142, 144; Gowlland-Debbas, *Collective Responses to Illegal Acts in International Law* (1990), 249. Later in the book, Gowlland-Debbas discusses the principle of non-recognition in the context of specific international crimes mentioned in Article 19 of the ILC's draft and analyses the operation of that principle using the example of specific crimes, emphasizing that the acts amounting to a crime in specific situations lead to a duty of non-recognition of such acts, id., 282 ff. See also Sorel, L'Avenir du 'crime' en droit international à la lumière de'l' expérience du *jus cogens*, 23 *Polish Yearbook of International Law* (1997–98), 69.

[160] Gowlland-Debbas, *Collective Responses to Illegal Acts in International Law* (1990), 240–241.

[161] Abi-Saab, The Concept of international Crime and Its Place in Contemporary International Law, in Weiler, Cassese and Spinedi (eds), 143.

At the same time, the Commission has been unwilling to qualify every breach of *jus cogens* as an international crime, which among others follows from the emphasis in Article 19 on the criterion of seriousness and massiveness of breaches. The Commission furthermore emphasized that

It would be wrong simply to conclude that any breach of an obligation deriving from a peremptory norm of international law is an international crime and that only the breach of an obligation having this origin can constitute such a crime. It can be accepted that obligations whose breach is a crime will normally be those deriving from the rules of *jus cogens*, though this conclusion cannot be absolute. But above all, although it may be true that failure to fulfil an obligation established by a rule of *jus cogens* will often constitute an international crime, it cannot be denied that the category of international obligations admitting of no derogation is much broader than the category of obligations whose breach is necessarily an international crime.[162]

Perhaps not every violation of peremptory norms can qualify as an international crime. In national legal systems, for instance, certain labour laws are part of public order and their violation receives the sanction of nullity, but does not involve criminality.[163] As Rosenstock points out, it is 'one thing to have a policy safeguarding certain interests of the national or international community and quite a separate act to denominate particular conduct contrary to that policy as criminal.'[164]

The concept of international crimes of States has met fierce opposition both in doctrine and in the Sixth Committee of the United Nations. This has influenced the ILC's decision to abandon this concept and delete Article 19 from its Articles on State responsibility. This deletion had no unanimous support in doctrine. Abi-Saab had suggested from the outset that no deletion of Article 19 was necessary, as the defects in its content could be perfected through good draftmanship.[165]

It is true that the concept of international crimes of States under Article 19 has met serious opposition from States. But similar developments took place with regard to the concept of serious breaches of peremptory norms proposed and adopted by the Commission at the later stage of the codification, and also with regard to the very notion of *jus cogens* when it was proposed by the Commission in draft articles on the law of treaties. It is a general

---

[162] YbILC, 1976, vol. II, part 2, 120.

[163] Barboza, State Crimes: A Decaffeinated Coffee, in L. Boisson de Chazournes and V. Gowlland-Debbas (eds), *The International Legal System in Quest of Equity and Universality. Liber Amicorum Georges Abi-Saab* (2001), 370.

[164] Rosenstock, R., Crimes of States—an Essay, in Ginther, Hafner, Lang, Neuhold, Suchapira-Behrmann (eds), *Völkerrecht zwischen normativem Anspruch und politischer Realität. Festschrift für Karl Zemanek* (1994), 324.

[165] Abi-Saab, The Uses of Article 19, 10 *EJIL* (1999), 339; see also Bos (2002), 235–236.

phenomenon that every juridical initiative concerning the categories of public order restraining States' freedom of action and attaching aggravated consequences to some of their conducts is expected to meet substantial opposition among States. Every public order notion produces a concern for States that they will be restrained in their freedom of action to a greater degree than in the past and they are reluctant to let this happen. This circumstance dictates that all notions as to the aggravation of State responsibility regime must be examined on their own merits and in accordance with their objective value.

The recognition of the concept of State crimes in relation to what are known as serious breaches of *jus cogens* is not alien to State practice. In the State practice of the interwar period, a number of multilateral treaties and resolutions of international organizations, including the League of Nations, defined the war of aggression as an international crime[166] (and so did the UN General Assembly Resolution 3314(1974) on Definition of Aggression). The UN General Assembly Resolution 37/69A (1982) declared the bantustanization and denationalization of the black majority in South Africa to be an international crime.

The Commission acknowledged in 1976 that the difference between the regimes of responsibility was not explicitly affirmed in judicial practice. It merely reiterated that the judicial and arbitral practice did not explicitly contradict the assumption that different wrongful acts entail different regimes of responsibility.[167] The Commission, however, linked its difference between delicts and crimes to the distinction in United Nations practice between systematic, persistent, serious and grave human rights violations and other, less serious violations of human rights. The Commission emphasized that such serious and grave breaches are viewed as international crimes.[168]

It seems that judicial practice has since then to some extent affirmed the distinctions and analogies upheld by the International Law Commission. As the ICTY emphasized in *Furundzija*, 'If carried out as an extensive practice of State officials, torture amounts to a serious breach on a widespread scale of an international obligation of essential importance for safeguarding the human being, thus constituting a particularly grave wrongful act generating State responsibility.'[169] This is in fact the differentiation between different types of wrongful acts and regimes of State responsibility, in a language very similar to that of Article 19.

In the case concerning *Promulgation and Enfocrement of Laws*, the Inter-American Court dealt with the issue of aggravation of responsibility in

---

[166] YbILC, 1976, vol. II, part 2, 101.
[168] YbILC, 1976, vol. II, part 2, 110.
[167] YbILC, 1976, vol. II, part 2, 98 ff.
[169] *Furundzija*, 38 ILM 1999, 347.

consequence of the gravity of the breach of the American Convention on Human Rights. The Court took as a starting-point that the promulgation or enforcement of legislation contrary to the Convention would give rise to the international responsibility of a State.[170] If the enforcement of such laws results in crimes against peace, war crimes or crimes against humanity, this fact would also give rise to the individual responsibility of perpetrators.[171] 'If these violations were also to constitute international crimes, they would, in addition, give rise to individual responsibility' of 'the agents or officials who execute it to international responsibility.'[172]

This approach is based on an implicit assumption that individual responsibility can be involved when the breaches of the Convention are so serious as to constitute crimes under international law. The starting point is that the acts which give rise to individual responsibility are international crimes and they are attributable to States as violations of international law, in particular, the American Convention. In other words, acts denoted by the Court as 'international crimes' are committed by and attributable to States. The use by the Court of the words 'in addition' demonstrates that States remain responsible for what is denoted as international crimes. The act in question is not made a crime by the fact that individuals are involved but, on the contrary, once the enforcement of a law committed by and attributable to a State constitutes an international crime, the agents or officials who execute that law shall also be subjected to international responsibility.

All this largely accords with the International Law Commission's observation in 1976 that the instances where individuals are held responsible for acts criminal under international law must automatically be considered as an act entailing a special form of responsibility of a State to which the conduct of the individual in question is attributable.[173]

The concept of criminal responsibility of States has encountered multiple objections, which are based mostly on policy rather than on strictly legal considerations. It is suggested that, although the responsibility of individuals for international crimes may not generally exhaust responsibility of a State for a wrongful act, it may do so with regard to criminal aspects of responsibility. Since, as the Nuremberg Tribunal affirmed, crimes are committed by individuals and not abstract entities, and if those individuals are punished, there is not much space left for the criminal responsibility of a State.[174] But this ignores the context in which the Nuremberg Tribunal made the

---

[170] 116 ILR 335.   [171] 116 ILR 335–336.   [172] 116 ILR 336.
[173] YbILC, 1976, vol. II, part 2, 104.
[174] Barboza, International Criminal Law, 278 RdC (1999), 106; Barboza, State Crimes: A Decaffeinated Coffee, in L. Boisson de Chazournes and V. Gowlland-Debbas (eds), *The International Legal System in Quest of Equity and Universality. Liber Amicorum Georges Abi-Saab* (2001), 374.

above-mentioned statement, which was to justify the concept of individual criminal responsibility in face of the defences that the relevant criminal acts were committed as a matter of State policy and superior orders and the perpetrators were hence not individually responsible. But the Nuremberg Tribunal said nothing to prejudice the relevance of the aggravated, including criminal, responsibility in terms of the State conduct. If the Nuremberg dictum is stretched so far as to exclude by implication the graduation of the State responsibility regimes by asserting that once crimes are committed by individuals there can be no State responsibility for the pertinent crimes, it would lead to absurd results, making it possible to assert that there can be no State responsibility at all because every single wrongful act is committed by individuals and only then attributed to the State.

It is also argued that the concept of criminal responsibility of States can only be conceived in a certain institutional context that incorporates the due process guarantees. It is suggested that the concept of State crimes or aggravated responsibility regimes must be viewed in the context of due process and dispute settlement. Once the criminal responsibility is conceived, due procedural guarantees should be afforded and the procedures for investigation be provided for.[175]

The argument that the concept of international crimes is possible only within a certain institutional framework is reminiscent of the discussion at the Vienna Conference of linking the concept of *jus cogens* to compulsory international jurisdiction in order to preclude the abuses of this concept and support the stability of treaty relations. But the 1969 Vienna Convention does not establish the link between the *jus cogens* invalidity of treaties and compulsory judicial jurisdiction, as the use of the word 'may' in Article 66 of the Convention evidences. Moreover the *jus cogens* invalidity is a matter of general international law and operates even with regard to States that are not party to the Vienna Convention.

It is an extremely formalistic approach to require the existence for States of all procedural guarantees which individuals have in national legal systems. Owing to the peculiarity of the international legal system, States exist without having such procedural guarantees, at least as a matter of general international law, because there is no institutional jurisdiction unless consented to by States. International law suffers from the absence of effective procedural safeguards generally, and not only with regard to the regime of State crimes. Yet, nobody could seriously suggest that this factor should have a bearing on the substantive categories of the State responsibility regime in general.

---

[175] Crawford, Revising the Draft Articles on State Responsibility, 10 *EJIL* (1999), 443; Crawford, On Re-reading the Draft Articles on State Responsibility, *ASIL Proceedings* (1998), 296–297; Barboza, International Criminal Law, 278 *RdC* (1999), 107–109.

Moreover, the rights of due process and fair trial in national legal systems are not limited to the issues of criminal proceedings but also extend to civil litigation.

It is interesting whether the significance of the deletion of the ILC's Article 19 is crucial. It seems that despite the deletion of Article 19, the concept of international crimes of States remains a viable concept. In practical terms, if a State, or group of States, implementing the responsibility of the State which committed serious breaches of *jus cogens* such as an act of aggression view this as the responsibility for international crimes, there is little to object to this attitude. This holds true especially, and most importantly, to the underlying idea of the concept of the criminal responsibility of States—that the serious breaches of peremptory norms entail special consequences related to responsibility. There are several dimensions in which the viability of this concept can prove itself.

The concept of State crimes can be conceived as generating clear-cut and straightforward consequences, as was approved in the draft articles on State responsibility adopted on first reading,[176] and is reflected to some extent in the legal consequences of serious breaches of *jus cogens* which replaced the concept of State crimes. In addition, international law does not rule out punitive or exemplary damages but instead recognizes that reparation, especially payments of compensation, must reflect the scale of the breach. Thus, the consequences of international State crimes are in principle accepted in international law.

Alternatively, the concept of State crimes can be an interpretative guide in the law of State responsibility, for instance by serving as guidance in measuring the damages due for certain wrongful acts,[177] or in clarifying whether the illegality is duly redressed or can be cured.

Finally, the conceptual underpinnings of the concept of State crimes and their link to the breaches of peremptory norms are reflected in the concept of serious breaches of *jus cogens* as the successor of the State crimes concept.

It is conceivably due to these factors that the definition of the category of serious breaches of *jus cogens* has been perceived as an alternative to the concept of international crimes of States. As suggested in doctrine, international crimes may be renamed into the breaches of substantive *jus cogens*

---

[176] Article 52 of the 1996 draft related to the issue of limitations on reparation. Article 53 included the duties of non-recognition and non-assistance to the State that commits international crime.

[177] cf former Article 45 of the ILC Articles on State Responsibility, which emphasized that in the case of gross infringements of the rights of the injured State, damages reflecting the gravity of the breach may be required.

norm, because the notion of crimes largely corresponds in scope to *jus cogens*. But the regime of responsibility would still be dual.[178]

3.2. The ILC's specific consequences for serious breaches of peremptory norms

The ILC Articles on State responsibility provide for specific consequences of serious breaches of *jus cogens* (Articles 40–41). Article 41(1) stresses that States, whether or not directly affected, are under a positive duty to cooperate to counteract such breaches and their effects.[179] According to Article 41(2), no State shall recognize as lawful the situation established through a serious breach, nor render any aid or assistance to an author State.

Recognition is normally considered in terms of the emergence of States. But in fact this is the more general concept related to 'evaluation of State conduct in face of facts which may relate to legal titles, liabilities or immunities'.[180] But the duty of non-recognition of the breaches of peremptory norms extends not only to State-creation but to every kind of illegality. It refers to the general duty to refrain from acts and actions, or from taking attitudes, that imply the recognition of the acts offending against peremptory norms in a variety of international legal relations.

As for the duty of non-assistance, it bears some similarity to the general aspects of complicity in internationally wrongful acts. But the duty of non-assistance in the context of peremptory norms applies not to the process of commission of a wrongful act and the ensuing determination of its attribution, but to situations where the wrongful act offending against peremptory norms is already committed and hence emphasizes the effect-oriented or consequential profile of peremptory norms. As the International Law Commission emphasized, the duty not to assist the State which commits breaches of peremptory norms deals with conduct 'after the fact' which has to ensure that the potential legality of breaches of peremptory norms and situations arising therefrom is barred *erga omnes*.[181]

---

[178] Abi-Saab, The Uses of Article 19, 10 *EJIL* (1999), 349; Gaja also considered that the notion of crimes should have been replaced by a more neutral term, in order to avoid the impression of connotations involving penal sanctions, Gaja, Should All References to International Crimes Disappear from the ILC's Draft Articles on State Responsibility?, 10 *EJIL* (1999), 369. Dominice, The International Responsibility of States for Breach of Multilateral Obligations, 10 *EJIL* (1999), 359; Pellet, Can a State Commit a Crime? Definitely, Yes!, 10 *EJIL* (1999), 428. Pellet did not propose to abandon the notion of crimes, but instead suggested that when a State commits a wrong against the international community as a whole, it never acts by chance or intentionally. Therefore, the elements of intent and of fault, which are not necessarily present in other internationally wrongful acts, are part of the crimes. Moreover, even without organized adjudication, the community reaction may involve a punitive element. Thus the notion of crime is acceptable and defensible. Pellet, Can a State Commit a Crime? Definitely, Yes!, 10 *EJIL* (1999), 434.

[179] *ILC Report*, 2001, 286–287; Brownlie (2003), 492.

[180] Brownlie, Recognition in Theory and Practice, 53 *BYIL* (1982), 200–201.

[181] Commentary to Article 41, para. 11, *ILC Report* 2001, 290–291.

Such character of the duty of non-assistance causes this duty to go beyond the mere obligation to refrain from complicity in wrongful acts and is mainly aimed at the prohibition of acts and actions of third States that can help the State that has committed a breach of *jus cogens* in consolidating the effects of that breach and the gains that such breach can potentially produce. Therefore, this duty can be applicable in a variety of fields and outlaw acts of various kinds.

The ILC approach met criticism in the Sixth Committee because the seriousness of a breach arguably entails consequences different in degree, not in kind, from the ordinary regime of State responsibility.[182] Nevertheless, these consequences reflect the specific effects of *jus cogens* arising in different fields of general international law. The duty to cooperate in counteracting effects of breaches of *jus cogens* seems most relevant for repression of *jus cogens* crimes with consequent prosecution or extradition.[183] The duty of non-recognition is clearly established for breaches of *jus cogens*.[184]

Therefore, the special consequences of breaches of peremptory norms apply to every pertinent case where the actions and attitudes of States are capable of recognizing or consolidating the effects of such breaches. One such field is the law of State immunity and it is arguable that the recognition of State immunity for breaches of peremptory norms amounts to their recognition as sovereign acts of States. This is manifested in the jurisprudence of Greek and Italian courts on this subject. While denying State immunity to German atrocities in Greece during the Second World War, the Court of Levadia referred to the peremptory character of the prohibition of war crimes to which the German atrocities amounted and specified that 'the recognition of immunity for an act contrary to peremptory international law would amount to complicity of the national court to the promotion of an act strongly condemned by the international public order'.[185]

The Italian Supreme Court denied immunity to Germany for its atrocities committed in Italy during the Second World War by explicit reference to ILC's Articles 40 and 41, thus viewing the denial of immunity for the breaches of *jus cogens* as the compliance by States with their obligation not to recognize the effects of such breaches and not to assist the State which committed them.[186] As Bianchi emphasized, 'consideration of the legal

---

[182] Crawford (2002), 35–36; Crawford, *Fourth Report*, A/CN.4/517, paras 43–53.

[183] See below, Chapter 9.

[184] The ILC has not specified the instances in which the duty of non-assistance applies. This duty operates in several fields, such as the impact of *jus ad bellum* on the law of neutrality or the prohibition to assist a State engaged in a breach of self-determination or serious human rights violations. These issues are beyond the scope of this analysis. On the relevance of *jus cogens* in the field of recognition see below, Chapter 11.

[185] Case No. 137/1997, Multi-member Court of Levadia, 30 October 1997, 50 *Revue Hellénique* (1997), 599.

[186] *Ferrini*, Judgment, para. 9.

consequences stemming, under the law of State responsibility, from a serious violation of a *jus cogens* rule may well lead, by way of interpretation, to the non-recognition of a State's jurisdictional immunity'.[187]

This reflects the doctrinal argument that acts contradicting *jus cogens* and subject to non-recognition cannot attract State immunity. 'If a domestic court grants sovereign immunity to a State that has violated a rule of *jus cogens*, it is recognising a sovereign right which does not exist.'[188]

All this confirms that if the mandatory duties for States arising from the breach of peremptory norms are to operate meaningfully, they must operate in relation to every relevant field of international law in which such breach may be committed and consolidate its effects. Because of this, it seems opportune to focus on the ILC's specific consequences of serious breaches while dealing with respective fields of effects of *jus cogens*.

That the specific consequences of the breaches of peremptory norms fit conceptually into the effect of international public order has been confirmed by the International Court's treatment of the legal consequences of the construction of the wall in the Occupied Palestinian Territory. The Court considered that, owing to the character and the importance of the rights and obligations involved, which it denoted as *erga omnes* obligations, 'all States are under an obligation not to recognize the illegal situation resulting from the construction of the wall in the Occupied Palestinian Territory, including in and around East Jerusalem.' The Court furthermore concluded that States 'are also under an obligation not to render aid or assistance in maintaining the situation created by such construction'.[189]

Judge Higgins approached the Court's treatment of this issue with a certain degree of criticism, stating that the dictum on *erga omnes* obligations from *Barcelona Traction* 'is frequently invoked for more than it can bear'. She denied that 'the specified consequence of the identified violations of international law have anything to do with the concept of *erga omnes*'. Judge Higgins criticized the Court's reference to *erga omnes* obligations in terms of the *Barcelona Traction* dictum, stating that 'that dictum was directed to a very specific issue of jurisdictional *locus standi*. . . . It has nothing to do with imposing substantive obligations on third parties to a case'.[190] Similarly, Judge Koojmans had 'considerable difficulty in understanding why a violation of an obligation *erga omnes* by one State should necessarily lead to an obligation for third States.'[191]

---

[187] Case-note on *Ferrini*, 99 *AJIL* (2005), 247.

[188] Belski *et al.* (1989), 401; a further reference is made to the approach of F.A. Mann that 'he who assists in the consummation of an illegal act must be treated as a party to it', 415. This perspective contradicts the assumption that the wrongfulness of the act is the issue different from whether it is covered by State immunity as a procedural issue.

[189] *Wall*, Advisory Opinion, para. 159, and the operative paragraph 3(D).

[190] Separate Opinion, para. 37.   [191] Separate Opinion, para. 40.

Judge Higgins also criticized the reference to the *erga omnes* nature of obligations in terms of the violations of humanitarian law, submitting that the intransgressible principles of humanitarian law are generally binding because they are customary international law, no more and no less.[192] The question before the Court was, however, not only whether the norms and principles of humanitarian law are 'generally binding' and their violation generates the secondary obligations in the field of State responsibility, but also, and crucially, what are the specific legal consequences of serious breaches of those norms and principles with regard to the construction of the wall in the Palestinian territory. The fact that a norm is 'generally binding' does not explain the specific consequences it may generate in case of its breach. A norm can be binding and yet allow a bilateral or multilateral settlement through the recognition of its breaches. The recognition of breaches of the norm is not precluded just because that norm is generally binding and this requires searching for some alternative justifications. Therefore, the specific consequences that the Court elaborated upon are due to the normative character of a rule, as opposed to its binding character. As the International Law Commission suggested, the International Court's passage in the *Nuclear Weapons* Advisory Opinion on the intransgressible character of basic norms of humanitarian law refers to their peremptory character.[193] This factor can justify the Court's application of the principle of non-recognition to the breaches of relevant humanitarian norms.

Judge Koojmans also tried to distinguish the instant case from *Namibia*. He submitted that 'the situation is completely different from that in the *Namibia* case where the question was exclusively focused on the legal consequences for States, and logically so since the subject-matter of the request was a decision by the Security Council'.[194] However, the breaches of peremptory norms *ipso jure* entail the legal consequences both with regard to the State which has breached the relevant peremptory norm and also other States. The consequences as regards other States, which form an integral part of the effects of the given substantive norm, must be deemed to have formed part of the request of the General Assembly for the Advisory Opinion. The fact that such consequences were not the only object of the request for the Opinion, as emphasized by Judge Koojmans, does not mean that they were excluded from its ambit. The Court was asked to state the consequences of breaches of certain fundamental norms as they stand in substantive law and this necessarily included, contrary to Judge Koojmans' approach, the consequences as regards other States.

The Court itself never expressly mentioned the concept of peremptory

---

[192] Separate Opinion, para. 39.
[193] *ILC Report* 2001, Commentary to Article 40, para. 5, at 284.
[194] Separate Opinion, para. 39.

norms, but spoke of *erga omnes* obligations. Judge Koojmans acknowledged that the legal consequences for third States as stated by the Court were similar to those expressed in Article 41 of the ILC's Articles on State Responsibility. However, Judge Koojmans avoided the question 'whether obligations *erga omnes* can be equated with obligations arising under a peremptory norm of general international law'.[195] But it is widely recognized in doctrine that *jus cogens* and obligations *erga omnes* are but two sides of the same coin: they are virtually coextensive—obligations *erga omnes* follow from peremptory norms and are concerned with their enforcement.[196] It is also recognized that the International Court implied *jus cogens*, without explicitly referring to it, when it spoke of *erga omnes* obligations in *Barcelona Traction*.[197] Therefore, it is not the *erga omnes* nature of an obligation following from a rule of international law which confers an imperative character on that rule or itself determines any of the consequences of its breaches. On the contrary, the *erga omnes* nature of an obligation merely refers to the invocability of legal consequences of the violation of the rule, as these consequences themselves are determined by the *jus cogens* nature of a rule from which the obligation in question follows.

This state of affairs could confirm that Judge Higgins is perhaps right in asserting that 'The obligation upon United Nations Members of non-recognition and non-assistance does not rest on the notion of *erga omnes*',[198] to the extent that, in the process of State responsibility, the phenomenon of *erga omnes* obligations does not by itself imply the mandatory consequential duties for the State which is the author of the violation or the third States. In the face of Judge Higgins' criticisms, one could only defend the Court by assuming that it referred to the *erga omnes* character of the pertinent obligations as the manifestation of the peremptory character of the rules which give rise to them.[199] This point is, as evidenced above, supported in doctrine and practice. However, if the Court did not refer to peremptory norms by implication, its treatment of the consequential duties on States arising from the construction of the wall in the Occupied Palestinian Territory can only be justified on the basis that the norms involved in this situation— the principle of self-determination and the basic norms of humanitarian law—anyway form part of *jus cogens* and their breaches generate legal consequences analogous to those embodied in the Court's Opinion. Had the

---

[195] Separate Opinion, para. 41.

[196] See above, Section 2 and the sources referred to there.

[197] Frowein, *Jus Cogens*, 7 *EPIL* 328; De Hoogh, The Relationship between Jus Cogens, Obligations Erga Omnes and International Crimes: Peremptory Norms in Perspective, 42 *Österreichische Zeitschrift für öffentliches Recht und Völkerrecht* (1991), 183; Malanczuk, First ILA Study Group Report on State Responsibility (2000), 44–45, para. 141.

[198] Separate Opinion, para. 38.

[199] It could be relevant in this context that the Court spoke about the character of the relevant obligations, not the relevant norms.

Court expressly followed the logic of this normative link, its findings could have been spared the criticisms by individual judges.

The Court in the *Wall* Advisory Opinion, having pointed out that all States are under the duty not to render any aid or assistance in maintaining the situation created by the construction of the wall in occupied Palestinian territories, emphasized that 'It is also for all States, while respecting the United Nations Charter and international law, to see to it that any impediment, resulting from the construction of the wall, to the exercise by the Palestinian people of its right to self-determination is brought to an end'.[200] This last formulation, as well as the preceding formulation on the duty of non-assistance, has been viewed by the Court as an implication of the *erga omnes* character of the obligations that were violated by the fact of the construction of the wall. However, the formulation of such duty 'to see to it' that the impediments to the exercise of Palestinian self-determination are brought to an end is new in international judicial practice. The Court's approach in *Wall* differs from the earlier approach in *Namibia* where South Africa, itself being in breach of its obligations under the Mandate Agreement, was required to end the occupation of the Namibian territory. However, in the *Wall* Advisory Opinion, the Court extended similar obligations to third States.

The postulation of such duties for third States is new and does not directly follow from the ILC's approach to the consequences of serious breaches or from international judicial practice. Nor does the duty proclaimed by the Court seem to be an inherent consequence of peremptory norms, unless it were understood in terms of a duty to adopt attitudes with regard to situations involving breaches of *jus cogens* to prevent validation of those breaches. The Court might indeed have meant to postulate limitations on the attitudes and behaviour of third States which could, under some circumstances, contribute to the validation of the situation surrounding the construction of the wall in Palestine.[201] In this narrow sense, the postulation of this duty can be explained in terms of effects of peremptory norms. If, however, this duty also requires the active behaviour of third States, then further developments must be awaited to see what implications the Court-proclaimed duty entails. One such potential implication could be the taking of third-party countermeasures with a view to ensuring that the relevant impediments to the Palestinian self-determination are brought to an end.

---

[200] Opinion, para. 159.   [201] cf below, Chapter 11.

9

Peremptory Norms and the Allocation of Jurisdiction to States

While the impact of peremptory norms on the law of remedies determines what specific remedies are due in case of breach of such norms, the impact of peremptory norms on the allocation of jurisdiction to States determines how these remedies must be obtained before national courts.

I. UNIVERSAL CRIMINAL JURISDICTION AND THE DUTY TO PROSECUTE *JUS COGENS* CRIMES

Crimes that offend the community interest are outlawed under *jus cogens*, and the international community as a whole has a legal interest in their prosecution. These are genocide,[1] torture,[2] war crimes,[3] and crimes against humanity.[4] As Goodwin-Gill suggests, the notion of international crimes 'is indeed distinguished by its foundation in a rule of *jus cogens*, and in the importance and universality of its basic moral content'.[5] These crimes entail objective illegality whose redress is a matter of community interest despite the attitudes of or prejudices to individual States.

Jus cogens criminalization therefore impacts on principles allocating jurisdiction through providing for universal jurisdiction. Traditional jurisdiction patterns—territorial, personal, or protective—imply a link between the crime and the forum State and hence its individual interest to prosecute the crime. Universal jurisdiction is exercised without any link of a State to a crime and enables States to prosecute *jus cogens* crimes in the community interest.

Both in theory and in practice there are objections to universal jurisdiction, either on a policy basis or by reference to the lack of State practice, although

---

[1] *Kayishema*, para. 88; *Roach*, para. 55; Steven, Genocide and the Duty to Extradite of Prosecute: Why the United States is in Breach of Its International Obligations, 39 *Virginia Journal of International Law* (1999), 438–439; Parker and Neylon, *Jus Cogens*: Compelling the Law of Human Rights, 12 *Hastings International and Comparative Law Review* (1989), 430.

[2] On torture see above, Chapter 2.

[3] Charney, Universal International Law, *AJIL* (1993), 541; Parker and Crew, Compensation for Japan's World War II War-Rape Victims, 17 *Hastings International and Comparative Law Review* (1994), 520–521.

[4] *Pinochet* (Belgium), 355; Bassiouni, *Crimes Against Humanity in International Criminal Law* (1999), 217; Stevens (1999), 436.

[5] Goodwin-Gill, Crime and International Law: Expulsion, Removal, and the Non-Derogable Obligation, in Goodwin-Gill and Talmon (eds), *The Reality of International Law, The Essays in Honour of Ian Brownlie* (1999), 213.

the weight of such approaches is decreasing. To start with, the International Court has at least implicitly recognized universal jurisdiction over serious international crimes in the *Arrest Warrant* case relating to the immunity of the incumbent foreign minister of a foreign State, as it joined the parties in not disputing its existence; furthermore, the Court stated that one State can try another State's foreign minister after his/her retirement and did not specify that any territorial or nationality link was required either with the accused or the victim.[6] The Court's reasoning implies that Belgium could have issued an arrest warrant against the Congolese Foreign Minister after his retirement, which is to exercise universal jurisdiction.

The *Arrest Warrant* case is the first case where the International Court faced the issue of universal jurisdiction in relation to crimes outlawed under *jus cogens*, such as war crimes, crimes against humanity and torture. It is therefore natural that, even if the question of jurisdiction was not at the heart of the controversy between the parties as presented to the Court, individual judges nevertheless addressed it. They did so as they considered that the issue of jurisdiction impacted on the issue of immunity which was central to the Court's decision. President Guillaume asserted that the issue of jurisdiction must be considered before the issue of immunity, and that the normal position in international law is that States can only exercise jurisdiction over a crime if it is linked to them in terms of the victim or perpetrator, or if it threatens their internal or external security; universal jurisdiction can be exercised only if specifically provided for in treaties. There is therefore limited universal jurisdiction over war crimes covering, under the 1949 Geneva Conventions, the cases where the accused is present in the territory of the State exercising jurisdiction, and there is no universal jurisdiction over crimes against humanity.[7]

Judge Guillaume's reasoning does not confront the textual meaning of the relevant clauses of the 1949 Geneva Conventions which impose on States-parties the obligation to search for war criminals without limiting this obligation in terms of their place of presence. It is also conceptually wrong to make universal jurisdiction dependent on the place of presence of the accused. The presence of an accused in the forum State's territory is a question not of principle, but of fact; the actual presence of an accused in the territory of the forum state is relevant only if there is, on independent grounds, universal jurisdiction. That is, although presence is a fact that facilitates a State's exercise of universal jurisdiction, it has no decisive relevance to the question of whether universal jurisdiction exists in any particular case as a matter of international law.

It is doubtful that there is a clearly crystallized requirement in international law that the accused must be present on the territory of the forum State to be

---

[6] *Arrest Warrant*, para. 61.　　　[7] Separate Opinion, paras 16–17.

subjected to universal jurisdiction. In the *Arrest Warrant* case universal jurisdiction was not disputed by the Respondent State even as it was exercised in
the absence of the accused.

By contrast to President Guillaume, the Joint Separate Opinion of Judges
Higgins, Koojmans and Buergenthal admitted in principle that there is universal jurisdiction over war crimes, crimes against humanity and torture both
under conventional and customary law.[8] Judge Koroma also accepted that
there is universal jurisdiction over war crimes, crimes against humanity, slave-
trade and genocide.[9] Judge van den Wyngaert advanced similar conclusions.[10]

One could justify universal jurisdiction by reference to *Lotus*, according to
which a State could establish its jurisdiction over any case as soon as this is
not precluded by a prohibitive norm. In its specific context, *Lotus* affirmed
that there is no prohibitive norm precluding the establishment of jurisdiction
of a State over the situation which takes place outside its territory and
involves the act committed by foreign nationals. But the broader significance
of *Lotus* is its presumption of the legality of the establishment of jurisdiction
in the absence of the norm prohibiting doing so.[11] Despite possible criticism,
the *Lotus* principle is still a valid principle, as it best reflects the decentralized
and sovereignty-oriented nature of the international legal system. It was in
fact approved by individual judges as one of the justifications for universal
jurisdiction over international crimes.[12]

But it is also necessary to focus upon the distinctive conceptual basis
of universal jurisdiction. The Joint Separate Opinion in *Arrest Warrant*
recognizes that in exercising universal jurisdiction, States act as agents of the
international community and that 'this vertical notion of the authority of
action is significantly different from the horizontal system of international
law envisaged in the *Lotus* case'.[13] But the judges do not enquire why States
are considered to be acting as community agents in such cases and what
makes the legal framework vertical rather than horizontal. The answer must
be sought in the status of primary rules entailing universal jurisdiction, that is
the peremptory status of criminalization of the crimes in question.

---

[8] Joint Separate Opinion, paras 42–52.   [9] Separate Opinion, para. 9.
[10] Dissenting Opinion, paras 52–67.
[11] PCIJ Series A, No. 10, 18–19. The Israel Supreme Court accepted the *Lotus* approach as it
held that there was no rule of international law prohibiting States to exercise extra-territorial
jurisdiction and that the universal jurisdiction over crimes against humanity was 'vested in the
State of Israel on its establishment in 1948 as a sovereign State,' 36 ILR 279. In *Polyukhovich*
before the Australian High Court, Brennan J justified the federal power to enact legislation to
punish war criminals, among others on the universality basis, by pointing out that 'Australia's
international personality would be incomplete if it were unable to exercise a jurisdiction to try
and to punish offenders against the law of nations whose crimes are such that their subjection to
universal jurisdiction is conducive to international peace and order'. 91 ILR (577).
[12] Joint Separate Opinion, paras 49–50; Dissenting Opinion of Judge van den Wyngaert,
para. 51.
[13] Joint Separate Opinion, para. 51.

The ICTY recognized in *Tadic* that certain international crimes such as war crimes and crimes against humanity offend the community interest transcending the interest of an individual State and shock the conscience of mankind, and hence justify the action in the community interest to prosecute and suppress these crimes.[14] The German Constitutional Court likewise affirmed that the universality principle covers actions that threaten the interests of the entire international community of States.[15] The rules on prosecution of *jus cogens* crimes serve the interests of the international community as a whole. The effects of *jus cogens* in this field are reflected in conventional and customary law.

Treaty provisions on universal jurisdiction can be reflective of the effects of *jus cogens*, especially if they criminalize conduct as an offence against the community interest,[16] pursuant to their general nature as treaties embodying objective obligations safeguarding the community interest as distinct from individual State interests. These are the 1948 Genocide Convention, the 1949 Geneva Conventions and 1977 First Additional Protocol, and the 1984 Torture Convention.

Criminalization of conduct in the community interest in such treaties differs from other treaty-based crimes based on 'universal' jurisdiction, such as those outlawed under anti-terrorist conventions.[17] Criminality established under these conventions and ensuing jurisdictional principles applies not to each and every crime capable by its nature of falling within the ambit of the relevant convention, but only to those whose commission extends—in terms of victims or perpetrators—beyond the frontiers of a single State-party and affects the interests of another State-party.[18] These conventions declare relevant acts punishable not as such, but only if committed in a situation giving rise to a bilateral legal relation involving direct and individual interests of a State-party, such as its link to a crime. Such treaties are multilateral treaties on mutual legal cooperation, instruments exchanging mutual rights and obligations; they relate only to crimes linked to States-parties and their enforcement is a matter for their reciprocal interest. They provide for jurisdiction in the interest of individual States-parties affected directly or through

---

[14] *Tadic* (Trial Chamber), 10 August 1995, para. 42. [15] 1290/99, para. 38.

[16] Parker and Neylon (1989), 455, refer to the 1949 Geneva Conventions as 'a major step in developing universal jurisdiction for *jus cogens* violations'.

[17] Jurisdiction here is not strictly universal as Judge Guillaume has pointed out. Goodwin-Gill (1999), 206 distinguishes between crimes which are crimes generally recognized under international law and crimes which States may, from time to time, agree should be subject to universal jurisdiction. See also Schabas, *Genocide in International Law* (2000), 355–357.

[18] Article 4, Montreal Convention on Suppression of Unlawful Acts against the Safety of Civil Aviation (1971); Article 4, Convention for the Suppression of Unlawful Acts against the Safety of Maritime Navigation (1988); Articles 3 and 6, Convention for the Suppression of Terrorist Bombings (1998); Article 3, Convention for the Suppression of the Financing of Terrorism (1999).

their nationals, through acts outlawed under the Conventions. Thus, the 1998 Convention on Terrorist Bombings would not establish jurisdiction over a bombing perpetrated by ETA in Spain or the IRA in England, while the Convention against Torture criminalizes each and every mistreatment of a person committed in any State-party regardless of the nationality of the perpetrator or victim.

Criminalization and ensuing universal jurisdiction under humanitarian treaties reflect the fact that *jus cogens* crimes are subject to prosecution wherever and by whomever committed, independent of any link of the forum State to the crime in question. This universal jurisdiction reflects the nature of universal jurisdiction for *jus cogens* crimes—prosecution without link to a crime. This runs parallel to the fact that humanitarian treaties operate in the community interest and embody integral obligations not divisible into bilateral relations, that is they embody *jus cogens* and provide for universal jurisdiction for its breaches which they declare objectively reprehensible.

Universal jurisdiction is provided for in several treaty clauses. Articles 5 and 7 of the 1984 Torture Convention provide for the prosecution of persons accused of torture in the courts of a State which has no territorial or personal link with the crime. Article 49/50/129/146 of the 1949 Geneva Conventions provides for the prosecution of persons accused of grave breaches of these Conventions, by States not linked to the crime.[19] As the Joint Separate Opinion in *Arrest Warrant* emphasized, the jurisdiction to prosecute or extradite under the Geneva Conventions is based on the heinous nature of the crime rather than on links of territoriality or nationality.[20] Article VI of the 1948 Genocide Convention provides that persons charged with genocide shall be tried in the courts where the act was committed or by an international penal tribunal. This provision arguably falls short of establishing universality but, even if so, this should not create a false impression that the Genocide Convention does not provide for or imply universal jurisdiction.

The argument widely supported in doctrine and judicial practice is that the Convention does not negate but implicitly acknowledges universal jurisdiction over genocide existing under general international law and must be read accordingly.[21] The parties did not intend to abrogate, through Article VI, their jurisdictional prerogatives under customary law. Article VI postulates

---

[19] Provost, Reciprocity in Human Rights and Humanitarian Law, *BYIL* (1995), 388; Pictet, *Commentary to the First Geneva Convention of 1949* (1952), 366; the relevant provisions of the Geneva Conventions reflect 'the jurisdictional power of the international community to try war criminals', *R v Finta* (High Court), 82 ILR 446.

[20] Joint Separate Opinion, para. 46.

[21] *Pinochet* (Spain), 336; Bassiouni (1999), 234–235; Parker and Neylon (1989), 456; Steven (1999), 452; *per contra* Schabas (2000), 367–368.

only one possible jurisdictional basis and genocide remains under customary law as a crime triggering universal jurisdiction.[22]

Textual and teleological interpretation (under Article 31 of the 1969 Vienna Convention) of the Convention also justify universal jurisdiction. First, even if Article VI does not explicitly establish universality, it upholds it implicitly both singly and together with Article VII. While Article VI says that persons charged with genocide shall be tried in the country where an act was committed, it is addressed not only to the territorial State, but also to all other parties who may not be linked to the crime but in whose territory the accused is present. If so, then not only the territorial State but also these other States are obliged to ensure that the accused is indeed tried in the territorial State. For this, they would need to establish jurisdiction over the accused, *inter alia* with a view to extradition to the territorial State, and this may well be universal jurisdiction. This approach is reinforced by the duty to extradite under Article VII.

From a teleological perspective, it is also implausible that Article VI establishes only territorial jurisdiction. If so, the Convention falling short of imposing any other jurisdictional standard over States-parties, it would have to be interpreted as tolerating impunity for genocide in cases where an accused is found in a State other than the territorial State. Such interpretive outcome would be inadmissible as incompatible with the Convention's object and purpose.

Yet another interpretive rule requires interpreting Article VI as not conflicting with customary law under which *jus cogens* requires universal jurisdiction over genocide.[23] The International Court rejected the territorial limitation of jurisdiction under the Convention by stating that 'the rights and obligations enshrined by the Convention are rights and obligations *erga omnes*. The Court notes that the obligation each State thus has to prevent and to punish the crime of genocide is not territorially limited by the Convention.'[24]

The German Constitutional Court engaged with the argument of whether Article VI of the Genocide Convention includes universal jurisdiction, in terms of the interpretation of the Convention. The court initially noted that Article VI does not regulate jurisdiction in an exclusive way because it does not explicitly mention the active or passive personality principles either. It then stressed the need to interpret the Convention in terms of its object and purpose, which consists of the effective prosecution of the perpetrators.

---

[22] *Eichmann*, 36 ILR 277; Byrnes and Kamminga, ILA Final Report on the Exercise of Universal Jurisdiction in Respect of Gross Human Rights Offences (2000), 5; Randall, Universal Jurisdiction under International Law, 66 *Texas Law Review* (1988), 835–836; Steven (1999), 459, adding that obligation under Article VI is a minimum rather than an exclusive obligation.

[23] Steven (1999), 460.   [24] *ICJ Reports*, 1996, para. 31.

Therefore, the lack of reference to universal jurisdiction only means that the Convention itself does not impose the duty to exercise universal jurisdiction, but States-parties retain their right to exercise universal jurisdiction over genocide. Genocide is, according to the court, the heaviest violation of human rights and it requires the application of universal jurisdiction to ensure the prosecution of the perpetrators without gaps.[25]

Similarly, Judge Lauterpacht in the *Bosnia* case considered that the purpose of the Genocide Convention is to authorize the exercise of universal jurisdiction by States over the crime of genocide, even if the crime is committed outside their borders and by non-nationals against non-nationals.[26]

At the preparatory stage of the Genocide Convention the principle of universality was seriously opposed, by both the United States and the Soviet Union, the latter on the basis that respect for State sovereignty required that there should be only territorial title of jurisdiction. Some States have supported the universality principle.[27] State practice is also familiar with the interpretative declarations by States acceding to the Genocide Convention expressing against the existence of universal jurisdiction under Article VI.[28] Judge Kreca in *Bosnian Genocide* denied that universal jurisdiction is available under the Genocide Convention, which he considered as limited to providing territorial jurisdiction.[29]

It seems that the relevance of both preparatory work and State practice is limited in the context where the plain meaning of the Genocide Convention as understood in terms of its object and purpose does not exclude, and even facilitates, the concept of universal jurisdiction. The objections in preparatory materials express the will of certain States that the treaty shall not include universal jurisdiction, but the interpretative relevance of these materials is only secondary. Likewise, the attitudes of the newly acceding States against universal jurisdiction cannot change much in the outcome if the text of the agreement allows for the opposite attitude to prevail. The outcome reached in judicial practice is furthermore preferable as it contains the coherent reasoning based on the character of the Convention and relevant rules of international law as to why the Convention must be deemed to include the principle of universality.

It is thus clear that the principal treaties that deal with outlawing and prosecution of what are *jus cogens* crimes under international law all provide for universal jurisdiction over respective crimes.

General international law upholds both the concept of universal jurisdiction and also its link to the community interest safeguarded by *jus cogens*.[30]

---

[25] 1290/99, para. 40.   [26] Separate Opinion, *ICJ Reports*, 1993, 325.
[27] Schabas (2000), 355–356.   [28] Id., 363.   [29] *ICJ Reports*, 1996, 535.
[30] Wolfrum, National Prosecution of International Offences, 24 *Israel YbHR* (1994), 185–186, 197; Parker and Neylon (1989), 455.

The Joint Separate Opinion in *Arrest Warrant* states that there is no signifi-cant practice affirming universal jurisdiction.[31] This statement unfortunately does not reflect the actual practice. There is quite consistent practice of affirmation, as a matter of general international law, of the existence of universal jurisdiction for *jus cogens* crimes by national and international bodies.[32]

A specific feature of this practice is that it does not view universal juris-diction over core international crimes as something dependent on, and the product of, the consensus and agreement between States. It rather views uni-versal jurisdiction as an inherent consequence of the universal nature of the respective crimes and thus links universal jurisdiction to some predetermined factors related to the nature of crimes rather than to empirical evidence. In other words, the practice of universal jurisdiction is the elaboration on, and illumination of, the pre-existing principle.[33]

In *Eichmann*, the exercise of universal jurisdiction was justified by reference to the community interest to prosecute crimes against humanity.[34] The Supreme Court of Israel dismissed the plea that by exercising universal jurisdiction Israel violated the sovereignty of other States. Jurisdiction in *Eichmann* was asserted not simply over the crimes committed abroad by and against non-nationals, but over crimes at the commission of which the State of Israel did not yet exist. The Supreme Court emphasized that the relevant crimes were recognized under customary international law as crimes damaging vital international interests, impairing the foundations of the international community and violating universal moral values and humani-tarian principles. Therefore, every State can try these crimes wherever com-mitted.[35] In *Demjanjuk*, the universality principle is justified, as some crimes are so universally condemned that the perpetrators are the enemies of all people. Therefore, any nation having custody of the perpetrators may punish them according to its law applicable to such offences.[36] In the case of exer-cising universal jurisdiction, 'neither the nationality of the accused or the victim(s), nor the location of the crime is significant. The underlying assumption is that the crimes are offences against the law of nations or against humanity and that the prosecuting nation is acting for all nations,' and vindicates their interest.[37]

---

[31] Joint Separate Opinion, paras 19 ff., 45.

[32] See, eg, German Practice, Wirth, Germany's New International Crimes Code: Bringing a Case to Court, 1 *Journal of International Criminal Justice* (2003), 161–162; Swiss Practice, Reydams, Case-note on *Niyonteze v Public Prosecutor*, 96 *AJIL* (2002); Dutch Practice, the *Bouterse* Decision of the Amsterdam Court of Appeal and *Hoge Raad*.

[33] It should be stated that this is similar to the affirmations of universal jurisdiction on an alternative basis, such as the implication of sovereignty in terms of *Lotus*, in not searching for the consensual evidence but rather pointing to the character of specific legal relations.

[34] 36 ILR 50.   [35] *Eichmann*, Supreme Court, 36 ILR 279, 291–292.

[36] *Demjanjuk*, 79 ILR 545.   [37] *Demjanjuk*, 79 ILR 545–546.

In *R v Finta*, the High Court of Canada emphasized that the principle of universal jurisdiction 'recognises that with regard to certain types of international crimes a country has the right to prosecute an offender irrespective of the fact that the offence was not committed on its territory'.[38] In England, *Pinochet* clarified that universal jurisdiction is available in case of breaches of *jus cogens*, having demonstrated the clear link between the two notions.[39] The decision of the Australian Supreme Court in *Polyukovich* also suggests that universal jurisdiction 'is based on the notion that certain acts are so universally condemned that, regardless of the situs of the offence and the nationality of the offender or the victim, each state has jurisdiction to deal with perpetrators of those acts.'[40] *Nulyarimma* affirms that the customary *jus cogens* crime of genocide empowers all States to exercise jurisdiction over it. It was considered established that the crime of genocide 'which has acquired the status of *jus cogens* or peremptory norm' and consequently 'States may exercise universal jurisdiction over such a crime'. This has been the legal position since at least 1948.[41] Finally, the ICTY in *Furundzija* affirmed that perpetrators of torture can be held criminally responsible for torture, whether in a foreign State, or in their own State under a subsequent regime. It further specified, without referring to any territorial or nationality link to the crime, that 'one of the consequences of the *jus cogens* character bestowed by the international community upon the prohibition of torture is that every State is entitled to investigate, prosecute and punish or extradite individuals accused of torture, who are present in a territory under its jurisdiction'. The inherently universal character of the crime based on its peremptory status gives all States universal jurisdiction.[42]

In more general terms, the Inter-American Commission of Human Rights affirmed the link between universal jurisdiction and international public order, by emphasizing that any State has the authority 'to prosecute and sanction individuals responsible for such international crimes, even those committed outside of a State's territorial jurisdiction, or which do not relate to the nationality of the accused or of the victims, inasmuch as such crimes affect all of humanity and are in conflict with public order of the world community'.[43] The *amicus curiae* brief of the European Commission presented to the United States Supreme Court also regarded universal criminal

---

[38] *R v Finta*, 82 ILR 444; see also the Supreme Court's decision in *Finta*, [1994] 1 SCR, 811.

[39] Crimes implicating breaches of *jus cogens* justify States in taking universal jurisdiction over them wherever committed, because offenders are common enemies of mankind and all nations have an equal interest in their apprehension and prosecution, Lord Browne-Wilkinson, *Pinochet*, 2 All ER (1999), 109; Lord Millett, ibid., 177–178. Court of First Instance of Brussels, 119 ILR, 356–357.

[40] Toohey J, *Polyukhovich v Commonwealth*, 91 ILR 118.

[41] *Nuliarimma*, 632 (Whitlam J); 641 (Merkel J).   [42] *Furundzija*, paras 155–156.

[43] *Universal Jurisdiction and the International Criminal Court*, Recommendation of the Inter-American Commission, 1998.

jurisdiction as well established and derived from the character of the relevant crimes in whose suppression and punishment every State has a legitimate interest.[44]

Doctrine also accepts the principle that the *jus cogens* nature of an international crime provides a basis for the exercise by States of universal jurisdiction over a crime wherever committed.[45]

In some cases, admittedly, courts have failed to exercise universal jurisdiction, but this practice does not deny the existence of universal jurisdiction, as, apart from a few isolated cases,[46] national courts do not dispute the existence of universal jurisdiction over *jus cogens* crimes as a matter of international law but merely state that they are prevented from acting owing to the rules of national law, which do not always reflect international standards.[47] States also narrow down their legislative provisions on universal jurisdiction, but for pragmatic reasons rather than their legal conviction against that jurisdictional title.[48] Furthermore, distinction should be made, as it was by the Canadian Supreme Court, between the existence of universal jurisdiction as a matter of international law and the constraints imposed by the national statute on the exercise of this jurisdiction within the national legal systems.[49]

Arguments against universal jurisdiction become less and less plausible. But it is debated whether universal jurisdiction is permissive or mandatory. There is a doctrinal argument that for *jus cogens* crimes affecting the community interest there is a general duty to extradite or prosecute the perpetrators.[50] Special Rapporteur Waldock viewed it as an incidence of *jus cogens* that in cases of slave-trade, piracy and genocide, international law 'places a general obligation upon every State to co-operate in the suppression and punishment of certain acts'.[51]

While judging on the existence of the duty to prosecute certain international crimes and the impact of *jus cogens* on the outcome, it is necessary to examine all relevant and available evidence, not just pick and choose the pronouncements conducive to one specific attitude. The relevance of specific

---

[44] EC *Amicus Curiae* Brief in *Sosa v Alvarez-Machain*, 23 January 2004, 15.

[45] Barboza, International Criminal Law, 278 *RdC* (1999), 188; Seiderman, *Hierarchy in International Law: The Human Rights Dimension* (2001), 106; Randall (1988), 830–831; Evans, International Wrongs and National Jurisdiction, Evans (ed.), *Remedies in International Law: The Institutional Dilemma* (1998), 180; Byrnes and Kamminga (2000), 8.

[46] eg *Pinochet* (Luxembourg), 119 *ILR* 361–367.

[47] Byrnes and Kamminga (2000), 5, on Swiss practice; Stern (1999), 525, on French practice; Cassese (2003), 303.

[48] Belgium's amendment of its universal jurisdiction law (42 *ILM* 2003, 1258) was caused by completely non-legal factors such as pressure by a foreign Government, including the threat that Belgium would cease to be the host of the NATO headquarters. Also, the US pressure was based not on legal conviction but on practical concerns not to have its officials prosecuted in Belgium.

[49] *R v Finta* (Supreme Court), 104 ILR 354–356; the Senegalese court adopted a similar approach *Habre* (Court of Cassation), 125 ILR 579.

[50] Bassiouni (1999), 219; Steven (1999), 441–442.   [51] Waldock, 2 YbILC, 1963, 53.

pronouncements for judging whether the prosecution of *jus cogens* crimes is mandatory should also be assessed with care, especially with regard to the cases which do not as such pronounce on this specific issue.[52] It is true that in certain pronouncements of the International Court and individual judges in the *Arrest Warrant* case the mandatory jurisdiction over *jus cogens* crimes was not affirmed. But this was so in the first place because the mandatory character of jurisdiction was not at all the subject-matter of the dispute.[53] The dispute concerned the instance of jurisdiction actually exercised by the relevant State (not the failure to exercise jurisdiction) and there was an agreement between the litigating parties that there was no problem with exercising universal jurisdiction over the relevant crimes. In addition, this dispute was concerned with the immunity of the incumbent foreign minister, which is a conceptually different issue from whether there was a duty to exercise jurisdiction over him. Norms on jurisdiction form the set of norms separate from norms on immunity and judging on the latter, whatever the final outcome, by no means involves judgment on the former.

Similarly, the decision of the European Court of Human Rights to uphold the immunity of a State for the acts of torture in *Al-Adsani* was not concerned with criminal jurisdiction, even though it in fact affirmed that the situation in the field of criminal prosecutions can result in denying State immunity to the perpetrators of *jus cogens* crimes. Therefore, neither of these two decisions speaks against the mandatory character of the jurisdiction over *jus cogens* crimes, and cases like these should not be considered as relevant, at least not crucially relevant, in judging the pertinent issues.

The issue of the duty to prosecute international crimes is crucial both in conceptual and practical terms. If international law only permits but does not oblige the prosecution of *jus cogens* crimes, then it in fact approves that such prosecution can be avoided either through inaction or as a matter of deals and transactions at national and international levels and thus approves, to some extent, the state of impunity. To consider that the duty to prosecute *jus cogens* crimes is not peremptory means to affirm that those crimes can go unpunished.

The duty to prosecute *jus cogens* crimes is an issue independent from universal jurisdiction, as where it exists it can be complied with through the exercise of jurisdiction under any heading, whether territorial, personal or universal, and such a duty would make the exercise of every relevant jurisdictional title mandatory. As individual criminal responsibility for *jus*

---

[52] For the treatment of some such pronouncements as relevant see Cryer, *Prosecuting International Crimes* (2005), 110–117.

[53] As the Separate Opinion of Judges Higgins, Koojmans and Buergenthal points out, the question in the *Arrest Warrant* case was whether Belgium had the right to issue and circulate the arrest warrant in pursuance of the universality principle if it so chose, para. 44.

cogens crimes is part of *jus cogens*, the rest of the jurisdictional framework such as universal jurisdiction and the duty to prosecute are merely specific implications of this fact and it follows that there is a duty to prosecute including the duty to establish universal jurisdiction. It must be examined whether this conclusion is supported under international law.

From a traditional *Lotus* perspective, all types of jurisdiction are permissive. But the duty to prosecute *jus cogens* crimes has a different conceptual basis. It is one thing to view *jus cogens* crimes as giving rise to a specific jurisdictional principle (such as universal jurisdiction). It is another thing to view *jus cogens* as making mandatory all kinds of jurisdiction as soon as they are exercised over *jus cogens* crimes, through prescribing the duty to prosecute. The essence of the duty to prosecute is to ensure that the perpetrators of *jus cogens* crimes will find no safe haven and enjoy no impunity. Such a duty would be a necessary corollary to *jus cogens* crimes to ensure that States are required to act in a way not undermining criminality. The essence of universal jurisdiction is, on the other hand, to ensure that persons accused of international crimes can be prosecuted even without a link with the forum State, which in fact appears as a conceptual accessory to the duty to prosecute, providing it with a clear jurisdictional basis linked to the *jus cogens* nature of a crime. In sum, the duty to prosecute and universal jurisdiction are two separate, though interconnected and mutually supportive consequences of the *jus cogens* nature of a crime. If and to the extent the duty to prosecute applies, traditional permissive patterns of jurisdiction are overtaken.

Humanitarian conventions impose on States the obligation to prosecute or extradite persons accused of certain *jus cogens* crimes. Article 7 of the Torture Convention obliges States-parties to bring persons accused of torture before its competent organs of prosecution,[54] a universal obligation to exercise criminal jurisdiction.[55] Articles 49/50/129/146 of the 1949 Geneva Conventions oblige States to search for and try persons accused of grave breaches of these Conventions. The same obligation is extended to breaches of the First Additional Protocol under its Article 85. Article VI of the Genocide Convention also compellingly requires the prosecution of persons accused of genocide. The exercise of universal jurisdiction is not only permitted but also required under the Genocide Convention to give substance to the parties' overall commitments under the Convention.[56] This is particularly true if the prosecution obligations established under the Genocide Convention are viewed as a system: compliance with the duties to ensure the

---

[54] The UN Committee against Torture considered that the prosecution of Senator Pinochet in the UK, if he was not extradited to another country, would satisfy the UK obligations under CAT, CAT/C/SR.360, 5.

[55] Burns and McBurney, Impunity and the United Nations Convention against Torture: A Shadow Play without an Ending, in Scott (ed.), *Torture as Tort* (2001), 281.

[56] Steven (1999), 461.

prosecution of the perpetrators in the place of the commission of the crime will under certain circumstances require the establishment of universal jurisdiction over the perpetrators, with the eventual purpose of extradition to the relevant forum.

Humanitarian instruments protect the community interest, not individual State interests. Therefore, prosecution clauses are not reciprocal obligations but objective obligations protecting the community interest, which cannot be divided into bilateral relations. Failure to comply with these duties is an offence not only towards individual States-parties but the international community as a whole. This is further evidenced by the establishment of true universal jurisdiction reflecting the rationale of universal jurisdiction with regard to *jus cogens* crimes—the absence of any link between the forum State and the crime. Therefore, duties under humanitarian conventions to prosecute *jus cogens* crimes can qualify as *jus cogens*.

Involvement of the community interest in conventional duties to prosecute reflects the *jus cogens* nature of criminality and indicates that these duties operate not just as treaty obligations but are also linked to general international law. This is even more relevant as the applicability of humanitarian treaties is limited *ratione materiae*. It is only the Genocide Convention which envisages prosecution for genocide wherever and by whomever committed. Geneva Conventions apply only to armed conflicts between States-parties (Article 2) and the scope of prosecution clauses (Articles 49/50/129/146) is limited accordingly. CAT envisages prosecution of torture linked to States-parties (Article 5). Of course, none of these affect the existence of universal jurisdiction under these treaties, or weigh against the objective and non-bilateralizable nature of duties to prosecute. But the fact remains that they do not, as treaty provisions, apply to situations not involving States-parties. In addition, no treaty regulates the prosecution before national courts of war crimes in internal conflicts and crimes against humanity.

State practice arguably does not yet affirm that States are under a duty to prosecute serious international crimes; instead references are made to evolving trends and directions of international law, in terms of treaties, UN resolutions and judicial practice, that could ultimately neutralize the lack of consistency in State practice.[57] Dugard observes in the same spirit about crimes against humanity that, 'although State practice may not provide sufficient evidence of the required usus or settled practice for such an obligation under customary international law there is at least a prima facie case for an obligation to prosecute.'[58]

---

[57] Edelenbos, Human Rights Violations: A Duty to Prosecute? 7 *LJIL* (1994), 20; Cassese, *International Criminal Law* (2003), 301–303.

[58] Dugard, Is the Truth and Reconciliation Process Compatible with International Law? The Unanswered Question, *South African Journal of Human Rights* (1997), 264.

Some cases of State practice do affirm that the prosecution of core international crimes is mandatory. The 2002 German Code of Crimes against International Law, which extends to international crimes such as genocide, war crimes and crimes against humanity, not only allows world-wide prosecutions under the principle of universal jurisdiction which it comprehensively implements, but also contains the principle of mandatory prosecution, which means that the prosecutor must prosecute.[59] An exception from the principle of mandatory prosecution is admitted only if either the accused is not present in Germany and such presence is not anticipated or, specifically in the case of German suspects, the case is also being prosecuted outside Germany. The reason for providing these exceptions is that judicial resources can be applied efficiently, that is only those suspects are indicted which can in fact be brought before German courts, and that impunity can be prevented. There are no other exceptions to the principle of mandatory prosecution.[60] This legal position corresponds to the conceptual basis of the duty to prosecute international crimes, and also is framed in a way corresponding to the alternatives this duty offers.

The Australian Federal Court, having affirmed the *jus cogens* character of the prohibition of genocide in international law, also affirmed the obligation imposed by customary law on each nation 'to extradite or prosecute any person, found within its territory' who has committed any act of genocide as specified in Article II of the Genocide Convention.[61] This statement of legal position under international law clearly points to mandatory universal jurisdiction over genocide under customary law, as it refers to the prosecution of *any* person, and also to the link of that mandatory jurisdiction to the peremptory status of the primary prohibition of genocide. It was also established that 'the acceptance under international law of a universal crime which has attained the status of *jus cogens* obliges a nation State to punish an offender or to extradite that offender, who is within its territory, to a State that will punish the offender.'[62]

It is questionable whether the status of the duty to prosecute *jus cogens* crimes in general international law should be determined only by reference to the traditional criteria of custom-generation. State practice mainly consists of national legislation and judicial practice. Treatment of this issue in legislative instruments and judicial decisions is diverse and hence cannot build a uniform rule. In addition, the relevance of State practice is diminished if it involves facts and conduct incompatible with humanitarian treaties. This must be viewed not as valid State practice but as a violation of international obligations. This holds true, as duly emphasized in doctrine, for the US legislation excluding universality and merely upholding territoriality and

---

[59] Wirth (2003), 151, 157.   [60] Id., 158–160.
[61] *Nulyarimma*, 627, *per* Wilcox J.   [62] Id., 656, *per* Merkel J.

personality with regard to genocide and war crimes, despite the requirements of the Genocide Convention and the Geneva Conventions.[63]

It is also argued that the numerous instances of granting amnesties to the perpetrators of core international crimes militates against regarding the duty to prosecute these crimes as an obligatory or peremptory norm.[64] But one should be careful not to rely in judging the precise legal position under customary law to acts of doubtful legality and validity, given in particular that many of the amnesties are of blanket character. The potential of the amnesties absolving the perpetrators of the core crimes to contribute to the custom-generation process is negligible because they have never won the recognition of the international community, being on the contrary regularly denounced by national and international bodies as amnesties that either are not genuine pardons or contradict the obligations under treaties or peremptory norms.[65] The mere fact that amnesties for core crimes happen is not sufficient for regarding them as relevant in determining the pertinent legal position. More generally, it is highly implausible that under current international law the acts and situations condoning impunity for core international crimes can have the relevance capable of impacting on the general legal situation.

Therefore, factors other than the traditional criteria of custom-generation—that is, instruments which embody not decentralized responses of individual States but the community response to and attitude on prosecution of *jus cogens* crimes—are also relevant. There is a strong presumption that the humanitarian treaty clauses establishing the duty to prosecute reflect customary international law. For instance, the *Genocide* Opinion suggests that the principles of the Genocide Convention, while they protect the community interest, bind States even in the absence of any conventional obligation. The Opinion speaks of the Convention as a whole and does not exclude any provision from the principle it states, which justifies assuming that jurisdictional principles under the Convention shall also be deemed to be part of general international law. Provisions in the 1949 Geneva Conventions providing for the prosecution of grave breaches are also accepted as customary law.[66] The same could apply to the Torture Convention which, like the Genocide Convention, reflects *jus cogens* criminality and declares it punishable in the community interest.

In line with this approach, in its decision regarding the prosecution for the acts of torture committed during the Argentine dirty war, the Committee against Torture emphasized that even before the entry into force of the

---

[63] Cassese (2003), 306; Steven (1999), 464–466.

[64] Naqvi, Amnesty for War Crimes: Defining the Limits of International Recognition, 85 *International Review of the Red Cross* (2003), 611–612.

[65] cf above, Chapter 7.   [66] Joint Separate Opinion, *Arrest Warrant*, para. 46.

Torture Convention there existed a general rule of international law requiring the prosecution and punishment of acts of torture.[67]

Yet another confirmation of the duty to prosecute *jus cogens* crimes as a matter of legal conviction of the international community as a whole can be found in the Preamble of the ICC Statute, which emphasizes the role of national prosecution and related international cooperation in combating impunity and recalls that 'it is the duty of every State to exercise its criminal jurisdiction over those responsible for international crimes'.[68] This provision seems to refer to general international law and not just to treaties as it recalls that the duty to prosecute is incumbent on *every State*.

Recognition by the international community as a whole of the duty to prosecute *jus cogens* crimes is also mirrored in General Assembly resolutions 2840(1971) and 3074(1973).[69] Resolution 3074 requires that States shall assist each other in detecting, arresting and bringing to trial persons suspected of having committed war crimes and crimes against humanity (para. 4). This statement implies the requirement that jurisdiction shall be exercised with a view to prosecution or extradition. Resolution 2840 is more categorical in stating that the refusal of States to cooperate in the arrest, extradition, prosecution and punishment of persons guilty of war crimes and crimes against humanity is 'contrary to generally recognised norms of international law'. Even if such resolutions are recommendatory, this last resolution definitely goes beyond that, as it not only recommends a course of action but states the law by identifying generally recognized norms of international law requiring prosecution of war crimes and crimes against humanity, and identifies the failure to prosecute them as incompatible with those generally recognized norms. The intention of the General Assembly has clearly been not to make recommendation but to state the law in force, and its assessment represents the legal conviction of the international community as a whole as to the content of relevant legal norms—the community *opinio juris* with regard to custom as distinct from individual State convictions.[70]

This factor reinforces the point that the relevance of State practice in determining the customary status of the duty to prosecute *jus cogens* crimes is limited, as the very practice falling short of compliance with the duty to

---

[67] Communications No. 1-3/1988, Decision on Admissibility of 23 November 1989.

[68] Preambular paras 4 and 6; this was so interpreted in *Ghaddafi* (Court of Appeal of Paris), 125 ILR 497–498. In *Prosecutor v Gbao* (25 May 2004), the Special Court for Sierra Leone expressly affirmed that 'under international law, States are under a duty to prosecute crimes whose prohibition has the status of jus cogens'.

[69] Normative resolutions of the General Assembly can serve as evidence of customary law, *Nicaragua, ICJ Report*, 1986, 14.

[70] Such community legal conviction is also expressed in specific situations. The UN Human Rights Commission Resolution 1999/1 emphasized that all countries are under an obligation to identify and punish crimes committed in non-international armed conflict in Sierra Leone.

prosecute may itself be viewed as illegal, under either conventional or customary international law. There is every reason to suggest that an action deplored as illegal by the international community as a whole, such as giving safe haven to perpetrators of war crimes and crimes against humanity, cannot be a valid basis for State practice.

The duty *aut dedere aut judicare* is imposed on the custodial State in whose territory an alleged offender is present and activates as State gains control over the offender. From this moment the duty to exercise jurisdiction over him becomes mandatory, whatever the jurisdictional title. The custodial State is in a 'unique position' to implement that duty by virtue of the presence of the alleged offender in its territory, and shall take steps to apprehend and prosecute him.[71] Before gaining control over the offender, universal jurisdiction, like any other jurisdiction, remains permissive.

It must be examined whether the duty to prosecute *jus cogens* crimes, and universal jurisdiction for that matter, is itself part of *jus cogens*. If traditional criteria of law-making are employed, State practice could be seen as the relevant factor in determining the peremptory character of a rule. But it is also plausible to suggest that the *jus cogens* character of a crime can imply a similar character in respect of the consequential duty to prosecute. The substance of a norm is often sufficient to warrant viewing that norm as peremptory.

The Belgian court in *Pinochet* has recognized that universal jurisdiction with regard to crimes against humanity is of *jus cogens* character.[72] The French Court in *Ghaddafi* accepted that the duty to prosecute international crimes is based on *jus cogens*. Prosecution of such acts should not be subject to any derogation.[73] As Judge Van den Wyngaert suggested, 'the *ratio legis* of universal jurisdiction is based on the international reprobation for certain very serious crimes such as war crimes and crimes against humanity. Its *raison d'être* is to avoid impunity, to prevent suspects of such crimes finding a safe haven in third countries.'[74] If, as a matter of fact, this statement is correct— there seeming no plausible way of challenging it—the inescapable conclusion follows that universal jurisdiction as attached to those serious crimes is peremptory as such, for the reason it exists is to prevent impunity and to exclude the possibility that criminals find a safe haven, in all circumstances

---

[71] ILC Code of Crimes against the Peace and Security of Mankind, 1996, commentary to Article 9, para. 3. The physical presence of an accused on a prosecuting State's territory as a prerequisite for the exercise of the duty *aut dedere aut judicare* is also recognized in the Byrnes and Kamminga Report (2000), 2.

[72] 119 ILR 357.

[73] *Ghaddafi* (Court of Appeal of Paris), 125 ILR 496; the Cour de Cassation did not contradict this.

[74] Dissenting Opinion of Judge Van den Wyngaert, the *Arrest Warrant* case, ICJ General List No. 121, 2002, para. 46. id., para 28 on peremptory status of international crimes. The majority of the Court avoided the issue of universal jurisdiction, having considered that the case could be decided even without focusing on it.

and without any exception; in order to achieve this, this principle vests with jurisdiction all States even if they have no individual link with a crime, and in circumstances even obliging them to exercise such jurisdiction. Having imperative purpose, emanating from imperative norms and envisaging community response, that norm cannot be portrayed except as part of *jus cogens*.

This is further affirmed by Judge Al-Khasawneh, who reiterates that 'The effective combating of grave crimes has arguably assumed a *jus cogens* character reflecting recognition by the international community of the vital community interests and values it seeks to protect and enhance.'[75]

The German *Bundesvervassungsgericht* also confirmed that the universal jurisdiction over *jus cogens* crimes, such as genocide, and also that jurisdiction's mandatory character, is part of *jus cogens*. It determined that there can be no rule of international law contradicting universal jurisdiction over genocide whose prohibition is peremptory both under customary and conventional law.[76] The Hungarian Constitutional Court determined that the regulations on the punishment of war crimes and crimes against humanity 'form peremptory norms of international law (*jus cogens*). Those States which refuse to assume these obligations cannot participate in the community of nations,'[77] which is nothing short of an emphasis on the *jus cogens* nature of the duty to prosecute. Lord Hope in *Pinochet* emphasized the peremptory character of the duty to prosecute *jus cogens* crimes by stating that *jus cogens* imposes on all States an *erga omnes* obligation to punish certain international crimes.[78] According to *Nulyarimma*, duties with regard to universal crimes, such as the duty to prosecute or extradite, are non-derogable and the only discretion is to choose between prosecution and extradition.[79]

The ICTY in *Kupreskic* considered that the liability for grave breaches of humanitarian law is 'absolute and may in no case be set aside by resort to any legal means such as derogating treaties or agreements' or 'thwarted by recourse to arguments such as reciprocity'.[80] A clearer description of a peremptory principle is hard to imagine.

This approach is conceptually coherent. If *jus cogens* crimes are outlawed in the community interest, the same interest persists in their due prosecution. If *jus cogens* crimes are peremptorily outlawed as crimes, then the duty to prosecute or extradite their perpetrators must be viewed as peremptory. The duty to prosecute or extradite perpetrators of *jus cogens* crimes fulfils all relevant criteria of a peremptory norm: it protects the community interest as distinct from individual State interests, operates as an obligation of a State towards the international community as a whole and is not bilateralizable. According to Bassiouni and Wise, the peremptory nature of the duty to

[75] Dissenting Opinion of Judge Al-Khasawneh, *Arrest Warrant*, para. 7.
[76] 1290/99, Decision of the 4th Chamber, 2nd Senate, 12 December 2000, para. 17.
[77] Decision No. 53/1993, para. V.1.   [78] Lord Hope, *Pinochet*, 2 All ER (1999), 147.
[79] *Nulyarimma*, 661.   [80] *Kupreskic*, para. 517.

prosecute *jus cogens* crimes follows from the need not to allow perpetrators of large-scale human rights violations to escape with impunity.[81]

If States explicitly or implicitly agree that a person having committed an international crime shall not be punished, they in fact legitimize their crimes and negate the fact that the norms outlawing the very crimes are peremptory, as they act against the requirement of a norm that war crimes must be punished. As Bassiouni and Wise make clear, to consider the principle *aut dedere aut judicare* as a peremptory norm is dictated by the need of effective oppression of international offences. If this principle is peremptory, States are unable to contract out of it, because the prohibition of the offences involved is in the paramount interest of international public order. States are not entitled to acquiesce in the violations of this principle. Any State holding the violator without prosecuting or extraditing him impermissibly acquiesces in the violation of a peremptory norm.[82] Bassiouni and Wise add that failure to prosecute vitiates the authority of a primary prohibition and is itself a violation of international law. Whatever the domestic political reasons, the international wrongfulness may not be evaded.[83]

This approach is in accordance with the non-derogable character of the duty to prosecute. States are not permitted to derogate from the *aut dedere aut judicare* rule with regard to *jus cogens* crimes, and no derogation has ever been attempted. If States could *inter se* opt out of the duty to prosecute a *jus cogens* crime, they could also opt out *inter se* from its very criminal character as they would treat the criminal action as not prosecutable in their *inter se* relations. Such would be the outcome whether derogation happens explicitly or implicitly through practice and conduct. If a State is bound by the attitude that a given action is peremptorily criminal (which means that it *must* be prosecuted), it can no longer take a view that it is free to give safe haven to an accused, as such an attitude would mean that, for that State or for the given situation, a given action is no longer peremptorily criminal—and this latter factor must be enough to prevent a practice consolidating such an attitude from being valid.

The *Genocide* Opinion emphasized the universal character of prohibition of genocide and the equally universal character of the duty to cooperate in repressing genocide.[84] As the Opinion is understood as what today is known as *jus cogens*,[85] it supports the idea that the duty to prosecute genocide is peremptory. As Rosenne submitted to the ILC, the Opinion established a *jus*

---

[81] Bassiouni and Wise, *Aut Dedere Aut Judicare: The Duty to Extradite or Prosecute in International Law* (1995), 52–53.

[82] Bassiouni and Wise (1995), 52, 69. Seiderman (2001), 110, suggests that when the violation of a *jus cogens* norm engenders criminal liability, the universal enforcement measures may be seen as necessary to the fulfilment of the correlative obligation of non-acquiescence in the commission of an international crime in violation of a peremptory norm.

[83] Bassiouni and Wise (1995), 53–54.   [84] *ICJ Reports*, 1951, 23–24.

[85] See above, Chapter 3.

cogens duty of all States to cooperate in the suppression of genocide, and that this duty was quite independent of the Genocide Convention itself and derived from the General Assembly resolutions on the subject.[86] *Bosnian Genocide* also indiscriminately affirms that the rights and obligations under the Genocide Conventions are rights and obligations *erga omnes*, presumptively also its jurisdictional principles. Similarly, Schindler affirms that the duty of States to prosecute the Geneva Conventions violators is not only a duty related to *erga omnes* obligations, but itself a duty *erga omnes*, despite the fact that States show little readiness to prosecute such crimes effectively.[87]

According to Goodwin-Gill, in the case of crimes deriving from *jus cogens*, the legal implications are peremptory: States are not only entitled but also obliged *erga omnes* to try an offender or extradite to a State with a stronger claim to do so. *Jus cogens* makes prosecution unavoidable as a matter of duty.[88] For instance, the duty to extradite or prosecute for genocide is peremptory because it is the inherent condition of the underlying peremptory norm. 'The only way the prohibition of genocide can have any concrete meaning as a *jus cogens* norm—that is, as a rule of paramount importance to the maintenance of the international order and from which no derogation is allowed—is if this norm is supported by a *jus cogens* duty to prosecute. The absolute prohibition of genocide has no meaning unless all States have an absolute obligation to bring offenders to justice.'[89]

The peremptory character of *aut dedere aut judicare* with regard to *jus cogens* crimes can also be inferred from the ILC's consequences of breaches of peremptory norms. In its commentary on Article 41 on State responsibility the ILC mentions the duty of States to cooperate to counteract the effects of a serious breach of *jus cogens*. Impunity can certainly be viewed among such effects and the required form of cooperation is the arrest, prosecution and extradition of perpetrators.[90]

2. UNIVERSAL CIVIL JURISDICTION AND THE DUTY TO REMEDY BREACHES OF *JUS COGENS*

A breach of *jus cogens* offends the community interest and to remedy it is in the community interest, as is the avoidance of original breaches. This very factor justifies States in asserting universal civil jurisdiction for the purpose

---

[86] YbILC, 1963, I, 74.

[87] Schindler, Erga omnes-Wirkung des humanitären Völkerrechts, Beyerlin, Bothe, Hofmann and Petersmann (Hrsg.), *Recht zwischen Umbruch und Bewahrung. Festschrift für Rudolf Bernhardt* (1993), 211.

[88] Goodwin-Gill (1999), 220.

[89] Steven (1999), 443, 447–448, 450; Seiderman (2001), 110.

[90] *ILC Reports* 2001, commentary to Article 41, 287, para. 3.

of enforcing civil remedies for breaches of peremptory norms.[91] Owing to the status of primary norms, universal civil jurisdiction can exist even without a specific provision.[92] In addition, unless otherwise provided, jurisdiction must be viewed as comprehensive, covering both criminal and civil aspects: if an act attracts universal criminal jurisdiction, it is unclear why it cannot attract universal civil jurisdiction.

This follows directly from the findings of the Italian Supreme Court in *Ferrini* with regard to universal civil jurisdiction. The Court emphasized that certain international crimes are subject to universal criminal jurisdiction and not subject to statutory limitations. These factors suffice to view the same actions capable of generating universal civil jurisdiction.[93]

While the basis in international law of universal criminal jurisdiction is inferable from numerous textual instruments expressing the community will and interest, universal civil jurisdiction is arguably not supported by the same amount of textual authority.[94] The textual evidences are, however, not difficult to find if the proper treaty interpretation methods are applied. In addition, there are enough instances of affirmation of universal civil jurisdiction in practice.

In the proceedings before the US Supreme Court, the European Commission stated in general terms that unlike universal criminal jurisdiction, the existence and scope of universal civil jurisdiction is not well established in international law.[95] Nevertheless, the European Commission admitted that universal civil jurisdiction can exist for the same category of violations as is covered by universal criminal jurisdiction, and also be subject to the same limitations, such as the presence of the defendant on the territory of the forum State.[96]

Universal civil jurisdiction is recognized in *Furundzija* where the ICTY suggested that the victims of torture, where they are unable to get remedies in a country where they have allegedly been tortured, are entitled under general international law to bring a civil suit in a foreign court.[97] National courts also affirm the same principle.[98] In *Filartiga*, the District and Circuit Courts of the United States condemned torture committed in Paraguay, by a Paraguayan against a Paraguayan, and awarded punitive damages to the victims.[99] Similar decisions in civil cases have been taken by courts in several other cases

---

[91] Swan, International Human Rights Torts and the Experience of US Courts, in Scott (ed.), *Torture as Tort* (2001), 91.

[92] McGonville, Taking Jurisdiction, in Scott (ed.), *Torture as Tort* (2001), 173.

[93] Bianchi, Case-note on *Ferrini* (Supreme Court of Italy), *AJIL* (2005), 244.

[94] McGonville (2001), 172.

[95] EC *Amicus Curiae* Brief in *Sosa v Alvarez-Machain*, 23 January 2004, 17.

[96] Id., 21–22.   [97] *Furundzija*, IT-95-17/I-T, para. 155.

[98] For an overview see Dodge, Which Torts in Violation of the Law of Nations? 24 *Hastings International and Comparative Law Review* (2001).

[99] 77 ILR 169.

affirming that the customary prohibition of torture entitled domestic courts to award damages to the victims tortured abroad, despite the fact that the forum State had no connection with the actual torture of victims. In *Trajano v Marcos* and *Hilao v Marcos*, the Court of Appeals for the Ninth Circuit dealt with the issue of extraterritorial torture, as conduct outlawed under *jus cogens*, which provided the basis for the Court's jurisdiction to award money damages in a civil case.[100] In *Trajano v Marcos* the US court faced the plea that the Alien Tort Claims Act (ATCA) did not cover the acts of torture having no nexus with the United States. However, the court felt constrained by what the statute showed on its face: 'no limitations as to the citizenship of the defendant, or the locus of the injury.'[101] In *Xuncax v Gramajo* the US court linked the jurisdiction thus construed to wrongs perpetrated in contravention of peremptory norms of international law.[102]

All these cases are based on universal customary law, and the peremptory status of norms. In addition, *Filartiga* suggests that a torturer is a *hostis humani generis* for the purposes of civil liability,[103] in the same way as in cases of criminal prosecution. The inference of Judge Edwards in *Tel-Oren* was that persons may be susceptible to civil liability under the ATCA universal jurisdiction 'if they commit *either* a crime traditionally warranting universal jurisdiction *or* an offence that comparably violates current norms of international law'.[104] This is an emphasis on the parallelism of criminal and civil jurisdiction over the breaches of peremptory norms.

This practice confirms a logical conclusion that if conduct is outlawed by *jus cogens*, all States may assert jurisdiction to vindicate the breach. The US courts often use the *jus cogens* character of the norms involved to affirm that the universal jurisdiction can be exercised over the relevant torts as a matter of international law and thus triggering the applicability of section 1350 ATCA.[105]

In Canada the starting-point principle which is embodied in the *Tolofson* decision is that a Canadian court has jurisdiction over a tort where there is 'a real and substantial connection between the subject matter of the litigation and the forum'. Under this view, Canadian courts will in principle not hear the cases of human rights violations committed against non-Canadians.

---

[100] 103 ILR 526–527, 530, 104 ILR 126–128; See also *Forti v Suarez-Mason*, 81 ILR 631–633, *Xuncax v Gramajo*, 104 ILR 183–184, and *Alvarez-Machain v US*, 41 ILM (2002), 130, supporting the same principles.

[101] *Trajano v Marcos*, 527.   [102] *Xuncax v Gramajo*, 183.   [103] 77 ILR 184.

[104] *Tel-Oren v Libyan Arab Republic*, 77 ILR 210 (emphasis added).

[105] It is probably the case that not in all cases do the relevant breaches need to be qualified as breaches of *jus cogens* to attract universal jurisdiction under ATCA. As this statute refers to universal, definable and obligatory norms, the customary law status of the norm would probably suffice, and this is indeed the case in some judicial decisions. See Dodge (2001). The point is, however, that in a great many cases it is exactly the concept of peremptory law that is used as justification of universal civil jurisdiction.

However, in *Bouzari* the Ontario Superior Court of Justice admitted exception for torture because the plaintiff could not pursue such claims in Iran where he was tortured.[106] Such indirect circumvention of the requirement of a link to the forum on alternative grounds suggests that Canadian courts are in principle ready to exercise universal jurisdiction over breaches of international *jus cogens* on the basis of the assessment of specific situations. This differs from the ATCA jurisdiction in the United States as it is based not on statutory jurisdiction but on judicial assessment.

The Court of Appeal in *Bouzari* was more straightforward in coming closer to recognizing universal civil jurisdiction over the breaches of peremptory norms. As by torturing Bouzari Iran had committed a breach of peremptory norms, it eliminated itself as a possible forum, the appellant was left without the forum and hence the application of the requirement that the tort shall have a real and substantial connection with the forum was not easy.[107] This line of reasoning demonstrates that although the Canadian courts generally seem reluctant to accept universal civil jurisdiction and maintain that the link to the forum should be demonstrated, they show some readiness to exercise such jurisdiction if the relevant tort offends against the international *jus cogens*.

The Italian Supreme Court in *Ferrini* affirmed that the principle of universality of jurisdiction which is available over international crimes also extends to civil actions arising out of such crimes. The court's decision was generally motivated by the relevance of peremptory norms.[108]

It seems that universal civil jurisdiction with regard to breaches of *jus cogens* is mandatory. The Convention against Torture contains the grant of universal civil jurisdiction over torture in mandatory terms. According to Article 14, States-parties must ensure in their legal systems that 'the victim of an act of torture obtains redress and has an enforceable right to fair and adequate compensation'; in the event of the death of the victim, 'his dependants shall be entitled to compensation'. This provision establishes not only universal jurisdiction as an entitlement but also the obligation to

---

[106] *Bouzari*, paras 15–17, *per* Swinton J.

[107] *Bouzari* (Court of Appeal for Ontario), paras 36–38, *per* Goudge JA. Although the Court stated in para. 38 that it did not need to finally clarify this issue because the adjudication was refused on the basis of State immunity, which is the issue separate from the issues of jurisdiction and relevant forum, it nevertheless acknowledged most pressing reasons favouring the exercise of universal jurisdiction as outlined above and did not quote any specific reason contrary to those, which could mean that there is not much on the opposite side in the process of balancing the conflicting considerations that could prevent the exercise of universal jurisdiction in the cases like this.

[108] Judgment, paras 9 and 12, quoted in De Sena and De Vittor, State Immunity and Human Rights: The Italian Supreme Court Decision on the *Ferrini* Case, 16 *EJIL* (2005), 97, 103.

exercise jurisdiction,[109] and does not require the occurrence of an original act of torture within the territory or under the jurisdiction of the forum State, nor does it require any other link between the forum and the act.[110]

The scope of obligations under Article 14 is crucial in this process for several reasons. This provision provides for the jurisdictional clause to enforce treaty obligations which are laid down in pursuance to the superior community interest and are thus non-bilateralizable. In addition, the Convention against Torture introduces the treaty framework for the prosecution of what in general international law is a *jus cogens* crime and the scope of obligations under this Convention can be indicative of the state of general international law, given especially, as noted on occasions, that the Convention itself restates and embodies customary law on its subject-matter.

The alleged uncertainty of Article 14 is noted and doubts are admitted whether Article 14 grants civil jurisdiction in the same way as Articles 5 and 7 of the Torture Convention grant criminal jurisdiction, especially because the reference to civil jurisdiction in Article 14 is ambiguous.[111] But the ambiguity cannot be so easily attributed to the treaty clause which on its face lays down a clear obligation of States to provide remedies, that is exercise jurisdiction. It is true that the criminal jurisdiction provisions of the Torture Convention are more detailed and Article 14 is stated in more simple and straightforward terms, but this is by no means the same as ambiguity, because a treaty provision does not have to be drafted in a complex way to produce a foreseeable effect.

Doubts are expressed whether States-parties would have lightly agreed to assume jurisdictional obligations involving among others the provision of national compensation funds.[112] But this argument suffers from conceptual deficiency. It should be clear that the duty to provide jurisdiction does not imply the duty of the territorial State to provide compensation funds for extraterritorial torture, because compensation would be due from the foreign actor which commits torture abroad. In addition, it is erroneous to judge the content of a treaty provision such as Article 14 by abstract speculations as to what the States-parties would or would not have lightly assumed. The proper way is rather to clarify what obligations they have assumed by reference to what Article 14 suggests on its face.

The textual interpretation of Article 14 produces clear results and also accords with the general international law framework developed by national

---

[109] Adams, In Search of Defence of the Transnational Human Rights Paradigm: May Jus Cogens Norms be Invoked to Create Implied Exceptions in Domestic Immunity Statutes?, in Craig (ed.), *Torture as Tort* (2001), 251–252.

[110] Orakhelashvili, *EJIL* (2003), 551–555.

[111] Byrnes, Civil Remedies for Torture Committed Abroad: An Obligation under the Convention Against Torture?, in Scott (ed.), *Torture as Tort* (2001), 542; see also Adams (2001), 252, 262–264.

[112] Byrnes (2001), 543.

and international bodies. It further evidences a contrast to similar provisions in other treaties and proves that if States-parties to a treaty wish to provide for a territorially restricted jurisdiction, they will do so explicitly.[113]

The result is very much the same if Article 14 is interpreted in terms of the object and purpose of the Convention against Torture. Such interpretation, it is admitted, would imply that the Convention is aimed at eliminating impunity and facilitating effective compensation for victims, and hence supports the expansive interpretation of Article 14 to cover universal civil jurisdiction.[114] Such interpretation is more than appropriate. As shown above, the German Constitutional Court read into Article VI of the Genocide Convention, which expressly subscribes to territorial jurisdiction only, the inherent entitlement of States-parties to exercise universal jurisdiction and this conclusion was reached by reference to the overarching goal of the Genocide Convention to ensure prosecution and prevent impunity. If the similar interpretation is applied to the Convention against Torture, universal jurisdiction is even easier to justify than in the case of Article VI of the Genocide Convention, because Article 14 does not on its face limit the jurisdiction of States to any particular mode such as territorial jurisdiction.

Those eager to prove that Article 14 does not provide for universal jurisdiction resort to arguments based on the preparatory work of the Convention combined with the subsequent practice of its application. The special reference is made to the attitude of the US Government at the time of the ratification of the Convention by the Senate that Article 14 only obligates States-parties to provide remedies for torture committed on the territory under its jurisdiction. During the preparatory work, what is now Article 14 was indeed qualified in such terms but the limitation of jurisdiction to the acts of torture committed under the jurisdiction of the State-party was dropped. The US Government maintained that this happened by mistake.[115] But it is unjustified to attribute to a mistake the change of a normative provision which causes a substantial change in the jurisdiction of States-parties transforming it from territorial into extraterritorial. Such a line of reasoning implies that States-parties did not know what they were doing while drafting the Convention.

It may also be thought that the lack of Application of Article 14 by States-parties in a way of exercising universal jurisdiction can weigh against the existence of such jurisdiction under that provision. The answer to that concern is simple, as the practical application of a treaty provision does not prejudice its inherent content, apart from the cases where the positive

---

[113] cf Article 6 of the 1968 Convention on the Elimination of All Forms of Racial Discrimination obligating States-parties to provide remedies for racial discrimination in territories under their jurisdiction. This is noted by Byrnes (2003), 548, but without acknowledgment of the consequences thereof.

[114] Byrnes (2001), 547–548.   [115] Byrnes, 546.

evidence is inferable that an agreement to modify the relevant treaty provision is clearly established among States-parties. The relevance of this factor would be even less likely with the treaty such as the Convention against Torture whose provisions are not bilateralizable and their modification would need the positive expression of the views of the entire membership which remains only a hypothetical option.

It is thus clear that the relevance of the action and attitudes of the individual States-parties is limited. It is nevertheless opportune to examine the treatment of jurisdiction under Article 14 by British and Canadian courts. The Court of Appeal in *Jones v Saudi Arabia* declined to see universal civil jurisdiction following from Article 14. The court started with the assumption that Article 14 had 'no explicit jurisdictional ambit' and it seemed 'unlikely that it can have been intended that every State should ensure that its legal system provided redress for every act of torture' wherever committed and whoever the victim. The court also touched upon the factors that militate against assuming the exclusively territorial character of the obligation under Article 14, by pointing out that this provision can also extend to torture committed abroad by officials of the forum State and thus effectively subsuming extraterritorial, along with territorial, personal jurisdiction within the ambit of Article 14. Nevertheless the court refused to apply Article 14 to torture committed abroad and by foreign officials, asserting that Article 14(1) is not designed to *require* every other State to provide redress in its civil legal system for acts of torture committed by another State.[116] These findings were related to the claims against the foreign State and the Court of Appeal would not admit the foreign State itself getting impleaded as the defendant. The Court of Appeal, however, accepted with regard to claims against the foreign State officials that Article 14(1) can justify assuming jurisdiction over torture committed abroad by another State when the victim cannot pursue his claims in the State where torture occurred. Otherwise, the right to access to a court would be deprived of its real meaning.[117] This finding echoes the rationale advanced by the Canadian Court of Appeal in *Bouzari* in support of universal civil jurisdiction over acts contrary to peremptory norms.[118]

As can be seen, *Jones* effectively disapproves the attitude of the US Government that Article 14 extends only to acts of torture committed under the jurisdiction of the forum State. This demonstrates that if it is sought to establish that Article 14 does not provide for universal civil jurisdiction, this must be done on grounds other than the bare assumption of territoriality unsupported by the text. But apart from that, and presumably for the very reason that justifying the absence of universality on the alternative basis is hardly possible in the text of Article 14, the court's treatment of Article 14 is

---

[116] *Jones*, paras 18, 20–21, *per* Mance LJ.
[117] *Jones*, paras 84–85, 92, *per* Mance LJ.   [118] Above, notes 106–107.

inconsistent and self-contradictory. At the cost of ignoring the plain meaning of Article 14 as interpreted in terms of the object and purpose of the Torture Convention, the court subscribed to the false approach that Article 14 has 'no explicit jurisdictional ambit' which, once again, is incorrect in the face of the text of Article 14. If one proceeds from the territoriality restriction approach, then the jurisdictional ambit of Article 14 is quite clear and is territorial. But as this is not the case, which the court itself acknowledged, it proceeded to dismiss the universality principle on the basis that Article 14 had no explicit ambit. It is exactly here that the court's approach proved most inconsistent. It did not subscribe to the territoriality limitation, included extraterritorial personal jurisdiction within Article 14 and did so because the text of Article 14 did not exclude such personal jurisdiction. As a matter of fact, that text does not exclude universal civil jurisdiction any more than it excludes personal jurisdiction, and the court's conclusion that for some mysterious reasons one type of jurisdiction is in and another is out is indeed arbitrary for not properly considering the text and purpose of the Convention. *Jones* merely justifies its approach by what is 'likely' that 'can have been intended' by the Convention and for what Article 14 of the Convention is 'designed', instead of what the Convention actually says and what its purposes require. Subjective appreciation of treaty provisions cannot replace the value of their plain meaning and amount to proper judicial exercise.

Another conceptual inconsistency of *Jones* is that it construed Article 14 differently depending on the identity of the defendant, suggesting that extraterritorial, and *a fortiori* universal, jurisdiction is not available in proceedings against States but is available over State officials. This distinction is even more questionable as the concerns of the impossibility of pursuing torture claims in Saudi Arabia still persisted whoever the defendant was. As a matter of treaty obligations, Article 14 requires establishment of jurisdiction over torture whoever the defendant is. It is true that jurisdiction over States in the UK is prevented by the State Immunity Act, but the issue of immunity is different from the issue of jurisdiction. Immunity, here as a matter of national legislation, can prevent the exercise of jurisdiction but does not prejudice its existence in the first place.

In *Bouzari v Iran* the Ontario Superior Court of Justice also commented on Article 14 of the Torture Convention and found it inapplicable to the acts of torture of a foreign national committed abroad. The court accepted that the text of Article 14 contains no specific territorial limitation, but it nevertheless subscribed to the exclusively territorial character of jurisdiction under Article 14 by reference to the practice of certain States, namely the US attitude on territoriality (effectively disapproved, as demonstrated above, by the English court) met by the response of Germany which can only ambiguously, if at all, be considered as the acceptance of the US view, the silence of other States-parties, and Canada's own attitude before the Committee against

Torture.[119] The Court of Appeal for Ontario vigorously reaffirmed the lower court's determination that Article 14 applies only to the acts of torture committed within the territory of the forum State. It further approved the lower court's understanding of State practice as crucially influenced the meaning of Article 14, by reference to Article 31(3)(b) of the 1969 Vienna Convention on the Law of Treaties regarding the relevance of subsequent practice in treaty interpretation.[120]

The Canadian courts thus effectively accepted that the attitude of the three States-parties, on occasions themselves ambiguous, coupled with the silence of the other States-parties, can overrule the textual meaning of Article 14 as acknowledged by that court itself. The courts did not make any effort to prove that the silence of other States-parties was necessarily meant to establish the agreement to reduce the scope of Article 14 to the provision that provides merely for territorial jurisdiction. In addition, the Court of Appeal referred to the 1969 Vienna Convention to justify its interpretative approach, but did not bother to enquire into whether the same Convention had anything to say on the relevance of the plain meaning of the treaty text as understood in terms of its object and purpose. Furthermore, the Court of Appeal insisted on the territoriality of Article 14 while having accepted that the breaches of peremptory norms can in principle give rise to universal civil jurisdiction as a matter of general international law. Most importantly, Canadian courts have subscribed to territoriality of jurisdiction under Article 14, while the English court has not.

That the reasoning of *Bouzari* and, *a fortiori*, of *Jones* is inconsistent and defective was demonstrated in the proceedings before the Committee against Torture regarding the compliance of Canada with its obligations under Article 14 of the Torture Convention. The representatives of Canada defended the attitude of their courts by insisting that Article 14 only requires the establishment of jurisdiction over the acts of torture committed in the forum State's territory. The arguments they used were much the same as those of the courts.[121] The Committee did not share this approach as it dealt with it in the context of 'subjects of concern', one of which is 'the absence of effective measures to provide civil compensation to victims of torture *in all cases*'. It furthermore insisted that 'the State-party should review its position under Article 14 of the Convention to ensure the provision of compensation through its civil jurisdiction *to all victims of torture*'.[122] Thus the Committee clearly and effectively disapproved the approach of national courts to view Article 14 as restricted to territorial jurisdiction or as excluding universal jurisdiction.

---

[119] *Bouzari*, paras 49–51, *per* Swinton J.

[120] *Bouzari* (Court of Appeal), paras 72–82, *per* Goudge JA.

[121] Committee against Torture, Summary Record of the 646th Meeting, CAT/C/SR.646/Add.1, at 8, 13, paras 41–44, 74.

[122] CAT/C/CO/34/CAN, paras 4(g) and 5(f) (emphasis added).

It seems that the Committee against Torture is better placed than individual States-parties to pronounce on the scope of the provisions of the Convention. If conclusive weight were given to the assertions of the British and Canadian courts that Article 14 does not provide for universal jurisdiction, this would imply the recognition of the powers of auto-interpretation by individual States-parties. The interpretation by States of their treaty obligations sometimes complies with, and sometimes contradicts, the genuine meaning of those obligations. It is exactly for avoiding interpretative confusions that the Committee against Torture is entrusted with the task of determining whether the interpretation by States of a provision such as Article 14 is consistent with its genuine meaning. The relevance of the role and attitude of the Committee becomes even more pressing as the interpretations advanced by national bodies are likely to differ from each other and fail to provide uniform guidance.

Apart from that, the involvement of *jus cogens* can have an impact in clarifying whether Article 14 grants universal jurisdiction, because it can provide interpretative guidance favouring universal jurisdiction.[123] If *jus cogens* otherwise entails universal jurisdiction, a treaty provision on its face compatible with that must also be taken to reflect universality.

Thus, it must be concluded that Article 14 of the Torture Convention provides for mandatory universal civil jurisdiction over the acts of torture, and not, as sometimes assumed, for territorially restricted jurisdiction or a mere implied entitlement to accept or encourage the exercise of universal jurisdiction.[124]

The situation is similar in contexts other than the Torture Convention. Article 7 ICCPR has been construed by the UN Human Rights Committee in a way that in cases of torture, 'the alleged victims must themselves have effective remedies at their disposal, including the right to obtain compensation'.[125] The Committee does not require that an initial act of torture must occur within the jurisdiction of a State in question for triggering applicability of these consequences. These provisions confirm the mandatory character of universal civil jurisdiction.

The state in customary law of the mandatory civil jurisdiction for breaches of *jus cogens* such as torture is potentially derived from, and in any case consistent with, the relevant multilateral treaties. It seems agreed, among others by the Human Rights Committee, that the prohibition of torture includes an obligation for States to make remedies available for the victims of torture without territorial limitation. The customary prohibition of torture would be meaningless without including a similar obligation.

---

[123] Adams (2001), 264.   [124] cf Byrnes (2001), 548–549.
[125] General Comment 7, para. 1.

As for the breaches of *jus cogens* other than torture, US courts apply universal civil jurisdiction to them as well. With regard to these breaches, there is on the one hand no specific reason for assuming that the universal civil jurisdiction over them is not mandatory, while on the other hand the absence of the provision similar to Article 14 of the Torture Convention signifies the insufficiency of factors that could promote the crystallization of the customary rule that makes universal jurisdiction over those other breaches mandatory. However, Article 19 of the UN Declaration on Forced Disappearances,[126] framed in terms similar to Article 14 of the Torture Convention, could strengthen the case for mandatory universal civil jurisdiction over disappearances under customary law.

On a more general plane, the fact that States are obliged to provide effective remedies for breaches of *jus cogens*, coupled with the existence of universal civil jurisdiction, is sufficient for treating such jurisdiction as mandatory. As the duty to make reparation for breaches of *jus cogens* is itself peremptory, jurisdiction established over such breaches is mandatory as well.

The award of civil remedies for breaches of *jus cogens* takes place primarily in the community interest. States are not allowed to derogate by treaties from their duty to grant remedies for violations of *jus cogens*. Certain treaties which intended such effect have been upheld by some national courts which in the first place ignored the very relevance of peremptory norms, or referred to factors of national and not international law.[127]

3. SPECIFIC CONTEXT OF HUMAN RIGHTS TREATIES

It must be examined how the specific context of human rights law responds to the general legal framework on prosecuting *jus cogens* crimes and remedying the breaches of *jus cogens*, to the principle that the peremptory nature of effects of *jus cogens* is inherent in substantive peremptory norms. The interpretation of human rights treaty provisions suggests that human rights and humanitarian norms have consequential effects, consequential civil remedies and criminal prosecution being inherent parts of primary prohibition.

In general terms, a serious human rights violation places on States the duties to investigate the facts, to take action thereon as appropriate, to bring the persons responsible to justice, to provide appropriate, including medical, treatment to victims, and to pay compensation to them and their families.[128] This is also part of general international law, as affirmed by the ICTY in *Furundzija* that State responsibility ensues as a result of State

---

[126] GA Res 47/133 (1992).
[127] See above, Chapter 8 and below, Chapter 10.
[128] Van Boven, E/CN.4/Sub.2/1993/8, 26, 30, 37 ff., 57–58.

officials engaging in torture, and for the failure of a State to punish tor-
turers.[129] Furthermore, 'the requirement that States expeditiously institute
national implementing measures is an integral part of the international obligation to prohibit torture'.[130]

General human rights treaties such as ICCPR, ECHR and ACHR do not
lay down the explicit obligation for States to investigate the breaches and
prosecute the perpetrators. The absence of such express clause has not prevented inferring these obligations from the general obligation clauses as well
as the object and purpose of these treaties.

Although the European Convention on Human Rights does not explicitly
elaborate upon this issue, the European Court considers that consequential
obligations are inherent to substantive Convention human rights. In *Cyprus v
Turkey* and *Assenov*, the Court emphazised that Articles 2 and 3 of the
European Convention, in conjunction with Article 1, impose on States not
only obligations to abstain from breaches of the right to life and freedom
from torture, but also to take consequential steps to punish perpetrators.[131]
In *Aksoy*, *Kaya* and *Yasa* the European Court interpreted Article 13 of the
European Convention as requiring the criminal responsibility of perpetrators, along with the duty to award civil remedies.[132] Similarly, the
European Court in *Kelly* underlined the need for absolute performance of the
right to life. Article 2 of the European Convention implies in its content that
those responsible for unlawful killing must be found and punished.[133]

The UN Human Rights Committee has gradually developed the approach
that serious breaches of the ICCPR cause consequences in terms of criminal
prosecution and civil remedies.[134] In earlier decisions the Committee asserted
that the International Covenant on Civil and Political Rights does not provide for an individual to require that the State-party criminally prosecute
another person.[135] But in *Rodriguez* the Committee reversed that approach by
pointing to multiple consequential duties of the State including the duty to
prosecute the perpetrators and the duty to give remedies to the victims.[136]

The Inter-American Court confirmed this principle in *Velasquez-
Rodriguez*.[137] The Inter-American Commission in *Las Hojas* considered as
a breach of Article 1 of the American Convention the failure of El Salvador
to ensure the due prosecution of the perpetrators of the violations. The
prosecution of the perpetrators has thus been an inherent aspect of guaranteeing under Article 1 the 'free and full exercise of human rights and funda-

[129] *Furundzija*, IT-95-17/I-T, para. 142.   [130] *Furundzija*, 38 ILM 1999, 348.
[131] *Cyprus v Turkey*, para. 131; *Assenov*, paras 90–106.
[132] *Aksoy*, para. 98; *Kaya*, para.105; *Yasa*, para. 74.
[133] *Kelly*, para. 105.   [134] Rodley (1999), 112.
[135] *HCMA v The Netherlands*, Communication No. 213/1986, Decision of 30 March 1989,
para. 11.6; *SE v Argentina*, Communication No. 275/1988, Decision of 26 March 1990, para. 5.5.
[136] *Hugo Rodriguez*, paras 12.3, 14.
[137] *Velasquez-Rodriguez*, 95 ILR 232.

mental guarantees of all persons subject to [the State-party's] jurisdiction'.[138] The Inter-American Commission has affirmed more generally that Article 1 of the American Convention obligates States-parties 'to prevent, investigate, and punish any violation of the rights recognised therein'. These obligations, together with the identical obligations under the Inter-American Convention on Forced Disappearances, 'expressly provide that a State-party should take the measures necessary to establish its jurisdiction over the crimes provided for in those instruments when the alleged offender is within its jurisdiction and it does not extradite him/her.'[139]

Thus, the practice of human rights organs affirms that substantive human rights inherently include the consequential obligations with regard to criminal prosecution of perpetrators and civil remedies for victims. If a substantive prohibition is part of *jus cogens* and consequential duties are integral to it, then these consequential duties are also peremptory. The specific context of human rights norms both reflects and reinforces the peremptory nature of criminal and civil sanctions for breaches of *jus cogens* in general international law and especially in international criminal law.

---

[138] *Las Hojas*, 170–171.
[139] *Asylum and International Crimes*, Recommendation of the Inter-American Commission, 108th Session, 20 October 2000.

10

Peremptory Norms and State Immunity

I. GENERAL QUESTIONS

In empirical terms, the immunity of a foreign State[1] and that of foreign State officials are different in terms of who appears as the defendant. Nevertheless, both categories refer to State immunity as such. When a person acting on behalf of a State is impleaded in a foreign State, an action against that person impleads the State.[2] Historically, the original concept of immunity of high-level State officials, such as head of State, arose from the fact that they represent their States and 'to sue him was tantamount to suing an independent State'.[3] In addition, in their evolution the rationales and scopes of the two categories of immunities are quite similar,[4] in accordance with the evolution of the concept and scope of the sovereign authority of a State, the latter influencing justification and scope of both categories of immunities, regardless of the identity of the defendant in the court.

The normal result of a successful immunity plea is that a State or its officials sued in a foreign court are immune from any kind of prosecution or execution proceedings. On the other hand, it has to be realized that, very often, certain violations of international law—universally condemned as offending the common conscience of mankind and elementary considerations of humanity—are perpetrated by persons exercising the official authority of a State and using the State machinery. The immunity of a State and its officials arises as an impediment to the prosecution of the accused or the award of remedies to the victims, when a State and its officials are sued in foreign courts.

An unconditional deference to the immunity of a State and its officials is hardly justified. It must not be forgotten that as amounting, in effect, to the denial of a legal remedy in respect to what may be a valid legal claim, 'as

[1] This study is concerned with the immunities before national courts. Immunities before international or internationalized tribunals, such as the ICC or the Special Court for Sierra Leone, are beyond its scope.
[2] Jennings and Watts, *Oppenheim's International Law* (1992), 342.
[3] Lord Slynn, *Pinochet*, 4 All ER (1998), 909; Lord Phillips, *Pinochet*, 2 All ER (1999), 186. State immunity grew out of the personal immunity of the monarch, Lord Browne-Wilkinson, *Pinochet*, 2 All ER (1999), 111.
[4] Joint Separate Opinion, *Arrest Warrant*, paras 72 ff.

such, immunity is open to objection'.[5] In addition, immunities are a source of controversy between sovereignties of the defendant State and the forum State; it involves the proposition that immunity of a foreign sovereign, as deduced from his sovereignty, is an exception to the otherwise absolute rule of territorial sovereignty and jurisdiction.[6] This is something which cannot easily or routinely be assumed, but has to be justified in every specific case, by reference to all relevant juridical considerations which may require States to grant immunity or, on the contrary, withhold immunity and exercise jurisdiction. These conflicting circumstances must be weighed, and their relevance duly assessed. Such circumstances cannot be uniform and identical in all cases, since the concrete situations differ in terms of underlying facts, as well as the interplay of various rules and obligations, which may in certain cases entail different, and sometimes mutually conflicting, juridical requirements. All rules of international law exist and operate in the context of their interaction with other rules; their scope and applicability may depend on how those other rules affect or qualify that scope and applicability. This latter question depends, in its turn, on whether those other rules possess a capacity so to affect or qualify the scope and applicability of that rule, for example by virtue of their being a *lex posterior*, *lex specialis* or *lex superior* in relation to that norm.

The argument regarding the impact of peremptory norms on State immunity is affected by multiple considerations regarding the character of State immunity or that of peremptory norms. It thus seems opportune to consider the relevance of State immunity within the realm of *jus cogens* from three different perspectives, each of them reflecting the conceptual and practical debates and independently capable of affecting the outcomes of the debate as to whether State immunity can be available in cases of breaches of peremptory norms.

The functional perspective focuses on the scope of State immunity as dependent on the difference between sovereign and non-sovereign, official and non-official acts as the criterion for judging whether the given act attracts immunity. The normative perspective focuses on starting-point issues of whether the principle of the immunity of a State or its officials is positively recognized under international law, that is, whether immunity is available in the first place. The hierarchical perspective, based on the presumed existence of the customary norms on State immunity and without prejudging the outcomes that are reached under normative and functional perspectives,

---

[5] Jennings and Watts, *Oppenheim's International Law* (1992), 346. For a negative approach to State immunity see H. Lauterpacht, The Problem of Jurisdictional Immunities of Foreign States, 28 *BYIL* 1951, 220–271, and R. Garnett, Should the Sovereign Immunity be Abolished? 20 *Australian YBIL* (1999), 190.

[6] O'Connell, *International Law* (1970), 842; Caplan, State Immunity, Human Rights and *Jus Cogens*, 97 *AJIL* (2003), 771, suggesting that there is thus no inherent right to State immunity.

examines whether the rules on State immunity can apply in the face of superior peremptory norms which prevail over inconsistent norms.

2. THE FUNCTIONAL PERSPECTIVE: THE SCOPE OF STATE IMMUNITY IN INTERNATIONAL LAW

2.1. The immunity of States

Under classical international law, a State may not be impleaded before a foreign court, because States are equal and have no authority over each other (*par in parem non habet imperium*). This approach, based on a State's status as a sovereign entity, had already been replaced in the early twentieth century by the restrictive approach, making immunity dependent upon the nature of the action complained of before a foreign court. The courts began to distinguish between acts *jure imperii* and acts *jure gestionis*. In case of the latter, unlike the former, a State does not act in the exercise of its sovereign powers, but acts like an ordinary legal person. This distinction has laid the basis for the functional, as opposed to the status-based or sovereignty-oriented, concept of State immunity. The emanating principle means, therefore, that a State is not precluded from being impleaded before a foreign court, but that whether or not it may be so impleaded depends upon the nature of the act complained of before that court.[7] It must be demonstrated that 'the act is truly an act of sovereignty. One must look at the precise act complained of', because 'there is no answer which is consistent right across the board'.[8]

The functional difference between acts *jure imperii* and *jure gestionis* undoubtedly impacts on the normative quality of the rules and principles related to State immunity. These seem to be merely the reference rules and not substantive ones, since, as we have seen, 'there is no answer which is consistent right across the board'. The distinction based on the nature of acts does not itself resolve the question whether the act in question attracts immunity; this question must be decided in every specific case due to the nature of an act complained of and the circumstances of its performance. The concept of an act *de jure imperii*, while lacking a scope of its own, must be construed in the context of its interaction to all relevant juridical considerations, which may influence the scope of sovereign authority.

---

[7] Higgins, *Problems and Process* (1994), 78–79; O'Connell, *International Law* (1970), 844–845. As emphasized, 'there is no obvious impairment of the rights of equality, or independence, or dignity of a State if it is subjected to ordinary judicial processes within the territory of a foreign State', Jennings and Watts, *Oppenheim's International Law* (1992), 342. Consequently, it is an outmoded fashion to ground State immunity on principles of equality and non-interference, Bianchi, Denying State Immunity to Violators of Human Rights, 46 *Austrian Journal of Public and International Law* (1994), 200.

[8] *I Congreso* (HL), I AC 1983, 252, 262–264. The House of Lords follows in this regard the approach of the German *Bundesverfassungsgericht* in *Empire of Iran*, 45 ILR 57, 80.

This requires undertaking a descriptive analysis in specific cases to clarify whether an act complained of forms part of State immunity. It is not decisive that an act is done by a State or its instrumentalities. It is rather decisive whether an act in question has been claimed by the respective State to be an act performed in pursuance of its governmental authority and, most importantly, whether international law permits characterizing this act as an act of State authority. For example, the House of Lords in *I Congreso* held that the conduct of a State is not a sovereign act and attracts no immunity if it is an act which could be performed by any private actor, and a State invokes no governmental authority, even if the situation had to do with a highly contingent political context.[9] Under such a view, the category of *acta iure imperii* would encompass only a narrow category of acts inherent to the sovereign authority of a State.[10] *I Congreso* laid down a fundamental test of clarifying whether the given act is a sovereign act and this has been so accepted in later jurisprudence.[11]

It may be important how an act is characterized under international law, and some evidence suggests that in cases of violation of international law, immunity may be unavailable.[12] But it is not clear whether there is an international rule to that effect. Though wrongful, acts still may be sovereign in nature. The existence of some practice does not oblige States not to accord immunity to wrongful acts properly falling within the sovereign authority of a State. States cannot be expected to provide a forum for redress of any internationally wrongful act, unless either their clear interest is involved, or they are under a clear and specific obligation to that effect, under either a treaty or a peremptory norm requiring the forum State to adjudicate.

It would be better to suggest that acts which by their nature are outside the State prerogatives cannot attract immunity. There is a difference between the legality of an act—whether on the national or international plane—and its exercise in pursuit of sovereign authority. To illustrate, it is established that the enactment of a law, conclusion of a treaty, declaration of war, expropriation of property—whether illegal under international law or not— may *prima facie* fall within the sovereign authority of a State, while torture, enslavement, rape, unlawful killing and racial discrimination may not.

It is enquired whether the actual involvement of State apparatus in the performance of an act may render irrelevant considerations as to the nature of that act, and consequently immunize it. The English case of *Littrell* and

---

[9] *I Congreso* (HL), I AC 1983, 268.

[10] Higgins (1994), 84.

[11] In *Holland v Lampen-Wolfe* Lord Millett followed Lord Wilberforce's test in *I Congreso*, 3 All ER (2000), 845.

[12] *Von Dardel v USSR*, 77 ILR 265. Other instances in practice are concerned with the law of neutrality and prize, overviewed in Bianchi, 201–202, 212, and Karagiannakis, State Immunity and Fundamental Human Rights, 11 *Leiden Journal of International Law* (1998), 13.

the American case of *Nelson* are understood in this way.[13] But the first case hardly involved any serious breach of international law, let alone a breach of *jus cogens* or an international crime;[14] while the latter case related to the interpretation of a commercial activities exception provision in a domestic statute only, and has in no way prejudiced whether torture may be a sovereign act and thus immune under international law.[15] Moreover, in *Letelier*, Chile contended that assassination of a former ambassador by a car bomb, even if committed or ordered by the Chilean government, was an act *jure imperii*, as an act of 'policy judgment and decision' immunized under the US legislation. The court responded that 'whatever policy options may exist for a foreign country, it has no "discretion" to perpetrate conduct designated to result in the assassination of an individual or individuals, action that is clearly contrary to the precepts recognized in both national and international law',[16] thereby affirming that the involvement of State machinery or policy may be irrelevant as soon as the act is unacceptable under the law or public policy.

Once again, the test is not whether an act is lawful, but whether an act would by its nature fall within the sovereign powers of a State: an enactment of a law or expropriation of property may involve an international illegality, but it cannot be doubted that States generally do possess a power to enact laws and expropriate property. Unlawful acts may attract State immunity. In order not to attract immunity, illegality must be a characterizing feature of an act itself and not merely a circumstance of its performance or a result it brings about. In other words, the illegality of an act must be substantive and

---

[13] The Report of the Human Rights Committee of the British ILA Branch 'Civil Actions in the English Courts for Serious Human Rights Violations Abroad', 7 *European Human Rights Law Review* (2002), 153.

[14] 1 WLR 82 (1995), 100 ILR 452, dealing with personal injury as a result of negligent medical treatment in a United States military hospital in England. Case-note by Christopher Staker, 65 *BYIL* 1994, 491.

[15] The applicant contended that the facts of his beatings and torture by police were covered by the commercial activities exception, as related to the American employee's reporting a local hospital's safety hazards to a competent governmental commission, and thus to his employment contract. But as the suit itself was based on beatings and torture, the Supreme Court declined to regard them as commercial acts. Supreme Court, *Saudi Arabia v Nelson*, 100 ILR 551–554. The *amici* from Human Rights Watch referred only to the commercial nature of the acts complained of, and so did individual justices who disagreed with the majority on this point, 100 ILR 554–565. None of them considered these acts immune under international law. Similarly, the Canadian court in *Bouzari* understood a sovereign act under the Canadian State Immunity Act as a non-commercial act and did not enquire into whether the nature of the relevant act and the circumstances of its performance made it possible to assert its sovereign nature, *Bouzari* (Ontario Superior Court of Justice), paras 28–29, *per* Swinton J. The Court of Appeal in *Bouzari*, facing the plea that torture is not a State function and hence cannot be accorded State immunity, simply stated, without engaging into clarifying the substance of the plea, that acts such as torture did not fall within the exceptions provided in the Canadian SIA, *Bouzari* (Court of Appeal for Ontario), paras 89–90, *per* Goudge JA.

[16] *Letelier*, 63 ILR 388. Chile considered that the act involved was immune under section 1605 of the US Foreign Sovereign Immunities Act (FSIA) of 1976. For the text of the act see 64 ILR 654.

not merely ensuing. It must be demonstrated that a State is not even *prima facie* permitted under international law to perform a particular act in relation to which immunity is claimed, since it would be outside its sovereign powers. These criteria are not least dictated by humanitarian considerations increasingly incorporated into international law during the last century, which arguably provide for certain inherent limits beyond which a State cannot claim that it acts in the exercise of its sovereign authority. Humanitarian considerations are supplemented by those of a more pragmatic character: the conduct outlawed under humanitarian norms, such as torture, enslavement or war crimes, may be committed even by a private person, and is thus more similar in nature to acts *jure gestionis* than to acts *jure imperii*. On the other hand, a typical case of acts *jure gestionis*, such as the breach of contract, may be said to be outside State prerogatives in the same way as torture or enslavement, and the same criteria may apply to certain commercial and non-commercial acts.[17] All these considerations make it necessary to agree with O'Connell, who suggests that the international law of State immunity, if it exists at all, 'covers only a very narrow field of governmental activity'.[18]

One reason why certain serious breaches of international law cannot be considered as belonging to the functions of States is that they are outlawed by peremptory norms which are endowed with a superior status that expresses the determination of the international community that those breaches must be unconditionally outlawed. It is therefore correctly suggested that if foreign courts adjudicate a breach of *jus cogens* such as torture they do not infringe on the sovereignty of the State in which that breach took place; a violation of *jus cogens* is not a sovereign act and attracts no immunity.[19] As Judge Wald emphasized in *Princz*, '*jus cogens* norms are by definition non-derogable, and thus when a State thumbs its nose at such a norm, in effect overriding the collective will of the entire international community, the State cannot be performing a sovereign act entitled to immunity'.[20]

---

[17] As *Empire of Iran* (*Bundesverfassungsgericht*) 48 ILR 80 demonstrates, the distinction between sovereign and non-sovereign acts does not depend 'on whether the State acted commercially. Commercial acts of States are not different in their nature from other non-sovereign activities.' According to *Krajina v The TASS Agency*, reported in Lauterpacht, *BYIL* 1952, 220, non-sovereign acts are not limited to commercial acts. Already in the League of Nations work was it recognized that non-sovereign acts may give rise to actions for a tort or quasi-tort, as distinguished from purely commercial transactions. See also Panezi, 56 *Revue Hellénique* (2003), 209.

[18] O'Connell, 846.

[19] Adams, In Search of Defence of the Transnational Human Rights Paradigm: May Jus Cogens Norms be Invoked to Create Implied Exceptions in Domestic Immunity Statutes? in Craig (ed.), *Torture as Tort* (2001), 253, 272; Reinmann, A Human Rights Exception to Sovereign Immunity: Some Thoughts on *Princz v Federal Republic of Germany*, 16 *Michigan Journal of International Law* (1995), 421.

[20] 33 *ILM* (1994), 1500. In this case the immunity was upheld on the basis of US, not international, law.

The US Court of Appeals in *Siderman de Blake* has noted the clear and straightforward argument that 'International law does not recognise an act that violates *jus cogens* as a sovereign act. A State's violation of the *jus cogens* norm prohibiting official torture therefore would not be entitled to the immunity afforded by international law,' and said nothing to contradict the substance of that argument.[21] As pointed out, because *jus cogens* is the set of non-derogable rules, 'a State act in violation of such a rule will not be recognised as a sovereign act by the community of States'.[22]

The link with *jus cogens* conceptually reinforces the standing of certain breaches of international law in the framework of the functional perspective of international law. The fact that a breach of *jus cogens* offends against the interests of the international community as a whole and hence entails absolute illegality translated into nullity prevents its recognition in any way within the international legal system and thus considering it as a sovereign act for the purposes of sovereign immunity.

All this demonstrates that it is hardly possible to justify treatment of the breaches of peremptory norms as sovereign acts for the purposes of State immunity. This explains that the courts which uphold State immunity for breaches of peremptory norms mostly ignore the question of the nature of the act in question and do not address it. The European Court of Human Rights justified the UK in not permitting the person tortured in Kuwait to claim damages from Kuwait before English courts. The treatment by the Court of the rationale of State immunity is surprisingly short in space, and represents the Court as thinking of something which is very well and clearly established in international law, both in scope and effects, and needs no further enquiry:

Sovereign immunity is a concept of international law, developed out of the principle *par in parem non habet imperium*, by virtue of which one State shall not be subject to the jurisdiction of another State. The Court considers that the grant of sovereign immunity to a State in civil proceedings pursues the legitimate aim of complying with international law to promote comity and good relations between States through the respect of another State's sovereignty.[23]

The first thing which is striking here is that the Court does not attempt to distinguish between sovereign and non-sovereign acts. This approach is based on a false premise of absolute immunity. The Court avoids the task of determining whether torture can be considered as a *jure imperii* act, which in all probability would make it more difficult to uphold immunity in this case. Unlike national courts, the European Court would have had to determine whether torture is an act *jure imperii* and attracts sovereign immunity under international law as such, and regardless of what domestic statutes say on the

[21] *Siderman de Blake v Argentina*, 103 ILR 474.
[22] Belski *et al.* (1989), 377.   [23] 34 EHRR 11 (2002), 289, para. 54.

subject. Indeed, domestic laws are merely facts to be assessed in the context of international rules.

But the Court, through the use of a simpler, but more doubtful, approach based on the concept of absolute immunity, infers existence of a requirement under international law to grant immunity to foreign States even in the face of allegations of torture. The soundness of this approach is very difficult to justify.

The Canadian Court of Appeal in *Bouzari* justified State immunity for torture by invoking 'the principle that States must treat each other as equals not to be subjected to each others' jurisdiction'.[24] The Court did so having refused to enquire into whether torture is a State function under international law, stating that it was immunized under domestic law.[25] This is yet another instance of the absolute understanding of State immunity not distinguishing between sovereign and non-sovereign acts.

The Greek court in the case related to the massacre carried out by the German forces in Greece during the Second World War expressly adopted the view that these actions which contradicted the basic principles of humanitarian law and consequently *jus cogens* were not sovereign acts and could not qualify for State immunity.[26] The Supreme Court of Greece similarly considered that German atrocities in Distomo were in breach of peremptory norms and hence were not acts *jure imperii*.[27]

The approach of the Levadia court was opposed by the German Supreme Court (*Bundesgerichtshof*) in the case related to the same events. The *Bundesgerichtshof* expressly stated, with regard to the acts of mass executions and destruction of property by German forces, that these acts indisputably constituted sovereign acts (*ein hoheitliches Handeln*). It furthermore suggested that the Levadia court's determination that war crimes are not sovereign acts was not convincing.[28] The *Bundesgerichtshof* set no firm criteria in that case for distinguishing between sovereign and non-sovereign acts, nor did it examine whether, in the face of the earlier German jurisprudence such as *Empire of Iran*, the acts involved in the *Distomo* case were sovereign acts. Under this test the ruling of the *Bundesgerichtshof* is unsustainable. In the end, if anything is not convincing, it is the assertion of the *Bundesgerichtshof* that under international law Nazi atrocities still count as sovereign acts shielded by State immunity.

---

[24] *Bouzari* (Court of Appeal for Ontario), para. 95, *per* Goudge JA.

[25] Id., para. 90.

[26] Case No. 137/1997, Multi-member Court of Levadia, 30 October 1997, in 50 *Revue Hellénique* (1997), 599.

[27] Case No. 11/2000, *Prefecture of Voiotia v Federal Republic of Germany*, case-note by M. Gavouneli and I. Bantekas, 95 *AJIL* 2001, 200.

[28] III ZR 245/98, paras B.I.2.a and B.IV.2.b.

2.2. *The immunity of State officials*

As already explained, the immunity of State officials serves the same purpose as the immunity of States, namely preservation of the integrity of the sovereign powers and functions of a State. It seems to be accepted in practice that State immunity protects an official as long as he acts within the scope of his official duties,[29] and this holds true even in the case of high-ranking officials, such as a head of State, inviting classification of the acts as sovereign or non-sovereign.[30] Since State immunity is not afforded just because an act is done by a State as such, it is logical that a public official should not be immune just because he has been acting as part of a State apparatus,[31] unless an act is performed in pursuit of the sovereign powers of a State.

Involvement of the State apparatus or policy in an act is a highly factual question, depending upon the very relative criteria, inviting the enquiry whether an act of torture, killing or genocide is immunized because of the actual involvement of State machinery, or the policy purpose related to it, such as countering 'enemies' of a State or nation.[32] Apart from possibly involving judicial cynicism, such reasoning amounts to saying that whatever States and their officials actually do is their function, regardless of the content of the act. But common sense would dictate that State or official functions are those for the performance of which the State and its officials exist.[33]

Another perspective would enquire into whether the act complained of may also be performed by a private person or group and prevent immunization of any of the acts of commission of international crimes. There may be some uncertainty in cases of massive and large-scale activities, but it is clear that genocide or crimes against humanity may be committed by a private army or rebels and thus performed by private actors as well.

An even more objective test is that of the legitimate scope of State functions, in accordance with what national or international law considers a permissible function of a State. The House of Lords in *Pinochet* considered that acts such as torture, hostage-taking and crimes against humanity, disavowed as abhorrent by all States and outlawed as international crimes under specific conventions, cannot be official functions of a public official, even a head of

---

[29] *Chuidian*, US Court of Appeals, 92 ILR 491–492.

[30] Lord Steyn, *Pinochet*, 4 All ER (1998), 944–945.

[31] *Per contra* Lord Slynn, *Pinochet*, 4 All ER (1998), 908, and Lord Goff, *Pinochet* 2 All ER (1999), 119, submitting that even if a Head of State commits torture or genocide, he still may be acting within his functions.

[32] So it was submitted to the House of Lords by Senator Pinochet, see Lord Hutton, *Pinochet*, 2 All ER, (1999), 155.

[33] Function is understood as meaning 'The special kind of activity proper to anything; the mode of action by which it fulfils its purpose', with particular reference 'to a person as belonging to a particular class, *esp.* to the holder of any office', VI *The Oxford English Dictionary* (2nd ed., 1989), 263.

State, and the immunity normally available to State officials, including heads of State, does not arise in relation to, and does not attach to, such acts.[34] As Lord Browne-Wilkinson clarified, 'the existence of the international crime of torture as *jus cogens* was enough to justify the conclusion that the organisation of State torture could not rank for immunity purposes as the performance of an official function.'[35] A similar result was reached by a US Court of Appeals, expressly refusing to immunize acts of torture, killings and disappearance performed by, under direction or in connivance of, a head of State, and implicating systematic use of State machinery, because no public official, even the head of State, can claim these as his functions.[36] The English Court of Appeal in *Jones* refused to immunize the conduct of Saudi State officials having engaged in torture, asserting that, pursuant to the outcomes reached by the House of Lords in *Pinochet*, torture was a breach of *jus cogens* and hence could not form part of State functions for which immunity can be claimed.[37] Therefore, a public official, regardless of his rank, would not be immune under international law for such acts, as they do not fall within the sovereign authority of a State.

Despite the similarity with State immunity in terms of subject-matter, the immunity of State officials must also respond to certain different concerns. In a certain limited number of cases, State officials may claim immunity attached to their status, thereby enabling them to invoke in a foreign court both immunities *ratione materiae* and *ratione personae*. However, immunity *ratione personae* is not available to a public official sued in a foreign court, unless his position is of such a nature as to itself attract immunity. One may speak in this context of a very special status of heads of State as supreme representatives of States.[38] Heads of governments and foreign ministers are not ordinary officials, but their representative capacity is not as all-encompassing as that of heads of States either, and they do not personify the State,[39] though foreign ministers are in charge of international relations, the

---

[34] Lord Nicholls, *Pinochet*, 4 All ER (1998), 939–940; Lord Steyn, *Pinochet*, 4 All ER (1998), 945–946; Lord Hutton, *Pinochet*, 2 All ER (1999), 165–166. See also Lord Millett, 2 All ER (1999), 179, submitting that for the offence of torture, no immunity *ratione materiae* could possibly be available. For a similar attitude see the decisions of the Amsterdam Court of Appeal in *Bourtese*, para. 4.2. The *Hoge Raad* of the Netherlands has not contradicted this approach. See also Yang, State Immunity in the European Court of Human Rights: Reaffirmations and Misconceptions, *BYIL* (2003), 359–360.

[35] Lord Browne-Wilkinson, *Pinochet*, 2 All ER (1999), 113–114.

[36] *Hilao v Marcos*, US Court of Appeals (Ninth Circuit), 104 ILR 122–125, involving civil litigation against ex-dictator of the Philippines Marcos and his family. Since the head of State as such was not immunized under the FSIA, there was no domestic law obstacle to adjudicating certain violations of international law which would be 'as adjudicable and redressable as would be a dictator's act of rape'.

[37] *Jones*, para. 31.

[38] Watts, The Legal Position in International Law of Heads of State, Heads of Government and Foreign Ministers, 247 *RdC* (1994-III), 36, 53.

[39] Id., 100, 102.

conduct of diplomatic communications, and treaty-making.[40] Consequently, it may be arguable that these officials enjoy some immunities *ratione personae*, though the scope thereof is hardly indisputable,[41] especially given that there is no uniform State practice to support the immunities for such officials.

In addition, it would be unjustified to construe the scope of the immunity *ratione personae* in a way frustrating the rationale of the immunity of States and its agents *ratione materiae*, based on the difference between sovereign and non-sovereign acts. Immunity *ratione personae* cannot permanently immunize acts which are not immune *ratione materiae*, ie non-sovereign acts. Consequently, any immunity *ratione personae* should be limited in time to the official's presence in office. This would follow from the functional justification of immunities to enable certain officials to carry out their functions; but the legal validity of such an approach depends in its turn upon the validity of legal principles of those functional considerations, which, as we have seen, are far from settled.[42]

The scope of the immunity of State officials was faced by the International Court in the *Arrest Warrant* case involving the issuance of an arrest warrant by Belgium against the incumbent foreign minister of the Democratic Republic of the Congo. The Court found that the rationale of a foreign minister's immunity is that he must be able to represent his government without impediment, and communicate with it, as well as with diplomatic representatives of his State, and the governments of other States. Thus, the immunity of an incumbent foreign minister is unlimited, encompassing non-official acts, and even extending to the allegations of war crimes and crimes against humanity.[43] The Court emphasized that it had to 'consider the nature of the functions' exercised by a foreign minister, in order to determine the extent of his immunities.[44] The Court seems to affirm that the principles and rules on immunity of State officials in general international law, if any, are not substantive rules, but possess the character of reference: if an official exercises certain functions, he may be immune from foreign prosecutions; if he does not, his official position is irrelevant.

---

[40] Id., 100–101.

[41] Sir Arthur Watts does not provide a specific justification for the case of heads of government, id. The rationale for immunity of heads of government and foreign ministers follows from the functional considerations in context when they are on official visits, and their ability to carry out functions needs to be preserved, id., 102, 106. While a head of State also enjoys immunity in private visits, there is no similar legal rule concerning heads of governments and foreign ministers, whose cases seem to be based not on the law but on courtesy, id., 110. In its recent resolution, the Institute of International Law upheld the idea of a *ratione personae* immunity of heads of States and governments only, but not of foreign ministers; see H. Fox, The Resolution of the Institute of International Law on the Immunities of Heads of State and Government, 51 *ICLQ* (2002), 120.

[42] See above, notes 38–41 and the accompanying text.

[43] *Arrest Warrant*, paras 52–56. [44] *Arrest Warrant*, para. 53.

This is confirmed by the Court's reference to foreign ministers' need to be representing their countries in order to justify their full immunity. There is no attempt to ground the decision on a conceptual understanding of the principles of the international legal order, such as sovereign equality of States. The Court's adherence to this functional, rather than status-based, concept of State immunity is not without consequences, and indicates that any other State official, however high ranking, may be tried in foreign courts if and insofar as he is not protected by the immunity afforded to foreign ministers. And taking into account the arguments that the Court has presented to justify the immunity of a foreign minister while in office,[45] one may predict that not many other officials—possibly none except for the head of State or government—may qualify for the same degree of protection. These other officials would not be protected by immunity just because they are State officials; they would have to plead justification for immunity by reference to the sovereign nature of the acts of which they are accused.

In paragraph 61 of the Judgment, the Court delimited the scope of the immunities of a foreign minister, portraying prosecution of an ex-minister for private acts as one of the options. This approach is a welcome one, but the problem persists how to understand the scope of official and non-official, or private, acts, and which criteria of delimitation between the two categories of acts the Court is referring to. Does the Court emphasize the involvement of State machinery or elements of policy in performance of an act? Or is the Court linking the distinction to the nature of an act itself and its legitimacy? Since paragraph 61 fails to define the terms 'official' and 'private', the answer must be sought in the context of the case.

The common picture of the submissions of parties, the Court's approach and individual opinions seem to demonstrate that the proper understanding of the scope of immunity is to understand it not as comprising international crimes in the case of a retired official. The Congo claimed the foreign minister's immunity only as long as he remained in office, but recognized that he could be subject to criminal prosecution in another country when he was no longer a minister. This 'purely functional' approach is required to enable the foreign minister to perform his functions freely.[46] The Congo referred to the contemporary position of Yerodia and not the nature of the acts complained of, nor the fact of action by a State, implication of State policy, or use of State facilities.

---

[45] Id., paras 53–56.

[46] Id., 47–48; *The Princeton Principles on Universal Jurisdiction* (2001) arguably differ from this approach, as it does not distinguish between the cases of incumbent and retired officials. Principle 5 reads as follows: 'With respect to serious crimes under international law . . . the official position of any accused person, whether as head of state or government or as a responsible government official, shall not relieve such person of criminal responsibility nor mitigate punishment.'

The attitudes of the parties were quite helpful in enabling the Court to portray immunity as a functionally and temporally limited principle. The understanding of immunity by individual judges makes it difficult to assume that the Court would be ready to support a notion of immunity broader than described above. Judges Van den Wyngaert and Al-Khasawneh considered that the Court should have further clarified that international crimes cannot be covered by the notion of official acts.[47] On the other hand, the Joint Separate Opinion made it abundantly clear that the scope of official acts may not shield international crimes, because the latter are outside State functions and 'State-related motives are not the proper test for determining what constitutes public State acts'.[48]

In view of this analysis, and the entire context of the case, the 'private acts' referred to in paragraph 61 seem to denote acts exceeding the competence of a foreign minister, or acts performed in a private capacity, or acts which Yerodia would be able to perform even if he were not a foreign minister. One does not need to be a foreign minister to incite racial hate and propaganda. Alternatively, 'private acts' may refer to the acts outside the definition of the functions of a State and its officials, such as international crimes.

A different perspective was suggested in *Gaddafi*, dealing with the immunity of the incumbent head of State, where the Cour de Cassation of France held that the crimes of terrorism of which Gaddafi was accused 'did not constitute one of the exceptions to the principle of jurisdictional immunity of foreign Heads of State in office'.[49] This position is based among others on the uncertainty of the status of terrorism-related crimes in international law and, as is clear, does not subscribe to the absolute view of the head of State immunity, which knows of no exceptions. This would *a fortiori* extend to other officials placed in the hierarchy below heads of State.

To sum up, the functional understanding of the immunity *ratione personae* of the very limited number of State officials such as heads of State and government and foreign ministers as expounded by the House of Lords in *Pinochet* and later by the International Court in *Arrest Warrant* are arguably based on sound functional explanation. This understanding refers to the exceptional role of those officials and links immunity to the limited time period that is necessary for the performance of their official functions. Nevertheless, this outcome, arguably sound in itself, should not be viewed as ready-made and easily generalizable. Its relevance can be contested and set aside by reference to the lack of normative justification for the rule consisting

---

[47] Dissenting Opinion of Judge Al-Khasawneh, para. 6; Dissenting Opinion of Judge Van den Wyngaert, para. 36.

[48] Joint Separate Opinion, para. 85. See also para. 74, referring to prosecution for international crimes, 'which are often committed by high officials who make use of the power invested in the States'.

[49] *Gaddafi* (Court of Cassation), 125 ILR 509.

in the lack of clear and uniform State practice, or the normative hierarchy dictating that even if the given high-level official enjoys immunity, such immunity can no longer be available if it conflicts with the superior peremptory rule requiring the exercise of jurisdiction over the relevant official. If a national or international organ were to deny immunity along one of the above lines, the outcome thus produced would not by itself contradict the current state of international law.

3. THE NORMATIVE PERSPECTIVE: STATE IMMUNITY AND THE SOURCES OF INTERNATIONAL LAW

The reasoning of courts which uphold immunity is based on their attitude that certain sources of law, giving rise to certain rules and principles on immunity of States and their officials, justify that line of reasoning. In *Al-Adsani*, the European Court grounded its decision both on conventional and customary law. On the one hand, it considered that the legislation of the United Kingdom was in conformity with the 1972 Basle Convention on State Immunity. On the other hand, it referred to generally recognized customary rules on State immunity.[50] In *Arrest Warrant*, the International Court considered as 'firmly established' in international law that certain high-ranking State officials, such as Heads of State and government, as well as foreign ministers, enjoy immunities from jurisdiction in other States, both civil and criminal.[51] Both judgments reach these conclusions without due examination of practice and legal conviction of States; nothing in the texts of the judgments suggests that the courts performed such an examination. But the existence of generally recognized or firmly established rules may not simply be assumed; it must be established through careful evidence.

The issue whether international law, especially customary law, requires States to grant immunity to foreign States before their courts can be resolved by evidencing that the relevant norms indeed exist and have been created through the normal law-making processes. This is especially important given that international law no longer subscribes to absolute State immunity and excludes certain acts from its ambit, especially those it considers definitionally outside the functions of a State, such as breaches of international *jus cogens* including serious violations of the rights of an individual. It would thus be a logical contradiction to argue that international law categorically excludes certain acts from the ambit of State immunity and yet it contains customary norms that justify granting immunity to States for such acts. It is for this reason that the standing of the State immunity claims in terms of the available sources of international law must be examined.

---

[50] *Al-Adsani*, 289, para. 56.   [51] *Arrest Warrant*, para. 51.

This is even truer for *Al-Adsani*, because of the European Court's adherence to the theory of absolute immunity. Since the immunity not based on the difference between sovereign and non-sovereign acts is hard to justify under international law, the Court had a greater responsibility to duly support its approach with the appropriate sources of law.

Although the functional justification in paragraph 53 of the judgment in *Arrest Warrant* is not without logical foundation, the International Court's careful examination of the rationale for upholding a foreign minister's immunity itself demonstrates that there was not much evidence available at the disposal of the Court to support the assumption that States are legally bound to respect a foreign minister's immunity.[52] All this invites a due examination of the sources, preferably to examine the status of immunities first under conventional, and afterwards under general, or customary, international law.

3.1. The immunity of States

Certain authors consider that there is an established and generally consistent State practice supporting the existence of customary law on State immunity.[53] Others refer to the lack of uniformity of practice as a circumstance which may possibly lead to questioning the existence of a general rule on State immunity.[54] As for the reasons of such an approach,

> it is now almost impossible to speak of 'customary international law' of foreign State immunity given the divergences in State practice. Immunity has, in fact, become little more than a sub-branch of each State's domestic law. In particular, there is disagreement among States subscribing to the restrictive theory as to the circumstances in which immunity should be excluded.[55]

It seems that this approach correctly points to the surrounding legal context and draws adequate conclusions from it.

---

[52] As Judge Van den Wyngaert submitted, identifying a common *raison d'être* for a protective rule is one thing, elevating this protective rule to the status of a legal rule is quite another thing. *Arrest Warrant*, Dissenting Opinion, para. 11.

[53] Jennings and Watts, *Oppenheim's International Law* (1992), 342–343. Admitting that national decisions allegedly forming that practice vary in points of detail and even in substance, id. 342. See also R. Jennings, The *Pinochet* Extradition Case in the English Courts, L. Boisson de Chazournes and V. Gowlland-Debbas, *The International Legal System in Quest of Equity and Universality. Liber Amicorum Georges Abi-Saab* (2001), 677.

[54] O'Connell, *International Law* (1970), 846. Lack of uniformity and consistency of practice is also emphasized in Higgins, *Problems and Process* (1994), 81. See also 1 Lauterpacht (ed.), *Oppenheim's International Law* (1955), 274, expressing doubts on whether the question may be regarded as affirmatively regulated by international law and whether a State would incur international responsibility for its courts' assumption of jurisdiction. See also Caplan, 97 *AJIL* (2003), 761–765.

[55] Garnett, 175.

In practice, the existence of international legal rules on State immunity has been vigorously asserted by Lord Millett, who suggested that immunity is a creature of customary international law, not a self-imposed restriction on the jurisdiction of the courts which a State chooses to adopt, but a limitation imposed from without upon the sovereignty of a State,[56] without elaborating upon evidences supporting this view.

In the period when the absolute understanding of State immunity prevailed, there was little doubt as to the customary law character of that straightforward and general principle which was not disputed by anyone.[57] But after the absolute understanding of immunity has been replaced by restrictive immunity, it is not clear beyond doubt that immunity as such continues to exist, since 'it is possible that international law has not prescribed an alternative rule'.[58] Caution is urged as to the holding that State immunity in any form is established as a rule of customary law, due to the absence of a necessary consensus.[59]

These doubts may be justified. Judicial practice stems predominantly from national courts, each of which operates on the specific basis of substantive and procedural law under respective national legislations. Although it may be true that national legislative instruments on State immunity were aimed at the time of their enactment to reflect what is called the restrictive approach to State immunity, they nevertheless provide national rather than international law guidance as to which acts attract immunity and which do not. Their impact is not to immunize what by its nature is a sovereign activity but to immunize what the legislator has decided to immunize. National statutes are clear by their terms and prevent the courts from expressing their attitude as to how the matter is governed under international law.[60] Thus,

---

[56] *Holland v Lampen-Wolfe*, 3 All ER (2000), 847–848. Lord Millett also referred to the 1972 European Convention on State Immunity as evidence of general international law and the 1978 State Immunity Act of the UK, id., 843.

[57] cf *Schooner-Exchange v McFadden*, 11 US 116 (1812), referring to State immunity as an undisputed principle of customary international law.

[58] Karagiannakis, State Immunity and Fundamental Human Rights, 11 *Leiden Journal of International Law*, 1998, 13.

[59] Watts, The Legal Position in International Law of Heads of States, Heads of Governments and Foreign Ministers, *RdC 247*, 1994, 36, 53.

[60] In *Letelier*, 63 ILR 386–387, Chile wanted the Court of Appeals to hold 'that the character of a given tortuous act be judicially analysed to determine whether it [. . .] should be classified as *jure imperi*'. But the Court decided that 'the other provisions of the Act mandate that the Court not do so, for it is made clear that the Act and the principles it sets forth in its specific provisions are henceforth to govern all claims of sovereign immunity by foreign States'. See *Amerada Hess v Argentina*, 81 ILR 664; *Siderman de Blake v Argentina*, 103 ILR 455; *Princz v Federal Republic of Germany*, 33 ILM (1994), 1483; *Smith et al. v Libyan Arab Jamahiriya*, 36 ILM (1997), 100; *Al-Adsani v Kuwait*, 107 ILR 536. The exception may be the cases where the domestic statute itself requires the assessment of the (sovereign) nature of an act; see the treatment of section 14(2) of the UK State Immunity Act in *Kuwait Air Corp.*, 103 ILR, 401, 412, and *Letelier* (note 16 above and accompanying text). Alternatively, the nature of the act is assessed where the domestic legislation contains the clause that it does not apply. Thus, in *Holland v Lampen-Wolfe*, the

judicial practice hardly offers compelling international law guidance on the subject.[61]

As regards other possible evidences of custom, there are certain conventions on the subject, such as the European Convention on State Immunity of 1972. But whether and to what extent they embody customary international law is to be decided by reference to the State practice on the subject, supplemented by respective *opinio juris*, as well as the nature of a conventional instrument. Apparently for such reasons, Lord Wilberforce refused to treat the 1972 Convention and the 1926 Convention on the Immunity of State Owned Ships as evidence of customary law on State immunity. In order to be capable of generating custom, a convention must, according to Lord Wilberforce, 'bear a legislative character and there must be a wide general acceptance of it as law-making, before that condition is satisfied'.[62]

In addition, there is hardly any convincing evidence that States adopt their legislation on State immunity in belief of an international obligation. True, in certain cases, national legislatures may take into account what is required or permitted under international law,[63] but even here, a uniform legal conviction of States can hardly be inferred. It is a reality that States adopt legislation on the immunity of foreign sovereigns; it is equally a reality that they are at liberty not to adopt such legislation (many States indeed do not have it), or even abolish or modify the existing legislation, under whatever reason or pretext they please.[64]

Consequently, judicial practice is hesitant to take domestic statutes on immunity as evidence of international legal rules. In *I Congreso*, the House of Lords was asked to consider that the State Immunity Act of 1978, which was not directly applicable to the case because of its non-retroactivity, nevertheless embodied applicable international law. Lord Wilberforce refused, con-

---

House of Lords confronted the situation that section 16 of the State Immunity Act excluded the applicability of that Act to the actions of foreign military forces. Lord Millett considered that the case was to be decided under common law and 'accordingly the question is whether, in accordance with the law laid down in the *I Congreso* case, the act complained was jure imperii or jure gestionis'. Lord Millett held that the publication of defamatory materials in the course of his duties by an official employed at the foreign military base was an official or governmental act; 3 All ER (2000), 845–846. Had the SIA been applicable, the nature of the act would have been irrelevant.

  [61] Further evidence that national statutes do not quite reflect the international law distinction between sovereign and non-sovereign acts is provided by provisions regarding torts that occur within the forum's jurisdiction, UK SIA Section 5, Canadian SIA Section 6. These provisions can be applied indiscriminately to the act irrespective whether it is commercial, sovereign or anything else in nature.

  [62] *I Congreso* (HL), I AC 1983, 260–261.

  [63] Higgins, *Problems and Process* (1994), 81.

  [64] The very fact of the amendment by the US Congress of the FSIA in a way removing immunity from certain acts which earlier attracted it (so-called *Flatow* amendment) evidences that the United States does not consider itself bound in terms of international law by the 'rules' on State immunity and considers that it may withdraw immunity from any act at its pleasure. See below, note 74 and accompanying text.

sidering that 'to argue from the terms of a statute to establish what international law provides is to stand the accepted argument on its head', and added that 'if one State chooses to lay down by enactment certain limits, that is by itself no evidence that those limits are generally accepted by States. And particularly enacted limits may be (or presumed to be) not inconsistent with general international law—the latter being in a state of uncertainty—without affording evidence what that law is.'[65] Similarly, the Irish Supreme Court remarked in *McElhinney* that 'statutes are evidence of domestic law in the individual States and not evidence of international law generally'.[66]

Obviously, it was these circumstances that led Lord Denning to question whether the doctrine of sovereign immunity finds its place in general international law. Facing the assumption that the doctrine of sovereign immunity is based on international law and commands the consensus of civilized nations, he observed the following:

> To my mind this notion of a consensus is a fiction. The nations are not in the least agreed upon the doctrine of sovereign immunity. The courts of every country differ in their application of it. Some grant absolute immunity. Others grant limited immunity, with each defining the limits differently. There is no consensus whatever. Yet this does not mean that there is no rule of international law upon the subject. It only means that we differ as to what that rule is. Each country delimits for itself the bounds of sovereign immunity. Each creates for itself exceptions from it.[67]

Lord Denning's reasoning shows that if one tries to find in international law a general rule requiring States to grant immunity to other States in certain circumstances, one should at least support such a finding with a uniform and coherent practice affirming that international law itself obliges States to grant immunity to a foreign State for certain acts. This has still to be awaited and consequently at present there is no customary international law on State immunity.

The absence of a general rule on State immunity in international law evidences the lack of a specific rule in general international law itself *requiring* States to grant immunity to foreign States for one act or another. By the same token, there is no specific rule of general international law itself determining the scope of acts with respect to which a State is *empowered* to grant immunity to foreign States. States indeed happen to grant immunity to foreign States, for acts both *jure imperii* and *jure gestionis*, but in doing so they should be seen as acting not in the context of 'rules' on State immunity,

---

[65] *I Congreso* (HL), I AC 1983, 260.

[66] *McElhinney*, 104 ILR 701.

[67] *Trendtex Trading v Bank of Nigeria*, 1 QB 1977, 552–553. For example, national legal systems differ in their criteria determining whether an act is commercial. The US legislation refers to the nature of the act and not its purpose while the Canadian Supreme Court refers to nature as well as purpose of the act, cf *Bouzari* (Ontario Superior Court of Justice), para. 29; and so do French courts, Caplan, 97 *AJIL* (2003), 761.

but in a more general context of rules governing jurisdiction of States, as masters of their general territorial jurisdiction, and as acting on the basis of considerations such as interest, comity or reciprocity. While so acting in this context, States, owing to the absence of a general rule on State immunity, are not mandated by customary law to exercise their jurisdictional rights, *inter alia*, through granting immunity to a foreign State, in a way contradicting their specific obligations under international law.

This legal position makes it difficult to justify State immunity for serious breaches of international law such as torture. But the courts who take such an attitude do not seem to bother with justifications. *Al-Adsani* refers to 'generally recognized rules of public international law on State immunity',[68] without, however, illustrating the ways in which those rules acquired their 'generally recognized' character. The Court of Appeal in *Bouzari* considered that 'the immunity of States from civil proceedings in the courts of foreign jurisdictions is an example of a principle of customary international law',[69] and also supplied no evidence to support this view. Both courts thus adhered to a now-abandoned absolute approach to State immunity, and insisted upon the existence of a rule justifying absolute deprivation of remedies to the victims of torture. As the analysis here has shown, the state of customary law can in no way be understood as supporting this view. It is not enough for courts to state customary norms: they have to prove their existence as well.

3.2. The immunity of State officials

The International Court in the *Arrest Warrant* case held that immunities of an incumbent foreign minister are 'firmly established' in international law.[70] But the Court, as well as individual judges supporting the judgment, did not examine State practice and *opinio juris*. The Court found that there is no exception to immunity even in cases of war crimes and crimes against humanity, but before one speaks about exceptions to a rule, one has first to demonstrate that the rule as such exists. As the analysis below shows, the examination of State practice and *opinio juris* might have given some trouble to the International Court in terms of its preferred approach.

The Court referred to the *Pinochet* and *Gaddafi* decisions, the latter focusing on immunity of a serving head of State and not a foreign minister and the former only suggesting that serving heads of State, which are placed higher than foreign ministers, are immune. Moreover, as the ruling of the Cour de Cassation in *Gaddafi* suggests, there are certain crimes under

---

[68] *Al-Adsani*, 34 EHRR 11 (2002), 289, para. 56.

[69] *Bouzari* (Court of Appeal for Ontario), para. 86, *per* Goudge JA.

[70] *Arrest Warrant* case, Judgment, para. 51. For a similar assumption without examining evidence see Lord Slynn, *Pinochet*, 4 All ER, 1998, 908, 913–915, 917, and Lord Phillips, *Pinochet*, 2 All ER 1999, 182–183.

international law the prosecution of which may lead to an exception from immunity even for an incumbent head of State,[71] and the International Court has erred in referring to this case to justify the absolute immunity of foreign ministers. *Gaddafi* does not uphold the rule that the International Court upheld. Furthermore, even if relevant in terms of subject-matter, it is difficult to agree that these two decisions are sufficient to identify the *opinio juris* necessary for the establishment of a general customary rule accepted by the community of nations.

In addition, there is another part of practice, portraying things quite differently from what the Court thought to be the actual state of law, demonstrating that States do not always view themselves as legally bound to respect immunity of high-ranking foreign officials. For example, a US court in *Noriega* considered that the immunity of a head of State may be influenced by the question whether the forum State recognizes a person in that capacity.[72] In that case, as well as in *Lafontant v Aristide*, the US courts have clearly emphasized that 'the grant of immunity is a privilege which the United States may withhold from any claimant'.[73] *Lafontant v Aristide* also suggests that a head of State is immune in the US courts 'unless that immunity has been waived by statute'.[74] This means that the US courts consider the United States entitled to deprive, by adopting respective legislation, foreign heads of State of their immunity, and cannot be understood as anything other than the absence of a legal conviction of being bound to respect the immunity of heads of State as a matter of international law.

This state of practice justifies Judge Van den Wyngaert's criticism of the Court's approach. The Court is to be blamed for simply having assumed the existence of a rule granting immunity to incumbent foreign ministers in disregard of its own practice of identifying existence of customary rules, consisting of examination of elements of custom formation.[75] The fact that States have often abstained from prosecuting foreign ministers or other comparable officials of other States may be explained by reasons other than the belief of obligation, eg by considerations of courtesy or policy.[76] Consequently, in issuing the arrest warrant against the Congolese foreign minister, 'Belgium might have acted contrary to international comity, but has not infringed international law'.[77]

---

[71] *Gaddafi* (Court of Cassation), 125 ILR 509; Zappala, Do Heads of State Enjoy Immunity from Prosecution for International Crimes?, 12 *European Journal of International Law* (2001), 601–607.

[72] *United States v Noriega*, 99 ILR 162–163.

[73] *Lafontant v Aristide*, 103 ILR 586. [74] Id., 584–585.

[75] *Arrest Warrant*, Dissenting Opinion of Judge Van den Wyngaert, paras 10–12, 23, referring to the *North Sea Continental Shelf* cases (*Federal Republic of Germany v Denmark*; *Federal Republic of Germany v Netherlands*), Judgment of 20 February 1969, *ICJ Reports* 1969, 4, where the Court laid down certain strict criteria of identification of customary rules.

[76] Id., para. 13. [77] Id., para. 23.

4. THE HIERARCHICAL PERSPECTIVE:
THE IMPACT OF PEREMPTORY NORMS

4.1. Conceptual aspects

There is sufficient evidence that peremptory norms prevail over the rules of general (customary) international law. Vattel recognized that the immutable law provides criteria to distinguish not only lawful treaties from those that are not lawful, but also innocent and rational customs from those that are unjust or censurable.[78] The primacy of *jus cogens* has been recognized by Judge Lauterpacht in *Bosnia*,[79] the ICTY which placed *jus cogens* above the special and also general customary law,[80] the Inter-American Commission of Human Rights,[81] and also reaffirmed by writers.[82]

It is pointed out that there is no real conflict between *jus cogens* and immunities, because State immunity, not being a rule of customary law, is not recognized under international law, and the real conflict is between *jus cogens* and the adjudicatory jurisdiction of States.[83] More precisely, the real conflict is between peremptory norms and national legislative instruments. This being so, this analysis goes on to examine the impact of peremptory norms on immunities assuming that immunities are part of customary law. This is without prejudice to the outcomes of the previous section on normative perspective, but it is necessary to focus on the hierarchical perspective because courts often assume that State immunity is based on custom.

It is contended that there is no conflict between *jus cogens* and State immunity. The argument follows that as sovereign immunity for the breach of a peremptory norm would not require the abolition or violation of that peremptory norm, but would merely oppose its enforcement before the domestic forum, it remains unaffected by its superior force and is invocable even in the face of *jus cogens*. The starting-point argument for this approach is that substance and enforcement of *jus cogens* are different things, and while peremptory norms are accepted in international law and bind States, they do not possess superior force with regard to their effect and enforcement. In other

---

[78] Wolff, *The Law of Nations Treated according to a Scientific Method*, in Scott (ed.), *Classics of International Law* (Oxford 1934), 10; Vattel, *The Law of Nations, or the Principles of Natural Law applied to the Conduct and to the Affairs of Nations and of Sovereigns*, in Scott (ed.), *Classics of International Law* (Washington 1916), 4.

[79] Separate opinion of Judge Lauterpacht, *ICJ Reports* 1993, 440.

[80] *Furundzija*, para. 153.

[81] *Victims of the Tugboat '13 de Marzo'*, para. 79.

[82] Verdross, *Forbidden Treaties in International Law, AJIL* (1937); cf Simma and Alston, The Sources of Human Rights Law: Custom, Jus Cogens, and General Principles, 12 *Australian Yearbook of International Law* (1992), 105; Christenson, *Jus Cogens*: Guarding Interests Fundamental to the International Society, 28 *Virginia Journal of International Law* (1988), 611; Saulle, Jus Cogens and Human Rights, *International Law at the Time of its Codification, Essays in Honour of Roberto Ago*, vol. II (1987), 392.

[83] Caplan, 97 *AJIL* (2003), 771–773.

words, while peremptory norms regulate substantive conduct, immunities relate to procedural norms. The peremptory status of a norm does not carry with itself the peremptory obligation on the forum State to provide the victim with civil remedies for acts committed abroad and by the foreign State.[84]

This argument is flawed for several reasons. First, limiting the relevance of peremptory norms to primacy prohibitions of conduct is justified neither by the concept of *jus cogens* nor its practical application. It is generally accepted that peremptory norms have inherent consequential effects, among others in terms of State responsibility and reparation, jurisdiction, and prosecution of international crimes. This proves that peremptory norms are not limited to the primary prohibitions of conduct. In addition, even if it is perhaps right to view, as a matter of national law, the issue of immunity as the preliminary or procedural issue determining whether the national court can proceed with considering the claims, under international law, which knows of no inherent and clear-cut distinction between substantive and procedural rules, viewing immunities as inherently procedural and hence outside the ambit of *jus cogens* is not justified.

Second, the scope of State immunity in international law precludes viewing the substance and enforcement of peremptory norms as two different things. Breaches of *jus cogens* are definitionally outside the scope of acts *jure imperi*. This effectively confirms that peremptory norms have inherent consequential aspect and their relevance extends to the process of enforcement including the issues of the relevant forum.

Third, the practice of the application of universal jurisdiction over *jus cogens* crimes and torts rejects the substance/effects distinction. The views of Law Lords in *Pinochet* are among those referred to below to illustrate this practice.

Consequently, the distinction between the substance and enforcement of *jus cogens* and the ensuing contention that State immunity should be available because it does not affect the former but merely affects some aspects of the latter is conceptually flawed. It is the natural effect of peremptory norms as superior norms that they trump the 'rules' or principles on the immunity of States and their officials, if and to what extent such rules actually exist. Apart from having no conceptual coherence, the substance/enforcement distinction only points to abstract categories, misjudging the implications for individual cases in practice, where the failure to enforce the relevant peremptory norm before the domestic forum effectively renders that norm non-existent from the position of individuals whose rights that norm is meant to protect in that case.

---

[84] ILA British Branch Report (2002), 150; Fox, *The Law of State Immunity* (2002), 524–525; Tomuschat, L'immunité des états en cas de violations graves des droits de l'homme, *Revue general de droit international public* (2005), 51–74; Akande, International Law Immunities and the International Criminal Court, 98 *AJIL* (2004), 407, at 414; De Wet (2004), 109–110.

This principle cannot be prejudiced by reference to the lack or rarity of its application in practice (even though, as the relevant practice demonstrates, courts, when judging independently on the basis of international rather than national law more often than not deny State immunity for the breaches of peremptory norms). As Cassese affirms, 'it is not always necessary to have a wealth of authorities available before asserting that *jus cogens* norms override contrary customary rules. This in particular holds true when peremptory norms are intended to protect the fundamental values of the international community that are currently regarded as more imperative and indeed overriding than traditional State concerns protected by rules on State immunities.'[85]

A cognate argument against the impact of *jus cogens* on immunities is that peremptory norms and principles governing State immunity are two separate legal institutes developing parallel to, but not intercepting, each other.[86] As a matter of the sources of law and their hierarchy, this view is hard to sustain, because no rule or principle operates in isolation. As soon as there are two different sets of legal rules and each of them requires a juridical outcome different from what the other may require, the conflict between these allegedly separate and self-contained sets of rules emerges. Considerations of the hierarchy of norms are considered legitimate in every legal system to deal with such normative conflicts.

In addition, the arguments advancing the separate and independent nature of different sets of principles of international law fail to demonstrate that a set of principles, such as immunities, is intended to constitute an exception from the effect of peremptory norms; or that a peremptory norm, such as that outlawing and requiring prosecution of and remedies for torture or crimes against humanity, in itself contains an exception when a plea of immunity of a State or its officials is involved. As soon as peremptory rules can in principle prevail over conflicting rules, acts and transactions, it is unclear why they cannot take such effect with regard to sovereign immunity. To argue the contrary is to portray immunities as a special class of rules somehow comparable to *jus cogens*.[87] But this is not easy to prove: immunities may be waived, renounced, derogated from or breached by way of reciprocity or countermeasures. Thus, immunities, if and to the extent they exist in international law, are subject to the operation of the international public order in the same way as any other norm is.

---

[85] Cassese, *International Law* (2005), 107–108.

[86] Zimmermann, Sovereign Immunity and the Violations of International *Jus Cogens*—Some Critical Remarks, 16 *Michigan Journal of International Law* (1995), 438; Akande, International Law Immunities and the International Criminal Court, 98 *AJIL* (2004), 414.

[87] This is indeed suggested by Jennings, The *Pinochet* Extradition Case in the English Courts, L. Boisson de Chazournes and V. Gowlland-Debbas, *The International Legal System in Quest of Equity and Universality. Liber Amicorum Georges Abi-Saab* (2001), 677 at 684–685.

All these considerations require acknowledgment that under international law peremptory rules such as core norms of human rights law prevail over non-peremptory norms of immunities.[88] Also in the case of international crimes outlawed under *jus cogens*, such as crimes against humanity, it must be accepted that the principles of immunity have no peremptory status and the conflict between the two sets of norms must be resolved considering the framework of normative hierarchy giving primacy to the relevant peremptory norms.[89]

4.2. Peremptory norms and the immunity of States

In *Al-Adsani*, the principal question before the European Court of Human Rights was whether the grant of immunity to the foreign State for the acts of torture violated Article 6 of the European Convention on Human Rights, which guarantees the right to access to a court. Whether Article 6 was qualified by the limitation of State immunity required interpreting this provision in terms of the applicable rules of general international law, as required under Article 31(3)(c) of the 1969 Vienna Convention on the Law of Treaties. This approach of the Court is itself controversial because Article 6, requiring Al-Adsani's access to the court, contradicted and prevailed, as a treaty norm, over any possible rule of general international law, such as on State immunity, that may have required that Al-Adsani should not have such access to the court. But the Court chose to engage with the *jus cogens* argument as the prohibition of torture is peremptory.

The Court acknowledged that torture is prohibited in absolute terms, and this prohibition has a *jus cogens* character, as particularly emphasized by the ICTY, and takes primacy over general customary law, the character of which the European Court attributed to the rules on State immunity. However, the Court considered that, unlike the cases dealt with by the ICTY, the case before it did not concern criminal liability of an individual for the acts of torture, but the immunity of a State in a civil suit, and concluded that

notwithstanding the special character of the prohibition of torture in international law, the Court is unable to discern in the international instruments, judicial authorities or other materials before it any firm basis for concluding that, as a matter of international law, a State no longer enjoys immunity from civil suit in the courts of another State where acts of torture are alleged.[90]

---

[88] M Reinmann, Human Rights Exception to Sovereign Immunity, 16 *Michigan Journal of International Law* (1995), 407.

[89] Clapham, National Action Challenged: Sovereignty, Immunity and Universal Jurisdiction before the International Court of Justice, in Lattimer and Sands, *Justice for Crimes Against Humanity* (2003), 323–326.

[90] *Al-Adsani*, 34 EHRR 11(2002), 291, para. 61. Judge Zupancic's Opinion is inspired by the same point, id., 23–24

This statement of the Court results in a contradiction; for if it is assumed that a *jus cogens* rule as such prevails over an inconsistent norm of general, or customary, international law, it is rather curious to require existence of an additional norm—supported in a convention or judicial practice—enabling a given peremptory norm to take effect in specific cases.

Moreover, the Court seems to have assumed that a *jus cogens* prohibition of torture may override State immunity with regard to criminal liability of an individual. The reasons for assuming that the same is not true for civil proceedings may not logically be inferred from the nature of the peremptory prohibition of torture. The basic question is that of the hierarchy of norms. The Court's attitude, if correct, would undeniably lead to the result that the civil proceedings aspect of State immunity is in a position to achieve a result in its relation to *jus cogens* which its criminal proceedings aspect is not able to achieve, namely to prevail over *jus cogens*. One must admit that the Joint Dissenting Opinion of six judges is rightly based on a premise denying that 'the standards applicable in civil cases differ from those applying in criminal matters when a conflict arises between the peremptory norm of international law on the prohibition of torture and the rules on State immunity.'[91]

The Court has hardly examined the issue of the hierarchy of norms, and thus focused upon *jus cogens* without respecting its most peculiar characteristics—capacity to prevail over other norms. The paragraphs of the judgment dealing with the relevance of *jus cogens* lack any focus on the hierarchy of norms, and discuss merely evidentiary rather than normative aspects of *jus cogens*.

Jus cogens prevails over conflicting rules of international law, whether general or particular. Therefore, the prohibition on torture prevails over State immunity and this happens because of the normative characteristics of that prohibition, not because the 'rules' on State immunity shall or actually do allow this. If the Court decided to interpret Article 6 by reference to 'relevant rules' of general international law in terms of Article 31(3)(c) of the Vienna Convention, it would have to accord due importance to how general international law itself perceives the hierarchy of norms when they conflict with each other and especially that once one norm prevails over another the hierarchy becomes a matter of principle which operates by itself and without the need to find additional evidence to that effect.

This underlines the fact that 'the *jus cogens* character of the prohibition against torture may have rendered void any rule of customary international law which might otherwise have required English courts, when applying common law of State immunity, to grant immunity to foreign States'.[92] As

---

[91] Joint Dissenting Opinion, *Al-Adsani*, 34 EHRR 11(2002), 297–298 (introductory paragraph).

[92] Therefore, the English courts, when dealing with the areas not covered by a statute, should take into account the development of the concept of *jus cogens* and the fact that certain customary norms possess such status. Case-note by Byers, 67 *BYIL* 1996, 539–540.

rightly stressed in the Joint Dissenting Opinion, 'the majority, while accepting that the rule on prohibition of torture is a *jus cogens* norm, refuse to draw the consequences of such acceptance'. The procedural bar of State immunity does not produce legal effects as soon as it conflicts with a hierarchically superior norm.[93]

In order to justify its attitude, the Court referred to the attitude of the Working Group on State Immunity of the UN International Law Commission concerning the argument increasingly put forward that immunity should be denied in the case of acts in violation of human rights norms having the character of *jus cogens*. However, the Court construed the attitude of the Working Group as supporting the immunity of States even in the case of torture, since that Group emphasized that in most cases where *jus cogens* was pleaded, the plea of sovereign immunity had succeeded.[94]

Regrettably, the European Court misinterpreted the attitude of the ILC's Working Group. Although the Working Group acknowledged that in the majority of cases, the plea of immunity had succeeded, this did not prejudice its final view. Rather, the Working Group, instead of proposing that international law upholds immunity for *jus cogens* breaches in civil proceedings, submitted that the recent developments with regard to the plea of immunity in cases of *jus cogens* are so significant that their impact cannot be ignored.[95]

Apart from this general misinterpretation of the ILC Working Group's attitude, the Court did not properly assess how the domestic judicial decisions could impact the issues before it. The Court took as conclusive that in most domestic proceedings, the plea of State immunity has succeeded with regard to civil claims arising out of torture. But this can hardly evidence the state of international law as such, because national courts, notably English and American courts, uphold immunity pleas on the basis of national statutes, such as the US Foreign Sovereign Immunity Act (1976) and the UK State Immunity Act (1978), which are exclusive sources of jurisdiction over foreign States. The national legislature, while requiring the courts to grant immunity to foreign States, has not admitted exception from this requirement in case of *jus cogens*, and the Courts refuse to exercise jurisdiction by reference to State immunity to which they accord predominance as required by their domestic law.[96] It would suffice to indicate that, when the case of *Al-Adsani* was considered by the English courts, the reasoning of Mantell J,

---

[93] Joint Dissenting Opinion, *Al-Adsani*, 297–298 (introductory paragraph and para. 4).

[94] *Al-Adsani*, 291, para. 62; De Wet, The Prohibition of Torture as an International Norm of *Jus Cogens* and Its Implications for National and Customary Law, 15 *EJIL* (2004), 112, similarly misinterprets the *Princz* decision.

[95] Annex to the Report of the Working Group on State Immunity, UN Doc. A/CN.4/L.576 (1999), 56–58.

[96] See, eg, *Siderman de Blake v Argentina*, 103 ILR 455; *Princz v Federal Republic of Germany*, 33 ILM 1483 (1994); *Smith et al. v Libyan Arab Jamahiriya*, 36 ILM 100 (1997).

Stuart-Smith LJ and Ward LJ did not show the slightest indication that, under international law, Kuwait would be entitled to immunity for the acts of torture. Their reasoning rather acknowledges that an act of torture could hardly attract immunity under international law, but the 'comprehensive code' embodied in the 1978 State Immunity Act would not have allowed a solution dictated by international law to be implemented in English domestic law.[97] On the same facts, immunity might not have been available at common law.[98]

The intellectual weakness of the European Court's majority reasoning in *Al-Adsani* is demonstrated by the fact that it was acquainted with national court decisions pointing to the difference of the outcomes between national and international law, even to the conflict between national and international regulations of immunity for breaches of peremptory norms, and yet it took those very same decisions as evidence of international law recognizing the immunity for the acts like torture.

The logical and conceptual confusion generated in *Al-Adsani* showed its impact in the decisions of some national courts, such as the Canadian court in *Bouzari*, whose principal basis of the decision was the wording of the Canadian State Immunity Act (SIA) not admitting the exception from immunity for the pleas based on torture. The Canadian court treated the issue of the impact of *jus cogens* on State immunity in the context of the principle that, in accordance with the primacy of domestic statutes, the wording of the SIA, even as it conflicted with international law, prevailed, within the Canadian legal system, over international *jus cogens*. As the text of the SIA was clear and immunized the acts of torture, there was 'no need to read in a further exception to comply with international law'.[99] The Court of Appeal in *Bouzari* was even more accurate in describing the legal position. The court acknowledged that international *jus cogens* produces effects in the law of Canada, but if the Canadian legislation contradicts those effects, it will prevail 'although it would put Canada in breach of its international obligations'. Consequently, even if international law requires Canada to provide a civil remedy for breaches of *jus cogens*, the State Immunity Act was clear in not permitting Canadian courts to assume jurisdiction over such breaches.[100]

As a matter of Canadian law that would suffice for deciding the case, but the court, following *Al-Adsani*, further elaborated on whether international law and practice admits an exception to immunity based on peremptory

---

[97] *Al-Adsani* (High Court), 103 ILR 427–431; *Al-Adsani* (Court of Appeal), 107 ILR 538–547.

[98] Therefore, the English courts, when dealing with the areas not covered by a statute, should take into account the development of the concept of *jus cogens* and the fact that certain customary norms possess such status. Case-note by Byers, 67 *BYIL* 1996, 539–540.

[99] *Bouzari* (Ontario Superior Court of Justice), paras 39–42.

[100] *Bouzari* (Court of Appeal for Ontario), paras 65–66, *per* Goudge JA.

norms. It argued that, pursuant to *Al-Adsani*, such exception was not available, without considering the lack of consistency in the European Court's majority approach. Consequently, the Canadian court argued, on the one hand, that despite the state of international law the Canadian SIA, which contradicts international law, must be given primacy and shield the acts of torture, and on the other hand, that the very same Canadian SIA is actually consistent with international law and the latter provides for immunity for breaches of *jus cogens* such as torture.[101] But this last argument supported by two Canadian courts, which substantially contradicts the former one, was irrelevant for judicial decision-making in the legal system which subscribes to the primacy of domestic statutes over international law, because whatever the outcome on this issue, the Canadian courts would still remain bound by SIA to uphold State immunity; it was furthermore inconsistent with how most national courts see the obstacles to giving effect to *jus cogens* in the face of conflicting domestic legislation and thus with the fact that the current state of international law on the subject did not actually reflect the Canadian courts' vision.

The Court of Appeal affirmed that *jus cogens* prevails over conflicting customary law, to which in the court's view State immunity belonged, but maintained that in view of State practice customary international law still provides immunity for acts of torture.[102] This overstretched statement neglected that the only case actually affirming this attitude was the European Court's decision in *Al-Adsani*, which itself was defective both in terms of treatment of normative hierarchy and of State practice. All national decisions in which State immunity was affirmed, which were available for the attention of Canadian courts, did so by reference to national legislation, which took primacy, *not* to international law.

The Court of Appeal in *Bouzari* further justified its support for the immunity of States for torture by emphasizing the difference between civil and criminal cases to the effect that while the perpetrators of torture can be held criminally accountable, State immunity with regard to civil suits arising out of torture still persists, and referred in this regard to the view of the Law Lords in *Pinochet* regarding the difference between civil and criminal cases.[103] But the Canadian court did not bother to ascertain which reasons prompted the Lords to emphasize the difference between civil and criminal cases: this reason was certainly not based on international law, but the Lords were constrained by the fact that the UK State Immunity Act precludes, as a matter of domestic law, the civil claims against the State for torture committed abroad. Such inconsistencies of reasoning and poor treatment of

---

[101] *Bouzari* (Ontario Superior Court of Justice), paras 38–42, 68–73; the Court of Appeal upheld this argument, *Bouzari* (Court of Appeal for Ontario), para. 68, *per* Goudge JA.

[102] *Bouzari* (Court of Appeal for Ontario), paras 86–88, *per* Goudge JA.

[103] *Bouzari* (Court of Appeal for Ontario), para. 91 *per* Goudge JA.

evidence make it impossible to regard the decisions of Canadian courts in *Bouzari* as references of any useful value for identifying the position of international law with regard to State immunity.

The approach of the European Court and Canadian courts was followed up by the Court of Appeal in England in *Jones v Saudi Arabia*.[104] This case differs from other English decisions, which referred merely to the State Immunity Act as the national law obstacle of giving due legal effect in the English legal system to the prohibition of torture. In *Jones* there is arguably a shift from this position whose sustainability will only be checked by subsequent developments. This shift consists in the fact that the court did not close the matter by pronouncing, unlike other English and also American courts, that the State Immunity Act immunizes the breaches of *jus cogens* as the comprehensive code on the subject-matter.[105] It left this issue open and proceeded to explain the state of international law on the relevant issues, thus leaving a further possibility open that the relevant issues are determined by international law and should the Act potentially contradict international law its wording might as well be disregarded. This approach is an important shift from, or at least qualification to, the doctrine of statutory supremacy over common and hence international law.

As shown above, the European Court misconstrued the relevance of these decisions through describing them as evidence of the international legal position justifying a similar outcome. The Court of Appeal in *Jones*, instead of deciding the case on traditional grounds of statutory supremacy, went on to incorporate the European Court's reasoning into its own decision and asserted that civil immunity for torture was required under international law.

The Court of Appeal engaged in justifying State immunity in civil proceedings for torture by suggesting an artificial distinction between the substance of peremptory norms and the consequences of their breaches. The Court suggests that

The recognition under general principles of international law of civil immunity on the part of a State from civil suit in a State other than that of the alleged torture does not sanction the torture or qualify the prohibition upon it. It qualifies the jurisdictions in which and means by which the peremptory norm may be enforced.[106]

This approach, even though popular among some writers, is not the usual one which is judicially used to defeat *jus cogens* pleas against immunity. The European Court in *Al-Adsani* has not expressly subscribed to such general distinction between substance and enforcement of peremptory norms, even if

---

[104] *Jones*, paras 13–14, *per* Mance LJ.

[105] cf the suggestion that in this case the claimants argued their claims, and the Court decided the case, outside the 1978 Act; see the case-note on *Jones* by X Yang, Universal Tort Jurisdiction over Torture? 64 *CLJ* (2005), 2.

[106] *Jones*, para. 17, *per* Mance LJ.

some would justify its decision from this perspective—it spoke instead in evidentiary terms, and so did Canadian courts in *Bouzari*. The fact that the general distinction between the substance and enforcement of norms is not judicially subscribed to apart from isolated instances seems to confirm the inborn deficiency of such argument and that, if viewed in context, it can produce more questions than it resolves.

To begin with, this question was not the one on which the English court, constrained by the letter of national legislation, had to pronounce. But once the court chose to pursue this issue, it did not bother to enquire how the inferior norm on immunity is to retain its applicability in the context where the superior norm on the enforcement of the prohibition of torture comes into play. It further did not ask how the prohibition of torture is to operate as a legal norm in situations where it is construed as having only the 'conduct' aspect but not the consequential aspect. The norm that cannot be enforced is not a norm. Consequently, the view that the prohibition of torture cannot be enforced before the otherwise available forum means that for the purposes of that forum and the relevant case there is no prohibition of torture.

The court's approach that the enforcement of a peremptory norm can be qualified by the operation of a non-peremptory norm implies that the enforcement aspects of a peremptory norm are not peremptory. As evidenced by the relevant normative framework and supported by the jurisprudence of national and international bodies, the enforcement aspect of peremptory norms is also peremptory and constitutes the inherent part of its substantive, or 'conduct', aspect.

The distinction between substance and legal consequences of peremptory norms fails also because of the functional limits on State immunity. It is crucial that immunity is unavailable for acts contrary to *jus cogens* because they are categorically outside the scope of sovereign functions. In this specific perspective it does not matter which aspect of the given *jus cogens* norm is peremptory—substantive or consequential. For breaches of *jus cogens*, immunity is not available as a matter of principle and cannot prevent any exercise of jurisdiction.

Any contention that with regard to immunities the substance and enforcement aspects of *jus cogens* are different from each other is necessarily based on the blanket and absolute understanding of State immunity which does not distinguish between sovereign and non-sovereign acts, and considers the breaches of *jus cogens* which also constitute international crimes as part of sovereign functions of States. The very exclusion of the breaches of *jus cogens* from the scope of sovereign functions covered by State immunity implies that the peremptory character of the norm is relevant not only in terms of the substance of that norm but also when the breach of that norm is adjudicated before the foreign court; in this field peremptory norms have the inherent consequential aspect.

The court's distinction in *Jones* between the substance and enforcement of peremptory norms also contradicts its own reasoning regarding the immunity of State officials engaged in serious human rights violations. With regard to this issue the court easily conceded that the breach of *jus cogens* is outside the scope of State immunity and the otherwise available immunity will not shield the defendant.[107] This renders the Court of Appeal's reasoning even more questionable. If, as a matter of international law, the immunity of a State from civil proceedings 'qualifies the jurisdictions in which and means by which the peremptory norm may be enforced', why does it not qualify the jurisdictions in the same way when State officials are sued? Or more broadly, why does State immunity not shield the perpetrators of international crimes from prosecution? The argument that immunity does not question the validity of substantive prohibition of international crimes but merely qualifies the jurisdictions in which the perpetrators can be prosecuted could, if applied consistently, prevent adjudication also with regard to individual State officials. This was even perhaps implied in Lord Goff's opinion in *Pinochet*, but no court has ever subscribed to this view. As Cassese explains,

if the violation of the general rule of *jus cogens* entails that the individual author is no longer protected by the customary rule on functional immunity (a corollary of the general rule on State immunity from any foreign interference in the internal organisation of the State), why should the rule on State immunity from jurisdiction not yield to *jus cogens* in the same or similar cases?[108]

This demonstrates the inconsistency of assuming that peremptory norms can trump the norms with the same rationale in one context but not in another. As further observed, 'to uphold the immunity of foreign States while lifting that of their organs for the same violations calls into question the consistency of the whole normative system.'[109]

One reason that this artificial distinction between the substance and enforcement of *jus cogens* is developed with regard to the immunity of States is the misunderstanding of the relevance of national statutes in this process. Once it is properly understood that these statutes are merely the sources of national, *not* international law and prescribe immunity for the breaches of peremptory norms as a matter of national law, it will be more easily understood that there is no State practice (of which these statutes would form part) justifying, as a matter of international law, immunity of States for the breaches of *jus cogens*. The argument of distinction between the substance and enforcement of *jus cogens* would then no longer be relevant.

There is practice affirming this approach and demonstrating that when not constrained by the wording of national statutes, domestic courts do not

---

[107] *Jones*, para. 31.   [108] Cassese, *International Law* (2005), 108.
[109] Bianchi, case-note on *Ferrini* (The Supreme Court of Italy), 99 *AJIL* (2005), 247.

hesitate to reject immunity pleas for acts offending against *jus cogens*. The Court of Levadia refused to grant immunity to Germany for the acts committed by German forces in Greece during the Second World War.[110] The court started its analysis with construing State immunity as the functionally limited principle covering sovereign acts only. It then affirmed that Germany as the occupying power was obliged under the Fourth Hague Convention of 1907 to respect the local laws and especially the lives, family honour and property of the inhabitants of the occupied territory. These norms constitute customary law of peremptory status (*jus cogens*) for the violation of which a State cannot invoke immunity.[111]

The Court of Levadia provided the conceptual explanation of the approach it adopted. A State committing the breach of *jus cogens* waives the entitlement of sovereign immunity for those breaches. These acts cannot qualify as sovereign acts. Instead, these acts are null and void and cannot generate legal benefits for the wrongdoer such as immunity, pursuant to the general principle *ex injuria jus non oritur*. The court further affirmed that 'the recognition of immunity for an act contrary to peremptory international law would amount to complicity of the national court to the promotion of an act strongly condemned by the international public order'.[112] The Greek Supreme Court affirmed this judgment and its underlying principle that the breaches of peremptory norms attract no immunity.[113] This reasoning provides a coherent argument which considers all relevant factors including the hierarchy of norms and the inherent limits on the scope of State immunity.

The Special Supreme Court of Greece has later overturned the ruling of the Levadia Court and the Supreme Court, and immunized German war crimes. The Special Supreme Court decided the case by following certain prior decisions, such as the European Court's decision in *Al-Adsani*, without examining the actual merit of the pertinent issues of State immunity such as the distinction of sovereign and non-sovereign acts and the impact of the hierarchy of norms. The relevant passages of the court's decision contain not much more than a survey of the sources the court considers supportive of its approach, and hardly any analysis of the pertinent legal principles and categories is developed. Also, the fact that the court heavily relied on the outcomes suggested by the 1972 European Convention on State Immunity suggests that its decision does not unconditionally affirm that in customary law immunity persists even for the violations of peremptory norms.[114] In any

---

[110] Case No. 137/1997, Multi-member Court of Levadia, 30 October 1997, in 50 *Revue Hellénique* (1997), 594.

[111] Id., 598–599.

[112] Id., 599.

[113] Case No. 11/2000, *Prefecture of Voiotia v Federal Republic of Germany*, case-note by M. Gavouneli and I. Bantekas, 95 *AJIL* 2001, 198–204.

[114] Case No. 6/2002, The Special Supreme Court, 17 September 2002, reported in 56 *Revue Hellénique* (2003), 56.

case, it does not contain anything *a priori* contradicting the consequential impact of peremptory norms on State immunity.

The Italian Supreme Court decided in the *Ferrini* case that Germany could not claim immunity for the actions of German occupying forces in Italy during the Second World War.[115] The Supreme Court drew proper conclusions from the hierarchy of norms by concluding that peremptory norms as superior norms 'prevail over all other norms, either statutory or customary in nature . . . and therefore also over norms concerning immunity'.[116] Significantly, the Italian Supreme Court viewed the normative hierarchy as an expression of the balance of values that different norms protect: the superior substantive values protected by peremptory norms prevailed over the values of individual State sovereignty as the principle of State immunity may protect.[117]

The Italian Supreme Court has furthermore elaborated on the nature of normative conflicts arising out of the hierarchy of norms, and effectively disapproved the view that the norms of State immunity do not conflict with peremptory norms or they build a separate set of norms which does not intercept with *jus cogens*. The court affirmed that the norms on State immunity must be interpreted systematically, considering their interaction with other norms of international law. Legal norms are not 'to be interpreted independently of one another, because they complete and integrate each other, influencing one another in their application'. Such interaction with other norms causes recognition to the exceptions to immunity, among which is the exception to give 'priority to hierarchically superior norms' of *jus cogens*, because this is necessary to safeguard the values essential to the entire international community.[118]

The *Ferrini* decision thus expounds the basics of normative hierarchy involving peremptory norms: as peremptory norms embody the values fundamental to the international community as a whole, they prevail over State immunity which protects the interests of individual States and prevents its invocation to the extent of the enforcement of the relevant peremptory norm. *Ferrini* thus differs from *Al-Adsani* or *Bouzari* which examined the state of international law on the subject without properly addressing the crucial question of the hierarchy of norms, viewing the effect of such hierarchy in terms of the evidences in practice. The judges in *Al-Adsani* and *Bouzari*, as well as *Jones*, do not seem to have understood the basic principle that when a

---

[115] Judgment No. 5044, 6 November 2003; reviewed and analysed by P De Sena and F De Vittor, State Immunity and Human Rights: The Italian Supreme Court Decision on the *Ferrini* Case, 16 *EJIL* (2005), 89–112.

[116] Judgment, para. 9, quoted in De Vittor and De Sena, 101; see also Bianchi, Case-note on *Ferrini*, 99 *AJIL* (2005), 244.

[117] De Vittor and De Sena, 101.

[118] Judgment, para. 9.2, quoted in De Vittor and De Sena, 102.

peremptory norm is involved and prevails over an inconsistent norm, this produces the case of *a priori* hierarchy which operates by itself and without any need to clarify whether there is sufficient practice supporting such outcome.

The Greek and Italian decisions consistently affirm that it is not possible to view State immunity as an absolute or free-standing principle, but the principle that operates within the entire context of the international legal system and is consequently subject to important qualifications. The actual or possible criticisms, such as the view of Tomuschat, are therefore unsustainable. In fact, while Tomuschat disagrees with this area of practice, he does not advance any sound or consistent reason based on the scope of State immunity or the hierarchy of norms, apart from reiterating the misconceived difference between the substance and enforcement of peremptory norms.[119] Instead, as Bianchi explains, the argument that State immunity, because of its procedural nature, does not conflict with *jus cogens*, is conceptually flawed because it ignores the fact that immunities are likewise affected and qualified by their limited scope, as well as the general obligation not to recognize acts contrary to peremptory norms.[120]

To conclude, the area of judicial practice which follows the primacy of peremptory norms over the inconsistent claims of State immunity expounds the consistent reasoning regarding the hierarchy of norms and demonstrates in contextual terms the primacy of *jus cogens*. It consistently analyses the factors that cause such primacy: the scope of sovereign immunity and its place within the normative hierarchy. That part of practice which upholds immunity pleas consists mostly of the obedient repetition by courts of each other's reasoning, instead of building up an independent argument. The *Al-Adsani–Bouzari–Jones* thread of judicial decisions has produced a jurisprudence of doubtful quality which is based not only on the misunderstanding of the hierarchy of norms and its implications, but also on serious confusions between international and national law factors and between the concepts of jurisdiction and immunity in determining which immunity pleas are positively supported under international law.

4.3. *Peremptory norms and the immunity of State officials*

The impact of peremptory norms on the immunity of State officials was dealt with in the *Arrest Warrant* case before the International Court involving the immunity pleas on behalf of the incumbent foreign minister, in terms of the relevance of universal jurisdiction over the crimes that were alleged to

---

[119] Tomuschat, L'immunité des états en cas de violations graves des droits de l'homme, *Revue général de droit international public* (2005), 51–74.

[120] Bianchi, case-note on *Ferrini*, 99 *AJIL* (2005), 247.

have been committed. The International Court decided not to examine the issue of universal jurisdiction. But by ignoring the issue of universal jurisdiction, the Court also ignored its legal character and effect.

The Joint Separate Opinion criticized the Court, acknowledging that immunity, providing exception to an otherwise valid jurisdictional title, represents an interest that must always be balanced against the interest of the norm to which it is an exception. Consequently, immunity depends not only upon the status of an official, but also upon the type of jurisdiction.[121] The judges would seem to allow certain types of jurisdiction, depending on their specific basis, to potentially override immunity. They recognized that in exercising universal jurisdiction, States act as agents of the international community and that 'this vertical notion of the authority of action is significantly different from the horizontal system of international law'.[122] But they did not enquire why States act as community agents in such cases and what makes the legal framework vertical rather than horizontal.

The answer must be sought in the factors underlying universal jurisdiction, which is exercised without any territorial or otherwise direct link to the relevant acts. The fact excusing absence of such a link or interest is the nature of the primary norms the violations of which are prosecuted through the exercise of universal jurisdiction. It is established that universal jurisdiction is available over *jus cogens* crimes. States are in some circumstances under a duty to exercise universal jurisdiction through extraditing or prosecuting the accused. In the *Arrest Warrant* case this was affirmed by Judges Van den Wyngaert and Al-Khasawneh, who both emphasized the peremptory character of the duty to prosecute *jus cogens* crimes.[123]

The criteria suggested in the Joint Separate Opinion do not properly appreciate the hierarchy of norms but instead suggest their balancing test: 'On the one scale, we find the interest of the community of mankind to prevent and stop impunity for perpetrators of grave crimes against its members; on the other, there is the interest of the community of States to allow them to act freely on the inter-State level without unwarranted interference.'[124] But this ignores that these two considerations stand at different levels of normative hierarchy in international law. Immunities under international law do not possess the same characteristics as peremptory norms. When the State's immunities are violated, there would be no injured State except that State itself. The interests to be balanced are that of the international community as a whole in punishing war crimes and crimes against

---

[121] Joint Separate Opinion, paras 3, 71.

[122] Id., para. 51.

[123] Dissenting Opinion of Judge Van den Wyngaert, para. 46; Dissenting Opinion of Judge Al-Khasawneh, para. 7; for more extensive treatment of these passages see above, Chapter 9.

[124] Joint Separate Opinion, para. 75.

humanity, and that of individual States in ensuring that their foreign ministers perform their functions.

What would be the impact of the hierarchy of norms in such a normative conflict? The Joint Separate Opinion somewhat unhelpfully contends that international law seeks the accommodation of immunity with the fight against impunity, 'and not the triumph of one norm over the other'.[125] The Opinion ignores, however, the hierarchy of norms, and ends up submitting that 'no exercise of criminal jurisdiction may occur which fails to respect the inviolability or infringes the immunities of the person concerned', categorically subordinating any kind of jurisdiction to any kind of immunities. By contrast, Judge Al-Khasawneh considers that 'when this hierarchically higher norm comes into conflict with the rules on immunity, it should prevail'.[126] Judge Van den Wyngaert also submitted that if war crimes and crimes against humanity offend against *jus cogens*, there would be even greater tension between the 'status of the rules punishing these crimes and the rules protecting suspects on the ground of immunities for incumbent foreign ministers, which are probably not part of *ius cogens*'.[127]

The approach of Judges Al-Khasawneh and Van den Wyngaert differs from the approaches of the majority and other individual judges in that the two judges spoke not only about the conflict between different rules, but about resolving that conflict according to the hierarchy of norms. Had the Court taken the approach of the two judges and duly considered the legal foundation for, and hierarchical position of, universal jurisdiction, it might have reached a different outcome on whether the Congolese foreign minister enjoyed immunity from Belgian jurisdiction.

There is evidence that the exercise of universal jurisdiction on the basis of *jus cogens* prevails over immunities. The authorities opposing the immunity for the perpetrators of international crimes, whether within the International Court or national courts, refer to peremptory norms rather than the mere issue of criminality of the conduct under international law. The *jus cogens* argument is the central factor in practice towards denying immunity, as a matter of general international law, to the perpetrators of serious international crimes.

In *Pinochet*, the majority of Lords supported the hierarchical superiority of *jus cogens* in relation to immunities, although distinguishing between the cases of actual and former heads of State (but without prejudice to the case of an incumbent foreign minister). Lord Hutton affirmed that even in cases where the immunity of the high-level State officials applies and persists, it does not operate if the relevant officials have violated rules that achieved the status of *jus cogens*.[128] As Lord Millett suggested, 'International law cannot

---

[125] Joint Separate Opinion, para. 140.
[126] Dissenting Opinion, para. 7.
[127] Dissenting Opinion, para. 28.
[128] Lord Hutton, *Pinochet*, 2 All ER (1999), 158.

be supposed to have established a crime having a character of *jus cogens* and at the same time to have provided an immunity which is co-extensive with the obligation it seeks to impose.'[129] According to Lord Phillips, torture is outlawed under *jus cogens*, and State immunity cannot coexist with it.[130]

In *Gaddafi*, the Cour de Cassation, having decided the case on other grounds, did not pronounce on the hierarchy of norms and *jus cogens*. The Court of Appeal had affirmed that Heads of State cannot claim immunity for international crimes. The Advocate-General in *Gaddafi* accepted in principle that *jus cogens* norms can prevail over the norms of custom, such as the immunity of heads of State. But he pointed out that France did not recognize *jus cogens*; it did not accede to the 1969 Vienna Convention which defines *jus cogens*. Hence, *jus cogens* cannot produce for France the obligations to prosecute overriding the head of State immunity.[131] It seems that if not these obstacles, the Advocate-General would have affirmed that peremptory norms preclude conflicting immunity in terms of obligations of France, and has indeed implicitly affirmed the same in general, in terms of obligations of other States who recognize *jus cogens*.

The reasoning of the Advocate-General with regard to France's obligations has two aspects to focus upon. First, the Advocate-General's opinion claims the validity of the persistent objection argument against *jus cogens*. Second, his argument implies the claim that the 1969 Vienna Convention is the sole source of *jus cogens*. As examined in the respective places of this book, both of these suggestions are wrong as a matter of principle as well as practice and thus they cannot justify the Advocate-General's position. France is bound by *jus cogens* as any other State is and if the consequential link to the duty to prosecute and primacy over immunity is in principle acknowledged by the Advocate-General, the consequences must be construed accordingly.

In addition, the ILC's Draft Code on Crimes against Peace and Security of Mankind, while laying down rules about jurisdiction of national courts with regard to prosecution of war crimes and crimes against humanity and the irrelevance of the official position of an accused, whether head of State or other official,[132] evidences the requirements of specific peremptory norms in terms of prosecution of a *jus cogens* crime.

Whether liked or not, the impact of *jus cogens* is, in principle, indiscriminate in its effects, and may trump immunity of incumbent officials in the same way as that of former officials. But there can be factors that keep this effect within its proper limits, thus avoiding the undue harassment of

---

[129] Lord Millett, *Pinochet*, 2 All ER (1999), 179.
[130] Lord Phillips, *Pinochet*, 2 All ER (1999), 189–190.
[131] *Gaddafi* (Opinion of the Advocate-General), 125 ILR 507.
[132] Draft Code, Articles 7–8. As the commentary to Article 7 suggests, it excludes any immunity.

serving heads of State and foreign ministers. This can happen either by considering the immunity *ratione personae* of heads of State and government as merely temporary exemption from prosecution, as the International Court has done, or by considering the immunities *ratione personae* lifted only when the relevant official enters the forum State's territory.[133] While both options are conceptually viable, it remains far from assured that they are, or will be, accepted in international law. The factors preventing them from being so accepted are related to the hierarchical factor of the supremacy of *jus cogens*, and the normative factor requiring the proof that State immunity, in whichever shape or scope, is affirmatively regulated in international law.

4.4. *Immunity from execution*

In *Al-Adsani*, Judges Pellonpää and Bratza contend that if the claims based on peremptory norms are allowed to proceed against the claims of State immunity, then they will prevail not only over immunity from jurisdiction but also 'over rules concerning immunity from execution', including immunity of bank accounts intended for public purposes, real estate used by cultural institutes and perhaps even of embassy buildings.[134] It seems that such fears are based on artificial concerns and misconceptions. The execution measures against the State property situated abroad are part of international practice and occur frequently. It is a general practice that while national courts allow execution against the property of foreign States, they will not allow this with regard to public property such as the bank accounts of diplomatic missions, while property used for commercial purposes is not immune from enforcement.[135] Whether such measures of execution are taken pursuant to *jus cogens* claims or to anything else is not crucial.

In addition, the immunity from execution, like immunity from jurisdiction, is based on the distinction between sovereign and non-sovereign, that is private and commercial, acts of States. The first category of assets is immune, while the second category is not.[136] There are also what Brownlie denotes as considerations of principle emphasizing the consequential link between adjudicatory jurisdiction and enforcement jurisdiction: if the former can be exercised, then the latter can be exercised as well.[137]

Nevertheless, there is a conceptual difference between immunity from jurisdiction and immunity from execution in terms of their subject-matter.

---

[133] In accordance with the ILC's Commentary to Article 9 of the Draft Code, pointing to the 'unique position' of the territorial State in prosecuting the relevant crimes.

[134] Concurring Opinion of Judges Pellonpää and Bratza, 34 EHRR 11 (2002), 295–297; see also de Wet (2004), 109–110.

[135] Cassese, *International Law* (2005), 109–110; Brownlie, *Principles* (2003), 339.

[136] Cassese, *International Law* (2005), 109.

[137] Brownlie, *Principles* (2003), 338.

The former relates to the types of conduct over which jurisdiction can be exercised; the latter relates to the types of property and assets which can be covered by domestic enforcement measures. The fact that immunity from jurisdiction is not available for breaches of peremptory norms because they hierarchically prevail over State immunity does not entail that the property or assets used strictly for sovereign purposes shall be subject to execution. The primacy of *jus cogens* over immunities ensures the absence of impunity through the exercise of jurisdiction over the foreign State. This goal simply does not require affecting the inviolability of assets used strictly for sovereign purposes such as embassy funds or buildings, or other similar assets. Upholding the immunity from jurisdiction for breaches of peremptory norms entails the recognition of these breaches as sovereign acts and contradicts their nullity, thus giving rise to an impermissible normative conflict, while upholding the immunity of the assets used for strictly sovereign purposes does not entail such recognition and entails no normative conflict. Thus, the otherwise applicable standards and practice of execution are relevant also in the case of breaches of *jus cogens*.

5. CONCLUSION

The impact of peremptory norms on immunities is designed to avoid impunity for breaches of these norms. It is sometimes asserted, among others by the International Court in *Arrest Warrant*, that immunity is not tantamount to impunity. But this depends on circumstances. The outcome of *Arrest Warrant* can be open to criticism in various ways, but the International Court, while upholding the incumbent foreign minister's immunity, did so on clearly defined terms and also enumerated alternative possibilities through which a State official accused of international crimes may be prosecuted. This solution postpones, on the basis of functional immunity *ratione personae*, the enforcement of a peremptory norm until the person accused of an international crime retires from office. The impact of peremptory norms on immunities of individual State officials in criminal and civil proceedings seems to be respected, in terms of the context of the relevant cases, in *Pinochet* and in *Jones*.

The situation is different in cases which uphold the immunity of States. Although it is suggested that granting immunity is not the same as impunity because 'the former is a procedural matter while the latter is a substantive one',[138] the reality proves exactly the opposite because individuals who face the hurdle of State immunity have no other option to vindicate their rights. The European Court in *Al-Adsani*, and the Canadian and English courts in

---

[138] Yang (2003), 343.

Bouzari and *Jones*, not only portrayed the immunity of a State as a blanket principle but also ignored the basics of normative hierarchy. The reasoning in *Al-Adsani* and *Bouzari* based on the reluctance to acknowledge the overriding effects of peremptory norms results in the affirmation of impunity for torture. The facts and reasoning in both cases affirm this. The European Court had ascertained that Al-Adsani would get no remedy in Kuwait, while Canadian courts acknowledged that Bouzari would get no remedies in Iran and positively affirmed this in their judgments. Therefore, the affirmation of immunity in the case of breaches of peremptory norms necessarily leads to impunity, and sends the message to the State that has perpetrated the relevant violation reassuring that it will not face legal responsibility for that violation.

The line of reasoning that immunity is not affected by the *jus cogens* character of the relevant breaches because it affects only the norm's enforcement before domestic courts, not its substance, suffers from inherent inconsistency, leaving open the question why the same substance-enforcement distinction does not apply to civil proceedings against State officials or to criminal prosecutions. Every healthy debate on these issues needs to concentrate on the issues of hierarchy proper, acknowledge the difference between national and international legal positions, and, above all, refrain from spreading the panic that floods of litigation are likely if courts follow the primacy of *jus cogens* over immunities.

Practice continues to witness the adherence to the substance-enforcement dichotomy in some situations and its rejection in other situations. This conceptual controversy can only be resolved either through final and conclusive recognition in practice of the primacy of peremptory norms over immunities, or the definite end of the movement towards the practical implementation of the principle that no immunity is available for the breaches of *jus cogens*. Whatever the present position, the latter option is certainly less likely to materialize than the former one.

11

Problems of Subsequent Validation
of Breaches of *Jus Cogens*

I. GENERAL ASPECTS

1.1. The concept of subsequent validation and its applicability to jus cogens

The issue of subsequent validation of violations of *jus cogens* relates to the alleged contrast between the peremptory nature of norms and the decentralized nature of the international community. How, it may be asked, can international law steadfastly refuse to admit any derogation from certain norms when international law-applying processes are so diffuse and decentralized? This issue tests the nature of *jus cogens* rights, such as individual rights, and their disposability by States.

There is no uniform concept of subsequent validation of violations of peremptory norms, nor has there been any thorough comparative analysis of the concepts belonging to this field in terms of public order. The subject overlaps with the effect of *jus cogens* on treaty invalidity and interpretation, unilateral acts and actions, and customary law. What is examined here is the group of acts or actions with the common feature that they purport to validate breaches of *jus cogens*.

The relevance of validation devices in the realm of *jus cogens* requires clarification in a number of dimensions. The first of these is the relationship between the validation of illegality before and after breach. It could be asked, provided that a State can excuse illegality through consent, why it cannot subsequently cure illegality. What comes to mind is the use of force on a State's territory with its consent. A State may consent to the deployment or use of foreign armed forces on its territory. That would not necessarily involve a breach of *jus cogens* in the first place as the action on the basis of valid consent would not be the use of force against a State's territorial integrity and political independence under Article 2(4) of the UN Charter but by reason of the consent given would involve an exercise of that sovereignty and independence. There would only be a breach of *jus cogens* if a State were to abandon in advance its right to decide whether foreign armed forces can be deployed on its territory and hence enable another State to perform that action without the territorial State's consent.[1] This distinction is further

---

[1] Crawford, Second Report, A/CN.4/498/Add.2, 14; Gaja, *Jus Cogens* beyond the Vienna Convention, 172 *RdC* (1981), 295; Roth, The illegality of 'pro-democratic' invasion pacts, in Fox

highlighted by the context of the law of State responsibility where the consent given prior to the performance of the act, that is the consent proper, is the issue of circumstances precluding wrongfulness, while the 'consent' given afterwards is really the issue of subsequent validation, conceivably of waiver.[2] The situation in which no wrongful act has been committed is conceptually different from that in which such act is committed, and cannot determine its effects.

There are therefore different types of consent in terms of their compatibility with peremptory norms. There is no general standard that breaches of peremptory norms can be excused before their commission, and this has implications for the question whether they can be excused after their commission. *Jus ad bellum* is clear that while a State can consent to the use of force on its territory, its consent is valid only if consistent with a relevant peremptory norm.

The next dimension focuses on whether, provided that the prior validation of a breach is excluded, one or several States can excuse a breach of a norm protecting the community interest and generating objective illegality, for example in the context of a settlement of the underlying dispute. There is no clear rule or principle that what is not permitted in terms of public order before a breach is permitted after it.[3] Such an approach would be a mere presumption and would leave unanswered a crucial question: why the opposite is not true; why cannot peremptory norms have their effect in one area while they can have it in another. The preferable approach is that peremptory norms have effect with regard to conflicting acts regardless of the time factor. This approach can be consolidated by examining the effects of *jus cogens* on specific validation devices, and asking whether they can override the effects of *jus cogens*.

The third dimension relates to a purported *ex post* validation by the international community of States as a whole. Since this community, on terms defined in Article 53 of the Vienna Convention, creates and modifies peremptory norms, it is worth enquiring whether it can excuse a specific breach of *jus cogens* while maintaining the rule itself.

Some scepticism may be expressed as to the nature of validation devices in general. According to Judge Spender, the concepts of acquiescence, estoppel and recognition are not legal principles, but just 'factual situations to which

---

and Roth (eds), *Democratic Governance and International Law* (2000), 342. This issue is also relevant in terms of the voidness of treaties authorizing forcible action, above Chapter 6, section 3.

[2] Lowe, Precluding Wrongfulness or Responsibility: A Plea of Excuses, 10 *EJIL* (1999), 407.

[3] As long as the given peremptory norm continues in force—one must distinguish between validation of a breach of the peremptory norm and modification of the norm in terms of Article 53 of the Vienna Convention.

certain general principles of international law may apply and in so doing operate so as to affect legal rights and obligations as between States'; they may also be 'the reasons which underlie certain legal principles and rules'.[4] Such an approach may seem an exaggeration to those treating validation doctrines as clear legal principles. But there is nevertheless some merit in Judge Spender's view, which demonstrates that validation devices must be seen not in a vacuum, as self-contained concepts, but within the overarching legal context. The best way to reconcile conflicting approaches is to consider that validation devices are perhaps recognized in international law, but that they are subordinated, in both their nature and their effects, to the governing legal framework, and that it is the latter which is determinative.

Since the law of treaties excludes subsequent validation with regard to treaties offending against *jus cogens*, and since these treaties are invalid because *jus cogens* absolutely forbids, outlaws and invalidates the acts they justify, it would be a logical consequence that subsequent validation should also be excluded in the case of non-treaty acts offending against peremptory norms.

Fitzmaurice treats validation as a matter of the rights and responses of directly involved States, but emphasizes that 'overriding rules of *jus cogens* produce a situation of irreducible obligation and demand that illegal actions be ignored or not allowed to affect the obligations of other States'. In such cases, the validation of illegality does not really occur.[5] As Brownlie states, it is plausible that certain illegal activities can best be settled on a bilateral basis, but this principle does not extend to situations governed by *jus cogens*.[6] According to Hannikainen, the *jus cogens* invalidity 'is incurable in character. A treaty or title does not become valid in the course of the time but its invalidity can be invoked at any time, even decades later.'[7]

Jus cogens applies and invalidates unilateral acts and other actions of States involving manifestation of will contrary to *jus cogens*. Validation devices fall, by their nature, within the category of such acts and actions, and are subject to normal conditions of validity. It is therefore unwarranted to hold that they are immune from the effect of superior norms.[8]

---

[4] Dissenting Opinion, *Temple, ICJ Reports*, 1962, 143.

[5] Fitzmaurice, The general principles of international law considered from the standpoint of the rule of law, 92 *Recueil des cours* (1957), 119–122.

[6] cf Brownlie, *Principles* (2003), 63, 67, 85–86, 615.

[7] Hannikainen, The case of East Timor from the perspective of jus cogens, *International Law and the Question of East Timor* (1995), 105.

[8] See, eg, Rodriguez-Cedeno, *Sixth Report on Unilateral Acts*, A/CN.4/534, 20, recognizing that the conditions of validity applicable to legal acts in general, and particularly conditions stated in the 1969 Vienna Convention, apply fully to acts of recognition. Also Pfluger, *Die Einseitigen Rechtsgeschäfte im Völkerrecht* (1936), 138, Suy, *Les actes juridiques unilateraux* (1962), 196, define validation devices such as recognition in terms of acts of States in general.

1.2. Conceptual basis

The conceptual basis of validation devices relates to the principle of effectiveness, which has undergone serious doctrinal and practical transformation. The principal impact of the reasoning putting emphasis on effectiveness is to view legal phenomena in terms of relativity and consequently deny the existence of any firm line separating legality from illegality, or any principle preventing the transformation of the latter into the former.

The relativist pattern of thinking of the legally relevant changes to some extent based on the concept of effectiveness has to do with the pattern that dominated the process of territorial changes in and around the nineteenth century. In that period, territorial changes were considered as a matter to be resolved between the interested States. Any centralized power over States absent, everything depended on their claims and responses. Even if in many, if not most, cases no final reconciliation of those claims, protests and responses would take place, the controversies would allegedly be cured and resolved with the passage of time. In other words, where express validation has not been granted, implicit and tacit validation was presumed to have taken place. Factual situations would succeed in bringing about legal changes. While this was predominantly, though not exclusively, part of the political process, international lawyers also tended to view the legal developments as derived from and subjected to the overriding norm-creating force of facts and hence explained by the principle of effectiveness some developments that would not have been explainable otherwise. In other words, the principle of effectiveness has been the factor that somehow conflicted with the positivist conception of international law dictating that the creation and change of norms and legal relations in the international system depends solely on the expression of the will of States.

If one tends not to see this matter as the mutual contradiction of principles, it would be possible to view the process of operation of effectiveness as involving the implicit expression of State will. But this position would not be perfectly correct as several territorial changes took place without the consent of the relevant States and international lawyers tended to accept these changes as conclusive regardless.

Be that as it may, the nineteenth century witnessed a constant process of territorial modifications. The inclusion of Krakow in the Austrian Empire was challenged, but then allegedly acquiesced to. The neutralization of the Black Sea, which was based on the 1856 Paris Treaty, was abrogated by Russia, to which the Western Powers did not fail to protest, though later they acquiesced to this new situation through the 1871 London Treaty. The settlement that was solemnly proclaimed at the 1878 Berlin Conference was not free from such subsequent developments either. Contrary to the terms of the Berlin Treaty, Britain proclaimed the protectorate over Egypt, and France did the same with regard to Tunisia, while Russia abolished the free port status of Batumi, and Austria in 1908 annexed Bosnia, which had hitherto been its protectorate pursuant to the Berlin Treaty. The most usual follow-up to those steps were protests and disapprovals, but in most cases the subsequent acceptance would end the matters of controversy.

While evaluating this process it is also material that the means through which legal changes were brought about were not considered illegal in the first place. In some cases, moreover, the original settlements that were breached or abrogated subsequently were not considered fair and equitable enough to command the right for long-term, still less permanent, existence.[9] Alternatively, writers such as Lorimer relied on the cultural and racial superiority of European nations to justify their annexation or otherwise of the non-European States by reference to the principle of effectiveness. Lorimer suggested that 'Barbary States' such as Algeria were burdened by their criminal intention and the act of their annexation, performed in this case by France, was 'an act of discipline which the bystander was entitled to exercise in the absence of police'. If a European State annexed a non-European State, then 'Law follows fact very closely, and a very short prescription will give an international title'.[10]

Thus, the relativist pattern of validation was linked to, indeed originated from, the absence of a clear regulation of the relevant illegalities, and to some extent was based on prejudicial attitudes. In the twentieth century, however, normative developments have brought about a qualitatively different framework of the norms that operate in an absolute way and their violations produce objective illegality independent of the individual attitudes of States, and give rise to nullity. This position was inaugurated with the adoption of the League of Nations Covenant and the 1928 Paris Pact on the Renunciation of War, and further developed with the emergence of the cluster of treaty and customary norms on *jus ad bellum*, self-determination, human rights and humanitarian law that possess peremptory status. These developments, as originally evidenced by the Stimson Doctrine, require abandoning the relativist pattern of legal changes, the pattern which emerged and operated in the substantially different system of international law. The

---

[9] Brierly, *The Law of Nations* (1949), 243, defends the Russian decision to abrogate the commitments regarding the neutralization of the Black Sea. While Brierly notes that claims could have arisen on both sides, he quotes the following passage of John Stuart Mill to show that the Russian action was justified: 'If a lawless act has been committed in the present instance, it does not entitle those who imposed the conditions to consider the lawlessness only, and to dismiss the more important consideration whether, even if it was wrong to throw off the obligation, it would still not be more wrong to persist in enforcing it. If, though not fit to be perpetual, it has been imposed in perpetuity, the question when it becomes right to throw it off is but a question of time. No time being fixed, Russia fixed her own time, and naturally chose the most convenient.' J.S. Mill further emphasized that nations 'should abstain from imposing conditions which, on any just and reasonable view of human affairs, cannot be expected to be kept.'

[10] Lorimer, *The Institutes of the Law of Nations*, vol. I (1883), 161.

principal feature of the norms of present public order is that they imperatively separate legality from illegality, which is something that nineteenth century international law never did.

In practical terms too, the relativist pattern developed in the nineteenth century has not proved conducive to general peace and stability in international relations, as this very pattern culminated in the outbreak of two World Wars. This experience demonstrates that a stricter approach and framework is required when the continued operation of fundamental international norms is at stake.

The doctrinal essence, and internal consistency, of the relativist views of effectiveness is a separate issue. W.E. Hall developed his view of effectiveness by taking as his example the case of territorial title by prescription, stating that prescription serves not the interest of a lawful owner but 'stability of international order which is of more practical advantage than the bare possibility of an ultimate victory of right'.[11] The law can 'lend itself as a sanction for wrong, when wrong has shown itself strong enough not only to triumph for a moment, but to establish itself permanently and solidly'.[12] Therefore, Hall submitted, prescription must be effective not only with regard to lawful settlements,

but also to give title where an immoral act of appropriation, such as that of the partition of Poland, has been effected, so soon as it has become evident by lapse of time that the appropriation promises to be permanent, in the qualified sense which the word permanent can bear in international matters, and that other States acquiesce in the prospect of such permanence.[13]

Hall went on, however, to point out that the title thus acquired was not necessarily good for the inhabitants of the territory, who may even have to free themselves from a foreign yoke. But, this liberal proviso notwithstanding, he held it to be good internationally, so that neither the wronged State nor other States have the right to attack such a title.[14]

To begin with, Hall's views are incoherent, as he had previously recognized that treaties with an immoral object are void.[15] It is difficult to reconcile this with the view just quoted, especially if the outcome of prescription he considers permissible can also be achieved by treaty.

Hall's view assumes that the rights gained through effectiveness can be opposable to the wronged State without its having accepted that effectiveness through its conduct or attitude and this in fact asserts that effectiveness can operate without establishing estoppel, which, as we shall see throughout the analysis following, is wrong.

Hall's view resembles the Hobbesian view of law, as it does not distinguish between the lawful and the unlawful in defining what is safeguarded by the

---

[11] Hall, *A Treatise on International Law* (1924), 143.
[12] Id.   [13] Id., 143–144.   [14] Id., 144.   [15] Id., 405.

law. The difference from Hobbes is that, by reference to the anarchical nature of the international society dominated by power, Hobbes denied that the law of nations could exist, while Hall tries to sell lawlessness as law. Furthermore, Hall's analysis is outdated as, when it was made, international law knew no actual limitation on the freedom of States in terms of say, the prohibition of force, still less its peremptory status. The evolution of law has modified the very concept of effectiveness and its effects and made the blanket view of effectiveness irrelevant.

Another, and similar, view of effectiveness is developed by Guggenheim, consistently with his refusal to accept the relevance of peremptory norms in international law. Guggenheim admits the validation on the basis of effective operation of acts that are subject to non-recognition, suggesting that social reality admits of no permanent separation between validity and effectiveness. Validity of the norm should correspond to its effectiveness and its nullity to its ineffectiveness. Therefore, the *fait accompli* of the annexation of the State against its will can be transformed into the lawful situation.[16]

Subsequent views of effectiveness acknowledge the law-creating force of facts, and accept, to some extent, the possibility of transformation of an illegality into legality. But this approach is not a blanket one. It not only refers to the decentralized nature of international law, but also on some specific developments in jurisprudence, such as the principles upheld in *Anglo-Norwegian Fisheries*. The authors supporting such a view of effectiveness do not place it above the law, still less reveal an intention to consider it as superior to public order considerations. This is the view of effectiveness derived from the law and placed within the context of the normal patterns of international law-making, which involves not only the factual background of the situation but also the element of will as the psychological element.

According to Visscher and Jennings, effectiveness compensates for the absence of centralized international law-enforcement.[17] But that principle is not unqualified. Lauterpacht acknowledges that facts have a law-creating influence. However, 'unless law is to become a convenient code for malefactors', it must be recognized that 'the legal effectiveness and validity of its obligations are unaffected by individual acts of lawlessness'.[18] Furthermore, 'It is one thing to say that law is ultimately based on the facts of life and that it is a body of rules established by a system of force; it is another thing to say that breaches of the law, if they are repeated and remain unpunished, become

---

[16] Guggenheim, La validité et la nullité des actes juridiques internationaux, *RdC* (I-1949), 231. Hence Guggenheim's views as to the legality and validity of puppet States in Croatia, Slovakia, and the Italian annexation of Abyssinia.

[17] Visscher, *Les effectivités du droit international public* (1967), 20; Jennings, *The Acquisition of Territory in International Law* (1967), 65, 67.

[18] Lauterpacht, *Collected Papers* (1970), 342.

part of the legal order.'[19] This approach makes a clear distinction between effectiveness in terms of facts and illegality.[20]

Lauterpacht, while bearing in mind the absence of centralizsed law-enforcement, considers that the law of invalidity is even more important to uphold the law. Lauterpacht acknowledged the absence of centralized law-enforcement, but also sought alternatives to it, such as the law of invalidity and the principle of non-recognition.[21]

If conflicting categories are to be reconciled, the relevance of invalidity and recognition as public order devices would qualify a more general principle of effectiveness. In fact, there is no inherent conflict between the maxims *ex factis jus oritur* and *ex injuria jus non oritur*, as the maxim that facts can generate law does not necessarily mean that every kind of illegality can be a source of rights in every kind of situation.

Lauterpacht's view best reconciles conflicting assumptions in terms of the decentralized character of the international community. International law accepts this approach. The concept of effectiveness has witnessed a heavy transformation, given especially that the blanket view of effectiveness mainly has to do with doctrinal conjectures based on the denial of the role of nullity and public order. Effectiveness is placed within and not above the law. To illustrate, the judgment of the International Court in *Cameroon–Nigeria* has assigned a rather qualified role to the principle of effectiveness.[22]

1.3. Overlapping relevance of specific validation devices

Validation devices—recognition, waiver, acquiescence and prescription—overlap in their character and effects. While each concept is arguably independent, in practice its operation can be intertwined with that of another concept.[23]

Some similarity between the concepts of acquiescence and estoppel has been noted.[24] In *Gulf of Maine*, Canada submitted that estoppel is an *alter ego* of acquiescence. The Court itself found no estoppel because there was no acquiescence imputable to either party. The same facts were relevant both for acquiescence and estoppel.[25] Earlier, Judge Ammoun characterized acquiescence as estoppel by conduct.[26] As Judge Fitzmaurice noted, 'acquiescence

---

[19] Lauterpacht (1970), 342.

[20] Without prejudice to Lauterpacht's views on recognition examined below. For a more cautious view see Dinstein, *War, Aggression and Self-Defence* (2001), 155.

[21] Lauterpacht, *Recognition in International Law* (1947), 418.

[22] Judgment, paras 211–223; reviewed by Orakhelashvili, *CLJ* 2003, 9–12.

[23] cf Judge Spender, *ICJ Reports*, 1962, 131.

[24] Spender, Dissenting Opinion, *ICJ Reports*, 1962, 137, 162.

[25] *ICJ Reports*, 1982, 304 ff.

[26] *ICJ Reports*, 1969, 120–121. See also Judge Urrutia in *King of Spain, ICJ Reports*, 1960, 222; Swiss Federal Tribunal in *Valais v Tessin*, 118–119.

can operate as a preclusion or estoppel in certain cases, for instance where silence, on an occasion where there was a duty or need to speak or act, implies agreement, or a waiver of rights.'[27]

As Brownlie notes, acquiescence has the same effect as recognition,[28] and F.A. Mann considers that acquiescence can amount to waiver.[29] McNair holds that recognition of a title is akin to estoppel, while a refusal of recognition is akin to a protest.[30] Schwarzenberger suggests that estoppel is present in several validation devices, such as waiver, recognition and prescription, whether extinctive or acquisitive.[31]

Different validation devices are conceptually similar because they are all based on the principle of good faith. The Swiss Federal Tribunal affirmed that point as between estoppel and acquiescence.[32] The International Court affirmed this with regard to both devices in *Gulf of Maine*.[33]

A further common feature of validation devices is that they operate in a bilateralist context. The concept of validation is essentially bilateralist, as evidenced in *Island of Palmas*, *King of Spain*, *Anglo-Norwegian Fisheries*, or *Temple*. The Court in *Gulf of Maine*, after having concluded that the 1958 Convention on Continental Shelf did not apply to the case, had to ascertain 'whether, *as between the parties*, any other factors intervened which might, independently of any formal act creating rules or instituting relations under special international law, nevertheless give rise to an obligation of this kind'.[34] Jurisprudence treats validation devices as tools of establishing *inter se* relations when such relations are in principle permissible and does not suggest that validation devices can cure illegalities offending against the community interest involving *jus cogens*.

In terms of both the general nature of validation devices and their subjection to *jus cogens*, it is important to note that they also share their character with general law-making devices. Most notably, Judge Sorensen has noted

[27] Separate Opinion of Judge Fitzmaurice, *ICJ Reports*, 1962, 62. Judge Ajibola also found estoppel on the basis of Libya's acquiescence in *Territorial Dispute, ICJ Reports*, 1994, 81–83. 1 Schwarzenberger (1957), 565 sees acquiescence as a waiver of claim. Elias, *Modern Law of Treaties*, 411; McNair (1961), 485.

[28] Brownlie, *Principles* (2003), 151; Brownlie, Recognition in Theory and Practice, 53 *BYIL* (1982), 201.

[29] Mann, Reflection on the Prosecution of Persons Abducted in Breach of International Law, in Y. Dinstein and M. Tabory (eds), *International Law at a Time of Perplexity. Essays in Honour of Shabtai Rosenne* (1989), 409.

[30] McNair, The Stimson Doctrine of Non-Recognition, *BYIL* (1933), 67. This view is widely shared: Judge Ajibola in *Territorial Dispute*, stating that 'recognition is also considered as an aspect of estoppel'. *ICJ Reports*, 1994, 78; McGibbon, Estoppel in International Law, 7 *ICLQ* (1958), 473; Suy (1962), 208.

[31] Schwarzenberger, Title to Territory: Response to a Challenge, 51 *AJIL* (1957), 51–52; 1 Schwarzenberger, *International Law* (1957), 299–300, 535.

[32] *Valais v Tessin*, 118–119.

[33] *ICJ Reports*, 1982, 309.   [34] *ICJ Reports*, 1982, 303 (emphasis added).

that acquiescence is related to custom-formation.[35] As validation devices give rise to new law *inter partes*, they hence derogate from otherwise applicable general law. This fact, in conjunction with the interdependent overlap between the concepts of specific validation devices, logically dictates that if one device is subject to *jus cogens* due to its nature and effect, the presence of some of its elements in another device naturally raises the question whether the latter itself is, for the same reason, qualified by *jus cogens*.

1.4. The concept of estoppel

Before examining specific validation devices, it is worth pausing over the concept of estoppel, as it is consequential upon all validation devices: a State to which a statement or conduct validating an action or situation is imputable is estopped from disputing such action or situation. Conversely, if *jus cogens* applies to estoppel, then a State is entitled to challenge certain situations even despite its previous statement or conduct.

One of the most classical applications of the principle of estoppel took place in the *Temple* case, where the International Court ruled that sovereignty over the temple of Preah Vihear belonged to Cambodia, due to the attitude inferable from the conduct of Thailand in relation to the relevant map of the area that has been used in bilateral communications.[36] Judge Alfaro in *Temple* referred to a generally accepted principle that 'a State-party to an international litigation is bound by its previous acts or attitude when they are in contradiction with its claims in the litigation'. A State must not benefit from its own inconsistency.[37] As Cheng, McGibbon and Dominice demonstrate, estoppel is applied in practice to a wide variety of situations.[38]

It is thus suggested that estoppel as a principle has no coherence in international law, its incidence and effects not being uniform.[39] According to Judge Ajibola, estoppel is a developing principle and it may be difficult to classify.[40] Estoppel can bind a State to what does not amount to its intention. This concept, understood in such a way, should be treated with caution,

---

[35] Sorensen, *ICJ Reports*, 1969, 248; see below, note 233, on the primacy of *jus cogens* over custom.

[36] *Temple of Preah Vihear*, Merits, Judgment 15 June 1962, *ICJ Reports*, 1962, 6.

[37] *ICJ Reports*, 1962, 39, 40; See also *Argentine–Chile Frontier*, Award of 24 November 1966, 38 ILR 77, reiterating the same principle by reference to Judge Alfaro. In the specific context of the ECHR case-law on preliminary objections estoppel is almost routinely applied.

[38] Bin Cheng (1953), 141–149; McGibbon (1958), 471 ff.; Dominice, A propos du principe de l'estoppel en droit des gens, *Recueil d'études de droit international en hommage à Paul Guggenheim* (1968), 327.

[39] Brownlie, *Principles* (2003), 616. In *Gulf of Maine*, Canada acknowledged that the doctrine of estoppel was 'still developing', *ICJ Reports*, 1982, 131

[40] *ICJ Reports*, 1994, 77

especially with regard to territorial disputes.[41] But estoppel in terms of recognition, waiver and acquiescence is always based on the clear (whether explicit or implicit) intention of a State.

Estoppel has been defined by the Swiss Federal Tribunal as follows:

Estoppel is created where a party, in reliance on assurances or conduct implying intention on the part of another party, has been induced to perform acts which have a legal significance and which will be prejudicial to that party if the other party were subsequently allowed to retract. The characteristic effect of estoppel is that, where the conditions mentioned above are fulfilled, the subsequent attitude of the other party cannot be taken into consideration, regardless of whether that attitude is justified or not.[42]

The requirement that a State cannot take an attitude conflicting with its earlier attitude on which other State(s) relied characterizes estoppel, but also waiver, acquiescence, prescription and recognition.

Thirlway considers estoppel not as an expression of consent but as the absence of consent.[43] Judges Spender and Wellington Koo in *Temple* required the element of detriment and advantage for an estoppel to be there.[44] Both judges disagreed with the Court as the latter found that Thailand was estopped from contesting the boundary with Cambodia due to long acquiescence by the former. Judge Fitzmaurice has supported the strict view of estoppel, but recognized that it is not often employed in practice.[45] Similarly, Thirlway recognizes that the strict approach is not adhered to in practice.[46] *Temple* involved initial acquiescence and consequent estoppel.[47] In addition, the factor of 'reliance upon' the statement or conduct of a State, expounded by Fitzmaurice,[48] is inherently present in all other validation devices.

At a conceptual level, it is arguable that the elements of detriment and

---

[41] Brownlie (2003), 152; as the International Court pointed out, 'It is apparently in the Judgment in the *North Sea Continental Shelf* cases that gave the most precise definition of the conditions for invoking the doctrine of estoppel; but even disregarding the element of detriment or prejudice caused by a State's change of attitude, which distinguishes estoppel *stricto sensu* from acquiescence, it never presupposes clear and consistent acceptance,' *Gulf of Maine, ICJ Reports*, 1982, 309; see also *ICJ Reports*, 1969, 26.

[42] Swiss Federal Tribunal, *Canton of Valais v Canton of Tessin*, 75 ILR 119–120.

[43] Thirlway (1989), 45–46.

[44] In their Dissenting Opnions, *ICJ Reports*, 1962, 94, para. 47 (Wellington Koo), and 144 (Spender).

[45] *ICJ Reports*, 1962, 63; Judge Spender, *ICJ Reports*, 1962, 144.

[46] Thirlway, The Law and Procedure of the International Court of Justice, *BYIL* (1989), 45, refers to the *Gulf of Maine* pronouncement (305) and concedes that even where estoppel is pleaded, in fact the acquiescence or conduct was sought to be established. He refers to a theoretical difference between the two concepts which has not manifested itself in practice during the last few decades.

[47] Thirlway (1989), 46.

[48] *ICJ Reports*, 1962, 63; the strict requirement of representation and detriment is mirrored in *El Salvador/Honduras, ICJ Reports*, 1990, 92.

advantage are just circumstances leading to estoppel, not its effect on legal relations *inter partes* once it is clarified that estoppel is there. Therefore, it is arguable that estoppel is a consequential principle, dictating that a State cannot change an attitude previously expressed which another State relied on and benefited from. Unless this approach is adopted, the establishment of the precise content of the principle will be difficult for the very reason that it is applied in radically different situations.

A general feature of different situations involving estoppel is that a previous concordance of the wills of two or more States cannot subsequently be undermined by a State which has been part of such concordance. Estoppel can follow from recognition, acquiescence and waiver, and form another side of the coin in relation to them: once a State has exercised a valid recognition, waiver or acquiescence, it is estopped from contesting the situation thus established. In some cases estoppel by acquiescence is found, in others it is not, but all is determined primarily not by factors like detriment and prejudice, but by formal and normative requirements such as conduct by an authorized subject and duration.

If the Court was correct that estoppel by acquiescence was inferable in *Temple*, the merit in Judge Spender's view is unclear, as even if, under the strict application of the concept, estoppel was not to be found in the case, this would hardly affect the outcome, because acquiescence would operate by itself and bring about the same effect as estoppel normally does. On the other hand, if the strict view of estoppel is correct, then the legal effect of different validation devices, which is similar to that of estoppel, should be summarized under some other name, or considered as ramifications of a broader principle of good faith.

Estoppel is not easily found in jurisprudence and its use is more exceptional than usual. The reluctance of the International Court to refer to the principle of estoppel or related doctrines must be noted. In *Tunisia–Libya*, the Court stated:

It should be made clear that the Court is not here making a finding of tacit agreement between the parties—which, in view of their more extensive and firmly maintained claims, would not be possible—nor is it holding that they are debarred by conduct from pressing claims inconsistent with such conduct on some such basis as estoppel.[49]

It has to be the government's conduct or inaction to amount to estoppel, as expounded in *Barcelona Traction*.[50] But in some legal relations, where the traditional diplomatic protection model does not apply exclusively, it is

---

[49] *Tunisia-Libya, ICJ Reports*, 1982, 84; In *Gulf of Maine* the Court also found no estoppel, *ICJ Reports*, 1982. See also *Nicaragua, ICJ Reports*, 1984, 414–415; The Arbitral Tribunal decided not to address estoppel in *Guinea/Guinea-Bissau*, 77 ILR 669.

[50] *ICJ Reports*, 1964, 24.

non-State actors who are protected and whose positions cannot be prejudiced by the States concerned.

Not least for this reason, estoppel is a concept most conveniently shaped to operate in the field of bilateral relations. Judge Alfaro underlined that, referring to 'necessity for security in contractual relationships' and 'harmonious and undisturbed exercise of the rights of each party and faithful discharge of contractual obligations'.[51] It is clear that the concept protects individual State interests only.

The effect and operation of estoppel seems to be subject to the principles which govern treaty validity: duress, error, or fraud.[52] This naturally provokes the question whether estoppel is also subject to *jus cogens*. In English law, estoppel is not invocable to legitimize an illegal act.[53] If, within a legal system, agreements against public order norms are void, then it is possible to regard a representation serving as a basis for estoppel as void. The very existence of *jus cogens* means that an international tribunal should reject an estoppel based on or involving a breach of *jus cogens*.[54]

2. THE IMPACT OF *JUS COGENS* ON SPECIFIC VALIDATION DEVICES

2.1. Recognition

2.1.1. The impact of peremptory norms on the validity of recognition

Recognition is a device used not just for the recognition of States and governments, but also with regard to any situation involving legally relevant change without any limitation in terms of subject-matter.[55]

Recognition is a manifestation of the will of a State, whereby it considers that a given situation is legitimate.[56] Recognition is relevant if the legality of a title or situation is doubted.[57] If so, then as a validation device, recognition is constitutive rather than declaratory (although recognition of States is generally declaratory). The constitutive theory, as generally applied to the recognition of States, is conceptually incompatible with the notion of *jus cogens*. When statehood is established on the basis of a peremptory norm, as in the case of lawful exercise of the right to self-determination, it becomes

---

[51] Separate Opinion of Vice-President Alfaro, *Temple, ICJ Rep*, 1962, 42.

[52] Cheng, *General Principles of Law* (1953), 148.

[53] Martin, *L'Estoppel en droit international public* (1979), 327.

[54] Id., 327–329; Kadelbach, *Zwingendes Völkerrecht* (1992), 337. Jennings (1967), 64 considers that the failure to protest a violation of fundamental norms can never work as estoppel.

[55] Suy (1962), 189; Rodriguez-Cedeno, *Sixth Report on Unilateral Acts*, A/CN.4/534, 19; Brownlie (1982), 200–201.

[56] Suy (1962), 191.   [57] Lauterpacht, *Recognition in International Law* (1947), 411.

imperatively opposable to all States, and the latter may not validly challenge it through withholding recognition. If an entity claims statehood in violation of *jus cogens*, here too the constitutive theory fails, since the illegality created is imperatively opposable to all States, which are duty-bound not to recognize it. As for the declaratory theory, it can be relevant in terms of the recognition of States established pursuant to the relevant peremptory norms; but it can have no relevance in cases where the statehood or legal regime is purported to be established in contravention of the relevant *jus cogens*, through acts and tools that are illegal and void. All this dictates that the role of recognition should be viewed as limited. If recognition transforms illegality into legality, it may cause derogation from otherwise applicable rules and thus is inherently subject to the operation of *jus cogens*.

In the spirit of the traditional approach, Visscher considers that recognition is an act of free discretion by a recognizing State.[58] Sztucki acknowledges that in situations like the Munich Treaty and the Stimson Doctrine, the international community has not recognized the outcome of illegality, but holds that non-recognition, which is a free political act, is not an incidence of *jus cogens*.[59] It is submitted that this statement is a misapprehension.[60] The Arbitration Commission on Yugoslavia affirmed that while recognition is generally a discretionary act, it must be exercised in compliance with the peremptory norms of general international law such as the prohibition of the inter-State use of force or safeguarding the rights of minorities.[61] Article 4(c) of the 2005 African Union Non-Aggression and Common Defence Pact proclaims in quite comprehensive terms that 'States parties undertake not to recognise any territorial acquisition or special advantage, resulting from the use of aggression.'

The structure of this phenomenon can be explained by analysing its elements. As Castaneda points out, 'non-recognition cannot be interpreted as a *sanction* in the same sense as embargo, the severance of relations, or other measures provided for in Article 41 [of the UN Charter]. The duty of non-recognition is rather the result of a juridico-political evaluation of a given situation, which is normally made by each State individually. If, as a result of that evaluation, the conclusion is reached that the change in a situation was the consequence of an illicit use of force, the legal duty of non-recognising the change exists, on the basis of and in compliance with a rule of general international law.'[62] According to Cassese, the inability of the United Nations to act effectively in remedying the illegalities arising out of the occupation of the Palestinian territory 'forces international law to confine

---

[58] Visscher (1967), 39.
[59] Sztucki (1974), 36; see also Mann, The Consequences of an International Wrong in National and International Law, *BYIL* (1977), 101.
[60] cf Cassese, *International Law* (2005), 207.   [61] 4 *EJIL* (1993), 90.
[62] Castaneda, *Legal Effects of United Nations Resolutions* (1969), 191.

itself to an essentially negative stand, that is to withholding its endorsement of the *de facto* situation'.[63] This attitude emphasizes that although, as is the case in the decentralized international legal system, the judgment regarding non-recognition is made by individual States, the entire process of non-recognition follows from the relevant rules of general international law.

There are different applications of the principle of non-recognition: with regard to territorial acquisitions, customs lines, property acquired in disregard of the Hague Convention, delimitation, domestic legal proceedings, conflicting domestic laws etc.[64] Sztucki considers in bilateralist terms that a State towards which an international obligation is breached can insist that it will not recognize consequent effects.[65]

But non-recognition in case of illegality must be distinguished from non-recognition where the situation of fact is itself not contrary to the law, and is withheld from a new entity for political or diplomatic reasons; it also must be distinguished from cases where recognition is withheld for legal reasons, namely in cases where an entity in question does not possess the attributes of statehood and its recognition can be premature.[66] Such premature recognition is an injury to and an interference with the internal affairs of the country concerned.[67] This would be a matter of bilateral relations of the States concerned and accordingly entail a mere subjective illegality.

The practice of the nineteenth century was familiar with the doctrine of non-recognition solely in the context of the rights of individual States under particular treaty or customary rules, and demonstrates that the basis of illegality is solely the violation of such rights; moreover, the States concerned affirm, explicitly or implicitly, that the illegality could have been avoided had they been consulted or given their agreement in advance.[68] Such attitudes affirm that the illegality which exists at the time of making the protest exists merely because the States affected made the protest, and could have been cured had these States decided to remain silent. This involves a mere subjective illegality relevant in a bulk of legal relations. A State may consider that it does not recognize an entity or situation because of its illegality, but in such cases it is acting in the exercise of discretion, and the non-recognition in question is the product of free will, and not the duty, of that State.

In order to affect the freedom of States to recognize certain situations, a norm must have special normative characteristics. Non-recognition as a public order concept operates over and above the bilateralist framework. The rationale underlying the principle of non-recognition is that an entity or

---

[63] Cassese (1986), 37.

[64] Overviewed in Lauterpacht (1947), 409 ff., and Gowlland-Debbas, *Collective Responses to Illegal Acts in International Law* (1990), 238 ff.

[65] Sztucki (1974), 35.   [66] Gowlland-Debbas (1990), 275.

[67] Fitzmaurice (1957), 124.   [68] Overview in Lauterpacht (1947), 414 ff.

situation seeking validation is brought about through an act in violation of a fundamental norm, and the continuing operation of such a rule prevails over the capacity of States to recognize such situations.

Once a norm serves the community interest and is part of *jus cogens*, it is the duty of States not to recognize sovereign acts offending against it. In the case of norms serving the individual State interest and having the character of reciprocal exchange, that compelling duty is absent and everything would depend on reciprocal relations between the wronged and recognizing States.[69] As further affirmed, 'Since peremptory norms cause the invalidity of rules, treaties and titles which are in conflict with them, and invalidity is incurable in character, third States must be under obligation not to recognise such a rule, treaty or title as valid and legal.'[70] Gowlland-Debbas rightly emphasizes the difference between ordinary non-recognition policy and a duty not to recognize an illegal regime.[71] As Visscher and Brownlie affirm, the prohibition of force under Article 2(4) of the United Nations Charter not only empowers but also obliges States not to recognize situations established through the use of force.[72] Such obligatory non-recognition of acts like unlawful forcible acquisition of territory could only be explained by reference to the fundamental nature of the primary rule thus breached, whether the prohibition of force or the principle of self-determination.[73]

A decision not to recognize may be a political decision, but in face of fundamental illegalities it has to be based on some objective legal criteria. This is clear from the Dutch attitude with regard to recognition of the Transkei. As the Dutch foreign minister stated, the decision not to recognize the Transkei was based 'on political grounds', as there is no duty to recognize a State and maintain relations with it. However, his statement went beyond that and laid down some objective criteria of political judgment, particularly the fact that until abolition of racist policies and establishment of equality between whites, blacks and coloureds it was impossible for the Netherlands to review its decision of non-recognition.[74]

It is worth examining when such objective criteria of non-recognition emerged. The original standard was contained in the statement of the US Sectretary of State Stimson addressed to Chinese and Japanese Governments in the wake of the Japanese aggression against China that the United States did not intend to recognize any situation, treaty, or agreement which may be

---

[69] Jaenicke, Zur Frage des Internationalen Ordre Public, 7 *Berichte der Deutschen Gesellschaft für Völkerrecht* (1967), 122.

[70] Hannikainen (1995), 106.

[71] Gowlland-Debbas (1990), 299.

[72] Visscher (1967), 25; Brownlie, *International Law and the Use of Force by States* (1963), 410–423, also examining the practice during the Second World War.

[73] Gowlland-Debbas (1990), 240–245, 324.

[74] Netherlands State Practice, *NYIL* 1976, 192–193.

brought about by means contrary to the covenants and obligations of the 1928 Pact of Paris.[75]

Lauterpacht considered that the Stimson Doctrine did not imply the obligation of non-recognition. Despite the argument that the doctrine was a reaffirmation of obligations enshrined in the Paris Pact, Lauterpacht considered that the obligation was only a moral one, adding that 'A State signing a treaty does not automatically undertake a legal obligation to contribute to its enforcement by a refusal of recognition or otherwise.'[76] Lauterpacht focused on complementary effects of the League of Nations resolution on Manchukuo, stating that it was intended to be binding on Member States and thus constitutive of the duty of non-recognition.[77]

But Lauterpacht acknowledged that the Stimson Doctrine had a more general scope, and the main practical application of the doctrine of non-recognition was concerned with the non-recognition of conquest and other forcible territorial changes violating the League of Nations Covenant and the Pact of Paris.[78] The communication of the US to Japan and China[79] was an earlier precedent of action in the community interest, since it involved the non-recognition of violation of China's territorial integrity—an action as such unrelated to the individual interests of the US.[80]

Since the Stimson Doctrine, the principle of non-recognition was associated with the violation of one or another fundamental norm of international law. Non-recognition of territorial status or changes in cases of Namibia, Cyprus, the Middle East, or East Timor, as well as the non-recognition of the statehood of South African homelands and of the declaration of independence by Rhodesia was based on the prevailing effect of substantive norms on the use of force, human rights and self-determination.

The non-recognition of Rhodesia was based on the fact that its government was not representative of the majority of the people; it was an illegal racist minority regime.[81] As Dugard observes, the non-recognition in the case of Rhodesia targeted the racist minority regime in that country, not the independence itself.[82] This accords with the fact that the British colony of Southern Rhodesia was entitled to self-determination and hence its independence was not as such objectionable under international law.[83] The

---

[75] For the text see Keith (ed.), *Speeches and Documents in International Affairs 1918–1937*, vol. I (1938), 256; for an analysis of the development and implications of the Stimson Doctrine see Turns, The Stimson Doctrine of Non-Recognition: Its Historical Genesis and Influence on Contemporary International Law, 2 *Chinese Journal of International Law* (2003), 105.

[76] Lauterpacht (1947), 416–417.   [77] Lauterpacht (1947), 417–418.

[78] Lauterpacht (1947), 414, 425.   [79] Reported in Lauterpacht (1947), 415.

[80] Even though the US attitude was also motivated by its interests in China.

[81] UNGA Res 2022(XX); UNSC Res 202(1965), 216(1965), 277(1970).

[82] Dugard (1987), 93–94

[83] The context was pointing exactly to the opposite, as the UN General Assembly repeatedly affirmed that the people of Zimbabwe had the right to self-determination. GA Res 2151(XXI), 2262(XXII), 2383(XXIII), 2508(XXIV), 2652(XXV).

illegality was involved only in the manner of declaration of its independence and conflicted with the very right to self-determination to which the population of Southern Rhodesia was entitled.

Non-recognition of the Rhodesian minority regime was both in doctrine and practice associated with the impact of the Declaration on Granting Independence to Colonial Territories embodied in the UN General Assembly Resolution 1514(XV), which lays down the basic parameters of the modern law of self-determination.[84] Given the peremptory status of the right to self-determination, this fact also reinforces the role of the General Assembly resolutions as vehicles of (customary) peremptory norms.

The non-recognition of the South African homelands of Transkei, Bophuthatswana, Venda and Ciskei was based on the illegality of the policies of apartheid and the violation of the rights of peoples to self-determination[85]—the illegalities that the independence of those homelands was meant to consolidate. As Dugard points out, the establishment of these homelands not only resulted in the territorial fragmentation of the self-determination units but also caused the violation of individual human rights by resulting in the deprivation to eight million black South Africans of their South African nationality.[86] The non-recognition of the South African administration over Namibia was based on the violation of human rights obligations and the right to self-determination.[87]

The Turkish Republic of Northern Cyprus was denied recognition on the basis of its being established in consequence of the illegal use of force against the Republic of Cyprus and the consequent violation of the territorial integrity of Cyprus.[88] The non-recognition of Israeli sovereignty over the West Bank and East Jerusalem is also due to the impermissibility of the forcible acquisition of the territory,[89] and the same holds true for the Israeli annexation of the Golan Heights.[90]

The doctrine had not originally acknowledged this normative reality. McNair examines non-recognition not in the context of public order, but in an extremely bilateralist context in the light of the costs and benefits of adopting specific policies. A principal concern he expresses is the preservation of the rights, interests and benefits of a third State which it had in the annexed territory before the annexation and the necessity of preserving

---

[84] Dugard, *Recognition and the United Nations* (1987), 96–98.

[85] UNGA Res 31/6A, 32/105 N; UNSC Res 402(1976), 407(1977); SC Presidential Statements S/13549, S/14794.

[86] Dugard (1987), 104–107.

[87] *Namibia, ICJ Reports*, 1971, 16, elaborating upon the relevant normative standards.

[88] UNSC Res 541(1983), 550(1984), and the European Court's decision in *Loizidou*, ECtHR Series A–310.

[89] UNSC Res 242(1967), 252(1968), 267(1969), 465(1980).

[90] UNSC Res 497(1981).

existing treaty relations, such as those in the field of commerce, extradition, diplomatic protection and intellectual property.[91]

McNair concludes that 'It is difficult to see how such a policy [of non-recognition] can do more harm to the wrongdoing State than to the non-recognising States'.[92] But making this a central point ignores the hierarchy of rules and their impact on the issue of non-recognition. If certain rules are peremptory, the need to preserve them prevails over the interest of individual States in obtaining material or economic benefits from cooperation with the entity concerned.

Lauterpacht was the first to link the principle of non-recognition to international public order. His analysis emphasizes that not all situations involving recognition can be treated alike as a matter of State discretion, due to the different interests and values involved.

Lauterpacht considered that the doctrine of non-recognition is 'an instrument for maintaining and, indirectly, for enforcing international law and morality'.[93] Therefore,

From the jurisprudential point of view the acceptance of the policy or of the obligation of non-recognition is of interest as a vindication of the legal character of international law against the law-creating effect of fact. In a society in which the enforcement of the law is in a rudimentary stage there is a natural tendency for breaches of the law to be regarded, for the sole reason of their successful assertion, as a source of legal right. Non-recognition obviates that danger to a large extent.[94]

Acts of non-recognition, such as the Stimson Doctrine and the League of Nations declarations on Manchukuo, do not themselves make contested acts illegal and void. They assume the existence of obligations, according to which the acts in question would be anyway devoid of legal validity.[95] Thus, Lauterpacht considers non-recognition as declaratory of original invalidity.

As for situations where such voidness can take place, Lauterpacht submits that when an illegal act in question is in violation of individual rights of a State, that State may waive its rights and recognize the situation thus established, and the latter becomes the situation in conformity with international law. However, the illegal act in breach of general international law requires, he submits, recognition of a quasi-legislative character, to be validated.[96] Thus, Lauterpacht has taken initial steps to establish the scope of the doctrine of non-recognition though he fell short of fully ascertaining the relevance of *jus cogens*.

Dugard has formulated the modern doctrine of non-recognition based on *jus cogens*. When the practice of States and organizations refers to a certain entity or situation by using the language of 'illegality', 'invalidity' or 'nullity',

---

[91] McNair (1933), 72–73.   [92] McNair (1933), 73.
[93] Lauterpacht (1970), 340–341.   [94] Lauterpacht (1970), 347; Lauterpacht (1947), 427.
[95] Lauterpacht (1970), 341.   [96] Lauterpacht (1947), 412.

this is the evidence that the recognition is withheld from an entity not because that entity lacks the ingredients of statehood, but because it is illegally brought about.[97] South African homeland-States arguably met the requirements of statehood laid down in the Montevideo Convention, but no State except South Africa recognized them.[98] 'A cluster of fundamental principles inherent in the two fundamental norms of the prohibition of the use of force and the right to self-determination provide a legal basis for the refusal of the United Nations to recognise Israel's sovereignty over East Jerusalem.'[99]

Jus cogens gives a new doctrinal coherence to the doctrine of non-recognition.[100] Dugard formulates this doctrine as follows:

An act in violation of a norm having the character of *jus cogens* is illegal and is therefore null and void. This applies to the creation of States, the acquisition of territory and other situations, such as Namibia. States are under a duty not to recognise such acts.[101]

This is so, because

Jus cogens is a central feature in the modern doctrine of non-recognition as the violation of a norm having the character of *jus cogens* is a prerequisite for the illegality that results in the nullity and non-recognition.[102]

Non-recognition applies to situations involving nullity for conflict with *jus cogens*.[103] In all these cases the invalidity of titles as confirmed by UN organs is implementing and declaratory of the *jus cogens* nullity, not just a discretionary action.[104] This is further confirmed by the wording of UN resolutions, such as those adopted on the Middle East or Cyprus, that link the declaration of nullity to the breach of one or more fundamental norms that happen to be of peremptory character. The pronouncements of UN organs are aimed at upholding the original nullities and the consequent duty of

---

[97] Dugard (1987), 130–131.

[98] Dugard (1987), 100.   [99] Dugard (1987), 115.

[100] Dugard (1987), 132; *per contra* Mann (1977), 100, rejecting the link between *jus cogens* and non-recognition.

[101] Dugard (1987), 135.

[102] Dugard (1987), 137; Kadelbach (1992), 82.

[103] Dugard, Collective Non-Recognition: The Failure of South Africa's Bantustan States, *Boutros Boutros-Ghali—Amicorum Discipulorumque Liber—Peace, Development, Democracy*, vol. I (1998), 400–402. Talmon accepts that *jus cogens* applies to the recognition of the situation that violates it, but refuses to acknowledge the relevance of nullity as bringing about the duty of non-recognition, cf Talmon, The Constitutive versus the Declaratory Theory of Recognition: *Tertium Non Datur?*, *BYIL* (2004), 134. In the end, Talmon accepts that the difference between void situations and situations subject to non-recognition is merely theoretical, id., 136. It is clear that there is certainly no normative difference between these two categories. In addition, if the duty of non-recognition applies to the situation, this is in fact the duty to treat that situation as lacking legal effect, that is null and void. From this perspective, even the theoretical distinction seems to be misconceived.

[104] Dugard (1998), 402; see further below, Chapter 13.

non-recognition and preventing third States from disregarding them; at inducing the relevant States to revert to the correct legal position; at reminding States that the issues in question are imperatively governed by public order norms, there being no room for bilateral and multilateral transactions on this subject, among others in terms of validation.

Rozakis explains that *jus cogens* transforms the principle of non-recognition into a more effective principle emanating from the concept of objective illegality and its subject-matter is determined not by subjective determinations but by peremptory norms.[105]

Substantive peremptory norms have a twofold impact on the doctrine of non-recognition, determining in what cases non-recognition is applicable and what the effect of non-recognition is. Unlike Lauterpacht, Dugard clearly formulated the principle of non-recognition linked to the operation of peremptory norms as such, independently of explicit or implicit affirmation in conventional provisions or State practice.

2.1.2. Peremptory norms and the types of recognition outlawed

Some qualifications to the principle of non-recognition are put forward. Jennings considers that recognition by third States may qualify the *jus cogens* nullity.[106] But Brownlie rejects that option, affirming that the loser would still be able to challenge the title thus purported to be established.[107] According to Lauterpacht, the obligation of non-recognition may not last for ever and be adjusted to the requirements of international peace and stability. It may merge in a general international settlement. 'But there is a difference between this procedure and the automatic incorporation of any breach of international law as part of the law of nations.'[108]

According to Jennings and Brownlie, the obligation of non-recognition could give way to international settlements and procedures most likely involving Great Powers, validating even forcible territorial changes through recognition. In their view the legality of the situation would stem from such collective recognition, not from illegalities as such.[109] As Cassese pointed out, the Israeli authority over occupied territories is 'internationally illegal (except as a belligerent occupant), until such time as the overwhelming majority of States (or the competent organs of the United Nations) decide legally to recognise the change of status of the territory'.[110]

---

[105] Rozakis, *The Concept of* Jus Cogens *in the Law of Treaties* (1976), 27.

[106] Jennings, Nullity and Effectiveness in International Law, *Cambridge Essays in International Law* (1965), 74; Fitzmaurice (1957), 120.

[107] Brownlie (2003), 160.

[108] Lauterpacht, I *Collected Papers* (1970), 348.

[109] Lauterpacht (1970), 348; Jennings (1967), 62–64; Brownlie (2003), 160. But Jennings, 64, accepts that it is unlikely that States explicitly recognize illegal territorial changes.

[110] Cassese, Legal Considerations on the International Status of Jerusalem, 3 *Palestinian Yearbook of International Law* (1986), 31.

But such views are highly controversial, being based on an artificial distinction. The assumption that a title would not be based on illegal action is wrong, as the subsequent collective recognition would itself be a confirmation of that illegal action. To assume that forcible territorial acquisitions are void but can nevertheless be recognized, is to approve the fragmentation of the prohibition of the use of force and to ignore its peremptory character.

Another question is whether the international community as a whole can recognize a breach of *jus cogens* or the effects of such a breach.[111] It is arguable that once this community is the creator of peremptory norms, it can also excuse, through the device of recognition, their specific breaches.

There is some conceptual coherence in this reasoning. But the peculiarity of the recognition device is also relevant. The community's recognition of illegality can never be presumed and must involve a clear, uniform and unequivocal expression of the will of the community as a whole, not just some parts of it. This places a serious burden of proof on those attempting to find community recognition of *jus cogens* illegalities in specific cases.

Practice disapproves the 'collective recognition' approach. It is impossible to find a single case where the international community has recognized a serious breach of *jus cogens*. Rather, the duty of non-recognition has been adhered to, without qualifications such as are advanced by authors favouring 'collective recognition'. Despite the assertions that the duty of non-recognition cannot last for ever and will eventually have to capitulate to contrary facts,[112] there is no single case of validation of a situation to which the *jus cogens* duty of non-recognition applies. On the contrary, invalidation has been applied to situations quite widely recognized as apparently 'permanent' (eg the 'extinction' of Ethiopia or the Baltic States).

Even where a State's conduct or attitude may resemble collective or community recognition, such conducts and attitudes (even of many States) have not normally altered the legal picture. For instance, Dugard speaks of the failure of non-recognition in cases of Manchukuo and Ethiopia,[113] though such 'failure' has not entailed any conclusive effect in terms of legally upholding 'recognized' situations. In the case of East Timor, third States recognized *de facto* incorporation of East Timor in Indonesia as a *fait accompli*, but questioned its validity or the method of incorporation, also maintaining that the people of East Timor had the right to

---

[111] cf Rozakis (1976), 128. Jennings (1967), 62–64, speaks technically of the community recognition but in essence about the collective recognition through some procedure. But he also refers to the position expressive of the will of the international community, id., 67.

[112] Tomuschat, International Crimes by States: An Endangered Species?, in Wellens (ed.), *International Law: Theory and Practice. Essays in Honour of Eric Suy* (1998), 259; Dinstein (2001), 154.

[113] Dugard (1987), 134–135; Craven, The European Community Arbitration Commission on Yugoslavia, *BYIL* (1995), 364.

self-determination.[114] In its statement to the UN General Assembly Fourth Committee, Malaysia recognized that East Timor was part of Indonesia and had in this way already exercised its right to self-determination in accordance with Resolution 1514(XV).[115] The US considered, in recognizing *de jure* the Indonesian incorporation of East Timor, that no valid act of self-determination had taken place.[116] This attitude seems to imply a certain link between the substance of legal norms and their legal effects and differs from the suggestion that even if the people is the proper self-determination unit, its annexation and consequent incorporation by another State can nevertheless be recognized, that is, the primary norm of self-determination shall at some stage cease to be operative in determining the status of the relevant territory and the entitlements of the annexing State as well as third States in relation to it.

Whatever the pretext of recognition, the subsequent independence of East Timor, opposable to all States, confirms that every *de facto* or *de jure* recognition of the incorporation into Indonesia was devoid of legal validity.

This provokes the further question what kinds of recognition are outlawed by the principle of non-recognition. The classical distinction between *de facto* and *de jure* recognition is somewhat archaic in terms of public order illegalities, such as unlawful territorial acquisitions. The doctrine of non-recognition is contingent upon the validity of a title. On its face, the so-called *de facto* recognition that a given territory is under the actual control of a given State would just acknowledge the obvious, and would not imply an intention to recognize the title. But the actions, such as establishment of treaty relations, can be tantamount to implicit *de jure* recognition of a title, even if a State maintains that its recognition is just *de facto*. For in State practice we can meet instances where such *de facto* recognition is regarded as a basis for, and is followed by, actions which are practically equal to *de jure* recognition of an illegality and its legal consequences, especially the authority of a given State with regard to the unlawfully acquired territory, and hence is indistinguishable from recognition *de jure*.

In the matter of East Timor, the Australian Government held that it was unrealistic to continue to refuse to recognize that East Timor had in fact become part of Indonesia,[117] 'the incorporation of East Timor into Indonesia is now a reality and that the Indonesian Government is the authority in effective control'.[118] But it is difficult to interpret this statement just as *de facto* recognition. First, it states that not Indonesian actual control, but Indonesian *incorporation* of East Timor is a reality. Second, from the context of this

---

[114] Antonopoulos, Effectiveness v. the Rule of Law Following the *East Timor* Case, 27 *Netherlands Yearbook of International Law* (1997), 97 ff.

[115] Cited in Cassese, *Self-Determination of Peoples* (1994), 226, n. 30.

[116] Hannikainen (1995), 113.

[117] Hannikainen (1995), 113.   [118] 8 *AYIL*, 273; cf also Craven (1995), 363.

statement it is clear that it is not easily separable from *de jure* recognition, as it was made in explanation of Australia's vote against the UN resolutions on East Timor, which confirmed the illegality of East Timor's incorporation and demanded that Indonesia withdraw. Referring to reality and thereby justifying a vote against the UN resolution which demands redress of invalid annexation is nothing but acknowledgment that those realities have brought about a legal title of Indonesia in East Timor.

This is confirmed by the subsequent attitude of Australia to give *de jure* recognition to Indonesia's acquisition of East Timor, and again referred to 'reality with which we must come to terms', despite the fact that the means which brought about the Indonesian control were 'critical',[119] ignoring applicable legal principles. Furthermore, Australia contended that 'there is no binding international legal obligation not to recognise the acquisition of territory that was acquired by force'.[120] It was Australia's attitude that Australian–Indonesian negotiations on delimitation of the seabed boundary would signify *de jure* recognition.[121] In fact, these were negotiations which led subsequently to the conclusion of the 1989 Timor Gap Treaty, coming to terms with the reality of almost one-third of the East Timorese population having been slaughtered during the Indonesian occupation.

Therefore, whether recognition is *de facto* or *de jure* depends not on the stated intention of the recognizing State but on the context of recognition, on preceding and subsequent steps, the relation of acts of the recognizing State to the actual enjoyment by the wrongdoer State of the benefits from its illegal action, and its legality or validity is to be assessed accordingly. Even if Australia had not explicitly recognized the annexation of East Timor subsequently, its original '*de facto*' recognition was still in breach of the principle, as it supported the validity of actual annexation.

Yet another attempt to override the operation of the duty of non-recognition is associated with the US policies in the Middle East. Despite the prevailing characterization of the status of East Jerusalem as the occupied territory, in the 1990s the US started to object to such characterization. This process included the US ambassadorial statements before the United Nations and culminated with the 1994 statement of the US Vice-President that united Jerusalem including the Western and Eastern parts was the capital of Israel.[122] Such State views cannot amount to valid State practice. They cannot generate, and have not generated, as most recently confirmed in the International Court's *Wall* Opinion, any change in the status of East Jerusalem as occupied territory.

---

[119] 8 *AYIL*, 273; 10 *AYIL*, 279.
[120] Turns (2003), 133; Hannikainen (1995), 114.   [121] 10 *AYIL*, 281.
[122] Quigley, The Israel–PLO Agreements versus the Geneva Civilians Convention, 7 *Palestinian Yearbook of International Law* (1992–1994), 52.

The overarching legal framework and the legal outcome of the relevant situations evidence that the validation device of recognition cannot operate in a way supporting the assumption of the separateness between peremptory norms and their legal effects.[123] Instead, where the primary norm affected by the illegality is peremptory, it produces a consequential effect depriving the recognition of illegality of its legal effects. The application of this principle has so far always prevailed over the conflicting practice.

2.1.3. Peremptory norms and the implications of the duty of non-recognition

It is commonly accepted that recognition is relative and effective only between the recognizing and the recognized States, and has no effect with regard to other States.[124] This questions whether the recognition of an *erga omnes* illegality may cure it, as the effects, if any, would concern only relations between recognizing and benefiting States.

As one option, it is suggested that the recognition of fundamental illegalities is always subject to revocation of recognition.[125] While this is correct, this is merely the consequence of the original invalidity of recognition. According to Suy, recognition cannot validate an act illegal *erga omnes*;[126] and hence it has no effect. According to Special Rapporteur Rodriguez-Cedeno, recognition of acts contrary to *jus cogens*, such as illegal annexation of a State, would be invalid and produce no legal consequences.[127] Acts such as annexation are void in themselves, and recognition cannot give them any effect, even recognition by third parties.[128] Rodriguez-Cedeno does not qualify this principle with any exception of collective recognition. At the same time, the voidness of the recognition of illegalities offending against peremptory norms, which is itself equivalent to the negative effect of public order, also entails a positive effect, namely the unimpeded operation of the existing legal relations. An example is provided by the legal position, affirmed by the international community, that the Turkish Republic of Northern Cyprus, whose establishment is void, shall not be recognized, and the only

---

[123] That such separation is without foundation is also witnessed by the fact that some States recognizing the illegal situation deny the relevance of the substantive peremptory norm in the first place.

[124] Mann (1976–77), 41; Suy (1962), 207.

[125] Brownlie (1963), 421–422; Mann (1976–77), 41; an example of the revocation of recognition is observable in the case of the annexation of Austria by Germany. Sztucki (1974), 27, suggests, though without pointing to any evidence, that Britain, USA and USSR had in 1938 recognized the legal consequences of the annexation. If this were so, the 1943 Declaration that emphasized the nullity *ab initio* of this annexation could be qualified as the case of revocation of that alleged recognition.

[126] Suy (1962), 211.

[127] Rodriguez-Cedeno, *Sixth Report on Unilateral Acts*, A/CN.4/534, 19.

[128] Id.; for an identical view see Hannikainen (1995), 106, especially with regard to the recognition of Indonesia's title to East Timor.

legitimate government of Cyprus is the government of the Republic of Cyprus based at Nicosia.

It is clear that the fact of recognition of a breach of *jus cogens* cannot cause modification of a violated peremptory norm, because it is concerned merely with validation of a single conduct or situation, and not a general modification of a rule. This is more a derogation in terms of refusal to apply a given rule to a given situation. The inevitable link between substance and enforcement is clear: if the group of States considers that a rule exists on the plane of substantive law, and governs a given situation as a peremptory norm, they cannot hold that their refusal or failure to give effect to that norm with regard to that situation is not a derogation. For if a *jus cogens* norm exists and applies, it must so apply, even if the States involved disagree. If a peremptory norm requires that territory X shall belong to State A, but the group of other States recognizes that territory as independent or as belonging to State B, then the group of States must either be pretending that that peremptory norm does not exist or does not apply to that situation, or expresses its intention not to allow that norm to take effect with regard to that situation, that is to replace the regime it requires by their own regime, which is the same as derogation.

Recognition is in fact an agreement between recognizing and beneficiary States to substitute the existing legal framework by a new one, based on a newly recognized title. It cannot be argued that the recognizing States merely depart from the effect of a given peremptory norm in the given case and not from its content or general effect. But on the other hand, the recognition of a new title is tantamount to the emergence of, or at least the attempt to create, new rules governing the intended new title with the effect to be applicable *inter partes* with regard to recognizing and beneficiary States; this is an attempt to replace the otherwise applicable *jus cogens*, and hence a derogation from it. This means that such recognitions are void as derogations from the substantive *jus cogens* which applies to the given situation.

The doctrine of non-recognition as such has been successful in laying down uniform principles whose impact is never seriously disputed by any State or group of States, except directly interested States.[129] In practice following the inauguration of the principle by the Stimson Doctrine, and after *jus cogens* has emerged, no illegal situation has been recognized with final force, even in cases where the applicability or effect of the principle was doubted or incoherently applied in practice, such as Manchukuo, Ethiopia or East Timor.

Once the *jus cogens* duty not to recognize certain situations is established, specific implications of that duty must be considered, which are as relevant in

---

[129] Such as Turkey in case of Turkish Republic of Northern Cyprus, Armenia in case of Nagorno-Karabakh, Japan in case of Manchukuo.

terms of public order as the original duty is. Judge Petren's statement in *Namibia*, that non-recognition implies not positive action but abstention from acts signifying recognition, seems to hold the key to the outcome.[130] McNair, Guggenheim and Lauterpacht, partly due to their bilateralist approach, approved the recognition of certain acts emanating from what is a change contradicting *jus cogens*, but they wrote before the major developments related to the doctrine, and their views have not been approved in practice, as confirmed by *Namibia* and *Loizidou*. This practice takes a consequential approach, so that the original illegality bars subsequent co-operation or recognition. This has further been confirmed by the European Court of Justice in *Anastasiou*, where the Court stated that the Agreement of Association between EEC and Cyprus

must be interpreted as precluding acceptance by the national authorities of a Member State, when citrus fruit and potatoes are imported from the part of Cyprus to the north of the United Nations Buffer Zone, of movement and phytosanitary certificates issued by authorities other than the competent authorities of the Republic of Cyprus.[131]

The Court took this consequential approach by reference to principles and practice on non-recognition of fundamental illegalities. The Court also rejected the submissions that certain kinds of cooperation with the non-recognized State are possible in a way not implying its non-recognition.[132]

Talmon criticizes *Anastasiou* by submitting that 'international non-recognition does not necessarily preclude cooperation between the authorities of the non-recognising State and those of the unrecognised State'.[133] But Talmon fails to locate the principle of non-recognition in the context which is assigned to it in international law, namely, the effects of violation of *jus cogens*. It must be understood that this principle is not self-sufficient, but comes into play only when certain overarching rules are violated through the creation of a non-recognized entity or situation. Non-recognition is merely a logical outcome of the continuing operation of those norms, not of the non-recognizing State's whim.

The principle of non-recognition, if it has any meaningful value, may not be reduced to the formal acts and condemnations by non-recognizing States which subsequently would retain the discretion to enter into such relations with a non-recognized entity which would make the privileges of statehood available to that entity and, consequently, grant to it the benefits from the violation of the principles and rules which are the very basis of its non-recognition.

---

[130] *ICJ Reports*, 1971, 134.   [131] *Anastasiou*, 100 ILR 302.   [132] 100 ILR 296.
[133] Talmon, The Cyprus Question before the European Court of Justice, 12 *EJIL* (2001), 743.

In addition, if, as Talmon suggests, non-recognition does not exclude cooperation with the non-recognized entity, it would be hard to portray non-recognition as a legal principle with clearly defined content. If, as a starting-point, cooperation is not excluded, it would be open to scholars and practitioners to attempt to find other activities which the principle of non-recognition would not, in their view, 'necessarily preclude'. An endless list of permitted activities could obtain, and the principle of non-recognition would be reduced to mere declarations capable of being refuted in practice.

To denote the European Court's approach as being 'out of touch with reality'[134] is to ignore the essential point that the very function of the principle of non-recognition is to preclude legitimation of factual situations which succeed in reality through serious breaches of public order norms. This principle is a clear exception to the general pattern that the violation of law may create new law. If the rationale of the principle is accepted, it is unclear why that rationale is not relevant in the course of the practical operation of that principle.

Talmon's approach clearly contradicts international judicial practice, especially *Namibia* and *Loizidou*, which clearly emphasize that no acts of non-recognized entities in the exercise of their 'State' prerogatives may be recognized and given legal effect. Non-recognition has to be extended to all acts adopted by those entities in pursuance of their 'State' interests as distinguished from the acts adopted solely in the interests of the inhabitants of the territory in question. Thus, it is an error to attribute to the European Court the misjudgment of the scope of the principle of non-recognition. The European Court's approach follows the prevailing approach accepted in the practice of States, international organizations and tribunals.

Nor is the argument correct that air communication with the non-recognized entity does not imply its recognition. It is true that several States introduced direct flights into East Germany and Macedonia before they recognized these States.[135] But it is also the case that those States were not subject to the duty of non-recognition and by introducing flights, the relevant States did not offend against any legal requirement.

As for indirect flights, there is some practice that Turkish Cypriot planes can communicate with Europe either through being registered in Turkey or through landing in Turkey before reaching Cyprus.[136] While several States have tolerated these flights in and from their airports, only the Republic of Ireland has objected by refusing permission for flights from Dublin through Antalya to Northern Cyprus. Although it is suggested that this decision was based on political rather than legal considerations as it was meant to send a

---

[134] Talmon (2001), 743.

[135] Talmon, Luftverkehr mit nicht anerkannten Staaten. Der Fall Nordzypern, 43 *Archiv des Völkerrechts* (2005), 17, 22.

[136] For an overview of this practice see Talmon (2005), 3–5, 17–35.

political signal,[137] in fact the opposite is true because the Irish government clearly referred to the need for compliance with UN resolutions, which is no doubt a legal requirement.

The approach that the principle of non-recognition requires little more than the expression of the formal attitude that the given entity is not a State, would be misguided. The statehood is not merely the formal status but it is the phenomenon displaying its effects and implications in time and space. When an illegal entity claims statehood, it claims not merely the formal status but also the practical ability to exercise, as a matter of real life, a variety of rights, powers and privileges which it considers as derived from its sovereignty, whether related to diplomatic intercourse, trade, valid issuance of documents and certificates, or administration in general. If the principle of non-recognition had no impact on the lawfulness of such exercise of the rights and powers, it would be a rather curious principle that would legitimize the hypocrisy of formal non-recognition accompanied by the cooperation with the non-recognized entity that enables that entity to effectively exercise what it claims as its sovereign powers.

The practice affirms that the principle of non-recognition is meant to apply not only to formal status but also to its implications in real life. The requirements that are implications of the duty of non-recognition of the South African presence in Namibia are stated in the *Namibia* case in quite comprehensive terms. The Court addressed the duties it postulated *inter alia* to the States which had economic or related interests in Namibia. States were obliged, in relation to the Namibian territory, not to apply their treaties with South Africa, not to maintain diplomatic or consular relations with it, and not to enter 'into economic and other forms of relationship or dealings with South Africa'. Furthermore, they were obliged 'to refrain from any acts and in particular any dealings with the Government of South Africa implying recognition of the legality of, or lending support or assistance to, such presence and administration.'[138] The refusal of several States to move their embassies in Israel to Jerusalem is caused by their refusal to take any action that could imply the recognition of the Israeli acquisition of East Jerusalem. This is a further instance that confirms the comprehensiveness of the duty of non-recognition.

The International Court in *Namibia* ruled that States were bound to abstain from establishing diplomatic and consular relations with South Africa in the way extending such relations to Namibia.[139] The non-recognition of Rhodesian UDI was signified through maintenance of existing British and US consulates in Salisbury, which were not accredited to

---

[137] Talmon (2005), 22.   [138] *ICJ Reports*, 1971, 16, paras 122–124, and operative para. 2.
[139] *ICJ Reports*, 1971, 55, para. 123.

Southern Rhodesia. This was the US and UK view.[140] US judicial practice did not recognize the Soviet annexation of the Baltic States and continued to recognize the capacity of the officials of those States, such as consuls.[141] The US representative, in the process of adoption of UN Security Council Resolution 277, referred to the independence of the judiciary under the American constitutional system and emphasized that the courts would be free to take judicial notice of the legal acts of Southern Rhodesia.[142] However, as Gowlland-Debbas rightly suggests, States have a duty to refuse cognizance at all levels and of all acts.[143] The above practice in fact accords with the requirements of *Namibia*.

The only exception from this principle can be formed by reference to the acts and transactions which relate to the interests of individuals rather than States, and hence cannot amount to validation. The International Court has recognized this exception in *Namibia* with regard to registration of births and marriages. The exception of everyday transactions is necessary to avoid unnecessarily inhumane results.[144] This does not support the illegalities involved, nor does it benefit the wrongdoer.

The International Court considered in the Advisory Opinion on *Wall* that, due to the character and the importance of the rights and obligations involved, 'all States are under an obligation not to recognize the illegal situation resulting from the construction of the wall in the Occupied Palestinian Territory, including in and around East Jerusalem.'[145]

The Court's approach to the duty of non-recognition raises thoughts in terms of the implications of that duty. Judge Koojmans in the *Wall* case had a 'difficulty . . . in understanding what the duty not to recognize an illegal fact involves.' As no State considered the Israeli wall as legal, he concluded that 'the duty not to recognize amounts, therefore, in my view to an obligation without real substance.'[146] But Judge Koojmans' criticism is unsustainable, considering that the duty of non-recognition is designed to prevent factual situations from being transformed into legal reality and hence it must be viewed as a principle capable of dynamic application to changing circumstances. The mere fact that, at the point the Court's Opinion was delivered, no State considered the wall as legal does not by itself ensure

---

[140] Gowlland-Debbas, *Collective Responses to Illegal Acts in International Law* (1990), 300.
[141] Overview see in Lauterpacht, 432, n. 2.
[142] See in Gowlland-Debbas (1990), 303–304.
[143] Gowlland-Debbas (1990), 311. The Security Council declared in Resolution 550 (1984) that all secessionist actions, such as the exchange of ambassadors between Turkey and TRNC were illegal and invalid.
[144] Gowlland-Debbas (1990), 306–307.
[145] Opinion, para. 159, and the operative paragraph 3(D).
[146] Separate Opinion, para. 44.

that contrary attitudes cannot emerge in the future.[147] The continuous operation of the duty of non-recognition prevents such possible attitudes from consolidating a legally problematic change.

Furthermore the fact that no State as such considered the wall as legal is not sufficient in explaining the effect of peremptory norms in this case, as certain, or indeed many, States could have acted out of their political discretion in declaring that the wall is illegal. This conclusion is further reinforced by the fact that the decisions of the UN principal organs are largely based on political discretion and consensus, and as such are subject to the possibility of change. This cannot by itself satisfy the imperative requirements of international public order. But the Court's treatment of the issue has provided a statement of the law independent of processes based on political discretion. Furthermore, the General Assembly finding on the illegality of the wall and the related consequences, though authoritative, is not binding as such: by contrast according to the Court the duty of non-recognition is binding as such, ie *ex lege*. As Judge Koroma stated, 'The Court's findings are based on the authoritative rules of international law and are of an *erga omnes* character.'[148] This is due to the fact that the Opinion's findings affirm 'that the international community as a whole bears an obligation towards the Palestinian people . . . not to recognize any unilateral change in the status of the territory brought about by the construction of the wall.'[149]

2.2. Waiver

Waiver is a validation device. It can validate an act or situation either before or after it occurs; it can amount to a situation where what was wrongful is no longer so *inter se*.[150]

It is conventional wisdom that waiver cannot be presumed.[151] Apart from general contexts, *Clipperton Island* has affirmed this in terms of the waiver of territorial sovereignty. In *Nauru*, Australia argued that Nauruan authorities waived before independence the claims for phosphates, but the Court disagreed, having found no definite proof of waiver.[152]

The concept of, and limitations on, the operation of waiver in the law of treaties, as codified in Article 45 of the Vienna Convention on the Law of

---

[147] Consider, especially, the attitudes of certain States concerning the alleged impossibility of return to their homes of certain Palestinian refugees, due to the alleged irreversibility of some changes resulting from the Six Day War in 1967; or the attitudes of certain States concerning the absence of the act of valid self-determination by the people entitled to such self-determination under international law.

[148] Separate Opinion, para. 8.

[149] Separate Opinion, para. 7.

[150] For an overview see Rodriguez-Cedeno, Seventh Report on Unilateral Acts, A/CN.4/542.

[151] Mann (1989), 410; Suy (1962), 159 ff.   [152] *ICJ Reports*, 1992, 240, 253–255.

Treaties, could conceivably be applied by analogy to the entire international law.[153] The ILC's earlier work on State responsibility did not refer to the nature of rules in the context of waiver or settlement; the principal focus concerned the attitude of the States involved,[154] despite the fact that the Vienna Convention analogy was clearly acknowledged. It was also examined whether there is a difference between subsequent consent to the breach and the consent to waive consequences of the breach.[155] But in the final Articles, the ILC formulated an unqualified bar on waiver in terms of *jus cogens*.[156]

In terms of operation of *jus cogens*, waiver can give rise to conceptual concerns, as States can try to dispose of the non-disposable rights of certain actors protected by non-derogable norms, and sometimes do that by treaty. The most explicit case of humanitarian dimension to be examined in terms of express waiver rather than some other validation devices is perhaps the case of the Asian comfort women.

It is well known that the Korean and Philippinese comfort women, abused by the Japanese military in the Second World War, did not mention their plight for decades. When they finally overcame their inhibitions, they faced the difficulty that their governments, acting with a view to bring about peace in their mutual relationships, might have renounced any possible claims against Japan resulting from the war.[157] With regard to reparations to be paid by Japan, South-East Asian countries took different views. While Vietnam claimed reparations and a settlement was reached, Cambodia and Laos announced their intent to waive reparations.[158] Korea and the Philippines concluded treaties with Japan containing purported waivers.[159]

This contrasts with settlements reached with Germany with regard to the Second World War. The Governments of Poland and Russia agreed not to assert further claims of Polish and Russian citizens that arose in connection with Nazi persecution, but considered that this created no limitations of the

---

[153] cf Crawford, Third Report, A/CN.4/507/Add.2, 12.

[154] Crawford, Third Report, A/CN.4/507/Add.2, 12 ff.; *ILC Report*, 2000, 75, para. 248.

[155] Crawford, Third Report, A/CN.4/507/Add.2, 13.

[156] *ILC Report* 2001, commentary to Article 45, para. 4, at 308, and commentary to Article 41, 289–290, para. 9, specifying that the peremptory character of a rule excludes waiver. Gattini, To What Extent are State Immunity and Non-Justiciability Major Hurdles to Individuals' Claims for War Damages?, 1 *Journal of International Criminal Justice* (2003), 366–367, affirms that the ILC Articles do not leave to the injured State any faculty of waiving *jus cogens* breaches and any settlement on reciprocal waiver of such is void.

[157] Tomuschat, Individual Reparation Claims in Instances of Grave Human Rights Violations, in Randelzhofer and Tomuschat (eds), *State Responsibility and the Individual. Reparation in Instances of Grave Violations of Human Rights* (1999), 6–7.

[158] Ito, Japan's Settlement of the Post-World War II Reparations and Claims, 37 *Japanese Annual of International Law* (1994), 53.

[159] 9 May 1953, 1 Japanese Annual (1967), 132; 22 June 1965, 10 *Japanese Annual* (1966), 284. For an overview of treaty clauses see Parker and Crew (1994), 537–538.

individual rights of citizens of both nations.[160] In cases where governments presumably consider themselves entitled to waive certain claims, they exercise this power with caution and limitations.[161] Such practice is far from affirming the entitlement to dispose the claims of individuals. Generally, one would support the permissibility, and indeed desirability, of waivers for past wrongs with the argument that governments should prefer getting over past wrongs to the revival of old disputes. This approach is indeed utilized in practice by some governments but is not always seen as the factor that should require the permanent renunciation of rights and claims.[162] In addition, the argument against the revival of old disputes does not always confront the concerns that may be raised by the specific situations influencing the relevance of waivers.

In terms of the traditional approach, every kind of waiver is lawful. Briggs refers to unlimited control of the State over the claims of nationals. A State may refuse to espouse a claim, abandon it, or make any other disposition of it which it finds expedient, with or without compensation.[163] In terms of bilateral and reciprocal legal relations, States can do the same through treaties and there is a solid treaty practice of reciprocal waivers of claims arising from nationalization of property and assets.[164] But there must be some limits on the legal position under which States can dispose the rights of individuals through inter-State transactions. The practice related to Litvinov Agreements is a good illustration of this. Under these Agreements,[165] the Soviet Union ceded to the United States the assets of Russian companies that were covered by Soviet nationalization decrees and were present in the United States. With these assets the United States would compensate its nationals that were affected by the measures of the Soviet government. This settlement was motivated by the desire to end past frictions. Nevertheless some conceptual, if not strictly normative, concerns arose as to how far the practice of such deals could go. As Jessup observed, if no limits are imposed on the freedom of States to reach such deals, the outcome could be quite troubling. For instance, could the US government reach with Germany, after its defeat in

---

[160] Polish–German Framework Treaty, 16 October, 1991; Note of the Russian Government, 30 March 1993. But the Seim of Poland has nevertheless requested the government to present to Germany the claims for compensation for the damage caused in the Second World War, Schweisfurth, Reparationen an Polen?, *Frankfurter Allgemeine Zeitung*, 20 September 2004.

[161] The 1953 Soviet Declaration freeing East Germany from the war reparations was based on the fact that Germany had already fulfilled some of its reparation obligations and, as seen below, did not cover the claims of individuals.

[162] The statement of the Prime Minister of Estonia regarding the claims for the Soviet occupation, made on 6 October 2005, is relevant in this context. The Prime Minister renounced the claims of apology against Russia. As for monetary compensation, the Prime Minister stated that 'no State can live with the past, it is necessary to move forward instead of presenting the bills'. However, the actual renunciation statement confirms only that there are no compensation claims at present, but the Prime Minister stated that he is not responsible for future occurrences.

[163] Briggs, *The Law of Nations* (1953), 722–723.

[164] Jaenicke (1967), 107 ff.   [165] 28 *AJIL Supplement* (1934), 1.

war, the deal that would assign to it Germany's claim to the confiscated properties of its Jewish citizens?[166] Jessup of course did not make a parallel between this hypothetical agreement and the agreements actually concluded, but instead pointed out that there is the need of some limits on the governments' disposal of private rights. In fact, the Litvinov Agreement is not impeachable under international law as it governs only matters of bilateral relations. The crucial issue is how far the approach that this agreement embodies can go.

Waiver has been applied by national courts in terms of bilateral international legal relations, where the rights involved were those properly falling under the concept of diplomatic protection. For instance, in *Togen Akiyama*, the District Court of Tokyo found that the 1951 Peace Treaty with Japan validly disposed of the rights of applicants encroached upon by seizure of their property by the Canadian government, and under the same Treaty Japan validly waived its right of diplomatic protection with regard to such actions.[167] A similar approach was taken by the Supreme Restitution Court of Berlin in *Abel*, which dealt with bonds deposited in the bank of Vienna. It was held that the 1955 Austrian State Treaty validly waived these rights.[168] US courts applied a similar approach in a case concerning the seizure of property.[169]

In another case, it was stated that 'International law has developed a rule that it is within the discretion of States to make agreements with other States regulating the private legal relations of their citizens, and to do so without their consent, and that right includes the right of the contracting State to waive a claim of its citizens without the latter's consent.'[170] A rather blanket approach to waiver is suggested in the *Hungarian Restitution* case dealing with actions of Germany during occupation of Hungary with regard to Hungarian Jews.[171]

In *Shimoda*, the District Court of Tokyo agreed that the use of atomic bombs was illegal under the then applicable laws of war, but concluded that the victims of the Hiroshima bombing could not claim damages from the United States as these claims were waived under Article 19(a) of the Peace Treaty with Japan.[172] The Court went on to State that claims waived by Japan under the Treaty included claims arising out of hostilities, and also claims

---

[166] Jessup, The Litvinov Assignment and the Pink Case, 36 *AJIL* (1942), 282.

[167] 32 ILR 233; for the similar approach see also Decision of the Tokyo District Court, February 25, 1963, 9 *Japanese Annual of International Law* (1965), 163, and Decision of the Hiroshima High Court, 11 May 1966, 13 *Japanese Annual of International Law* (1969), 110.

[168] 32 ILR 151–153.

[169] *Tag v Rogers*, 28 ILR 467; see also *Neri v US*, 20 ILR 223.

[170] *Austrian Citizen's Entitlement to Compensation (Germany)*, 32 ILR 156; see also *Shareholders of the Z. AG v A. Bank, Kammergericht Berlin*, 45 ILR 439.

[171] 44 ILR 301.

[172] 32 ILR 627. The Court also held that individuals had no right to claim damages under international law.

of nationals as distinct from the State.[173] In addition, the Court took a broad view of the power to waive a national's right, and made in particular a statement well illustrating the conceptual basis of the concept of waiver:

As for the contention that a State cannot waive the claims of its nationals, who are different subjects of law, the contention would surely be justified if the claims of nationals referred to mean the rights of nationals under international law. However, it must be pointed out that a State has the power to waive all claims of its nationals under municipal law. A State has, as a function of its sovereignty, the power to create, modify and extinguish rights and duties of its nationals in accordance with the due process of its municipal law; it is therefore possible in theory for a State to undertake, as against another State, to waive the rights of its nationals which have such character in relation to the State, setting aside the question of the propriety of such undertaking.[174]

This statement illustrates the indispensable link between the substance of legal relations and the ensuing legal consequences: waiver is possible precisely because the substantive legal relations, in this case the rights of individuals, are disposable by States. This must be qualified when the nature of legal relations so requires. The approach that international law knows no rights of individuals as such, that such rights are entirely dependent on the will of States, and therefore waiver is permissible, was no longer correct both at the time of the litigation and even at the time of the waiver, when international law already included the catalogue of human rights of individuals protecting them as such, and not as nationals of a given State.

The claims against the impact of the waiver contained in the 1952 Treaty between Japan and New Zealand on the rights of individuals were submitted to the UN Human Rights Committee but could not be considered because the case was declared inadmissible. The substance of the claim was that the 1952 Treaty could not have validly disposed the applicants' rights because in doing so it placed them in the state of discrimination and thus contradicted *jus cogens* norms on non-discrimination. The discrimination consisted in the fact that those New Zealanders who had been to Japanese concentration camps could not get proper compensation, unlike those New Zealanders who had been to German concentration camps.[175]

Waiver contains an inherent limitation as to which rights may be renounced and which may not, particularly in terms of rights protecting interests going beyond the interests of individual States. As Schwarzenberger states, 'provided that treaty rights are granted to a party in its own interest, a party may also renounce expressly its rights under a treaty.'[176] Suy also states that one can only waive his own rights.[177]

---

[173] Id., 640.   [174] Id., 641.
[175] *Evan Julian*, paras 5.3, 5.4, 7.2; the communication was considered inadmissible *ratione temporis*.
[176] 1 Schwarzenberger, *International Law* (1957), 535.   [177] Suy (1962), 166.

There is a distinction between absolute and relative rights of States, and only relative rights are renunciable.[178] Such a category of absolute rights also covers the inherent rights of a human person which a State cannot waive.[179] According to Doehring, peremptory norms related to human dignity cannot be waived even by the interested subject.[180]

Hersch Lauterpacht has linked the criterion of renunciability with fundamental illegalities following from the breaches of public order norms:

> In case of a violation of a multilateral treaty laying down rules of conduct whose observance is in the interest of all contracting parties, it is difficult to see how waiver on the part of one of them—even if such a waiver is juridically possible in the circumstances, e.g. in case of duress—can free the act of the stigma of unlawfulness and its results of the taint of invalidity. If the invalidity is due, for instance, to the breach of the General Treaty for the Renunciation of War, how can the consent of the defeated State conceivably influence the legal situation?[181]

The view of Jennings is also relevant:

> If the *injuria* is merely a wrong against a legal person, it would seem to follow that that person would have the capacity to qualify any resulting nullity by waiver. . . . But if the *injuria* is truly a breach of a *jus cogens*, whether or not there be also a wrong in respect of a particular legal person, there should in principle be no question of qualifying the resulting nullity by waivers or estoppels resulting from the conduct of a particular legal person.[182]

If an alleged waiver is enshrined in a treaty, and if it is as such impermissible and without effect, it necessarily affects the validity of the treaty. Article 53 of the Vienna Convention can be applicable. This factor may further necessitate interpreting a treaty in accordance with the international law standard that a State may renounce only its rights and not the rights of non-State actors; this would cause a narrow reading of waiver clauses and save a treaty from invalidation.

The practice varies in understanding the relevance of waivers in post-war treaties. Japan consistently argues that the 1951 Peace Treaty closed the door to all individual claims.[183]

The German *Bundesgerichtshof* in *Distomo* refused to see in the 1953 London Debt Agreement the intention to exclude the claims of victims of the 1944 Distomo massacre in Greece.[184] American courts, however, consider that

---

[178] Suy (1962), 167; Pfluger (1936), 265–267.   [179] Suy (1962), 167.

[180] Doehring (1997), 102.   [181] Lauterpacht (1970), 345.

[182] Jennings (1965), 74; Thirlway, (1990), 102, emphasizes that *jus cogens* shall be observed in all cases and cannot be subject to waiver. Virally, Reflexions sur le 'jus cogens', 12 *Annuaire Français de Droit International* (1966), 9; Gaja (1981), 296.

[183] Shelton, The World of Atonement: Reparations for Historical Injustices, 50 *NILR* (2003), 316; Parker and Crew, Compensation for Japan's World-War II War-Rape Victims, 17 *Hastings International and Comparative Law Review* (1994), 538.

[184] III ZR 245/98, 26 June 2003, Section 3, paras 1–3, at 13–17.

the slave labour claims are overridden by the settlement clauses of the post-war treaties. In *Burger-Fischer*, the US court considered that the reparations to individuals belong to the exclusive competence of the State of their nationality, that in the negotiation of peace treaties States have complete control of their nationals' claims and that, most significantly, that approach is not disputed by plaintiffs.[185] However, in this case the court failed to invoke the specific and clear treaty clause demonstrating the intention of States to consider the private claims as waived, that is they actually exercised their right to control private claims. If the court had adduced the evidence, the further issue of the validity of these waivers under *jus cogens* would arise.

The US court in *Iwanowa* referred to the 1953 waiver of the Soviet Union in favour of Germany but found, among others by reference to the practice of German courts, that it only extinguished inter-State claims, not private claims. The London Debt Agreement was perceived not as extinguishing claims but limited their relevance to inter-State channels.[186]

In general, this practice reduces a multilateral obligation to a bilateral one. It is suggested that American courts, while dismissing the slave labour claims by reference to the post-war treaty clauses of waiver and settlement, failed to consider the importance of violations of peremptory norms when interpreting whether an agreement is valid.[187]

With regard to the waiver of claims against Japan, it is noted that the treaty-based waivers must be interpreted restrictively, in accordance with the general concept of waiver in international law, which dictates that a State can only waive its own rights or the right of diplomatic protection, but not the substantive rights of individuals themselves.[188] In particular, such waivers do not extinguish individuals' rights to claim compensation at the national level,[189] nor address the private claims, such as the war-rape claims.[190] This contradicts the approach of the Japanese courts.

Parker and Crew convincingly state that

even if language in the treaties could be found that extinguished private claims, the parties to these treaties had no legal authority to do so. First of all, the underlying

---

[185] *Burger-Fischer*, 273–276; Christopter (2000), 1230 ff. See also *World War II Era Japanese Forced Labour Litigation*, where the Californian court rejected the claims of the former US prisoners against Japan due to the waiver under Article 14 of the Peace Treaty, 9–10.

[186] *Iwanowa*, 468–469, 456–461 (stating that the private claims are cognizable under the agreement but can be pursued only by the State of nationality), 491; the final outcome was prejudiced by the fact that the applicant's claims were time-barred.

[187] Christopher, *Jus Cogens*, Reparation Agreements, and Holocaust Slave Labour Litigation, 31 *Law and Policy in International Business* (2000), 1232.

[188] Ito (1994), 68.

[189] Igarashi, Post-War Compensation Cases, Japanese Courts and International Law, 43, *Japanese Annual of International Law* (2000), 78.

[190] Parker and Crew (1994), 538.

claims arise from violations of *jus cogens* norms and *erga omnes* obligations which require an appropriate remedy—compensation. The right to seek a remedy is itself a *jus cogens* right. If any provision of either the allied Treaty or the Korean Treaty effectively nullifies these *jus cogens* norms or allows violations of *jus cogens* to go uncompensated, then that provision would be void.[191]

Accordingly, Japan may not rely on its treaties with the allied powers or Korea to circumvent its liability or its duty to remedy individual claimants for acts governed by *jus cogens*.[192]

In the end, the argument about renunciability by a State of the rights of other (non-State) entities, and the *jus cogens* argument are practically based on the same conceptual precept. The argument that a State cannot renounce certain individual rights reinforces the argument about the normative quality of such rights as rights beyond a State's control and protected by international law for the sake of an individual itself.

The specific context of human rights and humanitarian law also contributes to outlawing waivers with regard to certain humanitarian norms. Peremptory norms, especially humanitarian law, prohibit waivers of claims, especially with regard to reparations.[193] The directly injured State has no right to waive breaches of the laws of war and it is left to its discretion when it will present its claims.[194]

One consequence of the 1949 Geneva Conventions protecting the protected persons as individuals is that individual rights may not be waived. 'If the belligerent occupant prevails on the ousted sovereign to agree to a forfeiture of rights of the occupied population, the Convention deems such forfeiture to be a nullity. Despite any such agreement, the rights of individuals under belligerent occupation remain in place.'[195] As the Pictet commentary to the Geneva Conventions suggests, 'The States may not by special agreement restrict, ie waive, their obligations under the Convention.'[196] Furthermore, the purpose of the Common Article 51/52/131/148 is 'to prevent the defeated party from being compelled in an armistice agreement or peace treaty to abandon all claims due for infractions committed by persons in the service of the victor.'[197]

---

[191] Parker and Crew (1994), 538.

[192] Id., 539.

[193] Kadelbach, *Zwingendes Völkerrecht* (1992), 71, 337.

[194] Kadelbach (1992), 245; Gattini (2003), 366, considers that a settlement contrary to peremptory humanitarian law is invalid and illustrates that both by the ILC's treatment of the issue of waiver in terms of *jus cogens* and by the Common Article 51/52/131/148 of the 1949 Geneva Conventions.

[195] Quigley (1992–1994), 46.

[196] Pictet, *Commentary to the First Geneva Convention of 1949* (1952), 74 (on Article 6).

[197] Pictet (1952), 373 (on Article 52).

2.3. Acquiescence

Acquiescence, unlike waiver and recognition, involves no explicit statement of attitude but is inferable from the conduct of a State. Acquiescence arises from conduct and the absence of protest.[198] Silence can undoubtedly produce legal effects.[199] As Judge Fitzmaurice stressed, when there is a duty or need to speak or act, and this is not done, it implies agreement.[200] If so, then such agreement replaces an existing legal regime through a derogation.

According to the Swiss Federal Tribunal, acquiescence is a passive acceptance of a situation giving rise to a binding legal relationship:

The term 'acquiescence' is understood to mean silence observed in response to a legal claim advanced by another subject of law, with the result that, according to the principle of good faith, this passive attitude can only be interpreted as constituting tacit recognition.[201]

While equating the effects of acquiescence to that of recognition, the Tribunal gives a further reason for assuming that acquiescence is as such subject to peremptory norms.

Acquiescence presupposes the legal conviction of involved States that nothing in their behaviour offends against the general legal conscience and their practice is in conformity with the general principles of international law.[202] This implies the conviction of States that under international law they are entitled to acquiesce to a given situation.

Acquiescence is a validation device. As McGibbon states, 'Rights which have been acquired in clear conformity with existing law have no need of the doctrine of acquiescence to confirm their validity.'[203] Acquiescence sets the seal of legality upon rules which were formerly in process of development and upon rights which were formerly in process of consolidation. It relates to recognition of legality and condonation of illegality.[204]

The law of acquiescence developed long ago and applies to a wide variety of situations. There is so far no general theory of acquiescence; it has not yet been constructed on the basis of existing practice.[205] Such a theory should be based not only on individual manifestations of acquiescence, but also with due account to the governing legal framework, not only on the concept of acquiescence, but also on the conditions and limits on its operation.

---

[198] Judge Ammoun, *North Sea*, *ICJ Reports*, 1969, 120–121; Brownlie (2003), 157.

[199] Rodriguez-Cedeno, *Fifth Report on Unilateral Acts*, A/CN.4/525, 14 17.

[200] Fitzmaurice, *ICJ Reports*, 1962, 62.

[201] Swiss Federal Tribunal, *Canton of Valais v Canton of Tessin*, 75 ILR 118–119.

[202] McGibbon, The Scope of Acquiescence in International Law, *BYIL* (1954), 145.

[203] McGibbon (1954), 143.

[204] McGibbon (1954), 145.

[205] McGibbon, although noting that acquiescence can validate practices which were originally illegal (1954: 182), focuses on title, historic rights etc., generally on substantive legal situations, not on acquiescing to illegal situations whose substantive illegality is not doubted.

Mere silence cannot amount to acquiescence; it can exceptionally have such effect, if it is prolonged and deliberate.[206] As the International Court stressed in *North Sea*, acquiescence presupposes a 'clearly and consistently evidenced acceptance'.[207] Uniform practice embodying a definite expression of will, free of ambiguity, is required.[208] It is unclear how many years of silence justify a conclusion of acquiescence.[209] All this naturally means that acquiescence can never be presumed and is always subject to heavy proof.

In *King of Spain*, the International Court considered that Nicaragua had acquiesced to the binding force of the defective arbitral award and could no longer contest its validity.[210] The same was held in *Temple* with regard to the border between Thailand and Cambodia, based on a map prepared by French colonial authorities. Circumstances called for some reaction, within a reasonable period, on the part of the Siamese authorities, if they wished to disagree with the map. They did not do so, either then or for many years, and thereby must be held to have acquiesced.[211]

Owing to the high standard of proof, tribunals often refuse to find acquiescence. No acquiescence was found by the International Court in *Gulf of Maine*, as the high standard of proof was not met.[212] No acquiescence was found in *Libya/Malta*, as the Court was 'unable to discern any pattern of conduct on either side sufficiently unequivocal to constitute either acquiescence or any helpful indication of any view of either Party as to what would be equitable'.[213]

The process of acquiescence takes place exclusively on a bilateral plane, in terms of purely inter-State relations. There can be a process of acquiescence involving a community dimension, such as in *Anglo-Norwegian Fisheries*, but such a process is still related to a bundle of bilateral relations. No practice can be identified where acquiescence validates acts and practices void as a matter of public order. All cases involving acquiescence relate to bilateral relations between the involved States and nowhere are public order norms involved. This justifies the ILC's decision to exclude the relevance of acquiescence from the ambit of *jus cogens*. As the Commission stated, as the breach of peremptory norms 'engages the interest of the international community as a whole, even the consent or acquiescence of the injured State does not preclude that interest from being expressed in order to ensure the settlement in

---

[206] Mann (1989), 409–410.   [207] *ICJ Reports*, 1969, 26.

[208] 83 ILR 81; Judge Ammoun, Shelf, *ICJ Reports*, 1969, 121.

[209] Thirlway, The Law and Procedure of the International Court of Justice, *BYIL* (1989), 46.

[210] *ICJ Reports*, 1960. the Award was published in Nicaragua's official Gazette. See also Judge Spender, Separate Opinion, *ICJ Reports*, 1960, 219.

[211] *Temple, ICJ Reports*, 1962, 23; Judge Alfaro, *ICJ Reports*, 1962, 40; Judge Fitzmaurice, *ICJ Reports*, 1962, 62; but see Dissenting Opinion of Judge Wellington Koo, *ICJ Reports*, 1962, 96–97.

[212] *ICJ Reports*, 1982; see also Guinea, 77 ILR, 667, para. 63.

[213] *ICJ Reports*, 1985, 261.

conformity with international law'.[214] This statement not only refers to the contexts in which bilateralism does not work but also, especially mentioning the need that settlements shall conform to international law, to the limits on derogation.

In *King of Spain*, Judge Urrutia enquired into possible limits of acquiescence, particularly whether it is within the power of acquiescence to revive the non-existent effects of a void award.

In civil law there are acts which are null and void which cannot be given life even by subsequent acceptance of the parties. In international law, however, States are sovereign and are bound by no limitation upon their acceptance of or agreement to anything whatsoever.

States may agree, if they think fit, to the carrying out the provisions of a null and void award, but in that case the cause and the legal basis of the provisions of the award are not to be found in the award which is a nullity, but in the valid agreement between two Sovereign States.[215]

This statement assumes that international law is a flat system with no hierarchy of norms constraining the capacity of States to make agreements: acquiescence is allowed in cases where, and precisely because, States can cure illegality by an agreement. It follows that if Judge Urrutia had recognized that peremptory norms constrain the treaty-making power, he could extend the same to acquiescence.

According to Fitzmaurice, territorial acquisitions null in their inception could be validated by prescription or acquiescence.[216] But this view is not supported by practice or the governing legal framework. Lauterpacht acknowledges that 'The absence of protest may . . . in itself become a source of legal right inasmuch as it is related—or forms a constituent element of—estoppel or prescription.'[217] Therefore, owing to the absence of centralized law-enforcement machinery, a protest by a State could be a useful tool of preservation of rights and it might be prudent for States to follow such a line if needed.[218] However,

the absence of protest is irrelevant if the action of the State claiming to acquire title is so wrongful in relation to any particular State or so patently at variance with general international law, as to render it wholly incapable of becoming the source of a legal right. . . . In such cases protest may be advisable; it is not essential. . . . *Ab injuria jus non oritur*. There are acts which are so tainted with nullity *ab initio* that no mere negligence of the interested State will cure it.[219]

---

[214] *ILC Report* 2001, commentary to Article 45, 308, para. 4.
[215] *ICJ Reports*, 1960, 222. [216] Fitzmaurice (1957), 121–122.
[217] Lauterpacht, Sovereignty over Submarine Areas, *BYIL* (1950), 395.
[218] Lauterpacht (1950), 396–397. cf also McGibbon (1954), 180–182.
[219] Lauterpacht (1950), 397–398, adding that rights related to submarine areas do not fall within such a category.

This approach is reflective of peremptory norms whose violation causes the objective illegality and nullity of conflicting acts. It is well-advised to hold that the doctrine of acquiescence is suitable in the contexts of bilateralism and breaches not involving objective illegality.

It is a rule of international law that a State must not perform acts of sovereignty on the territory of another State, and hence the extraterritorial arrest of a fugitive criminal is a violation of international law. But some writers hold that if the State of asylum acquiesces in the arrest, there is no breach of international law.[220] This view has been mirrored in practice. In *Alvarez-Machain*, a case involving abduction of a Mexican citizen from the territory of Mexico, the US court held that only Mexico had the standing to object to breaches of its sovereignty.[221] In *Lujan*, a US court stressed that the failure of Argentina and Bolivia to protest against the abduction of an Argentine citizen 'preclude any violation which otherwise might have occurred'.[222] But as F.A. Mann observed, 'every step in this argument is open to criticism.' The absence of protest would not heal these breaches.[223] This approach of the US courts is inadequate in terms of international public order. As the violations in question offended against *jus cogens* and gave rise to objective wrong against the international community as a whole, it is unjustified to make the matter dependent upon the subsequent reaction of a State from whose territory the abduction took place.

If States cannot recognize a situation through explicit will, it is unclear how their silence can bring about such an effect; a contrary assumption implies that an implied and silence-based attitude of a State has weightier effects than its express attitude.

A State obviously can in any case, through its protests or representations, interrupt the period consolidating acquiescence. But this approach is conceptually incorrect in terms of public order violations entailing objective wrongs, as it assumes that it is still the will of an aggrieved State on which illegality exclusively depends. As far as *jus cogens* is involved, this cannot be reasonable or correct, and this requires reappraisal of the very concept of acquiescence as traditionally understood.

Some scholars have developed the idea that practice commanding the assent of a great number of States can entail acquiescence. McNair held that the Japanese annexation of Korea commanded 'concurrence of the whole or the main part of the international community'.[224] Furthermore,

---

[220] O'Higgins, Unlawful Seizure and Irregular Extradition, 36 *BYIL* (1960), 280.

[221] *Alvarez-Machain v US*, 41 ILM (2002), 133.

[222] 61 ILR 67.

[223] Mann, Reflection on the Prosecution of Persons Abducted in Breach of International Law, Y. Dinstein and M.Tabory (eds), *International Law at a Time of Perplexity. Essays in Honour of Shabtai Rosenne* (1989), 410.

[224] McNair (1933), 71.

The benefits which accrue to a State annexing territory from the active recognition or passive indifference of other States are plain. The expression of approval or the absence of protest tends to confirm her title.[225]

According to Lauterpacht, there is nothing precluding collective acquiescence to illegal acts if the members of the community act in the general interest of peace and stability. In this context, recognition of the Italian annexation of Abyssinia by the UK and other States was justified by the reasons of pacification in Europe and the general interest.[226] Sztucki similarly claims that the Members of the League of Nations have acquiesced to the annexation of Ethiopia and to the Munich Agreements.[227] But to make such a claim it must be demonstrated that the silence of the Members of the League involved the legal conviction as to the legality of the relevant territorial changes, which is far from established. Also, apart from the fact that these annexations have never received full validity or recognition, the implication of such policy in terms of Second World War events was far from the 'pacification' Lauterpacht attributed to it, and the value of such general 'acquiescence' should be assessed accordingly. This is so also because, as was clarified above, the failure to protest is not the same as tacit recognition or acquiescence. It cannot be taken for granted that the so-called 'collective acquiescence' is genuine and the individual State attitudes in this 'collective' process are not motivated by considerations of political expediency rather than legal judgment. For instance, the failure of the US to question the incorporation of East Timor into Indonesia in 1976 did not represent a legal judgment but was rather based on political expediency (amounting in truth to some form of complicity in the breach). Thus, owing to its national interests, and also because the reaction was not likely to bring about any changes, the US decided to act on the basis of the prevailing factual situation, although legally it was committed to the principle of self-determination.[228]

It seems that in general while States sometimes fall short of direct recognition of illegalities, as some States did in the case of annexation of East Timor, their conduct can be interpreted as *de facto* acquiescence. Nevertheless, the standard of proof on finding acquiescence is quite high and combines material and psychological elements, which perhaps also motivate States to take ambiguous attitudes which they can reinterpret later, and therefore conducive conduct cannot by itself amount to acquiescence.

Jennings has acknowledged that *jus cogens* does not permit validation through acquiescence, but he further referred to third-party acquiescence, which could operate even in cases of public order wrongs.[229] Jennings tries to

---

[225] McNair (1933), 71.   [226] Lauterpacht (1947), 429–430.

[227] Sztucki (1974), 35–36.   [228] Department of State Bulletin, 5 September 1977, 326.

[229] Jennings (1967), 64; Gomez Robledo, Le ius cogens international: sa genèse, sa nature, ses fonctions, 172 *Recueil des cours* (1981), 197, suggesting that the passivity of the community can legalize the state of things contrary to peremptory norms.

take into account public order considerations, but still applies old criteria developed by McNair when international law was less familiar with peremptory norms. Hence, Jennings' view rests unsatisfactorily on an inconvenient combination of the dictates of bilateralism and the community interest. The concept of third-party acquiescence is doctrinally incoherent and does not operate in practice.

Brownlie repeatedly states that acts offending *jus cogens* cannot be validated through acquiescence or prescription, and does not refer to the exception suggested by Jennings.[230] Similarly, Cassese states that no serious breach of self-determination can be validated by the States concerned, as it involves *jus cogens*.[231]

As the international community as a whole is the creator of peremptory norms, it is conceptually imaginable that it can validate breaches of *jus cogens* through acquiescence.[232] However, finding the community's acquiescence is not an easy task. Any acquiescence must involve an unequivocal expression and evidence of the community will to validate a given breach, as opposed merely to the attitude of some parts of that community. The normal features of acquiescence obviously apply, which requires that the community's acquiescence shall satisfy the time factor and involve a belief of legal change which is never presumed, but must always be evidenced.

At the same time, bearing in mind the close similarity between the processes of acquiescence and custom-generation, it is arguable that any community acquiescence to a breach of *jus cogens* must satisfy criteria to be met by the emergence of a general customary norm. That involves uniform, consistent and continuous State practice accompanied with a clear, even if implied, *opinio juris*. The custom-generation criteria elaborated in *Asylum* or *North Sea* would be highly relevant in this context.

There is a logical possibility for arguing that the international community has acquiesced to breaches of peremptory norms on occasions, for example to the South African Truth and Reconciliation process which is at variance with the duty to prosecute *jus cogens* crimes, and this validates the illegalities this process may involve. This cannot be ruled out, but cannot be assumed either, because every instance of community acquiescence requires proof of the legal conviction of the community as a whole and that is far from clear in this case.

In general, so-called collective acquiescence has a conceptual problem. The expression of attitude of third States or the international community as a

---

[230] Brownlie (2003), 67, 157, 488, 615.   [231] Cassese (1994), 179–180.
[232] Rozakis (1976), 128 refers to validation not by conduct of the State concerned but by 'the general conduct of the international community as a whole.'

whole falls better within the concept of custom-generation—a process itself subject to *jus cogens*.[233]

The doctrine of acquiescence has the same ingredients as the general doctrine of customary law. McGibbon states that 'the doctrine of acquiescence is as significant a factor in the development of a customary right as is the *opinio juris* in the formation of a customary obligation'.[234] Emergence of customary rights for a State necessarily implies customary obligations for other States to respect those customary rights; and in terms of acquiescing States, acquiescence performs a role fairly similar to *opinio juris*.

If peremptory norms trump conflicting custom, there is no reason to assume that they cannot trump practices allegedly involving acquiescence, which share the nature and ingredients of custom-generation. However, this still should be reconciled with the conceptual possibility that community acquiescence established with an intention to validate *jus cogens* breaches could perhaps escape the effect of *jus cogens*, provided that the proof criteria are met.

Community acquiescence is difficult to establish as the burden of proof is high and hence it is virtually without incidence. In addition, what this writer takes as superior community norms are by their essence incompatible with the concept of validation which could weigh in the balance when the proof of community acquiescence to a given breach is sought to be established.

2.4. Prescription

Acquiescence and prescription are two sides of a coin.[235] The ILC Articles on State Responsibility mention acquiescence in the context of extinctive prescription of claims.

International law is familiar with the concepts of acquisitive and extinctive prescriptions. The former is more often involved in terms of territorial acquisitions,[236] and has often to do with situations involving acquiescence. In terms of *jus cogens*, and also generally, acquisitive prescription deals with legitimation of a wrong through passage of time. So does extinctive prescription and hence these concepts are similar.

The notion of prescription is applied more often to personal rights, such as fisheries or compensation claims, while acquiescence is more often used in

---

[233] The primacy of *jus cogens* over customary law is recognised by Vattel (1916), 4–5; Verdross (1937), 573; Christenson (1988), 611; Saulle (1987), 392. In practice the primacy of *jus cogens* over customary law has been confirmed by Judge Lauterpacht in *Bosnia*, Separate Opinion, *ICJ Reports*, 1993, 440; the Inter-American Commission in *Victims of the Tugboat '13 de Marzo'*, para. 79; and the US court in *Siderman de Blake v Argentina*, 103 ILR 472.

[234] McGibbon (1954), 151.

[235] cf 1 Jennings and Watts (1992), 527; Jennings (1967), 67, speaking interchangeably of acquiescence and recognition.

[236] *Rann of Kutch*, 381–384, ILR 50; Lauterpacht (1929), 116–118; Johnson (1950), 332.

terms of consolidation of the legality of situations, including territorial ones. But both kinds of situations relate to loss of the right to invoke certain entitlements, transformations of illegality into legality.

According to Lauterpacht, illegality can be legitimized if the rigid conditions of the lapse of time and prescription are complied with.[237] Bin Cheng regards prescription as a general principle of law.[238] Lauterpacht defended the principle of prescription in support of his thesis that private law concepts are influential in international law.[239] McNair would probably respond that no automatic transfer of general principles into international law is advisable. Pure international law reasons and evidences must be found, and these, as will be seen, are far from certain and uniform. In particular, nothing in the practice discussed by Lauterpacht indicated that the principle applies to public order violations.

There is some case-law claimed in support of prescription.[240] As noted in *Ambatielos*, 'it is generally admitted that the principle of extinctive prescription applies to the right to bring an action before an international tribunal.'[241] But it is noted that 'There is, of course, no rule of international law putting a limitation of time on diplomatic action or upon the presentation of an international claim to an international tribunal.'[242]

As the Mixed Arbitral Tribunal noted, 'Positive international law has not so far established any precise and generally adopted rule either as to the principle of prescription as such or as to its duration. Neither do arbitral decisions or opinions of writers yield any agreed solution.'[243] *Ambatielos* states there is no rule laying down any precise prescription time-limit, except in cases of special agreements to that effect.[244] The 1925 International Law Institute Resolution stated that tribunals 'must be able to detect, in the facts of the case before it, the existence of one of the grounds which are indispensable to cause prescription to operate'.[245] If tribunals have such

---

[237] Lauterpacht (1947), 421–428.   [238] Cheng (1953), 375.

[239] Lauterpacht (1929), 116–119, 217–265. Visscher (1960), 525–533.

[240] 4 AD 265.

[241] Ambatielos, 23 ILR 314; Re Jennings and Watts, para. 155. On early practice see King (1925), 82.

[242] George W. Cook (No. 2) Case, US–Mexico: General Claims Commission, 3 June 1927, 4 AD 264–265. cf also *Nauru, ICJ Reports*, 1992, 253–254, *LaGrand*, Merits, paras 53–57.

[243] *Sarropoulos v Bulgarian State*, Greco-Bulgarian MAT, 1927, 4 AD 263; French State Railways, 20 ILR 483–484.

[244] Ambatielos, 23 ILR 315; see also Vadapalas, Codification of the Law of International Responsibility by the International Law Commission: Breach of International Law and Its Consequences, 23 *Polish Yearbook of International Law* (1997–1998), 37, pointing out that 'general international law does not contain any exact time limits for prescription, except if it is established by international treaty binding the parties to the dispute or responsibility'. The example of this is the six-month limit on the time period that can pass before the seising the European Court of Human Rights after the last national decision has been taken on the issue.

[245] *BYIL*, 1925, 315.

discretion, they are unlikely to use it in a way upholding strict and fixed time limits for the presentation of a claim. In *Ambatielos*, the Arbitration Commission gave no effect to prescription claims.

The absence of a fixed time limit for prescriptibility of claims complicates the principle itself, as if there are no fixed time limits, it will always be difficult to find in specific cases whether prescription has taken place. Consequently, even if there is a rule on prescription it can be merely a reference rule and not a substantive one; the principle cannot determine whether prescription takes place, but it is necessary to look at peculiarities of specific situations and see whether they would admit the principle to operate.

A tribunal would in such cases have to balance conflicting factors, and it is likely that the community interest will be one of them, which could strengthen the presumption against prescription. It is clear that tribunals will not apply classical standards of prescription in cases of aggression, torture or genocide as they possibly will in the case of a breach of a bilateral treaty or fisheries claims.

As we saw, one extreme view is that prescription as a rule is not recognized and that everything depends on specific legal relations; another extreme is to consider prescription as a device operating in a blanket manner. One might reconcile the two conflicting approaches in the following way: prescription could perhaps operate as a validation device, but apply only where the nature of legal relations so permits, that is where the development of that relation depends on the view of involved States only, and does not entail any conflict with public order considerations.

Differentiation of the situations to which prescription could apply is desirable, and one may note the suggestion that prescription requirements are more exacting in the case of contractual claims than non-contractual ones.[246] This is logical, as non-contractual claims can involve radically different situations and some situations are more likely than others to militate against strict time limits for presenting a claim.

Lauterpacht states that prescription may be prevented by 'the patent illegality of the purported acquisition combined with continued protests on the part of the dispossessed State',[247] and prescription cannot be invoked in support of forcible territorial acquisitions.[248] More cautiously, Jennings submits that the prescription period cannot run if the policy of non-recognition is adopted.[249] If it is accepted that non-recognition of breaches of *jus cogens* is a matter of duty not policy, that may exclude the relevance of prescription

---

[246] Fleischhauer, Prescription, in Bernhardt (ed.), 3 *Encyclopedia of Public International Law* (1997), 1107.
[247] Lauterpacht (1970), 345.
[248] Lauterpacht (1947), 428.   [249] Jennings (1967), 67–68; Dinstein (2001), 154.

altogether. Consequently, Brownlie suggests that the obligation of non-recognition prevails over prescription.[250] That may dictate that claims arising out of breaches and involving voidness subject to the principle of non-recognition of *jus cogens* are categorically imprescriptible.

With regard to human rights law, it is inconceivable that time prescription bars the claims of victims of gross human rights violations.[251] One may also invoke the imprescriptibility of international crimes.[252] If international law does not allow prescription for trying certain international crimes, it is doubtful that it allows the claims arising from the very conduct causing such crimes to be subject to prescription at inter-State level.[253]

The final issue with regard to prescription is its relation to the process of custom-generation. Lauterpacht made a distinction between prescription and custom-generation just in the time element, asserting that while prescription needs a long time to crystallize, this is not necessarily so in case of custom where the general practice may cure the lack of time element.[254] But Lauterpacht has not otherwise distinguished between custom-generation and prescription. According to McGibbon, 'prescriptive and customary rights share a common process of development which involves, on the one hand, constant assertion of the right in question, and, on the other hand, consent in that assertion on the part of the affected States. As in prescriptive rights, so in customary rights the two elements are complementary and mutually independent.'[255]

According to Fitzmaurice, both customary and prescriptive rights, although one general and other particular in nature, both depend on practice

---

[250] Brownlie (1963), 422, speaking of the example of the unlawful use of force, and also excluding prescription with regard to illegal territorial acquisitions, Brownlie (2003), 150, and more generally id., 490. Crawford, *The Creation of States* (1979), 82, with a special emphasis on *jus cogens*.

[251] Van Boven, para. 135; Paolilo, On Unfulfilled Duties: The Obligation to Make Reparation in Cases of Violation of Human Rights, in V. Götz, P. Selmer, R. Wolfrum (eds), *Liber Amicorum Günther Jaenicke—Zum 85. Geburtstag* (1998), 298–299. Non-gross violations also cannot be time-barred. Id., 300.

[252] *Furundzija*, para. 157; *Pinochet* (Belgium), 358. Brownlie (2003), 567; Van den Wyngaert and Dugard, Non-applicability of Statute of Limitations, in Cassese, Gaeta & Jones (eds) *The Rome Statute of the International Criminal Court—A Commentary* (2002), 887–888; Degan, Responsibility for International Crimes, in Sienho Yee and Wang Tieya (eds), *International Law in the Post-Cold War World—Festschrift Li Haopei* (2001), 205; Simma and Paulus, The responsibility of Individuals for Human Rights Abuses in Internal Conflict: A Positivist View, 93 *AJIL* (1999), 302. According to the Italian court in *Haas and Priebke*, this is a *jus cogens* principle.

[253] Joinet, Revised Final Report on Impunity, para. 31; Kadelbach (1992), 65, doubts that prescription can cure breaches of *jus cogens*.

[254] Lauterpacht (1950), 393.

[255] McGibbon (1954), 150. McGibbon, Customary International Law and Acquiescence, *BYIL* (1957), 119, stressing in particular that acquiescence is involved on the part of respective States.

or usage, and on 'general acceptance in the one case, and in the other specific recognition or tacit acquiescence'. The only significant difference is a time factor, while the method (practice and assent) is the same both for customary and prescriptive rights.[256]

As the emergence of prescriptive rights is 'contrary to the existing (and otherwise still subsisting) international order', the passage of time is relevant at least in all cases where an express agreement cannot be shown.[257] This factor makes the process of prescription even more similar to custom-generation (and emphasizes that it embodies agreement). Though prescription most typically applies to situations where one party benefits and another is burdened and custom-generation applies in a way benefiting and burdening all, the material and psychological elements giving rise to rights and duties are shared similarly by both concepts, even though prescription is about a specific claim and custom is about a general rule. This confirms that prescription is subject to *jus cogens*, as it shares the nature of custom-generation.

3. CONCLUSION

The character of validation devices does not require that they should operate in each and every situation without any limitation. It is inherent to *jus cogens* that its effects apply even if contradicted by another rule or principle. This requires viewing validation devices as qualified in scope when public order norms are at stake.

As the capacity of States to perform certain acts is always subject to *jus cogens*, validation devices fall within the same principle. It is also clear that some validation devices are subject to *jus cogens* because they share the nature and effect of other devices and processes which are obviously subject to *jus cogens*. Validation devices mostly also share the characteristics of treaty and custom—both of which are subject to *jus cogens*—and this reinforces the view that they are subordinated in their scope and effects to peremptory norms.

The governing legal framework requires agreeing with the view that no act contrary to *jus cogens* 'can be legitimated by means of consent, acquiescence or recognition; nor is a protest necessary to preserve rights affected by such an act'.[258]

Validation of the breaches of peremptory norms by one or several States is excluded as a matter of principle. There can be conceptual room for the community validation of such breaches. But that is contingent upon the

---

[256] Fitzmaurice, The Law and Procedure of the International Court of Justice, 29 *BYIL* (1953), 31.

[257] Fitzmaurice (1953), 31, 68–69.   [258] 1 Jennings and Watts (1996), 8.

specificities of individual validation devices. In order for the *jus cogens* illegalities to be recognized, there must be manifest community recognition in the first place, involving a clear and unequivocal expression of the community will to that effect. In order for the *jus cogens* illegalities to be acquiesced in, there must be a valid community acquiescence involving the proper time element and the belief of a legal change similar to the process of general custom-generation. Therefore, although the community validation of *jus cogens* illegalities cannot be excluded and can even carry a certain degree of conceptual coherence, the burden of proof is always very high, which negatively impacts upon the practical possibilities of the international community as a whole validating specific breaches of peremptory norms.

PART III

Peremptory Norms and the Powers of International Organizations

Preliminary Questions

International organizations are established by States for dealing with problems of global or regional importance which cannot be resolved without the coordination of State activities through the establishment of bodies separate from States. The very existence of international organizations and their powers is derived from agreements between States, and there can be no international organization unless States want it to be there. International organizations are thus based on constitutions of limited powers, derived from the agreement of Member States, and thus bound by international law standards.[1] Some organizations are more powerful than others, but their powers, extensive as they are, nevertheless derive from their founding instrument consented to by Member States.

Apparently in line with this approach, the ILA Report on the Accountability of International Organisations refers to the principle of constitutionality and affirms that, since international organizations are based on the Rule of Law, they cannot avoid a review as to whether the decisions and measures adopted by them are in conformity with the constituent instrument. Organizations cannot overstep the restraints laid down in the constituent instrument and determining how they exercise their powers.[2] The Member States, organs, officials and staff members of an international organization have a fundamental obligation to secure the lawfulness of the actions and decisions of the organization, and to take all precautionary measures to prevent the occurrence of any harm as a result of these actions and decisions.[3] But, apart from such general considerations, there are some factors underlining the special relevance of peremptory norms.

As international organizations are based on agreements between States, nothing in principle precludes the organs of such organizations to act in

---

[1] Franck, *Fairness in International Law and Institutions* (1995); Reinisch, Developing Human Rights and Humanitarian Law Accountability of the Security Council for the Imposition of Economic Sanctions, 95 *AJIL* (2001), 858; E. Lauterpacht, The Legal Effect of Illegal Acts of International Organisations, *Cambridge Essays in International Law* (1965), 89. The fact that international organizations are bound by general international law was emphasized by the International Court in the Advisory Opinion on *WHO Regional Office, ICJ Reports*, 1980, 90. For a similar view see M. Shaw and K. Wellens, Third ILA Report on Accountability of International Organisations (2002), 11–13.

[2] M. Shaw and K. Wellens, ILA Second Report on Accountability of International Organisations (2000), 7; M. Shaw and K. Wellens, ILA Final Report on Accountability of International Organisations (2004), 13.

[3] M. Shaw and K. Wellens, Second Report, 18.

disregard of ordinary norms of international law (*jus dispositivum*), pro-vided and to the extent that the constituent instrument confirms the inten-tion of Member States to enable an organization to act in disregard of certain norms of international law while exercising its functions. Here, the extent of the intention of the Member States is crucial. But if a norm is peremptory, then States are not allowed to derogate from it and establish organizations entitled to act in disregard to *jus cogens*. It follows that *jus cogens* is an inherent limitation on any organization's powers, and binds an organization even if the opposite could be inferred from its constituent instrument. In addition, a breach of *jus cogens* causes specific legal con-sequences in terms of the validity and interpretation of relevant acts or transactions, and these consequences are not characteristic to ordinary rules.

International organizations violate peremptory norms quite often in the fields such as *jus ad bellum*, self-determination of peoples, or human rights and humanitarian law. As the ILA Final Report on the Accountability of International Organisations confirms, human rights and humanitarian norms bind international organizations in different areas. For instance, organizations are bound to make a human rights impact assessment when imposing non-military coercive measures. The same principle applies to structural adjustment and development projects.[4] But the consequences related to the responsibility of international organizations for breaches of peremptory norms come into play not because the organization violates *jus cogens*, but simply because it acts illegally.[5]

The relevance of peremptory norms for powers of international organiza-tions is determined by the non-derogable character of these norms. The contexts in which the issue of derogation can be conceived with regard to international organizations have to do either with the question whether the constituent instrument of an organization permits acting in violation of *jus cogens*, or whether that instrument provides for the adoption by the organiza-tion of decisions that contradict *jus cogens*. Examples of the first option are hard to find. However, if an organ of the organization or its member claim that its conduct contradicting *jus cogens* is justified by its mandate to

---

[4] Final Report (2004), 23–24, 28.
[5] The responsibility of international organizations is currently among the subjects being studied by the UN International Law Commission. See, in this regard, the reports of the Special Rapporteur G. Gaja, *First Report*, A/CN.4/532, and *Second Report*, A/CN.4/541. See especially *First Report*, 8–9, emphasizing that the responsibility of international organizations follows from their international legal personality and their consequent ability to be bound by international obligations. The ILA Final Report affirms that 'the principles that international organisations may be held internationally responsible for their acts is nowadays part of customary international law', Shaw and Wellens, ILA Final Report on Accountability of International Organisations (2004), 26.

adopt such decisions, then, along with the issues of responsibility, the issue of validity of the respective provisions would arise.

This framework suggests that the action derogatory from *jus cogens* is to be expected in the first place from the organization which can adopt binding decisions impacting the rights and duties of States. International financial institutions such as the International Monetary Fund and the World Bank are certainly bound by general international law and peremptory norms as other organizations are. But their participation in breaches gives rise to responsibility rather than acts derogating from peremptory norms.[6] These institutions do not possess the competence to adopt binding decisions. A theoretical argument can still be made about the derogation from *jus cogens* through the lending agreements concluded between the World Bank and its members. The conceptual significance of this issue is reinforced by the fact that if the Inspection Panel pronounces that the Bank has violated its policies and procedures, the fact that these actions were based on a treaty concluded between the Bank and its members does not alter the legal position. But this matter has never so far been treated as one of *jus cogens* invalidity. Therefore, on balance, it seems that it is premature, though by no means unjustified, to deal with this issue at this point.

As for UN organs, the General Assembly does not issue binding decisions, at least not in relation to States,[7] and it is unlikely that its resolutions would offend against peremptory norms, the only possibility of this being the decisions expressing the attitude of this organ regarding certain legal positions. However, the Security Council can not only bind States, it can also establish authorities and offices with the power to take binding decisions. This makes the Council's role most relevant in terms of compliance with peremptory norms and the relevant consequences for the Council's decisions, and it is preferred to place principal emphasis on this organ.

The specific focus on the Security Council is justified for several reasons. The Council is established under the UN Charter as a powerful organ; it possesses the power to issue binding decisions not only internally, but also externally, with regard to Member States of the United Nations, thereby entering the field of general international law. It could even override certain international obligations, which provokes thoughts about the impact of *jus cogens*. Its practice affects a wide variety of legal relations and is hence particularly rich in instances in which a violation of international law in general or peremptory norms in particular can be alleged. Such a specific

---

[6] The establishment of the World Bank Inspection Panel serves as evidence that the Bank is accountable for violations of its policies and procedures and the Panel implements this accountability. cf Orakhelashvili, *IOLR* (2005), 57–102. There is no similar structure in the IMF.

[7] The General Assembly can issue operative decisions, as confirmed in *Namibia, ICJ Reports* 1971, 16. But operative decisions are not meant to impose obligations on States, though they can impact some legal positions.

position provokes the question whether and to what extent the Council could be subject to legal norms and particularly to non-derogable peremptory norms. On its face, the problem could even be conceived as a conflict between two different intentions of the international community: to endow peremptory norms, as a special category of norms, with special status impacting with specific legal consequences on conflicting acts and transactions, and to endow the Security Council with certain powers by virtue of its special hierarchical position in order to enable it to fulfil its primary responsibility with regard to maintenance of international peace and security. It is the mutual interaction of these arguably conflicting circumstances which needs to be examined and explained.

The broad nature of the Council's powers becomes even more explicit if the doctrine of implied powers is considered. Practice has affirmed in many instances that in order to meet their tasks fully, international organizations have certain powers implied in their legal personality or their purposes.[8] The conceptual basis of this approach is explained by Judge Alvarez in the *Admissions* case, stating that 'an institution, once established, acquires a life of its own, independent of the elements which have given birth to it, and it must develop, not in accordance with the views of those who created it, but in accordance with the requirements of international life'.[9] This factor has been crucial in the development of the powers of the Security Council, which is empowered under Chapters VI and VII of the UN Charter to deal with situations endangering international peace and security. The powers of the Council are largely discretionary, as under Article 39 of the Charter it can determine the existence of a threat to, or breach of, international peace, and under Articles 41 and 42 it can take enforcement measures to deal with such a threat or breach. In practice, both the concept of threats to peace under Article 39 and enforcement measures under Articles 41 and 42 have been interpreted extensively, thus enabling the Council to cope with situations originally not envisaged to be subsumable within its competence.[10]

It is therefore argued that as the decisions of the Security Council are discretionary, they are not as such based on legal judgment and are hence

---

[8] *Reparation for Injuries*, ICJ Reports, 1949, 174, 182, 184; *Effect of Awards*, ICJ Reports, 1954, 47, 57; *Certain Expenses*, ICJ Reports, 1962; *Legality of the Threat or Use of Nuclear Weapons*, ICJ Reports, 1996, 226, 240; *Cumaraswamy*, ICJ Reports, 1999, 62, 82. For a sceptical approach, see the dissenting opinion by Judge Hackworth in the *Reparation* case, stating that 'powers not expressed cannot freely be implied' due to the delegated nature of the powers of the United Nations, *ICJ Reports*, 1949. In some fields, such as in international employment law, organizations are expected to take only decisions expressly authorized by law, Akehurst, *The Law Concerning Employment in International Organisations* (1967), 132.

[9] *Admission to the United Nations*, ICJ Reports, 1947–48, at 68.

[10] It will suffice to mention that the International Criminal Tribunal for the Former Yugoslavia is established under Article 41. Although this is not expressly provided for in the text of the Article, the Tribunal held in the *Tadic* case that this Article may serve as the legal basis of its establishment, *Prosecutor v Tadic*, Case IT-94-1-AR72, 35 ILM 32, 44–45 (1995).

political in character. Kelsen considered that the Security Council is there to preserve peace and not to enforce law.[11] But the crucial question is whether the political character of decisions of the Council makes this process of decision-making free of legal constraints.

In other words, it is not doubted that the Council's substantive powers are broad; but it is another issue to consider legal limitations on the exercise of such substantive powers, particularly bearing in mind the specific legal position of the Council. Therefore, before going on to examine specific aspects, some preliminary factors regarding the legal nature of the Council's powers should be examined.

The International Court gave a clear solution to this issue by stating that the political character of the organ of an international organization does not release it from the observance of legal provisions which constitute limitations on its powers or criteria for its judgment.[12] Similarly, Bernhardt suggested that even if the issues of legality of political institutional decisions involve highly political issues, they still are legal questions subject to analysis of international lawyers.[13] Judge Jennings clearly adopted such view in *Lockerbie* by stating that

all discretionary powers of lawful decision-making are necessarily derived from the law, and are therefore governed and qualified by the law. This must be so if only because the sole authority of such decisions flows itself from the law. It is not logically possible to claim to represent the power and authority of the law, and at the same time, claim to be above the law.[14]

Consequently, Judge Jennings rejected the view that the Security Council resolutions adopted under Chapter VII of the Charter are immune from review according to applicable legal principles. A similar view seems to have recently prevailed within the Council itself. In the process of adoption of Resolution 1483(2003), which confirmed the status of the occupying powers in Iraq, the President of the Security Council emphasized that

under the Charter the powers delegated to the Security Council under this resolution are not open-ended or unqualified. They should be exercised in ways that conform

---

[11] Kelsen, *The Law of the United Nations* (1951), 294; see also Gill, Legal and Some Political Limitations on the Power of the UN Security Council to Exercise its Enforcement Powers under Chapter VII of the Charter, XXVI *Netherlands Yearbook of International Law* (1995) 46.

[12] *Admission of a State to the Membership of the United Nations* (Advisory Opinion), *ICJ Reports*, 1947–48, 64.

[13] Bernhardt, *Ultra Vires* Activities of International Organisations, in Makarczyk (ed.), *Theory of International Law at the Threshold of the 21st Century. Essays in Honour of Krzysztof Skubiszewski* (1996), 608.

[14] *ICJ Reports*, 1998, 110; see also Brownlie, General Course, 228 *RdC* (1995), 217, stressing that discretion can exist only within the law. The ILA Final Report (2004), 28, affirms that international organizations may 'incur international legal responsibility if the exercise of discretionary powers entails a sufficiently serious breach of a superior rule such as the right to life, food and medicine of the individual or guarantees for due process of law.'

with 'the principles of justice and international law' mentioned in article 1 of the Charter, and especially in conformity with the Geneva Conventions and the Hague Regulations, besides the Charter itself.[15]

Such a situation needs to be reconciled with the fact that the Security Council can adopt decisions which can impact on the rights and duties of State and non-State actors. It has even been contended, both by writers and the representatives of States in the Security Council, that this organ has on some occasions exercised legislative competence.[16] At the same time, the membership of the Council has offered serious resistance to the idea of the Council's role as legislator. The ICTY also emphasized that there is no organ within the UN system empowered to legislate for Member States.[17]

This widely debated issue cannot be examined here fully, but a few observations are necessary. The claims portraying the Security Council as the legislative organ do not reflect the normal essence of legislature, which involves the competence to establish the rules regulating all possible aspects of social life. The Council's role is far from this, its mandate being limited to actions where the threats to peace arise under Article 39. It is also clear that no specific intent is inferable either from the UN Charter or from its preparatory materials to establish the Council as a legislative organ. In addition, the 'legislative' measures adopted by the Council, with the possible exception of antiterrorist resolutions such as Resolutions 1373(2001) or 1540(2004), which prescribed a number of measures to combat international terrorism, have so far addressed only specific situations, such as for example the situation of the demarcation of the Iraq–Kuwaiti border. It is therefore difficult to see sufficient evidence of the Council acting as a legislator.

Even if it were assumed that the Council is a legislator, this factor would not exempt it from the constraints of legal standards under the Charter and general international law. The issue of the legislative character of the Security Council's competence is simply moot, because it does not alter anything in terms of the scope of the Council's powers or limits on those powers. The question whether the Council's specific measure is of legislative character is not likely to make any difference in terms of the application of that measure. Denoting the Council's measures as legislation brings about no consequences that are not otherwise available, nor removes the consequences otherwise arising. The principal, and only real, question is that of the operation of the

---

[15] S/PV.4761, at 11–12.

[16] Kirgis, The Security Council's First Fifty Years, 89 *AJIL* (1995), 506 at 520; Szasz, The Security Council Starts Legislating, 96 *AJIL* (2002), 901–905; Talmon, The Security Council as World Legislature, 99 *AJIL* (2005), 175–193. But see Angelet, International Law Limits to the Security Council, in Gowlland-Debbas (ed.), *United Nations Sanctions and International Law* (2001), 79, submitting that the Council may not create new obligations for a target-State of its Chapter VII action, and it can act only as a law-enforcing and not a legislative body.

[17] Appeal Chamber, 2 October 1995, para. 40.

legal framework that includes the Charter and the relevant rules of general international law. As for the general character of certain resolutions, they must be viewed in the interpretative framework as the incidences of application the Council's powers to determine and respond to the threats to peace. The legality of such measures ultimately depends not on whether the Council can exercise 'legislative' powers, but whether those measures properly fit into the scope of delegated treaty powers of this organ.

The instances involving the enactment of norms of general applicability do not necessarily involve legislative competence. Akehurst considers it 'generally admitted' that international organizations have legislative power over their staff, and refers to the general character of norms laid down in staff regulations: 'When a body is able to lay down general and permanent rules applicable to a class of people who are not parties to an agreement providing for those rules, the conclusion is inevitable that such a body has a legislative power.'[18] However, the legislative character of the body enacting norms requires not merely the general character of those norms, but the basic question is about the status of the organ, whether it has been designated as legislature, because even in national legal systems the rules of general applicability are often enacted by executive or administrative organs and are denoted as administrative regulations. Therefore, nothing proves the assumption that the relevant international organizations are endowed with legislative powers. The proper difference needs to be made between legislative and regulatory powers. It is the latter that international organizations possess within the framework of their general powers, among others implied powers necessary to enable them to meet their purposes.

Apart from the issue of law-making, it has also been debated whether the Council, even if not originally so empowered, can enter the sphere of the law by adopting decisions impacting on the rights and duties of Member States. Such a proposition has been put forward by the International Court in *Namibia*, where the Court dealt with the status of Namibian territory and the ensuing legal consequences.[19] Judge Fitzmaurice disagreed with the Court, stating that it is not the Council's function to perform such functions, as it is only designed to adopt measures preserving and restoring peace.[20] Despite the fact that this view has not been accepted by the Court, it is strongly represented in doctrine. Bowett has doubted that States, while ratifying the Charter, empowered the Security Council to modify their legal rights, and adds that the Council is not a legislature.[21] Graefrath similarly submits that the Security Council may suppress breaches of peace, such as the illegal

---

[18] Akehurst, *The Law Concerning Employment in International Organisations* (1967), 199–200.
[19] *ICJ Reports*, 1971, 15.
[20] Dissenting Opinion, *ICJ Reports*, 1971, 294, para. 115.
[21] Bowett, The Impact of Security Council Decisions on Dispute Settlement Procedures, 5 *EJIL* (1994), 92.

use of force, but may not impose the solution of a conflict which caused the use of force, as this would be beyond its competence.[22] Klein likewise submits that no authority to impose territorial settlements follows from the power of the United Nations to maintain international peace and security.[23]

It is also occasionally contended that the Security Council acting under Chapter VII or the General Assembly acting with an overwhelming majority of States may legally impose a comprehensive territorial settlement on States, and such a settlement may become valid against all States; or that the Council can make other similar arrangements through the use of powers under Article 41, such as the establishment of permanent no-fly zones.[24] In the case of the Iraq–Kuwait boundary, however, the members of the Council took care to emphasize that the Council was merely performing the technical task of demarcating an already existing boundary,[25] as it would not be competent to do more than that.[26] It is emphasized that neither the Council nor any other UN organ is given the power to permanently allocate rights or impose the terms of a settlement.[27] In particular, these organs have no rights to order the dispositions of territory.[28] As is illustrated by the views referred to, such an approach seems to dominate the doctrinal debate.

It suffices to state that, in maintaining or restoring international peace and by virtue of its long practice as considered and tolerated by the community of States, the Security Council is perhaps generally empowered to take decisions affecting the legal rights and duties of State and non-State actors, though the limits of this general power remain to be determined, and could be constrained, in specific situations. (The exclusion of the power to effect a permanent settlement is an instance of these limitations.) But this is not the same as having the Security Council exempted from the operation of law. That could not be reconciled with the Charter framework, or with practice. The International Court in *Namibia*, while interpreting the Council's powers broadly, was careful to emphasize that in adopting its decisions, the Council is subject to certain legal standards.[29] This approach

---

[22] Graefrath, International Crimes and Collective Security, in Wellens (ed.) *Festschrift Suy* (1998), 243.

[23] Klein, *Statusverträge im Völkerrecht* (1980), 354.

[24] Subedi, Objective Regimes and UN Settlements, 37 *German YIL* (1994), 200–201; Matheson, United Nations Governance of Postconflict Societies, 95 *AJIL* (2001), 84–85, advocates the power of the Council to adopt permanent settlements. For a criticism of Matheson see Kirgis, Security Council Governance of Postconflict Societies: A Plea for Good Faith and Informed Decision Making, 95 *AJIL* (2001), 579–582.

[25] Graefrath (1998), 244; cf also Subedi, Objective Regimes and UN Settlements, 37 *German YIL* (1994), 197–198; Nolte, The Limits on the Security Council's Powers and its Functions in the International Legal System: Some Reflectons, in Byers (ed.), 322.

[26] Brownlie, General Course, 228 *RdC* (1995), 220.

[27] Irmscher, Legal Framework of the Activities of UNMIK, 44 *German YIL* (2001), 364.

[28] Cassese, Legal Considerations on the International Status of Jerusalem, 3 *Palestinian Yearbook of International Law* (1986), 32.

[29] *ICJ Reports*, 1971, 50–52.

has been more vigorously confirmed by the ICTY Appeals Chamber in *Tadic*, which stated that the Council is not *legibus solutus* (unbound by law).[30]

The principle that the Security Council is subject to international law in general or to *jus cogens* in particular could be challenged by reference to the classical debate on interaction of the concepts of peace and justice in international relations. But, apart from the fact that the Council is not *legibus solutus*, its practice would not justify the assumption that the maintenance of peace justifies the neglect of the law; rather, the practice of the United Nations conceives justice as a necessary part of peace. In its resolutions regarding the Middle East, the UN General Assembly clearly stated that the maintenance of international peace is integrally linked with the enforcement of legal norms violated in a given situation, such as the withdrawal from occupied territories and return of displaced persons.[31] Similarly, the Security Council itself has stated in several resolutions that for the restoration of international peace in former Yugoslavia the enforcement of certain legal norms, such as those imposing individual criminal responsibility on those perpetrating international crimes, was a necessary precondition.[32] Therefore, the view of conflict between the concepts of peace and justice and the primacy of the former over the latter, manifested in compromising legal principles or the enforcement of fundamental rules of international law for the sake of peace, is supported neither by the normative framework underlying the UN system, nor by practice of the UN organs.

The idea of a 'conflict' between peace and justice is even more untenable when the legal norms at stake pertain to international public order, and could sometimes lead to absurd results. This has been convincingly illustrated by Bowett, asking whether the Council could decide that a State must transfer territory to an aggressor in the interests of peace and security. Obviously, this question has to be answered in the negative as such a decision of the Council would clearly be *ultra vires*.[33]

The very idea of applying peremptory norms to determine the legality and legal consequences of the Security Council's decisions is at variance with the traditional pragmatic approach, which would prefer to keep international law flexible and adaptable to political interests and political compromises made between States. This question becomes even more sensitive considering that the Council is a body arguably representing the will of the international community: Article 24 of the UN Charter suggests that the Council is there to ensure prompt and effective action on behalf of the UN membership, in pursuance of the goals the organization is established for. But the view that

[30] *Prosecutor v Tadic*, Case IT-94-1-AR72, 35 ILM, paras 20–28 (ICTY 1995).
[31] GA Res 41/162 (1986), paras 2–3; GA Res 39/146A (1984); GA Res 34/65 (1979) A, para 2.
[32] UNSC Res 771(1993), 817(1993), 827(1993).
[33] Bowett, The Impact of Security Council Decisions on Dispute Settlement Procedures, 5 *EJIL* (1994), 93, 96.

the Council is not unbound by the law is indisputable even in view of the representative character of the Council.

The following analysis will focus upon more specific questions. These are: the nature and scope of *jus cogens* limitations on the Security Council's powers; the ways in which the Council's action could come into conflict with *jus cogens*; and the legal consequences arising in cases of such normative conflict with *jus cogens*.

12

The Nature and Scope of *Jus Cogens* Limitations on the Security Council's Powers

The Security Council can be prevented from adopting the resolutions contrary to peremptory norms by various factors, such as the lack of a required majority or a veto cast by a Permanent Member. The right to veto can be criticized, but no viable alternative has been suggested so far. Although veto prevents the Council from adopting decisions, it also prevents the adoption of decisions expressing the majority dictatorship. This likelihood is clear in the context of the Council decisions which would affect the most basic rights of States and non-State actors. But once the required majority supports the decision, the latter can only be resisted on the basis of relevant normative requirements.

In the *Namibia* case, the International Court pronounced that a resolution of the Security Council that complies with the conditions of its adoption 'must be considered to have been validly adopted'. The language of presumption in this statement can evidence that the legality of resolutions is not just about the compliance with procedural requirements. Compliance with some substantive standards is also required. In addition, if, as Sir Robert Jennings suggests, a treaty offends against *jus cogens* not because of the defect of will of States-parties but precisely because it is a treaty, then the decision of the Security Council does not conflict with peremptory norms because of the defects in the process of its adoption but precisely because it is a properly adopted Security Council resolution, that is, through its substance.

I. SUBSTANTIVE CONTENT OF *JUS COGENS* LIMITATIONS

There are views that *jus cogens* cannot apply to the Security Council resolutions as its scope is limited to the law of treaties.[1] It is however widely affirmed that the invalidating capacity of *jus cogens* is not limited to the law of treaties. There are in any case many authorities confirming the relevance of *jus cogens* in this field. The ILA Final Report unambiguously affirms that peremptory norms of international law are applicable both to Member States and international organizations.[2] Judge Lauterpacht in the *Bosnia* case has

---

[1] Martenczuk, The Security Council, the International Court and Judicial Review: What Lessons from Lockerbie? 10 *EJIL* (1999), 517.
[2] M. Shaw and K. Wellens, Final Report (2004), 13.

clearly expressed the view that *jus cogens* unconditionally binds the Security Council.

The conceptual basis of this approach is clearly explained in legal doctrine. According to Reinisch, 'the Council must respect peremptory norms of international law because the core values protected by the concept of *jus cogens* are simply not derogable in the sense of *jus dispositivum*'.[3] Doehring refers to the direct relevance for the Security Council's decisions of the fact that peremptory norms are not subject to derogation and waiver.[4] One may perhaps tolerate disregard of dispositive norms if the interests of the maintenance of peace so require, but this cannot extend to *jus cogens*.[5] In this regard, a Council resolution adopted in violation of *jus cogens* would in fact be a derogation from *jus cogens*, as it would be an attempt to use the UN system for the establishment of a new legal regime through a resolution contrary to *jus cogens*.

After ascertaining the general applicability of peremptory norms to decisions of the Security Council, it remains to examine specific peremptory norms in terms of their applicability to such decisions.

It is undeniable that the peremptory prohibition of the use of force constitutes a full-fledged limitation on the powers of the Security Council. The International Law Commission asserted that the prohibition of the use of force, which binds international organizations, is the most credible example of *jus cogens*.[6] This prohibition, as proclaimed both under Article 2(4) of the Charter and general international law, is linked to the powers of the Council itself, which is entitled to authorizse the use of force under Chapter VII in order to maintain or restore international peace and security. Such Charter exceptions, also including the inherent right of States to self-defence under Article 51, are the qualifications to the prohibition, and there is arguably nothing in general international law contradicting this principle.

However, the fact that the Council may authorize force under Chapter VII does not mean that it is entirely free to disregard the basic prohibition of the use of force; it rather means that the prohibition as such is qualified to the extent of the specific Charter exceptions. The use of force is legal as soon as it is authorized by the Council, *inter alia* in compliance with the principle of proportionality; it is illegal unless it is so authorized, and authorization cannot be presumed unless there is an explicit intention of the Council. In

---

[3] Reinisch, Developing Human Rights and Humanitarian Law Accountability of the Security Council for the Imposition of Economic Sanctions, 95 *AJIL* (2001), 859; Dugard, Judicial Review of Sanctions, in Gowlland-Debbas (ed.), *United Nations Sanctions and International Law* (2001), 89.

[4] Discussed in Doehring, Unlawful Resolutions of the Security Council, 1 *Max Planck YBUNL* (1997), 102–103.

[5] Doehring, Unlawful Resolutions of the Security Council, 1 *Max Planck YBUNL* (1997), 99, 108.

[6] *UNCLT Official Records* II (1986), 39.

this latter circumstance, the Council remains bound by the prohibition and its actions have to be consistent with it.

This approach is required by the very rationale of the Charter mechanism of collective security. The authorization of force presupposes a determination by the Council that there is a threat to, or breach of, peace, and that forcible measures are required for the maintenance or restoration of peace and security. The Council cannot be presumed to have passed such a two-stage judgment, unless there is definite evidence affirming the opposite. Therefore, in the absence of such definite evidence, the use of force remains illegal, and the value of a decision of the Council conducive to such a use of force is to be assessed accordingly.

The right of peoples to self-determination is part of *jus cogens* and hence constitutes a full-fledged limitation on the Council's powers. According to Tomuschat, the Security Council is bound by the right of peoples to self-determination and shall respect it in all circumstances.[7] This is further signified by the fact that the members of the Council, as was the case in the process of adoption of Resolution 1483(2003), clearly consider that not to infringe on the principle of self-determination.[8]

It is axiomatic that the Security Council can never be entitled to infringe upon the rights that protect individuals.[9] The UN Charter obliges the organs to respect human rights. But the standards to be respected by the organs are not necessarily limited to those implicitly or explicitly enshrined in the Charter. As submitted, the human rights limitations on the Security Council's powers are inferable from universal human rights instruments such as the Universal Declaration on Human Rights, the International Covenant on Civil and Political Rights, the Convention on the Rights of the Child, and other instruments. These lay down certain basic human rights which may be vulnerable in case of the Council's action and hence constitute limitations on such action.[10]

---

[7] Tomuschat, Yugoslavia's Damaged Sovereignty over the Province of Kosovo, in Kreijen *et al.* (eds), *State, Sovereignty and International Governance* (2002), 341.

[8] This point was the most acute in deliberations, and the need to safeguard the permanent sovereignty of Iraq over its natural resources has been explicitly emphasized by representatives of the United Kingdom, Spain, Mexico, Russian Federation, Guinea, Chile, Angola and Pakistan. S/PV.4761, at 5–15. The Representatives emphasized that Iraqi people are the owners of their oil resources, and some of them even linked this issue with the right of peoples to self-determination (Guinea, Russian Federation, Spain). S/PV.4761, at 6–9. The representative of Mexico was more specific in saying that Resolution 1483 'does not authorize the establishment of long-term commitments that would alienate the sovereignty of the Iraqi people over its petroleum resources.' S/PV.4761, 7.

[9] Tomuschat, Yugoslavia's Damaged Sovereignty over the Province of Kosovo, in Kreijen *et al.* (eds), *State, Sovereignty and International Governance* (2002), 340.

[10] M. Bossuyt, The adverse consequences of economic sanctions on the enjoyment of human rights. Working paper, E/CN.4/Sub.2/2000/33, 9; E. de Wet, Human Rights Limitations to Economic Enforcement Measures Under Article 41 of the UN Charter and the Iraqi Sanctions Regime, 14 *LJIL* (2001), 284, 286–289.

It may be contended that the Security Council is bound to respect rights that are non-derogable under instruments such as ICCPR and have the status of *jus cogens*. Due process is not part of *jus cogens*, as most human rights treaties permit derogation from it and the Security Council could override that right.[11] This argument is flawed above all because of misconceiving the scope of *jus cogens* in human rights law.

The rights which serve as limitations on the Security Council's powers are not limited to rights expressly stated to be non-derogable under specific human rights instruments. The rights that are formally derogable under human rights instruments, such as the freedom from retroactive laws or civil imprisonment, freedom of thought, religion and conscience, nevertheless bind the Council as non-derogable rights and this organ is not empowered to take a different attitude.[12] The decision of the ICTY Appeals Chamber in *Tadic* gives an impression that the right to fair trial is an unconditional limitation on the powers of the Security Council and that the observance of the right to fair trial and the related procedural safeguards was a *sine qua non* for the validity of the Council's measures such as the establishment of the International Criminal Tribunal for the Former Yugoslavia.[13] This is confirmed by the analysis of Brownlie, who as a counsel for Libya in *Lockerbie* has submitted that the right to fair trial entailed a limitation on the Council's powers. At the outset, Brownlie submitted with regard to the extradition demands regarding the two Libyan suspects that there were substantial grounds for the view that a fair trial was not possible either in Scotland or in the United States; the right to a fair trial is considered to be a fundamental human right. The ambit of the Security Council resolutions was to be determined by reference to the principles of human rights including those embodied in the United Nations Charter. Even the reference to Article 103 of the Charter, which would *prima facie* support the primacy of the Security Council's measures, would not empower the Council to trump the right to fair trial as a fundamental right, as the 'resort to Article 103 does not produce a single outcome or ready-made prioritization of obligations'.[14]

---

[11] Aust, The Role of Human Rights in Limiting the Enforcement Powers of the Security Council: A Practitioner's View, in De Wet and Nollkaemper (eds), *Review of the Security Council by Member States* (2003), 34.

[12] E. de Wet, Human Rights Limitations to Economic Enforcement Measures Under Article 41 of the UN Charter and the Iraqi Sanctions Regime, 14 *LJIL* (2001), 286.

[13] *Tadic* (Appeals Chamber), paras 41–47; it is submitted that the right to fair hearing in criminal proceedings is part of *jus cogens*, E. de Wet and A. Nollkaemper, Review of Security Council Decisions by National Courts, 45 *German YIL* (2002), 182–183. See id., 183–184, for the practice affirming such assumption. See also De Wet, The Role of Human Rights in Limiting the Enforcement Power of the Security Council: A Principled View, in De Wet and Nollkaemper (eds), *Review of the Security Council by Member States* (2003), 22; Herdegen, Review of the Security Council by National Courts: A Constitutional Perspective, in De Wet and Nollkaemper (eds.), *Review of the Security Council by Member States* (2003), 79.

[14] Brownlie, CR 97/24.

Within the scope of margin of appreciation States perhaps can impose, pursuant to the Security Council's decision, some limitations on the exercise of the rights that can be justified by circumstances that can normally justify States in adopting such measures unilaterally under human rights treaties. This would further be subject to the requirement of proportionality. In other words, the so-called 'derogable' provisions can be impacted upon by the Council to the extent that the content of the relevant right allows. However, the Council cannot adopt the decision that goes against the content of the relevant human right.

The Council's compliance with economic and social rights is also crucial for the legality of its measures, particularly economic sanctions.[15] A similar approach has also been affirmed in practice. General Comment No. 8 of the UN Committee on Economic and Social Rights clearly states that when the Security Council imposes sanctions under Chapter VII, the economic and social rights still serve as limitations on the permissible scope of those sanctions. The provisions of the ICESCR, 'virtually all of which are also reflected in a range of other human rights treaties as well as the Universal Declaration of Human Rights, cannot be considered to be inoperative, or in any way inapplicable, solely because a decision has been taken that considerations of international peace and security warrant the imposition of sanctions'.[16] The Committee reached this conclusion even though economic and social rights are not treated as non-derogable under specific instruments. It is particularly noteworthy that the Committee seems to speak in terms of a normative hierarchy. It focuses on two separate legal regimes: the regime underlying economic sanctions, as based on the Charter, and economic and social rights, and it concludes that the former is subject to the latter.

In any case, it is clear that the scope of *jus cogens* in human rights law is not limited to rights that are non-derogable under specific treaties and this is important for construing the scope of human rights limitations on the powers of the Security Council. The character of individual human rights as limitations on the power of the Security Council reinforces their peremptory character. If a human right must be imperatively observed by a treaty-based organ like the Security Council, the inescapable conclusion follows that that specific right stands above the treaty-making capacity of States, that is, it possesses peremptory status.

The relevance of humanitarian law as a limitation on the Security Council's powers is clear. The principal areas in which humanitarian law is relevant involve the UN-authorized military operations and the regime of UN economic sanctions.

---

[15] Reinisch, Developing Human Rights and Humanitarian Law Accountability of the Security Council for the Imposition of Economic Sanctions, 95 *AJIL* (2001), 861–863.
[16] ICESCR Committee, General Comment No. 8 (1997), para. 7.

Some doctrinal suggestions have been made that in case of collective or institutional military action there is no room for the operation of general rules of war and hence international police actions should be governed by rules totally different in nature.[17] But the law and practice have developed in a different way. The UN Secretary-General is clearly of the view that UN forces are bound by existing humanitarian law.[18] In the 1971 Zagreb Resolution and the 1975 Wiesbaden Resolution, the Institute of International Law clearly stated that humanitarian law applies to the United Nations and must be complied with in every circumstance by the United Nations Forces engaged in hostilities; the rules relevant in this context are the rules embodied in the Geneva Conventions, such as the rules protecting civilians and their property, and those relating to distinction between military and non-military objectives (Article 2, Zagreb Resolution, Article 2, Wiesbaden Resolution). The UN is obliged to issue appropriate regulations to its forces and give adequate instruction to the personnel (Articles 3 and 4, Zagreb Resolution); it is liable for the damage caused by UN forces without recourse to the State to whom the unit in question belongs (Article 8, Zagreb Resolution, Article 6, Wiesbaden Resolution).[19]

According to the ILA Report on the Accountability of International Organisations, the UN economic sanctions are subject to peremptory norms, particularly the fundamental humanitarian rules, such as the principles of proportionality and necessity under international humanitarian law.[20] The ILA Final Report emphasizes that when taking and implementing decisions such as those concerning the use of force, temporary administration of territory, imposition of coercive measures, launching of peacekeeping or peace-enforcement operations, international organizations shall observe basic human rights obligations and applicable norms and principles of humanitarian law.[21] Of particular importance is the positive duty of occupying powers to ensure the protection and survival of the civilian population.[22] It is also recognized in doctrine that humanitarian law applies not only to belligerents, but also to the Chapter VII measures taken by the Security Council. This primarily implies an obligation not to deprive civilians of

---

[17] Jessup, *A Modern Law of Nations* (1948), 188 ff; H. Lauterpacht, The Limits of the Operation of the Law of War, *BYIL* 1953, 206.

[18] UN Secretary-General's Bulletin on 'Observance by United Nations Forces of International Humanitarian Law', UN Doc ST/SGB/1999/13 (6 August).

[19] Conditions of Application of Humanitarian Rules of Armed Conflict to Hostilities in which United Nations Forces May be Engaged, Session of Zagreb, 1971; Conditions of Application of Rules, other than Humanitarian Rules, of Armed Conflict to Hostilities in which United Nations Forces May be Engaged, Session of Wiesbaden, 1975.

[20] M. Shaw and K. Wellens, Third ILA Report on Accountability of International Organisations (2002), 11, 15.

[21] Final Report (2004), 23.

[22] Reinisch, Developing Human Rights and Humanitarian Law Accountability of the Security Council for the Imposition of Economic Sanctions, 95 *AJIL* (2001), 861.

access to the goods necessary for their survival.[23] Any sanctions regime is governed by humanitarian law, above all by norms essential for the survival of the civilian population, to secure food, water, shelter, medicines and medical care.[24] The measures of the Security Council may not lead to the starvation of the civilian population. Such a consequence would characterize the measures as disproportional.[25] The Martens clause test also applies,[26] which means that the Council's measures cannot result in offending the laws of humanity and dictates of public conscience.

2. THE INTERACTION OF SUBSTANTIVE *JUS COGENS* LIMITATIONS WITH THE POWERS OF THE SECURITY COUNCIL

It is one thing to outline substantive standards of *jus cogens* applicable to the acts of the Security Council; it is another thing to examine the interaction between those substantive standards and those acts. There are different ways in which peremptory norms could apply to, and serve as a limitation on, the action by the UN Security Council. Peremptory norms may be embodied in the UN Charter and thus bind the Security Council; peremptory norms may apply to the Council through the law of treaties; and peremptory norms can have a direct or autonomous effect on the Council's decisions, as it applies to acts of legal persons, thus determining the validity and legal consequences of such acts.

2.1. The purposes and principles of the UN

The UN Charter is clear in subordinating the Security Council to the purposes and principles of the United Nations. Article 24 clearly requires that the Council shall act in accordance with such purposes and principles; Article 25 makes the binding force of the Council's acts conditional upon such compliance.[27] It is suggested that Articles 24 and 25, based on their ordinary meaning, establish compliance with *jus cogens* as the *sine qua non* for

---

[23] Gasser, Collective Economic Sanctions and International Humanitarian Law, 56 *ZaöRV* (1996), 885–887; Reinisch, Developing Human Rights and Humanitarian Law Accountability of the Security Council for the Imposition of Economic Sanctions, 95 *AJIL* (2001), 860–861.

[24] M. Bossuyt, The adverse consequences of economic sanctions on the enjoyment of human rights. Working paper, E/CN.4/Sub.2/2000/33, 10.

[25] Gasser, Collective Economic Sanctions and International Humanitarian Law, 56 *ZaöRV* (1996), 882.

[26] M. Bossuyt, The adverse consequences of economic sanctions on the enjoyment of human rights. Working paper, E/CN.4/Sub.2/2000/33, 12.

[27] Delbrück, On Article 25, in Simma (ed.), *The Charter of the United Nations. A Commentary* (2002), 455. It could be added that the wording of Article 25 is clear and it would anyway be absurd to consider that States have established an organ to serve the purposes and principles of the Charter and yet this organ has the mandate to disregard the Charter.

binding and valid Security Council action.[28] Bowett particularly emphasizes the importance in Article 25 of the phrase 'in accordance with the present Charter', which indicate that the decisions are binding only insofar as they are in accordance with the Charter.[29] It is therefore clear that no act of the Security Council is exempt from the requirement that it must be in conformity with the purposes and principles of the United Nations.[30]

The UN purposes and principles importantly overlap in scope with the peremptory norms of general international law. As Doehring states, the Charter itself is a treaty referring to peremptory norms such as prohibition of force and human rights.[31] The clearest examples are Article 2(4) prohibiting the use of force and Article 51 relating to inherent right to self-defence, which cannot be overridden by the Council's action. Besides, the preamble and Article 1 of the Charter clearly confirm that the principle of self-determination is part of the purposes and principles of the organization. It is also generally accepted that fundamental human rights form part of the principles of the United Nations Charter.[32]

It is suggested that the principles and purposes of the United Nations restrain the UN organs in their action because these organs would be estopped from behaviour that violates the rights referred to in the purposes and principles.[33] It does not seem, however, that the concept of estoppel, in whichever form, is essential in explaining the legal constraints on the Security Council under the UN Charter or general international law. The concept of estoppel operates when the given actor creates certain expectations by its own action or expression of attitude,[34] thus implying that in the absence of such factors there would be no legal obligation or constraint operating. It would be pointless to require the presence of estoppel where the relevant actor is anyway bound to respect the identical predetermined legal restrictions that exist on grounds other than that actor's action and expression of attitude. This is exactly the situation with regard to the legal limitations of the Security Council's powers. Although the Council occasionally announces its allegiance to certain principles of international law,[35] it is hardly disputable that the principal ground of the Council's being bound by the relevant standards lies elsewhere than the expression of its attitude or of commitments.

---

[28] C. Scott *et al.*, A Memorial for Bosnia, 16 *Michigan Journal of International Law* (1994), 126.
[29] Bowett, The Impact of Security Council Decisions on Dispute Settlement Procedures, 5 *EJIL* (1994), 92.
[30] M. Bossuyt, The adverse consequences of economic sanctions on the enjoyment of human rights. Working paper, E/CN.4/Sub.2/2000/33, 7.
[31] Doehring, Unlawful Resolutions of the Security Council, 1 *Max Planck YBUNL* (1997), 98.
[32] *Namibia* (Advisory Opinion), *ICJ Reports*, 1971, 57; *Tehran Hostages*, *ICJ Reports*, 1980, 42.
[33] De Wet, *Chapter VII Powers*, 195–198; De Wet, in De Wet and Nollkaemper (eds), 10–13.
[34] De Wet, id., 12, accepts this.
[35] Such as the respect for human rights obligations in Resolution 1456(2003).

Of course, estoppel is a ramification of the principle of good faith, which is generally considered as one of the limitations on the Security Council's powers. But the principle of good faith binds the Council, or so it would seem from the analysis of the legal framework, in a way different from requiring the respect of the commitments assumed. The relevance of the principle of good faith rather is to ensure that the delegated powers of the Council are exercised in a proper way. This principle limits the Council's freedom, but not in terms of what it has committed, but in terms of what binds it externally and as a condition of its existence.

2.2. The law of treaties

The basic question in this field relates to the *jus cogens* limitation on the treaty-making power of States: are States empowered to establish an institution with the powers to act in contravention of *jus cogens*? The law of treaties, as codified in the 1969 Vienna Convention on the Law of Treaties, applies to the constituent instruments of international organizations, such as the UN Charter.[36] Even if the Vienna Convention has no retroactive force, it embodies customary law on the subject, and nothing in the nature of the constituent instruments of international organizations precludes the applicability of the Vienna Convention. Therefore, *jus cogens* must be deemed applicable to the powers of the UN because it is established by a treaty.

This means that a treaty like the UN Charter is subject to the effect of Articles 53 and 64 of the Vienna Convention, dealing with voidness and termination of treaties conflicting with *jus cogens*. But *jus cogens* is relevant not only in terms of the validity, but also in terms of the interpretation of treaties. While concluding a treaty, whatever its subject-matter, States cannot be presumed to authorize acts contrary to *jus cogens*, unless a treaty contains an explicit clause to that effect (in which case the entire treaty would be void). As the UN International Law Commission emphasized, States cannot escape the operation of *jus cogens*, particularly its invalidating capacity, through the establishment of an international organization.[37] As long as that principle

---

[36] Article 5 VCLT. See also Gowlland-Debbas, The Functions of the UN Security Council in the International Legal System, in Byers (ed.), 305–306, suggesting that the law of treaties governs the relationship of the Charter to customary law, including peremptory norms from which treaties cannot derogate.

[37] II *UNCLT Official Records* (1986), 39; the relevance of *jus cogens* is similarly affirmed by reference to the principle that States cannot delegate to international organizations powers more than they themselves can exercise. In addition, after an institution is established, its powers are qualified by subsequent development of *jus cogens*, E. de Wet and A. Nollkaemper, Review of Security Council Decisions by National Courts, 45 *German YIL* (2002), 181–182. See also M. Shaw and K. Wellens, Third ILA Report on Accountability of International Organizations (2003), 11, affirming that if the Members transfer to an international organization the power to impose coercive economic measures, their obligation to comply with peremptory norms is not affected. Jenks observed that 'each international organisation must regard itself as being bound

applies, it must equally be presumed that an entity or institution established on the basis of a treaty is not endowed with powers to act in contravention to *jus cogens*, still less to override the operation of *jus cogens*. Acts contrary to *jus cogens* are beyond the powers of an institution (*ultra vires*). This is the only possible approach to avoid the application of Articles 53 and 64 of the Vienna Convention.

Therefore, the provisions of the UN Charter dealing with the powers of the Security Council, particularly the binding force of its decisions, have to be interpreted and executed in a way compatible with *jus cogens*; they must be deemed to contain implicit limitations on that organ's powers, thereby placing it under the strict limits of peremptory norms.

This is also the position in the case of institutions other than the UN. *Jus cogens* finds full application within the legal system of the World Trade Organization. The WTO legal system is not itself concerned with peremptory norms, such as human rights, but the measures adopted within the WTO are subject to the operation of *jus cogens* in their content and operation. In case of normative conflict, *jus cogens* enjoys primacy either through the duty to adopt interpretation of the WTO agreements conducive to *jus cogens*, or through invalidating a contrary WTO provision.[38]

The situation is similar with regard to the European Union. The European Commission on Human Rights referred to a general principle that States-parties to the European Convention are responsible for the violation of the Convention, even if the act or omission in question is a consequence of the necessity to comply with international obligations, and especially noted that this limits the effect of obligations assumed within an international organization.[39] Otherwise, the Commission continued, 'the guarantees of the Convention could wantonly be limited or excluded and thus be deprived of their peremptory character'. Therefore, the transfer of powers to an international organization is effective only to the extent fundamental human rights are adequately protected within that international organization.[40]

In *Waite and Kennedy* the European Court of Human Rights further affirmed the primacy of the obligations under the European Convention over the obligations under the treaties establishing international organizations:

in the first instance by its own constitution and will naturally apply instruments which it is itself responsible for administering,' but added that this principle is not unqualified, it can be limited by the operation of the hierarchical principle. Jenks, The Conflict of Law-Making Treaties, 30 *BYIL* (1951), 448.

[38] Marceau, WTO Dispute Settlement and Human Rights, 13 *EJIL* (2002), 753.

[39] *M & Co v FRG*, Application No. 13258/87, 9 February 1990, 33 *YB ECHR* 1990, 51–52.

[40] Id., 52; for the repeated emphasis on the peremptory character of the Convention obligations in the context of the powers of international organizations, see the *Bosphorus* case, para. 154.

Where States establish international organisations in order to pursue or strengthen their cooperation in certain fields of activities, and where they attribute to these organisations certain competences and accord them immunities, there may be implications as to the protection of fundamental rights. It would be incompatible with the purpose and object of the Convention, however, if the Contracting States were thereby absolved from their responsibility under the Convention in relation to the field of activity covered by such attribution.[41]

The reference to the object and purpose of the Convention is further evidence that the primacy of human rights treaties follows from the non-bilateralizable character of the obligations they embody.

The European Court affirmed the identical principle in the *Bosphorus* case, where it concluded that State action taken in compliance with the legal obligations assumed within the framework of the relevant organization 'is justified as long as the relevant organisation is considered to protect fundamental rights'. If this was not the case, the interest of international cooperation would be outweighed by the Convention's public order character.[42] Judge Ress further clarified this principle in the same case, by pointing out that 'The importance of international cooperation and the need to secure the proper functioning of international organisations cannot justify Contracting Parties creating and entering into international organisations which are not in conformity with the Convention'.[43]

In *Matthews*, the European Court of Human Rights considered that the Treaty on European Union and the acts of EU organs are subject to scrutiny in terms of their compatibility with the European Convention on Human Rights.[44] This does not fit within the regime of application of conflicting treaties in terms of Article 30 of the Vienna Convention on the Law of Treaties, as it assumes that one treaty applies despite the requirements of another. This perhaps has to do with the superior, or objective, non-derogable and non-bilateralizable character of humanitarian or human rights treaties, which share the nature of *jus cogens* as being protective of the interests of the community rather than individual States. Obligations under such treaties are non-derogable, which requires the construction of other treaties, including constituent instruments of international organizations, so as to be compatible with the human rights treaty. In addition, it must be seen that the European Commission of Human Rights has clearly emphasized that the obligations under the European Convention are peremptory, and moreover has done so in the context of normative conflict between different sets of obligations—a classical field of application of *jus cogens*. As the obligations under other humanitarian instruments, such as the ICCPR or the Genocide Convention, are similar in nature, their implications must also be similar.

---

[41] *Waite and Kennedy v Germany*, 18 February 1999, para. 67.
[42] *Bosphorus*, paras 155–156.   [43] Concurring Opinion, *Bosphorus*, para. 5.
[44] *Matthews v UK*, ECHR 24833/94, 18 February 1999, paras 26–35.

The relevant jurisprudence of the European Court is in accordance with, and indeed follows from, the more general approach taken by human rights treaty organs in the matters of the conflict between human rights treaties and other treaty obligations. As seen, the rules of conflict under Article 30 of the Vienna Convention do not find an application to human rights treaties, which confirms that human rights treaties constitute one of the hierarchical limitations on what other treaties can contain or how what they contain can be applied. This, in its turn, is translated into the specific context of international organizations as a limitation on the exercise of the treaty-based institutional powers. In fact, the pronouncement in *Namibia* that the Council measures regarding the suspension of treaty relations with South Africa did not apply to humanitarian treaties[45] must be viewed as confirmation that such treaties constitute limitations on the Council's powers with regard to the maintenance of peace.

There is nothing in international law suggesting that the United Nations Charter is exempt from a regime of *jus cogens* which applies to all international organizations. The ultimate categorical conclusion reached on the basis of the law of treaties is that a treaty such as the UN Charter cannot be construed as authorizing any organ to act in violation of *jus cogens*.

The most likely objection to the construction of the Charter as not prejudicing *jus cogens* remains Article 103 of the Charter, according to which in the case of conflict between the Charter obligations and obligations of members under other international agreements, the former prevail over the latter. Those admiring the strong and powerful Security Council can find this provision helpful. However, serious problems of interpretation remain, which cast doubt on the view that the Charter or the resolutions of the Security Council can be construed as prevailing over general international law and especially *jus cogens*.

Article 103 relates to the obligations under the UN Charter[46] and it is doubted whether the Council's resolution is an obligation under the Charter, as it is not part of the Charter. Bowett suggests that according to Article 103, the Charter provision prevails over other treaty obligations, but the decision of the Security Council is not *per se* a Charter obligation. The obligation to comply may be, but the decision itself is not.[47] On the other hand, it may be possible to understand a resolution as a Charter obligation, as soon as its binding force derives from Article 25 of the Charter. This question may be debatable, but even if Article 103 is construed broadly as covering the effect

---

[45] *ICJ Reports*, 1971, 55–56.

[46] See M. Shaw and K. Wellens, Third ILA Report on Accountability of International Organisations (2003), 13, considering that Article 103 'establishes the primacy of the obligations contained in the Charter itself'.

[47] Bowett, The Impact of Security Council Decisions on Dispute Settlement Procedures, 5 *EJIL* (1994), 92.

not only of the Charter itself but also of binding resolutions adopted pursuant to it, its effect would still be limited. The obligation to comply with the Council's resolutions is itself conditional upon the Council's compliance with the Charter's principles, and this is crucial in seeing whether a decision falls within the purview of Article 103. In other words, Article 103 cannot make a resolution unlawful under the Charter to prevail over other rules of international law.[48]

The issue also arises whether Article 103, which refers to obligations under international agreements, extends to the rights of States. It could perhaps extend by implication to the rights of States which correspond to treaty obligations to which Article 103 applies expressly so that this provision is fully effective with regard to the obligations which are covered by its scope.

Another, more serious problem with the role of Article 103 in this field concerns its clear wording, which states that the Charter is to prevail over international agreements, but does not state that it prevails over general international law, of which *jus cogens* forms part. The clear text does not support the opposite view,[49] and those who wish to see Article 103 as making the Charter prevail over general international law cannot rely on evidence, but only on wishful thinking.

As Bowett suggests, the function of Article 103 is concerned with the compatibility with the Charter of obligations under any other international agreement, and its reasoning would not apply where a Member State relies on its rights under general international law.[50] The classical commentary to the UN Charter is clear in stating that the primary purpose of Article 103, as

---

[48] As Jenks affirms, 'Article 103 cannot be invoked as giving the United Nations an overriding authority which would be inconsistent with the provisions of the Charter itself.' Jenks, The Conflict of Law-Making Treaties, 30 *BYIL* (1951), 439.

[49] Alvarez argues that Article 103 makes the Council decisions prevail both over treaties and custom, referring in this regard to the International Court's pronouncement in *Nicaragua, ICJ Reports*, 1986, 14, on the interrelated character of treaty and customary law, and seems to suggest on that basis that if the Security Council resolution prevails over the treaty obligations on human rights, it also prevails over their customary counterparts. Alvarez, De Wet and Nollkaemper (eds), 133. But Alvarez' argument is defective as it neglects the clear distinction between treaty and custom as expounded by the Court in *Nicaragua* when it expressly emphasized that when treaty and customary norms overlap in their content, they still maintain their separate existence, *ICJ Reports*, 1986, 94–95. Given that, it is more plausible that if the Council measure were to prevail over treaty obligations, it is unlikely to affect their customary counterparts.

The other point of Alvarez, id., that the UN membership has acquiesced into the reading in Article 103 the primacy over customary law in the case of Security Council sanctions on Libya, is also not free of problems. The amount of protests and disagreement with the Security Council's attitude in the *Lockerbie* crisis demonstrates that no genuine acquiescence to the Council's attitude could have taken place. On this see below, Chapter 14, Section 4.

[50] Bowett, The Impact of Security Council Decisions on Dispute Settlement Procedures, 5 *EJIL* (1994), 92. In this regard, Bowett criticizes the 1992 Order on *Lockerbie*, suggesting that 'the Court's reasoning is disturbing in its possibilities.' See also Sassoli, Sanctions and Humanitarian Law, in Gowlland-Debbas (ed.), *United Nations Sanctions and International Law* (2001), 264, making a similar point in terms of both customary law and *jus cogens*.

following *inter alia* from the attitude of the General Assembly, is to ensure that that States should be freed from legal liability for any non-performance of their obligations under other international agreements entailed by the carrying out of United Nations coercive measures.[51] No suggestion is made that the primacy over the rights of States or general international law is envisaged. All this justifies concluding that Article 103 makes the Charter prevail over obligations under international agreements, and rights corresponding to such obligations, but not over general international law.

The issue of conflict between Article 103 and *jus cogens* has been clearly addressed by Judge Lauterpacht in *Bosnia*. Even if the Charter prevails over other international agreements, the same is not true for norms which are part of *jus cogens*. Therefore, 'the relief which Article 103 may give the Security Council in case of one of its decisions and an operative treaty obligation cannot—as a matter of simple hierarchy of norms—extend to a conflict between a Security Council resolution and *jus cogens*.'[52] Similarly, Professor Gasser considers that 'Article 103 makes it clear that there is also no way for the Security Council to disregard international obligations other than those enshrined in international treaties, i.e. general principles of law or customary law.' *Jus cogens* norms including the considerations of humanity constitute absolute prohibitions which bind the hands not only of States but also of the Security Council.[53]

The outcome of the interpretation of Article 103 is clear. It only needs to be added by way of alternative that even if Article 103 were to extend to general international law and not merely to agreements, it would still be a treaty provision and hence unable to prejudice the operation of *jus cogens*. The reference by Judge Lauterpacht to the issue of hierarchy of norms is a clear confirmation that the effect of *jus cogens* is above all due to its normative superiority, rather than to empirical ways of construction, as the entire process must be seen as subject to the overarching operation of peremptory norms. This is confirmed by the Third ILA Report on Accountability of International Organisations, which states that although Article 103 establishes the primacy of the Charter obligations, the Member States cannot be required to breach peremptory norms of international law.[54]

---

[51] Goodrich, Hambro and Simmons, *The Charter of the United Nations* (1969), 615–616; as Sztucki (1974), 40–41 further comments on Article 103, 'An inconsistency of obligations under a treaty with those under the UN Charter may be purely occasional and transitory, and need not result in the voidness of the treaty in question.'

[52] Separate Opinion, *ICJ Reports*, 1993, 440.

[53] Gasser, Collective Economic Sanctions and International Humanitarian Law, 56 *ZaöRV* (1996), 881; E. de Wet and A. Nollkaemper, Review of Security Council Decisions by National Courts, 45 *German YIL* (2002), 191.

[54] M. Shaw and K. Wellens, Third ILA Report on Accountability of International Organisations (2003), 13; M. Shaw and K. Wellens, Final Report (2004), 19.

2.3. Direct and autonomous effect of jus cogens with regard to the Security Council resolutions

The direct and autonomous effect of *jus cogens* is the most usual way in which *jus cogens* applies to conflicting acts and transactions. The applicability of *jus cogens* to conflicting treaties or non-treaty acts consists in its direct and autonomous effect and is aimed to resolve normative conflicts through the immediate effect of the former upon the latter. This means that *jus cogens* applies to the acts of the Security Council directly, as distinguished from the modalities of applicability through the UN Charter or treaty interpretation.[55] What is meant here is that the acts of the Council are subject to *jus cogens* in the same way as acts or actions of any actor within the international legal system. This perspective involves not the analysis whether a given act of the Council is in accordance with the constituent treaty, or whether the Council has been empowered by Member States to adopt such acts, but purely and simply the assessment of direct and immediate effect of *jus cogens* as such on the acts of the Council as such.

The 1986 Vienna Convention confirms that international organizations are bound by *jus cogens* in the context of the validity and termination of treaties (Articles 53 and 64). Thus, they have no capacity to conclude treaties conflicting with *jus cogens* and are subject to it as independent legal persons. In addition, international organizations seem to be subject to peremptory norms in all aspects of the law of treaties in the same way as States, as is exemplified by the fact that the relevant provisions of the 1969 and 1986 Vienna Conventions have identical content. In the case of States, it is clear that besides the law of treaties, their acts and actions are also subject to *jus cogens* and their validity is conditional upon compliance with *jus cogens*. Therefore, the fact that international organizations are bound by *jus cogens* with regard to the validity of treaties, invites the same argument, namely that peremptory norms also apply to unilateral acts or actions of international organizations, particularly to the resolutions of the Security Council. Of course, one may argue that international organizations have different capacities and are subject to different constraints than States, but this would not be enough to consider that acts of an organ such as the Security Council are exempt from the immediate effect of *jus cogens* and this has not so far been seriously suggested. On the contrary, the ILC and the 1986 Vienna Conference did not hesitate to extend to international organizations the operation of *jus cogens* in terms of coercively imposed treaties and treaties

---

[55] See N. Angelet, International Law Limits to the Security Council, in Gowlland-Debbas (ed.), *United Nations Sanctions and International Law* (2001), 75–76, submitting that *jus cogens* can bind the Council either by virtue of the principle *nemo plus juris transfere quam ipse habet*, or just by virtue of the nature of *jus cogens*.

conflicting with *jus cogens*, even if the difference is capacities has been mentioned there as well.[56]

The reasoning of Judge Lauterpacht in *Bosnia* seems, at least implicitly, to proceed from such a basis and to focus on the autonomous effect of *jus cogens* on Resolution 713(1991), which imposed the arms embargo on former Yugoslavia. Judge Lauterpacht seems to refer to the immediate and direct effect of the prohibition of genocide, as a peremptory norm, on that resolution, and not to any intermediate modality bringing about such effect.[57]

---

[56] For the reasoning of such extension see 1986 UNCLT Official Records, vol. II, 37 ff.

[57] Separate Opinion, *Bosnia*, *ICJ Reports*, 1993, 440–441. Judge Lauterpacht did not link the issue of the observance of the Charter to the issue of *jus cogens*, and did not engage in examining the intention of the drafters of the Charter.

13

The Normative Conflict between a Security Council Resolution and *Jus Cogens*: The Practice of the Security Council

I. THE CONCEPT OF NORMATIVE CONFLICT

Clarification of the issue of whether a specific resolution of the Security Council offends against *jus cogens* depends upon whether there is a normative conflict between a peremptory norm and a resolution. The identification of such a normative conflict is a task separate from the identification of peremptory norms as a limitation on the Council's powers.

The conflict of the Council decision with *jus cogens* means an attempt to legitimize acts contrary to *jus cogens* and thus hinder the integral and non-fragmentable operation of a given peremptory norm, to aim at a result outlawed under a peremptory norm, to allow or oblige States to do what peremptory norms prohibit or abstain from what peremptory norms require them to do. A normative conflict necessarily involves the operation of two different norms, which for our purposes would be a peremptory norm and a provision in a Security Council resolution. It is important to clarify not only whether they conflict with each other on their face, but also whether these two sets of norms, with the effects they have and the results they require, contradict each other. When two conflicting sets of norms operate, it is the stage of their practical operation which is often most instructive in understanding whether there is a normative conflict. This practical and operative aspect assumes predominance, as exactly in this area the emergence of conflicting rights and duties of States is most likely. On a general plane, a given violation of *jus cogens* may be qualified either as a derogation from *jus cogens* or as its simple breach; however, the fact of involvement of a Security Council resolution in such a situation would most likely involve an attempt of derogation from *jus cogens* consisting in an attempt to exempt a given behaviour from the general regime of a peremptory norm as is applicable and subject it to a regime designed by the Council itself.

Thus, a decision of the Security Council can conflict with *jus cogens* explicitly or implicitly. Consequently, whether there is a conflict of a treaty with *jus cogens* depends upon an objective and dynamic interplay of the provision in question or of the resolution as a whole, with a relevant peremptory norm. Not only the clear wording and the stated intent of a resolution should be studied, but also the necessary result of possible application following from, or compatible with, the wording of its relevant clauses, because the Council may conceal its intent to offend against *jus cogens* through stating totally neutral purposes or even the purpose of maintenance or restoration of peace and security. A clause in the resolution may appear innocent on its face, but could at the same time result in legitimating or justifying the conduct contrary to peremptory norms. This necessitates the objective examination of how a provision in the resolution and a given peremptory norm interact to each other, and of the real juridical impact of an action or inaction by the Security Council on the legal consequences of violation of peremptory norms.

2. SPECIFIC TYPES OF NORMATIVE CONFLICT OF THE SECURITY COUNCIL RESOLUTION WITH *JUS COGENS*

2.1. *The Council's implicit support for the breach of a peremptory norm*

It has happened that the Security Council, aware of the fact that a violation of a peremptory norm is taking place, nevertheless adopts a decision which practically supports the cause of a State which pursues that cause through the violation of *jus cogens*. This can happen when the Council positively adopts a certain attitude or measures without explicitly stating the intention to contravene *jus cogens*.

A clear example can be found in the fact of the adoption of Resolutions 731(1992) and 748(1992), which required Libya to extradite to the United States or the United Kingdom two suspects of the Lockerbie aircraft bombing, and imposed an air and arms embargo on Libya until it complied with such demands. While demanding extradition, the US and the UK had embarked upon the policy of the threat to use force against Libya, in order to induce it to comply with such demands, which clearly contradicts the peremptory prohibition of the use or threat of force as particularly embodied in Article 2(4) of the Charter. Professor Brownlie, as a counsel for Libya before the ICJ in *Lockerbie*, has demonstrated that such threats were made at various levels of UK and US governments and were directed at Libya.[1] This happened in a context where the Council itself had not considered that circumstances it dealt with under Resolutions 731 and 748 required the authorization of the use of force. The Council was not asked to authorize the use of force under Chapter VII, and the threats took place in a bilateral context only; nor were these threats subsumable under Article 51 of the Charter. But Resolution 748 unconditionally supported the action and attitude of States which demanded extradition, and the Council's attitude

---

[1] CR 97/21, and CR 97/24 (Brownlie).

itself resulted in an assumption that even if it was not suggested that circumstances warranted the authorization of force under Chapter VII, it supported the threat or potential use of force by certain States on a bilateral basis. The Council obviously was aware that the use of force was threatened and Libya had made several complaints in this regard, particularly during the *Lockerbie* proceedings before the International Court. The Council was also aware that such threats were aimed at inducing Libya to adopt a certain line of behaviour, but it supported and demanded precisely the same line of behaviour from Libya, backed this demand with coercive measures and in fact acted in a way to promote the success of those unlawful threats of the use of force. It is not suggested that the Council was under a duty to condemn the threat of the use of force, just that it had no power to adopt the attitude and measures supporting such a threat.

Another issue of conflict with *jus cogens* is that Resolution 748 was adopted despite the contention that the extradition of the suspects could deprive them of their right to a fair trial, as Libya expressed doubts that a fair trial would be possible in Scotland or the United States.[2] But the Council did not examine whether this allegation was true and whether compliance with its resolution could result in a serious human rights violation.

There are other examples in practice where the Council has acted in a way supporting a breach of *jus cogens*. This is particularly the case where it is required to differentiate between the conduct of States in terms of the legal merits of such conduct and the Council nevertheless acts in an indiscriminate way.

At the early stage of the conflict in Cyprus, the Council acted nonselectively in the sense that it did not distinguish between aggressor and victim. As a political organ, the Council is perhaps not obliged to condemn every act of aggression, but it is a different question whether the Council can deprive a State of its inherent right to self-defence. Its first resolution on the matter, Resolution 186(1964) referring to Article 2(4) of the UN Charter, called on 'all Member States' to refrain from actions 'likely to worsen the situation in Cyprus or to endanger international peace'. So, although the Council invoked the prohibition on the use of force, it did not address this issue as such in the operative paragraphs of the resolution, limiting itself to broader references to notions of threatening the peace and worsening the situation, which have no precise legal content. But the real contradiction with *jus cogens* was to come with Resolution 193(1964) in which the Council demanded the cessation of the use of force again in a non-selective way. Turkey was called upon to cease the use of force and bombardment of Cyprus, and Cyprus 'to order forces under its control to cease firing immediately'. Here the Council again acted in a way inconsistent with *jus ad bellum*.

---

[2] Brownlie, CR 97/24.

The use of force by Turkey was to be considered as contrary to Article 2(4), while the use of force by Cyprus was an act of self-defence, but the Council placed them on a similar footing. It is true that the Council is perhaps not obliged to make determinations of illegality on each and every occasion. It is also true that the Council is generally empowered to demand a ceasefire from both parties to the conflict. But in this situation what the Council actually did was to demand from a State not to resort to its inherent right to self-defence, which is clearly beyond the mandate of this organ.

At a later stage of the conflict, after the Turkish invasion, the Council by Resolution 354(1974) demanded that all parties cease firing and hostilities. It is obvious that this demand was addressed not only to Turkey, but also to Cyprus, which was acting in exercise of the right to self-defence under Article 51 of the UN Charter. Such a non-selective approach was clearly beyond the powers of the Council and was very unlikely to override the operation of the right to self-defence. It may be argued that the Council did not think it was overriding the right to self-defence, but its demands as addressed to Cyprus specifically resulted in precisely that. In addition, the Security Council made no use of its power under Article 51 for maintenance and restoration of international peace and security. It is therefore clear that the Security Council has not duly respected the need to observe the Article 2(4) prohibition. Once again, the assessment of the Council's action requires bearing in mind the elementary distinction between the failure to condemn the aggressor and the positive demand that the victim of an aggression stops defending itself.

Finally, there are situations where the Security Council has perhaps not intended to act in a way offending *jus cogens*, but the events subsequent to adoption of a given measure give rise to such inconsistency. This has been the case in terms of Resolution 713(1991), which imposed an arms embargo on Yugoslavia before its disintegration.[3] However, after disintegration, the situation arose in which, if the resolution were complied with, Bosnia was hindered in the exercise of its right to self-defence and prevention of genocidal practices. In this case, it was perhaps the Council's failure to lift the embargo after disintegration of the SFRY which caused the principal contradiction with peremptory norms.

2.2. *The relevance of the Council's failure to act in the face of a breach of* jus cogens

It is an important question whether the inaction of the Security Council in the face of a clear violation of *jus cogens* is tantamount to implicit validation

---

[3] For a comprehensive description of developments related to arms embargo on Bosnia, see Gray, Bosnia and Herzegovina: Civil War or Inter-State Conflict? Characterisation and Consequences, *BYIL* (1996), 155–199.

of such violation. The basic, and logically anterior, issue is whether peremptory norms take their effect in the absence of the action of the Security Council. These issues involve multiple aspects of proof of intention and interpretation.

At a general level, the issue of inaction of UN organs has been raised in *Nauru* by Professor Bowett who, as a counsel for Australia, asked if, in terms of the use of Nauru phosphate resources, 'there was a breach [of the Trusteeship Agreement on Nauru], why did not the Trusteeship Council and the General Assembly detect it? . . . why did not the General Assembly declare that there was a breach?'[4] The International Court has not expressed its view on the subject, as it adjudicated on preliminary objections only, and this was followed by a settlement with decent monetary compensation. But conceptually, the issue is still important, and it is clear that the silence of the General Assembly as a political organ could not have been determinative of a strictly legal factor whether the breach of the Trusteeship Agreement had occurred.

The issue arose more acutely in *East Timor*, even though it received no direct judicial consideration there either. In this case, Australia defended its decision to enter into negotiations with Indonesia and conclude the controversial Timor Gap Treaty of 1989, in the face of the fact that Indonesia's occupation of East Timor was a grave breach of the principle of self-determination. But Australia referred to the fact that the Security Council in the first place, and also the General Assembly, had stopped short of condemning the Indonesian occupation of East Timor.

Australia especially considered the right to self-determination to be dependent on the decisions of the United Nations, since without such a central determination the content of a right and its beneficiaries may be unclear.[5] It submitted that Resolutions 384 and 389 of the Security Council 'contained no guidance as to the behaviour expected—even less imposed—on third States'.[6] Moreover, Australia's submissions went so far as to consider that the fact that the General Assembly in Resolution 34/40 of 12 November 1979 did not refer to its previous resolutions was indicative of the fact that the earlier resolutions were no longer to be regarded as operative.[7]

In addition, Australia claimed that it could enter into the Treaty with Indonesia concerning East Timor because there was no United Nations resolution which would curtail that right.[8] Furthermore, it was argued that 'The various resolutions—which say nothing at all about treaty-making, or non-recognition by third States, or the illegality of Indonesia's presence—

---

[4] CR 91/16 (Bowett), 14; also distinguishing Nauru's case from South-West Africa where a breach was found and thus the mandate was terminated, 16.

[5] Counter-Memorial of Australia, *East Timor*, 145, para. 322.

[6] Counter-Memorial of Australia, *East Timor*, 148, para. 330.

[7] Counter-Memorial of Australia, *East Timor*, 151, para. 338.

[8] CR 95/8, 55–56 (Crawford).

ceased in 1982. They certainly do not constitute a finding, or a *donnée*, in relation to the entry into the Treaty in 1989.'[9] Australia also attempted to distinguish the case from previous situations. Thus, the history of the issue demonstrates that the UN did not intend precluding Australia from dealing with Indonesia concerning East Timor. And there is, so it was contended, a fundamental difference between the Security Council's and the General Assembly's response to the East Timor issue and the other issues, such as Rhodesia, the Turkish Republic of Northern Cyprus, Namibia, or Israel's claim on East Jerusalem.[10]

Australia also acknowledged that certain States who voted for Resolution 34/40—eg Canada, Australia, France, Sweden, and Japan—recognized that the integration of East Timor into Indonesia was a reality and moreover an accomplished and irreversible fact. They later submitted that they were not ready to support further resolutions on East Timor.[11] In further Resolutions 35/27 and 36/50, the General Assembly took these views into account and refrained from judging Indonesia's actions, and from imposing the consequent obligations on third States.[12] Furthermore, States did not challenge the Indonesian statement that only about 30 per cent of the UN membership questioned East Timor's integration with Indonesia.[13] All this was considered by Australia as highly relevant, as in its view it depends solely on the decision of the General Assembly whether third States are prevented from dealing with the power in control of a territory, even if that control is illegal under international law.[14]

Australia in fact referred to the attitudes of Indonesia and other States which considered East Timor's integration with Indonesia as irreversible and thus affirmed the validity of a forcible territorial acquisition. Even if some arguments were made to distinguish between the initial validity of incorporation and further consequences, these arguments were nevertheless made parallel to each other, and were in fact treated as mutually complementary.

If a territorial acquisition is wrongful, it must be the case that no rights, such as the treaty-making power and the right to stay in the territory, which are the prerequisites of such treaty-making power, may arise from it. The International Court's affirmation that East Timor had the right to self-determination[15] meant that Indonesia had no right to stay in East Timor, and consequently no right to make treaties in relation to it. The Court was of course aware of such a logical and consequential link, and it was not deterred

---

[9] CR 95/8, 72; CR 95/14, 51 (Crawford).
[10] Counter-Memorial of Australia, *East Timor*, 155–156, para. 347–348.
[11] Counter-Memorial of Australia, *East Timor*, 152–153, paras 339–341; 153–154, paras 344–345.
[12] Counter-Memorial of Australia, *East Timor*, 153, para. 343.
[13] Counter-Memorial of Australia, *East Timor*, 154, para. 346.
[14] Counter-Memorial of Australia, *East Timor*, 147, para. 327.
[15] *ICJ Reports*, 1995, para. 36.

by the contrary practice outlined above to affirm East Timor's right to self-determination. In addition, this practice of States or UN organs has not been treated as relevant in the subsequent processes of the gaining by East Timor of independence as an entity entitled to self-determination.

A similar situation has been confronted in the case of Jordanian and Israeli annexation of East Jerusalem and the question was posed whether the silence of the United Nations has constituted their acquiescence to the territorial title. As Cassese pointed out, mere silence cannot be interpreted as an expression of attitude resulting in the grant of title.[16] A similar approach is upheld by Bowett with regard to the failure of the Council to condemn, in some cases, armed reprisals as illegal, which entails the discrepancy between the principle of illegality of all armed reprisals and the actual practice. But once the principle is part of the broader prohibition of the use of force as *jus cogens*, 'no spasmodic, inconsistent practice of one organ of the United Nations could change a norm of this character'.[17]

In 1964, the Republic of Cyprus argued before the Security Council that the 1960 Cyprus Guarantee Treaty between Greece, Turkey, Cyprus and the UK was void, as it authorized forcible intervention into the country and thus offended against *jus cogens*. The Council has not expressed a view on this. It has not upheld the Treaty explicitly and the mere fact of the failure to reject it explicitly does not suffice to assume that it has upheld the Treaty implicitly. Jacovides correctly notes that the Council did not follow the proposal of Turkey to affirm the Guarantee Treaty, but simply noted the views of the parties in relation thereto and also referred to Article 2(4) of the Charter, which could also be interpreted as negating the validity of claims of the forcible intervention.[18]

The view of the General Assembly was clearer. In 1965, in Resolution 2077(XX), the General Assembly asked the guarantor powers not to intervene in Cyprus, without pronouncing on the validity of the Guarantee Treaty. The General Assembly affirmed that the Republic of Cyprus was entitled to enjoy full sovereignty and independence without outside interference. It called upon on all States to refrain from any intervention directed against the independence or territorial integrity of Cyprus.[19] It is submitted that such an attitude of the General Assembly, aware of the existence of the Guarantee Treaty and its clauses on intervention, in fact ignored them and demanded

---

[16] Cassese, Legal Considerations on the International Status of Jerusalem, 3 *Palestinian Yearbook of International Law* (1986), 25.

[17] Bowett, Reprisals Involving Recourse to Armed Force, 66 *AJIL* (1962), 22.

[18] Jacovides, *Treaties Conflicting with Peremptory Norms of International Law and the Zurich–London 'Agreements'* (1966), 25.

[19] Jacovides, *Treaties Conflicting with Peremptory Norms of International Law and the Zurich–London 'Agreements'* (1966), 26; Paul, Legal Consequences of Conflict between a Treaty and an Imperative Norm, 21 *ÖZÖR* (1971), 28; Schwelb, Some Aspects of International *Jus Cogens*, 61 *AJIL* (1967), 952–953.

behaviour opposite to the right to intervene under that Treaty, thus in fact treating the Treaty as non-existent.

In Resolution 541(1983), the Council seems to have considered that the 1960 Guarantee Treaty was valid, as it pronounced that the proclamation of an independent State of Northern Cyprus is incompatible with the 1960 Treaty establishing the Republic of Cyprus. However, this pronouncement does not necessarily imply the validity or legality of Article IV. If the view is taken that the principle of the total invalidity of treaties conflicting with *jus cogens* applies only to the treaties concluded after the 1969 Vienna Convention on the Law of Treaties entered into force,[20] it becomes clear that the 1960 Treaty as a whole has probably survived while Article IV had been void and it is only as much in the Treaty that the Council seems to have endorsed.

The most recent situation of the inaction of the Security Council in the face of violations of *jus cogens* arose in 1999 with regard to the conflict in Kosovo, where the Council did not support the draft resolution submitted by Russia, China and India condemning the armed attack against the Federal Republic of Yugoslavia. The Council had neither itself authorized such armed attack, nor found circumstances under Chapter VII that would justify it.

It has been submitted quite convincingly that 'the failed adoption of the draft resolution calling for the immediate cessation of the air strikes cannot be treated as an implied authorisation'.[21] A clear distinction should be made between the absence of explicit condemnation of the NATO action and the acceptance that the intervention was in conformity with international law.[22] The political nature of the motives of non-condemnation combined with the criticism of the essential number of States both within and outside the Security Council demonstrates that no implicit acceptance or authorization took place.[23] Unlike the practice examined in Section 2.1, the practice analysed in this section does not disclose any intention of the Council to adopt the attitude or measures whose practical effect would be the perpetration, support or condonation of the breaches of *jus cogens*, not least because the practice considered in this section does not refer to any clear provision in a Security Council resolution offending against *jus cogens*.

This approach is supported in jurisprudence. In *Namibia*, the International Court clearly emphasized that 'The fact that a particular proposal is not adopted by an international organ does not necessarily carry with it the inference that a collective pronouncement is made in a sense opposite to that proposed'.[24]

---

[20]   Above, Chapter 6.

[21]   Gazzini, NATO Coercive Military Activities in the Yugoslav Crisis, 12 *EJIL* (2001), 431.

[22]   Hilpold, Humanitarian Intervention: Is There a Need for a Legal Reappraisal? 12 *EJIL* (2001), 460.

[23]   Id.   [24]   *Namibia, ICJ Reports*, 1971, 36, para. 69.

In general, the process of decision-making in the Security Council is greatly influenced by political factors and the entire process of negotiations and voting is subjected to heavy bargaining based on political self-interest. In such circumstances, it is difficult to find conclusive evidence that the Council is ready to excuse or validate retrospectively certain breaches of peremptory norms, and particularly that the members of the Council act with respective legal conviction and not out of political considerations.

The issue of the relevance of the Security Council's attitude for the effects of peremptory norms arose in the *Wall* case with regard to the effects of the duty of non-recognition of breaches of *jus cogens*. Judge Higgins suggested that in terms of the *Namibia* Advisory Opinion, 'The obligation upon United Nations Members not to recognize South Africa's illegal presence in Namibia, and not to lend support or assistance' relied on the principle that 'A binding determination made by a competent organ of the United Nations to the effect that a situation is illegal cannot remain without consequence'.[25] Under this view, the invalidity of acts and actions contradicting fundamental obligations under the norms of international public order would be sustainable only if supported by the institutional determination to that effect. As Castaneda suggests, if the determination of non-recognition of forcible territorial acquisitions is made by the Security Council or the General Assembly, 'this determination would be obligatory' and the members would have a duty of non-recognition.[26] Does this imply that otherwise there is no duty of non-recognition of the breaches of peremptory norms? In conceptual terms, linking non-recognition to institutional determinations is the negation of the existence of respective duties under general international law.

On the other hand, as Judge Skubiszewski observed, 'the obligation not to recognise a situation created by the unlawful use of force does not arise only as a result of a decision of the Security Council ordering non-recognition. This rule is self-executory'.[27] It seems that this view better reflects the existing legal position.

The argument that arguably there have been no instances of the consistent application of the duty of non-recognition in the absence of UN resolutions must be acknowledged and confronted.[28] At the same time, the relevance of this argument is merely descriptive because in all serious cases relevant in terms of non-recognition the UN organs have actually expressed its support for the principle, and never contradicted it. In addition, in the practice of the principal organs of the United Nations, whether the General Assembly or the Security Council, the application of the principle of non-recognition

---

[25] Separate Opinion, para. 38; see also Legal Consequences of the Continued Presence of South Africa in Namibia (South-West Africa) notwithstanding Security Council Resolution 276 (Advisory Opinion), *ICJ Reports*, 1971, 16.

[26] Castaneda, *Legal Effects of United Nations Resolutions* (1969), 191.

[27] Dissenting Opinion, *East Timor, ICJ Reports*, 1995, 263.   [28] Turns (2003), 134.

to the specific situations is always linked to and justified by the requirements of one of the legal norms which possess the peremptory status in general international law.[29] The action of the UN organs is perceived not as the discretionary action based on purely political or related considerations (even as the decision-making in these organs is generally a political process), but the consistent application, and statement of the legal consequences of, the fundamental norms of peremptory status. In other words, the UN organs have not considered, and could not conceivably consider, their action and decisions as constitutive of the duty of non-recognition. Conversely, the fact that in some cases the UN organs fall short of stating the legal implications of the duty of non-recognition with regard to the specific situation is not necessarily an indicator that these organs, or the majority of their membership, regard this duty as inapplicable in that situation.

Although in *Namibia* the International Court referred to the binding determination of illegality by the Security Council, this cannot be an unconditional acceptance of the constitutive character of the Council's pronouncements. It matters in the first place that the Council has not viewed its role as constitutive but implementing the relevant norms of customary law.[30] In fact the Court, having pronounced that 'A binding determination made by a competent organ of the United Nations to the effect that a situation is illegal cannot remain without consequence', proceeded, on an independent basis, to determine the effect of the illegality of the South African presence in Namibia with regard to non-members of the United Nations which are not subject to Articles 24 and 25 of the Charter, and did not suggest that the UN organs can bind non-members. The Court upheld the duty of non-members not to recognize the South African presence because such presence involved illegality of such kind as to bar *erga omnes* its recognition by any State.[31] In other words, the illegality operated on its own, independently of institutional determinations.

The Court further referred to the respective duties of all States, and to the fact of the declaration of illegality by the Council.[32] This means that the Council declared the illegality and ensuing consequences such as non-recognition rather than constitute it. The Court's pronouncements, placed in the common context, admit of such state of general international law which

---

[29] See above, Chapter 11. Dugard, *Recognition and the United Nation* (1987), 102–103 suggests that the General Assembly and Security Council Resolutions related to non-recognition 'are to be viewed as authoritative interpretations of the Charter and serve as a reminder to States of their duty to refrain from recognising such an illegality under the Charter and customary law'. Dugard considers that this approach is preferable to basing the duty of non-recognition on Article 25 of the Charter, because in some cases the Security Council does not speak in obligatory terms and the door is opened for selectivity.

[30] cf Opinions of Judge Petren, *ICJ Reports*, 1971, 133–137, and Judge Onyeama, id., 147–149.

[31] *ICJ Reports*, 1971, 56, para. 126.   [32] Id., 56, paras 126–127.

imposes on States the duty not to recognize certain illegalities independently of the pronouncements of the United Nations organs.

As Dugard explains, the resolutions barring the recognition of Northern Cyprus did not refer to Article 25 of the Charter or Chapter VII.[33] This moves things closer towards viewing that these resolutions reflected the judgment of the Security Council on the legal situation in general international law rather than expressed its intention to apply the duty of non-recognition that would not otherwise exist. Therefore, the view that the non-recognition of certain illegal situations is effective only if and as far as upheld by the UN principal organs simply does not stand if tested against practice. No duty of non-recognition can exist and operate unless it is viewed as part of general international law as opposed to that of the process of political decision-making in the United Nations organs.

The approach that the duty of non-recognition in situations like that involved in the case at hand can only follow from the institutional determinations of the principal organs of the United Nations is not justified from the perspective of international public order. The existing practice and doctrinal opinion confirms that once the breach of a peremptory norm is capable of causing a legally relevant change, the nullity of the relevant acts or actions follows and the duty of non-recognition is among the natural consequences of the breach, independently of any institutional determination to that effect. If the opposite were the case, then peremptory norms would not be able to take their effect in the face of fundamental illegalities, unless the principal organs of the United Nations decide accordingly. This perspective would reduce peremptory norms to a dead letter.

2.3. The claims of subsequent validation of the breaches of jus cogens

This section will consider whether the adoption of a resolution by the Security Council, as opposed to its non-adoption, can subsequently validate a breach of peremptory norms and particularly whether such a result can be present if the Council approves through its decision the factual or legal consequences of a given breach of *jus cogens*. The most significant instances in the Council's practice arose from the conflict in Kosovo with regard to which the Council adopted several resolutions in 1998 and 1999.

In October 1998, the Federal Republic of Yugoslavia (FRY) signed an agreement providing for the return of refugees in Kosovo and the verification role for the OSCE. It was clear that these agreements were obtained through deliberate military threat and may be regarded as void *ab initio* in accordance with Article 52 of the Vienna Convention on the Law of Treaties.[34] The

---

[33] Dugard (1987), 110.

[34] Gazzini, NATO Coercive Military Activities in the Yugoslav Crisis, 12 *EJIL* (2001), 430.

United States admitted that the credible threat of force was necessary to conclude these agreements.[35] NATO, through its Secretary-General, has openly stated that it would resort to the threat and use of force.[36] It is therefore clear that these agreements were void, as coercively imposed treaties are void unconditionally and absolutely. This is recognized in respect of treaties concluded both by States and international organizations,[37] and this conclusion is identical in terms of conventional law as embodied in the 1969 and 1986 Vienna Conventions, customary law[38] and judicial practice.[39] The Security Council manifestly lacks the competence to validate the agreements imposed through coercion.[40] This is so not least because the peremptory prohibition of the use of force is a manifest limitation in the Council's powers and the voidness of coercively imposed treaties is the clear consequence of *jus cogens*.[41]

The fact of the adoption of Resolution 1203(1998), which approved the terms of the settlement reached with the FRY, has sometimes been interpreted as a validation of coercively imposed agreements. In the process of adoption of the resolution, France considered Resolution 1203 as necessary to legitimate agreements signed by the FRY.[42] The resolution itself did not explicitly support such reasoning. In fact, the opposite view is justified. Far from affecting the legal value of 1998 agreements, Resolution 1203 imposed on the FRY 'entirely new obligations having an identical substantive content

[35] Gazzini, NATO Coercive Military Activities in the Yugoslav Crisis, 12 *EJIL* (2001), 430, n. 293, (S/PV.3937, 24 Oct 1998, 15) (also S/PV.3955).

[36] Hilpold, Humanitarian Intervention: Is There a Need for a Legal Reappraisal? 12 *EJIL* (2001), 440.

[37] In codifying the law of treaties applicable to international organizations, the ILC decided to use the formulation which is used in VCLT 1969 applicable to States, 1986 *UNCLT Official Records*, vol. II, 37–39. The formulation was so adopted as part of VCLT 1986.

[38] It is implied that the voidness of coercively imposed treaties is also recognized under customary law, Cassese, *International Law* (2005), 176–177. The 1966 ILC Report on the Law of Treaties, YbILC (II-1966), 246–247, clearly states that the voidness of forcibly imposed treaties is the result of the evolution of international law in general and particularly emphasizes that any other stance is incompatible with the state of general international law on the use of force.

[39] *Fisheries Jurisdiction (UK v Iceland)*, *ICJ Reports*, 1973, para. 24. Dissenting Opinion of Judge Schwebel, *Nicaragua, ICJ Reports*, 1984, 615.

[40] Gazzini, NATO Coercive Military Activities in the Yugoslav Crisis, 12 *EJIL* (2001), 430.

[41] The UK view at the Vienna Conference on the Law of Treaties was that a peremptory norm embodied in Article 49 of the ILC draft which later became Article 52 VCLT would render any conflicting treaty void, UNCLT First Session (1969), 304 (UK). Judge Schwebel in *Nicaragua* referred to Article 52 VCLT in the context of the peremptory nature of the prohibition of the use of force, Dissenting Opinion of Judge Schwebel, *ICJ Reports*, 1984, 615. This is also affirmed in legal doctrine. According to Virally, there is a parallelism between *jus cogens* and invalidity of treaties procured through threat or use of force. Virally, Reflexions sur le 'jus cogens', 12 *Annuaire Français de Droit International* (1966), 13. In addition, as the International Court stressed in *Fisheries Jurisdiction (UK v Iceland)*, *ICJ Reports*, 1973, para. 24, the voidness of coercively imposed treaties is implied in the UN Charter itself and this seems therefore to be a clear limitation on what the Council can do.

[42] Gazzini, NATO Coercive Military Activities in the Yugoslav Crisis, 12 *EJIL* (2001), 406; (S/PV.3937, 12).

to those included in the agreements. It rendered the illegal procurement of the agreements irrelevant and, more importantly, replaced the alleged consensual basis of the monitoring missions with a mandatory decision under Chapter VII of the Charter.'[43]

Thus, it is suggested that the Security Council has on occasion chosen to replace agreements of doubtful validity by a binding resolution rather than retrospectively validate them. But it must also be ascertained that the Council in Resolution 1203 has welcomed the conclusion of the agreements of 15–16 October 1998 with the FRY, explicitly endorsed these agreements and demanded the 'full and prompt implementation of these agreements by the Federal Republic of Yugoslavia' on which they were forcibly imposed. The preamble and paragraph 1 of the Resolution are very clear in this regard. All this took place despite the fact that the Council lacked the competence to validate the forcibly imposed agreements. The only conclusion in this situation could be that such validation is void *ab initio* for its conflict with the peremptory prohibition of force embodied both in the Charter and general international law.

Similar issues arose with regard to Resolution 1244(1999), whereby the Council approved the international security presence in Kosovo and defined the mandate of KFOR. This has been interpreted by some as a retrospective approval of the armed attack on Yugoslavia, although nothing in the text of the resolution approves this, and it is also clear that a resolution approving the war against the FRY would not have commanded the necessary votes under Article 27 of the Charter. (This situation is contrasted to Resolution 1203 where the Council explicitly supported the void agreements.) Besides, the Council had not found that the situation around Kosovo mandated the authorization of force, and it would be absurd to assume that it later validated such use of force; such judgment would justify the Council in offending against the clear terms of the Charter which outlaws the use of force in absolute and unconditional terms. The use of force was not authorized when it was employed and hence remained illegal both under the Charter and general international law. When the Council initially authorizes the use of force under Chapter VII, such use of force is *legal*; but when the force is used without the authorization, it becomes *illegal* in terms of both the Charter and general international law. Therefore, it cannot be argued that once the Council can initially authorize the use of force it can also retrospectively validate the use of unauthorized force. The two situations are radically different in nature. In the first situation the Council would act in accordance with the clear mandate delegated to it by States under the Charter; in the second case it would validate an action which the States considered in the Charter as absolutely illegal, and this is beyond the

---

[43] Gazzini, NATO Coercive Military Activities in the Yugoslav Crisis, 12 *EJIL* (2001), 430.

Council's mandate. If it is also understood that the use of force is absolutely and peremptorily outlawed under general international law, it becomes clear that no treaty organ could be deemed to be established by States with the powers to override such prohibition and ensuing illegalities.

Nevertheless, Pellet and Wedgwood consider that the Council's endorsement of the outcome of the conflict is tantamount to a validation of the NATO action.[44] Pellet also considers that Resolution 1244 dramatically changed the picture and retrospectively legitimated the action against the FRY, which Pellet characterizes as an international crime.[45] But if the issues are accurately examined, it is far from established that the Council was willing to provide retrospective validation of the NATO action against the FRY. It would be more appropriate to say that the Council decided to act in the face of a new reality: the vacated territory of the Yugoslavian province of Kosovo was to be placed under a certain kind of authority which would be able to maintain law and order before the solution of the conflict would be found, ensure the safe return of refugees and prevent further instances of inter-ethnic conflict. Therefore, 'the fact that [in Resolution 1244] the Security Council does not refer to the NATO military action can hardly be seen as evidence for an acquiescence to the intervention'.[46] The outcome here seems to be the same as with regard to the Council's inaction in the face of the claims of invalidity of the Cyprus Guarantee Treaty as focused upon above in Section 2.2.

Pellet himself recognizes that such subsequent validation, if it happened, was deeply repugnant to the function of law in any society.[47] Similarly, Gray convincingly characterizes the idea of retrospective authorization of illegal armed actions as a dangerous idea with no adequate support in State practice.[48] The idea of subsequent validation is also rejected with regard to illegal armed actions in the UNGA Resolution 3314(1974) on the Definition of Aggression, which requires the express determination by the Security Council that an act is not to be condemned as an aggression.

The implausibility of some claims of subsequent validation of illegal actions in the case of Kosovo has become so clear that when, after the Second Gulf War, the Council adopted Resolution 1483(2003) governing the status of occupying powers in Iraq, it was not seriously contended that this resolution could be understood as a subsequent validation of the use of force against Iraq.

---

[44] Wedgwood, Unilateral Action in the UN System, 11 *EJIL* (2000), 358–359; Pellet, Brief Remarks on the Unilateral Use of Force, 11 *EJIL* (2000), 387 ff.

[45] Pellet, Brief Remarks on the Unilateral Use of Force, 11 *EJIL* (2000), 389.

[46] Hilpold, Humanitarian Intervention: Is There a Need for a Legal Reappraisal? 12 *EJIL* (2001), 441.

[47] Pellet, Brief Remarks on the Unilateral Use of Force, 11 *EJIL* (2000), 389.

[48] Gray, *International Law and the Use of Force* (2000), 195.

2.4. *Resolutions explicitly approving breaches of* jus cogens

Apart from the situations considered above, measures taken by the Security Council may result in a direct approval of a violation of *jus cogens*, when the intent to do so is clearly inferable from the text of the Council's Resolution. This is the case with the Council's approval of enhanced powers of the High Representative in Bosnia.

The position of the High Representative was initially introduced by the Dayton Agreement. Annex 4 of that Agreement confirmed the political independence and sovereignty of Bosnia; its Article I(4) affirmed that Bosnia and Herzegovina should have such symbols as are decided by its Parliamentary Assembly and approved by the Presidency; Article III(1) determines the matters for responsibility of the institutions of Bosnia-Herzegovina.

Article II of Annex 10, which lists the powers of the High Representative, does not empower it to make binding decision on any of the above-mentioned matters, and states that the High Representative has only monitoring, consultative, coordinative and conciliatory powers. It is not given any power of public authority within or with regard to Bosnia. Article V of Annex 10 makes the High Representative 'the final authority in theatre regarding interpretation of this Agreement on the civilian implementation of the peace settlement'. However, there is a difference between interpretation and revision of treaty provisions, and the High Representative is the final instance in interpreting its powers which it has been granted under the treaty, not in arrogating new powers to itself. It was in this way that the Security Council originally upheld the Dayton Agreements and ensuing powers of the High Representative in its Resolution 1031(1995).

This difference has somehow been neglected in subsequent practice, which supported the expansionist reading of his powers by the High Representative. The Bonn Decision of the Peace Implementation Council (PIC), adopted on 10 December 1997, particularly welcomed the High Representative's intention to use its authority of final interpretation, and in particular exercise some functions not conferred to it under the Dayton Treaty: organization of meetings of common institutions, interim measures with regard to governmental decisions, and dismissal of public officials 'who are found by the High Representative to be in violation of legal commitments made under the Peace Agreement or the terms of its interpretation'. Thus, the High Representative is given the powers not foreseen under the Peace Agreement. These powers conferred are very broad, and the PIC Decision empowers the High Representative to exercise these powers 'as he judges necessary'.

In practice, the High Representative used these powers to effect dismissal of a great number of officials of various levels, including popularly elected high-level officials such as presidents,[49] and to adopt laws (on the ombudsman,

---

[49] Numerous decisions of this kind are available at www.ohr.int.

State Border Protection, criminal procedure etc),[50] State symbols, and a procedure for the adoption of laws.[51] These powers and the manner of their exercise went to the core of State sovereignty and, most importantly for the purposes of this analysis, to the right of peoples to self-determination, which consists in the entitlement of peoples to decide freely on their political organization and future.

This factor has been neglected by the Security Council, which, in its Resolution 1305(2000), paragraph 4, and Resolution 1491(2003), paragraph 4, expresses full support for the High Representative to make binding decisions as elaborated in the PIC Bonn Decisions. It seems that this provision clearly offends against the principle of self-determination, and on this account its legal effect is doubtful in view of the overriding status of the principle of self-determination.

This conclusion with regard to the High Representative's powers is not easily generalizable. It differs from the situation with regard to UNMIK,[52] which assumes some powers substantially comparable to the powers exercised by the High Representative.[53] However, UNMIK is operative in a province of the FRY, and not in an entire State, and hence its powers do not come into conflict with the principle of self-determination of any country or people— any entity which would have such right.[54] The difference between these two situations affirms that while the Security Council is empowered to establish territorial administrations with broad powers, it must do so with full respect for the principle of self-determination. In addition, the legality of the arrangements like UNMIK has to do with their temporary nature, which by itself guarantees that these arrangements are not intended to violate the territorial integrity of States. If such an arrangement were imposed in perpetuity, serious problems of their validity would arise.

2.5. *Resolutions generating the breaches of* jus cogens

It is possible that the action of the Security Council itself serves as a source of breach of *jus cogens*. The possible instances of such violation of peremptory rules directly by the Council's action relates to situations where the

[50] Decision imposing the Law on the Human Rights Ombudsman of Bosnia and Herzegovina, 14 December 2000; Decision on the Law on State Border Service, 13 January 2000; Decision Amending the Law on Special Witness Protection in Criminal Proceedings in the Federation of BiH, 2 March 2001.

[51] Decision on Law-signing Procedures in the Republika Srpska During a Presidential Vacancy, 25 June 1999.

[52] On UNMIK generally, see Irmscher, Legal Framework of the Activities of UNMIK, 44 *German YIL* (2001), 353 ff., and Stahn, Territorial Administration in the former Yugoslavia, 61 *ZaöRV* (2001), 107 ff.

[53] Stahn, 134 ff.

[54] Stahn, 134–135, clearly emphasizing that the functions of UNMIK are provisional and transitional, without affecting the sovereignty of any State.

Council adopts coercive measures under Chapter VII. Like other situations, it is States which would actually act in violation of *jus cogens*: but it is the Council which explicitly provides an excuse to do so. The norms which are offended in such circumstances pertain to human rights and humanitarian law.

There are several familiar examples of sanctions which in the first place affect the innocent civilian population.[55] The economic sanctions against Iraq reached their exhaustion point in causing suffering to the civilian population. The perpetuation of those sanctions caused severe hardship to the Iraqi population, including the Kurdish minority, without having any effective influence on the Iraqi elite which took the decisions to invade Kuwait.[56] Sanctions against the FRY have also not avoided placing a heavy burden upon the civilian population.[57] It can hardly be disputed that sanctions against Haiti, the FRY and Iraq contributed to an increase in infant mortality and impaired access to food and medicines.[58] In Iraq, child mortality increased twice after the imposition of UN sanctions.[59] Besides, such sanctions have not proved effective. As Damrosch concludes, 'presumably, the theory of applying comprehensive economic sanctions to a State (or para-State) is that infliction of hardship on the people living there will induce changes in the practices that the senders of sanctions deem unacceptable. The causal mechanism by which economic pressure on a population could produce behavioural change in the leadership is far from evident.'[60]

This problem being evident, the Security Council has approved humanitarian exceptions to sanctions it has imposed on certain States,[61] but such

---

[55] Reinisch, Developing Human Rights and Humanitarian Law Accountability of the Security Council for the Imposition of Economic Sanctions, 95 *AJIL* (2001), 851–852; The UN Sub-commission on Human Rights in its Resolution 2000/1 expressed its concern that UN embargoes and sanctions result in severe hardship for innocent population, such as children and elderly people, and appealed to the Security Council to alleviate such suffering through alleviating sanctions regimes (preamble and para. 2).

[56] White, *The Law of International Organisations* (1996), 188; Damrosch, Enforcing International Law through Non-Forcible Measures, 269 *Recueil des Cours* (1997), 117, 121.

[57] Id., 127.

[58] Damrosch, Enforcing International Law through Non-Forcible Measures, 269 *Recueil des Cours* (1997), 139, 147–148.

[59] E. de Wet, Human Rights Limitations to Economic Enforcement Measures Under Article 41 of the UN Charter and the Iraqi Sanctions Regime, 14 *LJIL* (2001), 289.

[60] Damrosch, Enforcing International Law through Non-Forcible Measures, 269 *Recueil des Cours* (1997), 129. A similar approach is embodied in CESCR General Comment No. 8, para. 3, emphasizing that UN sanctions regimes often reinforce the power of elites through generating black markets and causing enhancement of their control of populations in terms of oppressing political opposition. See also Reinisch, Developing Human Rights and Humanitarian Law Accountability of the Security Council for the Imposition of Economic Sanctions, 95 *AJIL* (2001), 851.

[61] For an overview of such humanitarian exceptions see E. de Wet, Human Rights Limitations to Economic Enforcement Measures Under Article 41 of the UN Charter and the Iraqi Sanctions Regime, 14 *LJIL* (2001), 281–284.

measures have not been particularly effective, as particularly emphasized in General Comment No. 8 of the UN Committee on Economic and Social Rights. Exceptions are limited in scope and do not address such human rights issues as primary education, access to health care or drinkable water.[62] As Gasser submits, humanitarian exceptions established by Resolutions 661, 666 and 757 on Iraq and Yugoslavia are in accordance with international humanitarian law as embodied in the Geneva Conventions. But the Iraqi and Yugoslav civilian population have unquestionably suffered hardship under the embargoes despite the humanitarian exceptions.[63] The problem may consist either in the given sanctions regime itself or the problem of the scope or enforcement of specific humanitarian exceptions. In both cases, however, the Security Council has to undertake assessment in terms of foreseeability of adverse humanitarian consequences. In addition, Gasser properly observes that the Council should allow more than the elementary standards embodied in the Geneva Conventions to be enforced in the course of the Chapter VII measures.[64] The 'unintended' or 'unavoidable' effects on the civilian population could thereby be limited to a strict minimum.[65]

Another example of resolutions that directly entail the breach of peremptory norms is the preventive freezing of assets of those suspected of involvement with terrorism. Under Resolution 1333(2000), the Council ordered freezing assets but has neither provided for any forum where such freezing could be reviewed, nor authorized national courts to do so. Such a decision would reverse the presumption of innocence as the burden would be on suspects to prove that they are not involved with terrorism.[66] The Council has violated Article 14 of the ICCPR and arguably a *jus cogens* norm by not providing for a fair hearing in Resolution 1333(2000). The Council therefore acted illegally.[67]

3. SOME GENERAL OBSERVATIONS

The instances examined above illustrate the fact that the Council may act in contravention of *jus cogens* in various ways; and the governing legal framework requires assessing the value of such actions accordingly. It must

[62] General Comment No. 8, para. 5; see also Reinisch, Developing Human Rights and Humanitarian Law Accountability of the Security Council for the Imposition of Economic Sanctions, 95 *AJIL* (2001), 863.

[63] Gasser, Collective Economic Sanctions and International Humanitarian Law, 56 *ZaöRV* (1996), 892–894.

[64] Gasser, (1996), 901.   [65] Gasser, (1996), 902.

[66] De Wet, The Role of Human Rights in Limiting the Enforcement Power of the Security Council: A Principled View, in De Wet and Nollkaemper (eds), *Review of the Security Council by Member States* (2003), 18.

[67] De Wet, id., 23, 29.

be emphasized that the analysis of practice confirms the approach to normative conflict as formulated above, in terms of practical and operative interaction of the terms of a resolution to *jus cogens*. This approach would clarify that in many cases where the Council's action or inaction *prima facie* looks as though it may conflict with *jus cogens*, it has no such effect in reality as is demonstrated in cases of the so-called 'retrospective validation'. On the other hand, a resolution can be qualified as offending *jus cogens* even if *prima facie* it reveals no such intent, being based on some neutral purpose. For example, Resolution 748(1992) is aimed at combating the State-sponsored terrorism, but in fact it is conducive to the unlawful threat of the use of force.

As far as the effects of a resolution offending against *jus cogens* are concerned, it must be borne in mind that the illegality emanating from the breach of *jus cogens* is objective, which means that the basis of the illegality is the breach of a rule as such, regardless of the attitude of specific actors. This is so because, as Jennings suggests, the objective wrongs are breaches of *jus cogens* offending against the community interest, and the consequent nullity is not qualified by subsequent attitudes.[68] According to Rozakis, objective illegality means the objective recognition of an illegality, as such, which can be invoked with a view of its extinction by all members of the international community.[69] This means that the attitude of an international body with regard to such illegality is not crucial. The applicability of peremptory norms to a given situation, or the legality of a given fact or action, is not prejudiced by the fact of how a body such as the Security Council treats such an act or situation. To hold otherwise would mean that the rules of international law do not, in the case of their violation, independently generate legal consequences but that such consequences arise only in the event of a subsequent determination of illegality by one or other international body. Such an outcome would result in the fragmentation of legal relations, and defeat the primary purpose of *jus cogens*, which is to avoid such fragmentation.

Some specific issues arise from claims of subsequent approval or validation of certain conduct by the Security Council or its acquiescence in certain acts. It must be understood, however, that the concept of acquiescence is not unqualified. International tribunals always apply a very high standard of proof in terms of acquiescence and in most cases decline to find it.[70] It is never justified to presume acquiescence: it must be inferred from convincing evidence, including the clarity of attitude and the time factor. To find these in the Security Council's practice outlined above is an impossible task. In

---

[68] R.Y. Jennings, Nullity and Effectiveness in International Law, *Cambridge Essays in International Law* (1965), 74.

[69] Rozakis, *The Concept of* Jus Cogens *in the Law of Treaties* (1976), 24.

[70] Acquiescence was found in *Temple* due to the situation being unchallenged for decades, *ICJ Reports*, 1962. It was, however, not found in a number of cases, such as *Gulf of Maine*, *ICJ Reports*, 1982, *Libya–Malta*, *ICJ Reports*, 1985, 261, *La Bretagne*, 82 ILR 652.

particular, the non-condemnation of an act does not mean its approval, as confirmed by the *Namibia* Opinion. In addition, the concept of acquiescence does not operate in the face of overriding *jus cogens*, and there are categorical problems with subsequent approval where *jus cogens* is involved. There is no valid precedent of the acquiescence into acts or situations *contra juris cogentis* and the legal doctrine rejects the idea that in such situations the acquiescence can be validly involved.[71] No act contrary to *jus cogens* 'can be legitimated by means of consent, acquiescence or recognition; nor is protest necessary to preserve rights affected by such acts.'[72]

There could be more practical problems with such acquiescence, when some States consider that the action 'approved' by the Council still remains illegal as, for instance, the FRY and many other States consider with regard to the NATO action against the FRY. The opposite conclusion would mean that the Council is master of the Charter and of *jus cogens* rather than an organ subjected to the Charter.

In all instances where the Council acts contrary to *jus cogens*, or where its action is so interpreted, this is tantamount to accepting the fragmentation of *jus cogens* and derogation from it as this would mean that the action contrary to *jus cogens* can become legal through subsequent validation. Such fragmentation of *jus cogens* has no lawful foundation. The particular regime of an organization may warrant derogation from ordinary norms and empower it to act contrary to them in certain cases; but with regard to *jus cogens* such contention is not tenable.

---

[71] Sir Hersch Lauterpacht considered that acquiescence cannot cure acts which are void *ab initio*, Lauterpacht, Sovereignty over Submarine Areas, *BYIL* (1950), 397–398. F.A. Mann also clearly asserted that no acquiescence could heal serious violations of State sovereignty, even if the affected State does not raise the issue, Mann, Reflection on the Prosecution of Persons Abducted in Breach of International Law, in Dinstein and Tabori (eds), *Festschrift Rosenne*, 410.

[72] 1 Jennings and Watts, *Oppenheim's International Law* (9th ed., 1996), 8.

14

Legal Consequences of the Conflict of a Security Council Resolution with Peremptory Norms

I. *JUS COGENS* AND THE INTENTION OF THE SECURITY COUNCIL

It is clear from the previous analysis that *jus cogens* is a limitation on the Security Council's actions, and the latter may come in conflict with the former in different ways. This naturally raises the issue of legal consequences in case of such conflict.

To understand whether a decision of the Council offends against *jus cogens* requires ascertaining the intention of the Council behind a given decision through the careful analysis of the text of a resolution, to find whether, in acting or failing to act, the Council intends to derogate from a peremptory norm or its effects, or legitimate the non-compliance with it, and then judging the established intention in terms of applicable peremptory norms. This is basically a task of finding whether there is a normative conflict between *jus cogens* and a Security Council resolution.

The ascertainment of the intent of the Council serves the need to preserve the stability of decision-making and supports the presumption of the validity of resolutions. Before conclusions are made as to the validity of a given resolution, it must be ascertained through the analysis of the text whether the Council itself intended to enact a resolution which would become void for conflict with peremptory norms.

It is clear that the encroachment on *jus cogens* is outside the Council's competence. It is established that the conduct outlawed under *jus cogens* is outside the functions and sovereign prerogatives of States. The national and international jurisprudence on sovereign immunity has clearly reached that conclusion.[1] Even if this jurisprudence is on a different matter, it clearly demonstrates that it is not part of the functions of a State to offend against *jus cogens*. International organizations, established by States, cannot be deemed to be endowed with functions which States themselves are not entitled to exercise in any circumstances, even if they act through powers invested in international organizations. This brings us to the issue of excess of competence (*ultra vires*) and ensuing legal consequences. But in the first

---

[1] Above, Chapter 10.

place the Council is aware of such limitations of its competence, and must be presumed to respect it, unless the opposite appears true from the clear wording of a resolution.

This raises the issue of interpretative methods. It is contended that the interpretation of the Security Council's resolution should give effect to the will of Member States, but at the same time the resolutions should be interpreted in accordance with the UN Charter.[2] As far as general international law is concerned, it is suggested that

> The extent to which Security Council Resolutions should be interpreted taking into account applicable rules of international law, whether general international law or particular treaties, depends on the analysis of the intentions of the Security Council (as evidenced by the text of the resolution and the surrounding circumstances). If it appears that the Council was intending to lay down a rule irrespective of the prior obligations of States, in general or in particular, then that intention would prevail; if, conversely, it appears that the Council was intending to base itself on existing legal rules or an existing legal situation, then its decisions ought certainly be interpreted taking those rules into account.[3]

This statement could be perfectly true if international law were a flat system where none of its norms possess the distinctive characteristics of public order. But there is a hierarchy in international law, with direct impacts on the scope of the Council's powers. Not only are the Council's resolutions part of secondary law subjected to the Charter, but also part of a system which in its entirety is subordinated to *jus cogens*. Therefore, the task of interpretation of resolutions is to ensure compliance of a given conduct not only with the text of the resolution, but also with the standards which govern the powers of the Council and thus the meaning of its resolutions.

It is true that by virtue of Article 103 of the Charter, the Council could perhaps override international law in some respects:[4] but this does not extend to *jus cogens*. This factor would be relevant for voiding incompatible resolutions. But it is even more relevant for the question of interpretation, and supports the presumption that the Council, mindful of limitations on its powers, would not intend to hamper operation of a peremptory norm.

As Cassese suggests, the need to construe treaties in a way avoiding their conflict with peremptory norms also applies to the resolutions of the Security Council which is bound by *jus cogens* as States are.[5] Judge Lauterpacht suggested in *Bosnia* that the Security Council would not deliberately adopt a resolution violating a peremptory norm such as that prohibiting genocide, but suggested that such contradiction may be involved in an unforeseen

---

[2] M. Wood, The Interpretation of Security Council Resolutions, 2 *Max-Planck YBUNL* (1998), 95.

[3] Id., 92.   [4] Id.   [5] Cassese, *International Law* (2005), 106.

manner.[6] The question of validity of the Council's resolution would not come into play if a direct normative conflict may be avoided through a careful interpretation qualifying the effect of resolutions in a way compatible with *jus cogens*, which would preserve a given resolution.

Apart from the cases of imposition of economic sanctions foreseen under Article 41 of the Charter, which may prevail over inter-State agreements, such as trade agreements, the Security Council hardly ever expresses any intention of disregarding existing rules of international law. As the ICTY observed in *Tadic*,

It is open to the Security Council—subject to peremptory norms of international law (*jus cogens*)—to adopt definitions of crimes in the Statute which deviate from customary international law. Nevertheless, as a general principle, provisions of the Statute defining the crimes within the jurisdiction of the Tribunal should always be interpreted as reflecting customary international law, unless an intention to depart from customary international law is expressed in the Statute, or from other authoritative sources.[7]

This approach has further been shared in *Akayesu*, where it was concluded that, through establishment of the *ad hoc* criminal tribunals, the Council did not derogate from customary law, and the fact that the concept of crimes against humanity was linked to an armed conflict in *Tadic* and to a discriminatory intent in *Akayesu* was due not to the intention of the Council to change the composition of these crimes as recognized under general international law, but just to the intention to provide the ICTY and ICTR with the accordingly limited jurisdiction. The normal regime of international criminal law, and the normal legal consequences arising within it, including the duty of States to extradite and prosecute perpetrators of international crimes, remained unaffected.[8] This must be the key criterion presuming that the Council does not deviate from general international law unless the contrary intent is clear. But again, even if on rare occasions the intent to contradict peremptory norms clearly appears from a resolution, interpretive methods could be used which would qualify such an intention so as to make it consistent with *jus cogens*.

It should be mentioned in the first place that certain resolutions contain explicit clauses on humanitarian exceptions to sanctions, requiring respect for human rights and humanitarian law in terms of the fight against terrorism, such as Resolution 1456(2003), or for respect of territorial integrity and sovereignty of a State, such as Resolution 1244(1999), and this demonstrates that the Council does not intend to offend *jus cogens* in these specific ways. Resolution 1373(2001) requires certain measures of identifying terrorist suspects in the process of asylum-seeking, in conformity with the relevant

---

[6] *ICJ Reports*, 1993, 440–441.
[7] Tadic, Appeals Chamber, 2 October 1995, para. 296.　　[8] *Akayesu*, para. 466.

human rights norms. However, in other cases one could wish for more certainty, and the overall interpretation of the resolution has to be performed in order to ascertain the Council's intention.

The terms of a resolution, in case of vagueness, must be construed as requiring an outcome consistent with international public policy as embodied in *jus cogens*. According to Gasser, 'doubtful' wording of the Council's resolutions must always be construed in such a way as to avoid conflict with fundamental international obligations.[9] For example, Resolution 242(1967) called for 'a just settlement of the refugee problem' in Palestine. The Security Council's insistence on a 'just settlement' is more plausibly read as affirming a right of Palestinians to return. 'Just settlement' refers to what the United Nations found to be a just outcome, namely the return of displaced Palestinians, and other interpretations of this notion may be hazardous.[10] The Council must be presumed not to have intended any outcome preventing the displaced persons from returning to their homes and it is indeed hazardous to assume that the Council could adopt decisions validating mass deportation or displacement of people. More so, if it is borne in mind that expulsion or deportation is defined as a crime against humanity or war crime. Under Article 18(g) of the ILC's Draft Code on Crimes against Peace and Security of Mankind and Article 7.1(d) of the ICC Statute, the arbitrary deportation or forcible transfer of a population is a crime against humanity, and under Article 8.2(e VII) of the ICC Statute 'ordering the displacement of the civilian population for reasons related to the conflict' is an exceptionally serious war crime. This would naturally suggest that the violation of *jus cogens* is involved, with all due effects and consequences,[11] and the Council cannot validly intend to preclude such effects and consequences.

In its various paragraphs, and especially in relation to the disposal of the Iraqi oil resources, Resolution 1483(2003) refers in its paragraphs 16, 20 and 21 to 'a properly constituted, internationally recognised, representative government of Iraq', without defining any further requirements such a government would have to satisfy. This question is even more acute bearing in

---

[9] Gasser, Collective Economic Sanctions and International Humanitarian Law, 56 *ZaöRV* (1996), 883.

[10] Quigley, Displaced Palestinians and a Right to Return, 39 *Harvard JIL* (1998), 192; this is further affirmed by the judgment of the General Assembly as to what constitutes 'just settlement'. In Resolution 39/146A (1986), the General Assembly emphasized that 'peace in the Middle East in indivisible and must be based on a comprehensive, just and lasting solution of the Middle East problem ... which ensures the complete and unconditional withdrawal of Israel from the Palestinian and other territories occupied since 1967, including Jerusalem, and which enables the Palestinian people, under the leadership of the Palestine Liberation Organisation, to exercise its inalienable rights, including the right to return and the right to self-determination, national independence and the establishment of its independent sovereign State in Palestine.'

[11] As Special Rapporteur Waldock suggested, one of the criteria for determining a norm's peremptory status is the criminality of the conduct it outlaws, see (1963-II), 52–53.

mind that recently the provisional council consisting of 25 members has been constituted in Iraq as the country's provisional government.

The principal thing missing here is the reference to a government constituted on the basis of democratic elections, and the requirements suggested in the resolution are anyway ambiguous. 'Properly constituted' may be a term which may be subjectively interpreted; people may differ on what is proper in given circumstances. 'Internationally recognised' is no less relative—it is unclear by whom, and by how many States the future Iraqi government must be recognized. 'Representative' may resemble something democratically elected, but may also be different from it—for example a government which includes representatives of different parties or ethnic, religious and social groups, but is still not elected by the population of the country.

Apart from the ambiguity of these basic requirements, it is also unclear whether these three factors can be balanced against each other. Could, for example, the fact that a government is 'internationally recognised' allow for a liberal interpretation of the requirement that it has to be 'properly constituted', and legitimize an unelected government? By the same token, could the fact that a government is duly elected by people and is therefore 'properly constituted' and 'representative' without any doubt, excuse the fact that it is not, or not sufficiently 'recognised internationally', or is recognized by some States but not others? It is clear that some outcomes of this analysis may allow for the recognition of a government which is not based on popular support, or for suppression of a truly representative government which is not politically acceptable to some.

This ambiguity could be deliberate and aimed at ensuring flexibility in the political processes in Iraq. At the same time, the requirements listed in the resolution cannot be understood as trumping the basic rights of Iraqi people under international law, including the right to govern themselves and decide on their natural resources. It is exactly here that the principle of self-determination steps in, and requires the construction of the Security Council's intent in clear accordance with the Charter and general international law, which include the peremptory principle of self-determination. Resolution 1483 must therefore be interpreted in a way favouring the existence and operation of a government in Iraq which is based on free will and election by the population, even if some requirements laid down in paragraphs 16, 20 and 21 of the Resolution need to be liberally interpreted in order to give way to full operation of the principle of self-determination. The intention of the Council must be construed accordingly, and the requirement of recognition, which is anyway declaratory rather than constitutive under international law, must be interpreted broadly, flexibly and liberally, to accommodate the requirement for an elected government. Consequently, the resolution cannot be understood as treating the requirements which are imperative under general international law as optional, and vice versa.

The requirement of an elected government is perhaps not clearly established in international law. As the International Court affirmed in *Nicaragua*, a State is not under a duty to have a particular form of government.[12] But cases like the one at hand are special in that the government in question may be required to commit the Iraqi people in terms of natural resources over which they have permanent sovereignty, and allocate oil contracts. To commit the Iraqi people validly, the government in question must be elected by the people, and only this option can guarantee the observance of their right to self-determination and the attendant permanent sovereignty over natural resources. The question of democratic legitimacy is therefore crucial, as it is linked with sovereignty over natural resources.

The next tool could be an evolutionary interpretation of resolutions. For instance, one could ask, using the example of Resolution 713(1991), whether the subsequent changes in the situation made this resolution incompatible with *jus cogens*, and whether Bosnia, despite the terms of the resolution, would be entitled to receive military support to exercise its right to self-defence. Several States have contended before the Security Council that Resolution 713 must be interpreted in a way not applicable to Bosnia because the contrary solution impaired the right to self-defence of that State.[13] One could perhaps advance the concept of functional non-compliance in this regard, which means that the resolution should not be observed in the part in which it offends against *jus cogens*, or with regard to a State which is the victim of the breach of *jus cogens*. Such a concept of functional non-compliance is based on the assumption that had the Council foreseen the outcome, it would not have ordered the arms embargo as it did, and even if it did, this would trigger the issue of validity of its action, as an arms embargo deprives a victim of armed attack of the practical possibility to exercise the right to self-defence. A similar functional non-compliance could perhaps be justified in case of economic sanctions against Iraq and Yugoslavia, as soon as it became clear that the Council would not intentionally inflict such severe hardship on populations in violation of human rights and humanitarian law.

In certain cases, the circumstances surrounding the acceptance of a resolution can confirm that the Council did not intend to offend against *jus cogens*. For instance, Resolution 1260(1999) welcomed the signing of the Peace Agreement in Sierra Leone, and called upon on all parties to implement it fully. At the signing, the UN Secretary-General made the statement

---

[12] *ICJ Reports*, 1986, 133. Also, according to the Friendly Relations Declaration, UNGA Res 2625(1970), 'Every State has an inalienable right to choose its political, economic, social and cultural systems, without interference in any form by another State.'

[13] Gray, Bosnia and Herzegovina: Civil Law or Inter-State Conflict? Characterisation and Consequences, *BYIL* (1996), 186–187.

that the amnesty provided for in the agreement would not extend to perpetrators of international crimes. Therefore, the Council cannot be presumed to have endorsed or required immunity for perpetrators of international crimes. Although the Secretary-General cannot speak for the Security Council, the latter must be presumed to have been aware that the former committed the United Nations while expressing the attitude that no impunity for the perpetrators of international crimes was warranted. As the Council has not contradicted the Secretary-General's conclusion, it must be presumed to have shared it in terms of the scope of the Peace Agreement.

In such cases, there would be no need to assert the invalidity of a resolution as it can be construed as consistent with *jus cogens*. The duty to comply with a resolution can be understood as qualified by the need to ensure observance of peremptory norms with regard to a State or a non-State actor whose rights under peremptory norms would be affected were the resolution strictly and indiscriminately implemented.

However, once the intention to offend against *jus cogens* cannot be excluded, because of the textual clarity in a resolution, there is no way other than raising the issue of invalidity. The same approach would be necessary where a resolution, despite its terms, is clearly supporting the action of States that are themselves offending against *jus cogens*. Resolution 748(1992) on Libya could be an example, as the sanctions it imposed on Libya were parallel to unlawful threats of force, and perhaps to a potential violation of the right to fair trial. This resolution is so closely linked to the context of those illegalities that it is difficult to conceive it as having a rationale other than the support of and participation in those illegalities. Also, the terms and the drafting process of Resolution 1203(1998) on the Federal Republic of Yugoslavia are very clear in supporting and affirming the coercively imposed agreements and it is beyond doubt that the Council intended that.

2. INVALIDITY OF RESOLUTIONS OFFENDING AGAINST *JUS COGENS*

Invalidity can in principle apply to all kinds of international acts, whether individual or collective, adopted by international organs, including even so-called legislative acts.[14] There seems to be nothing to exempt the acts of international organs, such as the UN Security Council, from the operation of invalidity. To illustrate, while Resolution 713(1991) has been viewed in practice as subject to the interpretation denying its applicability to Bosnia because otherwise Bosnia's right to self-defence would be impaired, in

---

[14] Verzjil, Actes juridiques internationaux, 15 *Revue de droit international* (1935), 306–307; Guggenheim (1949), 197–198.

addition and in alternative to that, several members of the Council considered that Resolution 713 was invalid for the very reason of its conflict with the inherent right to self-defence.[15] This confirms that the issues of interpretation and validity go hand in hand and if the former, as an aspect of the proof of the Council's intention, does not remove the problem of normative conflict, the latter comes into play.

The problem of invalidity of institutional acts is not adequately explored,[16] and much of the existing material on the subject was written at a time when the relevance of *jus cogens* was not seriously contemplated in doctrine in the context of the Security Council actions.[17] However, any analysis of this issue must consider the fact that there is a normative hierarchy in international law, and different norms produce different types of consequences in terms of the invalidity of acts conflicting with them.

A preliminary issue is that of the implied powers, by reference to which the Council may adopt certain decisions. It is crucial to clarify the scope and extent of such powers as well as to establish whether certain actions not covered by express powers may be based on implied powers or must be considered as acts *ultra vires*. The relevance of the *ultra vires* doctrine is much wider than the question of the implied powers' doctrine: an act of an international organization may be in excess of implied powers as well as of powers explicitly enshrined in a constituent instrument. It should also be stressed that the doctrines of implied powers and of *ultra vires* are sometimes considered to be two sides of one coin,[18] and this was indeed so in the *Certain Expenses* case.

In *Certain Expenses*, the Court concluded that 'when the Organisation takes action which warrants assertion that it was appropriate for the fulfilment of one of the stated purposes of the United Nations, the presumption is that such action is not *ultra vires* of the Organisation'.[19] Judge Fitzmaurice spoke also about the merely *prima facie* presumption of the validity of the organization's acts adopted in pursuance of its purposes.[20] The same approach was adopted in the Court's Order in *Lockerbie*,[21] where the Court did not consider the resolution of the Security Council adopted under Chapter VII as absolutely valid, but held that it was *prima facie* binding upon

[15] Gray (1996), 187, 191.

[16] But Guggenheim (1949), 198, affirms that the decision of the Security Council contradicting the Charter is invalid.

[17] See, eg, E. Lauterpacht, The Legal Effect of Illegal Acts of International Organisations, *Cambridge Essays in International Law* (1965), 88–121.

[18] White, *The Law of International Organisations*, 1996, 128.

[19] *ICJ Reports*, 1962, 168.

[20] Fitzmaurice, Separate Opinion, *ICJ Reports*, 1962, 204.

[21] Lockerbie (Provisional Measures), *Libya v US, ICJ Reports*, 1992, 126; *Libya v UK, ICJ Reports*, 1992, 15.

Libya and thus confirmed that validity of this resolution could become the subject of consideration by the Court on the phase of merits. This happened not least due to the stage that the proceedings had then reached as the final determination of legality of a Security Council measure would be most appropriate at the stage of merits.

In these cases, the Court focused only on the substantive legality of the measures in question; it did not prejudge the issue of invalidity or of its applicable types. The Court's presumption relates to substantive legality, to the issue of whether there has been an excess of competence, and not to legal consequences such as invalidity. Once it is clear that no excess of power has taken place, the issue of validity does not arise, and this was precisely the situation in *Certain Expenses*. The Court merely held that the measures were within the *vires* of the organization. This justifies a presumption that if the measure of the organization were not in accordance with the purposes and principles of the Charter, then the presumption of *prima facie* validity and bindingness of that measure would be undermined, and the law of invalidity would apply to that measure. In terms of our analysis, the question of acting pursuant to UN purposes and principles can only be a substantive question of determining if there is a conflict with *jus cogens*. It does not determine what happens after such conflict is established. This is not least so because the acts contrary to *jus cogens* cannot be authorized under the purposes and principles of the Charter, as such acts are by definition beyond the competence of UN organs.

The issue of validity has received some attention in individual opinions. Judge Morelli in *Certain Expenses*, while agreeing with the final findings of the Court, asserted that the acts of the UN enjoyed absolute validity, since within the international community and within the UN system in particular, there is no competent body empowered to decide on validity of acts of the organization.[22] The same reasoning led President Winiarski to consider that in the absence of provision for judicial review of acts of the organization it was only the individual Member States who could decide on the validity of those acts and, consequently, refuse to comply with them if they were *ultra vires*.[23] The Court's approach seems to be balancing opinions expressed by Judges Morelli and Winiarski. For the Court, the validity of an act of an organization is primarily connected not with any institutional prerequisites, such as existence of the body competent to review, but with the purposes of the organization as part of the substantive law. The Court does not assert absolute validity of an organization's acts: it speaks about presumption of validity. Therefore, despite the diversity of opinions expressed in the

---

[22] Morelli, Separate Opinion, *ICJ Reports*, 1962, 222–223.
[23] Winiarski, Dissenting Opinion, *ICJ Reports*, 1962, 232; see also the Separate Opinion of Judge Gros in *WHO/Egypt* Advisory Opinion, *ICJ Reports*, 1980, 104.

operative paragraphs of the Advisory Opinion, the Court's approach to the principles governing the competence of international organizations is more easily reconciled with the approach of Judge Winiarski than with that of Judge Morelli. Both the Court and Judge Winiarski seem to hold that the *ultra vires* acts of international organizations may be invalidated despite the non-existence of designated judicial remedies in this regard. In fact, Judge Morelli's view means that UN organs are *legibus solutus*, which was so vigorously rejected by the ICTY in *Tadic*, and earlier by the International Court in *Namibia*.

In *Certain Expenses*, the Court did not link its analysis to the type of invalidity, but only to the primary issue of legality. That said, it must be clarified what kind of invalidity applies if a resolution of the Security Council is *ultra vires*, especially in a case where the *ultra vires* character arises because of its conflict with *jus cogens*. The excess of competence by an organ can mean different things in different contexts. In some circumstances it may involve encroachment on interests of individual States only, while in other circumstances it may involve a breach of *jus cogens*, thereby infringing the community interest and giving rise to objective illegality. This factor could determine the applicable types of invalidity. The Court's presumption of validity does not mean that, in a case where this presumption is rebutted, the relative invalidity, or voidability, of the resolution is the necessary consequence.

In certain cases, such as the European Community or international administrative tribunals, institutional regimes include specific provisions concerning the process for determining the invalidity of *ultra vires* acts.[24] Such voidability in an institutional context can be understood to be a concept different from voidability in general international law. In general international law, voidability means that an interested party must challenge a given act in order to trigger its invalidity. This would be voidability in terms of the Vienna Convention on the Law of Treaties, for instance, which deals with a bilateralist framework of international law and would not be useful in the case of *jus cogens*. In an institutional context, voidability is sometimes linked to the determination of invalidity by a competent institution. But there is no ordinary way to challenge the Security Council's resolutions and the seising of the International Court can only result in an incidental review, subject to the usual jurisdictional requirements under the Court's Statute. The absence of a regular means of review may either mean that the Council's resolutions are not in practice subject to challenge and hence enjoy *de facto* absolute validity, or that their validity has to be judged by States by reference

---

[24] Overviewed in E. Lauterpacht, The Legal Effect of Illegal Acts of International Organisations, *Cambridge Essays in International Law* (1965), 94–99.

to the criteria provided for in international law. The governing legal framework supports the latter option. This option is also supported by the analogy from the law of treaties; as Simma demonstrates, both the spirit of the Vienna Convention and the conclusions of the Vienna Conference reject the assumption that *jus cogens* invalidity is dependent on institutional determination.[25]

It is clear that an act offending against *jus cogens* cannot be voidable; it can only be void. Nothing in international law supports the voidability, or the relative invalidity, of acts offending against *jus cogens*. All kinds of acts and transactions, such as treaties, unilateral acts, and generally actions of States are, as soon as they offend against *jus cogens*, subject to voidness and not voidability. Bernhardt distinguishes between certain situations of invalidity of institutional acts. Where special procedures exist, such as the cases of dismissal of officials, the acts are voidable but not void.[26] But acts obviously *ultra vires* are void *ab initio*.[27]

It is understandable that, as soon as ordinary norms are involved, the issue of the validity of illegal acts can be linked to the existence and operation of institutional machineries. Such acts would be subject to the regime of relative invalidity, which is part of *jus dispositivum*, thereby enabling States to derogate from that regime by establishing special institutional regimes which should deal with such invalidity issues. But acts contrary to *jus cogens* are void as such and *ab initio*, and such invalidity is itself part of *jus cogens*. It is therefore unjustified to consider that this regime of general international law could be replaced by specific institutional regimes, on which *jus cogens* invalidity would be dependent, because *jus cogens* invalidity admits of no derogation. Consequently, States are not entitled to establish a treaty-based institutional regime in which the voidness of institutional acts contrary to *jus cogens* would be derogated from through making such voidness dependent upon the institutional determination. There is no precedent where States have attempted to effect such derogation, and it is not justified to presume that such derogation is effected, and particularly that the constituent instrument of an organization does not preclude the voidness of acts contrary to *jus cogens*. Therefore, whatever the constituent instruments of an international organization would say on the subject, or even if they say nothing about this, the general international law regime of *jus cogens* invalidity still applies fully to institutional acts.

---

[25] Simma, From Bilateralism to Community Interest, 250 *RdC* (VI-1994), 289; see also Rosenne, *Developments in the Law of Treaties 1945–1986* (1989), 351.

[26] Bernhardt, *Ultra Vires* Activities of International Organisations, in *Festschrift Skubiszewski* (1996), 608.

[27] Bernhardt, *Ultra Vires* Activities of International Organisations, in *Festschrift Skubiszewski* (1996), 608; Security Council resolutions shall be held invalid if they are manifestly *ultra vires* or if they clearly violate *jus cogens*, Herdegen, De Wet and Nollkaemper (eds), 80.

3. THE QUESTION OF SEVERABILITY OF IMPUGNED CLAUSES

Practice does not furnish clear guidance as to whether a Security Council resolution is void in its entirety, or the void clauses are severable so that the rest of the resolution is left intact. There is some practice illustrating that severability of illegal institutional acts is possible to some extent.[28] The law of treaties, in contrast, supports the entire invalidity of a treaty whose content or conclusion involves a violation of *jus cogens*, as is clear from the wording of Articles 44, 52 and 53 of both Vienna Conventions on the Law of Treaties.

On the other hand, it can be contended that non-severability in cases of transactions offending against *jus cogens* is not part of general, or customary, international law.[29] If this view were accepted, then a resolution of the Security Council offending against *jus cogens* would not be void in its entirety, and the 'innocent' clauses would be preserved. This option also could help to avoid invalidation of the Security Council resolutions in their totality, bearing in mind that some provisions in a relevant resolution could be part of the genuine measures of the Council to maintain international peace and have nothing to do with the breaches of *jus cogens*.

But in any case, even if the severability view is accepted, it would not produce ready-made consequences; it would require in each specific case the demonstration that the impugned clause of a resolution is not in integral connection with the rest of the document, and is severable. If, for example, there is an impunity clause in a resolution imposing a comprehensive peace settlement and thus covering a wide range of matters, it could be tenable to hold that only the impunity clause is void, and the rest of the instrument is not affected. Furthermore, in certain cases, severability would be excluded if the resolution as such were based on, or were conducive to, a breach of *jus cogens*, and this course of analysis seems acceptable in terms of Resolution 748(1992). As emphasized above, this resolution followed up the unlawful threat of the use of force addressed to Libya, demanded from it to follow the course of conduct which was demanded under such threats and backed them up with coercive Chapter VII measures. This demonstrates that Resolution 748 was through its total rationale offending against the peremptory prohibition of the threat or use of force and it is impossible to apply the regime of severability to it. The same could be said about Resolution 1203(1998), whose rationale was clearly linked to the approval of the agreements forcibly imposed on Yugoslavia.

---

[28] E. Lauterpacht, The Legal Effect of Illegal Acts of International Organisations, *Cambridge Essays in International Law* (1965), 120–121.

[29] Cassese, *International Law* (2005), 206; Marceau, 13 *EJIL* (2002), 753.

4. THE MEANS OF CHALLENGING RESOLUTIONS OFFENDING AGAINST *JUS COGENS*

4.1. Protest

Security Council decisions are presumed to be legal and the failure to comply is permissible only if a decision is challengeable on legal grounds.[30] This extends even to Chapter VII decisions.[31] As Bowett considers, although the function of the Security Council is political, the allocation of legal responsibility is a legal issue and thus subject to legal limits, challengeable by States.[32] A natural corollary of this is the right of States to protest against an illegal decision.

In *Certain Expenses*, the French Statement explicitly and the Opinion implicitly recognize the right of Member States to pass judgment on Security Council resolutions.[33] It seems that individual States may appreciate only specific cases, and their views, which must at any rate be compatible with the Charter and general international law, are without prejudice to the ultimate legality of particular types of action. Thus, the decision of an individual State can itself be judged in terms of compatibility with these standards. The very fact that a protest was made against a resolution is not decisive; rather, the grounds of the protest are decisive.

Therefore, as Angelet submits, under Article 25 of the Charter, Member States are under obligation to justify refusal to comply in legal terms.[34] Portugal and South Africa questioned the legal aspects of resolutions on Southern Rhodesia, and Iraq did so with regard to resolutions related to the UN Compensation Commission. But the Security Council apparently gave no satisfactory consideration to this issue.[35] On the other hand, the protest of a number of States and regional organizations against the arms embargo imposed on Bosnia under Resolution 713 and the sanctions imposed on Libya in the Lockerbie crisis have eventually led to the revision of the pertinent decisions of the Security Council.[36]

It is suggested that a protest may be directed only against the Council's infringement of legal rights of the Member States. No protest may be made against the Council's assessment of facts, such as the determination of the

---

[30] Angelet, Protest against Security Council Decisions, in Wellens (ed.), *International Law: Theory and Practice: Essays in Honour of Eric Suy* (1998), 278; Bowett, The Impact of Security Council Decisions on Dispute Settlement Procedures, 5 *EJIL* (1994), 93.

[31] Angelet, Protest against Security Council Decisions, *Festschrift Suy*, 278–279.

[32] Bowett, The Impact of Security Council Decisions on Dispute Settlement Procedures, 5 *EJIL* (1994), 94.

[33] Angelet, Protest against Security Council Decisions, *Festschrift Suy*, 279.

[34] Angelet, Protest against Security Council Decisions, *Festschrift Suy*, 281.

[35] Angelet, Protest against Security Council Decisions, *Festschrift Suy*, 280.

[36] See, eg, OIC Resolution 14/24-P.

threat to peace under Article 39.[37] The tool of protest ensures participation of the entire UN membership in the Council's decision-making.[38] In terms of decisions offending against *jus cogens*, protest is not a necessary requirement, as the *jus cogens* regime of voidness applies anyway. However, if many States protest against the decision, this may induce the Council to reconsider it.

4.2. *Refusal to carry out*

As a general rule, Member States do not have the power to terminate the binding Chapter VII enforcement measures of the Security Council. This generally follows from the constitutional principle that the organ that institutes the measure is, unless explicitly determined otherwise, solely competent to revoke it.[39] That is how the relatively consistent practice of the Council understands this issue.

The UK terminated the sanctions instituted in 1965 against Southern Rhodesia on 12 December 1979. The General Assembly responded, in line with the reaction of the African States, on 18 December by Resolution 192 (1979) affirming that it was within the exclusive competence of the Security Council to revoke the mandatory sanctions it introduced and their unilateral termination was a breach of obligations under Article 25 of the Charter. The support of this attitude by the overwhelming majority in the Assembly demonstrates their belief that unilateral termination contravenes the UN Charter.[40]

The UK explained its decision to terminate the Security Council sanctions against Southern Rhodesia by the fact that the situation determined by the Security Council as a threat to international peace and security ceased to exist with the resumption of the control over Southern Rhodesia by the British Governor, and the purpose of the measures imposed had been achieved.[41]

It is also mentioned that the UK did not challenge the general rule regarding the termination of sanctions but tried to justify its decision by reference to the intention of the Security Council, namely that the Council tied the sanction to certain factual occurrences. Reference is made in this regard to Resolutions 232(1966) and 253(1968), which proclaimed the end of rebellion in Southern Rhodesia as the aim that the Council was determined to achieve.[42] Nevertheless, the determination of this purpose was made by the

---

[37] Angelet, Protest against Security Council Decisions, *Festschrift Suy*, 282.

[38] Angelet, Protest against Security Council Decisions, *Festschrift Suy*, 283; cf also Bowett, The Impact of Security Council Decisions on Dispute Settlement Procedures, 5 *EJIL* (1994), 99–100.

[39] De Wet, in De Wet and Nollkaemper (eds) (2003), 24.

[40] De Wet, id., 24; Kreczko, The Unilateral Termination of UN Sanctions Against Southern Rhodesia by the United Kingdom, 21 *Virginia JIL* (1980), 99–100; The Security Council itself terminated sanctions by Resolution 460 of 21 December 1979.

[41] Kreczko (1980), 98–99.   [42] Kreczko (1980), 109, 116, 121.

Council in the exercise of its Charter powers and individual Member States do not seem to be entitled to make determinations on this issue until and unless the Council itself has determined that the measures it ordered have achieved their purpose and must be revoked. The Council has made such decisions in revoking the sanctions imposed on Iraq and Yugoslavia.

The combined effect of several factors, such as the institutional prerogative of the Security Council with regard to mandatory measures ordered by it, and the reaction of the General Assembly as the body most representative of the UN membership, reinforce and justify the general rule precluding unilateral termination of the sanctions ordered by the Security Council.[43] It must be stated that the General Assembly was not generally against the termination of sanctions in this case either. Moreover, it expressly called for such termination. But the Assembly acted in accordance with the principle that it is only the Security Council that can take such decisions.

The reaction of the international community as represented in and by the General Assembly against the United Kingdom's action in terminating the Rhodesian sanctions seems to be reflected in the attitudes of States and UN organs with regard to the termination of the arms embargo imposed on the Federal Republic of Yugoslavia by Resolution 713(1991), in relation to the applicability of that resolution to Bosnia.

As the conflict between the former Yugoslav republics escalated, the issue of lifting the arms embargo in relation to Bosnia, which arguably could not otherwise defend itself from external aggression, became the subject of intensive discussions, and caused wide divergences in the attitudes of Member States. Bosnia began to seek the lifting of the arms embargo, which interfered with the exercise of its right to self-defence under Article 51 of the Charter. Bosnia contended that if the United Nations maintained its embargo it should effectively defend Bosnia; if not, then it should revoke the embargo so that Bosnia could acquire the arms necessary for its self-defence.[44] The draft resolution to this effect failed to command the required majority in the Council, among the permanent members only the United States voting for it, while those who opposed the revocation of the embargo explained their approach by the need to preserve the negotiation process and prevent further escalation.[45] The arguments of Member States opposing the embargo were diverse, though guided by the single consideration of principle—the need to preserve the right to self-defence.

Some States such as Iran argued that Resolution 713 was adopted in totally different circumstances, though this attitude can contradict the fact that the Council itself repeatedly reaffirmed Resolution 713 on subsequent occasions, which can be seen as the confirmation of continuity of that resolution.[46] This

---

[43] Kreczko (1980), 128.   [44] Gray (1996), 179–181.   [45] Id., 185.   [46] Id., 186.

argument was also perceived in interpretative terms reflecting the concept of functional non-compliance developed above. Furthermore, Afghanistan contended in the Council that as the Resolution was invalid, States were entitled to ignore it and deliver arms to Bosnia. Most Member States, while accepting that the embargo must be lifted, have considered that the Council should lift it or adopt its interpretation in a way exempting Bosnia, rather than supporting the idea of non-compliance by individual States.[47] The US position is most illustrative. While the US was the most enthusiastic supporter of the embargo being lifted to enable the victim of aggression to defend itself, it did not consider doing that unilaterally, which can be contrasted with UK and US views in relation to the Rhodesian sanctions. The US President vetoed the Bill of the Congress that required the unilateral revocation of the arms embargo as this measure contravened the right to self-defence.[48] The embargo was eventually revoked by the Council on 22 November 1995. The US attitude in this case is not quite compatible with its attitude in the case of Rhodesia when it upheld the UK line.[49]

The General Assembly Resolution 47/121(1992) referred to the inherent right of Bosnia to self-defence. The Assembly did not consider taking any relevant measures itself, but it called upon the Security Council to authorize Member States to use all necessary means to protect the independence, integrity and unity of Bosnia in cooperation with the Bosnian government. Furthermore, the Assembly called on the Council 'to exempt the Republic of Bosnia and Herzegovina from the arms embargo as imposed on the former Yugoslavia under Security Council Resolution 713'.[50] The Assembly thus acted in accordance with the principle that the decision on this issue was a matter for the Council's prerogative.

Therefore, the practice outlined so far confirms the general principle, without prejudice to the correctness of its application to specific cases, that the measures ordered by the Security Council can only be terminated by this organ. The principle that the organ which introduces the measure is competent for its termination seems to be the generally accepted principle of international institutional law. The specific context of the powers of the Security Council with regard to the maintenance of peace and security also confirms that the introduction of the mandatory sanctions takes place because of the circumstances that are determined solely by the Security Council, namely those subsumable under Articles 39 and 41. Consequently, whether those circumstances cease to exist or still subsist is a matter for the Council itself to decide. It seems that Member States should have no say in whether the circumstances mentioned as justification of mandatory sanctions have ceased or continue.

---

[47] Gray (1996), 191.   [48] Id., 191–192.   [49] Kreczko (1980), 17–18.
[50] The General Assembly reiterated its attitude in Resolutions 48/88(1993) and 49/10(1994).

Something more is required to enable the States to refuse compliance and thus justify the exception to the general principle, namely the illegality of the Council's measures under the Charter and general international law. The most pertinent case from the viewpoint of the refusal to carry out Security Council decisions is the decision of several groups of States to oppose the Security Council sanctions against Libya, declare them illegal and refuse to comply.

In the Lockerbie crisis, the League of Arab States adopted decisions expressing solidarity with Libya and demanding that the suspects of the Lockerbie bombing be tried by Scottish judges in the Netherlands. In Resolution 5373(1994), the Council of the League reiterated this attitude, condemned the attitude of the three Western States, that is France, the UK and the USA, and deplored the maintenance in force and consequences of the sanctions as well as the refusal of the three powers to accept the proposals as to the place and manner of the trial of suspects.[51] The Non-Aligned States also deplored the unjust character of sanctions and condemned the attitude of the three powers. The Organisation of Islamic Conference expressly termed Resolutions 748 and 883 as unjust resolutions and condemned the maintenance in force of the sanctions despite the well-known international efforts to defuse the crisis.[52]

Most importantly, the Ouagadougou Decision of the Assembly of Heads of State and Government of the OAU expressed regret 'for lack of positive response by the United States of America and the United Kingdom to the International and Regional initiatives and efforts aimed at finding a solution to the dispute based on the principles of international law'. On the one hand, the OAU Assembly called on the Security Council to adopt a resolution on suspending the sanctions imposed on Libya under Resolutions 748 and 883, which is reminiscent of the attitude of the General Assembly regarding the termination of Chapter VII measures in the matters of Rhodesia and Bosnia, as well as the US attitude with regard to the Bosnian case. However, the OAU Assembly went further and decided

not to comply any longer with Security Council Resolutions 748 (1992) and 883 (1993) on sanctions, with effect from September 1998, if the United States of America and the United Kingdom refuse that the two suspects be tried in a third neutral country pursuant to the verdict of the International Court of Justice by July 1998, date on which sanctions will be due for review, owing to the fact that the said resolutions violate Article 27 paragraph 3, Article 33 and Article 36 paragraph 3 of the United Nations Charter, and the considerable human and economic

---

[51] Kalala, La décision de l'OUA de ne plus respecter les sanctions décrétées par l'ONU contre la Lybie: désobéissance civile des états Africains a l'égard de l'ONU, *Revue Belge de Droit International* (1999/2), 549–551.

[52] Id., 552–553.

losses suffered by Libya and a number of other African peoples as a result of the sanctions.[53]

Therefore, the OAU members not only viewed the Security Council's Chapter VII measures as illegal, but also actually decided not to comply with them because of their illegality. The Assembly's reference to the UN Charter provisions regarding the peaceful settlement of disputes reflects the wrongfulness of the Council resolutions which backed up the unlawful threats of the use of force directed against Libya throughout the dispute regarding the trial and extradition of the Lockerbie bombing suspects. At the same time, the concern of African States was also related to the character and impact of the sanctions which resulted in large-scale human suffering. These circumstances must be viewed as the legal basis for the decision not to comply with the sanction resolutions.

The consolidated attitude of several regional organizations and their members eventually influenced the attitudes in the Security Council and the US and UK ended up in isolation. This factor, in addition to the fact that the sanctions against Libya were neither of the extent to induce Libya to alter its will nor effectively enforceable (or enforced), was responsible for the outcome that the US and UK finally yielded by accepting the solution proposed by Libya which they kept opposing over the years, and the Security Council decided accordingly to lift the sanctions on these conditions.[54] The solution proposed by Libya has from the outset been a compromise solution as it went beyond what Libya was obliged to do under international law. The fact that in response to that Libya suffered severe sanctions and the use of the UN enforcement powers to back up the threats of the use of force directed to it has provided sufficient justification for the OAU Assembly to refuse to comply with the sanctions.

The whole practice of States and international organs shows the difference between the cases of Southern Rhodesia and Libya. While in the case of Rhodesia the international community as represented by the General Assembly held that unilateral termination was impermissible, in the case of Libya there was an important number of States that considered that sanctions could be disregarded whatever the Security Council's attitude. This difference of reaction broadly reflects the principal difference between the two cases, in one of which the Council's sanctions were lawful and in accordance with the Charter and in the other case they were illegal both for upholding illegal threats of the use of force and for inflicting unjustified damage on Libya.

---

[53] *The Crisis between the Great Socialist People's Libyan Arab Jamahiriya and the United States of America and the United Kingdom*, AHG/DEC127 (XXXIV), 8–10 June 1998, 6 *African Yearbook of International Law* (1998), 390–391.

[54] Kalala (1999), 557.

The conceptual basis of the principle that States shall not enforce institutional decisions offending against *jus cogens* is that even after an organ such as the Security Council enacts a wrongful decision, States continue to be bound by *jus cogens*, because the latter is non-derogable and a decision in question is consequently *ultra vires*, as no power to adopt such decisions can be delegated to an international organization. Such a line of reasoning was adopted by the European Court of Human Rights in *Matthews*, where the Court clearly stated that States-parties remain bound by the obligations enshrined in the European Convention on Human Rights, even if they are contradicted by the powers delegated to the European Communities. In such cases, obligations under the European Convention assume priority.[55] In other words, despite the institutional decisions, States are still bound by alternative superior sets of norms to which the powers of respective institutions are subordinated.

Doehring notes that 'When the Security Council enacts unlawful decisions—i.e. not in accordance with the Charter of the United Nations and the general rules of international law—the questions remain of whether the Charter must be interpreted in a way that even those decisions produce binding force upon its members.'[56] The meaning of Article 25 of the Charter is that the Security Council decision is binding on a State even without an *ad hoc* agreement, not that it is binding on States even if it is incompatible with the Charter. In such cases, Article 25 admits that States may refuse compliance.[57] This legal framework proves that the argument that Member States cannot declare invalid the Security Council resolutions because this would undermine the whole Charter collective security system[58] is flawed not only conceptually but also in the face of practice.

It is not acceptable to treat an international organ as the final judge of the legality of acts it adopts.[59] A residual power to determine the legality of the Council's action rests with individual States,[60] and this applies even to Chapter VII measures.[61] The obvious *ultra vires* acts may be

---

[55] *Matthews v UK*, ECHR 24833/94, 18 February 1999, para. 32.

[56] Doehring, Unlawful Resolutions of the Security Council, 1 *Max Planck YBUNL* (1997), 98.

[57] Angelet, Protest against Security Council Decisions, *Festschrift Suy*, 278; De Wet, *Chapter VII Powers*, 376–377; De Wet, in De Wet and Nollkaemper (eds), 29; Kagala (1999), 571.

[58] Aust, The Role of Human Rights in Limiting the Enforcement Powers of the Security Council: A Practitioner's View, in De Wet and Nollkaemper (eds), *Review of the Security Council by Member States* (2003), 36.

[59] Bernhardt, *Ultra Vires* Activities of International Organisations, *Festschrift Skubiszewski* (1996), 604.

[60] Nolte, The Limits on the Security Council's Powers and its Functions in the International Legal System: Some Reflectons, in Byers (ed.), 318.

[61] E. de Wet, Human Rights Limitations to Economic Enforcement Measures under Article 41 of the UN Charter and the Iraqi Sanctions Regime, 14 *LJIL* (2001), 279–280.

challenged.[62] Doehring criticizes the argument that the whole collective security system would be destroyed had the States the right to judge legality independently and considers that such a view is neither coherent nor convincing. 'This position would result in an obligation to do wrong.'[63] Bernhardt also considers that despite the fact that Security Council decisions are binding on members, the competence of the Council is limited and States can pass their judgment on legality.[64] Gasser observes with particular reference to humanitarian law that States must not comply with the sanctions imposed by the Security Council if they violate the absolutely binding obligations, such as those embodied in Geneva Conventions or additional protocols.[65] In particular, States are under an absolute obligation to authorize civilian population relief obligations in the sense of the Fourth Geneva Convention, even if the sanctions do not contain humanitarian exceptions.[66]

Doehring further refers to the fact that the Vienna Convention on the Law of Treaties invalidates treaties conflicting with peremptory norms. If the Charter were interpreted as obliging members to carry out even unlawful decisions of the Council, 'an evident conflict with the Vienna Convention would exist'. More so, because the Charter itself is a treaty dedicated to peremptory norms such as prohibition of force and human rights.[67] Even if extreme examples are invoked, such as starvation to genocide in case of embargo, this still illustrates the grave consequences the Council decisions may bring if in conflict with a peremptory norm.[68] It can be added that such 'extreme' examples are not very rare in the Council's practice.

It is stated that a State could be estopped from challenging the decision of the Security Council to which it itself consented.[69] It is generally true that non-binding resolutions of the United Nations organs can bind States if they accept them.[70] For these purposes, the resolutions which are intended to be binding, but which exceed the competence of the relevant organ among others by offending against the superior substantive standard that limits the

---

[62] Bernhardt, *Ultra Vires* Activities of International Organisations, *Festschrift Skubiszewski* (1996), 604; Frowein, Reactions by Not Directly Affected States to Breaches of Public International Law, 248 *RdC* (1994), 385 also draws the distinction between the illegal acts and void acts in the case of the Security Council.

[63] Doehring, Unlawful Resolutions of the Security Council, 1 *Max Planck YBUNL* (1997), 98; for a similar view see De Wet, *Chapter VII Powers*, 378; De Wet, in De Wet and Nollkaemper (eds) (2003), 27.

[64] Bernhardt, *Ultra Vires* Activities of International Organisations, *Festschrift Skubiszewski* (1996), 607.

[65] Gasser, Collective Economic Sanctions and International Humanitarian Law, 56 *ZaöRV* (1996), 883.

[66] Id.

[67] Doehring, Unlawful Resolutions of the Security Council, 1 *Max Planck YBUNL* (1997), 98.

[68] Id., 98–99.

[69] Bernhardt, *Ultra Vires* Activities of International Organisations, *Festschrift Skubiszewski* (1996), 607.

[70] Dissenting Opinion of Judge Winiarski, *ICJ Reports*, 1962, 233.

powers of that organ, can probably fall within the same category as non-binding, or recommendatory, resolutions, with the consequence that States could in some instances accept the resolutions which are *ultra vires*. This could legally happen only in cases where the subject-matter of the resolution affects only the individual interests of the relevant Member States and does not go beyond that. In other words, the outcome depends on who is the injured party—the other organ of the organization, the individual Member State, third States or the international community as a whole. This not only reflects the relevance of waiver and acquiescence in inter-State relations in general international law, but also emphasizes the limits to which these processes of validation are subject.

It happens in practice that States give consent to a resolution which would not *per se* bind them, including *ultra vires* decisions, and are hence considered to be bound by it.[71] The acceptance of the UN resolution by a Member State is to undertake a binding obligation,[72] that is to reach an agreement with the United Nations. A profound example is the acceptance by Israel of the Partition Resolution in 1948. However, this standard cannot apply to decisions contradicting peremptory norms, the acceptance of which would be the derogation from *jus cogens* effected through concordance of wills between the Council's action on the one hand and a State's acceptance on the other. In addition, the concept of estoppel has no place in the context of *jus cogens*.[73]

Doehring also submits that the Council is under a duty to consult a State unwilling to carry out the resolution conflicting with *jus cogens*. If no consensus is reached, no State may be considered to be bound by a resolution which is contrary to peremptory norms.[74] This is close to holding implicitly the absolute nullity. But the duty of consultation with a view to settling the issue through conciliation between the Council and the affected State is not always compatible with *jus cogens*. The limit on such conciliation is that any resolution conflicting with *jus cogens* is void, and this cannot be remedied through consultations if the outcome of such consultations amounts to derogation from *jus cogens*.

---

[71] Such cases are described by E. Lauterpacht as the instances of 'relative nullity'. E. Lauterpacht, The Legal Effect of Illegal Acts of International Organisations, *Cambridge Essays in International Law* (1965), 121.

[72] *Oppenheim's International Law*, vol. I (1955), 139.

[73] Above, Chapter 11. The same holds true for acquiescence. There is some practice arguably evidencing acquiescence by States to illegal decisions of international organizations, as overviewed in E. Lauterpacht, The Legal Effect of Illegal Acts of International Organisations, *Cambridge Essays in International Law* (1965), 117–119. However, no precedent of valid acquiescence has so far been identified which would legitimize an institutional act offending against more than the interests of individual Member States and contrary to *jus cogens*.

[74] Doehring, Unlawful Resolutions of the Security Council, 1 *Max Planck YBUNL* (1997), 108–109.

4.3. Judicial review

If, in certain cases, the individual States are entitled to refuse compliance with a Security Council resolution for its conflict with *jus cogens*, it may be asked whether the International Court of Justice, the principal judicial organ of the UN, is entitled to proclaim that the individual States are legally justified in their non-compliance, that is to exercise the judicial review with regard to a given resolution. This is not the proper place to give comprehensive consideration to a topic as complex as judicial review in the international legal order, particularly the issue of entities who can bring a case and of jurisdictional prerequisites. This issue is not crucial in terms of the effects of *jus cogens* as it would have only a declaratory and not a constitutive effect in this regard, as *jus cogens* invalidity, being absolute rather than relative, does not depend on the existence of a respective institutional determination. But some observations nevertheless seem necessary, just because if, in certain situations, the Member States are legally justified to refuse compliance with a resolution, it is important what the Court's powers are to state the law with regard to such situations.

The issue of judicial review is therefore that of procedural competence of the given tribunal; it is separate from the issues of the scope of the competence of the UN principal organs and from the issue under which circumstances States shall or shall not comply with their decisions. On the other hand, if the International Court were to uphold a Security Council resolution which is *ultra vires* and illegal, then the Court's own decision would be *ultra vires* as well, because it is the Court's task to state the law, not to transform illegality into legality.

Judicial review can relate to irregular motives behind the institutional act, that is the improper exercise of powers. In this field, as Akehurst submits, 'judicial review of the substance of administrative decisions is severely limited in its effectiveness by the very nature of discretionary powers'.[75] These discretionary powers follow from the need to enable the organizations to achieve their purposes. But the standards against which the regularity of motives and other related requirements of institutional decision-making can be tested still exist.[76] But the context of the review of acts causing or approving the breaches of peremptory norms is the review of acts in terms of their compliance with applicable legal standards. In this context, the role of discretion is limited because the basic question is whether the outcome of the institutional decision is in accordance with the outcome required under legal norms and principles which determine the competence of these organs or serve as limitations on those powers. This can normally comprise the

---

[75] Akehurst, *The Law concerning Employment in International Organisations* (1967), 148.

[76] Akehurst, 150–165; Jenks, *The Proper Law of International Organisations* (1962), 93–99.

compliance with substantive legal requirements and procedural legal requirements. The issue of compliance with *jus cogens* is that of substantive legal requirements.

As Akehurst suggests at the example of employment law, 'an administrative decision cannot be allowed to stand if it is forbidden by law.' This happens when 'the Administration may do something which it is forbidden to do, or it may refuse to do something which it is obliged to do.'[77] The case seems to be very much the same for the UN system. When the Security Council fails to observe the Charter or other relevant legal standards, this is the violation of prohibitions.

The power of judicial review can follow either from the court's specific powers conferred to it in the context of establishment of the system of judicial review or, as is the more plausible explanation in the case of International Court, from the interpretation and application of the tribunal's general adjudicatory powers. The issue whether judicial review of the UN acts amounts to constitutional control[78] or to judicial review of administrative acts for the purpose of checking their compliance with legislation, mirroring the categories of national administrative law, does not seem to be among essential questions. The latter perspective reflects better the character of the Security Council resolutions which are by their nature more similar to administrative acts than to legislation. These factors notwithstanding, the criteria offered by the comparative law perspective are not suitable for identifying the existence and parameters of the judicial review of the UN acts. The basic factor impacting the outcome is that of the proper interpretation of all the relevant international instruments involved to clarify whether and to what extent the judicial review of UN acts is permissible.

There are doctrinal objections against the concept of judicial review within the UN system. It is sometimes suggested that, as the strengthening of the Council after the Cold War is a positive sign, judicial review would decrease the Council's effectiveness.[79] It is also considered relevant that when the UN was created, the Belgian proposal on endowing the International Court with respective powers was not adopted.

This fact of the non-adoption of Belgian proposal is interpreted differently, and it is suggested that the outcome of this is not to exclude judicial review.[80] The International Court clearly stated in *Certain Expenses* that the

---

[77] Akehurst, 130.

[78] Orego Vicuna (2004), 27, suggests that there can be a Constitutional Court in the absence of a formal constitution.

[79] Dissenting Opinion of Judge Schwebel, *Lockerbie, ICJ Reports*, 1998, 73–81.

[80] Watson, Constitutionalism, Judicial Review, and the World Court, 34 *Harvard International Law Journal* (1993), 1, 8–14; Gowlland-Debbas, The Functions of the UN Security Council in the International Legal System, in Byers (ed.), 308–309.

fact of rejection of the Belgian proposal does mean the rejection of judicial review by the Court of other principal organs' actions.[81] Besides, the Charter and the Court's Statute, which entitles the Court to decide 'any question of international law', do not expressly exclude judicial review, nor can such outcome be inferred by necessary implication; more so, if borne in mind that the Council is not *legibus solutus*. Even if each principal organ remains *prima facie* a judge of its competence, the exercise of such competence undoubtedly involves questions of international law on which the International Court is empowered to adjudicate, subject to the usual jurisdictional preconditions. Therefore, the only arguments against judicial review are just two: one is a policy argument regarding the need to preserve the Council as a powerful organ and also questioning whether considerations of justice can prevail over those of peace, as narrowly understood; another argument derives from a specific reading of *travaux* which are in fact just secondary means of Charter interpretation. These two arguments may be weighty to those inclined to believe in them, but they are not sufficient to exclude, by themselves, the possibility of judicial review within the United Nations system.

It is arguable that different people would understand the concept of judicial review differently and the actual type of judicial action would be more important than the terms in which it is formally described in specific cases. A common meaning would be a verification of acts in terms of their compliance with the law. The 1992 Order in *Lockerbie* does not itself signify that the concept of judicial review is irrelevant; it merely signifies—rightly or wrongly—that judicial review could not perhaps be performed at that stage of the proceedings. This is especially inferable by the Court's reference to *prima facie* force of Resolution 748(1992). The 1998 judgment in *Lockerbie* Preliminary Objections does not directly deal with judicial review, but the very fact that the Court has not declined jurisdiction in the case involving a Chapter VII resolution has in fact been considered by Dissenting Judge Schwebel (who then served as the President and ended up in the minority) as an exercise of judicial review.[82]

The Court has come very close to judicial review in some cases, for instance in *Certain Expenses* or *Namibia*. In individual Opinions, different views have been expressed. Judge Jennings in *Lockerbie* opposed judicial review, requiring that the Court should support and protect the Council's action in maintaining peace.[83] It should be added that the Court is obliged to support only such action of the Council as is compatible with the Charter and

---

[81] *ICJ Reports*, 1962, 168.

[82] Dissenting Opinion of Judge Schwebel, *Lockerbie, ICJ Reports*, 1998, 71, 73, complaining that the Court's judgment obstructs the Council in fulfilling its primary responsibility under the Charter.

[83] Dissenting Opinion of Judge Jennings, *Lockerbie, ICJ Reports*, 1998, 110.

relevant general international law.[84] Judge Lauterpacht in *Bosnia* considered that the Court is entitled, and indeed bound, to ensure respect for the rule of law within the United Nations system, and therefore to insist, in cases properly brought before it, on compliance by UN principal organs with the rules governing their operation.[85] Judge Skubiszewski noted in his Dissenting Opinion in *East Timor* that the Court is entitled to examine the Security Council's resolutions and draw appropriate conclusions if they are *ultra vires*.[86] The ICTY in *Tadic* has also affirmed its power to review the Chapter VII measures of the Security Council.[87] Therefore, there is solid support in jurisprudence for the idea of judicial review.

It is submitted in legal doctrine that the powers of the Security Council under Chapter VII are not unlimited, but are bound by legal norms finally to be determined by the International Court.[88] The Court is competent to determine the binding force of the Council's decisions. Even if this happens through an Advisory Opinion, States and other organs are empowered to act on the basis of the Opinion.[89] But the Court can determine validity of the Security Council's decision involving legal responsibility either in contentious or advisory proceedings.[90] The Council possesses autonomy in the relevant field; but the Court determines the legal and constitutional boundaries of that autonomy.[91] In some cases the Security Council decisions can be null and void and 'under these circumstances the International Court of Justice would also be entitled to disregard a resolution as having no legal effect'.[92]

The treatment by the International Court of the resolutions of principal UN organs, as well as the practice of other international tribunals, clearly demonstrate that judicial review in relation to the Security Council resolutions is both feasible and legitimate. If the International Court is faced with

[84] A classical case of this would be the International Court's pronouncement that a 'binding determination made by the competent organs of the United Nations to the effect that a situation is illegal cannot remain without consequences'. The Court itself reaffirmed the findings of the Security Council on Namibia, as was the subject-matter of that case, *ICJ Reports* 1971, 173.

[85] Separate Opinion of Judge Lauterpacht, *ICJ Reports*, 1993, 439.

[86] Dissenting Opinion of Judge Skubiszewski, *ICJ Reports*, 1995, paras 70, 85–86.

[87] *Prosecutor v Tadic*, Case IT-94-1-AR72 (Appeals Chamber), 35 *ILM* (1996), 44–45. Similarly, The EC Regulations implementing the Security Council sanctions can be challenged before and reviewed by the European Court of Justice for violating the fundamental human rights that are parts of general principles of the Community law, Kapteyn, De Wet and Nollkaemper (eds), 60.

[88] Bernhardt, *Ultra Vires* Activities of International Organisations, *Festschrift Skubiszewski* (1996), 606.

[89] Bernhardt, *Ultra Vires* Activities of International Organisations, *Festschrift Skubiszewski* (1996), 606; for an overview of these options see also Bowett, The Impact of Security Council Decisions on Dispute Settlement Procedures, 5 *EJIL* (1994), 98–100.

[90] Bowett, The Impact of Security Council Decisions on Dispute Settlement Procedures, 5 *EJIL* (1994), 101.

[91] Bernhardt, *Ultra Vires* Activities of International Organisations, *Festschrift Skubiszewski* (1996), 607.

[92] Frowein (1994), 385.

two sets of legal obligations, one of which offends against peremptory norms, and another is the *jus cogens* itself, it would have to decide this normative conflict as required in international law. The refusal to exercise judicial review would merely be a refusal to express a view, and could not justify the Court in considering that the Council's measure offending against *jus cogens* is nonetheless valid and binding. Therefore, if there is no power of judicial review, this factor should not help affirmation of validity of invalid measures of the Security Council, because this very affirmation is already a substantive judgment on the validity of a resolution, and if a court is entitled to make it, then it is also entitled to reach an opposite conclusion, and both conclusions would amount to an exercise of judicial review.

5. CONCLUDING REMARKS

If it is accepted that *jus cogens* provides a full-fledged limitation on the action by the Security Council, it must also be accepted that this limitation shall have necessary consequences in terms of validity and interpretation of relevant measures: if one accepts the principle, one must also accept its consequences. Thus, the substantive conclusions as to the role of *jus cogens* themselves prompt conclusions as to its consequences. On the other hand, the relevance of *jus cogens* does not by itself prompt conclusions of an institutional nature, such as the existence of institutional powers of determination of voidness, or judicial review. Such institutional powers are not natural consequences of the operation of *jus cogens*, and the latter is also independent in its operation and consequences from the former.

The most likely argument against this logical chain, likely to be advanced by those unwilling to see the Security Council limited by legal standards, may contend that this logical reasoning is not always accepted in the real world. But, along with reference to reality, one should also bear in mind the special role of peremptory norms in contemporary international legal systems, and that the continuance in force of a resolution of the Council conflicting with *jus cogens* is nothing but the maintenance of a situation morally and ethically repugnant in the eyes of the international community. This last factor is a reality in itself. Another incontrovertible reality is that the Council is not *legibus solutus*, and this factor needs to be accepted with all consequences.

The heavy moral and humanitarian concerns involved in certain measures of the Security Council demand that the role of *jus cogens* should be acknowledged, to address properly some serious violations of international law involving the illegal use of force or grave human suffering. In the process of drafting the resolutions, in many cases compliance with *jus cogens* is not the principal concern of States who are the members of the Council, unless they are directly affected. But such a tendency is perhaps not irreversible, as the drafting process of Resolution 1483(2003) on Iraq revealed that States have expressed clear concerns in terms of compliance with relevant peremptory norms, such as permanent sovereignty over natural resources.[93]

Another significant factor is that the more difficult the political process to arrive at a consensus within the Security Council in adopting a resolution, the less is the likelihood that *jus cogens* will be infringed by the Security Council. It is most probably the political divergences between members which caused Resolution 1244(1999) to as be careful in terms of compliance with *jus cogens* as it is—indeed, as it could possibly have been.

---

[93] Above, Chapter 12.

PART IV

Peremptory Norms and the Powers
of International Tribunals

15

Peremptory Norms and International Judicial Jurisdiction

I. THE RELATIONSHIP BETWEEN PEREMPTORY NORMS AND JUDICIAL SETTLEMENT OF DISPUTES

Judicial settlement of disputes differs from conciliatory or amicable settlement in that it is based on international law. Conciliatory or amicable settlements[1] are in principle adequate for dispute settlement involving ordinary norms safeguarding individual State interests, as the nature of such norms tolerates adjustment of a dispute as the parties consider it acceptable. States may deviate from such norms, generally or with regard to a special case to any extent thought desirable. The more imperative the requirements of a norm and the more stringent the community interest it embodies, the more necessary the strict application of the law, independently of individual attitudes of States and their *inter se* agreements. Judicial function can provide solutions which concentrate on the enforcement of imperative norms as such; amicable and conciliatory settlements raise the spectre of bilateralization of disputes based on such norms.[2] Also, adjudication enables disputes involving public order norms to be settled with finality and completeness, thereby maintaining the integrity of the norms involved. As peremptory norms have specific effects different from ordinary norms and such effects are dictated by the requirements of the community interest, it must be examined what jurisdictional resources tribunals possess to reflect those effects, and to what extent the effect of peremptory norms requires tribunals to adopt specific jurisdictional policies.

But here we arguably face a fundamental difficulty. In the present state of international law, judicial jurisdiction depends upon the consent of States. Judicial settlement, like other dispute settlement methods, is consensual. Peremptory norms do not by themselves establish judicial jurisdiction in the absence of a jurisdictional instrument. A major issue of the impact of *jus cogens* on the powers of tribunals is the relationship between substance and jurisdiction in international law. The 'classical' view pronounced, for example, by the International Court in *Fisheries Jurisdiction* suggests that

---

[1] Such methods are flexible and involve mutually acceptable solutions, in contrast to 'win/lose' formulations in judicial settlements, Chinkin, Alternative Dispute Resolution in International Law, in Evans (ed.), *Remedies in International Law: The Institutional Dilemma* (1998), 124.

[2] Chinkin (1998), 130 speaks in this context of the bilateralism that might not satisfy others' perceptions of what the fundamental community obligations should entail.

'there is a fundamental distinction between the acceptance by a State of the Court's jurisdiction and the compatibility of particular acts with international law. The former requires consent. The latter question can only be reached when the Court deals with the merits, after having established its jurisdiction.'[3] This was reiterated in *Legality of the Use of Force*, as a reason for non-indication of provisional measures or decline to find jurisdiction, and again in *DRC v Rwanda* in the face of pleas based on *jus cogens*.[4] In *East Timor*, the Court asserted that 'the *erga omnes* character of a norm and the rule of consent to jurisdiction are two different things. Whatever the nature of the obligations invoked, the Court could not rule on the lawfulness of the conduct of a State when its judgment would imply an evaluation of the lawfulness of the conduct of another State which is not a party to the case.'[5]

This approach implies that the substance of norms does not at all weigh in the balance of different factors relevant in jurisdictional disputes. The Court uses this approach in very different situations involving issues of competence as a 'magic wand' to counter opposite factors. It is worth enquiring if such statements are well founded as a matter of principle, if they were correctly made in the cases concerned, and if so, what are their general implications. This requires us to examine the nature of the dividing line between substance and jurisdiction, to clarify whether these two spheres are as separate from each other as the Court has asserted, and to what extent the nature of substantive obligations can influence the extent and manner of exercise of judicial competence, including jurisdiction proper, admissibility of claims, indication of provisional measures and acceptability of friendly settlements.

The divergence between substantive law and the outcome of judicial process is not problematic in ordinary legal relations which safeguard individual State interests, as in such cases the outcome of a dispute, like the very substance of obligations, is the concern of the parties to the dispute only. But in the case of norms protecting the community interest it is arguable that tribunals must safeguard such community interest not only in terms of substance but also at the jurisdictional level. To assess the impact of *jus cogens* properly, it is necessary to distinguish between the legally distinct situations tribunals may deal with. It is one thing to ask whether *jus cogens* can establish judicial jurisdiction in the absence of an applicable jurisdictional instrument; it is quite another to ask whether *jus cogens* could influence the scope of an existing jurisdictional instrument. One must distinguish between claims portraying *jus cogens* as a free-standing basis of judicial competence, and claims viewing it as a relevant factor in the interpretative process.[6] This

---

[3] *Fisheries Jurisdiction, ICJ Reports*, 1998, para. 55.

[4] See eg *Legality of the Use of Force*, Judgment (Preliminary Objections), General List No. 105, 15 December 2004, para. 128.

[5] *East Timor, ICJ Reports*, 1995, para. 29.   [6] cf Orakhelashvili, *LPICT* (2003), 512–513.

holds especially true where jurisdiction is provided in the community interest (eg, with regard to Article IX of the Genocide Convention the claim that jurisdiction can be established over a non-party to the Genocide Convention is different from the claim that *jus cogens* can impact on jurisdictional decisions involving the parties).

The consensual approach implies that the existence of each type of judicial power is subject to evidentiary factors. In terms of public order, this may run counter to the inherent effects of *jus cogens* on remedies for wrongful acts and the validity of conflicting acts and transactions. This may also contradict the principle that tribunals have inherent powers to deal properly with disputes submitted to them and to resolve them with finality.[7] Extreme consensual approaches must be assessed cautiously, as one aspect of the judicial function in international relations is to support, or at least not to obstruct, the operation and enforcement of fundamental legal norms. It is also relevant that the principle of consent as a jurisdictional principle is not absolute and its relevance can be qualified by other factors involved in adjudication, including the character of substantive norms.[8]

The total irrelevance of substance for jurisdiction cannot be assumed. To illustrate: the International Court in jurisdictional disputes such as *Aegean Sea* and *Qatar v Bahrain* examined questions of substantive law in order to clarify whether it had jurisdiction: in particular, whether the instruments conferring jurisdiction were treaties under international law, namely the law of treaties.[9] The Court also hinted in *Bosnia* that the character of obligations can influence the scope of its contentious jurisdiction.[10]

Jurisdictional/procedural instruments themselves can create substantive law and are as subject to interpretation as any other instrument.[11] Agreements conferring jurisdiction are treaties. If similar interpretative principles apply, it is unclear why *jus cogens* cannot have overriding impact on jurisdictional instruments—through interpretation and in the extreme case through invalidity—in the same way as on other treaty clauses.

The characteristics of judicial competence are not self-explanatory, but owe their existence to the system of general international law. The consensual nature of jurisdiction follows from the fact that international law does not bind States without their consent; the lack of jurisdiction over a claim falling

---

[7] The impact of *jus cogens* on remedial powers are not examined here, as the doctrine of inherent powers can also explain that phenomenon. Orakhelashvili, *LPICT* (2003), 534–538, Orakhelashvili, *LJIL* (2002), 105–130; Orakhelashvili, *CYELS* (2002–2003), 260–269.

[8] See the discussion in Orakhelashvili, *LPICT*, 501–550.

[9] *ICJ Reports*, 1978, 39–40; *ICJ Reports*, 1994, 122.

[10] *Bosnia, ICJ Reports*, 1996, paras 31–34. Brownlie (2003), 568.

[11] Lauterpacht, *The Development of International Law by the International Court* (1958), 338–339.

ratione temporis outside the competence of a judicial tribunal follows from the principle that international obligations have no retroactive force; most of the conditions of admissibility of claims before tribunals, such as the scope of the rule of local remedies, the question of a legal interest to bring claims, operate because they apply to areas other than judicial settlement of disputes and inherently pertain to general international law.

Tribunals operate on the basis of their constituent instruments and general international law, which set the limits of their competence and provide criteria for their action. Tribunals must respect their constituent instruments and other norms applicable to their action. The very relevance of the principle of consent should be understood in accordance with, as qualified by and not overriding the framework in which it operates, including the hierarchy of norms. Analysis should be made not only of what tribunals actually say, but also of whether what they say is justified in the context of the overarching standards governing their activities and provided for in their constituent instruments and general international law.

2. THE CONSENSUAL PRINCIPLE AND JUDICIAL COGNIZANCE OF PEREMPTORY NORMS

It must be examined how a tribunal can take cognizance of peremptory norms and their effects in cases where they are not *prima facie* covered by jurisdictional instruments.

The principle of consent would arguably dictate that tribunals should exclusively apply the law chosen by the parties as it is the exclusive basis of the tribunals' consensual jurisdiction. However, if *jus cogens* applies to a dispute, then it applies peremptorily, despite the law chosen by the parties to apply to that dispute. The principle of consent comes here into apparent clash with the principle of non-derogability of *jus cogens*. As tribunals are bound to decide in accordance with international law, as particularly affirmed in Article 38 of the International Court's Statute and implied in the case of all other tribunals, they are supposed to respect the fact that the observance of international law means different things in different situations because public order norms have to be observed even in the face of a contrary agreement, and a dispute cannot be settled in accordance with international law unless such a hierarchy of norms is respected.

Different solutions are suggested in doctrine and practice. In *Oscar Chinn*, the Permanent Court gave effect to the 1919 Saint-Germain Convention which arguably derogated from the 1885 Berlin Treaty setting out the fundamental rights and duties of States with regard to the Congo basin. The Court considered that the 1885 Treaty was irrelevant to the dispute as no party had referred to it and it applied the 1919 Treaty exclusively, not least due to the implications of the consensual principle.[12] Now, whether the Court's approach ignored peremptory norms or merely offended the interests of third parties would depend on whether the substantive norms involved were peremptory in the first place and this cannot be assumed. But the correctness of the principle as upheld by the Court is a different issue.

Judge Van Eysinga criticized the Court for its exclusive application of the Saint-Germain Treaty which itself was something the parties could not do, namely modify the Berlin Treaty *inter se*.[13] Judge Schücking similarly disapproved the Court's approach, asserting that an *inter se* modification of the Berlin Treaty was inadmissible and, most significantly, that the Court could not apply conventions that are contrary to public morality, since such conventions are null and void. This substantive issue has, in Judge Schücking's reasoning, clear jurisdictional implications, as 'the attitude of the tribunal should ... be governed in such a case by considerations of international public policy even when jurisdiction is conferred on the Court by virtue of a Special Agreement'.[14] Thus, Judge Schücking clearly emphasized a link between substance and jurisdiction: the principle of consent cannot require the Court to apply what is void as a matter of substance.

This issue has received doctrinal attention. According to Hudson, a court must respect the choice of law by the parties whatever its substance.[15] But Reisman offers an outcome more compatible with public order considerations. Any tribunal owes an obligation to the international community to apply international public policy.[16] Inter-State agreements can be void for contravening public order and this is relevant in the cases where 'litigants set out in the compromise specific substantive norms that are contrary to either an international *jus cogens*, international morality, or superior rules of jurisdiction to which litigants would, under ordinary circumstances, be subject'. The faithful application of public order would acquit a tribunal of its obligations to the parties to apply the law chosen by them through compromise or otherwise, but nothing can acquit a tribunal of its mandate to apply public policy. A decision which fails to do so would only compound a nullity.[17] Reisman denotes Hudson's view as anachronistic and especially emphasizes the link between substantive and jurisdictional issues when he considers that Hudson's consensual view denies 'any play for *jus cogens* and community regulation of private agreements'.[18] In fact, international *jus cogens* is among the limitations of the tribunal's statutory powers.[19] When the course of following the applicable law as determined by the parties would

---

[12] PCIJ A/B63, 80, pointing out that the 1919 Treaty was an immediate source of the parties' contractual obligations.

[13] PCIJ A/B63, 136.   [14] Id., 148–150.

[15] Hudson, *The Permanent Court of International Justice* (1943), 601–604.

[16] Reisman, *Nullity and Revision* (1971), 542.

[17] Id., 545–546.   [18] Id., 546.   [19] Id., 547.

lead to the adoption of the decision conflicting with public order, the tribunal has two options, either to return a non-decision, which is hardly suitable, or to formulate an alternative decision consonant with facts and minimum public policy.[20] Reisman distinguishes between cases where courts can use agreements between the parties as the exclusive source of the law they apply because such cases are governed by rules whose application and effect are the 'exclusive concern of the litigants', and cases where courts cannot do so as they are governed not only by the norms the parties choose but also by peremptory norms, denoted by Reisman as 'inclusively prescribed norms', or 'cogentive community prescriptions', which are subject to 'inclusive supervision' by tribunals.[21]

Reisman's view is correct, as confirmed in *Oil Platforms*, where the International Court construed the essential security exceptions clause in the 1955 Iran–US Treaty in conformity with peremptory *jus ad bellum*. The US considered that the Court was barred from doing so as its jurisdiction, due to the consensual principle, covered only the Treaty itself, not any rule of general international law,[22] and Judges Higgins and Buergenthal also treated this matter in such a way. Judge Higgins argued that the Court simply could not enquire into whether the parties had contemplated the legality of measures involving the unlawful use of force when concluding the Treaty, doubting whether the Court's jurisdiction extended to the question whether a measure under Article XX.1(d) constituted an unlawful use of force.[23] Judge Buergenthal also referred to the Court's lack of jurisdiction to treat general international law as relevant, because the parties did not submit these issues to the Court under the dispute resolution clause of the 1955 Treaty, and even contended that it could not take into account whether a relevant rule of international law was a *jus cogens* rule.[24] Furthermore, Judge Buergenthal criticized the Court, stating that its interpretative outcome achieved through the use of Article 31.3(c) of the 1969 Vienna Convention was not interpretation but amounted 'to an unwarranted distortion of the meaning of the jurisdiction conferred on the Court' under Article XXI the 1955 Treaty. This was so, because the Court failed 'to seriously address the jurisdictional restraints on the Court's freedom of treaty interpretation, given the consensual nature of the Court's jurisdiction'.[25]

Judge Owada attempted to take a somehow intermediate attitude, but ended up by suggesting mutually exclusive outcomes. On the one hand, Judge Owada stated that the Court had no competence 'to examine and rule

---

[20] Id., 550.   [21] Id., 252, 550–551.
[22] CR 2003/18, 17–18 (Weil); Judgment, para. 39.
[23] Judge Higgins, Separate Opinion, paras 44–49.
[24] Judge Buergentahl, Separate Opinion, paras 11 ff., 22–23.
[25] Judge Buergenthal, para. 28.

on the issue of self-defence under international law'.[26] On the other hand, the Court was competent to 'get into examination of the scope and the relevance of the rules of general international law relating to the use of force', but—for reasons that Judge Owada did not explain—it would not be self-defence under general international law that the Court would have the competence to examine.[27] This approach is self-contradictory. The Court either can examine the issues of *jus ad bellum* under general international law, or it cannot. If it cannot, then no issue of *jus ad bellum* can be referred to in interpreting the 1955 Treaty; but if it can, then every relevant issue of *jus ad bellum* can be examined. Judge Owada has not provided any reliable criterion to enable us to conclude that there is some inherent dividing line separating the issues of general international law from each other in the context where the Court is in principle entitled, as Judge Owada also agreed, to consider *jus ad bellum* in judging compliance with the 1955 Treaty.

The judges that opposed, for alleged lack of jurisdiction, the Court's treatment of Article XX of the 1955 Treaty made, on its face, a jurisdictional argument. But in reality, and whether consciously or not, they have pronounced on substantive legal issues (even if sometimes disclaiming any intention to do so). In their judgment, the Court, on the basis of the lack of jurisdiction over the issues of general international law, should in fact have pronounced legal those acts that were illegal under general international law of the use of force—legal under the 1955 Treaty, that is in fact approve, as a matter of substantive law, that that Treaty effectively and justifiably derogated from *jus ad bellum*. This is, by the way, yet another instance affirming the essential link between the substance of disputes and their judicial treatments.

If the judges were genuinely concerned with the lack of jurisdiction, their insistence on the refusal to exercise jurisdiction would have been better. Although not necessarily correct, this outcome would at least be compatible with the mainline argument of those judges as to the alleged non-existence of jurisdiction over the issues of general international law. The Court would have refused to adjudicate, but at the same time it would have done nothing to proclaim as legal the attacks that offended against customary *jus ad bellum* or to construe the 1955 Treaty as derogatory from the norms related to the use of force. More specifically, the judges could have said that as the matter before them includes, in terms of interpretation of Article XX, not just treaty relations but also general international law, the Court should decline to adjudicate for the lack of jurisdiction, because it could not pronounce that Article XX authorized certain forcible actions. Under this approach the Court would not rule legal anything that contradicts the requirements of *jus ad bellum*.

---

[26] Judge Owada, Separate Opinion, para. 13.   [27] Id., para. 14.

However, the real issue was that, as jurisdictional provision is an accessory to the substantive provisions of the treaty, it includes treaty norms as they are interpreted. If there is an inherent link between the treaty clause such as Article XX and general international law, the jurisdictional clause must simply be considered to cover the entire legal relationship.

The Court decided as it did even in the face of objections of a jurisdictional character referring to the principle of consent. The Court's approach is consistent with the proposition that there are limits to the contractual autonomy of States. States cannot confer jurisdiction on the Court on the basis of a treaty which authorizes acts contrary to *jus cogens*, and contains a jurisdictional clause empowering the Court to rule such acts legal. This goes beyond the limits of the contractual autonomy of States: strict adherence to the principle of consent could result in disregarding such limits of contractual autonomy, possibly making the Court in effect approve a treaty provision which derogates from *jus cogens*. It is one thing to say that the Court cannot adjudicate on matters not covered by a treaty conferring jurisdiction, and it is quite another thing to argue that the Court should adjudicate on the matters covered by a treaty in a manner leading to the result which the parties to that treaty are not at all allowed to achieve through the exercise of their contractual powers. The Court's approach affirms that the effects of *jus cogens* can be relevant both in terms of substance and jurisdiction, and the principle of consent should be seen as limited in its relevance and effect in order not to preclude the proper effects of the overriding *jus cogens*.

The application of the hierarchy of norms in *Oil Platforms* was based on the proper respect for the jurisdictional relevance of *jus cogens* and reflects the approach of Judges Van Eysinga and Schücking in *Oscar Chinn*. If proper cognizance of *jus cogens* is taken, then some restrictions on the relevance of the consensual principle are inevitable.

3. PEREMPTORY NORMS AND JUDICIAL ACTION *PROPRIO MOTU*

If peremptory norms and their effect, such as the objective illegality of breaches and the nullity of conflicting transactions, apply to disputes regardless of the parties' will, then it is the tribunals' duty to take cognizance of them of their own motion and irrespective of the parties' submissions. This is yet another confirmation of the link between substance and jurisdiction and the jurisdictional relevance of *jus cogens*.

According to Verzijl, once the action or instrument a tribunal deals with involves contradiction with *jus cogens*, it is obliged to deal with the issue of its own motion, as the situation involves absolute invalidity.[28] For instance, if a tribunal is asked to adjudicate on the basis of a treaty providing for forced labour and the parties do not challenge its validity, the tribunal would nonetheless be bound to spell out the invalidity of the treaty on the grounds of conflict with *jus cogens*.[29]

Verzijl criticizes the Permanent Court's stance in *Oscar Chinn* for having refused to deal with the compatibility of the 1919 Treaty with the 1885 Berlin Treaty because no party had raised this issue.[30] Judge Van Eysinga also emphasized that the norms parties cannot modify must not be left out of the Court's attention just because the parties have not referred to them.[31] According to Special Rapporteur Lauterpacht, the issue of *jus cogens* invalidity must be judicially addressed even if no party refers to that, and action *proprio motu* is justified.[32]

As Fitzmaurice emphasized, 'The *non ultra petita* rule is not only an inevitable corollary—indeed, virtually a part of the general principle of consent of the parties as the basis of international jurisdiction—it is also a necessary rule, for without it the consent principle could constantly be circumvented.'[33] Rozakis expresses a controversial view that a court cannot decide on a treaty conflicting with *jus cogens* unless the parties request, because to do so without their consent would exceed jurisdiction.[34] It seems that these suggestions confuse two different things. The principle of consent relates to jurisdiction, to the issues that tribunals can adjudicate upon because they have been submitted to them under the relevant jurisdictional titles. The principle of *non ultra petita* relates to the process of the adjudication of the specific claim or case and can be raised only within the context of the specific proceedings. While the consensual principle determines on what issues tribunals can adjudicate, *non ultra petita* relates to the issue on whose request the issues which anyway fall within the tribunal's jurisdiction can be raised. The principle of consent is conceptually and logically anterior to *non ultra petita*. Consequently, the argument that *non ultra petita* is an element of the consensual principle is conceptually flawed.

---

[28] Verzijl, La validité et la nullité des actes juridiques internationales, 15 *Revue de droit international* (1935), 321–322, 327.

[29] Verdross, Forbidden Treaties in International Law, *AJIL* (1937), 577; Arechaga, International Law in the Past Third of the Century, 159 *RdC* (1978), 68; Lowe, The Role of Equity, *Australian YIL* (1992), 68. On the impermissibility of the *non ultra petita* rule in the ECHR proceedings see Van der Meersch, Does the Convention have the Power of 'Ordre Public' in Municipal Law?, in Robertson (ed.), *Human Rights in National and International Law* (1968), 114.

[30] PCIJ A/B63, 80.   [31] Id., 136.   [32] YbILC, 1953.

[33] Fitzmaurice, *The Law and Procedure of the International Court of Justice* (1986), 529; see also Fitzmaurice, *The Law and Procedure of the International Court of Justice, BYIL* (1958), 98, referring to the *non ultra petita* rule as 'a derivative of the consent principle'.

[34] Rozakis, The Law of Invalidity of Treaties, *AVR* (1974), 185; Rozakis, *The Concept of* Jus Cogens *in the Law of Treaties* (1976), 163.

Courts are justified not to act *proprio motu* if the relevant norms are not peremptory (as they presumably were not in *Oscar Chinn*). In *Cameroon–Nigeria*, the Court did not examine the legality of the 1913 Treaty ceding Bakassi peninsula to Germany for its alleged conflict with the 1885 Berlin Treaty, as this issue, though raised initially, was not further pursued by any party.[35] The matter was deemed to be bilateral.

But in other cases the Court's approach is of doubtful value. In *Gabcikovo-Nagymaros*, the Court emphasized that since none of the parties invoked *jus cogens* norms of environmental law, it would not examine the effects and scope of Article 64 of the Vienna Convention on the Law of Treaties.[36] The Court left open the issue whether certain environmental law rules might be peremptory. If so they could have invalidated the 1977 Treaty between Slovakia and Hungary. Whether *jus cogens* was involved in that case is a different issue, but the Court's approach is deficient as it presumed that even if a treaty is invalid for conflict with *jus cogens*, the parties, and the Court itself, are still entitled to treat it as a valid treaty which continues to govern their rights and obligations. The Court ought to have taken up this issue *proprio motu*, since it involved the question of objective invalidity. The 1977 Treaty was presumably not invalid for conflict with peremptory norms. But the Court must have made this clear as a matter of substance and not given an impression, as it did, that it is ready to uphold treaties despite their object just because no party challenges them.

In *Arrest Warrant*, the Court took note of the fact that the Congo stopped short of complaining about Belgium's allegedly unlawful exercise of universal jurisdiction and limited its submissions to the breach of immunity rules. The Court decided by reference to the *non ultra petita* principle not to address the issue of jurisdiction and limited its judgment to the issue of immunity, the result of which was to affirm that the Congolese foreign minister enjoyed immunity and Belgium's arrest warrant was a breach of international law.[37] By following the submissions and leaving aside the issue of universal jurisdiction, the Court ignored the effect that universal jurisdiction as a *jus cogens* principle may have on immunities. Had the Court addressed this issue, it could have reached a different conclusion in accordance with the overriding effect of peremptory norms.

Adherence to *non ultra petita* is not always justified as, according to Fitzmaurice, it may cause a legally incorrect outcome or neglect juridically relevant factors.[38] If peremptory norms imperatively apply to a dispute, tribunals must apply them whether or not parties so request: it is beyond the

---

[35] *Cameroon–Nigeria*, paras 194–195; Orakhelashvili, *CLJ* (2003), 9–12.

[36] *ICJ Reports*, 1998, 76.

[37] *Arrest Warrant*, para. 43; Orakhelashvili, *AJIL* (2002), 677–684; Orakhelashvili, *GYIL* (2002), 231–232, 262–263.

[38] Fitzmaurice (1986), 529–530.

parties' power to make such norms inapplicable to a dispute, and such a derogation would be one which tribunals have no power to approve.

The *non ultra petita* principle was asserted by Judges Higgins and Buergenthal (who criticized the use of the principle in *Arrest Warrant*) in *Oil Platforms*, contending that the Court should not have examined peremptory *jus ad bellum* as it was not covered by the 1955 Treaty which was the sole basis of jurisdiction.[39] But, apart from the fact that *non ultra petita* does not justify a tribunal refusing to apply *jus cogens*, there was no independent place for that principle in *Oil Platforms*. *Non ultra petita* is relevant in terms of the submissions of the parties, while these judges also associated it with the requirement that the Court should not go beyond examining the issues governed by jurisdictional instruments. In addition, *non ultra petita* was irrelevant as Iran explicitly referred to the relevance of peremptory *jus ad bellum* in the interpretation of the 1955 Treaty.[40]

However, even if *non ultra petita* had been relevant in the proceedings, the Court would still be entitled to pass judgment on the use of force and self-defence, in order not to allow the qualification of the acts that give rise to objective illegality to be replaced by the qualification contained in the bilateral treaty.

4. *JUS COGENS* AND THE INTERPRETATION OF JURISDICTIONAL CLAUSES

The link between the substance of *jus cogens* and jurisdiction over its enforcement is relevant in terms of the interpretation and application of jurisdictional clauses, especially if they include reservations limiting the jurisdiction thus accepted. The consent-based approach would dictate that, as jurisdiction is consensual, States can accept it with whatever limitations they please. But the nature of the problem compels us to draw a distinction between cases where jurisdiction is not accepted at all, and where it is accepted with qualifications; it is one thing to say that *jus cogens* cannot as such provide for jurisdiction where none exists, it is another to enquire whether *jus cogens* can influence the parameters of an existing acceptance. The principle of consent is of course a factor but it is not the only relevant one, and circumstances can be envisaged where it must be balanced by reference to norms protecting the community interest. This is relevant for courts deciding whether the intention of a State as it stands must be given effect or how that intention must be interpreted.

---

[39] Judge Higgins, Separate Opinion, paras 9–24; Judge Buergenthal, Separate Opinion, paras 3–10.
[40] See also Declaration of Judge Koroma in *Oil Platforms*.

The treaty character of jurisdictional reservations is especially important in considering that by establishing bilateral consensual relations within the system of adjudication the parties have to keep their transactions in the state that is compatible with the system.[41] This means that the parameters of the will and intention embodied in such declarations must be judged not in isolation, just by reference to the will of a declarant State, but also having regard to the applicable framework of international law—which would be true even if these declarations were understood as unilateral acts. Declarations are made in the context of other instruments and principles of international law, which may be superior in force to them. Thus, in general, the intention of a State featured in a duly interpreted jurisdictional instrument must be deemed to be the source of jurisdictional obligations of that State, as well as of the scope of such obligations *ratione materiae*, *personae* and *temporis*. This approach is expressed in *Fisheries Jurisdiction*, where the International Court gave effect to the Canadian reservation exempting from the Court's jurisdiction certain matters related to the enforcement of fisheries regulations,[42] and *Aerial Incident*, where the Court gave full effect to the Commonwealth reservation of India.[43]

So far, the intention of a declarant State as established through interpretation is perhaps crucial. But the situation may be different if the intention thus established runs contrary to a superior instrument or principle; and nothing in *Fisheries Jurisdiction* can be understood as enabling a jurisdictional reservation to prevail in such a case. True, the Court rejected the argument 'that interpretation in accordance with the legality under international law of the matters exempted from the jurisdiction of the Court is a rule that governs the interpretation of such reservations'.[44] However, it is not a question of the compatibility with international law of acts covered by a reservation, but of the compatibility with international law of a reservation itself (and of the underlying imputed intention). *Fisheries Jurisdiction* approves reservations which may exempt some illegal acts from the Court's jurisdiction, but presumably only to the extent that the reservation in question is valid as such and does not conflict with the tribunal's constituent instrument or any other superior rule.

The context of the *Fisheries Jurisdiction* case has been in principle quite suitable for maintaining the distinction between the substance of a legal relationship and its judicial enforcement. Although Canada had been bound

---

[41] Orakhelashvili, *LPICT*, 517–528. But even if jurisdictional reservations are viewed as unilateral acts, the outcome is still the same. The consensual and bilateral element cannot be disregarded here either, partly because in any case bilateral relations exist between the reserving and other States, and partly because such bilateral relations can arise between them on the basis of the techniques of validation, such as waiver and acquiescence.

[42] *Fisheries Jurisdiction, ICJ Reports,* 1998, paras 62–84.

[43] *Aerial Incident, ICJ Reports,* 2000, 12, paras 30 ff.

[44] *Fisheries Jurisdiction (Spain v Canada), ICJ Reports,* 1998, para. 54.

by certain norms of the law of the sea, it precluded, by its reservation, the adjudication on the measures it took in the NAFO Regulatory Area. This is explained by, among others, the character of the norms that governed the dispute. These norms of the law of the sea, and their application to the pertinent case, were only a matter for bilateral relations between the litigants, and susceptible of derogation *inter se*. The litigants could have derogated from the pertinent norms among others through Spain's acquiescence to the Canadian measures in the regulatory area and the consequent treatment of Spanish ships. Had Spain chosen to do this instead of insisting on compliance and bringing the case before the Court, there would be nothing in international law to disapprove this position. This is so above all because the pertinent legal relations were bilaterally disposable and their certain aspects were in fact validly disposed through the series of bilateral agreements originated on the basis of the Canadian declaration of acceptance of the Court's jurisdiction between Canada itself and the other parties to the Optional Clause.

Such a position cannot persist without limits. In the very case of *Fisheries Jurisdiction*, individual judges have emphasized, as shown below, that the Court's approach would not necessarily be the same if it faces the legal relations governed by the norms that are not disposable on a bilateral basis.

In *Chrysostomos* and *Loizidou*, the European Commission and the European Court of Human Rights had to resolve not only the question of whether the territorial application reservation to the instruments recognizing the compulsory jurisdiction of these organs expressed the proper intention of the respondent State, but also the issue of what were the legal consequences in cases where that intention runs counter to the European Convention of Human Rights—the constituent instrument of these organs. As expected, the respondent State vigorously pleaded in both cases that its reservation was expressive of its intention and was an essential condition of acceptance of judicial jurisdiction. But the Commission and the Court have nevertheless given precedence to the requirements, including the object and purpose, of their constituent instrument—the European Convention—and have severed reservations without prejudice to the entire underlying acceptance of the State-party.[45]

One may contend that such an approach follows from the specifically European character of the European Convention, and hence is inapplicable to other tribunals such as the International Court. But in *Loizidou*, the European Court's analysis of the difference between the two tribunals relates exclusively to the question *which reservations are allowed under the respective*

---

[45] The Convention organs also held that Turkey's intention to accept jurisdiction was a basic intention to which the intention embodied in the reservation was subordinated, *Chrysostomos*, 12 *HRLJ* (1991), 123, para. 46, and *Loizidou*, para. 95, Series A, 310, 31–32.

optional clauses and which are not, and not *what are the powers of the two tribunals in deciding on consequences of those reservations*. The European Court referred to 'fundamental difference in the *role and purpose* of the respective tribunals'[46] and not to a difference in the provisions governing their jurisdiction. This difference in role and purpose is said to arise from the fact that the subject-matter of disputes before the International Court may relate to any area of international law and that 'the role of the International Court is not exclusively limited to direct supervisory functions in respect of a law-making treaty such as the [European] Convention'.[47] Consequently, *Loizidou* merely affirms that certain reservations, which would be permissible to the jurisdiction of the International Court, are impermissible to the jurisdiction of the European Court; but it does not support the assumption that the International Court would not have the power to sever a reservation incompatible with its statute.

Similarly, the UN Human Rights Committee affirmed that a jurisdictional reservation contradicting *jus cogens* is inoperative and severable.[48]

There is some support for such an argument even in the International Court's practice. In *Fisheries Jurisdiction*, the Court considered that the reservation of Canada did not in any way conflict with the Statute of the Court. Otherwise, the Court clearly implied, it would refuse to give effect to such a reservation. In paragraph 86 of the Judgment, the Court clearly explained that the Canadian reservation did not contradict any provision of the Statute or interfere with any power of the Court.[49] As far as the consequences of an inconsistent reservation is concerned, the International Court has never directly addressed the issue, although in *Interhandel* it came very close to the view favouring severance without prejudice to entire acceptance.[50]

---

[46] *Loizidou*, Preliminary Objections, para. 85 (emphasis added).

[47] Id., para. 84.

[48] General Comment No. 24(52), para. 8; *Rawle Kennedy*, 7 *IHRR* (2000) 319, para. 3.15.

[49] The Court particularly noted in paragraph 86 that it 'has had full freedom to interpret the text of the reservation, and its reply to the question whether or not it has jurisdiction to entertain the dispute submitted to it depends solely on that interpretation'. *ICJ Reports*, 1998. See also Counter-Memorial of Canada, paras 84–110, 143; the respondent provided sufficient evidence to demonstrate that its reservation was not anti-Statutory. In para. 62, Canada remarked that 'The intention of the declaring State is critical, but confers no privileged status upon the declaring State in the interpretation of its declaration. That role belongs to the Court under paragraph 6 of Article 36 of its Statute.' Canada emphasized that the interpretation of its reservation by the Court was exactly the exercise by the Court of its power under Article 36(6) of the Statute, CR 98/11, 54 (Willis). See also Separate Opinion of Judge Schwebel, *ICJ Reports*, 1998, paras 2–5, drawing a strict difference between the Canadian reservation and automatic reservations and emphasizing that the former is not anti-Statutory. Separate Opinion of Judge Koroma, affirming that 'the Court's finding should in no way be viewed, let alone interpreted, as a licence for a State to make a declaration or reservation under the optional clause system which is inconsistent with the Statute', id., para. 7.

[50] *Interhandel*, *ICJ Reports*, 1959, 6. Significantly, at the provisional measures stage of *Interhandel*, the Court did not consider the automatic reservation of the United States as a factor impeding the exercise of the Court's *prima facie* jurisdiction, *ICJ Reports*, 1957, 105.

Among individual judges, Judge Lauterpacht has most vigorously argued, both in *Norwegian Loans* and *Interhandel*, that a reservation contrary to the Court's Statute must entail the invalidity of an entire jurisdictional instrument.[51] Judge Lauterpacht has argued that a State having made an automatic reservation is *ipso facto* not a party to the Optional Clause and cannot thus appear before the Court under it either as an applicant or as a defendant.[52] But in some other instances Judge Lauterpacht seems to be inconsistent in his reasoning, holding that the Court's jurisdiction is absent only in cases where an automatic reservation is invoked by a reserving party.[53] These suggestions are mutually contradictory.

Judge Lauterpacht's line of reasoning has been criticized in doctrine.[54] The Court has never subscribed to the approach that Judge Lauterpacht insisted upon. In *Norwegian Loans*, the Court did not touch the issue of validity because parties had not raised this issue.[55] In *Interhandel* the Court had an opportunity, both at the stages of provisional measures and jurisdiction, to follow Judge Lauterpacht's reasoning had it been justified, but the Court did not do that.

Other judges in the Court subscribed to the view of severability that Judge Lauterpacht dismissed. Judge Guererro in *Norwegian Loans* referred to 'the urgent necessity for a judicial decision on the validity of the reservations which go beyond what is permitted by Article 36 of the Statute' and concluded that 'such reservations must be regarded as devoid of all legal validity', while the declaration of acceptance can stand without that reservation.[56]

For Judge Klaestad, a reservation incompatible with the Statute prevents the Court from acting on it. But 'this circumstance does not necessarily

---

[51] Separate Opinion of Judge Lauterpacht, *Norwegian Loans, ICJ Reports*, 1957, 44, 46.

[52] Separate Opinion of Judge Lauterpacht, *ICJ Reports*, 1957, 34. Later in the same Opinion, Judge Lauterpacht comments on automatic reservations that '*as such* they are invalid', id., 46 (emphasis added); see also id., 61: 'invalidity is inherent in the Declaration of Acceptance formulated in that way. . . . The Declaration is invalid *ab initio*.'

[53] Separate Opinion of Judge Lauterpacht, *ICJ Reports*, 1957, 55. Lauterpacht expressed opinion that an automatic reservation 'operates automatically, irrespective of the merits of the dispute, by its own propulsion—as it were—as the result of the physical act of having been invoked', Dissenting Opinion in *Interhandel, ICJ Reports*, 1959, 100.

[54] According to Elkind, 'Judge Lauterpacht's position is the most intransigent and the Court will be very unwilling to accept it', Elkind, *Non-Appearance before the International Court of Justice* (1984), 158. Elkind concludes that Judge Lauterpacht's reasoning leads to an absurd result, id., 164. For the similar approach, see Guggenheim, Das sogenannte automatische Vorbehalt der inneren Angelegenheiten, in v.d. Heydte, Seidl-Hohenveldern, Verosta and Zemanek (eds), *Völkerrecht und Rechtliches Weltbild. Festschrift für Alfred Verdross* (1960), 129.

[55] *Norwegian Loans*, Judgment, *ICJ Reports*, 1957, 27.

[56] Dissenting Opinion of Judge Guererro, *ICJ Reports*, 1957, 69; for support of such understanding of Judge Guererro's Opinion, see Guggenheim, Das sogenannte automatische Vorbehalt der inneren Angelegenheiten, in v.d. Heydte, Seidl-Hohenveldern, Verosta and Zemanek (eds), *Völkerrecht und Rechtliches Weltbild. Festschrift für Alfred Verdross* (1960), 127 ff., and Jennings, Recent Cases on 'Automatic' Reservations to the Optional Clause, 7 *ICLQ* (1958), 357, 360, 362.

imply that it is impossible for the Court to give effect to the other parts of the Declaration of Acceptance which are in conformity with the Statute'. Klaestad considered therefore that the objection by the respondent consisting of making a determination under an automatic reservation should have been rejected.[57]

According to Judge Armand-Ugon, the 'Declaration consists of two parts: acceptance of the Court's jurisdiction and reservations to that acceptance. Those two elements of a single juridical act are separable. Nothing justifies us, when reading the text, in considering them as an indivisible whole.'[58] Armand-Ugon continued with the suggestion that a declaration under Article 36(2) of the Statute is a secondary act, based on the provisions of the Statute which 'provide it with a legal *substratum*'. And he concluded: 'The Court, whose duty is to safeguard its Statute, is certainly empowered to determine whether the secondary part of the declaration is in accord with the primary text; in doing so, it may appraise the legality of the different parts of the declaration in order to determine whether the relevant clauses of the Statute have been correctly applied.'[59] The Court must therefore regard an automatic reservation as unwritten and inoperative.[60]

The view that the incompatible jurisdictional reservation has to be severed leaving the entire acceptance intact has commanded more authority from within the Court than the entire invalidity view has solid support in the doctrine, mainly on the basis that that if a reserving party's determination under its automatic reservation before the Court goes clearly beyond the scope of that reservation—for instance not being in reality related to domestic or national jurisdiction—the Court may review that determination and consider the reservation in question as inoperative.[61] Along with express support by the European Convention organs and implicit support in the *Fisheries Jurisdiction* case, this view has been explicitly accepted by the UN Human Rights Committee in its General Comment 24(52) as a matter of general policy,[62] and in the case of *Rawle Kennedy* as a specific expression of

---

[57] Dissenting Opinion of Judge Klaestad, *ICJ Reports*, 1959, 77–78; in approaching the matter in this way, Klaestad held that the intention of the respondent was to make a valid declaration of acceptance and to safeguard itself from subjection to the Court's jurisdiction only in certain cases.

[58] Dissenting Opinion of Judge Armand-Ugon, *ICJ Reports*, 1959, 91.

[59] Id.   [60] Id., 93.

[61] Shihata, *The Power of the International Court to Determine Its Own Jurisdiction* (1965), 297, who also considers that improper invocation may be reviewed by the Court as an abuse of the power to invoke the reservation. Collier and Lowe, *The Settlement of Disputes in International Law* (1999), 145. Briggs, Reservations to the Acceptance of Compulsory Jurisdiction of the International Court of Justice, 93 *Recueil des Cours* (1958), 361–363, referring also to the review of correctness of a determination under an automatic reservation. Elkind, *Non-Appearance before the International Court of Justice* (1984), 168.

[62] General Comment 24(52), UN Doc. CCPR/C/21/Rev.1/Add.6 (1994).

that policy.[63] Therefore, the view favouring severability of an incompatible jurisdictional reservation without affecting the entire acceptance has the largest doctrinal and practical support, which perhaps evidences its fairness.

The severability of incompatible jurisdictional reservations is based on the same conceptual and jurisprudential basis in different tribunals. Although in *Chrysostomos* there was a clear intention in the respondent's reservation to exclude certain issues from the European Commission's jurisdiction, the Commission concluded that 'the main intention of a State must prevail'.[64] In *Loizodou*, the European Court applied the same approach by referring to the 'basic—albeit qualified—intention' of the respondent to accept the jurisdiction and to the respondent's 'awareness of the legal position' concerning the legal consequences of impermissible reservations, including their severance.[65] This reasoning follows the approach of Judge Klaestad in *Interhandel*. There seems thus to be no legal obstacle preventing the International Court to safeguard the provisions of its Statute in a similar way, by construing the reserving State's intention as not hindering it in performing this task.

Along with the conflict of a declarant State's intention with a court's constituent instrument, it is interesting to ask what could happen if such intention conflicts with some fundamental principles of international law. The question is not only about hypothetical cases of explicit normative conflict between a State's intention and a fundamental rule of international law, but more about the interpretation of such an intention when it does not explicitly conflict with such a rule. In *Fisheries Jurisdiction*, Judge Weeramantry referred to 'a telling example of the exclusion of commercial disputes under a hypothetical reservation. Could any application concerning the commercial exploitation of children be excluded under the reservation, on the argument that this constituted "a commercial issue"?'[66] Similarly, Judge Vereshchetin referred to situations 'when the actions whose examination by the Court a State seeks to avoid, by making a reservation, are clearly contrary to the Charter of the United Nations, the Statute of the Court or to *erga omnes* obligations under international law'. In this context, Judge Vereshchetin considered that the Court cannot consider the will and intention of a State as conclusive: 'The Court would be failing in its duties of an "organ and guardian" of international law should it accord to a document the legal effect sought by the State from which it emanates, without having regard to the compatibility of the said document with the basic requirements of

---

[63] *Rawle Kennedy v Trinidad and Tobago*, Communication No. 845/1999, CCPR/C/67/D/845/1999 (31 December 1999).

[64] *Chrysostomos*, 12 *HRLJ* (1991), 123, para. 46.

[65] *Loizodou*, para. 95, Series A, 310, 31–32.

[66] Dissenting Opinion of Judge Weeramantry, *ICJ Reports*, 1998, para. 27.

international law.'[67] The Canadian reservation in *Fisheries Jurisdiction* was related to the conservation or management of fishing resources and as it was not contrary to the Statute the Court gave effect to it. But, as Judge Vereshchetin remarked:

This does not mean, however, that from the position of international law we can characterize as conservation and management, for example, measures for the protection of straddling fish stocks taken by one State in the territorial waters of a neighbouring State without the consent of the latter. International law recognizes the importance and encourages the development of transborder co-operation for the protection of natural resources, including straddling fish stocks, but it does not admit the possibility of providing this protection by way of violation of fundamental principles of international law. The terms of art for the Court are the terms used in the context of international law, even though they may have a somewhat different meaning in other disciplines.[68]

Similarly, Judge Bedjaoui stated that the faculty of States to include reservations in their declarations of acceptance of the Court's jurisdiction must be exercised in compliance with the Statute and Rules of the Court, the Charter of the United Nations and, more generally, with international public order as part of general international law. This is so because in its conduct the State has to comply with the requirements of the system.[69] Consequently, the reservations that offend the system of adjudication or those that contradict international public order must be viewed as null and void.[70]

Judge Bedjaoui considered several options of the legal consequences of invalid jurisdictional reservations. Having noted the option of entire

---

[67] Dissenting Opinion of Judge Vereshchetin, *ICJ Reports*, 1998, para. 11.

[68] Id., para. 13.　　　　　[69] Dissenting Opinion of Judge Bedjaoui, para. 43.

[70] Id., para. 44, in which Judge Bedjaoui observed as follows:

'– je ne vois pas pourquoi la Cour devrait hésiter à écarter, ou à déclarer irrecevable, ou non opposable, ou même invalide ou nulle, une réserve qui aurait pour objet ou pour effet d'annihiler ou de dénaturer une ou plusieurs dispositions statutaires ou réglementaires qui régissent le procès international et d'établir une sorte de procédure judiciaire *ad hoc* à la convenance et au profit du seul auteur de ladite réserve;

– je ne vois pas pourquoi la Cour devrait hésiter à déclarer nulle et invalide *ab initio* toute réserve qui l'empêcherait de connaître d'un génocide, de l'esclavage, de la piraterie, ou de tout crime international;

– je ne vois pas pourquoi la Cour se permettrait d'accueillir toute réserve dite «automatique», dont la formulation serait telle que l'Etat qui l'a émise serait le seul à pouvoir décider qu'une conduite qu'il a tenue, ou qu'un acte qu'il a commis, entre ou non dans le cadre de sa réserve, privant ainsi la Cour de «la compétence de sa compétence» telle que prévue par l'article 36, paragraphe 6, de son Statut;

– je ne vois pas pourquoi la Cour accepterait de prendre en compte une réserve qui, sous couleur d'établir des limites spécifiques à la compétence de la Cour, apparaîtrait en fin de compte comme incompatible avec le respect de l'intégrité de la déclaration dans son ensemble, car si le droit international pose incontestablement la liberté du consentement et si la déclaration pose la reconnaissance de la compétence de la Cour, il faut aussi que la réserve faite dans ce cadre respecte la cohérence et l'intégrité du «système» de la clause facultative.'

invalidity, Judge Bedjaoui considered it far from being certain that the nullity of a reservation to the declaration entails the nullity of the entire act of declaration, above all because good sense would not support this option. The reservation limits the field of the consent given in the declaration. The improperly limited field does not become a non-existent field.[71] Judge Bedjaoui's approach, apart from being based on sound logical foundations, is in line with the approach that has commanded the largest doctrinal and practical support.

These positions, which are by no means in the inherent contradiction with the majority reasoning in *Fisheries Jurisdiction*, affirm also the limited role of the principle of consent depending on the systemic context within which the State expresses its will. By joining the system, or by inherently and regardless of consent being bound by certain public order norms, the State finds its faculty to issue consensual instruments limited. The principle of consent allows expressing the will on any relevant issue within the framework of the system, but not if that will contradicts the system itself.

In its judgment the Court avoided this issue and left open the question what would be the result if a jurisdictional reservation were detrimental to a fundamental principle of international law or to a peremptory norm which has a superior force with regard to a conflicting transaction. Perhaps it could be suggested that if the reservation entails a result which goes far beyond its textual meaning by endangering the proper applicability of fundamental international rules or *jus cogens*, the intention of a State must be interpreted in a way not conflicting with these superior norms. Thus, if the Court were faced with the attempt to exclude from its jurisdiction the issue of commercial exploitation of children under the rubric of a 'commercial transaction', it could simply clarify whether the international law in force regards this issue as commercial or as one involving fundamental human rights. To decide on an issue in accordance with international law is to take into account that aspect of the question with which international law is primarily concerned. The result must be similar if a reservation on fisheries management or conservation is used to exempt from the Court's scrutiny a situation where a State, under the pretext of enforcement of fisheries regulations, invades the maritime space of another State which it thinks is in breach of these regulations, and performs a variety of actions including the sinking of the merchant fleet and a blockade of ports, with a view to enforcing fisheries regulations. Here, the dispute would be about the use of force rather than fisheries regulations. As the proper enforcement of peremptory norms is a matter of interest to the international community as a whole, the Court

---

[71] Dissenting Opinion, paras 60–61, also supporting this argument by pointing to the acceptance of severability within the ECHR system and international commercial arbitration.

would be both warranted and required to adopt methods of interpretation and application of a jurisdictional instrument which support such enforcement rather than obstructing it.

To conclude, the intention of a State expressed in a jurisdictional instrument, though important and necessary, cannot be given effect if it conflicts with a rule, principle or instrument superior to that intention. The consent of States in accepting judicial jurisdiction is the consent to accede to the system of jurisdiction and thus comply with the requirements of that system. In the final analysis, the principle of consent, if properly interpreted, can accommodate the argument of normative hierarchy. The primacy of the Charter or Statute and their invalidating effect on jurisdictional reservations is as much the issue of the interpretation of the consent of the reserving State as it is the issue of normative hierarchy. This is the case of hierarchy due to the prior or pre-existing consent of the reserving States to the system that qualifies the scope of their acts performed within or in relation to that system.[72] The public order primacy over jurisdictional reservations is also based on the self-explanatory peremptory force of the relevant norms, the non-consensual hierarchy derived from public order norms.

5. *JUS COGENS* AND JURISDICTION OF THE INTERNATIONAL COURT UNDER 'TREATIES OR CONVENTIONS IN FORCE' (ARTICLE 36(I) OF THE STATUTE)

5.1. *Reservations to Article IX of the Genocide Convention*

Humanitarian conventions embodying *jus cogens* give the International Court jurisdiction over their interpretation, application or fulfilment. Among them are the Convention against Torture (1984), the Genocide Convention (1948) and the Convention on the Elimination of All Forms of Racial Discrimination (1966). Article IX of the Genocide Convention has received most attention in practice.

Article IX has been subject to reservations.[73] Those reservations have been objected to[74] and this factor is of some evidentiary value in assessing the legal

---

[72] As Judge Bedjaoui commented with regard to this specific category, every person is free to enter the system, but once one consents to enter, one should abide by the rules of the game. This is also the consequence of joining the system of the Court's jurisdiction, Dissenting Opinion, *Fisheries Jurisdiction*, paras 44–45.

[73] By Algeria, Bahrain, Bangladesh, China, India, Malaysia, Morocco, Singapore, the United States, Venezuela, Vietnam and Yemen, *Multilateral Treaties Deposited with the Secretary-General. Status as at 31 December 1999*, vol. I, 92 ff.

[74] By Ecuador, Mexico, Netherlands, Norway, the United Kingdom, *Multilateral Treaties Deposited with the Secretary-General. Status as at 31 December 1999*, vol. I, 95 ff.

consequences of these reservations, as is the fact that several States have withdrawn their reservations to Article IX.[75]

In practice the permissibility of reservations to Article IX has mostly been denied. The governments of Ecuador, Guatemala, Vietnam and Cambodia considered that the reservations made by the USSR, Ukrainian SSR, Byelorussian SSR, Bulgaria, Romania and Czechoslovakia, which included reservations to Article IX, did not apply to them.[76] These States disagreed with those reservations not at the time of signature or accession, but subsequently, after they were contacted by the UN Secretary-General. The position of Guatemala and France was that even from the fact of their initial silence it cannot be inferred that they accepted those reservations.[77] The UK and Australia also objected to these reservations, noting that 'the reservation must either be abandoned or the State making the reservation must remain outside the Convention'.[78] France, on the other hand, considered that reservations with which it did not agree were not applicable in relation to it, but made no reference to the invalidity of the entire acceptance.[79]

The Philippines considered that the objection to its reservations by certain States did not affect the validity of the entire acceptance of the Convention by the Philippines and that it was ready to bring a contentious case concerning this issue before the International Court under Article IX.[80]

The 1951 Opinion is silent on whether the reservations to Article IX are permissible. Although the whole Opinion is about the law of reservations and Article IX was arguably relevant in the process of its request, it does not specifically address Article IX. Pleadings hint that such reservations are impermissible. The UK considered that the jurisdictional obligation in Article IX is 'one of the prime guarantees of the due fulfilment of the basic obligation to prevent and punish the crime of genocide' and was so regarded in the process of preparation and adoption of the Convention.[81] 'Conventions of this kind are illusory unless there is some machinery as that of appeal to the International Court of Justice.'[82] The Court did not contradict that view, nor has anyone else during the proceedings.

---

[75] Soviet Union, Byelorussian SSR, Ukrainian SSR, Bulgaria, Hungary, Mongolia, Poland, Romania, *Multilateral Treaties Deposited with the Secretary-General. Status as at 31 December 1999*, vol. I, 99.

[76] Written Statement of the United Nations, *ICJ Pleadings*, 104–105, 108–109.

[77] Id., 105, 109. But subsequently Guatemala seems to have changed its approach by stating that reservations may affect the application of the clauses concerned, id., 105–106.

[78] Id., 106–107.   [79] Id., 109.   [80] Id., 110.

[81] Oral Statement by Sir Hartley Shawcross, *ICJ Pleadings*, 380.

[82] Id. Reservation to this article raises serious doubts as to the value of signature, ratification or accession. As Special Rapporteur Pellet accepts, 'it is self-evident that, if the commitment to obligatory dispute settlement is precisely the purpose of the treaty, a reservation excluding such settlement would, of course, be contrary to the object and purpose of the treaty', Pellet, Tenth Report on Reservations to Treaties, Addendum 1, A/CN.4/558/Add.1, 18.

The UK has consistently maintained the view that reservations to Article IX are impermissible. It has objected to reservations to Article IX by Rwanda, Vietnam, Yemen, Singapore, Malaysia and the US, having 'consistently stated that they are unable to accept the reservations in respect to Article IX . . . [because] this is not the kind of reservation which intending parties to the Convention have the right to make.'[83] These statements did not raise the issue of invalidity of the entire acceptance.

Thus, State practice is diverse and offers no uniform guidance for the consequences of incompatible reservations to Article IX. But it also by no means, not even on a single occasion, affirms that reservations to Article IX are permitted.

The object and purpose of the Genocide Convention, the nature of the obligations contained in it (both under the Convention itself and general international law) plays an important role in determining the fate of incompatible reservations to the Convention. The Convention is designed to protect the community interest as distinct from individual State interests and hence embodies *jus cogens*. The means of enforcement under the Convention, including the jurisdictional clause, are designed to serve that community interest and hence form part of international public order.

Certain factors justify the assumption that judicial settlement is not just an element of the object and purpose of the Genocide Convention, but indeed constitutes the very essence of that object and purpose. Unlike certain other treaties, judicial settlement is the only method of dispute settlement mentioned in the Convention.[84] This implies that judicial settlement is the primary method of dispute settlement connected with the interpretation and application of the Genocide Convention.

In addition, the object and purpose of a treaty is a dynamic concept varying according to the development of the legal environment in which a treaty operates. The Court affirmed that due to their character, the obligations under the Genocide Convention are binding on States 'even without any conventional obligation'.[85] Later, in *Application of the Genocide Convention*, the Court affirmed that the rights and obligations enshrined in the Convention are rights and obligations *erga omnes*.[86] The rules prohibiting genocide

---

[83] The UK statements of 21 November 1975, 26 August 1983, 30 December 1987, 22 December 1989 and 20 March 1996 are available at untreaty.un.org.

[84] The Convention against Torture (1984) establishes the Committee against Torture and foresees also the possibility of arbitration for the purposes of interpretation and application of that Convention (Article 30). Article 30(2) expressly empowers States-parties to make a reservation excluding the jurisdiction of the Court. The Convention on Elimination of All Forms of Racial Discrimination (1966) establishes also the treaty-based Committee entrusted with the task to enforce that Convention.

[85] *Reservations to the Genocide Convention*, Advisory Opinion, *ICJ Reports*, 1951, 23.

[86] *Application of the Genocide Convention*, Preliminary Objections, *ICJ Reports*, 1996, 616.

are clearly part of customary law. Also some rules about cooperation between States exist and bind States independently of the Convention.[87]

This circumstance helps to clarify the issue as to what must be regarded as the Convention's object and purpose. That object and purpose is supposed to be *the object and purpose of the Genocide Convention as such, as a treaty*. These *treaty-specific rights and obligations* constitute *inter alia* the essence of a given treaty, its object and purpose. Article IX of the Genocide Convention providing for the Court's jurisdiction belongs to such a category and no reservation may be entered to it.

To determine the consequences of reservations to Article IX, the Vienna Convention regime which is relevant to the process of reservation-acceptance/objection is not helpful as it applies only to compatible reservations in terms of Article 19 of the Vienna Convention and also only on the State-to-State decentralized plane. This was acknowledged by the ILC at the final stage of its work on the law of treaties:

The problem concerns only the cases where the treaties are silent in regard to reservations, and here the Commission was agreed that the Court's principle of 'compatibility with the object and purpose of the treaty' is one suitable for adoption as a general criterion of the legitimacy of reservations to multilateral treaties and to objections to them. The difficulty lies in the process by which that principle has to be applied, and especially where there is no tribunal or other organ invested with standing competence to interpret the treaty.[88]

The Commission thus acknowledged that if there is a tribunal with standing competence to interpret the treaty, it has the power to clarify the effect of reservations. Neither the ILC nor the Vienna Conference could finally settle this issue: to lay down standards on which supervisory bodies must act is to prejudge their constituent instruments.

The Court explained that the process of acceptance/objections cannot be decisive in clarifying the fate of incompatible reservations and the accepting/objecting States are not the ultimate judges of this issue:

it may be that certain parties who consider that the assent given by other parties to a reservation is incompatible with the purpose of the Convention, will decide to adopt a position on the jurisdictional plane in respect of this divergence and to settle the dispute which thus arises either by special agreement or by the procedure laid down in Article IX of the Convention.[89]

The Court makes it clear that the reactions to an incompatible reservation at a decentralized level do not prejudge the issue of permissibility of that

---

[87] Such as the duties with regard to jurisdiction and extradition under Articles VI–VII; see further Chapter 9.

[88] *Yearbook of the International Law Commission*, 1966, vol. II, 205.

[89] *ICJ Reports*, 1951, 27.

reservation and, whatever the States' reactions, such a reservation may still be declared incompatible by a judicial organ.

This reinforces the Court's power to deal with incompatible reservations under Article IX. The Court is the guardian of the integrity of public order obligations assumed by States under the Genocide Convention. When an instrument embodying public order obligations entrusts the Court with the mission to interpret, apply and ensure the fulfilment of that instrument, the Court has to find an appropriate balance between the two intentions concerning its jurisdiction: of the instrument conferring it and of a State denying it contrary to the object and purpose if not the actual provisions of the instrument. To safeguard the object and purpose of the Convention, the Court has to disregard the will of an individual State and sever the reservation purporting to preclude the exercise of jurisdiction under Article IX. Alternatively, the Court may sever such reservations by referring to the basic or main intention of a State-party, as evidenced by its consent to be bound by the Convention, which must prevail over the intention underlying a reservation.[90] Schabas, among others by reference to the ECHR practice, states that the opposition to Article IX reservations is growing and States making such reservations can be parties to the Convention without their reservation being valid. Schabas therefore disagrees with the Court's approach in *Legality of the Use of Force*.[91]

In *Legality of the Use of Force* (*Yugoslavia v United States*) the applicant invoked the Genocide Convention as the jurisdictional basis for adjudication. The respondent had made a reservation to Article IX of the Convention, consisting of a condition that the consent of the United States is necessary in each concrete case to be submitted to the Court's jurisdiction. During the proceedings, the respondent made an explicit statement that it 'has not given the specific consent [to the Court's jurisdiction, as required by its reservation and] ... will not do so'.[92] The Court acted upon this statement and considered itself without jurisdiction.

The applicant did not challenge the reservation of the respondent as contrary to the object and purpose of the Convention. The Court counted this as a relevant factor and emphasized that

Whereas Yugoslavia disputed the United States interpretation of the Genocide Convention, but submitted no argument concerning the United States reservation to Article IX of the Convention; Whereas the Genocide Convention does not prohibit reservations; whereas Yugoslavia did not object to the United States reservation to Article IX; and whereas the said reservation had the effect of excluding that Article

---

[90] As practised by the organs of the European Convention, above, note 38.
[91] Schabas, *Genocide in International Law* (2000), 536–538.
[92] *Legality of the Use of Force*, Order (*Yugoslavia v US*), paras 22–23, 38 ILM (1999), 1194.

from the provisions of the Convention in force between the Parties; Whereas in consequence Article IX of the Genocide Convention cannot found the jurisdiction of the Court to entertain a dispute between Yugoslavia and United States,[93]

the request was to be dismissed. But the Court's Order provides at least some evidence that the reservations to the Court's jurisdiction under Article IX of the Genocide Convention do not enjoy absolute validity and can be challenged, even if its deference to the parties' attitudes could be open to criticism.

In *DRC–Rwanda*, the DRC challenged Rwanda's reservation to Article IX as contrary to the Convention's object and purpose, submitting that to give effect to it is to provide Rwanda with complete immunity and exempt it from all supervision mechanisms under the Convention.[94] The Court, however, accepted Rwanda's claim that despite the substantive *jus cogens* nature of the Convention obligations, jurisdiction remains consensual, and upheld Rwanda's reservation. The Court considered Rwanda's reservation compatible because the Congo had not objected to it and because the jurisdiction under Article IX is not part of the object and purpose of the Convention.[95] These findings contradict State practice on Article IX reservations, which never justified such reservations, and the ILC attitude, which clarified that individual State reactions are not crucial for deciding on a reservation's compatibility.

It is clear that Rwanda denied jurisdiction which the Court duly noted. But the legality of such denial is a separate issue. The Court's treatment of Rwanda's attitude as decisive is in fact the recognition of the defendant's power of auto-interpretation of its jurisdictional obligations on the basis of the reservation. The Court did not properly examine whether Rwanda's reservation was contrary to the object and purpose of the Convention, having not opposed anything to the DRC's argument that upholding that reservation undermines that object and purpose through releasing Rwanda from any kind of supervision and in effect providing it with impunity. It just asserted that Rwanda's reservation was not contrary to the object and purpose as it related only to jurisdiction and not substantive obligations.[96] This approach undermines the role of Article IX within the Convention as confirmed at earlier stages. It furthermore fails to comprehend the normative reality that reservations to Article IX are not just consensual declarations, but consensual declarations made within, and in relation to, the system. The respondent's consent must be viewed as consent to the entire system that the Genocide Convention establishes in the community interest.

---

[93] Id., paras 23–25. [94] Order, paras 22, 25.
[95] Order, paras 36, 40, 71–72. [96] Order, para. 72.

The Court's approach in *DRC–Rwanda* was also specific in that the applicant had explicitly challenged the reservation. The Court treated the consensual principle as the only relevant principle and applied it in a blanket way to the exclusion of solutions under the law of treaties and in terms of the nature of the Genocide Convention. The Court's approach was incorrect in principle: this was not the case where there is no acceptance of jurisdiction, but a case where jurisdiction is accepted as a matter of a treaty and the legality of a reservation denying jurisdiction had to be judged in terms of the character of the Genocide Convention as a public order instrument. The consensual principle allegedly justifying reservations was to be balanced against other relevant factors that may have rendered it incompatible. The Court's approach precluded the proper exercise of jurisdiction established in the interest of the international community as a whole.

With its decisions on *Kosovo* and *DRC–Rwanda* the Court has given rise to a troubling trend ignoring the effects of peremptory norms embodied in a treaty and undermining the efficiency of the Genocide Convention. There was no practical need to initiate this troubling trend in *Kosovo* as the severance of the US reservation would have led to consideration of the merits which would have clarified that the US actions did not amount to genocide. That happening, in *DRC–Rwanda* the Court would have been able to tackle a situation coming closer to the ambit of the Convention. But with the Court's trend, it is likely to avoid dealing with even real situations of genocide which would question that institution's utility and credibility. A straightforward abandonment of the Court's deference to reservations to Article IX is not very likely. But there could be some exit strategies for the sake of the Court's own prestige and reputation. The Court could in the future adopt a differentiated approach and, in cases involving plausible accusations of genocide, distinguish the decisions on *Kosovo* and *DRC–Rwanda* on the basis that the more credible the accusations of genocide the more likely the Court's disregard of reservations to Article IX.

5.2. Jurisdiction with regard to the conflict of treaties with jus cogens *under Article 66 of the 1969 Vienna Convention*

5.2.1. The nature and scope of judicial jurisdiction under the Vienna Convention

Article 66(a) of the Vienna Convention on the Law of Treaties empowers 'Any of the parties to a dispute concerning the application or interpretation of Articles 53 and 64' to bring disputes concerning the conflict of treaties with *jus cogens* before the International Court. This provision establishes jurisdiction necessary for the effective operation of Articles 53 and 64. That only Articles 53 and 64 are covered by Article 66 reflects the community interest element inherent in peremptory norms.[97]

Allegedly jurisdictional relations under Article 66 of the Vienna Convention are bilateral in character. It is argued that under the Vienna Convention a conflict of a treaty with *jus cogens* 'should be settled exclusively between the parties to the treaty, no third State being allowed to invoke the nullity if none of the States-parties has come up with this claim'.[98] But the analysis of the text confirms the opposite.

Article 65 of the Vienna Convention refers to a 'party', defined under Article 2.1(g) as 'a State which has consented to be bound by the treaty and for which the treaty is in force'. It is also true that the International Court's jurisdiction under Article 66 may only be established 'if, under Article 65, no solution has been reached'. It has therefore been argued that *ratione personae* the parties to a dispute under Article 66 'are only the parties to the contested treaty' and that 'no State which is not a party to that treaty can invoke the machinery of Article 66'.[99]

Such an assumption is erroneous. The only thing Article 66 requires is that an attempt at a solution should have taken place before the Court is seised. It contains a limitation *ratione materiae* concerning the characteristics of the dispute and not *ratione personae* concerning the identity of parties to a dispute. Article 66 mentions 'parties to the dispute concerning the application or interpretation of Article 53 or 64',[100] and not parties to a dispute which, in the words of Rozakis, has 'already matured in the circumstances of application of Article 65, paragraphs 1 to 3'.[101] The requirement is that the dispute brought before the Court should already have matured in terms of Article 65 and not that the Court must necessarily be seised by a party to the dispute which has matured under Article 65. To assume the opposite is to rewrite Article 66 of the Vienna Convention.

It must be concluded that the faculty to seise the International Court under Article 66 of the Vienna Convention is not limited to the parties of the contested treaty, but extends to all parties to the Vienna Convention. As *jus*

---

[97] Rosenne, Bilateralism and the Community Interest in the Codified Law of Treaties, in Friedmann, W., Henkin, L., and Lyssitzin, O. (eds), *Transnational Law in a Changing Society: Essays in Honor of Philip C. Jessup* (1972), 221; Rosenne, *Developments in the Law of Treaties* (1989) 286, for State views supporting this approach.

[98] Tomuschat, Obligations Arising for States without or against Their Will, 241 *RdC* (1993), 363, referring to Article 65.

[99] Rozakis, *The Concept of* Jus Cogens *in the Law of Treaties* (1976), 170; Hannikainen, *Peremptory Norms in International Law* (1988), 272, 310.

[100] Note that several authors, while analysing Article 66(a) VCLT, just refer to the notion 'parties to a dispute' and do not attempt to limit this notion to the parties of the contested treaty; see Elias, Problems concerning the Validity of Treaties, 134 *RdC* (1974), 193; Sinclair, *Vienna Convention on the Law of Treaties* (1986), 232; Aust, *Modern Treaty Law and Practice* (2000), 259.

[101] Rozakis (1976), 170–171.

cogens safeguards the interests of the international community as a whole and not of particular States, it is quite conceivable that after the failure of parties to the contested treaty to reach a solution under Article 65, States other than those parties may seise the International Court under Article 66. Such an interpretation is required by the natural meaning of Articles 65–66 and the character of *jus cogens* which tolerates no bilateralist restrictions in terms of standing.

5.2.2. Reservations to Article 66

States-parties to the Vienna Convention have entered several reservations to Article 66, which purport to release the reserving States from jurisdictional obligations under that article.[102] These reservations have been objected to.[103] The reason for these objections is that the judicial settlement of disputes on Articles 53 and 64 cannot be separated from them.[104] Some States have withdrawn their reservations to Article 66.[105] The entire process is characterized by the conflict of legal attitudes and this demonstrates that the right to make a reservation to Article 66 is far from commonly established.

The relevant guidance is the compatibility of reservations to Article 66 with the object and purpose of the Vienna Convention. If reservations are compatible, then objections excluding the applicability of Article 66 successfully exclude the jurisdiction of the Court as between reserving and objecting States. If not, the existence of judicial jurisdiction is not prejudiced either by reservations or by objections. Such a view is consistent with Articles 19–21 of the Vienna Convention stating that only compatible reservations can be effective.

It is argued that since 'there is nothing inherent in *jus cogens* which requires that disputes relating to its application or interpretation should be submitted to impartial third-party determination',[106] reservations to Article 66 are not contrary to the Vienna Convention's object and purpose.[107] But it is also relevant that the treaty provides for compulsory jurisdiction linked to *jus cogens*. If one tries to identify the object and purpose of the Vienna Convention, one cannot avoid the conclusion that the dispute settlement system provided for under Part V is an element of that object and purpose.

---

[102] Algeria, China, Cuba, Guatemala, Soviet Union, Tunisia, *Multilateral Treaties Deposited with the Secretary-General. Status as at 31 December 1999*, vol. II, 266 ff.

[103] By Germany, Japan, the Netherlands, New Zealand, Sweden, the United Kingdom, the United States, *Multilateral Treaties Deposited with the Secretary-General. Status as at 31 December 1999*, vol. II, 270 ff.

[104] Verhoeven, *Jus Cogens* and Reservations or 'Counter-reservations' to the Jurisdiction of the International Court of Justice, in Wellens (ed.) *International Law: Theory and Practice: Essays in Honor of Eric Suy* (1998), 199–200.

[105] Bulgaria, Hungary, Mongolia, *Multilateral Treaties Deposited with the Secretary-General. Status as at 31 December 1999*, vol. II, 275.

[106] Verhoeven (1998), 202.   [107] Verhoeven, 202–203.

This is dictated by the circumstance that almost all substantive rules of the Vienna Convention are part of customary law and operate independently of it. To exclude the operation of the dispute settlement provisions is to deprive the Vienna Convention in a significant respect of its *raison d'être*.

If a treaty purports to establish judicial safeguards related to the rules forming part of international public order, as the Vienna Convention does through Article 66, this must be considered at least as one of the essential purposes of that treaty. There is thus no obstacle to the competence of the International Court to examine the reservations to Article 66 and sever them. Verhoeven goes too far in asserting that 'the dispute concerning the validity of a reservation does not in principle fall under the jurisdiction of the ICJ' because the regime of validity of reservations is governed by the provisions of the Vienna Convention (Articles 19–23) differently from the provisions governing the issues of *jus cogens* (Article 53).[108] This distinction seems to be mechanistic and oversimplified. While it is true that Article 66 confers on the Court jurisdiction concerning Article 53 and 64 and not Articles 19–23, this does not prevent the Court from exercising fully its jurisdiction concerning the interpretation and application of Article 66. This provision, together with the power to determine its own jurisdiction provided for by Article 36(6) of the Statute, enables the Court to judge the legal consequences of reservations purporting to limit its jurisdiction.

---

[108] Verhoeven, 206.

16

Jus Cogens and the Standing to Bring Judicial Claims

Normally, a State instituting proceedings for the protection of an individual must be his or her State of nationality.[1] This limitation follows from the concept of diplomatic protection[2] applicable to obligations which give rise to simple bilateral inter-State relations, not necessarily to disputes concerning peremptory norms. It has been clarified above that once a peremptory norm is breached, the legal consequences of the breach are invocable *erga omnes*, in line with the International Court's *Barcelona Traction* dictum.[3] This conceptual link confirms that in case of breaches of *jus cogens*, the requirements of direct injury and prejudice should no longer apply and States should be able to institute proceedings before the International Court whether or not the breaches involved directly relate to their interests. *Barcelona Traction*, having examined the nature of *erga omnes* obligations, suggests that 'obligations the performance of which is subject to diplomatic protection are not of the same category' as *erga omnes* obligations.[4] The violation of an *erga omnes* obligation may justify claims without the nationality link. This issue forms a part of the broader problem of the legal interest of an applicant State, in particular the admissibility of *actio popularis*.

But in doctrine and practice the link between the *erga omnes* nature of an obligation and the entitlement of individual States to act in protection of that obligation without an individual injury is not always considered to be that direct. A strange distrust of the concept of *actio popularis* ensues in practice. Although there exists no rule or principle precluding *actio popularis*, States tend to avoid that concept when they seise the International Court. In *Nuclear Tests* and *East Timor*, the applicants referred to their action in the public interest only as one of the causes of action.[5] Such hesitation is perhaps due to *South-West Africa*, where the Court refused the applicants the right to sue without an individual prejudice, claiming that international law admits

---

[1] *Nottebohm* (Second Phase), *ICJ Reports*, 1955, 22 ff.

[2] *First Report on Diplomatic Protection* by Special Rapporteur Dugard, in particular, the presented draft Articles 1 and 3, A/CN.4/506, 11, 22.

[3] cf above, Chapter 8.

[4] *Barcelona Traction* (Second Phase), *ICJ Reports*, 1970, 32–33.

[5] *Nuclear Tests* (*Australia v France*), *ICJ Pleadings*, vol. 1, 326–330; id., (*New Zealand v France*), *ICJ Pleadings*, vol. 2, 207–208. Australia clearly based its legal interests on the alleged violation of one of its subjective rights, while New Zealand did not refer to individual interest and injury, Tanzi (1987), 15. In *East Timor*, *ICJ Reports*, 1995, 94, Portugal's principal submission referred to its status as Administering Power.

no *actio popularis*.[6] The Court considered that international obligations of a humanitarian character enshrined in the mandate of South Africa over South-West Africa did not confer any legal interest on the applicants. In order to be qualified to bring a case before the Court, a State must demonstrate that a right to do so is 'clearly vested in those who claim them, by some text or instrument or rule of law'.[7] The Court even construed an inherent limitation on its jurisdiction under the Optional Clause by requiring that despite the comprehensive nature of recognition of the Court's jurisdiction by declarations under Article 36 of the Statute, the applicant must demonstrate its individual interest in the subject-matter of a given dispute.[8]

That judgment has been widely disapproved both in doctrine and in practice.[9] It surprised world opinion and for a time undermined Third World confidence in the Court.[10] The opinions of dissenting judges also suggest that the Court's decision was 'completely unfounded in law'.[11]

In *South-West Africa*, the Court based its decision not to admit *actio popularis* mainly on the idea that substantive international law does not confer on a State a legal right to sue in the absence of a direct legal interest.[12] However, as Judge Koretsky remarked, 'the question is how to define a notion of "interest".'[13] This was not an issue the Court was clear about in 1966.

The judges supporting this decision had no uniform or consolidated view as to why a suit in the public interest was inadmissible in that case. Discussion of this issue in individual opinions of the 1962 judgment makes this clear. Judge Morelli referred to the non-existence of the dispute; he considered that applicants were not guided by their individual interest and thus no dispute existed.[14] Judge Winiarski attempted to deduce the intention of the drafters of the Mandate and concluded that no evidence of existence of an *actio popularis* in international law was available;[15] if the framers were willing to admit *actio popularis*, 'they would not have failed to say so explicitly'.[16] Judges Spender and Fitzmaurice were ready to recognize that 'States, parties to a treaty or convention, or who have third-State rights under it, may in certain types of cases be held to have a legal interest in its due observance, even though the alleged breach of it has not, or not yet, affected

---

[6] *ICJ Reports*, 1966, 47.   [7] Id., 32.   [8] Id., para. 73 [50, para. 97].

[9] Dugard, *The South-West Africa/Namibia Dispute* (1973), 333 ff.; Dugard, 1966 and All That. The South West Africa Judgment Revisited in the East Timor Case, 8 *African Journal of International and Comparative Law* (1996), 549–551.

[10] Elias, Problems concerning the Validity of Treaties, 134 *RdC* (1971), 398.

[11] See, in particular, the Dissenting Opinions of Judges Koretsky, *ICJ Reports*, 1966, 239 ff., Tanaka, id., 250 ff., Jessup, id., 325 ff.

[12] *ICJ Reports*, 1966, 36, para. 57.

[13] Dissenting Opinion, *ICJ Reports*, 1966, 242.

[14] Dissenting Opinion, *ICJ Reports*, 1962, 571.

[15] Dissenting Opinion, *ICJ Reports*, 1962, 452.

[16] Dissenting Opinion, *ICJ Reports*, 1962, 453.

them directly'.[17] But they considered that the Mandate was not a treaty capable of establishing jurisdiction in terms of Article 36 of the Court's Statute.

The attempt to negate *actio popularis* was made in the context of the interpretation of jurisdictional clauses. Judges Spender and Fitzmaurice seem to have admitted that the textual interpretation of Article 7 of the Mandate would not exclude suing in the general interest without a specific material prejudice. However, they considered that literal interpretation was not a sufficient method of determining this and the reference to *travaux préparatoires* was 'justified'.[18] But they failed to demonstrate why this was 'justified', particularly whether the text of the clause led to an unambiguous, obscure or absurd result. Judge Winiarski referred to a principle 'that every conventional provision must be interpreted on the basis of general international law'. Thus, a jurisdictional clause, whatever its text, may not be deemed to confer upon a State a right of action which it would not possess under general international law, ie in the absence of that jurisdictional clause.[19] But then, the judge did not explain why, absent the overriding *jus cogens*, a treaty clause cannot be a *lex specialis*.

The choice of a suitable method of interpretation must be made not by reference to the possible outcome as compared with the possible outcomes of other interpretative methods, but by reference to the primacy of certain interpretative methods over others, irrespective of the outcome. That the textual method was a primary one cannot be questioned, and the judges were not justified in assuming that the primacy of the text may so easily be overridden.

Article 7 of the Mandate conferred on the Court jurisdiction concerning 'any dispute whatever between the Mandatory and another Member of the League of Nations relating to the interpretation or the application of the provisions of the Mandate'. The Court in its 1962 decision considered that jurisdiction under Article 7 extends to all provisions of the Mandate whether they are concerned with obligations of the Mandatory towards inhabitants of the territory or towards other Member States. It explicitly referred to 'the manifest scope and purport of the provisions of this article' as evidencing the existence of a legal right or interest of individual States in the observance by the mandatory of its obligations toward the inhabitants of the mandated territory.[20]

Article 7 of the Mandate satisfied the requirement laid down in the 1966 judgment, namely, that a legal interest to sue must be 'clearly vested in those who claim them, by some text or instrument or rule of law'.[21] Articles 2, 3 and

---

[17] Joint Dissenting Opinion, *ICJ Reports*, 1962, 548.
[18] Joint Dissenting Opinion, *ICJ Reports*, 1962, 550, 554.
[19] Dissenting Opinion, *ICJ Reports*, 1962, 455.
[20] *ICJ Reports*, 1962, 343.   [21] Id., 32.

4 of the Mandate stipulated obligations of the Mandatory based on interests other than what the Court called 'special interests'. The acceptance of jurisdiction under Article 7 extended to those provisions as well. On the face of this fact, the assertion of the Court that individual States could exercise their legal interest concerning these obligations 'only through the appropriate League organs, and not individually',[22] is also flawed. If this were so, no need for a separate jurisdictional clause in Article 7 would arise.

The Court devoted an extensive analysis to the question whether a jurisdictional clause is in position to confer substantive rights on States and answered this question in the negative.[23] However, the Court ignored the fact that the obligations undertaken in the Mandate were assumed towards the other Members of the League and this very fact, in conjunction with Article 7, gave them the respective procedural capacity.

Article 7 of the Mandate was clearly aimed at opening the channel of accountability of the Mandatory not only towards the organs of the League, but also towards individual States. Whether or not most of the substantive provisions of the Mandate embodied the rights and interests of other individual States, the latter were clearly vested with a legal interest in safeguarding observance of all provisions of the Mandate. The Court was clear on this in the 1962 judgment:

The manifest scope and purport of the provisions of this Article [7] indicate that the Members of the League were understood to have a legal right or interest in the observance by the Mandatory of its obligations both towards inhabitants of the mandated Territory, and towards the League of Nations and its Members.[24]

The concern of Judge Morelli[25] and of the Court in the 1966 judgment was that a jurisdictional provision in itself cannot confer a legal interest on a State, unless it would have such interest on the basis of any other legal rule. This assertion is flawed in face of the clear text of the Mandate and its underlying intention. But in any event there is no rule or principle of international law dictating particular methods or forms of how a legal interest should be conferred on a State; this may take place through any means that States decide. Thus the Court, by declining to adjudicate in 1966, has unjustifiably substituted the intention underlying Article 7 of the Mandate by its own understanding of that Article. By doing so the Court—although warning throughout its judgment that its task was to adjudicate and not to legislate—attempted to amend Article 7 without any power to do so. As Judge Tanaka emphasized, Article 7 permitted League members to sue in the general interest.[26] And Judge Koretsky remarked that the wording of

---

[22] *ICJ Reports*, 1966, 35.   [23] *ICJ Reports*, 1966, 39–42.
[24] *ICJ Reports*, 1962, 343.   [25] Separate Opinion, *ICJ Reports*, 1966, 61.
[26] Dissenting Opinion of Judge Tanaka, *ICJ Reports*, 1966, 258; see also Dissenting Opinion of Judge Koretsky, *ICJ Reports*, 1966, 248.

Article 7 'is quite clear to anyone who is not seeking to read into it what it does not contain'.[27]

In the second phase of *South-West Africa*, the Court overruled its holdings of 1962, over the strong dissent of certain judges that the Court's 1962 judgment was binding and final under Articles 59–60 of the Statute.[28] In effect the majority in 1962 has become a minority in 1966. Despite this, Judge Morelli argued that in the 1962 judgment the Court neither admitted the concept of *actio popularis* as a general proposition, nor applied it to that case.[29] It seems, however, that the Court, in its 1962 judgment, understood *actio popularis* as a natural consequence and continuation of the Mandate provisions; the nature and content of the obligations enshrined in the Mandate required the recognition of *locus standi* of the non-directly affected States. These obligations were laid down for the protection of the rights and interests of entities other than States. The combined effect of those substantive provisions and the jurisdictional clause was considered by the Court as a sufficient basis to admit *actio popularis*. The Court has done so without attempting to construe any inherent limitation on its competence. The 1966 judgment unjustifiably deviated from this reasoning, since there was no imperative legal requirement, following either from the Statute or text of the Mandate, dictating the necessity of construing an inherent limitation on its competence to adjudicate on the basis of Article 7 of the Mandate.

Whatever the substance of the 1966 decision, its authority and precedential value is doubtful due to the circumstances of its adoption. It is well known that President Sir Percy Spender forced Judge Zafrulla Khan to withdraw from the case, invoking the reason that the latter had made statements supporting South-West Africa in the UN organs. If this criterion applies fairly and equally, Sir Percy Spender would also have withdrawn, since he also had earlier made statements in the UN organs supporting South Africa. But he did not withdraw and continued to assume presidency. In case of not forcing Zafrulla Khan out, or in case of withdrawal of both judges, the 1966 decision not only could, but definitely would be different, since the judges supporting the claims of the applicants would constitute the majority. The 1966 decision is not something the actual majority of the Court would accept.

In its later practice the Court has reversed the approach of *South-West Africa*. In *Barcelona Traction*, the Court singled out obligations *erga omnes* assumed not merely towards the individual States but also towards the entire international community.[30] Most importantly, the Court observed with regard to *erga omnes* obligations that 'all States can be held to have a legal

---

[27] Dissenting Opinion, *ICJ Reports*, 1966, 248.
[28] Judge Koretsky, *ICJ Reports*, 1966, 240; Judge Tanaka, id., 261; Judge Jessup, id., 332 ff.
[29] Separate Opinion, *ICJ Reports*, 1966, 60.   [30] *ICJ Reports*, 1970, 32.

interest in their protection'.[31] This was a clear rejection of the approach taken in *South-West Africa* that an applicant State has to show its individual interest in every case. The Joint Dissenting Opinion of Judges Onyeama, Dillard, Jimenez de Arechaga and Waldock in *Nuclear Tests* touched on the issue of *actio popularis* with regard to vindication of the freedom of the high seas and massive atmospheric pollution, and considered that all States have a legal interest in the observance of the international obligations involved. They considered such a legal interest as 'implicit in the very concept of such freedoms'.[32] The majority did not contradict this proposition.

Despite this change in the Court's attitude, certain authors still consider that *Barcelona Traction* did not change anything from the procedural point of view:[33] they argue that *actio popularis* has not been introduced into international law, 'even for the protection of what are sometimes regarded as obligations *erga omnes*'.[34]

But these views fail to see that the difference between *South-West Africa* and *Barcelona Traction* relates to the procedural capacity of an applicant State. The difference between *erga omnes* obligations and other obligations in *Barcelona Traction* also related to the applicant's *locus standi*. The obligations involved in *Barcelona Traction* were not obligations *erga omnes* and therefore the Court considered it necessary that 'in order to bring a claim in respect of the breach of such an obligation, a State must first establish its right to do so'.[35] As Judge Higgins emphasized, the reference in *Barcelona Traction* to *erga omnes* obligations 'was directed to a very specific issue of jurisdictional *locus standi*',[36] which effectively means that the Court then accepted the concept of *actio popularis*. What the Court considered in *South-West Africa* to be applicable to all claims, it considered in *Barcelona Traction* to apply only to the claims which are not based on *erga omnes* obligations. Where the claims submitted by the applicant are based on *erga omnes* obligations, the Court would not require proof of any individual interest of an applicant State.[37] In both cases, the issue of *actio popularis* is treated on the basis of a

[31] Id., para. 33.　　　　[32] Joint Dissenting Opinion, *ICJ Reports*, 1974, 369–371.

[33] Lachs, The development and general trends of international law in our time, 169 *RdC* (1980), 341, suggesting that there is a long way between *Barcelona* and *actio popularis*; Chinkin, *Third Parties in International Law* (1995), 215; Gray, *Judicial Remedies in International Law* (1990), 214; Ragazzi, *The Concept of International Obligations* Erga Omnes (1998), 212; Frowein, Verpflichtungen *erga omnes* im Völkerrecht und Ihre Durchsetzung, *Voelkerrecht als Rechtsordnung—Internationale Gerichtsbarkeit—Menschenrechte: Festschrift Mosler* (1983), 259, arguing that this would be an interference with the legal relations of directly affected States.

[34] Rosenne, *The Law and Practice of the International Court* (1997), 1203. Rosenne considers necessary 'a major change of political sentiment' to allow *erga omnes* rights and obligations to be sustainable through action before the International Court, id., 568.

[35] *ICJ Reports*, 1970, para. 35, 32–33.　　　　[36] Separate Opinion, *Wall in OPT*, para. 37.

[37] Id.; Separate Opinion of Judge Ammoun, *ICJ Reports*, 1970, 326–327, explicitly affirming that if the claims in question were based on *erga omnes* obligations, the Court would not dismiss them. He referred to the special category of actions brought before the Court in defence of *jus cogens*, id., 325.

substantial and inviolable link between the substantive law and procedural capacity. If the Court said that it would admit claims arising out of *erga omnes* obligations even in the absence of an individual interest of the claimant, it is difficult to construe this attitude otherwise than as a rejection of its earlier attitude on the inadmissibility of *actio popularis*.

According to Judge Schwebel, the 1966 *South-West Africa* decision was 'rapidly and decisively displaced' in *Barcelona Traction*.[38] Mann and Schwelb submit that international law provides for *actio popularis* if the breach of *jus cogens* is alleged, it did so in 1966 too and that *Barcelona Traction* overruled *South-West Africa*.[39] No separate proof by an applicant State of its individual interest is thus necessary to make admissible the claims submitted to the Court. The requirements for the admissibility of *actio popularis* merely are that a rule on which a claim rests must be in force as between the applicant and respondent—in case of *jus cogens* this is not difficult to demonstrate—and there should be a proper jurisdictional link.

In 1969 Ago suggested that *Barcelona Traction* is 'still too isolated to permit the conclusion that a definite new trend in international judicial decisions has emerged'[40] (and thus implicitly acknowledged that *Barcelona Traction* overrules *South-West Africa*). But *Barcelona Traction* fits perfectly into the normative and jurisprudential framework admitting *actio popularis* wherever substantive obligations admit it. In *Barcelona Traction*, the Court integrated its approach into the framework provided by the earlier attitude of the 1962 *South-West Africa* decision. The position is rather that the 1966 *South-West Africa* decision, having no parallel in the jurisprudence, is itself 'too isolated' to evidence that States have no right to sue in the public interest.

Barcelona Traction clearly evidences change from *South-West Africa*, especially in emphasizing the link between substance and jurisdiction in terms of the capacity to sue. In *Barcelona Traction*, the Court decided that the question of *jus standi* of the applicant could not be disposed at the preliminary objections stage because the question was

one not simply of the admissibility of the claim, but of the substantive legal rights pertaining to the merits ... In short, the question of the *jus standi* of a government to protect the interests of shareholders as such, is itself merely a reflection, or consequence, of the antecedent question of what is the juridical situation in respect of shareholding interests, as recognised by international law.[41]

Thus, where a government seises a tribunal, it necessarily invokes rights it contends to be conferred upon it under substantive law:

---

[38] *ICJ Reports*, 1984, 169, 197.

[39] Mann, The Doctrine of *jus cogens* in international law, *Further Studies in International Law* (1977), 96; Schwelb, The *Actio Popularis* and International Law, 2 *Israel Yearbook of Human Rights* (1972), 46–55.

[40] 2 YbILC, 1976, part one, 29.   [41] *Barcelona Traction, ICJ Reports*, 1964, 55–56.

Hence the question whether international law does or does not confer those rights is of the essence of the matter. In short, a finding by the Court that the Applicant Government has no *jus standi*, would be tantamount to a finding that these rights did not exist, and that the claim was, for that reason, not well-founded in substance.[42]

This approach clearly evidences the direct link between substance and competence; the jurisdictional issue of standing depends on how the issue of legal interest is resolved in the substantive law.

In *Barcelona Traction*, the Court followed the earlier perspective of considering the issue of *jus standi* as one of extension of the substantive legal issues:

It is the existence or absence of a right, belonging to Belgium and recognised as such by international law, which is decisive for the problem of Belgium's capacity.[43]

Both stages of *Barcelona Traction* and *South-West Africa* of 1962 are unanimous in treating the link between the substantive law underlying the claims and *jus standi* with regard to those claims as inevitable and natural.

Judge Bustamante suggested that the 'existence of Belgium's *jus standi* in this case cannot be considered without prejudging the merits of the Application'.[44] Strangely enough, Judge Morelli also admitted that 'the question whether or not Belgium does or does not possess the capacity to bring the claim it has brought against Spain is nothing other than an aspect of the merits of the case. A judgment on this question would not be a judgment on the admissibility of the claim, it would on the contrary be a judgment on the merits . . . a judgment deciding the merits of the claim to the effect that Belgium's claim is without foundation.'[45] This acknowledges that the capacity to sue is itself governed by substantive law. Judge Morelli reached a different conclusion in 1966, having presented the question as one of the concept of dispute and interpretation of treaty jurisdictional clauses, thereby ignoring the link between substance and jurisdiction.

Even more clearly, Judge Armand-Ugon affirmed that

What is first necessary is to establish the rule governing the matter. Consideration should then be given to the question whether that rule ever contemplates the possibility, where prejudice has been caused to a company by a *foreign* State, of diplomatic protection being exercised by a State other than the national State of the company itself.[46]

Similarly, Judge Fitzmaurice affirmed that

---

[42] *Barcelona Traction, ICJ Reports*, 1964, 56.

[43] *Barcelona Traction, ICJ Reports*, 1970, 33.

[44] Separate Opinion of Judge Bustamante, *Barcelona Traction, ICJ Reports*, 1964, 82.

[45] Dissenting Opinion of Judge Morelli, *Barcelona Traction, ICJ Reports*, 1964, 111.

[46] Dissenting Opinion of Judge Armand-Ugon, *Barcelona Traction, ICJ Reports*, 1964, 165 (emphasis original).

The question of Belgium's right to claim on behalf of the Barcelona Traction Company's shareholders, in so far as Belgian, is really a question of substance not of capacity (because the underlying issue is what rights do the shareholders themselves have).[47]

These views accord with *Barcelona Traction* in assuming and confirming that the question of *actio popularis* evidences the direct link between substantive law and judicial competence: it is available when substantive norms entail it.

The ILC affirmed *actio popularis* by stating that in case of breaches of *erga omnes* obligations, responsibility is engaged not only towards the directly injured State, but also 'in regard to all other members of the international community, so that, in the event of a breach of these obligations every State must be considered justified in invoking—*probably through judicial channels*—the responsibility of a State committing the internationally wrongful act'.[48] This entire framework requires agreement with the view that in special circumstances, international law recognizes *actio popularis*.[49] That concept is consequential upon the substantive nature of respective obligations and it would be absurd to require the existence of a specific State practice or *opinio juris* in support of the contention that *actio popularis* is recognized under international law.

The evidence in favour of the existence of the right to sue in the public interest can follow from treaty clauses. Jurisdictional clauses based on treaty provisions embodying international obligations safeguarding the interests of the international community as a whole can themselves provide the basis for suing in the public interest. This follows from the combined effect of the nature of obligations and effective interpretation of jurisdictional clauses. Obligations *erga omnes* based on customary law equally serve as a basis for an *actio popularis*.

Actio popularis is envisaged under several international instruments, such as Article 33 of the European Convention on Human Rights,[50] Article 41 of the International Covenant on Civil and Political Rights and Article 44 of the American Convention on Human Rights. So were brought, for instance, cases against Greece and Turkey before the European Commission on Human Rights.[51] *Actio popularis* is inherently present in Article IX of the Genocide Convention, Article 22 of the Torture Convention and Article 66 of the Vienna Convention on the Law of Treaties. Similarly, the wording of

---

[47] Separate Opinion of Judge Fitzmaurice, *Barcelona Traction, ICJ Reports*, 1970, 65.

[48] 2 YbILC, 1976, part II, 99 (emphasis added). See also ILC Report 2000, 115, 375.

[49] Dinstein, The *erga omnes* Applicability of Human Rights, 30 *AVR* (1992), 18; Oellers-Frahm, The *erga omnes* Applicability of Human Rights, 30 *AVR* (1992), 33.

[50] On *actio popularis* in the ECHR system see Orakhelashvili, *CYELS* (2002–2003), 247–255.

[51] 3321/67, *Greek*, 11 *YB ECHR*, 726; 4448/70, *Second Greek*, 13 *YB ECHR*, 134; 9940-44/82, *Turkish*, 4 *HRLJ*.

Common Article 1 of the Geneva Conventions makes inferable that in case of violation, States are entitled to *actio popularis*.[52]

The view that the invocation of jurisdictional clauses in such treaties requires a nationality link, direct interest or prejudice is logically and normatively flawed. Substantive provisions on which jurisdictional clauses are based give rise to obligations *erga omnes* and are invocable in the public interest. Jurisdictional clauses safeguarding them must be deemed to serve an identical purpose.

Obligations *erga omnes* possess that character not because they are embodied in a treaty provision, but because they would bind as part of general international law even in the absence of a conventional obligation. All this suggests that the Court would be competent to admit an *actio popularis* in proceedings instituted on the basis of the Optional Clause declarations under Article 36(2) of its Statute. This provision, like declarations made pursuant to it, is drafted broadly, requiring no demonstration of individual State interest or prejudice. The presence of such interest is required in practice depending on the nature of legal relations in specific cases. As Meron suggests, States may bring claims before the Court under Articles 36 of the Statute if they are not directly affected, on the basis of the legal interest of all States in the observance of certain fundamental norms.[53] Also, if treaty-based jurisdictional clauses refer to the 'interpretation and application' of provisions of a given treaty, Article 36(2) more broadly refers to 'any question of international law'.

[52] Schindler, Erga omnes-Wirkung des humanitären Völkerrechts, Beyerlin, Bothe, Hofmann and Petersmann (Hrsg.), *Recht zwischen Umbruch und Bewahrung. Festschrift für Rudolf Bernhardt* (1993), 206; Schwelb (1972), 46–55.

[53] Meron, *Human Rights and Humanitarian Norms as Customary Law* (1989), 192; Hannikainen, *Peremptory Norms in International Law* (1988), 280.

17

The Impact of *Jus Cogens* on Friendly Settlement and Discontinuance of Cases

Friendly settlement and discontinuance put an end to adjudication before the judicial determination of a case. In a formal sense, friendly settlements are based on a previous agreement between litigating parties, while discontinuances derive from unilateral action by a party (though accepted by another party). The constituent instruments and rules of tribunals refer to the option of friendly settlement,[1] discontinuance[2] or both.[3] This fact calls for examination of friendly settlement in the light of interaction between agreements based on consent and legal effects of *jus cogens* rights, which by their very nature exclude the validating relevance of consent. In addition, friendly settlements are not only about the removal of a case, but mostly about the very substantive resolution of a dispute—in some cases contrary to what the substantive norm of *jus cogens* may require, and in fact result in agreements contrary to *jus cogens*. This is yet further evidence that a strict distinction between the substance of a dispute and its judicial consideration may be artificial.

The phenomenon of amicable settlement or discontinuance of cases is not included in the International Court's Statute and derives exclusively from the Rules of the Court and its jurisprudence. The Permanent Court described the traditional view on the relevance of amicable settlement in judicial proceedings as follows:

the judicial settlement of international disputes, with a view to which the Court has been established, is simply an alternative to the direct and friendly settlement of such disputes between the Parties; . . . consequently it is for the Court to facilitate, so far as is compatible with its Statute, such direct and friendly settlement.[4]

---

[1] Article 45, Rules of the Inter-American Commission.

[2] Articles 88–89, Rules of the International Court; Article 43, Rules of the Inter-American Court; Article 77A, Rules of Procedure of the Human Rights Committee; Article 52, African Charter of Human and Peoples' Rights.

[3] Articles 38–39 and Article 37 of the European Convention, respectively.

[4] Free Zones of Upper Savoy and the District of Gex, Order of 19 August 1929, *P.C.I.J.*, Series A, No. 22, 13.

The Permanent Court's approach is, despite the view of certain commentators,[5] not value-neutral. The Court affirms that it must not facilitate or uphold a settlement offending against the Statute. It may well be under a supervisory duty with regard to such settlements. Here the guiding rules of the Statute are relevant. The neutral wording of Articles 88–89 of the Rules of the Court, arguably warranting a value-neutral approach, must be read in the context of and in subordination to the Court's duty to ensure respect for its own Statute. This is so, as the Rules are inferior to the Statute.

The Court's function, according to Article 38 of the Statute, is 'to decide in accordance with international law such disputes as are submitted to it'. The responsibility of the Court to ensure that disputes are settled in accordance with international law is expressly limited by the Statute to cases where a dispute—whether a jurisdictional or substantive one—is submitted to the Court. This elementary principle imposes on the Court the duty to ensure observance of international law in jurisdictional or substantive disputes submitted to it irrespective of the fact that it would have no such responsibility if the case were not submitted to it.

The requirement of respect for substantive international law can have a direct impact on the admissibility of a proposed friendly settlement. The Court must ascertain whether the conditions of a settlement or discontinuance involve results tolerated by international law, that is it must enquire into the nature of the substantive legal relations involved. This would make clear that actions violating *jus cogens* may not be adequately resolved amicably; for if the claims consisting in violation of ordinary rules of international law may be validly waived by an applicant State, certain claims based on *jus cogens* may not. Determination of the legal consequences of a wrongful act contrary to *jus cogens* affects the legal interests not merely of an applicant State but also the international community as a whole. If an applicant State, by agreeing to a settlement or discontinuance, waives claims based on *jus cogens*, this is not the settlement of a dispute 'in accordance with international law'. The objective, non-reciprocal, nature of obligations requires the determination of wrongful consequences and the reparation and rehabilitation of victims irrespective of the attitude of parties. The Court is therefore bound to reject a settlement or discontinuance which fails to respect the legal consequences of peremptory norms, for the specific nature of *jus cogens* may well cause that a simple waiver of a claim does not ensure the settlement of a dispute 'in accordance with international law'. Since international law attaches different consequences to different rules and obligations, Article 38 of the Statute requires the Court to act differently in cases of *jus cogens* and

---

[5] Fawcett (1985), 375. It is also suggested that the Rules of the Court 'deal with the "how" and not with the "why" of discontinuance'. Rosenne (1983), 185.

other rules, to ensure that a dispute is decided 'in accordance with international law'.

In practice, the Court hardly observes this requirement. Cases involving important aspects of the application of peremptory norms—*Pakistani Prisoners*,[6] *Nicaragua*,[7] *Aerial Incident*[8] and *Lockerbie*—were amicably settled and discontinued. Those cases dealt with allegations of the unlawful use of force, genocide and serious violations of humanitarian law. But the Court merely noted the coincidence of the wills of the parties to end the proceedings, and showed no interest in whether the settlements achieved respected the effects of relevant peremptory norms. The only concern the Court has so far shown is whether a settlement is achieved and not whether it is 'in accordance with international law' as required by Article 38. This practice results in the Court's failure to implement its mandate.

The friendly settlement option under the European Convention,[9] which may relate either to the merits of the case or to the issue of just satisfaction,[10] has generally been considered as an inherent part of the Convention system and has moreover been characterized as a normal mechanism to protect human rights,[11] ideally satisfying the interests of applicants, governments and Convention organs,[12] and providing for remedies more effective than a judicial determination of the case.[13] But the objective nature of the obligations enshrined in the European Convention and the status of the Convention rights under general international law raise the issue of the legality of such settlements.

Friendly settlement and discontinuance of proceedings based on withdrawal of an application are institutions based on consent between the parties and are agreements under international law.[14] The issue of the hierarchy of norms acquires particular importance where the friendly settlement procedure is likely to result, under certain circumstances, in purely diplomatic negotiations, where parties (as well as the Convention bodies) try to achieve a settlement and compromise as such, taking into account, along with need for observance of the Convention, considerations based on expediency: to preserve reputation, to avoid costs, to save time, to reduce caseload, to escape confrontation with governments. Friendly settlement involves, therefore, a

---

[6] *ICJ Reports*, 1973, 347–348.   [7] *ICJ Reports*, 1991, 47–48.

[8] *ICJ Reports*, 1996, 9–10.   [9] Orakhelashvili, *CYELS* (2003), 255–260.

[10] Harris, O'Boyle and Warbrick, *The Law of the European Convention on Human Rights* (1995), 680; Robertson and Merrils, *Human Rights in Europe* (1993), 282.

[11] Kiss, Conciliation, in Macdonald, Matscher and Petzold (eds), *The European System of Protection of Human Rights* (1993), 703.

[12] Harris, O'Boyle and Warbrick (1995), 681.

[13] Jacobs and White, *European Convention on Human Rights* (1996), 373, 378–379.

[14] Frowein/Peukert, *EMRK-Kommentar* (1995), 626.

considerable risk that the compromise reached will not satisfy the requirements of the Convention.[15]

The Convention makes 'respect of human rights as defined in this Convention' a necessary prerequisite for a friendly settlement (Article 28). If this provision means anything, it means that some friendly settlements *are* in conformity with human rights while others *are not*, thus entailing an automatic limitation upon the relevance of the will of the parties in this process. The Convention does not admit a compromise at the cost of enforcement of human rights. A settlement should be aimed not at achieving compromise between the interests of applicant and respondent as such, but at ensuring compliance of the conduct of the parties and thus of that compromise with the Convention's provisions. An agreement between the parties is not in a position to replace the need to observe the Convention obligations embodying interests going far beyond the reciprocal relationships between applicants and respondents.

Friendly settlement under the European Convention on Human Rights is not subject to the free will of the parties, but is subject to the imperative principles of the objective legal order.[16] Under the Convention system, the parties who launch proceedings are not masters of it. Their disposal of proceedings is subject to the public interest. Such public interest is determined by the Convention organs, which excludes the discretion of parties.[17] As Nicoloudis suggests, the conciliation procedure before the European Convention organs can be abused in a way of achieving the settlement that contradicts international public order. In normative terms this can be conceived as the conflict between the unilateral act of an ECHR organ and the international public order.[18]

Not every settlement, whatever its economic terms, can satisfy the general interest. The settlement must address the substance of the dispute. For example, compensation is not always the only response to official ill-treatment. The Convention should not endorse the policy of 'torture now, pay later', but only a settlement effectively putting end to such practices can be based on respect of human rights.[19]

---

[15] Van Dijk and Van Hoof, *Theory and Practice of the European Convention on Human Rights* (1998), 179.

[16] Walter (1970), 104; Van der Meersch, Does the Convention have the Power of 'Ordre Public' in Municipal Law?, in Robertson (ed.), *Human Rights in National and International Law* (1968), 123–126; Styrdom, *Ius Cogens*: Peremptory Norm of Totalitarian Instrument? 14 *South African Yearbook of International Law* (1988–89), 56.

[17] Walter (1970), 117, 124; Van der Meersch (1968), 115–116; Rolin, Vers un ordre public réellement international, in *Hommage d'une génération des Juristes au President Basdevant* (1961), 462.

[18] Nicoloudis (1974), 134.

[19] Opsahl, Settlement Based on Respect for Human Rights under the European Convention of Human Rights, *Proceedings of the Sixth International Colloquy about the European Convention of Human Rights* (1985), 972.

The obligations imposed on the Convention bodies under Article 19 exclude them being bound by the withdrawal of an application by the parties.[20] The organs are bound only by the Convention, not by the attitude of a party.[21] The Convention organs may *ex officio* continue proceedings if they find that the friendly settlement does not correspond to the requirements of public order, even against the will of the parties.[22] In *Kornmann*, the European Commission considered that it was not bound by the withdrawal of the application in a case which may extend beyond the interests of a particular applicant.[23] The same applies to the powers of the European Court.[24] In *De Becker*, it is assumed, the end of proceedings was not ultimately based on the withdrawal of the application by the applicant.[25] As Judge Ross explains, 'the public interest requires that the question whether a violation has or has not taken place shall be decided regardless of whether the Applicant is or is not interested in the continuance of the proceedings.' In *Gericke*, the discontinuance was allowed because no general imperative order (*impératif d'ordre général*) opposed this. The European Commission would refuse the waiver of claims when they raise public order interests going beyond those of the parties.[26]

For the compatibility of a settlement with the Convention, the legal as well as the factual circumstances should be taken into account. The factual basis of a settlement is important. In certain cases the respondent governments refer to concrete actions already taken for improving human rights situations including actions to redress the breach of the Convention in question. To this category belongs, for instance, the case of *Alam*,[27] where the refused certificate to enter the territory of the respondent State had been granted after the proceedings in Strasbourg had been initiated, supplemented by *ex gratia* payments by the respondent government. Another example is *Pfleger*,[28] where the European Court of Human Rights approved a settlement between the applicant and the government concerning the alleged violation of the Convention based on the fact that judicial hearings affecting the rights and interests of the applicants had not been conducted publicly. After the Court in Strasbourg was seised, the respondent agreed to pay the applicant a sum covering both the substance of the claim and the costs of the proceedings. The Court approved this settlement. Similar circumstances were present in *Denmark v Turkey*, where the settlement involved the payment of

---

[20] Walter, *Die Europäische Menschenrechtsordnung* (1970), 119.   [21] Walter (1970), 133.

[22] Walter (1970), 113.

[23] Walter (1970), 114. No discontinuance will be allowed if the general interest is affected and in *Kornmann* such factors were involved which necessitated the further consideration of the case despite 'a valid declaration of withdrawal'. *Kornmann* (Eur Commn HR), 9.

[24] Walter (1970), 115–116.   [25] Walter (1970), 117.

[26] *Gericke* (Eur Commn HR), 314, 320.

[27] *Alam, Khan and Singh v UK*, 10 *YB ECHR*, 478.

[28] *Pfleger*, Judgment of 4 April 2000.

compensation.[29] But some cases involve not an effected redress of a breach, but merely promises by a respondent government to adopt certain measures for undoing the violation.

The friendly settlement in the *Turkish* case, involving substantiated allegations of gross and massive breaches of several provisions of the Convention including torture on a widespread scale,[30] was based on the 'determination of the Turkish Government to secure compliance with the rights and freedoms secured by the Convention'.[31] The Turkish government undertook also to report to the Commission on the steps taken for improvement of human rights in the country.[32] Reporting obligations of such a kind could hardly have served any real purpose, because, as emphasized, the commitments undertaken by Turkey in the settlement were extremely vague. The violations of several Convention provisions alleged in the application were not mentioned at all in the settlement conditions.[33] These conditions, being apparently based on a value-neutral compromise between the parties, cannot really be characterized as contributing to effective enforcement of the Convention. The Commission's report approving the settlement was merely the reproduction of the text of the settlement the parties had arrived at. By simply approving what the parties had suggested, the Commission failed to make its own judgment on the issues of fact and law in terms of compatibility of the settlement with the Convention. The settlement was for the most part, though not exclusively, based on promises rather than the redress measures already taken, for instance on the issues of martial law and amnesties,[34] and did not cover measures of reparation and rehabilitation for the victims of torture. The reporting procedure under the settlement was confidential, exclusively bilateral and did not foresee any possibility of determination or consequences of any failure by Turkey to comply with the terms of the settlement.[35] Such a solution did not guarantee respect for human rights enshrined in the Convention.

Similar circumstances were present in *Greece v UK*, where the 'withdrawal of the application was a matter which concerned the Commission as well as the parties and the Commission must satisfy itself that the termination of the proceedings was calculated to serve, not to defeat, the purposes of the Convention', in view of responsibilities of the Commission under Article 19 'to ensure the observance of the engagements undertaken by parties in the

---

[29] *Denmark v Turkey*, paras 25 ff., 39 *ILM* (2000), 790.
[30] *Turkish* case (Admissibility), 4 *HRLJ*, 1983, 534–536.
[31] *Turkish* case (Friendly Settlement), 6 *HRLJ*, 1985, 337.
[32] *Turkish* case (Friendly Settlement), 6 *HRLJ*, 1985, 335–336.
[33] Van Dijk and Van Hoof (1998), 188; Robertson and Merrils (1993), 284.
[34] *Turkish* case (Friendly Settlement), 6 *HRLJ*, 1985, 336.
[35] *Turkish* case (Friendly Settlement), 6 *HRLJ*, 1985, 335–336, see, in particular, settlement condition A, in para. 39.

Convention'.[36] It should be noted, however, that no attempt was made by the Commission to look for evidence (or even for assurances) of reparation in favour of victims of forty-nine cases of torture which were the substance of the application. This factor obviously has its impact on the value of the Commission's decision to agree to withdrawal.

One may conclude that the European Commission of Human Rights has failed to take due account of the nature and consequences of a wrongful act in adopting the friendly settlements, which is a serious drawback in terms both of enforcement of the Convention and of considerations of international public order. Whatever the motives and reasons of the Commission, its decisions in an objective sense have resulted in a failure to protect rights and freedoms enshrined in the Convention.

The Commission's practice has given rise to the evaluation that 'in inter-State cases . . . the friendly settlement procedure should be approached with a degree of scepticism and its value assessed accordingly'.[37] Cases of a general character are normally not suitable for friendly settlements.[38] Matters belonging to European public order are not eligible to be the object of transaction, compromise or renunciation.[39]

A value-neutral approach is used by the African Commission of Human Rights. In *Association pour la Défense des Droits de l'Homme*, the Commission has faced claims based on massive attacks against a civilian population involving extra-judicial executions, torture and rape.[40] 'Friendly settlement' was nevertheless based merely on the report of a Commissioner and the letter from the applicant in which it agreed to the settlement.[41] The Commission merely acknowledged the fact of reaching settlement, but it gave no details as to its terms. The Commission's report is silent on whether any measures have been taken by the respondent government with a view to reparation or rehabilitation of victims; it makes no reference even to any promise of the government to undertake these steps.

The mandate of the African Commission is to ensure that human rights enshrined in the African Charter are duly observed in the course of a friendly solution.[42] Once it is seised of a case, its duty is not to allow a settlement resulting in the violation of the Charter, since this is tantamount to acquiescence in the original breaches.

Contrary to the practice just described, the organs of the American Convention on Human Rights assume a more responsible role in issues of

---

[36] 299/57, 2 *YB ECHR*, 178.   [37] Robertson and Merrills (1993), 285.

[38] Fribergh and Villiger, The European Commission on Human Rights, in Macdonald, Matscher and Petzold (eds), *The European System of Protection of Human Rights* (1993), 612.

[39] Sudre, Existe-t-il un ordre public Européen? in Tavernier, *Quelle Europe pour les droits de l'homme?* (1996), 68; Van der Meersch (1968), 98; *Ben Yaacoub*, Series A, No. 127-A, 8–9.

[40] 8 *IHRR* (2001), 216–217.

[41] Id., 217.

[42] African Charter of Human and Peoples' Rights, Article 52.

friendly settlement, showing interest not only in factual settlement possibilities, but also in their contents and the likelihood in concrete cases of restoring effectively the violated rights through amicable solutions. According to Article 45(2) of the Commission's Rules, 'In order for the Commission to offer itself as an organ of conciliation for a friendly settlement . . . in the judgment of the Commission, the nature of the matter must be susceptible to the use of the friendly settlement procedure.' According to Article 43(3) of its Rules, the Inter-American Court, in disregard of the attitudes of parties and 'mindful of its responsibility to protect human rights, may decide that it should proceed with the consideration of the case'. As Judge Garcia-Ramirez emphasized, the legitimacy of the friendly settlement agreements under the Convention depends not on the will of a State but on its compliance with human rights, and the Court's verification authority is to serve that purpose. No settlement can be approved if it aims to 'alter, replace, diminish or supplant the natural and immutable duties' under the IACHR legal system, such as the duty to prosecute the perpetrators of serious human rights violations.[43] As Judge Garcia-Ramirez speaks of agreements which cannot alter or diminish immutable duties, the relevance of peremptory norms as the limit on friendly settlement becomes clear.

In certain cases, the Inter-American Commission expressly maintained that the friendly solution was inappropriate.[44] In *Velasquez Rodriguez*, the respondent argued that the Commission violated Article 48(1)(f) of the Convention by not promoting a friendly settlement.[45] The attitude of the Inter-American Commission was that 'the rights to life (Art. 4), to humane treatment (Art. 5) and to personal liberty (Art. 7) violated in the instant case cannot be effectively restored by conciliation'[46] and thus it was not bound to seek a friendly settlement. The Court held that the Commission did not breach the Convention by not attempting to reach a friendly settlement, by referring to the nature of violations involved. The Court held that

Irrespective of whether the positions and aspirations of the parties and the degree of the Government's cooperation with the Commission have been determined, when the forced disappearance of a person at the hands of a State's authorities is reported and that State denies that such acts have taken place, it is very difficult to reach a friendly settlement that will reflect respect for the rights to life, to humane treatment and to personal liberty.[47]

The Court maintained a similar approach in *Godinez Cruz* and *Cabalerro Delgado and Santana*. The latter case stated that the friendly settlement could

---

[43] Concurring Opinion, *Barrios Altos*, 30 November 2001, paras 7–11.

[44] *Neira Alegria et al.*, para. 19.   [45] *Velasquez Rodriguez*, para. 42.

[46] *Velasquez Rodriguez*, para. 43. See also Standaert, The Friendly Settlement of Human Rights Abuses in the Americas, 9 *Duke JCIL* (1999), 519, affirming that the nature of the case can prevent the permissibility of a settlement.

[47] *Velasquez Rodriguez*, para. 46; the similar observation was made in *Godinez Cruz*, para. 49.

be omitted in exceptional cases if this is warranted by substantive reasons.[48] The factual possibility of the settlement is thus not a circumstance outweighing the need to respond to grave and serious human rights violations.

In view of the aforesaid, it seems erroneous to assume that the American Convention 'expressly mandates an attempted friendly settlement in all cases' and that the nature of violations is not a factor which may render the friendly settlement option unsuitable.[49] The text of the Convention is explicit in requiring that any settlement to be reached must be based on the 'respect for the human rights recognised in the Convention'. The text and the Convention organs are common in recognizing that if the friendly settlement does not cause an effective restoration of the rights violated, it may not be considered as an option.

Thus, unlike the other courts and tribunals, the organs of the American Convention understand the friendly settlement option functionally and resort to it only where this may ensure due enforcement of the consequences of violation.

In later cases the respondent governments have not referred to the need for friendly settlement as a preliminary objection. The organs of the American Convention tend to accept friendly settlements in cases where the governments acknowledge their responsibility and agree to pay substantial amounts in reparation. In *Benavides*, the respondent government expressly acknowledged its participation at the disappearance and death of the victim, and considered itself bound to pay compensation amounting to 1 million US dollars.[50]

It must be concluded that the requirements of the constituent instruments of international tribunals are more or less identical in establishing a supervisory duty of a tribunal to safeguard the integrity of constituent instruments in the course of achieving the settlement. They are unanimous in requiring that the legal consequences of acts offending against *jus cogens* must be implemented objectively and without decisive regard to the attitudes of litigants. But the actual practice of tribunals is hardly in accordance with what their constituent instruments require from them.

The essence of amicable or friendly settlement is to achieve a solution that best suits the individual interests of parties and their mutual relations. It is a process based on bilateralism. In bilateral relations, States may waive certain rights arising out of the subject-matter of a dispute, such as the right to pursue claims or demand reparation, but the same does not hold true for

---

[48] *Godinez Cruz*, paras 45–49; *Cabalerro Delgado and Santana*, paras 27–30.

[49] Cerna, The Inter-American Commission on Human Rights: Its Organisation and Examination of Petitions and Communications, in Harris and Livingstone (eds), *The Inter-American System of Human Rights* (1998), 100, 102.

[50] 19 *HRLJ* (1998), 416 ff., paras 34 ff.

disputes involving peremptory norms, where the interests of the international community as a whole are involved.

A legal dispute involving ordinary norms is a matter of concern for disputing States only, and whether and how it is resolved affects nobody else's interests. But when a dispute involves compliance with norms protecting the community interest, then the international community has a proper interest not only in the resolution of such dispute but also in its resolution in a way maintaining the integrity of the norms involved, to ensure that the settlement obtained does not derogate from such norms. Amicable settlement is a purely *inter se* phenomenon and is not opposable to third States, which may have an independent legal interest in the enforcement of peremptory norms. As legal benefits in such relations may be claimed by individuals and groups as such and regardless of the will of a State, third States may still claim compliance with the obligations involved, including reparations. They may, despite the achievement of a 'settlement', resort to countermeasures against the wrongdoer State. Tribunals may place themselves in a ridiculous situation by agreeing to a settlement in a situation which may, under general international law, still warrant claims and sanctions by another States. In other words, what may usually appear as a settlement in ordinary cases, can be denoted as the absence of a settlement in cases involving peremptory norms.

If a treaty is void for conflict with *jus cogens* because it is a treaty, so a friendly settlement may be incompatible with *jus cogens* and thus possibly void merely because it *is* a friendly settlement, endowed with all the necessary characteristics thereof but tainted with illegality because of the conflict with *jus cogens*.

PART V

The Effect of Peremptory Norms
in National Legal Systems

18

Techniques of Interaction of International *Jus Cogens* with National Law

I. GENERAL QUESTIONS

The effectiveness of peremptory norms in practice depends significantly on what effect they are given not only within the international legal system, but also within national legal systems. The primacy of peremptory norms over incompatible acts and transactions in international law does not by itself entail the identical effect in national legal systems, because international law and national law are separate from each other. While a State can be responsible under international law for the state of its national law, the effect of international law in national law depends on the status the latter accords to the former. This determines whether and to what extent national legal systems are capable of accepting and following the effects such as the primacy of peremptory norms over other norms, the nullity and non-recognition of the acts and transactions contrary to peremptory norms, and jurisdiction established pursuant to such norms. Several techniques within national legal systems can facilitate the proper enforcement of international *jus cogens*, along with other norms of international law by directly recognizing its effect, while others indirectly acknowledge the same, and still others preclude its effect on the national plane.

At the same time, how the pertinent issues are treated under national law is not necessarily an indication of the relevant legal position under international law. This chapter is rather intended as an outline and analysis of the options through which international *jus cogens* can be enforced before national courts. Some outcomes reached by national courts can be true for international obligations in general as much as for *jus cogens* in particular. But even so, the reasoning behind the outcomes reached by national courts is useful in understanding the difference, in specific situations, between the national and international legal positions as to the existence, effects and enforcement of peremptory norms.

2. DIRECT EFFECT OF INTERNATIONAL LAW

The enforcement of peremptory norms in national legal systems is most facilitated by the doctrine of incorporation under which international law is part of the law of the land and thus has direct effect within the given national legal system. As pointed out, the incorporation approach enables the actions of States that command nullity under international law for conflict with *jus cogens* to face the relevant consequences in national legal systems.[1]

This approach is followed, as a matter of common law, in the legal systems of the United Kingdom and the United States which recognize international law as part of the law of the land. As the US Court of Appeals pointed out in *CUSCLIN*, peremptory norms such as the proscription of murder and slavery may have domestic legal effect in the United States, 'that is, they may well restrain our Government in the same way that the Constitution restrains it'.[2]

A similar position of general international law is guaranteed under Article 25 of the German *Grundgesetz*, affirming that the general rules of international law form part of federal law, prevail over the legislation and immediately produce the rights and duties for German nationals; and under Article 10 of the Italian Constitution, according to which the legal order of Italy shall correspond to the generally recognized norms of international law. The position in countries like Australia is more ambiguous, as there is no constitutional or legislative provision clarifying whether the operation of conventional or customary international law within the Australian legal system is subject to the incorporation doctrine or transformation doctrine. The outcome is very much left to judicial discretion. Until the decision of the Federal Court in *Nulyarimma v Thompson* there was no judicial authority in Australia whether customary international law is automatically incorporated into Australian law or some specific transformation is required.[3] Article 231(4) of the South African Interim Constitution incorporates both customary and conventional international law into the law of South Africa to the extent that these are compatible with the Constitution and acts of Parliament.[4]

These examples demonstrate that national legal systems differ not only in whether general international law is part of national law, but also in whether they place international law above or below national legislation. This issue can predetermine whether the effects of *jus cogens* related to hierarchical primacy, validity of conflicting acts or jurisdiction will be followed in national law.

That *jus cogens* serves as a limitation on sovereign treaty-making power, with appropriate effects in national law, has been confirmed by the German

---

[1] Saladin (1988), 73.

[2] *CUSCLIN*, Court of Appeals (DC), 85 ILR 261.

[3] Flynn, Genocide: It's A Crime Everywhere, But Not in Australia, 29 *Western Australian Law Review* (2000), 60.

[4] But see Mahomed DP asserting that conventional and customary norms do not become part of South African law unless and until they are incorporated by a legislative instrument, *AZAPO v President of the Republic of South Africa* (Constitutional Court), 4 SA (1996), 688. France has a similar approach, *Gaddafi* (Court of Appeal of Paris), 125 ILR 495.

Bundesverfassungsgericht, which acted in the context of Article 25 of the *Grundgesetz*. The case involved the claim that the German Statute on Tax Burden Equalization, which gave effect to the 1952 German–Swiss Agreement, was contrary to international law and void. Although the Court did not face direct claims with regard to *jus cogens*, it went on to consider whether the rule that no resort may be had to aliens for covering war expenditures was a peremptory norm and decided that it was not. As the matter was regulated by a treaty, it was no longer necessary to examine whether it was a rule of general international law.[5] Both the agreement, and consequently the German statute, were valid.

The *Bundesverfassungsgericht* thereby acknowledged the hierarchy in international law and the readiness to respect it in domestic law, especially to accept that the nullity of a treaty conflicting with *jus cogens* shall be recognized in domestic law. If the rule were peremptory, the court would have to disregard a treaty and apply the rule which would have precedence over a challenged statute.[6] This would give effect not just to substantive norms of international law, but also to *jus cogens* invalidity of treaties.

The German *Bundesverwaltungsgericht* recognized the domestic relevance of international *jus cogens* in another context, again in terms of Article 25 of the *Grundgesetz*. The court pointed out that an order given by the military commander to a subordinate is void if it conflicts with the generally recognized rules of international law and no obedience can be claimed. The Executive and Judiciary were under a direct duty not to perform any act contrary to such rules. All this extends in particular to international *jus cogens* of which the prohibition of the use of force is an example.[7] This ruling enables international *jus cogens* to directly constrain the powers of the government not only internationally, but also nationally.

A different approach was taken in the Australian case of *Horta*. The plaintiffs submitted that the 1990 Petroleum Act establishing the Australia–Indonesia Zone of Cooperation in the Timor Gap for the purpose of exploiting the mineral resources of East Timor were not laws as they were beyond the power of the Commonwealth to legislate in external affairs. This contention was based on the invalidity of a treaty on the basis of which the legislation was enacted—the Timor Gap Treaty between Indonesia and Australia—and the conflict of legislation with Australia's obligations under customary international law. It was submitted that the conclusion of treaties conflicting with *jus cogens* is outside the executive competence of a State.[8]

---

[5] *Entscheidungen des Bundesverfassungsgerichts*, 1965, 448–451; Riesenfeld, 60 *AJIL* (1966), 513–514.

[6] Schwelb, 61, *AJIL* (1967), 951–952. Similarly, from the perspective of German law, Security Council resolutions rank as treaty law and hence they are fully reviewable by national courts in the light of *jus cogens*, Herdegen, in De Wet and Nollkaemper (eds), 81.

[7] BverwG 2 WD 12.04, para. 4.1.2.6.

[8] *Horta v Commonwealth of Australia*, 104 ILR 450, 452–453.

The Commonwealth argued that the issue was non-justiciable and the limits of the Commonwealth's legislative powers were observed irrespective of whether the Timor Gap Treaty was valid or whether the legislation failed to comply with obligations under customary international law.[9]

The court refrained from examining directly either the issue of validity of a treaty or compliance of the Act with customary international law. It focused on whether the Act would still be valid even if it was adopted in violation of Australia's international obligations. The examination of this question rendered other questions moot.[10]

The High Court interpreted the notion of external affairs purely in the context of Australian law and ignored the limits international law places on the treaty-making power of States. Thus the High Court unconditionally accepted the determination of the Parliament that the exploitation of the petroleum resources of East Timor was a matter affecting Australia; and consequently, the Act was within Australia's power to legislate with regard to external affairs. The validity of the Act was unaffected by the fact whether there was any treaty. The excess of legislative powers was to be found only on the basis of Australia's constitution. Even if a treaty was void or the Act was contrary to customary international law, the Act would not be deprived of its validity, since the constitution does not make the validity of legislation conditional upon compliance with international law. Australia's legislative competence is not necessarily the same as the competence recognized under international law.[11] Finally, even if the compliance with international law mattered for the validity of the Act, the plaintiffs' claims would still be non-justiciable, as 'the propriety of the recognition by the Commonwealth Executive of the sovereignty of a foreign nation over foreign territory cannot be raised in the courts of this country'.[12]

The Australian High Court thus approved both the 1989 Timor Gap Treaty, which was void under international law for authorizing the exploitation of East Timor's natural resources, and the annexation of East Timor, which was a clear case of forcible territorial acquisition and subject to the principle of non-recognition. Also, apart from being wrong in terms of international law, *Horta* denies the principle that international law is part of the law of the land. The approach of the *Bundesverfassungsgericht*, which judged the validity of the relevant treaty in terms of international law as such, reflects better the specificity of international public order and for this reason must, as a matter of international law, be preferred to the attitude of the Australian High Court.

---

[9] *Horta v Commonwealth of Australia*, 104 ILR 453.

[10] *Horta v Commonwealth of Australia*, 104 ILR 454.

[11] *Horta v Commonwealth of Australia*, 104 ILR 455–456.

[12] *Horta v Commonwealth of Australia*, 104 ILR 456; for the analysis of this decision see Fitzgerald, *Horta v Commonwealth*: The Validity of the Timor Gap Treaty and Its Domestic Implementation, 44 *ICLQ* (1995), 643.

The comparison of these two cases justifies the suggestion that to deny that the actions under national law are not bound by international *jus cogens* is to accept the position of radical dualism between international and national law.[13]

The direct incorporation of international law in national legal systems is significant in terms of the action of national courts regarding the prosecution and punishment of the perpetrators of the *jus cogens* crimes. The state of international law on this subject can be reflected in national law through the existence of jurisdiction over these crimes as a matter of that national law. The Supreme Court of Israel in *Eichmann* was the first to affirm this. The court faced the appeal plea that the Israeli statute conferring jurisdiction over international crimes to Israeli courts was invalid because it authorized the prosecution retrospectively. The court referred to the universal nature of the relevant crimes and rejected the argument that these crimes can be tried in national legal systems only if committed after the national jurisdiction over them has been established by the statute. The court's affirmation that it could try crimes committed even before the State of Israel emerged is a further confirmation of this. Having concluded that individual criminal responsibility for core international crimes is mandatory, the court affirmed that international law authorizes 'the countries of the world to mete out punishment for the violation of its provisions, which is effected by putting these provisions into operation either directly or by virtue of municipal legislation which has adopted and integrated them'.[14] This reasoning affirms that the existence of universal jurisdiction over core crimes under international law can, as one of the options, entail a similar jurisdiction directly under national law.

A similar issue arose in the *Pinochet* litigation before the House of Lords. The question was whether individual criminal responsibility for torture on the basis of universal jurisdiction as based on *jus cogens* was part of English law as such and without statutory incorporation. The majority of the Lords held, pursuant to the approach adopted by Lord Browne-Wilkinson, that torture was criminally punishable under English law only after the Act incorporating the 1989 Torture Convention was adopted. Consequently, the UK jurisdiction over Pinochet covered only the crimes committed after 29 September 1988, that is the date of incorporation of the Torture Convention into English law.[15] Lord Hope also emphasized that the offences for which Pinochet could be extradited were to be punishable in England when they were committed and not just at the time of extradition proceedings, adding that even if torture was criminal in England before 29 September

[13] Saladin, Völkerrechtliches Jus Cogens und Schweizerisches Landesrecht, Jenny and Kälin, *Die Schweizerische Rechtsordnung in Ihren Internationalen Bezügen* (1988), 74.
[14] *Eichmann*, 36 ILR 291–292.   [15] *Pinochet*, 2 All ER (1999), 107.

1989, it was not an extra-territorial offence against the law of the United Kingdom.[16] But Lord Millett disagreed, and took the general international law approach, considering that since universal jurisdiction for torture is part of *jus cogens*, the responsibility of a person brought before the English courts should not depend *ratione temporis* on national legislative instruments, as the principle of criminal responsibility with regard to that crime is anyway part of English law. According to Lord Millett, whether national courts have extra-territorial jurisdiction depends on the constitutional arrangements of the State and the relationship between its jurisdiction and customary international law. With regard to the position in England, Lord Millett specified that

The jurisdiction of the English criminal courts is usually statutory, but it is supplemented by the common law, and accordingly I consider that the English courts have and always have had extra-territorial criminal jurisdiction in respect of crimes of universal jurisdiction under customary international law.[17]

Lord Millett referred to the outcome in *Eichmann* as justifying universal jurisdiction based on 'an independent source of jurisdiction derived from customary international law, which formed the part of the unwritten law of Israel, and which did not depend on the statute'.[18] Under this view, international law, while providing universal jurisdiction over *jus cogens* crimes, can independently justify the same jurisdiction as a matter of national law and the existence of statutory jurisdiction is not a necessary requirement.[19]

This approach was not supported by the majority of the Lords, who subscribed to the approach of statutory transformation. On the other hand, the House of Lords had no difficulty with finding that effect must be given before English courts to the principle that the prohibition of torture, as part of *jus cogens*, prevails over the immunity of the former head of State. In this latter case, the incorporation approach seems to have succeeded because the solution envisaged under international law was applied as part of English common law. In terms of the scope of the immunity of States and their officials, the identical approach was applied when immunity pleas were rejected by the Greek courts in *Distomo*, Italian Supreme Court in *Ferrini* and Dutch courts in *Bourtese* (in this last case also with regard to universal jurisdiction).

The standing of the norms on prosecution of *jus cogens* crimes in national

---

[16] Id., 136, 141–143. In *Habre*, the Court of Appeal of Dakar considered that Articles 4 and 5 of the Torture Convention which require criminalizing torture and establishing jurisdiction over it cannot have effect in Senegalese law without the requisite amendments in Senegalese Criminal Procedure law. *Habre* (Court of Appeal of Dakar), 125 ILR 573–574.

[17] *Pinochet*, 2 All ER (1999), 177.   [18] Id., 176.

[19] Id., 178; see also *The Princeton Principles on Universal Jurisdiction* (2001), according to which 'national judicial organs may rely on universal jurisdiction even if their national legislation does not specifically provide for it', Principle 3.

law was also addressed in *Nulyarimma* before the Australian court. All judges at the Federal Court affirmed that Australia had an international obligation, as a matter of customary international law and derived from the prohibition of genocide under international *jus cogens*, to prosecute the crime of genocide but added that it is another thing to say that, without national legislation to that effect, persons accused of genocide can be put to trial in Australia.[20] The crucial issue for the court was whether the crime of genocide, which attracts universal jurisdiction under international law, could become part of Australian law without a legislative act creating genocide as an offence.[21] This was effectively the issue whether customary international law is part of Australian law. The court was divided on this issue. Judge Whitlam concluded that Australian courts 'can have no authority for themselves to proscribe conduct as criminal under the common law simply because it has now become recognised as an international crime with the status of *jus cogens* under customary international law'.[22]

However, Judge Merkel followed the approach of Lord Millett in *Pinochet* and affirmed that there was no support for the contention that a statutory vesting of jurisdiction is essential in respect of universal crimes having the status of *jus cogens*; 'essentially it is the universality and *jus cogens* status that result in the vesting of jurisdiction in all nation States.' This follows from the fact that there is a mandatory and non-derogable duty to prosecute universal crimes and States have no discretion whether to fulfil that obligation; 'therefore a vesting under the common law, rather than discretionary exercise of legislative power, is consistent with the principles of international law.' This outcome was furthermore facilitated by the fact that Australian courts can prosecute common law offences. Therefore, Judge Merkel concluded, 'the offence of genocide is an offence under the common law of Australia'.[23]

This reasoning in the consistent thread of jurisprudence of *Eichmann*, Lord Millett in *Pinochet* and Judge Merkel in *Nulyarimma* affirms that the peremptory and mandatory character of the duty to prosecute *jus cogens* crimes translates into the legal position under national law whereby States can exercise jurisdiction over such crimes with or without specific authorization by national legislation. Indeed, according to Lord Millett and Judge Merkel they have to exercise such jurisdiction even where it is not statutorily provided.

Also, much depends on the constructions of national law and the clear difference between the approach of statutory exclusivity of the definitions of crime advanced by Judge Wilcox and the reliance on common law offences by Judge Merkel must be noted. The latter approach is obviously more conducive for the proper enforcement of international *jus cogens* before

---

[20] *Nulyarimma*, 628–629, *per* Wilcox J.
[21] Id., 642, *per* Whitlam J.   [22] Id., 638.   [23] Id., 658, 661, 663, 668.

national courts and it appears possible though not guaranteed in common law countries. In civil law countries courts will not be able to choose between different options because they have to obey the rule that only acts expressly criminalized by legislation can be treated as crimes. This explains the reluctance of the courts in France and to some extent in Luxembourg to exercise universal jurisdiction over international crimes where it is not statutorily provided. Similarly, the Senegalese Court of Cassation declined in *Habre* to exercise universal jurisdiction but did not contradict it as a matter of international law and even affirmed that international *jus cogens* provided the basis for such jurisdiction. Instead, it stated that 'there is no procedural legislation which recognises that Senegalese courts have universal jurisdiction' to prosecute the perpetrators of international crimes.[24]

The incorporation approach can enable national courts to deny State immunity for breaches of peremptory norms. The Italian Supreme Court in *Ferrini* observed that 'the general norms of international law which protect the freedom and dignity of the person as fundamental rights, and which recognise as "international crimes" such behaviour as would seriously damage the integrity of these values' are an integral part of Italian law and the violation of these norms produces the causes of action by individuals within the Italian legal system.[25] This approach enabled the Supreme Court to hold that Germany could not claim immunity before Italian courts for its activities performed during the Second World War which offended against international *jus cogens*.

In Canada, the Court of Appeal emphasized that 'customary rules of international law are directly incorporated into Canadian domestic law unless explicitly ousted by contrary legislation'.[26] This approach recognizes the enforceability within the Canadian legal system of general international law including *jus cogens* but qualifies it to the extent that the doctrine of statutory supremacy applies. This was the principal reason for which State immunity was upheld for acts of torture.

The doctrine of incorporation enables national legal systems to reflect the changes within international law without the respective legislation or judicial authority within the national legal system, and also to consider the evolution of international law. Lord Denning affirmed this in the *Trendtex* case focusing on the scope of State immunity in international law:

Under the doctrine of incorporation, when the rules of international law change, our English law changes with them. But, under the doctrine of transformation, the English law does not change. It is bound by precedent. It is bound down to those rules of international law which have been accepted and adopted in the past. It cannot develop as international law develops.

[24] *Habre* (Court of Cassation), 125 ILR 578–579.
[25] Judgment, para. 7.1, in De Sena and De Vittor, 98.
[26] *Bouzari*, Court of Appeal for Ontario, para. 65, *per* Goudge JA.

. . . I now believe that the doctrine of incorporation is correct. Otherwise I do not see that our courts could ever recognise a change in the rules of international law. . . .

Seeing that the rules of international law have changed—and do change—and that the courts have given effect to the changes without any Act of Parliament, it follows to my mind inexorably that the rules of international law, as existing from time to time, do form part of our English law. It follows, too, that a decision of this court—as to what was the ruling of international law 50 of 60 years ago—is not binding on this court today. International law knows no rule of stare decisis. If this court today is satisfied that the rule of international law on a subject has changed from what it was 50 or 60 years ago, it can give effect to that change—and apply the change in our English law—without waiting for the House of Lords to do it.[27]

Lord Denning applied this approach in that specific case to demonstrate that the absolute State immunity was no longer part of international, and hence English, law even if earlier English precedents have upheld it, and due to the evolution of international law, English law should adopt the restrictive approach.

In the context related to *jus cogens*, the incorporation approach has been used by US courts in a series of human rights litigation originated with *Filartiga*. The US Alien Tort Claim Act permits US courts to adjudicate on violations of international law, and the courts have interpreted this authorization evolutively, so as to enable them to deal with breaches of peremptory norms of human rights on the basis of universal civil jurisdiction, that is without the requirement of any link with the forum.

In clarifying what torts against the law of nations are covered by §1350, *Filartiga* points out that 'courts must interpret international law not as it was in 1789, but as it has evolved and exists among the nations of the world today'.[28] Hence, this provision provides the jurisdiction over universal, definable and obligatory norms of international law, these very norms mostly being identified by reference to their peremptory status. The scope of the jurisdictional provision of the national statute must be interpreted to encompass international law as it stands at the moment of interpretation, not adoption of the relevant statutory provision.

The opposite approach, as expounded by Judge Bork in the *Tel-Oren* case, would view ATCA as frozen in time and covering only those torts which were considered as violations of the law of nations when ATCA was adopted—the violations which Blackstone considered as including only the violations of safe-conducts, inviolability of ambassadors and piracy. Judge Bork especially insisted that in order to be actionable under ATCA, the norm of international law must itself provide for the cause of action before national courts and thus opposed the construction of ATCA advanced in *Filartiga*.[29] Judge

---

[27] Lord Denning, *Trendtex Trading v Bank of Nigeria*, 1 QB 1977, 553–554.
[28] *Filartiga*, 77 ILR 175.　　　[29] *Tel-Oren*, 77 ILR 240–245, 249.

Edwards in the same case adopted the approach supportive of *Filartiga* and opposite to Judge Bork, holding that 'the law of nations is not stagnant and should be construed as it exists today among the nations of the world'. No specific requirement of the cause of action existed.[30]

Apart from the objection of Judge Bork in *Tel-Oren*, this approach has not met serious challenge, and the evolutive interpretation of the US statute enables the US courts to uphold the evolutive understanding of international law to give due effect to *jus cogens* within US legal system. The subsequent ATCA jurisprudence consistently and continuously develops in accordance with *Filartiga*.[31] This attitude is further followed in other jurisdictions by the treatment of universal jurisdiction over *jus cogens* crimes as a matter of domestic law in the reasoning of the Supreme Court of Israel in *Eichmann*, Lord Millett's attitude in *Pinochet* and Judge Merkel's attitude in *Nulyarimma*, as they all considered that such jurisdiction must be deemed to be part of national law as soon as it becomes recognized in international law, independently of the intervention of domestic legislatures.

3. *JUS COGENS* AND THE PRIMACY OF DOMESTIC STATUTES

While the principle that every national act that conflicts with international *jus cogens* must be seen as null and void[32] is certainly correct as a matter of international law, the practice of national courts has not always followed this principle as a matter of national law. The doctrine of the primacy of national statutes over international law is the factor that accounts for this.

In terms of the relevance of international *jus cogens* as the limitation on national legislative and even constitutional process, the Swiss experience is most significant. In 1996, the Swiss Federal Council faced the legislative proposals based on popular initiative, according to which the asylum seekers who entered the country illegally would be summarily deported without the right to appeal. The Council noted the relevance of the peremptory prohibition of *refoulement* and considered that this prohibition would be violated if the proposed legislation were adopted, and consequently asked the Parliament to declare the People's Initiative invalid. The Parliament followed this proposal. At the later stage, the clause was inserted in the Swiss Constitution prohibiting the adoption of the People's Initiative if it conflicts with international *jus cogens* and requiring that the conflicting acts be declared null and void.[33]

---

[30] *Tel-Oren*, 77 ILR 205–211.

[31] And it has also been supported by the European Commission, see EC *Amicus Curiae* Brief in *Sosa v Alvarez-Machain*, 23 January 2004, 5–10, 26.

[32] Saladin (1988), 89.

[33] De Wet, The Prohibition of Torture as an International Norm of *Jus Cogens* and Its Implications for National and Customary Law, 15 *EJIL* (2004), 101–102.

The situation is different where there is a clear conflict between domestic statute and international law, where domestic statutes traditionally have priority. The conception of primacy of domestic statutes by reference to the doctrines such as parliamentary sovereignty precludes the outcome that is realized in the Swiss legal system. Exceptions to this principle are sometimes stated. In one case, Lord Denning was ready to hold a domestic statute invalid for its conflict with the European Convention on Human Rights.[34] But in the later case he abandoned this view.

In terms of *jus cogens*, the problem of conflicting domestic legislation arises in different contexts. One option is that, in case of conflict between international norm and domestic statute, the statute has to be interpreted to ascertain whether it has been intended to offend against international law. This issue was involved in the Australian High Court case of *Kruger*, which dealt with the claims of alleged genocide. The applicants argued that the prohibition of genocide is a peremptory norm of international law and con-stitutional grants of legislative power must be construed as not authorizing to make laws contrary to that norm.[35] The views of judges were divided. One judge held that there was no need to interpret domestic legislation in accordance with the Genocide Convention unless that legislation was intended to be implementing a treaty to which Australia was a party. If the legislation preceded the treaty in time, it could be interpreted regardless of the obligations under the treaty. The language of the legislation was crucial.[36]

It was accepted that the notion of genocide 'is so fundamentally repugnant to basic human rights acknowledged by the common law that, by reason of well settled principles of statutory interpretation, an intention to authorise acts falling within that definition needs to be clear beyond doubt before a legislative provision can be construed as having that effect'. The Australian constitution must be construed 'on the basis that it was not intended to extend to laws authorising gross violations of human rights' including genocide.[37]

It was found that there was nothing in the legislation, according to the ordinary principles of construction, which would justify a conclusion that it authorized acts of removing children 'with intent to destroy, in whole or in part' the plaintiffs' racial group.[38] It was added that, 'subject to a con-sideration of the existence of a time bar, if acts were committed with the intention of destroying the plaintiffs' racial group, they may be subject of an action for damages whether or not the Ordinance was valid'.[39] This seems to

---

[34] 61 ILR 250.

[35] *Kruger v Commonwealth of Australia*, 118 ILR 376 (Gaudron J).

[36] *Kruger v Commonwealth of Australia*, 118 ILR 373 (Dawson J).

[37] *Kruger v Commonwealth of Australia*, 118 ILR 374 (Dawson J), 377–379 (Gaudron J).

[38] *Kruger v Commonwealth of Australia*, 118 ILR 376 (Toohey J), 379 (Gaudron J).

[39] *Kruger v Commonwealth of Australia*, 118 ILR 379 (Gaudron J).

imply that the prohibition of genocide is part of the law of Australia and the domestic statute authorizing acts contrary to the Genocide Convention does not preclude compensation for genocide. If this interpretation is correct, then this case offers a technique of interpreting national statutes in accordance with international law. But in other cases interpretation may not resolve the controversy because the normative conflict can be too straightforward.

This issue arose, for instance, when the South African amnesty arrangements were challenged before the courts for their conflict with the peremptory norms regarding the prosecution of international crimes. The Cape Provincial Court rejected the argument that the Act establishing the Truth and Reconciliation Commission violated *jus cogens* in the field of humanitarian law. The court referred to Article 231(4) of the Interim Constitution, which grants domestic statutes primacy over conventional and customary international law and asserted that these provisions 'enable Parliament to pass a law even if such a law is contrary to *jus cogens*'. The court added that 'the intention to legislate contrary to *jus cogens* would, however, have to be clearly indicated by Parliament in the legislation in question because of the *prima facie* presumption that Parliament does not intend to act in breach of international law.'[40]

This approach was affirmed by the Constitutional Court, which emphasized that it was irrelevant whether the Act complied with international law. The only relevant issue for that court was whether the Act was consistent with the Constitution and the issue whether it complied with the duties under international law was irrelevant.[41]

The conflict between *jus cogens* and domestic statutes most acutely arises in terms of the application of State immunity legislation, and this has been illustrated by the practice of English and American courts. These courts normally recognize the hierarchical superiority of peremptory human rights norms over immunities as a matter of international law, but consider this irrelevant when the clear text of domestic legislation requires upholding immunity. The doctrine of implied waiver of immunity in case of peremptory norms has been advanced, but has not succeeded, as courts decide to follow the statutory text.

In *Siderman de Blake*, the US Court of Appeals accepted that *jus cogens* norms do not depend solely on the consent of States for their binding force and they enjoy the highest status within international law. It furthermore accepted that the breaches of *jus cogens* were not entitled to immunity under international law. But unfortunately, the court did not 'write on a clean slate'. It dealt not with customary international law, but with the domestic statute, the Foreign Sovereign Immunities Act, which applied to the claims against

---

[40] *AZAPO v Truth and Reconciliation Commission*, 3 All SA [1996], 26.
[41] *AZAPO*, 688–689.

the foreign sovereigns and did not provide for the specific exception with regard to the claims based on the breaches of *jus cogens*. Consequently, the court concluded, 'if violations of *jus cogens* committed outside the United States are to be exceptions to immunity, Congress must make them so'.[42] On an identical basis, the Court of Appeals for the District of Columbia in *Princz* and the Court of Appeals for the Second Circuit in *Smith* rejected the argument that the Third Reich had implicitly waived the immunity for its wartime atrocities that violate *jus cogens*, because the text of FSIA did not provide for such an exception.[43]

The argument of the *Siderman* court was expressly based on the distinction between international and national legal positions. The court faced the argument that 'because sovereign immunity derives from international law, *jus cogens* supersedes it'. But while the court did not contradict this line of reasoning as a matter of international law, and even implicitly subscribed to it while it affirmed that peremptory norms prevail over any inconsistent rule, it refused to follow that line of reasoning by reference to national law obstacles, namely that the FSIA did not specifically provide for the *jus cogens* exception to sovereign immunity.[44]

In other words, the functional argument leading to the absence of immunity for breaches of *jus cogens* succeeds where the case is decided on the basis of international law, as was the case in *Pinochet* or *Bouterse*, but not if the national court is bound to give primacy to its domestic legislation, as seen in the cases of application of British and American immunity statutes.

In *Bouzari*, the Canadian Court of Appeal emphasized that, so far as possible, domestic legislation should be interpreted consistently with international obligations under general international law which forms part of Canadian law. 'This is even more so where the obligation is a peremptory norm of customary international law.' However, 'it is open to Canada to legislate contrary' to international obligations. 'Such legislation would determine Canada's domestic law although it would put Canada in breach of its international obligations.'[45] This is the principal argument of Canadian courts when they uphold immunity for the breaches of *jus cogens* such as torture.

This practice clearly evidences that the enforcement of peremptory norms in national proceedings against States, while envisaged under international law, is precluded by national legislation which takes priority over international law within the national legal system. Domestic statutes on State

---

[42] *Siderman de Blake v Argentina*, Court of Appeals (Ninth Circuit), 103 ILR 471, 474–475.

[43] *Princz v Federal Republic of Germany*, 33 ILM (1994), 1483; *Smith v Libyan Arab Jamahyria*, 36 ILM (1997), 100, at 107–108.

[44] *Siderman de Blake*, Court of Appeals (Ninth Circuit), 103 ILR 474–475.

[45] *Bouzari*, Court of Appeal for Ontario, paras 65–66, *per* Goudge JA.

immunity similarly preclude, as seen above,[46] the assessment under international law of the nature of the act for which State immunity is claimed, unless the respective legislative instrument itself provides for such an option.

The statutory transformation doctrine cannot in principle work in legal systems which place international law above the statutes. Thus Article 25 of the *Grundgesetz* makes the rules of customary law including *jus cogens* prevail over ordinary federal law, apart from the Constitution, and *a fortiori* over treaties which form part of that federal law.[47] According to Article 25, the generally recognized norms of international law not only form part of German law but also prevail over the German legislation. In case of doubt as to whether the relevant norm of international law exists, Article 100 of the Constitution provides that the *Bundesverfassungsgericht* shall be seised to clarify the issue. Thus, if German courts acknowledge that, as a matter of international law, peremptory norms prevail over immunities, they shall enforce this outcome even against the German legislation. This probably explains why the only way for German courts to avoid adjudication of *jus cogens* claims is to follow the blanket understanding of immunities and hold, as the German Supreme Court did in *Distomo*, that the breaches of *jus cogens* such as torture or war crimes, committed as part of Nazi atrocities, constitute sovereign activities and are immune under international law.

In general terms, the issue of conflict between international *jus cogens* and national statute could, under certain circumstances, be a question of the interpretation of domestic law, but it can still be objectionable, as the English and American courts applying SIA and FSIA even in a way detrimental to *jus cogens*, act in the context where international law is part of the law of the land and directly adjudicable before national courts. In interpreting the scope of immunity granted to foreign States under domestic legislation, domestic courts have to bear in mind that sovereign immunity is derived from international law, and it exists only to the extent indisputably recognized under international law. This circumstance also involves the considerations as to whether and to what extent the operation of State immunity conflicts with other principles of international law and what would be the impact of this conflict on the scope of State immunity in specific cases. If international law, due to the impact of a peremptory norm on the principle of State immunity, renders the latter inapplicable, the question arises whether domestic courts have to respect such an outcome of the hierarchy of rules in international law.

---

[46] Above, Chapter 10.

[47] Herdegen, Review of the Security Council by National Courts: A Constitutional Perspective, in De Wet and Nollkaemper (eds), *Review of the Security Council by Member States* (2003), 81. The outcomes required under international *jus cogens* can also be reached in the German legal system by reference to human rights provisions of the *Grundgesetz*, which would bar the implementation in Germany of the conflicting UN sanctions, id., 82.

This reasoning is further reinforced by the growing consciousness of national courts that their application of national legislation to the detriment of the outcomes required under international law can put the forum State in breach of its international obligations.

Therefore, courts may be more inclined to base their reasoning on international law proper and for this purpose adopt the unorthodox interpretations of the scope of statutory provisions. This approach would reflect the doctrinal argument that national codifications of the law of State immunity must not be conceived as comprehensive, but as reflecting the developments in international law.[48] It seems that this direction has been embarked upon by the English Court of Appeal in *Jones*.

The court in *Jones*, while construing the scope of the immunity of State officials in English law, referred to the *Propend* case, which involved the interpretation of section 14(1) of the 1978 State Immunity Act. This provision, which extends State immunity to the activities of any department of a State, was construed in *Propend* as protecting the employees and officials of the State for actions 'in respect of which the State they were serving had immunity'. Otherwise, 'the protection afforded by the Act of 1978 to States would be undermined.' Facing this position, the Court of Appeal in *Jones* would, if it had followed it, affirm that the individual defendants were immune (because it affirmed, rightly or wrongly, that the State itself was immune). But, according to the court, it is common ground that systematic torture is a high international crime contrary to *jus cogens*—or peremptory international law—and 'neither *Propend* nor any other authority referred to in it was concerned with allegations of such fundamental wrongdoing'.[49] Therefore, individual defendants were not immune.

The court in *Jones* does not argue that the reasoning in *Propend* was wrong; it merely establishes an exception from the otherwise valid principle of *Propend*. In other words, the scope of the statute as construed in *Propend* can be interpreted restrictively to determine which persons and what acts are immunized statutorily, and to exclude the most severe violations of international law from the scope of immunity.

If, as *Jones* affirms, and despite the fact that the State Immunity Act is the comprehensive code of immunity in English law, statutory immunity can be interpreted restrictively as not covering breaches of *jus cogens* by individual defendants, there is no reason why it cannot be so interpreted with regard to the similar actions of a State. This is possible, provided that the *Jones* approach with regard to claims against individual defendants duly prevails and is consistently applied. *Jones*, which saw an implicit exception to

[48] Riesenfeld, Sovereign Immunity in Perspective, 19 *Vanderbilt JTL* (1986), 16–17.
[49] *Jones*, para 31, *per* Mance LJ.

statutory immunity based on *jus cogens*, lends conceptual support to the argument or implied waiver developed with regard to the US jurisprudence related to the application of the FSIA, that courts should read an implicit exception into the Act when most serious breaches of international law are involved.

But the alternative option is provided by what the Court of Appeal did in *Jones* with regard to the relevance of the State Immunity Act in the case of State defendants. The court in fact held that the claims before it were not governed by any of the provisions of SIA and decided the case outside the context of this Act. The court's treatment of the relevant international law was, as explained,[50] inconsistent and ill-founded, but its approach has nevertheless opened the door for the option of construing the entire instrument of national legislation restrictively to enable international law to intervene and apply to the case. Under this approach, the national State immunity legislation is not going to prevent the domestic enforcement of *jus cogens*, provided that the national courts accept that the claims based on *jus cogens* are justified under international law.

Jones has opened the door for possible judicial interpretations of the UK State Immunity Act as not extending to the claims of serious violations of human rights and humanitarian law and consequently for judging these claims in terms of international law only. This option, as opposed to viewing the SIA as 'comprehensive code' on State immunity and also to the attitude of US courts that every exception to State immunity in the FSIA must be proved by the clearly evidenced intention of Congress, leaves open the conceptual possibility that claims based on *jus cogens* will eventually trump State immunity before national courts through the use and development of the international legal argument.

It seems that the prevalence of the Court of Appeal's treatment of this question of relationship between international and national law can, if further followed in practice, gradually end the primacy of national statutes over international law or at least restrict such primacy to cases in which serious breaches of international law such as breaches of *jus cogens* would not be left without remedies. For all its poor analysis of the state of international law regarding immunities, *Jones* has provided a positive impetus to revise the doctrine of the primacy of statutes over international law and pointed to the increase of the potential to enforce international law before national courts.

---

[50] Above, Chapter 10.

4. THE REASONING ANALOGOUS TO THE NATURE OF *JUS COGENS*

The device of analogy refers to principles and doctrines which, although not referring to *jus cogens* or international law at all, provide doctrinal devices for national courts to give effect to *jus cogens*. Such analogy is sometimes developed by national courts in a way parallel to international law reasoning. Analogous reasoning is quite similar to domestic public policy argument, in that it refers to immorality, repugnancy and abhorrence of certain acts that ought not to be given legal effect, which makes this reasoning similar to the general justification of international *jus cogens* as the body of morality-inspired norms.[51] Furthermore, due to the parallelism of the substantive norms involved in such cases in domestic proceedings—such as freedom from torture and inhuman treatment, due process and the liberty of person in general—and human rights norms with peremptory status, the policies that domestic courts follow effectively signify the policy of not giving effect in domestic legal systems to the acts that constitute breaches of *jus cogens* on the international plane.

Such a device of analogy has been used in cases of inter-State abduction. In *Toscanino*, the US Court of Appeals construed an exception on otherwise absolute principle practised in the US jurisprudence that the way in which an accused was brought before the court is irrelevant for the exercise of jurisdiction; the court held that it could be otherwise if reference is made to the horrendous, shocking nature of acts and actions, which should not be given effect. The starting-point question in *Toscanino* was whether 'a federal court must assume jurisdiction over the person of a defendant who is illegally apprehended abroad and forcibly abducted by government agents of the United States for the purpose of facing criminal charges here'.[52] Having confirmed in general terms the dominant *Ker-Frisbie* Doctrine dictating the irrelevance of the means through which the accused is brought before the court, the court referred to the cases 'in which the conduct of law enforcement agents is so outrageous that due process principles would absolutely bar the government from invoking judicial processes to obtain a conviction'.[53] This is particularly so where the suspect's 'presence has been secured by force or fraud'.[54] In other cases, such as *Lujan* and *Klock v Cain*, US courts used the device of constitutional rights, to reach a similar outcome.[55] This is a reasoning similar to *jus cogens*, which is also morality-based, and refers to

---

[51] In US jurisprudence, *jus cogens* principles are used to determine whether government acts are acceptable, Parker and Neylon, *Jus Cogens*: Compelling the Law of Human Rights, 12 *Hastings International and Comparative Law Review* (1989), 460–461.

[52] 61 ILR 194.   [53] Id., 195–197.   [54] Id., 198.

[55] 813 F Supp 1433 (E.D. Cal. 1993).

such illegality as 'would absolutely bar' the exercise of the ensuing rights. The implications of *jus cogens* invalidity are not very much different.

The English court stated in *Bennett* that the participation of the prosecuting authorities in violations of international law and of the laws of another State is a triggering condition for refusing to allow the trial to go on.[56] In the UK, individuals brought before trial in breach of customary international law or a treaty may invoke the doctrine of abuse of process. The prevailing practice is that if the abuse of process has taken place, the discontinuance of criminal proceedings is discretionary. Such discretion provides for the avenue for protection of the defendant's interests rather than for the automatic stay of proceedings.[57]

But much depends on the manner in which this discretion should be applied in the context of peremptory norms. Human rights norms have the potential capacity to bring objective standards to bear and structure the exercise of the discretionary power of the court to order a stay.[58] In the words of Lord Griffiths, the crucial question is whether the judiciary has 'to oversee executive action and to refuse to countenance the behaviour that threatens either basic human rights or the rule of law', in situations where the trial of a person would not involve any other illegality.[59]

According to Lord Lowry, the power to stay is a discretionary power and a venial irregularity would not be followed by a stay.[60] This demonstrates that the breach of certain norms may bring about some specific consequences. In other words, there is a certain threshold which, if crossed by the State, would render the existing prerogative of that State inoperative. It would not be unjustified to link these substantive standards to the public order norms, even if they are not explicitly mentioned.

Most significantly, 'if violations of human rights are involved, the discretionary power which characterises the abuse of process determination may be overridden by a mandatory obligation to give relief to a defendant'.[61] This language resembles very much the hierarchy of norms argument in terms of international law. Here, it is the doctrine of the abuse of power which implements *jus cogens* through analogous reasoning.

Another analogy to *jus cogens* has been shown by US courts in extradition cases, where they try to avoid immoral results through intended extradition, and are ready to deviate even from the rule of non-enquiry into foreign legal systems, which is part of US law. This is explicitly stated in *Demjanjuk*, according to which, US courts 'do not supervise the conduct of another

---

[56] Lord Bridge in *Bennett*, 155g; Warbrick, Judicial Jurisdiction and Abuse of Process, 49 ICLQ (2000), 491.

[57] Warbrick, Judicial Jurisdiction and Abuse of Process, 49 ICLQ (2000), 490.

[58] Warbrick, Judicial Jurisdiction and Abuse of Process, 49 ICLQ (2000), 495.

[59] *Bennett*, 3 All ER (1993), 150 (per Lord Griffiths).   [60] Lord Lowry in *Bennett*, 164 f.

[61] Warbrick, Judicial Jurisdiction and Abuse of Process, 49 ICLQ (2000), 495.

judicial system'.[62] It was further stated that 'In the absence of any showing that Demjanjuk will be subjected to procedures "antipathetic to federal court's sense of decency," this court will not inquire into the procedures which will apply after he is surrendered to Israel.'[63] The *Atta* case also confirms that 'neither can another nation use our courts to obtain power over a fugitive intending to deny that person due process'.[64] The rule of non-enquiry is thus qualified by an exception to ensure avoidance of procedures and punishment contrary to the sense of decency and basic human rights.[65] This no doubt conforms to the international principle, applicable within the framework of the law of treaties, that extradition is to be denied if a violation of human rights based on *jus cogens* can be expected.[66]

To sum up, although these decisions of national courts do not expressly refer to international *jus cogens*, it is nevertheless clear that the outcomes are the same as would be with the faithful application of peremptory norms.

But there are also more explicit parallels to *jus cogens*. In *Suresh* the Canadian Supreme Court had to examine the compatibility of certain deportation actions and their statutory basis with the Canadian Charter of Human Rights, as well as constitutionality of these acts and measures. As the court emphasized, 'the only question is whether this deprivation is in accordance with the principles of fundamental justice'.[67] While these 'principles of fundamental justice' are to be found in basic tenets of the Canadian legal system, the enquiry into these principles 'is informed not only by Canadian experience and jurisprudence, but also by international law, including *jus cogens*'.[68] The question to be resolved in *Suresh* was whether the return of the person allegedly involved in terrorism to the country where he might face torture accords with those fundamental principles. Looking at this issue from the international perspective, because the Charter norms 'cannot be considered in isolation from the international norms which they reflect', the Supreme Court emphasized that

international treaty norms are not, strictly speaking, binding in Canada unless they have been incorporated into Canadian law by enactment. However, in seeking the meaning of the Canadian Constitution, the courts may be informed by international law. Our concern is not with Canada's international obligations *qua* obligations; rather, our concern is with the principles of fundamental justice. We look to international law as evidence of those principles and not controlling in itself.[69]

In this context, the peremptory status of the prohibition of torture weighed heavily in terms of, and in fact determined, the outcome that the return of the

---

[63] *Demjanjuk*, 79 ILR 546.   [62] *Demjanjuk*, 79 ILR 546.
[64] *Extradition of Atta*, 104 ILR 95.   [65] *Extradition of Atta*, 104 ILR 96, 98.
[66] See above, Chapter 6.   [67] *Suresh*, paras 43–44.
[68] *Suresh*, paras 44–45.   [69] *Suresh*, para. 60.

relevant person to the country where torture may be faced is contrary to Canadian 'principles of fundamental justice'.

While in the Canadian Supreme Court's decision in *Suresh* it is positively clear that Canadian 'principles of fundamental justice' are informed among others by international *jus cogens*, the similar argument in the relevant British and American decisions implicitly affirms the parallelism between the two concepts. However, due to the heavy overlap in terms of subject-matter, it is pretty clear that the result arrived at is the same.

19

Peremptory Norms and Acts of Foreign States in Private International Law

I. CONCEPTS AND CATEGORIES

Public policy is a useful device in that it has peremptory effects: the acts and laws against public policy are absolutely void. The starting-point issue is whether national public orders reflect international law, thus enabling national legal systems to respond to illegalities against international public order. The issue whether international law obliges States not to recognize foreign acts contrary to international law in general or *jus cogens* in particular is conceptually different from whether national public policies require the non-recognition and non-execution of the same acts. Developments in practice have demonstrated that national public policies can counter the effect of international illegalities.

Today it is safe to assume that national public policies are no longer informed only by the difference between the national and the foreign, but also by international law. The idea of justifying the recourse to public order by reference to universal values is quite old.[1] Reference is made, among others, to the concept of *ordre public vraiment international* as a minimum standard common to civilized States, against which national courts shall test the recognition and execution of foreign laws and acts, and it is based on generally accepted principles of international law in terms of Article 38 of the ICJ Statute.[2] But this leaves open the question of origin of such 'true international public order', namely whether it is based on a consensus of different national legal systems or international law proper.

The 'internationalization' of national public orders no doubt goes hand in hand with the requirement that national courts respect international law and refuse to give effect to international illegalities. More specifically, it is accepted that the true international public order which is part of public international law must be observed by national courts.[3] Arguably, public order in terms of public international law has no special meaning for private

---

[1] Batiffol, H., and Lagarde, P., *Traité de Droit International Privé* (Tome 1, Paris, 1993), 586; in rare cases the reference to natural law would also be possible, Meyer, *Droit International Privé* (1994), 144.

[2] Völker, *Zur Dogmatik des* ordre public (1998), 277–278.

[3] Niederer, *Einführung in die Allgemeine Lehren des Internationalen Privatrechts* (1956), 289.

international law.[4] Only in cases of grave breaches of international law does this legal system require that the relevant foreign laws and acts shall not be applied by the forum.[5] *Jus cogens* of public international law which voids conflicting international treaties also requires that national courts shall give no effect to the relevant illegalities. This is the public international law aspect of public order in private international law, national public order.[6]

Jaenicke's analysis of proper international public order of the international community as principally consisting of *jus cogens* is aimed at demonstrating the effect of such public order with regard to recognition of foreign laws and other foreign State acts. Such international public order shall be observed by national courts.[7]

While parallelism between national and international public policies is clear, it still remains to understand through which modality international law in general and international public order in particular can find their recognition in national legal systems. A national court's reference to 'international public policy' is not necessarily the reference to international law. For instance, a Belgian court declared in *Lavi v Asco* that arms sales were 'contrary to Belgian international public policy' by reference to 'general principles of law and humanity recognised by civilised nations', even though it acknowledged that international law does not regulate arms sales.[8] This justifies Lipstein's enquiry whether a breach of public international law itself offends the forum's public policy or whether it is merely a factor in determining whether the normally applicable foreign law must be applied to the specific case or whether a foreign executive act is to be recognized and given effect.[9]

This requires identifying two basic options through which international law and public order can have effect on public order in national legal systems. Either international law can be an independent factor outlawing incompatible transactions and foreign laws, or international law can form an element of national public policies.

---

[4] It is argued that the norms of international *jus cogens* such as the prohibition of the use of force are not particularly relevant for private international law, Völker, *Zur Dogmatik des ordre public* (1998), 278. But in practice the opposite is confirmed, for example in the *Kuwait Air Corp.* litigation.

[5] Kropholler, *Internationales Privatrecht* (1997), 51.

[6] Kropholler, *Internationales Privatrecht* (1997), 51, adding that in German law such effect is guaranteed by Article 25 of *Grundgesetz* which makes general norms of international law part of German law. From the Swiss perspective, international *jus cogens* which belongs to international public order, also belongs to Swiss public order, Saladin (1988), 70.

[7] Jaenicke, Zur Frage des Internationalen Ordre Public, 7 *Berichte der Deutschen Gesellschaft für Völkerrecht* (1967), 81–82.

[8] *Lavi v Asco*, Commercial Court of Brussels, 91 *ILR* 224–225. The court declared the relevant contract void.

[9] Lipstein, *Principles of the Conflict of Laws: National and International* (1981), 79.

2. THE DIRECT AND INDEPENDENT RELEVANCE
OF INTERNATIONAL LAW

National legislative clauses banning transactions against good morals refer to international law as well. Thus, Article 138 of the German Civil Code protects the general interest embodied in general norms of international law. For example, private contracts that support interference in a State's internal affairs through supporting rebellion or revolution, or provide an aggressor State with weapons, or limit the rights of prisoners of war are null and void.[10] When something is prohibited under international law, it can be against good morals at domestic level, for instance in terms of Article 138 of the German Civil Code or Article 30 of the *Einführungsgesetz*. Even if the relevant norms of international law are not transformed into national law, the public order clauses banning conflicting transactions could provide respective sanctions and safeguards at domestic level.[11]

The approach viewing international law as a factor separate and independent from national public order was championed a century ago by Zitelmann, suggesting that foreign laws can be rejected if they do not comply with the requirements of international law. He refers to laws providing for religious inequality. Such laws must not be applied, even if the public order clause such as Article 30 of the *Einführungsgesetz* does not specifically require this.[12] Although religious inequality laws can be rejected on the basis of immorality, Zitelmann nevertheless categorically emphasized that the conflict with international law gives rise to a separate heading, independent of immorality concerns, under which foreign laws must be denied recognition. Zitelmann went further and also considered that when public international law governs the issue in question and foreign law is contrary to international law, the relevant norm of international law must be viewed as part of the legal order of the relevant foreign State and applied by the forum as such and instead of the applicable norm of the foreign law.[13]

It seems that this approach was applied, in the context of private international law and with particular reference to international *jus cogens*, by the Court of Appeals for the Ninth Circuit *Doe v Unocal*. Unocal urged the Court to apply the law of Myanmar instead of international law. The Court responded that in this case the violations of *jus cogens* were alleged, and 'by definition, the law of any particular State is either identical to the *jus cogens* norms of international law, or it is invalid'. This required, as is established in US jurisprudence, assessing the character of the relevant tort in terms of international, not foreign, law.[14] This is an example of the acceptance, as a

---

[10] Bleckmann, A., *Sittenwidrigkeit wegen Verstoßes gegen den* ordre public international, 34 *ZaöRV* (1974), 128–130.
[11] Id., 130.   [12] Zitelmann, *Internationales Privatrecht* (Bd. I, 1897), 379–380.
[13] Id., 380.   [14] *Doe v Unocal*, 14214.

matter of private international law, of the principle of *jus cogens* invalidity of State legislation.

The tendency to view international law as an independent factor that bans incompatible acts and transactions at domestic level is derived from and encouraged by the fact that public policy is, or it would so seem at the relevant stages of legal development, relative and not comprehensive enough to encompass the national courts' responses to international illegalities. According to F.A. Mann, not every international delinquency contradicts public policy, nor does every violation of public policy involve an international delinquency.[15] Therefore, the true principle of decision is public international law itself. A municipal court which deals with international wrong ought to be bound by international law and disregard the incompatible foreign law.[16] National judges should be guided by international law as opposed to their public policies and for them a violation of international law by foreign States should be enough to refuse giving effect to relevant foreign laws.[17]

The preference of international law is justified, according to FA Mann, because 'the relative objectivity and uniformity of its standards, as compared with varying notions of public policy, makes public international law a more attractive guide to judicial decisions'.[18] '*Ordre public* is frequently designed to protect or assert the interests or values of the judge's nation, while public international law provides a more neutral and at the same time a uniform standard.'[19] Furthermore, *ordre public* is 'so limited and so national, perhaps even chauvinistic' that it can, by reference to the requirement of *Binnenbeziehung*, 'recognise and enforce foreign laws and transactions which international law would condemn—not necessarily because such laws and transactions meet with approval, but because they are not of a sufficiently close concern'.[20] The requirements of public international law, on the other hand, are 'absolute and leave no room for the relativity of public policy'.[21] According to Mann, if national courts face a foreign legislation prohibiting inter-racial marriage, they could reject it if they are guided by international law as such, because under international law such legislation is clearly and categorically illegal. But the same result would not necessarily be achieved if the courts were guided by public policy only.[22] This is correct at least in cases

---

[15] Mann, International Delinquencies before Municipal Courts, 70 *LQR* (1954), 191.

[16] Mann, International Delinquencies before Municipal Courts, 70 *LQR* (1954), 191–192.

[17] Mann, The Consequences of an International Wrong in International and National Law, *BYIL* 1976–77, 30.

[18] Mann, International Delinquencies before Municipal Courts, 70 *LQR* (1954), 193.

[19] Mann, The Consequences of an International Wrong in International and National Law, *BYIL* 1976–77, 29.

[20] Mann, The Consequences of an International Wrong in International and National Law, *BYIL* 1976–77, 35. See also Mann's conclusions id. at 38–39.

[21] Mann, International Delinquencies before Municipal Courts, 70 *LQR* (1954), 193.

[22] Mann, *BYIL* 1976–77, 37.

where public policy is only informed by the distinction between the national and the foreign.

Furthermore, F.A. Mann emphasizes that even if the foreign measures which do not affect the forum are not offending public policy, a judge can engage his own sovereign's responsibility by supporting a measure which is contrary to international law.[23] Conversely, a State cannot modify by its laws the scope of its international obligations, which requires that municipal courts respect international law in terms of the choice of laws.[24]

F.A. Mann does not suggest disregarding the relevance of public policy in countering fundamental international illegalities. Quite the contrary, public order and international law are alternatives for a judge who wishes to avoid giving effect to international delinquencies through application of foreign laws or acts 'and prima facie it does not matter which of the tools the judge may decide to employ, provided he reaches the correct result'.[25] However, Mann's approach preferring international law to public policy as such is understandable given the precedents in national courts with the outcomes recognizing grave breaches of international law. A response to this concern can be the alternative approach of integrating international law requirements into national public policies, which indeed happens in judicial practice.

3. INTERNATIONAL LAW AS AN ELEMENT OF NATIONAL PUBLIC POLICY

The fact that national clauses refer to national public orders does not exclude the consideration of internationally dominant attitudes.[26] It is doctrinally accepted that international *ordre public* can be a tool to reject foreign laws that are contrary to international law.[27] Furthermore, *ordre public international* includes not only domestic legal factors, but also international legal factors as well as international collective interests that have not quite achieved the rank of binding international law.[28]

Lipstein explains that when confronted with a plea that the foreign law or foreign executive act offends against public international law, courts in

---

[23] Mann, International Delinquencies before Municipal Courts, 70 *LQR* (1954), 193–194. On the responsibility of States, especially attribution to a State of actions of its organs such as judicial organs, see ILC Articles on State Responsibility, Report of the UN International Law Commission on the work of its Fifty-third session (2001), *Official Records of the General Assembly, Fifty-sixth session, Supplement No. 10* (A/56/10), 43.

[24] Mann, International Delinquencies before Municipal Courts, 70 *LQR* (1954), 194.

[25] Mann, The Consequences of an International Wrong in International and National Law, *BYIL* 1976–77, 29.

[26] Kropholler, *Internationales Privatrecht* (1997), 228.

[27] cf Völker, *Zur Dogmatik des* ordre public (1998), 276.

[28] Bleckmann, A., *Sittenwidrigkeit wegen Verstoßes gegen den* ordre public international, 34 *ZaöRV* (1974), 113.

different countries have considered the rules of public international law as a facet of a broader notion of local public policy. The substance of the contested foreign law or executive act and not the fact or violation of public international law shall determine whether that rule or act offends against the basic social, political or moral foundations of the *lex fori*.[29] In addition, the incorporation of international law standards into national public policies can neutralize, to a certain extent, the obstacles raised to the enforcement of international law in legal systems that adhere to a transformation approach requiring that if an international rule is to be given effect nationally, it must be transformed into national law through a statute. International law cannot prevail over a domestic statute in a country which adopts a transformation approach, but it can have effect with regard to foreign law through the tool of public policy. This is a difference between using international law as an authoritative expression of public policy and applying it directly as a rule of domestic decision.[30] This allows viewing the transformation doctrine as a tool ensuring supremacy of national statutes over international norms, not *per se* preventing the enforcement of international norms within national legal systems.

The English jurisprudence has developed a relatively consolidated approach incorporating international law into the forum's public policy. It was originally stated in *Helbert Wagg* that foreign exchange control laws are normally the product of State discretion as States are in the best position to know what sort of control is best suited to their particular needs. But public policy may cause non-recognition of a foreign law if it is inconsistent with the 'usage of nations',[31] for example if its true object is racial discrimination.[32] Upjohn J was clear both in emphasizing the basis for decision and in stating preferences: 'In my judgment the true limits of the principle that the courts of this country will afford recognition to legislation of foreign States in so far as it affects title to movables in that States at the time of the legislation or contracts governed by the law of that State rests in considerations of international law or in the scarcely less difficult considerations of public policy as understood in these courts. Ultimately I believe the latter is the governing consideration.'[33] Under this approach, international law is included in public policy.

This approach was further developed by the House of Lords in *Oppenheimer v Cattermole* dealing with the validity of the racially motivated

---

[29] Lipstein, Principles of the Conflict of Laws: National and International (1981), 79.

[30] cf on this point Brundner, The Domestic Enforcement of International Covenants on Human Rights, 35 *University of Toronto Law Journal* (1985), 241.

[31] 'Usage of nations' could be taken as synonym of the law of nations, or international law, namely customary or general international law.

[32] *Helbert Wagg* (*per* Upjohn J), 2 All ER (1956), 142.

[33] *Helbert Wagg* (*per* Upjohn J), 2 All ER (1956), 140.

confiscation decrees in Nazi Germany. It was initially emphasized that a judge should be very slow to refuse giving effect to legislation of a foreign State in the sphere in which that State has jurisdiction under international law. Judges may well have inadequate understanding of the circumstances of adoption of foreign laws and their action could embarrass the executive in its relations with foreign governments. However, 'it is part of the public policy of this country that our courts should not give effect to clearly established rules of international law.' International law may be uncertain in some points but the contradiction with international law of a decree that confiscates property on the basis of racial discrimination cannot be doubted. 'A law of this sort constitutes so grave an infringement of human rights that the courts of this country ought to refuse to recognise it as a law at all.' This should be the case even in face of certain 'practical objections'.[34] Such legislation should be null and void in the eyes of an English court.[35] That the English court is, as one element of evaluation of public policy, entitled to take into account international law, and that international human rights are part of English public policy has been affirmed by the House of Lords also in *Kuwait Air Corp.*[36] But the House of Lords was careful to emphasize that human rights were just an example of the broader heading of public order based on and inspired by international law. Thus, other peremptory norms such as the prohibition of the use of force can also be part of public policy.[37]

In *Kuwait Air Corp.*, the House of Lords recognized that the Iraqi seizure of KAC aircraft on the basis of a decree to give effect to the forcible integration of Kuwait into Iraq was a flagrant violation of fundamental norms of international law.[38] The act of the Iraqi government illegally confiscating the planes of KAC was in breach not only of the UN Charter but also of the principles prohibiting the use of force that are of *jus cogens* character, ie are part of peremptory public international law.[39] This is a clear affirmation that if a norm is part of international *jus cogens*, that is international public order, it also becomes part of English public policy.

International human rights treaties can be authoritative expressions of public policy to void discriminatory contracts or refusing to enforce incompatible foreign rules.[40] Domestic courts can refer to human rights

---

[34] *Oppenheimer v Cattermole* (HL), *AC* 1976, 278, reaffirmed in *Williams v Humbert*, 1 AC (1986), 379, *Seltebello*, 1 WLR (1985), 1056.

[35] Mann, The Consequences of an International Wrong in International and National Law, *BYIL* 1976–77, 45.

[36] *Kuwait Air Corp.* (High Court), 116 ILR 571, also reaffirming that Lord Wilberforce's assessment in *Buttes Gas* affirms that international law is an element of public policy.

[37] *Kuwait Air Corp.*, HL, 16 May 2002, paras 114 (*per* Lord Steyn), 137–139 (*per* Lord Hope).

[38] *Kuwait Air Corp.*, HL, 16 May 2002, para. 19 (*per* Lord Nicholls).

[39] *Kuwait Air Corp.*, HL, 16 May 2002, paras 114, 117 (*per* Lord Steyn).

[40] Brundner, The Domestic Enforcement of International Covenants on Human Rights, 35 *University of Toronto Law Journal* (1985), 240.

instruments as guides to principles of public policy and 'confirmation of the universal validity and hence peremptoriness of those principles'.[41] This seems to reflect the fact that human rights treaties form part of public order of the international legal system.

Several human rights treaties contain norms justifying the refusal to apply foreign laws.[42] For instance, French public policy includes several rights under the European Convention on Human Rights and its Additional Protocols, such as the respect for privacy (Article 8), freedom of marriage (Article 12), right to property (Article 1, First Protocol), equality between men and women (Protocol 7).[43] In the German legal system, the rights enshrined in the ECHR are part of national public policy and can avoid the requirement of the link of the relevant situation to the forum.[44] In England too, it would be against public policy to apply a foreign law in a way contradicting the ECHR.[45] Certain cases in which the applicability of foreign laws was denied on the ground of public policy were influenced by the impact of the ECHR.[46]

The effect of the ECHR in national law can be based either on its direct application (provided that the national legal system allows this) or its integration into the principles of *ordre public international*.[47] The public policy relevance of the International Covenant on Civil and Political Rights (1966) can offer a back door to give them effect even if they are not transformed into national law through a legislative instrument, as is required in countries that adhere to the transformation doctrine in the matter of treaties, such as the United Kingdom. Even if such treaties are not incorporated into national law, they shall nevertheless be taken into account by courts when assessing the scope of public policy.[48] Thus, while human rights treaties cannot prevail over domestic statutes, due to parliamentary supremacy, they can have effect with regard to foreign laws by virtue of their being part of public policy.

The international law element of national public policies modifies their reach. In particular, international law can justify the intervention of national public order and loosen the requirement of the link to the forum.[49] It is generally admitted that the graver the violation of international law is, the looser the link may be to justify intervention of *ordre public*. 'A flagrant international wrong should invariably be deemed to be so grave a matter as to

---

[41] Brundner, The Domestic Enforcement of International Covenants on Human Rights, 35 *University of Toronto Law Journal* (1985), 246.

[42] Batiffol, H., and Lagarde, P., *Traité de Droit International Privé* (Tome 1, Paris, 1993), 587.

[43] Meyer, *Droit International Privé* (1994), 141–142.

[44] Kropholler, *Internationales Privatrecht* (1997), 231.

[45] North and Fawcett, *Cheshire and North's Private International Law* (1999), 128.

[46] Dicey and Morris, *Conflict of Laws* (2000), 82.

[47] Mayer, La Convention européenne des droits de l'homme et l'application des normes étrangères, 80 *Rev. crit. dr. internat. privé* (1991), 662. Mayer, id. 655, suggests that States-parties are merely entitled, but not obliged, to exclude through *ordre public international* foreign laws contradicting ECHR.

[48] Mann, *BYIL* 1976–77, 37.   [49] Kropholler, *Internationales Privatrecht* (1997), 228.

be contrary to the public policy of the forum. It is an absolute wrong and leaves no room for the doctrine of relativity.'[50] When public policy refers to the norms recognized by the community of nations as part of the law of nations, there is no need to distinguish specific situations in terms of their link with the forum.[51] This can be reconciled with the idea that the relevance before national courts of *ordre public vraiment international* as a minimum standard common to civilized States shall not depend on relativity doctrines such as *Binnenbeziehung*.[52]

It is arguable that public policy under the heading of international law would not interfere with recognition of those foreign laws and acts which are originally arguably unlawful under international law but relate to legal claims which are bilaterally disposable, and validly disposed, as a matter of international law. An example is the mutual renunciation of property and other claims by Soviet Russia and Germany under the Rapallo Treaty of 16 April 1922. The effect of this Treaty was to stop challenging before German courts of the legality of Soviet laws and acts that affected the private rights of Germans. These courts have thus refused to consider that the encroachments on property rights in question were against German *ordre public*.[53] If the original illegality no longer persists on an international plane, it would be senseless to portray these as part of national public order.

The Rapallo Treaty had no direct effect on German territory. The reasoning justifying the approach of German courts seems to be based on international law: general norms of international law (to the extent that the norms related to illegality of property confiscation fall into this category) were part of the German legal order; but once these general norms were contractually disposable, and validly disposed, German courts were justified to consider them inapplicable to the specific situations involving the legality of Soviet confiscatory laws and acts. This confirms not only that national public order is often informed by public international law, but also that the scope of national public order is often influenced by whether a legal relation under international law is derogable, in other words by the distinction between *jus cogens* and *jus dispositivum*.

Similar circumstances were involved in the case of the Litvinov Agreements between the USSR and USA disposing the private property rights and they too can be justified as a matter of international law on the basis that their subject-matter was not beyond the contractual power of the

---

[50] Mann, *BYIL* 1976–77, 52.

[51] Bucher, L'ordre public et le but social des lois en droit international privé, 239 *RdC* (1993), 53–54.

[52] Völker, *Zur Dogmatik des* ordre public (1998), 277–278.

[53] Nussbaum, *Deutsches Internationales Privatrecht* (1974), 68, also referring to German judicial practice implementing a similar approach. See also Jaenicke, Zur Frage des Internationalen Ordre Public, 7 *Berichte der Deutschen Gesellschaft für Völkerrecht* (1967), 106–107.

States-parties. That there are limits on this approach is clearly proved by the concerns Philip Jessup expressed, suggesting that this principle cannot be applied in a blanket way. Otherwise it would have serious humanitarian repercussions.[54] But this can be prevented by the fact that the generally recognized principles of international law are incorporated in national public policies in terms of *Oppenheimer v Cattermole* and thus prevent extreme solutions.

4. PUBLIC POLICY, INTERNATIONAL LAW AND THE ACT OF STATE DOCTRINE

The doctrine of an Act of State, which is a subject of interest both from the viewpoint of private and public international law, is a more consolidated version of the general approach based on comity and is conceptually based on concerns to avoid, through judicial restraint, the embarrassment of other branches of the government in their foreign relations. Much of what has been considered above can fall within the purview of the relevance of this doctrine because the concept of the 'Act of State' eludes precise definition and can in principle encompass any law or act of a foreign State. But the separate treatment of this doctrine is justified by its treatment in practice, though this should not detract us from viewing this doctrine as a specific implication of some broader approaches.

To begin with, the Act of State doctrine is not universal. In France, this doctrine is not really accepted as a factor preventing courts judging foreign State acts because these courts do not judge those acts as such but merely refuse to give them effect in France.[55] In England we face a more consolidated approach. The Court of Appeal in *Luther v Sagor*, which involved the validity of Soviet Russian confiscatory decrees, refused to invoke public policy, because it would be a serious breach of international comity if a national court were to proclaim, on the basis of public policy, that the legislation of a foreign sovereign State is contrary to morality and justice.[56] Similar concerns were also expressed in *Oppenheimer* and *Kuwait Air Corp.*, where the Lords acknowledged that non-recognition of foreign acts can embarrass the executive in relation to foreign governments. English courts should not offend against the principle that they should not sit in judgment on the sovereign acts of a foreign State.[57]

In the United States, the Act of State doctrine is also strongly represented. In *Sabbatino*, the Supreme Court examined the issue whether it could

---

[54] Jessup (1937), 481; Jessup (1942), 282; and see further above Chapter 11, Section 2.2.
[55] Battifol and Lagarde, 573–574.   [56] *Luther v Sagor*, 3 KB (1921), 558.
[57] *Kuwait Air Corp.*, HL, 16 May 2002, para. 24 (*per* Lord Nicholls).

challenge the validity or otherwise of Cuban confiscatory acts for their incompatibility with international law. The Court concluded that 'the Judicial Branch will not examine the validity of a taking of property within its territory by a foreign government ... in the absence of a treaty or other unambiguous agreement regarding controlling legal principles, even if the complainant alleges that the taking violates customary international law'.[58] This approach basically confirms that the act of State doctrine could fail if it confronts clearly established principles of international law. Lord Wilberforce developed a similar approach in *Buttes*, suggesting that English courts will not judge foreign State acts unless they contradict certain judicially manageable standards.[59] Foreign acts of State can be refused recognition on the basis of public order when they offend against international law.[60]

In *Rose Mary*, which is exceptional in Anglo-American jurisprudence, the Supreme Court of Aden withheld recognition from the Persian act nationalizing without compensation an oil company on the basis that it was contrary to international law.[61] This case demonstrates that the international law factor should not indiscriminately interfere with acts of State; otherwise, it will be turned into a tool of parochial economic interests.[62] The act of State doctrine, though not itself part of international law,[63] can nevertheless be useful in some cases to avoid foreign judicial interferences with internal economic processes of foreign States given that, moreover, the now unequivocal affirmation of the permanent sovereignty of nations over their natural resources has seriously questioned and reduced the degree of international legal validity of principles specifying the standard of compensation for the expropriation of foreign property.[64]

Up to this point, the act of State doctrine should not be viewed as incompatible with international law. But there are cases where this assumption is reversed, namely the cases where a foreign act of State contradicts a clearly recognized norm of international law. For example, while the Act of

---

[58] 36 US 428 (1964). The Court referred to situations where the complainant alleges that the taking violates customary law, not where it *in fact violates it*. Also, the reference to 'other unambiguous agreement regarding controlling legal principles' might as well be a reference to an established customary norm. For human rights as an instance of this principle see Parker and Neylon (1989), 446.

[59] AC 1982, 938.

[60] Bleckmann, A., *Sittenwidrigkeit wegen Verstoßes gegen den* ordre public international, 34 *ZaöRV* (1974), 132.

[61] [1953] 1 WLR 246.

[62] Brundner, The Domestic Enforcement of International Covenants on Human Rights, 35 *University of Toronto Law Journal* (1985), 245.

[63] Brownlie, *Principles of Public International Law* (2003), 483; Jaenicke, Zur Frage des Internationalen Ordre Public, 7 *Berichte der Deutschen Gesellschaft für Völkerrecht* (1967), 100–101; Lipstein, 79.

[64] For a detailed analysis of this issue see Lowenfeld, *International Economic Law* (2002), 391–415. See also A. Orakhelashvili, The Position of the Individual in International Law, 31 *California Western International Law Journal* (2001), 241 at 256–264.

State doctrine can be relevant with regard to property confiscations carried out abroad, it loses its force when such confiscations are discriminatory and racially motivated. As Lord Steyn emphasized in *Kuwait Air Corp.*, 'Judicial restraint must be exercised. But restraint is what is needed, not abstention. And there is no need for restraint on the ground of public policy where it is plain beyond dispute that a clearly established norm has been violated.'[65] Lord Nicholls went on to clarify that *Buttes* does not mean that courts should ignore that clear breaches of international law have been committed and refuse adjudication when they face clearly manageable international law standards.[66] This emphasis on 'clearly established' and 'judicially manageable' standards looks similar to *Sabbatino*, which refers to 'controlling legal principles'. *Kuwait Air Corp.* and *Sabbatino* are common in suggesting that where the foreign State act is clearly governed by and violates international law, the Act of State doctrine would not be applied. In addition, *Kuwait Air Corp.* expressly refers to public policy, which in its turn includes international law and especially international *jus cogens*, as a limitation on the Act of State doctrine.

This responds to F.A. Mann's emphasis on international public order as an element of national public policy. When there is a clear and serious international wrong, courts shall resort to '*ordre public international* in the true and most direct sense, which would have allowed, and indeed compelled English courts to assist in the elimination of a plain international illegality'. This is neither a point of politics nor a matter dependent on the attitude of the executive, but a matter of morality and juridical conscience.[67]

The application of public policy in the face of likelihood of embarrassment of foreign government as the core issue of the Act of State doctrine has received sufficient judicial attention. In *Oppenheimer*, Lord Salmon observed with regard to the non-recognition of the Nazi confiscation decree that such non-recognition could embarrass the Crown in its relations with foreign governments.[68] But the House of Lords doubted if it could be embarrassing for foreign governments if an English court 'decide that the 1941 [Nazi confiscation] decree was so great an offence against human rights that they would have nothing to do with it'.[69]

In *Wiwa v Royal Dutch Petroleum*, which dealt with the involvement of European oil companies in gross and large-scale human rights violations including torture and persecutions, the US court refused to apply the Act of State doctrine by referring to the change of government in Nigeria: 'the military regime responsible for the alleged torts has been replaced by a democracy,' and 'any finding of improprieties on the part of the previous

---

[65] *Kuwait Air Corp.* (*per* Lord Steyn), para. 114.
[66] *Kuwait Air Corp.* (*per* Lord Nicholls), para. 26.
[67] Mann, *Foreign Affairs in English Courts* (1986), 158.
[68] *Oppenheimer*, 282 AC 1976.   [69] *Oppenheimer v Cattermole* (HL), AC 1976, 283.

regime would more likely be consonant, than at odds, with the present position of the [Nigerian] government.' Thus, the court added, 'the danger of hindrance or embarrassment is "dim indeed" ' and adjudicating plaintiffs' claims would not interfere with Nigerian-American relations.[70]

The case of *Doe v Unocal* before the US Court of Appeals involved the situation where the respondent corporation was accused to have caused and promoted, during its business activities in Myanmar, severe human rights violations on a massive scale, such as murder, rape, forced labour and torture. The Court found that these claims related to the breaches of peremptory norms of international law (*jus cogens*) falling within the scope of §1350 of the Alien Tort Claims Act (ATCA).[71] But the court had also to examine whether the plaintiffs' claims were barred by the acts of State doctrine. The court accepted that this doctrine is generally relevant in situations where the acts of foreign States are involved, but pointed out that:

murder, torture, and slavery are *jus cogens* violations, i.e. violations of norms that are binding on nations even if they do not agree to them. . . . [R]ape can be a form of torture and thus a *jus cogens* violation. . . . [F]orced labour is a modern form of slavery and thus likewise a *jus cogens* violation. Accordingly, all torts alleged in the present case are *jus cogens* violations. Because *jus cogens* violations are, by definition, internationally denounced, there is a high degree of consensus against them, which severely undermines Unocal's argument that the alleged acts by the Myanmar Military and Myanmar Oil should be treated as acts of State.[72]

The court did not directly refer to public policy of the forum. It merely emphasized international consensus regarding the violated norms that are part of international *jus cogens* and this case clearly affirms that the Act of State doctrine has no place where a violation of peremptory norms is alleged.

The court acknowledged that the condemnation of the acts of the Myanmar military would offend the government of that country, and consequently embarrass the US government in its foreign relations. That was, so the court suggested, the only factor favouring application of the act of State doctrine.[73] The court adopted the approach different from *Wiwa* in overruling the Act of State defence. Thereby the court in principle tolerated the embarrassment of a foreign government. It seems that, as was the case in *Doe v Unocal*, if human rights violations in a given country are internationally condemned, the concerns of embarrassments would not preclude domestic adjudication over such violations. This approach is more straightforward than *Wiwa* and more helpful for victims of serious human rights violations.

---

[70] District Court for the Southern District of New York, 2002 U.S. Dist. LEXIS 3293, 22 February 2002.

[71] *Doe v Unocal Corp.*, US Court of Appeals (9th Circuit), 18 September 2002, at 14192–14231.

[72] *Doe v Unocal Corp.*, US Court of Appeals (9th Circuit), 18 September 2002, at 14233.

[73] *Doe v Unocal Corp.*, US Court of Appeals (9th Circuit), 18 September 2002, at 14234.

Thus, while the Act of State doctrine can prevent adjudication where either a purely bilateral legal issue is involved or governing international law standards are unclear or disputed, it cannot have the same effect where the adjudication before a national court involves a higher standard of international law embodied in peremptory norms. Jaenicke considers that in cases where a foreign State act contradicts norms safeguarding the fundamental interests of the international community, such as *jus cogens* norms, the application of the Act of State doctrine is no longer justified, because States are not merely entitled but also obliged not to recognize acts contradicting such fundamental norms.[74]

The effect of international *jus cogens* in national legal systems in general and as an element of national public policies in particular is part of a broader issue of the consequential duties that peremptory norms impose on States. *Jus cogens* as public order of international law requires non-recognition of acts that contradict *jus cogens*.[75] Therefore, although the application of the act of State doctrine is as such not contrary to international law, individual States are nevertheless bound not to apply this doctrine to cases involving breaches of international *jus cogens*, that is not to recognize the effect of these breaches in their own legal systems. Such an outcome follows from two mutually supportive factors. Violations of *jus cogens* are unequivocally condemned in international law as gross illegalities and cannot be considered as Acts of State. In addition, international law prohibits recognizing the effect of breaches of *jus cogens*. National courts can comply with these imperatives of international public order either through direct reference to international law or indirectly by referring to national public policies. To illustrate, the French court refused to give effect to the Nazi expropriation decree in Czechoslovakia by emphasizing the illegality of the annexation of Czechoslovakia as a factor precluding recognition of German expropriation measures.[76]

5. EVALUATION

The effect of international law and international public order in national legal systems demonstrates that public policy, originally a national law concept, is well suited not only to safeguard the basic values and interests of national societies but also to enable national courts to adapt to the

---

[74] Jaenicke, Zur Frage des Internationalen Ordre Public, 7 *Berichte der Deutschen Gesellschaft für Völkerrecht* (1967), 118, 122, 130.

[75] Commentary to Article 41, ILC Articles on State Responsibility, *ILC Report* 2001, 289–291. On the principle of non-recognition as an aspect of the effect of *jus cogens* see Dugard, *Recognition and the United Nations* (1987).

[76] *Jellinek v Levi*, 11 *Annual Digest* 24–25.

fundamental requirements of international life by enforcing fundamental standards of international law.

National public policies, originally the concepts of private law and private international law, are useful tools to 'receive' international law standards into national legal systems. They can enable national courts to respond to illegalities under public international law. This also causes substantial expansion of the scope of national public policies to reflect the imperatives not only of national but also of international legal systems. Furthermore, along with the general concern of enforcement of international law before national courts, the enforcement of peremptory norms of international law (*jus cogens*) as international public order is reinforced by the more specific and equally peremptory obligation of States not to recognize the effects of breaches of peremptory norms. Beyond these limits, the reception of international legal standards into national public policies seems to be a matter for national priorities, not least dependent on comity and related doctrines.

The internationalization of the concept of public policy in national legal systems by reference to international law, especially international *jus cogens*— a phenomenon comparable to the movements towards assertion in national legal systems, even without any connection with the forum, of universal criminal jurisdiction over certain international crimes or universal civil jurisdiction over some serious breaches of international law as particularly evidenced by the US §1350 ATCA proceedings—necessarily evidences not only that public policy is a flexible, dynamic and ever-changing regime that can adapt to the necessities of national and international legal systems, but also (due to the reference to international law and international *jus cogens* as standards objectively embodying the consensus of the international legal community about certain basic legal values) that it is not designed to become a tool for some to impose their interests, values and perceptions on others.

20

Conclusion

The movement of international law towards the consolidation of the concept of international public order and its effects has been the product of experience accumulated from the period of the two World Wars onwards. Different phenomena, such as illegal wars and annexations, wartime atrocities, gross human rights violations in internal armed conflicts as well as in peacetime, exploitation of the resources of undefended peoples and the state of individuals who are left without remedies after having faced severe oppression, prompt the conclusion that the evils that mankind has long been facing recur and persevere if the legal relations in the relevant situations are considered from the perspective of bilateralism and the individualistic structure of international law. Hitler's increased self-confidence in proceeding with the Holocaust on the basis of having observed the toleration of the impunity for Armenian massacres through inter-State transactions is just one example. The purported or actual toleration of the outcome of aggression or atrocities, whether explained by reference to effectiveness, or the predominant importance of peace, or bilateralism, always has the impact of encouraging subsequent actions of a similar kind.

It is this social reality that underlines the inseparable link of peremptory norms to international public order. The need to have evils banished is the normal, indeed principal, function of any public order in any society, and international public order is not an exception.

The normative framework of peremptory norms was originally worked out in the ILC's work on the law of treaties and culminated in the adoption of Article 53 of the Vienna Convention. But it rapidly became clear (if it was not already so) that this normative framework could not be confined to the field of treaty law, and subsequent developments, in particular the vast practice of international organs, shows that the category of peremptory norms is now firmly established as a matter of general international law having a comprehensive scope. While the specific norms and effects of *jus cogens* can indeed be the subject of discussion and disagreement, a sound approach, while attempting to explain the limits on the scope of *jus cogens* and its effects, must necessarily consider the essence of the category itself.

Despite stiff opposition at the outset, *jus cogens* has emerged in international law as a body of superior rules controlling bilateral and multilateral transactions of every kind. It has gained significance in all the different fields to which it could logically be extended, and has found growing recognition in judicial and other practice. It is not just a theoretical concept. Its importance does not merely lie in its symbolic significance; it is not just of an aspirational character. Rather it is a phenomenon highly relevant in practice. Despite desires to the contrary,[1] it shows no sign of fading away.

This process is not over. The stage that has been reached at the present time already witnesses the contours set for those effects and implications of international public order that enable it to have a comprehensive impact on the variety of acts and transactions of international legal persons. The most real challenge that international public order faces at present is not its existence or its effects, but the translation and implementation of these effects in the areas where the compliance rate with the relevant norms and principles is less than satisfactory.

Jus cogens as a concept embodying the community interest and reinforced by its link with public morality exists in modern international law as a matter of necessity. It establishes a much-needed normative hierarchy based on material factors—the interests it protects—by contrast to the formal or consensual nature of other hierarchies. This was accepted by the principal proponents of the concept even before its recognition in the Vienna Convention: in particular, Verdross, Lauterpacht and McNair. This factor necessarily impacts on the criteria for identifying individual peremptory norms, meaning that if a norm by its substance protects the higher community interest, it should be deemed peremptory.

There has been an argument that the Vienna Convention rejected this understanding, requiring instead that the existence and peremptory character of a norm be subject to consensual acceptance by States and hence to a heavy burden of evidence in State practice. This approach, however, is not the only possible reading of Article 53 of the Vienna Convention, which can also be interpreted as requiring the community recognition of peremptory norms and hence absolving those norms from the burden of being established through consensual evidence based on State practice (even if practice can be accessorily significant in terms of evidence as it is in the case of a number of peremptory norms). This latter approach has been favoured by tribunals and other bodies in identifying peremptory norms, often disregarding traditional requirements of norm-creation. It is safe to assume that in practice the Verdross–Lauterpacht morality-based approach has prevailed in identifying which norms are peremptory, thereby confirming that the appropriate reading of Article 53 of the Vienna Convention is justified.

The nature of *jus cogens* and its specific effects is a matter of necessity which was reflected by the ILC decades ago when it faced the lack of practical evidence as to one specific effect of *jus cogens*: its impact on the defence of consent. The Commission decided that that specific effect must be recognized

---

[1] Weisburd (1995), 51.

even if not adequately reflected in practice, because that was logically required by the existence and operation of peremptory norms:

> the logic of the conclusions to be drawn from the existence in international law of the rules of *jus cogens* is so incontestable, that it compels acceptance . . . of an exception to the general principle that consent given by a State to the adoption of conduct not in conformity with what would be required by an international obligation incumbent upon it precluded the wrongfulness of such conduct.[2]

The different effects of *jus cogens* reinforce each other either because they are conceptually similar, or because of some normative requirement. As for conceptual similarity, as soon as it is accepted that *jus cogens* is a body of non-derogable norms barring conflicting transactions, it becomes clear that such derogatory transactions can take place in a variety of contexts, encompassing explicit transactions such as those covered by Article 53 of the Vienna Convention, informal transactions covering concordances of will in State practice including the validation of illegalities, and transactions in international judicial process. As a logical matter, all such transactions are intended to hamper the ability of peremptory norms to produce their effects as norms and if *jus cogens* bars some of them, it must impact on others too. Otherwise, the very category of *jus cogens* as a body of non-derogable norms would be in question.

As for normative requirements, it is clear that Articles 53 and 71 of the Vienna Convention justify the assumption that *jus cogens* also apply to non-treaty acts, and hint that the breaches of *jus cogens* shall have some special effects in the law of State responsibility, impacting on specific remedies. Article 53 itself reinforces the assumption that *jus cogens* bars each and every kind of derogation, whatever its form and timing.

Such comprehensive effects of peremptory norms supplement their role in safeguarding the interests of the international community as a whole, and do so in an integral way, not allowing fragmentation of the respective legal relations in any aspect. There are many aspects of the operation of *jus cogens*. Most are already widely recognized on their own merits, sometimes due to factors not totally or not clearly identical to *jus cogens*. But the purpose of this study has been to demonstrate that what is recognized in specific instances may be due to a more general phenomenon. *Jus cogens* may have a comprehensive impact in international law in the interests of the international community as a whole, and the respective effects of *jus cogens* should be examined in a consolidated way, thereby making clear the necessary link between the concept of peremptory norms and their specific effects.

---

[2] YbILC 1979, vol. II, part 2, 115.

Another implication of the complex developments in the relevant areas is the necessity of a broad understanding of international public order, encompassing not only the norms of general international law *per se* but also treaty obligations that embody certain general international law obligations of a non-bilateralizable character, such as humanitarian treaties. Such understanding of public order follows from the structural connection between the two categories of norms and was so seen at earlier stages by writers such as Jenks and Fitzmaurice. The acknowledgment of this structural connection is likely to remove several uncertainties regarding the scope of peremptory law, especially in the field of human rights. More so, as the issues raised by peremptory law in general international law are pretty similar to the issues raised by the objective character of certain treaty obligations, such as those related to the law of reservations and reciprocal termination of treaties. The principles of non-derogability and the absence of reciprocity underline the relevant concepts whether as a matter of human rights treaties or of general international law.

The principal issue of effectiveness of peremptory norms is that of the coherent and consistent application of the relevant standards. In other words, norms must be taken as producing their effect independently of some additional factors.

This means above all that the relevance of State attitudes is not unlimited, among others because all States are equal and have similar standing in framing the legal position, and hence it becomes difficult to identify the exact amount of State practice necessary for the legal change. If, for instance, a treaty conflicting with peremptory norms is concluded, such as post-war or territorial settlement compromising self-determination of the relevant group or the need to prosecute perpetrators of international crimes, third States can be reluctant to object to what does not directly concern them. The attitudes of such third States, if accorded legal significance, would undermine the operation of public order.

In practice such attitudes do not change legal positions in terms of the applicable law and legal consequences. The controversies with regard to the annexation of Abyssinia, East Timor, establishment of settlements in Occupied Palestinian Territories and other similar cases witnessed the abundance of State attitudes opposed to the coherent application to the relevant public order norms. This has not influenced the regime of illegality and invalidity arising out of the breaches of peremptory norms, as witnessed, in particular, in the International Court's pronouncements on self-determination of the people of East Timor, or the illegality of annexation of and settlements in the Occupied Palestinian Territories.

The requirement of consistent application of norms also compares preferably to the relevance of collective/institutional determinations of the legal position, which attempt to influence the legal position, for instance those related to territorial changes or prosecution of international crimes. The force of such collective/institutional decisions is always relative. The doctrine of objective regimes does nothing but demonstrate the relative legal effect of 'objective' settlements. To be effective, they must be approved by other States. Institutional decisions, such as those of the UN Security Council, are also relative as they are conditioned by limitations under the Charter and general international law; they can be invalidated or disregarded if *ultra vires*. To view them as acts of legislature or the world government, eg by asserting that the effects of *jus cogens* such as non-recognition extend only to those situations that have been addressed in institutional contexts, runs counter to the decentralized character of international law in which there is no authority over sovereign States. Instead, the objective and consistent application of public order norms can offer ways of settlement which would be both more stable and endowed with the confidence of States, because such a process is more compatible with the decentralized character of the international legal system by falling short of endorsing any idea that some States can legislate for others through agreements or within the institutions.

Such an approach is necessary if the effect-oriented profile of *jus cogens* is considered, if we are to establish and consolidate basic values, independent of specific exercises of power by particular actors. If peremptory norms are to operate as norms, not merely as aspirations, they must generate consequences that are themselves peremptory. This study has shown that this is indeed the case.

Appendix

1. *Ahmed Ali Yusuf and Al Barakaat International Foundation and Yassin Abdullah Kadi v Council of the European Union and Commission of the European Communities*, Judgments of the EC Court of the First Instance in Case T-306/01 and Case T-315/01, 21 September 2005

The background of the dispute related to the action by the EC Council involving the adoption of measures, such as Common Position 1999/727/CFSP and Regulation No. 377/2000 regarding the freezing of financial funds held abroad by the Taliban; these were later followed by other comparable Community measures.[1] These measures were adopted to implement UN Security Council Resolution 1267(1999) which was directed against the Taliban regime in Afghanistan.

The applicants challenged 'the argument that the Council was obliged to implement the sanctions decided on by the Security Council on the ground that they were binding on the Member States of the Community by virtue of the Charter of the United Nations'. According to them, there was 'no absolute obligation under Article 25 of the Charter of the United Nations'. The Security Council 'must always act in accordance with the purposes and principles of the United Nations'. The Council submitted 'that the Community, like the Member States of the United Nations, is bound by international law to give effect, within its spheres of competence, to resolutions of the Security Council, especially those adopted under Chapter VII of the Charter of the United Nations', and that 'those resolutions prevail over every other international obligation. In that way Article 103 of the Charter of the United Nations makes it possible to disregard any other provision of international law, whether customary or laid down by convention, in order to apply the resolutions of the Security Council, thus creating an "effect of legality".' The contested regulation 'was adopted with a view to implementing in the Community legal order Security Council Resolutions 1267 (1999), 1333 (2000) and 1390 (2002)' and that closed the matter, 'even if the contested regulation were to be regarded as violating the applicants' fundamental rights'. In this case, 'judicial review would risk undermining the system of the United Nations'.[2]

The Court made it clear that the matter before it was that of judicial review. Fundamental human rights fall within the scope of judicial review and could lead to the annulment of the contested regulation.[3] The Community's powers 'must be exercised in compliance with international law',[4] and this brought international law within the ambit of the issues that can trigger judicial review. The Court denied that it could not review the acts of the Security Council for its compliance with fundamental

---

[1] *Ahmed*, Case T-306/01, paras 10–16; *Kadi*, Case T-315/01, paras 10–16.
[2] *Ahmed*, paras 200–225; *Kadi*, paras 136–156.
[3] *Ahmed*, paras 226, 230; *Kadi*, paras 176, 180.
[4] *Ahmed*, para. 274; *Kadi*, para. 199.

rights as an aspect of the Community law *per se*.[5] The Court stated, most pertinently, that

It must therefore be considered that the resolutions of the Security Council at issue fall, in principle, outside the ambit of the Court's judicial review and that the Court has no authority to call in question, even indirectly, their lawfulness in the light of Community law. On the contrary, the Court is bound, so far as possible, to interpret and apply that law in a manner compatible with the obligations of the Member States under the Charter of the United Nations.

None the less, the Court is empowered to check, indirectly, the lawfulness of the resolutions of the Security Council in question with regard to *jus cogens*, understood as a body of higher rules of public international law binding on all subjects of international law, including the bodies of the United Nations, and from which no derogation is possible. . . .

International law thus permits the inference that there exists one limit to the principle that resolutions of the Security Council have binding effect: namely, that they must observe the fundamental peremptory provisions of *jus cogens*. If they fail to do so, however improbable that may be, they would bind neither the Member States of the United Nations nor, in consequence, the Community.

The indirect judicial review carried out by the Court in connection with an action for annulment of a Community act adopted, where no discretion whatsoever may be exercised, with a view to putting into effect a resolution of the Security Council may therefore, in some circumstances, extend to determining whether the superior rules of international law falling within the ambit of *jus cogens* have been observed, in particular, the mandatory provisions concerning the universal protection of human rights, from which neither the Member States nor the bodies of the United Nations may derogate because they constitute 'intransgressible principles of international customary law' (Advisory Opinion of the International Court of Justice of 8 July 1996, *The Legality of the Threat or Use of Nuclear Weapons*).[6]

This line of reasoning emphasizes the independent, and original, relevance of *jus cogens*, which includes human rights and humanitarian law, as an aspect of the hierarchy of norms in the international legal system. In relation to judicial review of the Security Council acts, *jus cogens* can achieve the result that other concepts and categories arguably cannot. The reason why *jus cogens* binds the Security Council and justifies judicial review relates to its hierarchical superiority over the powers of the treaty-based organ. If *jus cogens* prevails over treaties, then it also sets limits to the validity of the acts adopted by treaty-based organs.[7] The function of international tribunals is not to uphold invalid acts and the decision of the Court of First Instance confirms just this.

It is arguable that to review the Security Council decisions may be inappropriate for the EC courts the UN Charter enjoys hierarchically higher status and, as soon as this is the case, the EC legal system must follow. The key to judicial review is the normative standard that constrains the validity of the acts adopted by the Security Council and is *also* part of the law that imperatively binds the EC as the treaty-based institution. This is the distinguishing feature of *jus cogens* which is relevant in both fields and this makes it crucially relevant. Article 103 of the UN Charter does not appear to unsettle this position.

---

[5] *Ahmed*, paras 272–273; *Kadi*, paras 221–222.
[6] *Ahmed*, paras 276–277, 281–282, 337; *Kadi*, paras 225–226, 230–231, 282.
[7] See on this above, Chapter 12.

In addition, the decisions of the Court of First Instance proceed from the assumption that if the Security Council is bound by certain substantive standards of fundamental character, this by itself justifies judicial review. In other words, the substance of legal relations and the procedural power of review go hand in hand, which leaves hardly any room for the arguments that judicial review of the Security Council acts cannot be exercised, among others because it risks getting involved with political questions and undermining the effectiveness of the UN collective security system. The decisions of the Court of the First Instance have also reinforced, in a way similar to the ICTY Appeal Chamber decision on *Tadic*, the conception of judicial review in the context of the International Court of Justice.

Apart from the issues of judicial review, the Court of First Instance in fact affirmed that the argument upholding the peremptory status of all fundamental human rights is a viable argument. This is confirmed by the Court's observation that 'it is in principle by the sole criterion of the standard of universal protection of the fundamental rights of the human person falling within the ambit of *jus cogens* that the applicants' claims may appropriately be examined' to set aside the contested regulation. The crucial question was whether the contested regulation implementing the Security Council resolution infringed the applicants' fundamental rights.[8]

Several rights were at stake: the right to property, the right to a fair hearing, and the right of access to a court. With regard to the right to property, the Court emphasized, by reference to Article 17 of the Universal Declaration on Human Rights, that 'in so far as respect for the right to property must be regarded as forming part of the mandatory rules of general international law, it is only an arbitrary deprivation of that right that might, in any case, be regarded as contrary to *jus cogens*'. It was, however, clear that the deprivation in that case had not been arbitrary.[9] Therefore, *jus cogens* was not violated in this aspect.

In terms of the right to a fair hearing, the Court pronounced that 'no mandatory rule of public international law requires a prior hearing for the persons concerned in circumstances such as those of this case, in which the Security Council, acting under Chapter VII of the Charter of the United Nations, decides, through its Sanctions Committee, that the funds of certain individuals or entities suspected of contributing to the funding of terrorism must be frozen.'[10]

In terms of the right of access to a court, the Court held that the limitations that the Security Council act imposed on the exercise of that right 'is inherent in that right as it is guaranteed by *jus cogens*'.[11] There was no breach of *jus cogens* involved here either.

The decisions of the Court of First Instance undermine the doctrinal construct that not all fundamental human rights are, or could be, part of *jus cogens*. The Court's arguments regarding the scope of peremptory human rights can be approved or disapproved, but the spirit and the letter of the decisions emphasize that probably no human right can *a priori* be denied of having the status of *jus cogens*. Instead, the decisions confirm that whether the given action contradicts *jus cogens* depends on the

---

[8] *Ahmed*, paras 286, 288, 290; *Kadi*, paras 235, 237, 239.
[9] *Ahmed*, paras 292–294; *Kadi*, paras 241–243.
[10] *Ahmed*, para. 307.　　[11] *Ahmed*, para. 343; *Kadi*, para. 288.

freedom of action, denoted as margin of appreciation or otherwise, that the content of the given human right leaves to the State.[12]

The decisions also distinguish between two issues: whether the specific aspect of the given human right is part of *jus cogens* and whether the right as such and in its totality is part of *jus cogens*. The finding that no breach of *jus cogens* had taken place or that the specific aspects of the relevant human rights were not peremptory precluded, in the eyes of the Court, judicial review of the contested regulation. This implies, and was moreover affirmed by the Court, that if the right, or its element, is recognized as peremptory, judicial review will follow:

In this action for annulment, the Court has moreover held that it has jurisdiction to review the lawfulness of the contested regulation and, indirectly, the lawfulness of the resolutions of the Security Council at issue, in the light of the higher rules of international law falling within the ambit of *jus cogens*, in particular the mandatory prescriptions concerning the universal protection of the rights of the human person.[13]

2. *A (FC) and others (FC) (Appellants) v Secretary of State for the Home Department* (Respondent) (2004), House of Lords, [2005] UKHL 71, 8 December 2005

The question that the House of Lords was asked in this case was whether British courts, in this case the Special Immigration Appeals Commission, may 'receive evidence which has or may have been procured by torture inflicted, in order to obtain evidence, by officials of a foreign state without the complicity of the British authorities'.[14] Thus, the House had effectively to pronounce whether the evidence obtained through torture abroad is admissible in British courts. Having examined the available evidence under common law, international treaties and general international law, the House decided that the evidence obtained through torture is inadmissible wherever and by whomever the pertinent act of torture is committed. Consequently, the House allowed the appeal against the Court of Appeal decision and reversed it, remanding the case to the Special Immigration Appeals Commission for further decision in the light of its Opinion at hand.[15] The public international law aspect of the reasoning in this Opinion is most relevant in the present context.

The House of Lords affirmed that the 'international prohibition of the use of torture enjoys the enhanced status of a *jus cogens* or peremptory norm of general international law'.[16] It further referred to *Furundzija*, the case in which the ICTY emphasized the consequential effect of the peremptory prohibition of torture and emphasized that not only are States bound not to commit torture but they also are required not to recognize as valid any act that precludes the criminal responsibility of the perpetrators of torture, such as amnesty. This consequential and effect-oriented profile of peremptory norms is similarly adhered in *A v Secretary of State* and is moreover used as the rationale of this decision in its public international law aspect.

This can particularly be seen in the fact that, following *Furundzija*, the House of Lords affirmed that the peremptory status of the prohibition of torture 'requires

---

[12] See on this above, Chapter 2.   [13] *Ahmed*, para. 337; *Kadi*, para. 282.
[14] *A v Secretary of State*, para. 1 (*per* Lord Bingham).
[15] *A v Secretary of State*, para. 69 (*per* Lord Bingham).
[16] *A v Secretary of State*, para. 33 (*per* Lord Bingham).

Member States to do more than eschew the practice of torture'. In *Kuwait Air Corp. v Iraqi Airways Corp. (Nos 4 and 5)*, the House of Lords had refused recognition to conduct which represented a serious breach of international law. This was 'a proper response to the requirements of international law'.[17] To support this approach, the House of Lords further referred to Article 41 of the ILC Articles on State responsibility pointing to the prohibition of recognition by States of acts contradicting *jus cogens* that are committed by other States, and to the International Court's 2004 Advisory Opinion on *Legal Consequences of the Construction of a Wall in the Occupied Palestinian Territory*.[18] This confirms that the House of Lords envisaged the uniform legal framework established by international *jus cogens* which operates in different fields with the uniform effect of precluding the validity and recognition of acts contrary to peremptory norms. The doctrinal argument that the substance of peremptory norms and their effect are different becomes less tenable, being contradicted by the legal framework that is assuming the comprehensive dimension.

The combined reference in *A v Secretary of State* to *Furundzija* and *Kuwait Air Corp.*, especially given the House of Lords' reference in the latter case to the relevance of international *jus cogens* as the factor precluding the recognition of certain acts through their characterization in the English legal system under the Act of State doctrine, further affirms that the conceptual background for the operation of *jus cogens* in the contexts and situations involved in all three cases is uniform: the consequential and effect-oriented profile of *jus cogens*, the inescapable link between the substance of peremptory norms, and their peremptory effects with regard to the outcome of breaches of peremptory norms. States are obliged not only not to breach *jus cogens* by their own conduct, but also not to accept, approve or recognize any act committed by other States that contradicts *jus cogens*.

The conceptual and normative framework envisaged in *A v Secretary of State* also unsettles the treatment of the effects of international *jus cogens* by the Court of Appeal in *Jones v Saudi Arabia*, namely the assertion that the peremptory prohibition of torture does not entail the duty not to grant immunity to States that engage in torture. Given that granting immunity for torture amounts to the recognition of the act of torture and that the Court of Appeal has not been consistent in adopting its substance/legal consequences distinction line, as particularly evidenced by its different outcomes with regard to the immunity of States and State officials,[19] the reasoning and outcome in *A v Secretary of State* seriously contradicts and undermines the approach of the Court of Appeal in *Jones*.[20] If States are bound not only not to breach *jus cogens* by their own conduct, but also not to accept, approve or recognize any act committed by other States that contradicts *jus cogens*, then they are bound not to grant immunity to States for acts of torture.

As the House of Lords clarified, the acknowledgment of the consequential profile of *jus cogens* is 'a proper response to the requirements of international law'. The implementation of such an outcome in national legal systems, such as English law,

---

[17] *A v Secretary of State*, para. 34 (*per* Lord Bingham); see above, Chapter 19 regarding the pertinent issues dealt with in *Kuwait Air Corp.*

[18] See on this above, Chapters 8 and 11.

[19] See on this above, Chapters 8 and 11.

[20] It remains to be seen what the response of the House of Lords will be in *Jones*.

depends also on how and to what extent the national legal system accepts the enforceability of international legal requirements. If the doctrine of statutory primacy is followed, as is the case with regard to most British and American decisions on State immunity,[21] the implementation in English law of such 'a proper response to the requirements of international law' will be hampered by the primacy of the 1978 State Immunity Act over common law and consequently over international law. That neither *Kuwait Air Corp.* nor *A v Secretary of State* involved any domestic legislative instrument preventing the enforcement of international *jus cogens* in English legal system fits perfectly into this picture.

3. *Regina (Al-Jedda) v the Secretary of State for Defence*, Queen's Bench Divisional Court, Case No. CO/3673/2005, Judgment of 12 August 2005

This case concerned the claimant's arrest in Iraq on suspicion of his membership of a terrorist group involved in weapons smuggling and explosive attacks in Iraq. This was challenged as contrary to Section 5 of the 1998 Human Rights Act. The defendant contended that the detention was justified under UN Security Council Resolution 1546(2004), which displaced the Section 5 the Human Rights Act.[22] The court turned to the issue whether Resolution 1546 does have the effect of displacing Section 5, in terms of the natural meaning of the resolution, the impact of human rights and the relevance of Article 103 of the Charter.[23] The court also emphasized that the United Kingdom, as the belligerent occupant in Iraq, was subject to the obligations under the Fourth Geneva Convention, Article 78 of which deals with the internment and detention on the basis of imperative security needs.[24] At the same time, Resolution 1546 was silent as to the need for the participating States to derogate from their existing international obligations.[25] The court concluded that

UNSCR 1546 has the meaning and effect which are plain, particularly from paragraph 10 of the Resolution. The Resolution is designed to authorise the MNF to exercise the powers it previously exercised when in belligerent occupation.[26]

At the same time, the court faced the claimant's suggestion, based on the practice of the International Court, such as the *Namibia* case and the Opinion of Judge *ad hoc* Lauterpacht in *Bosnia* that the Security Council is not entitled to encroach upon fundamental human rights nor would have it intended to do that.[27] The Court countered these submissions by asserting that under Chapter VII of the Charter the Security Council is empowered to act against threats to or breaches of peace and take such action under Articles 41 and 42 as it deems necessary. Therefore,

The Security Council, charged as it is with primary responsibility for maintaining international peace and security, has itself determined that a multinational force is required. Its objective is to restore such security as will provide effective protection for human rights for those within Iraq. Those who choose to assist the Security Council in that purpose are authorised to take those steps, which include detention, necessary for its achievement.[28]

---

[21] See on this above, Chapters 11 and 18.   [22] *Al-Jedda*, paras 9, 14–15, 62.
[23] *Al-Jedda*, para. 75.   [24] *Al-Jedda*, para. 82.   [25] *Al-Jedda*, para. 90.
[26] *Al-Jedda*, paras 92–93.   [27] *Al-Jedda*, paras 96–97.
[28] *Al-Jedda*, paras 99–100, 104.

The court also emphasized that the Security Council has authorized such detention as is necessary for imperative reasons of security in accordance with Article 78 of the Fourth Geneva Convention.[29]

The question of *jus cogens* was raised only incidentally and was not pursued by the applicant in relation to the impact of Article 103. Therefore, the court did not examine this issue either.[30] The court concluded that 'Article 103 is not merely engaged by UNSCR 1546 but that the resolution does indeed, by virtue of Articles 25 and 103 of the Charter, in principle override Article 5 of the Convention in relation to the claimant's detention in Basra.'[31]

The court's reasoning raises more questions than it answers. Being clear in its outcome, it falls short of providing a consistent reasoning. By refusing to examine the issue of *jus cogens* just because the claimant did not vigorously insist on that, the court left the issue open whether Article 103 would be invocable if the *jus cogens* issue had been properly argued. In this respect, the decision has little precedential value. In addition, it was not necessary to examine the relevance of Article 103 at all, as the court had already concluded that the powers under Resolution 1546 were in accordance with the Fourth Geneva Convention, which is anyway *lex specialis* in relation to human rights law in armed conflicts. Finally, the court's decision misinterprets the legal framework regarding the limitation of the Security Council's powers by asserting that even as the Council's powers are limited by the UN Charter and fundamental human rights, it can nevertheless take discretionary actions under Chapter VII. The legal framework as construed in international jurisprudence is directly opposite: the Council has broad powers under Chapter VII but they must be exercised in accordance with the Charter, fundamental human rights and humanitarian law.[32] It is unclear why the court developed its line of reasoning on this issue in the way it did, because it had already found that the relevant actions of the Council were in accordance with the Fourth Geneva Convention.

4. *Case Concerning Armed Activities on the Territory of the Congo (New Application: 2002) (Democratic Republic of the Congo v Rwanda)*, Jurisdiction of the Court and Admissibility of the Application, Judgment of 3 February 2006, General List No. 126

In this Judgment, the International Court of Justice dismissed the claims of the Democratic Republic of the Congo that the Court had jurisdiction over the allegations of breaches of the Genocide Convention (under Article IX) and of several other treaties. The Judgment follows the Court's earlier order issued in 2002 in the same case in which the Court refused to find that it had *prima facie* jurisdiction.[33] The Court's treatment of reservations under Article IX of the Genocide Convention and its jurisdiction under Article 66 of the 1969 Vienna Convention on the Law of Treaties are most relevant for the purposes of the present study.

The Court's treatment of Rwanda's reservation to Article IX of the Genocide Convention is the most central issue in this case. The Democratic Republic of the Congo submitted to the Court that this reservation was invalid because it prevented adjudication over the breaches of the peremptory prohibition of genocide and also

[29] *Al-Jedda*, para. 108.   [30] *Al-Jedda*, para. 114.   [31] *Al-Jedda*, para. 122.
[32] See above, Chapter 12.   [33] See above Chapter 15.

because it was contrary to the object and purpose of the Genocide Convention, since 'its effect is to exclude Rwanda from any mechanism for the monitoring and prosecution of genocide, whereas the object and purpose of the Convention are precisely the elimination of impunity for this serious violation of international law'.[34]

Although these submissions appear on their face separate from each other, in the context of this particular case they essentially constitute one single submission, because the involvement of *jus cogens* and the permissibility of reservations to Article IX related not only to the same factual situation but also to the same normative framework of the prohibition of genocide which has peremptory status both under the Convention and under general international law. Therefore, although it is right to state that the involvement of peremptory norms does not by itself, and in the absence of any jurisdictional title, establish jurisdiction over the case, such had not in effect been contended by the Democratic Republic of the Congo. The relevance of peremptory norms has been advanced in parallel to the arguments based on the Convention which embodies, according to the Court's pronouncements in 1951 and 1996, norms that have peremptory status.

The Court reiterated that the substance of legal relations and jurisdiction over the case are two different things, further suggesting:

The same applies to the relationship between peremptory norms of general international law (*jus cogens*) and the establishment of the Court's jurisdiction: the fact that a dispute relates to compliance with a norm having such a character, which is assuredly the case with regard to the prohibition of genocide, cannot of itself provide a basis for the jurisdiction of the Court to entertain that dispute. Under the Court's Statute that jurisdiction is always based on the consent of the parties.[35]

The Court also observed that 'When a compromissory clause in a treaty provides for the Court's jurisdiction, that jurisdiction exists only in respect of the parties to the treaty who are bound by that clause and within the limits set out therein', and consequently 'the view of the Court, a reservation under the Genocide Convention would be permissible to the extent that such reservation is not incompatible with the object and purpose of the Convention'. As for the actual compatibility of the reservation, the Court asserted:

Rwanda's reservation to Article IX of the Genocide Convention bears on the jurisdiction of the Court, and does not affect substantive obligations relating to acts of genocide themselves under that Convention. In the circumstances of the present case, the Court cannot conclude that the reservation of Rwanda in question, which is meant to exclude a particular method of settling a dispute relating to the interpretation, application or fulfilment of the Convention, is to be regarded as being incompatible with the object and purpose of the Convention.[36]

It is of course right that the Court's jurisdiction depends on consent. But the real question that was before the Court was how to determine whether the consent had been given. The consensual principle has no relevance on its own. Its relevance rather depends on the individual context in which the Court happens to adjudicate. If, for instance, there is no jurisdictional title in relation to the case and the respondent State refuses to consent to jurisdiction, then it is possible to state that jurisdiction cannot be

---

[34] Judgment, paras 56–57.   [35] Judgment, para. 64.   [36] Judgment, paras 65–67.

exercised because it is consensual and no consent has been given. But not all cases deal with vacuums or clean slates. Judicial jurisdiction under the Genocide Convention is not a simple case of consent given on a clean slate, but the consent to jurisdiction which forms part of the system and the consent which has been given as part of that system. The issue of compatibility of jurisdictional reservation in such context cannot be judged by the criteria applicable to the cases where the act embodying the consent to jurisdiction is an isolated act.

It is especially troubling that the Court made no attempt to examine the scope of the object and purpose of the Genocide Convention. It just submitted that because Article IX is a procedural provision, the reservation to it does not contradict the object and purpose of the Convention. This approach not only fails to be based on empirical evidence but also is conceptually flawed. The treaty clause, even if procedural, can be part of the object and purpose if this so appears from the intention of parties and the structure of the treaties. As the study of the structure of the Convention and the practice of application of Article IX demonstrates,[37] this provision is indispensable for the functioning of the Convention and forms part of its *raison d'être*.

In addition, the issue before the Court has been not only the issue of consent to jurisdiction, but also that of the assessment of the compatibility of reservation to Article IX with the object and purpose of the Genocide Convention, that is the question of the law of treaties. The Court does not consider the fact that the law of treaties can offer the outcome on the issue of compatibility of Article IX with the Convention's object and purpose, which would be the independent outcome under the law of treaties. The fact that jurisdiction is consensual does not mean that there can be no such independent outcome.

The fact that the Court did not consider these factors makes its reasoning inconsistent and is in fact counterproductive to the purpose that the Court tried to achieve. While the Court has apparently sent the message that the venues for challenging and invalidating reservations to Article IX are closed, its Judgment and surrounding context have instead raised the issue of whether these venues are in fact closed and whether they ought to be closed. That this is so is evidenced not only by the incompatibility of the Court's reasoning with how the incompatible reservations are treated in other treaty mechanisms, such as the European and Inter-American Human Rights Conventions, but also by the concerns raised in the opinions of a significant number of the International Court's judges.

As the Dissenting Opinion of Judge Koroma points out, Article IX is part of the Convention's object and purpose, because 'it is the *only* avenue for adjudicating the responsibilities of States'.[38] Therefore,

a State which denies the Court's jurisdiction to enquire into allegations alleging violation of the Convention would not be lending the co-operation required to 'liberate mankind from [the] . . . odious scourge' of genocide or to fulfil the object and purpose of the Convention. Denying recourse to the Court essentially precludes judicial scrutiny into the responsibility of a State in a dispute relating to the violation of the Convention.[39]

---

[37] See above Chapter 15, Section 5.1.
[38] Dissenting Opinion, para. 13 (emphasis original). [39] Dissenting Opinion, para. 21.

Consequently, the Rwandan reservation being contrary to the object and purpose of the Convention, the Court had to adjudicate the case in disregard of the reservation.[40]

The Joint Separate Opinion of Judges Higgins, Koojmans, Elaraby, Owada and Simma, who voted for the Judgment, raise similar concerns. The Opinion expresses concern with the Court's construction of the difference between the substance of obligation and jurisdiction over the case and emphasizes that the outcome of disputes regarding the reservations to Article IX cannot be left to the discretion of States.[41] The law regarding the reservations to humanitarian treaties has been developed by the organs of European and inter-American human rights conventions, which have not followed the *laissez-faire* approach. This approach, together with the severability view expressed in the UN Human Rights Committee General Comment No. 24, is not creating a special regime which constitutes an exception from the otherwise applicable general regime of reservations, but is rather the development of the approach the International Court itself took in the 1951 *Reservations* Advisory Opinion.[42]

The Joint Separate Opinion affirms that the procedural character of the treaty clause does not preclude it from being part of the treaty's object and purpose.[43] A reservation to a specific 'procedural' provision could be contrary to the treaty's object and purpose.[44] Further to referring to the flaws in the Court's reasoning, the Joint Separate Opinion stresses that the Court should revisit this issue.[45]

It should be noted that, as an additional argument, the Court referred to the fact that, as a matter of the law of treaties, when Rwanda acceded to the Genocide Convention and made the reservation in question, the Democratic Republic of the Congo made no objection to it.[46] But this argument is contradicted by the humanitarian character of the Genocide Convention and the fact that the compatibility of reservations to Article IX cannot be proved. The presence or absence of objections is irrelevant, because under the 1969 Vienna Convention, the regime governing the consequences of the objections to the reservations applies only to those reservations which are compatible to the treaty's object and purpose (Articles 19–22).[47] Furthermore, as Judge Koroma observed, 'the failure of a State to object should not be regarded as determinative in the context of *human rights treaties like the Genocide Convention that are not based on reciprocity between States but instead serve to protect individuals and the international community at large.*'[48]

Overall, the Court's treatment of Article IX of the Genocide Convention contains serious flaws and sets standards which provide comfort to the governments that brutalize populations. This makes more cogent the suggestion to revisit the outcome on other occasion, made in the Joint Separate Opinion.

As for the application of Article 66 of the 1969 Vienna Convention on the Law of Treaties, the Court's approach is rather original. The Democratic Republic of the Congo submitted to the Court that while Article 66 allows the Court to rule on any dispute concerning 'the validity of a treaty which is contrary to a norm of *jus cogens*', reservations to a treaty form an integral part thereof, and that they must accordingly

---

[40] Dissenting Opinion, paras 22, 26, 29.
[41] Joint Separate Opinion, paras 2–5.
[42] Joint Separate Opinion, paras 14–16, 22.
[43] On this see above Chapter 4, Section 2.
[44] Joint Separate Opinion, para. 21.
[45] Joint Separate Opinion, paras 28–29.
[46] Judgment, para. 68.
[47] See further Chapter 6 above.
[48] Dissenting Opinion, para. 14 (emphasis added); see also Joint Separate Opinion, para. 22.

avoid either being in direct contradiction with a norm of *jus cogens*, or preventing the implementation of that norm. Therefore, the Court should use Article 66 for invalidating the reservation to Article IX of the Genocide Convention.[49] Rwanda contradicted this argument by submitting that Article 66 extends only to the disputes relating to the validity of treaties, and that Article 66 is anyway inapplicable because the Genocide Convention was contracted by the parties before the 1969 Vienna Convention entered into force for them (Article 4 of the Vienna Convention).[50]

The Court's Judgment dismissed the submission of the Democratic Republic of the Congo, but only by reference to Rwanda's argument as to the temporal scope of the Vienna Convention, by stating that Article 66, which had no customary status, could not apply to the case.[51] Therefore, the Court left uncommented, and did not contradict, the argument of the Democratic Republic of the Congo that Article 66 can extend to the disputes regarding reservations alleged to conflict with *jus cogens*. This approach seems to be innovative, but fits into the scope of Article 66, because reservations ultimately purport to generate the treaty within the treaty and their validity for consistency with *jus cogens* can be judged similarly to treaties in general. There is thus no reason why the validity, compatibility or otherwise of reservations cannot fall within the scope of Article 66. If followed in future practice, this approach can only enhance the effectiveness of Article 66 and enable it to safeguard the operation of peremptory norms in a variety of contexts.

---

[49] Judgment, para. 121.   [50] Judgment, paras 123–124.   [51] Judgment, para. 126.

Bibliography

Abass, A., 'Consent Precluding State Responsibility: A Critical Analysis', 53 *ICLQ* (2004), 211.

Abi-Saab, G., 'The Concept of *Jus Cogens* in International Law', 2 *Lagonissi Conference: Papers and Proceedings*, vol. II, Carnegie Endowment for International Peace (Geneva, 1967), 7.

—— 'The Concept of International Crime and Its Place in Contemporary International Law', Weiler, Cassese, and Spinedi (eds), *International Crimes of State: A Critical Analysis of Article 19 of the ILC's Draft Articles on State Responsibility* (Berlin, 1989), 141.

—— 'The Uses of Article 19', 10 *EJIL* (1999), 339.

Adams, W., 'In Search of Defence of the Transnational Human Rights Paradigm: May Jus Cogens Norms be Invoked to Create Implied Exceptions in Domestic Immunity Statutes?' Craig (ed.), *Torture as Tort* (Hart Publishing, Oxford, 2001) 247.

Akande, D., 'International Law Immunities and the International Criminal Court', 98 *AJIL* (2004), 407.

Akehurst, M., *The Law concerning Employment in International Organisations* (Cambridge, 1967).

—— 'Reprisals by Third States', *BYIL*, 1970, 1.

—— 'The Hierarchy of Norms in International Law', *BYIL*, 1974–75, 273.

Alexidze, L., 'Legal Nature of Jus Cogens in Contemporary International Law', 172 *RdC* (1981-III), 219.

Allain, J., 'The *jus cogens* nature of *non-refoulement*', 13 *International Journal of Refugee Law* (2002), 533.

Alvarez, J., 'The Security Council's War on Terrorism: Problems and Policy Options', De Wet and Nollkaemper (eds.), *Review of the Security Council by Member States* (Intersentia, Antwerp/Oxford/New York, 2003), 119.

Angelet, N., 'International Law Limits to the Security Council', Gowlland-Debbas (ed.), *United Nations Sanctions and International Law* (Kluwer, 2001), 71.

Annacker, C., 'Part Two of the International Law Commission's Draft Articles on State Responsibility', 37 *German Yearbook of International Law* (1994), 206.

Antonopoulos, C., 'Effectiveness v. the Rule of Law Following the *East Timor* Case', 27 *Netherlands Yearbook of International Law* (1996), 75.

Arechaga, E., 'International Law in the Past Third of the Century', 159 *RdC* (1978), 1.

Aust, A., *Modern Treaty Law and Practice* (Cambridge, 2000).

—— 'The Role of Human Rights in Limiting the Enforcement Powers of the Security Council: A Practitioner's View', De Wet and Nollkaemper (eds), *Review of the Security Council by Member States* (Intersentia, Antwerp/Oxford/New York, 2003), 31–38.

Barberis, J., 'La liberté de traiter des états et le *jus cogens*', 30 *Zeitschrift für ausländisches öffentliches Recht und Völkerrecht* (1970), 19.

Barboza, J., 'International Criminal Law', 278 *RdC* (1999), 9.

Barboza, J., 'State Crimes: A Decaffeinated Coffee', L. Boisson de Chazournes and V. Gowlland-Debbas (eds), *The International Legal System in Quest of Equity and Universality. Liber Amicorum Georges Abi-Saab* (2001), 357.

Barile, G., 'The Protection of Human Rights in Article 60, Paragraph 5 of the Vienna Convention on the Law of Treaties', *International Law at the Time of its Codification. Essays in Honour of Roberto Ago*, vol. II (Milan, 1987), 3.

Bass, G.J., *Stay The Hand of Vengeance—The Politics of War Crimes Tribunals* (Princeton and Oxford, 2002).

Bassiouni, C. and Wise, E., *Aut Dedere Aut Judicare: The Duty to Extradite or Prosecute in International Law* (Dordrecht/Boston/London, 1995).

—— 'International Crimes: *Jus Cogens* and *Obligatio Erga Omnes*', 59 *Law and Contemporary Problems* (1996), 63.

—— *Crimes Against Humanity in International Criminal Law* (2nd ed., Kluwer, 1999).

Batiffol, H. and Lagarde, P., *Traité de Droit International Privé* (tome 1, Paris, 1993).

Baxter, R., 'Multilateral Treaties as Evidence of Customary Law', *BYIL* (1963), 275.

Beatson, J., *Anson's Law of Contract* (Oxford, 2002).

Bell, C., *Peace Agreements and Human Rights* (Oxford, 2000).

Belsky, A., Merva, M., and Roht-Ariaza, N., 'Implied Waiver under the FSIA: A Proposed Exception to Immunity for Violations of Peremptory Norms of International Law', 77 *California Law Review* (1989), 365.

Bernhardt, R., '*Ultra Vires* Activities of International Organisations', Makarczyk (ed.), *Theory of International Law at the Threshold of the 21st Century. Essays in Honour of Krzysztof Skubiszewski* (1996), 608.

Bernier, J., 'Droit Public and Ordre Public', 15 *Transactions of the Grotius Society* (1930), 83.

Bianchi, A., 'Denying State Immunity to Violators of Human Rights', 46 *Austrian Journal of Public and International Law* (1994), 195.

—— 'Case-note on *Ferrini* (Supreme Court of Italy)', *AJIL* (2005), 242.

—— 'Dismantling the Wall: The ICJ's Advisory Opinion and Its Likely Impact on International Law', 47 *German Yearbook of International Law* (2004), 343.

Birnie, P. and Boyle, A., *International Law and the Environment* (Oxford, 2002).

Black's Law Dictionary (6th ed., St Paul, 1990).

Bleckmann, A., *Sittenwidrigkeit wegen Verstoßes gegen den* ordre public international, 34 *ZaöRV* (1974), 112.

Blom, J., 'Public Policy in Private International Law and Its Evolution in Time', 50 *Netherlands International Law Review* (2003), 373.

Blum, G., and Steinhardt, R., 'Federal Jurisdiction over International Human Rights Claims: the Alien Tort Claims Act after *Filartiga v Pena-Irala*', 22 *Harvard JIL* (1981), 53.

Bos, A., 'Crimes of State: In Need of Legal Rules?' Kreijen *et al.* (eds), *State, Sovereignty and International Governance* (Oxford, 2002), 221.

Bourgon, S., 'The Impact of Terrorism on the Principle of "*Non-Refoulement*" of Refugees: The *Suresh* Case before the Supreme Court of Canada', 1 *Journal of International Criminal Justice* (2003), 169.

Bowett, D., 'Reprisals Involving Recourse to Armed Force', 66 *AJIL* (1972), 1.

—— 'Reservations to Non-Restricted Multilateral Treaties', *BYIL* (1975–76), 68.

—— 'The Impact of Security Council Decisions on Dispute Settlement Procedures', 5 *EJIL* (1994), 89.

Briggs, H., *The Law of Nations* (London, 1953).

—— 'Reservations to the Acceptance of Compulsory Jurisdiction of the International Court of Justice', 93 *Recueil des Cours* (1958), 223.

Brownlie, I., *International Law and the Use of Force* (Oxford, 1963).

—— 'Recognition in Theory and Practice', 53 *BYIL* (1982), 197.

—— *The System of the Law of Nations. State Responsibility* (Oxford, 1983).

—— *Principles of Public International Law* (6th ed., Oxford, 2003).

Brundner, A., 'The Domestic Enforcement of International Covenants on Human Rights', 35 *University of Toronto Law Journal* (1985), 219.

Bryde, B., 'Verpflichtungen *Erga Omnes* aus Menschenrechten', Kälin, Riedel and Karl (eds) *Aktuelle Probleme des Menschenrechtsschutzes, Berichte der Deutschen Gesellschaft für Völkerrecht*, Bd. 33, 1993 (Heidelberg, 1994), 165.

Bucher, A., 'L'ordre public et le but social des lois en droit international privé', 239 *RdC* (1993-II), 9.

Buergenthal, T., 'Advisory Practice of the Inter-American Court of Human Rights', 79 *AJIL* (1985), 1.

Buffard, I., and Zemanek, K., The 'Object and Purpose' of a Treaty: An Enigma? 3 *Austrian Review of International and European Law* (1998), 311.

Burns, P., and McBurney, S., 'Impunity and the United Nations Convention against Torture: A Shadow Play without an Ending', C. Scott (ed.), *Torture as Tort* (Oxford-Portland, Hart Publishing, 2001), 278.

Byers, M., 'Conceptualising the Relationship between Jus Cogens and Erga Omnes Rules', 66 *Nordic Journal of International Law* (1997), 211.

Byrnes, A., 'Civil Remedies for Torture Committed Abroad: An Obligation under the Convention Against Torture?' C. Scott (ed.), *Torture as Tort* (Hart Publishing, Oxford, 2001).

Caplan, M., 'State Immunity, Human Rights and *Jus Cogens*', 97 *AJIL* (2003), 741.

Capotorti, F., 'Possibilities of Conflict in National Legal Systems between the European Convention and Other International Agreements', Robertson (ed.), *Human Rights in National and International Law* (Manchester, 1968), 72.

Carrasco, M., and Fernandez, J., Case-note on *Pinochet* (Spanish National Court), 93 *AJIL* (1999), 690.

Cassese, A., Legal Considerations on the International Status of Jerusalem, 3 *Palestinian Yearbook of International Law* (1986), 13.

—— *Self-Determination of Peoples* (Cambridge, 1994).

—— *International Criminal Law* (Oxford, 2003).

—— *International Law* (Oxford, 2005).

—— and Weiler, J. (eds), *Change and Stability in International Law-Making* (Berlin, 1988).

Castaneda, J., *Legal Effects of United Nations Resolutions* (New York and London, 1969).

Cerna, C., 'The Inter-American Commission on Human Rights: Its Organisation and Examination of Petitions and Communications', Harris and Livingstone (eds), *The Inter-American System of Human Rights* (Oxford, 1998), 65.

Charlesworth, H. and Chinkin, C., 'The gender of *jus cogens*', 15 *Human Rights Quarterly* (1993), 63.

—— *The Boundaries of International Law, A Feminist Analysis* (Manchester, 2000).

Charney, J., 'The Persistent Rule and the Development of Customary International Law', 56 *BYIL* (1985), 457.

—— 'Universal International Law', 87 *AJIL* (1993), 529.

—— and Alexander, L., *International Maritime Boundaries* (The Hague, 1993).

Cheng, B., *General Principles of Law* (London, 1953).

Chinkin, C., *Third Parties in International Law* (Oxford, 1995).

—— 'Alternative Dispute Resolution in International Law', Evans (ed.), *Remedies in International Law: The Institutional Dilemma* (Hart Publishing, Oxford, 1998), 123.

—— 'Case-note on *Pinochet* (House of Lords)', 93 *AJIL* (1999), 703.

Chitty on Contracts (London, 1999).

Christenson, G., 'The World Court and *Jus Cogens*', 81 *AJIL* (1987), 93.

—— '*Jus Cogens*: Guarding Interests Fundamental to the International Society', 28 *Virginia Journal of International Law* (1988), 585.

Christopher, D., '*Jus Cogens*, Reparation Agreements, and Holocaust Slave Labour Litigation', 31 *Law and Policy in International Business* (2000), 1227.

Clapham, A., 'National Action Challenged: Sovereignty, Immunity and Universal Jurisdiction before the International Court of Justice', Lattimer and Sands, *Justice for Crimes Against Humanity* (Hart Publishing, Oxford, 2003).

Collier, J., and Lowe, V., *The Settlement of Disputes in International Law* (Oxford, 1999).

Cox, M., 'The Dayton Agreement in Bosnia and Herzegovina: A Study of Implementation Strategies', *BYIL* 1998, 201.

Craven, M., 'The European Community Arbitration Commission on Yugoslavia', *BYIL* (1995), 333.

—— 'Legal Differentiation and the Concept of the Human Rights Treaty in International Law', 11 *EJIL* (2000), 489.

Crawford, J., *Creation of States in International Law* (Oxford, 1979).

—— 'On Re-reading the Draft Articles on State Responsibility', *ASIL Proceedings* (1998).

—— 'Revising the Draft Articles on State Responsibility', 10 *EJIL* (1999), 435.

—— *The International Law Commission's Articles on State Responsibility* (Cambridge, 2002).

Czaplinski, W., 'Concepts of *jus cogens* and Obligations *erga omnes* in International Law in the Light of Recent Developments', 23 *Polish Yearbook of International Law* (1997–1998), 87.

—— and Danilenko, G., 'Conflicts of Norms in International Law', *Netherlands Yearbook of International Law*, vol. 21 (1990), 3.

Danilenko, G., *Law-Making in the International Community* (Boston/Dordrecht/London, 1993).

Dannemann, G., *Schadenersatz bei Verletzung der Europäischen Menschenrechtskonvention* (Köln/Berlin/Bonn/München, 1994).

De Hoogh, A., The Relationship between Jus Cogens, Obligations Erga Omnes and

International Crimes: Peremptory Norms in Perspective, 42 *Österreichische Zeitschrift für öffentliches Recht und Völkerrecht* (1991).

De Hoogh, A., *International Crimes and* Erga Omnes *Obligations: A Theoretical Inquiry into International Responsibility of States* (The Hague, 1996).

De Sena, P., and De Vittor, F., 'State Immunity and Human Rights: The Italian Supreme Court Decision on the *Ferrini* Case', 16 *EJIL* (2005), 89.

De Wet, E., 'Human Rights Limitations to Economic Enforcement Measures under Article 41 of the UN Charter and the Iraqi Sanctions Regime', 14 *LJIL* (2001), 277.

—— 'The Role of Human Rights in Limiting the Enforcement Power of the Security Council: A Principled View', De Wet and Nollkaemper (eds), *Review of the Security Council by Member States* (Intersentia, Antwerp/Oxford/New York, 2003), 7–30.

—— *The Chapter VII Powers of the United Nations Security Council* (Hart Publishing, Oxford, 2003).

—— 'The Prohibition of Torture as an International Norm of *Jus Cogens* and Its Implications for National and Customary Law', 15 *EJIL* (2004), 97.

—— and Nollkaemper, A., 'Review of the Security Council Decisions by National Courts', 45 *German Yearbook of International Law* (2002).

De Zayas, A., 'Amnesty Clause', 3 *EPIL* (Amsterdam, 1982), 14.

Degan, V., Responsibility for International Crimes, Sienho Yee and Wang Tieya (eds), *International Law in the Post-Cold War World—Festschrift Li Haopei* (Routledge, London, 2001), 202.

Delbrück, J., 'Some Observations on the Foundations and Identification of *erga omnes* Norms in International Law', Götz, Selmer, Wolfrum (Hrsg.), *Liber Amicorum Günther Jaenicke—Zum 85. Geburtstag* (Berlin/Heidelberg, 1998), 17.

Dhokalia, R., 'Problems Relating to *Jus Cogens*', Agrawala (ed.), *Essays on the Law of Treaties* (Bombay/Calcutta/Madras/New Delhi, 1972), 149.

Dinstein, Y., 'The *erga omnes* Applicability of Human Rights', 30 *AVR* (1992), 16.

—— War, Aggression and Self-Defence (3rd ed., Cambridge, 2001).

Dodge, W., 'Which Torts in Violation of the Law of Nations?' 24 *Hastings International and Comparative Law Review* (2001), 351.

Doehring, K., 'Unlawful Resolutions of the Security Council and Their Legal Consequences', 1 *Max Planck YBUNL* (1997), 91.

Domb, F., '*Jus Cogens* and Human Rights' 6 *Israel Yearbook of Human Rights* (1976), 104.

Domb, F., 'Treatment of War Crimes in Peace Settlements—Prosecution or Amnesty?' Dinstein and Tabory (eds), *War Crimes in International Law* (Dordrecht, 1996), 305.

Dominice, C., 'A propos du principe de l'estoppel en droit des gens', *Recueil d'études de droit international en hommage à Paul Guggenheim* (Geneva, 1968), 327.

—— 'The International Responsibility of States for Breach of Multilateral Obligations', 10 *EJIL* (1999), 353.

Doswald-Beck, L., 'The Legal Validity of Military Intervention by Invitation of the Government', 56 *BYIL* (1985), 189.

Dugard, J., *The South-West Africa/Namibia Dispute* (Berkeley and London, 1973).

—— *Recognition and the United Nations* (Cambridge, 1987).

—— '1966 and All That. The South West Africa Judgment Revisited in the

East Timor Case', 8 *African Journal of International and Comparative Law* (1996), 549.

Dugard, J., 'Is the Truth and Reconciliation Process Compatible with International Law? The Unanswered Question', *South African Journal of Human Rights* (1998), 258.

—— 'Collective Non-Recognition: The Failure of South Africa's Bantustan States', *Boutros Boutros-Ghali—Amicorum Discipulorumque Liber—Peace, Development, Democracy*, vol. I (Brussels, 1998), 383.

—— and Van den Wyngaert, C., 'Reconciling Extradition with Human Rights', 92 *AJIL* (1998), 187.

—— 'Dealing With Crimes of a Past Regime: Is Amnesty Still an Option?' 12 *Leiden Journal of International Law* (2000), 1001.

—— 'Possible Conflicts of Jurisdiction with Truth Commissions', Cassese, Gaeta and Jones (eds) *The Rome Statute of the International Criminal Court—A Commentary* (Oxford, 2002), 693.

Dupuy, P-M., 'L'unité de l'ordre juridique international', 297 *RdC* (2002), 9.

Edelenbos, C., 'Human Rights Violations: A Duty to Prosecute?' 7 *LJIL* (1994), 1.

Eek, H., 'Peremptory Norms and Private International Law', 139 *RdC* (1973-II), 1.

Elias, T., 'Problems concerning the Validity of Treaties', 134 *RdC* (1971-III), 391.

Elkind, J., *Non-Appearance before the International Court of Justice* (Boston, 1984).

Evans, M., 'International Wrongs and National Jurisdiction', Evans (ed.), *Remedies in International Law: The Institutional Dilemma* (Hart Publishing, Oxford, 1998), 173.

Fahmi, A., 'Peremptory Norms as General Rules of International Law', 22 *Österreichische Zeitschrift für öffentliches Recht* (1971), 383.

Fawcett, J., *The Application of the European Convention on Human Rights* (Oxford, 1985).

Fitzgerald, B., '*Horta v Commonwealth*: The Validity of the Timor Gap Treaty and Its Domestic Implementation', 44 *ICLQ* (1995), 643.

Fitzmaurice, G., The Law and Procedure of the International Court of Justice, 29 *BYIL* (1953), 1.

—— 'The general principles of international law considered from the standpoint of the rule of law', 92 *Recueil des cours* (1957-II), 1.

—— 'The Law and Procedure of the International Court of Justice', 34 *BYIL* (1958), 1.

—— 'The Law and Procedure of the International Court of Justice', 35 *BYIL* (1959), 183.

—— 'Hersch Lauterpacht—The Scholar as Judge', 39 *BYIL* (1963), 133.

—— 'Judicial Innovation: Its Uses and Its Perils', *Cambridge Essays in International Law* (London, 1965), 24.

—— *The Law and Procedure of the International Court of Justice* (Cambridge, 1986).

Fleischhauer, K-A., 'Prescription', Bernhardt (ed.), 3 *Encyclopedia of Public International Law* (Amsterdam, 1997), 1105.

Flynn, M., 'Genocide: It's A Crime Everywhere, But Not in Australia', 29 *Western Australian Law Review* (2000), 59.

Ford, C., 'Adjudicating *Jus Cogens*', 13 *Wisconsin International Law Journal* (1994), 145.

Fox, H., 'The Resolution of the Institute of International Law on the Immunities of Heads of State and Government', 51 *ICLQ* (2002), 120.

—— *The Law of State Immunity* (Oxford, 2002).

Franck, T., *Fairness in International Law and Institutions* (Oxford, 1995).

Fribergh, E. and Villiger, M., The European Commission on Human Rights, Macdonald, Matscher and Petzold (eds), *The European System of Protection of Human Rights* (Martinus Nijhoff, Dordrecht, 1993), 605.

Frowein, J., 'Verpflichtungen *erga omnes* im Völkerrecht und Ihre Durchsetzung', *Voelkerrecht als Rechtsordnung—Internationale Gerichtsbarkeit—Menschenrechte: Festschrift Mosler* (Berlin/Heidelberg, 1983), 241.

—— *Jus Cogens*, 7 *EPIL* (Amsterdam, 1984), 327.

—— Nullity in International Law, 7 *EPIL* (Amsterdam, 1984), 361.

—— 'Staatengemeinschaftsinteresse—Probleme bei Formulierung und Durchsetzung', Hailbronner, Ress and Stein (Hrsg.), *Staat und Völkerrechtsordnung, Festschrift für Karl Doehring* (1989), 219.

—— 'Reactions by Not Directly Affected States to Breaches of Public International Law', 248 *RdC* (IV-1994), 345.

—— 'Male Captus Male Detentus: A Human Right', Lawson and De Blois (eds), *The Dynamics of the Protection of Human Rights in Europe: Essays in Honour of Henry G. Schermers* (1994), 175.

—— and Peukert, W., *Europäische Menschenrechtskonvention/EMRK Kommentar* (Engel Verlag: Kehl/Strasbourg/Arlington, 1995).

Frulli, M., 'When Are States Liable Towards Individuals for Serious Violations of Humanitarian Law?' The *Markovic* Case, 1 *Journal of International Criminal Justice* (2003), 406.

Gaja, G., '*Jus Cogens* beyond the Vienna Convention', 172 *RdC* (1981-III), 271.

—— '*Ius Cogens*, Obligations *Erga Omnes* and International Crimes: A Tentative Analysis of Three Related Concepts', Weiler, Cassese and Spinedi (eds), *International Crimes of State: A Critical Analysis of Article 19 of the ILC's Draft Articles on State Responsibility* (Berlin, 1989), 151.

Garnett, R., 'Should the Sovereign Immunity be Abolished?' 20 *Australian YBIL* (1999), 175.

Gasser, 'Collective Economic Sanctions and International Humanitarian Law', 56 *ZaöRV* (1996), 871.

Gattini, A., 'To What Extent are State Immunity and Non-Justiciability Major Hurdles to Individuals' Claims for War Damages?' 1 *Journal of International Criminal Justice* (2003), 348.

Gavouneli M., and Bantekas, I., 'Casenote on *Prefecture of Voiotia v Federal Republic of Germany*', Greek Supreme Court, 95 *AJIL* (2001), 198.

Gavron, J., 'Amnesties in the Light of Developments in International Law and the Establishment of the International Criminal Court', 51 *ICLQ* (2002), 91.

Gazzini, T., 'NATO Coercive Military Activities in the Yugoslav Crisis (1992–1999)', 12 *EJIL* (2001), 391.

Gill, T., 'Legal and Some Political Limitations on the Power of the UN Security Council to Exercise its Enforcement Powers under Chapter VII of the Charter', XXVI *Netherlands Yearbook of International Law* (1995).

Gomez-Robledo, A., 'Le ius cogens international: sa genèse, sa nature, ses fonctions', 172 *Recueil des cours* (1981-III), 9.

Goodrich, L., Hambro E., and Simmons, A., *The Charter of the United Nations. A Commentary* (1969).

Goodwin-Gill, G., 'Crime and International Law: Expulsion, Removal, and the Non-Derogable Obligation', Goodwin-Gill and Talmon (eds), *The Reality of International Law. Essays in Honour of Ian Brownlie* (Oxford, 1999), 199.

Goodwin-Gill, G., 'The Limits of the Power of Expulsion in Public International Law', *BYIL* 1976, 67.

—— *The Refugee in International Law* (Oxford, 1996).

Gormley, P., 'The Right to Life and The Rule of Non-Derogability: Peremptory Norms of *Jus Cogens*', Ramcharan (ed.), *The Right to Life in International Law* (Dordrecht/Boston/Lancaster, 1985), 120.

Gowlland-Debbas, V., *Collective Responses to Illegal Acts in International Law* (Martinus Nijhoff, Dordrecht, 1990).

—— 'The Functions of the UN Security Council in the International Legal System', Byers (ed.), *The Role of Law in International Politics* (Oxford, 2000), 277.

Graefrath, B., 'Responsibility and Damages Caused: Relationship between Responsibility and Damages Caused', 185 *RdC* (II—1984), 9.

—— 'International Crimes and Collective Security', Wellens (ed.), *International Law: Theory and Practice. Essays in Honour of Eric Suy* (The Hague, 1998), 237.

Graveson, R.H., *Conflict of Laws* (1974).

Gray, C., *Judicial Remedies in International Law* (Oxford, 1990).

—— 'Bosnia and Herzegovina: Civil Law or Inter-State Conflict? Characterisation and Consequences', *BYIL* 1996, 155.

—— 'The Choice between Restitution and Compensation', 10 *EJIL* (1999), 413.

Gros-Espiel, H., 'Self-Determination and *Jus Cogens*', Cassese (ed.), *UN Law/ Fundamental Rights* (Alphen aan den Rijn, Sijthoff and Noordhoff, 1979), 167.

Guggenheim, P., 'La validité et la nullité des actes juridiques internationaux', *RdC* (I-1949), 195.

—— 'Das sogenannte automatische Vorbehalt der inneren Angelegenheiten', v.d. Heydte, Seidl-Hohenveldern, Verosta and Zemanek (eds), *Völkerrecht und Rechtliches Weltbild. Festschrift für Alfred Verdross* (Berlin, 1960), 117.

Hall, W., *A Treatise on International Law* (8th ed. by P. Higgins, Oxford, 1924).

Hannikainen, L., *Peremptory Norms in International Law: Historical Development, Criteria, Present Status* (Helsinki, 1988).

—— 'The case of East Timor from the perspective of jus cogens', *International Law and the Question of East Timor* (1995), 103.

Harris, D., O'Boyle, M. and Warbrick, C., *The Law of the European Convention on Human Rights* (Butterworths, London, 1995).

Hartmann, J., 'The Gillon Affair', 54 *ICLQ* (2003), 745.

Henkin, L., 'The Legality of Pro-democratic Invasion', 78 *AJIL* (1984), 642.

—— *International Law: Politics and Values* (Nijhoff, 1995).

Herdegen, M., 'Review of the Security Council by National Courts: A Constitutional Perspective', De Wet and Nollkaemper (eds), *Review of the Security Council by Member States* (Intersentia, Antwerp/Oxford/New York, 2003), 77–84.

Higgins, R., *The Development of International Law by Political Organs of the United Nations* (London, 1963).

—— 'Derogations under Human Rights Treaties', *BYIL* (1976–77), 281.

—— *Problems and Process: International Law and How We Use It* (Oxford, 1994).

—— 'Introduction', Gardner (ed.), *Human Rights as General Norms and a State's Right to Opt Out* (London, 1997), 1.

Hilpold, P., 'Humanitarian Intervention: Is There a Need for a Legal Reappraisal?' 12 *EJIL* (2001), 437.

Horn, F., *Reservations and Interpretative Declarations to Multilateral Treaties* (Amsterdam/New York, 1988).

Hudson, M., *The Permanent Court of International Justice* (New York, 1943).

Hutchison, M., 'Solidarity and Breaches of Multilateral Treaties', *BYIL* (1988), 151.

Igarashi, M., Post-War Compensation Cases, Japanese Courts and International Law, 43, *Japanese Annual of International Law* (2000), 45.

Imseis, A., 'On the Fourth Geneva Convention and the Occupied Palestinian Territory', 44 *Harvard International Law Journal* (2003), 67.

Irmscher, T., 'Legal Framework of the Activities of UNMIK', 44 *German YIL* (2001).

Ito, T., 'Japan's Settlement of the Post-World War II Reparations and Claims', 37 *Japanese Annual of International Law* (1994), 38.

Jacobs, F., and White, R., *The European Convention on Human Rights* (Oxford, 1996).

Jacovides, A., *Treaties Conflicting with Peremptory Norms of International Law and the Zurich-London 'Agreements'* (Nicosia, 1966).

Jaenicke, G., 'Zur Frage des Internationalen Ordre Public', 7 *Berichte der Deutschen Gesellschaft für Völkerrecht* (1967), 77.

—— 'International Public Order', 7 *EPIL* (Amsterdam, 1984), 314.

Janis, M., 'The Nature of *Jus Cogens*', 3 *Connecticut JIL* (1988), 359.

Jellinek, G., *Die Rechtliche Natur der Staatsverträge* (Vienna, 1880), 59.

Jenks, W., 'The Conflict of Law-making Treaties', 30 *BYIL* (1951), 401.

—— 'State Succession in Respect to Law-making Treaties', 32 *BYIL* (1952), 105.

—— *The Proper Law of International Organisations* (London/New York, 1962).

—— *The Prospects of International Adjudication* (London/New York, 1964).

Jennings, R.Y., 'Recent Cases on "Automatic" Reservations to the Optional Clause', 7 *ICLQ* (1958), 349.

—— 'Nullity and Effectiveness in International Law', *Cambridge Essays in International Law* (London, 1965), 64.

—— *The Acquisition of Territory in International Law* (Manchester, 1967).

—— 'General Course on Principles of International Law', II *RdC* (1967), 327.

—— 'Treaties', Bedjaoui (ed.), *International Law: Achievements and Prospects* (Paris/ Dordrecht/Boston/London, 1991), 135.

—— 'The *Pinochet* Extradition Case in the English Courts', L. Boisson de Chazournes and V. Gowlland-Debbas (eds), *The International Legal System in Quest of Equity and Universality. Liber Amicorum Georges Abi-Saab* (2001), 677.

—— and Watts, A., *Oppenheim's International Law* (9th ed., London, 1996).

Jessup, P., 'The Litvinov Agreement and the Belmont Case', 31 *AJIL* (1937), 481.

—— 'The Litvinov Assignment and the Pink Case', 36 *AJIL* (1942), 282.

Johnson, D., 'Acquisitive Prescription in International Law', *BYIL* (1950), 332.

Kadelbach, S., *Zwingendes Völkerrecht* (Berlin, 1992).

Kalala, T., 'La décision de l'OUA de ne plus respecter les sanctions décrétées par l'ONU contre la Lybie : désobéissance civile des états Africains a l'égard de l'ONU', *Revue Belge de Droit International* (1999/2), 545.

Kälin, W., 'Menschenrechtsverträge als Gewährleistung einer objektiven Ordnung', Kälin, Riedel and Karl (eds) *Aktuelle Probleme des Menschenrechtsschutzes, Berichte der Deutschen Gesellschaft für Völkerrecht*, Bd. 33, 1993 (Heidelberg, 1994), 9.

Kamminga, M., 'Legal Consequences of an Internationally Wrongful Act of a State against an Individual', Barkhuysen *et al.* (eds), *Execution of Strasbourg and Geneva Human Rights Decisions in National Legal Orders* (The Hague, 1999).

Kapteyn, P.J.G., 'The Role of the ECJ in Implementing Security Council Resolutions, De Wet and Nollkaemper (eds), *Review of the Security Council by Member States* (Intersentia, Antwerp/Oxford/New York, 2003), 57.

Karagiannakis, M., State Immunity and Fundamental Human Rights, 11 *Leiden Journal of International Law* (1998), 9.

Kegel, G., *Internationales Privatrecht* (Munich, 1987).

Kelsen, H., *The Law of the United Nations* (London, 1951).

King, B., 'Prescription of Claims in International Law', *BYIL* (1925), 82.

Kirgis, F., 'The Security Council's First Fifty Years', 89 *AJIL* (1995), 506.

—— 'Security Council Governance of Postconflict Societies: A Plea for Good Faith and Informed Decision Making', 95 *AJIL* (2001), 579.

Kiss, A., 'Conciliation', Macdonald, Matscher and Petzold (eds), *The European System of Protection of Human Rights* (Martinus Nijhoff, Dordrecht, 1993), 703.

Klein, D., 'A Theory of the Application of the Customary International Law of Human Rights by Domestic Courts', 13 *Yale Journal of International Law* (1988), 332.

Klabbers, J., 'Some Problems Regarding the Object and Purpose of Treaties', 8 *The Finnish Yearbook of International Law* (1998), 138.

Koji, T., 'Emerging Hierarchy in International Human Rights and Beyond: From the Perspective of Non-derogable Rights', 12 *EJIL* (2001), 917.

Kolb, R., 'Formal Source of *Ius Cogens* in Public International Law', 53 *Zeitschrift für öffentliches Recht* (1998), 69.

—— *Théorie du* ius cogens *international* (Paris, 2001).

—— 'Théorie du *ius cogens* international', *Revue Belge de Droit International* (2003/1), 5.

—— '*Jus Cogens*, Intangibilité, Intransgressibilité, Dérogation "Positive" et "Negative" ', *RGDIP* (2005), 305.

Kontou, N., *The Termination and Revision of Treaties in the Light of New Customary International Law* (Oxford, 1994).

Kreczko, A., The Unilateral Termination of UN Sanctions Against Southern Rhodesia by the United Kingdom, 21 *Virginia JIL* (1980–81), 97.

Kropholler, J., *Internationales Privatrecht* (Tübingen, 1997).

Kwakwa, E., *The International Law of Armed Conflict: Personal and Material Fields of Application* (Dordrecht/Boston/London, Martinus Nijhoff, 1992).

Lachs, M., 'The Development and General Trends of International Law in our Time', 169 *RdC* (1980), 9.

Laursen, A., 'The Use of Force and (the State of) Necessity', 37 *Vanderbilt Journal of Transnational Law* (2004), 485.

Lauterpacht, E., 'The Legal Effect of Illegal Acts of International Organisations', *Cambridge Essays in International Law* (1965), 88.

Lauterpacht, H., *Private Law Sources and Analogies in International Law* (New York/ Toronto, 1927).

—— *Recognition in International Law* (London, 1947).

—— 'Sovereignty over Submarine Areas', *BYIL* (1950), 376.

—— 'The Limits of the Operation of the Law of War', *BYIL* (1953).

—— *The Development of International Law by the International Court* (London, 1958).

—— I *Collected Papers* (Cambridge, 1970).

Leonetti, A., 'Interprétation des traités et règles impératives du droit international général (*jus cogens*)', 24 *ÖZÖR* (1973), 91.

Levi, W., 'The International Ordre Public', 62 *Revue de Droit International* (1994), 55.

Li Haopei, 'Jus Cogens and International Law', Sienho Yee and Wang Tieya (eds), *International Law in the Post-Cold War World—Festschrift Li Haopei* (Routledge, London, 2001), 499.

Lorimer, J., *The Institutes of the Law of Nations* (1883), vol. I, 4.

Lowe, V., The Role of Equity, 12 *Australian Yearbook of International Law* (1992), 54.

—— 'Precluding Wrongfulness or Responsibility: A Plea of Excuses', 10 *EJIL* (1999), 405.

Lowenfeld, A., *International Economic Law* (Oxford, 2003).

Lutz, E., 'Responses to Amnesties by the Inter-American system for the Protection of Human Rights', Harris and Livingstone (eds), *The Inter-American System of Human Rights* (Oxford, 1998), 345.

Malanczuk, P., 'Counter-measures and Self-defence', Spinedi and Simma (eds), *United Nations Codification of State Responsibility* (New York/London/Rome, 1987).

Mann, F.A., 'International Delinquencies before Municipal Courts', 70 *LQR* (1954), 181.

—— 'The Consequences of an International Wrong in National and International Law', *BYIL* (1976–77), 1.

—— 'The Doctrine of *Jus Cogens* in International Law', Mann, *Further Studies in International Law* (Oxford, 1977), 84.

—— *Foreign Affairs in English Courts* (Oxford, 1986).

—— 'Reflection on the Prosecution of Persons Abducted in Breach of International Law', Y. Dinstein and M. Tabory (eds), *International Law at a Time of Perplexity. Essays in Honour of Shabtai Rosenne* (Dordrecht, 1989), 407.

Marek, C., ' "Jus cogens" en droit international', *Recueil d'études de droit international en hommage à Paul Guggenheim* (Geneva, 1968), 426.

Martenczuk, B., 'The Security Council, the International Court and Judicial Review', 10 *EJIL* (1999).

Martin, P., *L'Estoppel en droit international public* (Paris, 1979).

Matheson, M., 'United Nations Governance of Postconflict Societies', 95 *AJIL* (2001).

McGibbon, I., 'The Scope of Acquiescence in International Law', *BYIL* (1954), 143.

—— 'Customary International Law and Acquiescence', *BYIL* (1957), 115.

—— 'Estoppel in International Law', 7 *ICLQ* (1958), 468.

McGoldrick, D., 'The Human Rights Committee', Capps, Evans and Konstadinidis (eds), *Asserting Jurisdiction* (Hart Publishing, Oxford, 2003), 199.

McGonville, A., 'Taking Jurisdiction', Scott (ed.), *Torture as Tort* (Hart Publishing, Oxford, 2001), 157.

McGregor, L., 'Individual Accountability in South Africa: Cultural Optimum or Political Façade?' 95 *AJIL* (2001), 32.

McNair, A., 'The So-called State Servitudes', *BYIL* (1925), 111.

—— 'Function and Differing Legal Character of Treaties', *BYIL* (1930), 100.

—— 'The Stimson Doctrine of Non-Recognition', *BYIL* (1933), 65.

—— 'Severance of Treaty Provisions', *Hommage d'une génération des Juristes au President Basdevant* (Paris, 1961), 346.

—— *The Law of Treaties* (Oxford, 1961).

Meron, T., *Human Rights Law-Making in the United Nations* (Oxford, 1986).

—— *Human Rights in Internal Strife* (Cambridge, 1987).

—— 'The Geneva Conventions as Customary Law', 81 *AJIL* (1987), 348.

—— *Human Rights and Humanitarian Norms as Customary Law* (Oxford, 1989).

—— 'The Humanisation of Humanitarian Law', 94 *AJIL* (2000), 239.

—— 'International Law in the Age of Human Rights, General Course on Public International Law', 301 *RdC* (2003).

Meyer, P., *Droit International Privé* (Paris, 1994).

Minagawa, T., '*Jus Cogens* in Public International Law', 6 *Hirotsubashi Journal of Law and Politics* (1968), 16.

Mohr, M., 'The ILC's Distinction between International Crimes and International Delicts and Its Implications', Spinedi and Simma (eds), *United Nations Codification of State Responsibility* (New York, 1987), 114.

Mosler, H., 'Ius Cogens im Völkerrecht', 25 *Schweizerisches Jarhbuch für Inernationales Recht* (1968), 9.

—— 'International Society as a Legal Community', 140 *RdC* (1974-IV), 1.

Münch, F., 'Bemerkungen zum ius cogens', *Voelkerrecht als Rechtsordnung— Internationale Gerichtsbarkeit—Menschenrechte: Festschrift Mosler* (Berlin/ Heidelberg, 1983), 617.

Müllerson, R., *Ordering Anarchy* (The Hague/Boston/London, 2000).

Nahlik, S., The Grounds of Invalidity and Termination of Treaties, 65 *AJIL* (1971), 736.

Naqvi, Y., 'Amnesty for War Crimes: Defining the Limits of International Recognition', 85 *International Review of the Red Cross* (2003), 583.

Nash, M., 'US Contemporary Practice Relating to International Law', 74 *AJIL* (1980), 418.

Nicoloudis, E., *La nullité de jus cogens et le développement contemporain de droit international public* (Athens, 1974).

Niederer, W., *Einführung in die Allgemeine Lehren des Internationalen Privatrechts* (Zurich, 1956).

Nieto-Navia, R., 'International Peremptory Norms (*Jus Cogens*) and International Humanitarian Law', L.C. Vorhah *et al.* (eds), *Man's Inhumanity to Man. Essays on International Law in Honour of Antonio Cassese* (Kluwer, The Hague, 2003), 595.

Nolte, G., 'The Limits on the Security Council's Powers and its Functions in the

International Legal System: Some Reflections', Byers (ed.), *The Role of Law in International Politics* (Oxford 2001).

Nussbaum, A., *The Concise History of the Law of Nations* (New York, 1964).

—— *Deutsches Internationales Privatrecht* (Tübingen, 1974).

O'Connell, D.P., *International Law*, vol. 2 (London, 1970).

O'Higgins, P., 'Unlawful Seizure and Irregular Extradition', 36 *BYIL* (1960), 279.

Oellers-Frahm, K., 'The *erga omnes* Applicability of Human Rights', 30 *AVR* (1992), 28.

Onuf, N. and Birney, R., 'Peremptory Norms of International Law: Their Source, Function and Future', 4 *Denver Journal of International Law and Policy* (1974), 187.

Opsahl, T., 'Settlement Based on Respect for Human Rights under the European Convention of Human Rights', *Proceedings of the Sixth International Colloquy about the European Convention of Human Rights* (Strasbourg, 1985), 966.

Orakhelashvili, A., 'The Position of the Individual in International Law', *California Western International Law Journal*, vol. 31, Spring issue, 2001, 241–276.

—— 'Questions of International Judicial Jurisdiction in the *LaGrand* case', *Leiden Journal of International Law*, No. 1, 2002, 105–130.

—— 'The *Arrest Warrant* Case (*Congo v Belgium*), Case Review', *American Journal of International Law*, No. 3, July 2002, 677–685.

—— 'State Immunity in National and International Law: Three Recent Cases before the European Court of Human Rights', *Leiden Journal of International Law*, No. 3, 2002, 703–714.

—— 'State Immunity and International Public Order', *German Yearbook of International Law*, vol. 45, 2002, 227–267.

—— 'The European Convention on Human Rights and International Public Order', *Cambridge Yearbook of European Legal Studies*, vol. 5, 2002–2003, 237–270.

—— 'Restrictive Interpretation of Human Rights Treaties in the Recent Jurisprudence of the European Court of Human Rights', *European Journal of International Law*, No. 3, 2003, 529–568.

—— 'Peremptory Norms of International Law and Reparation for Internationally Wrongful Acts', *Baltic Yearbook of International Law*, vol. 3, 2003, 19–55.

—— 'Treaties and Title to Territory', *Cambridge Law Journal*, March issue, 2003, 9–12.

—— 'The Concept of International Judicial Jurisdiction: A Reappraisal', *The Law and Practice of International Courts and Tribunals*, vol. 3, Fall issue, 2003, 501–550.

—— 'The Post-War Settlement in Iraq: The UN Security Council Resolution 1483(2003) and General International Law', *Journal of Conflict and Security Law*, vol. 8(2), 2003, 307–314.

—— 'The *Oil Platforms* case (*Iran v USA*), Case Review', *International and Comparative Law Quarterly*, July issue, 2004, 753–761.

—— 'The Impact of Peremptory Norms on the Interpretation and Application of United Nations Security Council Resolutions', 16 *European Journal of International Law* (2005), 59–88.

—— 'Judicial Jurisdiction and Judicial Remedies in the *Avena* Case', *Leiden Journal of International Law*, No. 1, 2005, 31–48.

—— 'International Public Order and the International Court's Advisory Opinion on

Legal Consequences of the Construction of a Wall in the Occupied Palestinian Territory', *Archiv des Völkerrechts*, No. 2, 2005, 240–256.

—— 'The World Bank Inspection Panel in Context: Institutional Aspects of the Accountability of International Organisations', 2 *International Organizations Law Review* (2005), 57–102.

Orego Vicuna, F., *International Dispute Setlement in an Evolving Global Society* (Cambridge 2004).

Paavistra, E., 'Internationalization and Stabilization of Contracts versus State Sovereignty', *BYIL* 1989, 329.

Paolilo, R., 'On Unfulfilled Duties: The Obligation to Make Reparation in Cases of Violation of Human Rights', in V. Götz, P. Selmer, R. Wolfrum (eds), *Liber Amicorum Günther Jaenicke—Zum 85. Geburtstag* (Berlin/Heidelberg, 1998).

Parker, C., and Neylon, L., '*Jus Cogens*: Compelling the Law of Human Rights', 12 *Hastings International and Comparative Law Review* (1989), 411.

—— and Crew, J., 'Compensation for Japan's World War II War-Rape Victims', 17 *Hastings International and Comparative Law Review* (1994), 497.

Paul, W., 'Legal Consequences of Conflict between a Treaty and an Imperative Norm of General International Law (*jus cogens*)', 21 *Österreichische Zeitschrift für öffentliches Recht* (1971), 18.

Pauwelyn, J, *Conflict of Norms in Public International Law* (Cambridge, 2003).

Pellet, A., The Normative Dilemma: Will and Consent in International Law-Making, 12 *Australian Yearbook of International Law* (1992), 22.

—— 'Can a State Commit a Crime? Definitely, Yes!' 10 *EJIL* (1999), 425.

Pellonpää, M., 'Individual reparation claims under the European Convention on Human Rights', Randelzhofer and Tomuschat (eds), *State Responsibility and the Individual: Reparation in Instances of Grave Violations of Human Rights* (The Hague, 1999).

Pfluger, F., *Die Einseitigen Rechtsgeschäfte im Völkerrecht* (Zurich, 1936).

Pictet, J. (ed.), *Commentary to the First Geneva Convention of 1949* (Geneva, 1952).

Pillet, A., and Niboyet, J., *Manuel de Droit International Privé* (Paris, II-1924).

Pilloud, C., *et al.*, *Commentary on the Additional Protocols of 8 June 1977 to the Geneva Conventions of 12 August 1949* (Geneva, 1987).

Pisillo-Mazzeschi, R., 'Reparation Claims by Individuals for State Breaches of Humanitarian Law and Human Rights: An Overview', 1 *Journal of International Criminal Justice* (2003), 339.

Plender, R., 'The Role of Consent in the Termination of Treaties', 57 *BYIL* 1986, 133.

Provost, R., 'Reciprocity in Human Rights and Humanitarian Law', *BYIL* (1995), 383.

Quigley, J., The Israel–PLO Agreements versus the Geneva Civilians Convention, 7 *Palestinian Yearbook of International Law* (1992–94), 45.

—— 'Displaced Palestinians and a Right to Return', 39 *Harvard International Law Journal* (1998), 171.

Raape, L., *Internationales Privatrecht* (Berlin/Frankfurt, 1961).

Ragazzi, M., *The Concept of the International Obligations erga omnes* (Oxford, 1998).

Rakate, P., 'The South African Amnesty Process: Is International Law at the Crossroads?' 56 *Zeitschrift für öffentliches Recht* (2001), 97.

Randall, K., 'Universal Jurisdiction under International Law', 66 *Texas Law Review* (1988), 785.

Reinisch, A., 'Developing Human Rights and Humanitarian Law Accountability of the Security Council for the Imposition of Economic Sanctions', 95 *AJIL* (2001), 851.

Reinmann, M., 'A Human Rights Exception to Sovereign Immunity: Some Thoughts on *Princz v Federal Republic of Germany*', 16 *Michigan Journal of International Law* (1995), 403.

Reisman, M., *Nullity and Revision* (New Haven/London, 1971).

—— 'Termination of the USSR's Treaty Right of Intervention in Iran', 74 *AJIL* (1980), 144.

—— 'Legal Responses to Genocide and Other Massive Violations of Human Rights', 59 *Law and Contemporary Problems* (1996), 75.

Reuter, P., *Introduction to the Law of Treaties* (London/New York, 1972).

Reydams, L., 'Case-note on *Niyonteze v Public Prosecutor*', 96 *AJIL* (2002), 231.

Riesenfeld, S., '*Jus Dispositivum* and *Jus Cogens* in International Law in the Light of a Recent Decision of the German Supreme Constitutional Court', 60 *AJIL* (1966).

—— 'Sovereign Immunity in Perspective', 19 *Vanderbilt Journal of Transnational Law* (1986), 1.

Riphagen, W., 'State Responsibility: New Theories of Obligation of Inter-State Relations', MacDonald and Johnson (eds), *The Structure and Process of International Law: Essays in Legal Philosophy, Doctrine and Theory* (1983), 601.

—— 'From Soft Law to Ius Cogens and Back', 17 *VUWLR* (1987), 81.

Robertson, A.H., and Merrils, J., *Human Rights in Europe* (Manchester, 1993).

Rodley, N., *The Treatment of Prisoners in International Law* (Oxford, 1999).

Roht-Ariaza, N., 'State Responsibility to Investigate and Prosecute Grave Human Rights Violations in International Law', 78 *California Law Review* (1990), 451.

—— and Gibson, L., The Developing Jurisprudence on Amnesty, 20 *Human Rights Quarterly* (1998), 843.

Rolin, H., 'La rôle du requérant dans la procédure prévue par la Commission Européenne des Droits de l'Homme', 9 *Revue Hellénique de Droit International* (1956), 3.

—— 'Vers un ordre public réellement international', in *Hommage d'une génération des Juristes au President Basdevant* (Paris, 1961), 441.

Röling, B.V.A., 'The Law of War and The National Jurisdiction Since 1945', 100 *RdC* (II-1960), 329.

Ronzitti, N., 'Use of Force, Consent and *Jus Cogens*', Cassese (ed.), *The Current Legal Regulation of the Use of Force* (Dordrecht, 1986), 147.

Rosenne, S., 'Bilateralism and the Community Interest in the Codified Law of Treaties', Friedmann, Henkin and Lyssitzin (eds), *Transnational Law in a Changing Society: Essays in Honor of Philip C. Jessup* (New York, 1972), 203.

—— *Procedure in the International Court* (Boston, 1983).

—— *Breach of Treaty* (Cambridge, 1985).

—— *Developments in the Law of Treaties 1945–1986* (Cambridge, 1989).

—— 'War Crimes and State Responsibility', 24 *Israel Yearbook of Human Rights* (1994).

—— *The Law and Practice of the International Court, 1920–1996* (The Hague, 1997).

Rosenstock, R., 'Crimes of States—an Essay', Ginther, Hafner, Lang, Neuhold, Suchapira-Behrmann (eds), *Völkerrecht zwischen normativen Anspruch und politischer Realität. Festschrift für Karl Zemanek* (Berlin 1994), 319.

Roth, B., *Governmental Illegitimacy in International Law* (Oxford, 1999).

Roth, B., 'The illegality of "pro-democratic" invasion pacts', Fox and Roth (eds), *Democratic Governance and International Law* (Cambridge, 2000), 328.

Rozakis, C., 'The Conditions of Invalidity of International Agreements', 26–27 *Revue Hellénique de Droit International* (1973–1974), 221.

—— 'The Law on Invalidity of Treaties', 16 *Archiv des Völkerrechts* (1974), 150.

——'Treaties and Third States: A Study in the Reinforcement of the Consensual Standards in International Law', 35 *Zeitschrift für ausländisches öffentliches Recht und Völkerrecht* (1975), 1.

—— *The Concept of* Jus Cogens *in the Law of Treaties* (Amsterdam, 1976).

Rumpf, H., 'Zur Lehre von den "Zwingenden Völkerrechtsnormen" ', Brunner u.a. (Hrsg.), *Sowjetsystem und Ostrecht* (Berlin, 1985), 561.

Saladin, P., 'Völkerrechtliches Jus Cogens und Schweizerisches Landesrecht', Jenny and Kälin, *Die Schweizerische Rechtsordnung in Ihren Internationalen Bezügen* (Bern, 1988), 67.

Sassoli, M., 'Sanctions and Humanitarian Law', Gowlland-Debbas (ed.), *United Nations Sanctions and International Law* (2001).

—— 'State Responsibility for Violations of Humanitarian Law', 84 *International Red Cross Review* (2002), 401.

Saulle, M., 'Jus Cogens and Human Rights', *International Law at the Time of its Codification, Essays in Honour of Roberto Ago*, vol. II (Milan, 1987), 24.

Schabas, W., *Genocide in International Law* (Cambridge, 2000).

Schachter, O., *International Law: Theory and Practice* (Dordrecht, 1991).

Scharf, M., 'Swapping Amnesty for Peace: Was There a Duty to Prosecute International Crimes in Haiti?' 31 *Texas International Law Journal* (1995–96), 1.

—— 'The Letter of the Law: The Scope of the International Legal Obligation to Prosecute Human Rights Crimes', 53 *Law and Contemporary Problems* (1996), 41.

—— 'The Amnesty Exception to the Jurisdiction of the International Criminal Court', 32 *Cornell Journal of International Law* (1999), 507.

Scheuner, U., 'Conflict of a Treaty Provision with a Peremptory Norm of International Law and Its Consequences', 27 *Zeitschrift für ausländisches öffentliches Recht und Völkerrecht* (1967), 520.

—— 'Conflict of Treaty Provisions with a Peremptory Norm of General International Law', 29 *Zeitschrift für ausländisches öffentliches Recht und Völkerrecht* (1969), 28.

Schindler, D., 'Erga omnes-Wirkung des humanitären Völkerrechts', Beyerlin, Bothe, Hofmann and Petersmann (Hrsg.), *Recht zwischen Umbruch und Bewahrung. Festschrift für Rudolf Bernhardt* (Berlin/Heidelberg, 1993), 200.

Schütz, D., Der internationale *ordre public* (Frankfurt/Bern/New York, 1984).

Schwarzenberger, G., The Fundamental Principles of International Law, 87 *RdC* (1955), 191.

—— *International Law*, vol. I (3rd ed., London, 1957).

—— 'Title to Territory: Response to a Challenge', 51 *AJIL* (1958), 308.

—— 'The Problem of International Public Policy', 18 *Current Legal Problems* (1965), 191.

—— *A Manual of International Law* (5th ed., London, 1967).

Schweitzer, M., 'Ius cogens im Völkerrecht', 15 *Archiv des Völkerrechts* (1971), 197.

Schwelb, E., 'Some Aspects of International *Jus Cogens*', 61 *AJIL* (1967), 946.

—— 'The *Actio Popularis* and International Law', 2 *Israel Yearbook of Human Rights* (1972), 46.

—— 'The Law of Treaties and Human Rights', 16 *Archiv des Völkerrechts* (1973), 1.

Scrijver, N., *Sovereignty over Natural Resources* (Cambridge, 1997).

Seiderman, I., *Hierarchy in International Law: The Human Rights Dimension* (Antwerp/Gröningen/Oxford, 2001).

Shaw, M., *Title to Territory in Africa* (Oxford, 1986).

Sharp, W., 'International Obligations to Arrest War Criminals', 7 *Duke JCIL* (1997), 411.

Shelton, D., 'Reparations in the Inter-American System', Harris and Livingstone (eds), *The Inter-American System of Human Rights* (Oxford, 1998), 151.

—— 'Righting Wrongs: Reparations in the Articles on State Responsibility', 96 *AJIL* (2002), 833.

—— 'International Law and "Relative Normativity" ', Evans (ed.), *International Law* (Oxford, 2003), 145.

—— 'The World of Atonement: Reparations for Historical Injustices', 50 *NILR* (2003), 289.

Shihata, I., *The Power of the International Court to Determine Its Own Jurisdiction* (The Hague, 1965).

Simma, B., 'Reflections on Article 60 of the Vienna Convention on the Law of Treaties and Its Background in General International Law', 20 *Österreichische Zeitschrift für öffentliches Recht* (1970), 5.

—— 'Bilateralism and Community Interest in the Law of State Responsibility', Dinstein and Tabory (eds), *International Law at a Time of Perplexity—Essays in Honour of Shabtai Rosenne* (Dordrecht, 1989), 821.

—— 'Injury and Countermeasures', Weiler, Cassese and Spinedi (eds.), *International Crimes of State: A Critical Analysis of Article 19 of the ILC's Draft Articles on State Responsibility* (Berlin, 1989), 283.

—— 'From Bilateralism to Community Interest', 250 *RdC* (VI-1994), 217.

—— *The Contribution of Alfred Verdross to the Theory of International Law*, 6 *EJIL* (1995), 33.

—— and Alston, P., 'The Sources of Human Rights Law: Custom, Jus Cogens, and General Principles', 12 *Australian Yearbook of International Law* (1992), 82.

—— and Paulus, A., 'The responsibility of Individuals for Human Rights Abuses in Internal Conflict: A Positivist View', 93 *AJIL* (1999), 302.

Sinclair, I., *The Vienna Convention on the Law of Treaties* (Manchester, 1984).

Sorel, J-M., 'L'avenir du "crime" en droit international à la lumière de'l'experience du *jus cogens*', 23 *Polish Yearbook of International Law* (1997–1998), 69.

Stanbrook, I. and Stanbrook, C., *Extradition: Law and Practice* (Oxford, 2000).

Standaert, P., The Friendly Settlement of Human Rights Abuses in the Americas, 9 *Duke JCIL* (1999), 519.

Stavros, S., 'The Right to a Fair Trial in Emergency Situations', 41 *ICLQ* (1992), 343.

Stein, Ted, 'The Approach of the Different Drummer: The Principle of the Persistent Objector in International Law', 26 *Harv. Int'l L.J.* (1985), 457.

Stein, Torsten, 'Collective Enforcement of International Obligations', 47 *ZaöRV* (1987), 95.

Stein, Torsten, 'Terrorists: Extradition versus Deportation', 19 *Israel Yearbook of Human Rights* (1989), 280.

Stern, B., 'Case-note on *Re Javor* and *Re Munyeshyaka*', 93 *AJIL* (1999), 525.

Steven, L., 'Genocide and the Duty to Extradite or Prosecute: Why the United States is in Breach of Its International Obligations', 39 *Virginia Journal of International Law* (1999), 425.

Styrdom, H.A., '*Ius Cogens*: Peremptory Norm or Totalitarian Instrument?' 14 *South African Yearbook of International Law* (1988–89), 42.

Subedi, S., 'The Doctrine of Objective Regimes in International Law and the Competence of the United Nations to Impose Territorial or Peace Settlements on States', 37 *German YIL* (1994), 162.

Sudre, F., 'Existe-t-il un ordre public Européen?' Tavernier, *Quelle Europe pour les droits de l'homme?* (Brussels, 1996), 39.

Suy, E., *Les actes juridiques unilatéraux* (Paris, 1962).

—— 'The Concept of Jus Cogens in International Law', *Lagonissi Conference: Papers and Proceedings*, vol. II, Carnegie Endowment for International Peace (Geneva, 1967), 15.

Swan, M., 'International Human Rights Torts and the Experience of US Courts', Scott (ed.), *Torture as Tort* (Hart Publishing, Oxford, 2001), 66.

Swelb, E., The Law of Treaties and Human Rights, 16 Archiv des Folkerrechts (1973), 1.

Sztucki, J., Jus Cogens *and the Vienna Convention on the Law of Treaties* (Vienna, 1974).

Talmon, S., 'The Cyprus Question before the European Court of Justice', 12 *EJIL* (2001), 727.

—— 'The Constitutive versus the Declaratory Theory of Recognition: *Tertium Non Datur?*' *BYIL* (2004), 101.

—— 'Luftverkehr mit nicht anerkannten Staaten. Der Fall Nordzypern', 43 *Archiv des Völkerrechts* (2005), 1.

—— 'The Security Council as World Legislature', 99 *AJIL* (2005), 175.

Tanzi, A., 'Is Damage a Distinct Condition for the Existence of an Internationally Wrongful Act?' Spinedi and Simma (eds), *United Nations Codification of State Responsibility* (New York/London/Rome, 1987), 1.

Tenekides, G., 'Les effects de la contrainte sur les traités a la lumière de la Convention du Vienne du 23 Mai 1969', 20 *AFDI* (1974), 79.

Terwiesche, M., 'International Responsibility arising from the Implementation of a Security Council Resolution: The 2nd Gulf War and the Rule of Proportionality', 22 *Polish Yearbook of International Law* (1995–1996), 81.

Thirlway, H., 'The Law and Procedure of the International Court of Justice', *BYIL* 1989, 4.

—— 'The Law and Procedure of the International Court of Justice', *BYIL* 1990, 3.

—— 'Concepts, Principles, Rules and Analogies: International Law and Municipal Legal Reasoning', 294 *RdC* 2002 (2003).

—— 'The Sources of International Law', Evans (ed.), *International Law* (Oxford, 2003), 117.

Tomuschat, C., 'Obligations Arising for States without or against Their Will', 241 *RdC* (IV-1993), 195.

—— 'International Crimes by States: An Endangered Species?' Wellens (ed.), *International Law: Theory and Practice. Essays in Honour of Eric Suy* (The Hague, 1998), 253.

—— 'Individual Reparation Claims in Instances of Grave Human Rights Violations', Randelzhofer and Tomuschat (eds), *State Responsibility and the Individual. Reparation in Instances of Grave Violations of Human Rights* (Nijhoff 1999).

—— 'Yugoslavia's Damaged Sovereignty over the Province of Kosovo', Kreijen *et al.* (eds), *State, Sovereignty and International Governance* (Oxford, 2002), 323.

—— 'Reparation for Victims of Grave Human Rights Violations', 10 *Tulane Journal of International and Comparative Law* (2002), 157.

—— 'L'immunité des états en cas de violations graves des droits de l'homme', *Revue général de droit international public* (2005), 51.

Turns, D., 'The Stimson Doctrine of Non-Recognition: Its Historical Genesis and Influence on Contemporary International Law', 2 *Chinese Journal of International Law* (2003), 105.

Turpel M-E. and Sands, P., Peremptory International Law and Sovereignty: Some Questions, 3 *Connecticut JIL* (1988), 364.

Vadapalas, V., Codification of the Law of International Responsibility by the International Law Commission: Breach of International Law and Its Consequences, 23 *Polish Yearbook of International Law* (1997–1998), 35.

Van den Wyngaert, C., 'The Political Offence Exception to Extradition: How to Plug the "Terrorists' Loophole" Without Departing from Fundamental Human Rights', 19 *Israel Yearbook of Human Rights* (1989), 297.

—— 'Applying the European Convention on Human Rights to Extradition: Opening Pandora's Box?' 39 *ILCQ* (1990), 757.

—— and Dugard, J., 'Non-applicability of Statute of Limitations', Cassese, Gaeta and Jones (eds) *The Rome Statute of the International Criminal Court—A Commentary* (Oxford, 2002), 872.

—— and Ongena, T., '*Ne bis in idem* Principle, including the Issue of Amnesty', Cassese, Gaeta and Jones (eds) *The Rome Statute of the International Criminal Court—A Commentary* (Oxford, 2002), 705.

Van der Meersch, G., 'Does the Convention have the Power of "Ordre Public" in Municipal Law?' Robertson (ed.), *Human Rights in National and International Law* (Manchester, 1968), 97.

Van Dijk, P., and van Hoof, G.J.H., *Theory and Practice of the European Convention on Human Rights* (Kluwer, The Hague/London, 1998).

Van Hoof, G.J.H., *Rethinking the Sources of International Law* (Deventer, Boston, 1983).

Vattel, E., *The Law of Nations or the Principles of Natural Law applied to the Conduct and to the Affairs of Nations and of Sovereigns*, Scott (ed.), *Classics of International Law* (Washington 1916).

Verdross, A., 'Forbidden Treaties in International Law', 31 *AJIL* (1937), 571.

—— 'Jus Dispositivum and Jus Cogens in International Law', 60 *AJIL* (1966), 55.

Verdross, A. and Simma, B., *Universelles Völkerrecht: Theorie und Praxis* (Berlin, 1984).

Verhoeven, J., '*Jus Cogens* and Reservations or "Counter-reservations" to the Jurisdiction of the International Court of Justice', Wellens (ed.) *International Law: Theory and Practice: Essays in Honor of Eric Suy* (The Hague, 1998), 195.

Verhoeven, J., 'La reconnaissance internationale: declin ou renouveau?' 39 *Annuaire Français de Droit International* (1999), 7.

Verzijl, J., 'La validité et la nullité des actes juridiques internationales', 15 *Revue de droit international* (1935), 284.

Vierdag, B., 'Special Features of Human Rights Treaties', Barnhoorn and Wellens (eds) *Diversity in Secondary Rules and the Unity of International Law* (Brill, 1995), 119.

Virally, M., 'Réflexions sur le "jus cogens"', 12 *Annuaire Français de Droit International* (1966), 5.

—— 'Sources of International Law', Sorensen (ed.), *A Manual of International Law* (London/New York, 1968), 143.

Visscher, C., *Les effectivités du droit international public* (Paris, 1967).

—— 'Positivisme et "jus cogens"', 40 *RGDIP* (1971), 5.

Völker, C., *Zur Dogmatik des ordre public* (Berlin, 1998).

Von der Heydte, F., 'Die Erscheinungsform des zwischenstaatlichen Rechts: jus cogens und jus dispositivum im Völkerrecht', 16 *Zeitschrift für Völkerrecht* (1932), 461.

Walter, H., *Die Europäische Menschenrechtsordnung* (Cologne, 1970).

Warbrick, C., 'Judicial Jurisdiction and Abuse of Process', 49 *ICLQ* (2000), 489.

Watts, A., 'The Legal Position in International Law of Heads of State, Heads of Government and Foreign Ministers', 247 *RdC* (1994-III).

Wei, S., 'Reservations to Treaties and Some Practical Issues', 7 *Asian Yearbook of International Law* (1997), 105.

Weil, P., 'Towards Relative Normativity in International Law?' 77 *AJIL* (1983), 413.

—— 'Le droit international en quête de son identité. Cours général de droit international public', 237 *RdC* (1992-VI), 9.

Weiler, J., Cassese, A. and Spinedi, M. (eds), *International Crimes of State: A Critical Analysis of the ILC's Draft Article 19 on State Responsibility* (Berlin, 1989).

Weisburd, M., 'The Emptiness of *Jus Cogens* as Illustrated by the War in Bosnia-Herzegovina', 17 *Michigan Journal of International Law* (1995), 1.

Werksman, J., and Khalatschi, R., 'Nuclear weapons and the concept of jus cogens: peremptory norms and justice pre-empted?' Boisson de Chazournes and Sands (eds), *International Law, the International Court of Justice and Nuclear Weapons* (Cambridge, 1999), 181.

White, N., *The Law of International Organisations* (Manchester, 1996).

Whiteman, M., '*Jus Cogens* in International Law, with a Projected List', 7 *Georgia Journal of International and Comparative Law* (1977), 609.

Wirth, S., 'Germany's New International Crimes Code: Bringing a Case to Court', 1 *Journal of International Criminal Justice* (2003), 151.

Wittich, S., 'Awe of the Gods and Fear of the Priests: Punitive Damages and the Law of State Responsibility', 3 *Austrian Review of International and European Law* (1998), 101.

Wolff, Ch., *The Law of Nations Treated According to a Scientific Method*, Scott (ed.), *Classics of International Law* (Oxford 1934).

Wolff, M., *Das Internationale Privatrecht Deutschlands* (Berlin/Göttingen/Heidelberg, 1954).

Wolfke, K., '*Jus Cogens* in International Law (Regulation and Prospects)', 6 *Polish Yearbook of International Law* (1974), 145.

Wolfrum, R., 'National Prosecution of International Offences', 24 *Israel YbHR* (1994), 183.

Wood, M., 'The Interpretation of Security Council Resolutions', 2 *Max Planck YBUNL* (1998).

Yang, X., 'State Immunity in the European Court of Human Rights: Reaffirmations and Misconceptions', *BYIL* 2003, 333.

—— 'Universal Tort Jurisdiction over Torture?' 64 *Cambridge Law Journal* (2005), 1.

Zappala, S., 'Do Heads of State Enjoy Immunity from Prosecution for International Crimes?' 12 *European Journal of International Law* (2001), 595.

—— *Human Rights in International Criminal Proceedings* (Oxford, 2003).

Zemanek, K., 'The Unilateral Enforcement of International Obligations', 47 *ZaöRV* (1987), 32.

—— 'New Trends in the Enforcement of *erga omnes* Obligations', 4 *Max Planck Yearbook of the United Nations Law* (2000), 1.

Zimmermann, A., 'Sovereign Immunity and Violations of International *Jus Cogens*— Some Critical Remarks', 16 *Michigan Journal of International Law* (1995), 433.

—— *Staatennachfolge in völkerrechtlchen Verträgen* (Berlin, 2000).

Zitelmann, E., *Internationales Privatrecht* (Bd. 1, Leipzig, 1897).

Zotiades, G., 'Staatsautonomie und die Grenzen der Vertragsfreiheit im Völkerrecht', 17 *Österreichische Zeitschrift für öffentliches Recht* (1967), 90.

Zweigert, K., and Kötz, H., *An Introduction to Comparative Law* (3rd ed., Oxford, 1998).

Index